Working Americans 1880–1999

Volume II: The Middle Class

by Scott Derks

A Universal Reference Book

Grey House Publishing

MILLERTON, NY 12546

PUBLISHER: Leslie Mackenzie
EDITORIAL DIRECTOR: Laura Mars-Proietti
EDITORIAL ASSISTANT: Pamela Michaud
MARKETING DIRECTOR: Jessica Moody

AUTHOR: Scott Derks
CONTRIBUTOR: Carla Brown, Marshall Derks, Erika Watson DePaz
EDITORIAL ASSISTANT to the author: Cheryl Quick

COPYEDITOR: Elaine Alibrandi
COMPOSITION & DESIGN: Stratford Publishing Services

A Universal Reference Book
Grey House Publishing, Inc.
185 Millerton Road
Millerton, NY 12546
518.789.8700
800-562-2139
FAX 518.789.0545
www.greyhouse.com
e-mail: books @greyhouse.com

10 9 8 7 6 5 4 3 2

First edition published 2001

Printed in the USA

ISBN 1-89148272-6 hardcover

Table of Contents

Introduction

Working Americans 1880–1999 Volume II: The Middle Class is the second volume of what will be a multi-volume set. Like its predecessor, *Volume I: The Working Class, Volume II: The Middle Class,* looks, decade by decade, into the work, homes, and lifestyles that defined the Middle Class—from a railroad engineer in Pennsylvania to an airline captain from Illinois. This volume also looks at the society and history that shaped the world of the Middle Class from 1880–1999.

> "*. . . this volume engages and informs, contributing significantly and meaningfully to the historiography of the working class in America. . . . A compelling and well-organized contribution for those interested in social history and the complexities of working Americans.*"
>
> Library Journal

> "*. . .* Derks *adds to the genre of social history known as 'history from the bottom up,' which examines the lives of ordinary people. . . . Recommended for all college and university library collections.*"
>
> Choice

Volume III: The Upper Class, will explore these same topics for America's Upper Class population 1880–1999.

As in the first volume, the chapters in Volume II have been carefully designed to enhance our undertanding of the growth and development of the Middle Class over more than a century. This volume begins in the late 1800s at a time when the economy was shifting from the agrarian to the industrialized sector. Also, better record-keeping during this time, and the increase in gathering statistics, provided a wealth of archives from which to draw original material for this book.

From the many government surveys, social worker histories, economic data, family diaries and letters, newspaper and magazine features, this unique reference assembles a remarkably personal and realistic look at the lives of Middle Class Americans.

Family Profiles

Each chapter of *Working Americans 1880–1999 Volume II: The Middle Class* covers a decade, and opens with an overview of important events to anchor the decade in its time.

The Middle Class is then explored by examining the lives of a number of Middle Class working families. These Family Profiles examine income, expenses, life at home, life at work, and life in the community. The information is presented in narrative form, but hard facts and real life situations back up each story.

The basis of every Family Profile is a study that either details the family's finances, lifestyle, or struggle. In most cases, a governmental study identified the family statistically, and this data was used to form the base of the profile. Extensive research into the times, professions, and geographic locations pumped additional life into these families. To further identify each family with their community, we gave each a name. The Irish salmon cannery manager from the 1880s is Seamus Cavanagh, the Kincaid family from Chicago illustrates life in 1919, securities analyst and 1941 Wellesley College graduate is Rosemary Charrette, and the Ducker family own and operate a ski lodge in Winter Park, Colorado.

Economic Profiles

Each chapter also includes an Economic Profile. These are a series of statistical comparisons designed to put the family's individual lifestyles and decisions in perspective. These charts include the average wages of other professions during the year being profiled, a selection of typical pricing, and key events and inventions of the time. Enhancing some of the chapters are examinations of important issues faced by the family, such as how Americans coped with war and civil rights issues.

In addition to the detailed economic and social data for each family, each chapter is further enriched with Historical Snapshots, News Profiles, articles from local media, and illustrations derived from popular printed materials of the day, such as clippings from cereal boxes, campaign buttons, postcards, and posters. Each graphic was carefully selected to add depth to the understanding of the world that the families lived in. The material used in *Working Americans, Volume II* is a compilation drawn from many different sources, which are listed in detail at the back of the book.

In more than 600 pages, *Working Americans 1880–1999 Volume II: The Middle Class* offers 76 Profiles that cover 32 occupations and dozens of ethnic groups. Geographically, the text travels the entire country, from Alaska to Texas, from sophisticated cities to quiet country homes.

The Table of Contents provides a clear guide through each chapter, outlining each section, from Life at Home to Selected Prices, and quickly illustrates the wealth of information for each decade. In addition, Volume II includes a comprehensive index, providing the reader with easy access to the thousands of specific topics in this volume.

Preface

This is the second volume in a series focused on the social and economic lives of working Americans, using everyday terms to describe everyday people. The first volume of *Working Americans: 1880–1999* examined the struggles of the working class through the eyes and wallets of more than three dozen families. It studied what shaped their jobs, wages, family life, expenditures, and hobbies throughout the decade. The second volume captures the struggles of the middle class in a similar, but sometimes subtly different, way, profiling the lives of everyday families that played a quiet role in building the day-to-day economy of America from 1880 to 1999. Few were heroes, all felt the pressure of living, and most wanted more for themselves and their families.

The strength of the American middle class is at the core of our economic system and stability. Most of these men and women emerged from the working class through education, family connections, good fortune, proper marriages, the rise of corporations, and, of course, skill. As a result, they gained positions that allowed more discretionary spending, offered more options for spending their time, or provided them with prestige in the community. Most often these men and women separated themselves from the working class by taking jobs as managers, professionals, inventors, entrepreneurs, and business owners. As a result, they helped create a dynamic economy that gives great weight to competitive products, industrious people, changing corporate structures, and bold, new ideas. When people ponder what separates America's economy from those of many countries, the size and quality of the American middle class are integral to the ultimate answer.

The definition of what constitutes the middle class is as elusive as defining humor. Early in the twentieth century, when the middle class was relatively small, this group was largely composed of individuals in managerial positions or in recognized professions such as medicine, law, or engineering. As the decade progressed, the term grew more democratic. By the late 1930s—when the nation was still creeping out of the claws of the Depression—a vast majority of Americans considered themselves "middle class." According to surveys, even the wealthy considered themselves to be middle class—always aware, perhaps, of someone else more wealthy, thus adopting the more humble designation. As we moved past World War II, national brands and national companies emerged. With them came large numbers of managerial jobs, uniform benefits such as health and life insurance, and the promise that "our children will do better than we."

With the rise of the middle class came discretionary time and dollars for thousands—later millions—of families. These increased options spawned a wide range of economic changes such as increased college enrollment, suburbia, a lawyer glut, and expanded vacation air travel—only available in a society in which large numbers of people enjoyed the luxury of time off and money to spend.

Working Americans: 1880–1999, Volume II: The Middle Class details the lives of the middle class, attempting to tell the truth about a vast stream of people by intimately focusing on the economic and social life of a few dozen. Each profile explains the workings of a middle class family, describing what they did with their time both at work and at home and how they interacted with their community. It is economic and social history at its most revealing. We see families from Colorado or Alaska or Connecticut wrestling with work and family pressures, childhood diseases, and concerns about labor strikes. At the turn of the twentieth century, a small New England company must decide whether to continue making superior, hand-forged pocketknives or change its methods to compete with catalog companies such as Sears.

Each profile is different, just as each family is different. None of us is average and neither were our ancestors. Some profiles intimately study the family's life at home, detailing how they coped with the Depression in New York or the need for water on their expanding cattle ranch in Texas. Others peer intently on life at work, such as the writing career of an African-American reporter for the *Pittsburgh Courier*, or life as a sales manager with Welch's Grape Juice, or an executive with Union Carbide. Fascinating portraits appear of a highly secretive engineer struggling to perfect television in 1931, the West Virginia Methodist minister determined to create a pension fund for retired preachers, or the Air Force pilot, just returned from Korea, whose family is adjusting to life in Kansas.

Beyond describing economic life, *Working Americans* opens a window into families experiencing change: the only woman helping to design Mack trucks in a department of 20, the manager of a textile mill faced with cheap imports from the American South, the cartoonist in San Francisco who is pondering a move to New York, or the couple whose Colorado ski lodge is experiencing declining revenues, and who now must find ways to attract more vacationers.

In preparing this book, I found that all families—no matter their economic situation—experience loss, pain, and insecurity. They also experience immeasurable joy and freedom. The newspaper and magazine stories strategically placed throughout the book remind us all that many of yesterday's critical issues are still with us. Happily, some issues, such as the quality of wartime corsets, are less pressing today.

Ultimately, this volume and its predecessor represent the history and ancestry of the vast majority of Americans. At the turn of the twentieth century, 10- and 12-hour workdays were standard by dictum; as we reached the end of the century, workdays of the same length were often with us by choice. The American economy is complex, made all the more perplexing by people who insist on explaining the intricacies of money movement without mentioning the lives of the families whose earnings and spending drive the economy. *Working Americans* is not the total answer; it is simply a clue to understanding whence we came and where we are headed.

Scott Derks

For Martha and Wayne

Acknowledgments

The author wishes to thank Cheryl Quick for her editorial assistance, perseverance, and patience, while Elaine Alibrandi's sharp pencil kept the nouns and verbs shuffling in the same direction. As important, this book was created through the kindness of friends and strangers, who supplied information, photographs, inspiration, critiques, and strongly worded suggestions. This work would have been poorer without the research of Lucia Derks, Carla Brown, Malcolm Brown, Marshall Derks, Erika Watson DePaz, Carol Watson, Betty Hart, Linda Hart, Bob Lee, Maureen Boler, Sheila Keller, Jan and Robin Brown, Cotton and Stuart Brown, Jean Farmer, Sally Gaillard, Margaret Lumpkin, Dick Gottlieb, William Draffin, John and Joyce Pipkin, Reed Freeman, and most of all, Ellen Hanckel.

The publisher wishes to thank Kerry Keser, Director of Holley-Williams House Museum in Lakeville, Connecticut, for her insightful comments on the 1903 Profile that is based in Lakeville.

1880–1899

The last twenty years of the nineteenth century were marked by dramatic change—much of it culminating in the emerging technology of the times and the restless spirit of America's people. The rapid expansion of railroads and of technology that allowed the canning of foods for shipment nationwide created new industries, thanks to the expanding markets of America. At the same time, America was witnessing the movement of people from farm to factory, the rapid expansion of wage labor, and the explosive growth of cities and massive immigration. Farmers, merchants, and small-town artisans found themselves increasingly dependent on regional or national market forces and the shift in concentrations of power that was unprecedented in American history. At the same time, each of these changes played a key role in reshaping the economy, particularly the movement of professionals and entrepreneurs into the ranks of America's emerging middle class. It was an economy on a roll with few rudders or regulations.

Across America the economy—along with its work force—was running away from the land. Before the Civil War, the United States was overwhelmingly an agricultural nation. By the end of the century, non-agricultural occupations employed nearly two thirds of the workers. As important, two of every three Americans came to rely on wages instead of self-employment as farmers or artisans. At the same time, industrial growth began to center around cities, where wealth accumulated for a few who understood how to harness and use railroads, create new consumer markets, and manage a ready supply of cheap, trainable labor. Jobs, offering steady wages and the promise of a better life for workers' children, drew people from the farms into the cities, which grew at twice the rate of the nation as a whole. A modern, industrially-based work force emerged from the traditional farmlands, led by men skilled at managing others and the complicated flow of materials required to keep a factory operating. This led to an increasing demand for attorneys, bankers, and physicians to handle the complexity of the emerging urban economy. In 1890, newspaper editor Horace Greeley remarked, "We cannot all live in cities, yet nearly all seem determined to do so."

The new cities of America were home to great wealth and poverty—both produced by the massive migrations and influx of immigrants willing to work at any price. It was a time symbolized by Andrew Carnegie's steel mills, John D. Rockefeller's organization of the Standard Oil monopoly, and the manufacture of Alexander Graham Bell's wonderful invention, the telephone. By 1894, the United States had become the world's leading industrial power, producing more than England, France, and Germany—its three largest competitors—combined. For much of this period, the nation's industrial energy focused on the need for railroads requiring large quantities of labor, iron, steel, stone, and lumber. In 1883, nine tenths of the nation's entire production of steel went into rails. The most important invention of the period—in an era of tremendous change and innovation—may have been the Bessemer converter, which transformed pig iron into steel at a relatively low cost, increasing steel output 10 times from 1877 to 1892.

The greatest economic event during the last two decades of the nineteenth century was the great wave of immigration that swept America. It is believed to be the largest worldwide population movement in human history, bringing more than 10 million people to the United States to fill the expanding need for workers. In the 1880s alone, 5.25 million immigrants arrived, more than in the first six decades of the nineteenth century. This wave was dominated by Irish, German, and English workers. Scandinavia, Italy, and China sent scores of eager workers, normally men, to fill the expanding labor needs of the United States. To attract this much-needed labor force, railroad and steamship companies advertised throughout Europe and China the glories of American life. To an economically depressed world, it was a welcome call.

The national wealth in 1890 was $65 billion; nearly $40 billion was invested in land and buildings, $9 billion in railroads, and $4 billion in manufacturing and mining. By 1890, 25 percent of the world's output of coal was mined in the United States. Annual production of crude petroleum went from 500,000 barrels in 1860 to 63.6 million in 1900. This was more than the wealth of Great Britain, Russia, and Germany put together.

Despite all the signs of economic growth and prosperity, America's late-nineteenth-century economy was profoundly unstable. Industrial expansion was undercut by a depression from 1882 to 1885, followed in 1893 by a five-year-long economic collapse that devastated rural and urban communities across America. As a result, job security for workers just climbing onto the industrial stage was often fleeting. Few wage-earners found full-time work for the entire year. The unevenness in the economy was caused both by the level of change under way and irresponsible speculation, but more generally to the stubborn adherence of the federal government to a highly inflexible gold standard as the basis of value for currency.

Between the very wealthy and the very poor emerged a new middle stratum, whose appearance was one of the distinctive features of late-nineteenth-century America. The new middle class fueled the purchase of one million light bulbs a year by 1890, even though the first electric light was only 11 years old. It was the middle class also that flocked to buy Royal Baking Powder, (which was easier to use and faster than yeast) and supported the emergence and spread of department stores that were sprouting up across the nation.

This group was largely composed of people of old American stock or immigrants from the British Isles who worked as either self-employed businessmen or at professional jobs. Merchant tailors, who once labored alongside their employees, began to dress more elegantly, received their customers in well-appointed shops, and hid the actual manufacturing process in a back room.

1883 Family Profile

This 30-year-old man, Gareth Rowlands, has worked for the Pennsylvania Railroad for a dozen years, primarily as a construction engineer; his work requires that he determine the exact route of each new railroad line, a job requiring considerable construction knowledge and excellent negotiating skills. He and his wife, Margaret, have two small children.

Annual Income: $1,300

Annual Budget

The average per capita consumer expenditure in 1883 is not available.

Life at Home

- Gareth Rowlands was born in Montgomery County, Pennsylvania, on an estate that has been the home of his father's family for five generations.
- His ancestors arrived from Wales in the late 1600s; they have long been members of the Society of Friends.
- He began his education at the Lower Merion Academy, completing his early studies at the Rensselaer Polytechnic Institute, which he entered at age 15.
- After one year of postgraduate work, he completed his formal education at age 18.
- He married Margaret, a girl well-known to the family, when they both turned 20; they have two children.
- At her insistence, they attend the Roman Catholic Church, which has 12 million members nationwide.
- The number of immigrants flooding the city is taxing the ability of the church to care for everyone; many of the ethnic groups do not like worshipping together.
- Like many of their friends, they have collected several etchings from Winslow Homer, Joseph Baker, and Foxcroft Cole, displaying these prints in the parlor where they can be seen by visitors.

Gareth Rowlands has worked for the Pennsylvania Railroad for 12 years.

- In his spare time, he loves to sail and take excursion steamers to Cape May, south of the city.
- He and his wife especially enjoy taking time off at the Bryn Mawr resort, now connected to the city by the Pennsylvania Railroad; the development of the line was one of his projects.
- He dreams of building a summer home there, but cannot afford two houses; publisher George W. Childs just completed an enormous residence in the style of a Swiss chalet.
- The extension of the Pennsylvania Railroad to Chestnut Hill is generating similar excitement and development.
- Recently the Wissahickon Inn was completed; its architectural form is "Old English," now in vogue for suburban hotels.
- But not all change is acceptable. With the development of the telegraph and telephone, dozens of overhead wires now dangle from 4,000 poles across the city.
- Many in the city, including key officials with the railroad, believe the wires are a symbol of the city's progress; to control the proliferation of telegraph poles, the city has passed an ordinance prohibiting new poles without a city permit.
- Philadelphia's first telephone directory, published in 1878, contains 47 names.
- Already recognized for his expertise at work, Gareth is being urged by many within the railroad community to be more politically active as a way to get ahead, since many men are becoming rich overnight through their association with local politics.
- Recently he was asked to join a group informally called the "All Night Poker Players," composed of powerful business and political interests—evidence that his time has come.
- He is now in contact with men who have made fortunes investing in the refining of gasoline, the creation of a telephone network, and land development.
- His expertise and responsibility for determining where railroad lines will be laid could make him a valuable member of the group, some believe.
- At a recent gathering he met John Wanamaker, whose department store is the talk of Philadelphia, and listened to a talk by Edwin J. Houston, who produced the Thomson-Houston arc light.
- Just last year, the Brush Electric Light Company installed lighting on Chestnut Street at its own expense to demonstrate the value of electricity.

Life at Work

- Railroading as a whole is enjoying great prosperity; despite labor problems and complaints about rates, it operates a virtual monopoly.
- Railroad men are respected members of the community, a construction engineer especially so.
- In 1830 the United States had 41 miles of railway track, while in 1883, it boasts 115,000 miles. It currently costs about $40,000 per mile to lay track.
- Railroading is not simply part of the American infrastructure in 1883; it *is* the American infrastructure.

- The gross earnings of the American railway companies last year was $752 million; $552 million of which was from freight earnings and $173 million from passenger traffic.
- In the past 10 years, freight traffic has tripled, while passenger travel has doubled.
- The increases demand major improvements and additions to keep the traffic flowing.
- His first job on the railroad was as a rodman on an engineering corps to locate the line of Pennsylvania's Mountain Division, a particularly difficult section over the Allegheny Mountains.
- His next engineering assignment involved projecting a line from Philadelphia to Bethlehem, Pennsylvania.
- Despite continuing competition, the Pennsylvania Railroad Company continues to pay its stockholders a regular return.
- To meet customer demands, the Pennsylvania Railroad Company recently purchased the Philadelphia and Baltimore Central Railroad Company, which formed a back road between Philadelphia and the Susquehanna River.
- The rail line is considered a "farmers' railroad" because so much of the area through which it passes is agricultural; subscriptions from farmers paid for the road, guaranteeing that it would stop at certain farm towns.

Despite competition, the Pennsylvania Railroad pays a regular dividend.

Railways in the United States, by Simon Sterne, 1912:

"In many instances the seemingly excessive profits made in the United States by railway building were but a fair and natural return for the great risks incurred. In the event of success, the men who had the foresight and boldness to invest their capital in building lines like the Transcontinental Pacific through the territory of hostile tribes of Indians, across plains and over deserts, at the risk of life and fortune, deserved considerable remuneration for their boldness and their enterprise. Differences of opinion may honestly be entertained whether they have not been overpaid, and whether the methods adopted through the instrumentality of political chicanery were in the least justifiable. These matters apart, however, it must be conceded that, but for the inducement held out of every large profit through the instrumentality of fictitious capitalization and subsidies of land or money, many of the newer territories of the United States would have been unsupplied by railways."

A section of track is called The Farmer's Railroad because subscriptions from farmers paid for it.

- The Pennsylvania regularly carries oil from the western part of the state; some oil producers are so angry about freight rates they are talking about developing pipelines to ship their own oil. Rowlands is convinced the cost is too high and too impractical.
- Railroading's recent history is marked by bitter labor wars, increasing competition, and continuing reductions in freight rates.
- The Great Strike of 1877 stopped railroad traffic for a week in cities as distant as Pittsburgh and Chicago; French and German socialists, most railroad men believe, were responsible—not the recent wage cuts announced for the rail lines.
- Currently, many farmers are blaming the railroads for luring people away from the farms and small towns into the cities.
- The Pennsylvania has begun double tracking their lines to provide faster travel.
- Newer and stronger locomotives are presenting challenges; their ability to travel at faster speeds makes the tracks unstable on the curves.
- Safety devices, such as the automatic couplers invented by Eli Hamilton Janney following the Civil War, were installed on all trains and are saving lives.
- More important was the air brake which allows railroads to run faster and use heavier trains now that the hand brake could be eliminated.
- Rowlands' company is currently installing new signals to improve efficiency; the tracks have become so congested that movement must be controlled by space rather than time.
- Battery-operated circuit controls signal automatically within a block, allowing multiple trains to travel safely.

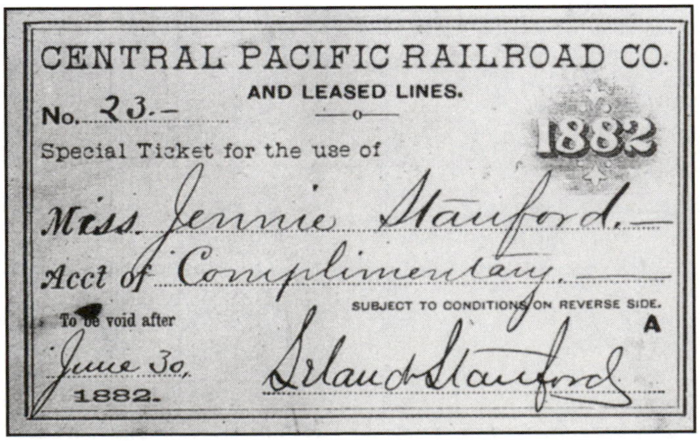
CENTRAL PACIFIC RAILROAD CO.
AND LEASED LINES.
No. 23.-
1882
Special Ticket for the use of
Miss Jennie Stanford.
Acct of Complimentary.
SUBJECT TO CONDITIONS ON REVERSE SIDE.
A
To be void after
June 30,
1882.
Leland Stanford

"Lorenzo Coffin, American Characters," by Richard F. Snow, *American Heritage Magazine*, October/November 1979:

"In 1874 an Iowa farmer named Lorenzo Coffin watched the train he was riding hook on to a freight car. A brakeman stood between the car and the train, ready to couple them. He miscalculated, and Coffin saw the man fall to the ground shrieking, two fingers sheared from his right hand.

Anyone would have been disturbed by that brutal vignette, but Coffin was more than disturbed; the brakeman's misfortune changed the course of Coffin's life and, in time, saved the lives of thousands. . . . He started talking to railroad men, and learned that the accident he had seen was hardly unique. The railroads used link-and-pin couplers, savage devices which were locked by a brakeman dropping a pin between two iron loops as they came together. It was easy enough for a brakeman, darting between approaching cars, to lose his fingers, his hand, his life. Moreover, when the trainmen weren't coupling cars, they were on top of them, bucking along unsteadily above the roadbed, setting hand brakes. In fact, a trainman had one of the most hazardous peacetime occupations on earth; 20,000 to 30,000 were maimed or killed each year.

Coffin, appalled, persisted: Were there no safety devices available to the railroads? Yes. Eli Janney had already patented an automatic coupler that locked like two hands clasping, and George Westinghouse had developed a workable air brake that could stop a train by controls in the locomotive.

Why weren't these in use? The railroad officials' bland, obdurate answer was that their installation was "impracticable"—that is to say, expensive. The dollar and fifty cents a day that the trainman earned made him responsible for his own injuries. Air brakes and automatic couplers cost the lines money; maimed railroad men cost nothing.

As Coffin asked his questions, his interest grew into fanaticism. At 51 years of age, he started off on a 20-year crusade. 'My first job,' he wrote, 'was to arouse the public to this awful wrong, this butchering of these faithful men who were serving the people at such a fearful risk of life and limb. Why, I discovered that it was taken as a matter of course that railroad men of necessity be maimed and killed.'

The public was not, he found, easily aroused. Coffin appeared in railroad offices, only to be thrown out. In an age when railroads could buy senators, they had little time to spare for a scrawny, bearded do-gooder. Coffin wrote to newspapers, but his stories were rarely printed. Religious and farming periodicals were the only platforms he could find, and there his vivid harangues appeared, in between essays on sheep dipping and accounts of parish goings-on.

Coffin kept on the move, traveling around the state, telling horror stories. In 1883 he managed to get himself appointed Iowa's first railroad commissioner. The commissioner wrote thousands of letters, and attended every gathering of railroad officials that did not forcibly reject him. The railroad managers knew him as the 'Air-Brake Fanatic' by now; he had at least attracted enough attention to get his arguments answered. Too expensive to install, a Chicago & Alton official told him once. 'But I note,' Coffin yelled back, 'that the Chicago & Alton and most other lines continue to pay their eight percent dividends regularly.'

Changing his tactics slightly, Coffin started badgering the Master Car-Builders' Association to test the air brakes on a freight train. Finally, in 1886, the trials were held—and were a total failure. . . . So yet another series of trials was scheduled late that summer. Again [George] Westinghouse was there, and Coffin stood next to him on a long grade outside Burlington. A Chicago, Burlington & Quincy locomotive started downgrade with 50 cars swaying behind it. When

(continued)

"Lorenzo Coffin, American Characters" . . . *(continued)*

the train hit 40 miles an hour, the engineer put on the air. The freight shuddered to a dead stop with scarcely a jar, and within 500 feet.

The gaunt old fighter stood watching it with tears on his face. 'I am the happiest man in all Creation,' he said.

Coffin's battle wasn't over, though. He drafted the first railroad safety appliance act, saw it become state law, and saw it universally ignored. He kept up the pressure, wrote and spoke, campaigned throughout the country. At last, in March of 1893, a bill requiring all American railroads to adopt air brakes and automatic couplers came before President Benjamin Harrison. The President signed it into law and gave the pen to Coffin.

The next year, casualties among trainmen dropped 60 percent."

Life in the Community: Philadelphia, Pennsylvania

- Philadelphia began as part of a quasi-religious utopian experiment of William Penn, who established the central area of the city in 1683.
- The grid pattern of streets and properties reflected both his aesthetic preference for order and his skill as a real estate developer.
- The city grew rapidly and Penn prospered.
- By 1800 rowhouses had become the dominant form of residence in the city.
- They were attractive and cheap to maintain with brick facades and attached party walls.
- The success of the Pennsylvania Railroad, incorporated in 1846 to build a line from Harrisburg to Pittsburgh, was considered an economic necessity if Philadelphia was to hold its own; the first Pennsylvania train to make the trip over its own tracks all the way from Philadelphia to Pittsburgh took place in July 1858.

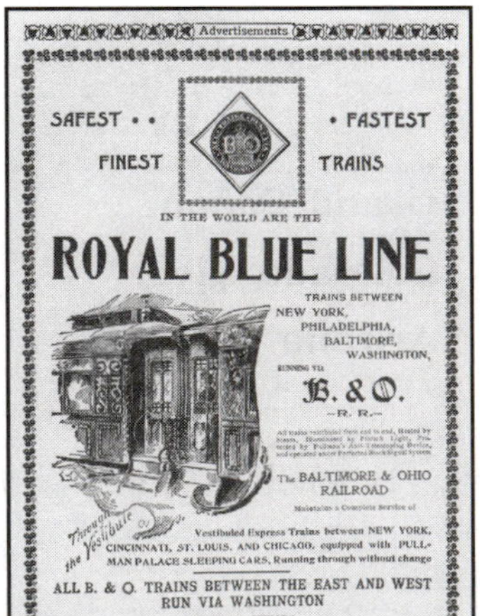

Rowlands loves to sail and takes excursions to Cape May in his spare time.

- The Philadelphia Bank was a key founder of the railroad, buying stock in the venture.
- When the industrial revolution occurred in Philadelphia, most of the available land close to the city was occupied by political, commercial, or residential activity.
- This historical development pattern spurred industrial development up and down the Delaware River.
- By 1880 the leading industry was clothing and textiles, employing 40 percent of the city's work force.
- Other key industries included machine tools and hardware, shoe and boot manufacturing, paper and printing, iron, and steel.
- Most establishments were small, the result of financial conservatives in Philadelphia, who preferred to operate on a cash basis instead of borrowing to finance plants, equipment, and inventories.
- Second in size only to New York, the population of the city in 1883 is approximately 1.3 million, largely as a result of massive foreign immigration.
- The city's favorite playground is Fairmount Park, visited in June by half a million people; in addition, 5,400 equestrians canter along its bridle paths, while 95,000 horse-drawn carriages parade down its drives.

Letter to the Editor, the *Philadelphia Public Ledger*, August 1882:

"No resident west of Broad Street desires the electric light. Would any one of the editors or owners of the daily paper like one in front of his private dwelling? Would Mayor King or any members of Council be delighted with one in front of his sleeping chamber? There is no city in the world where it would be tolerated in a street occupied almost entirely by private residences as West Chestnut Street is. Do you admire the six red poles in each square?"

Margaret Rowlands at afternoon tea.

- Squat little paddle-wheel vessels make regular runs from Fairmount landing, some by moonlight.
- Six ferry lines along the Delaware connect Philadelphia with opposite points on the Jersey shore; the cost is $0.03.
- Although the *Philadelphia Evening Bulletin* has the highest circulation in the city, residents have a choice of 17 newspapers, many in foreign languages to meet the needs of the new immigrants.
- Citizens of Philadelphia also may choose among 36 different banks.

Historical Snapshot
1883–1884

- The Brooklyn Bridge opened to traffic in New York
- The Northern Pacific Railroad line was completed
- The *Ladies' Home Journal* began publication; Cyrus H.K. Curtis was the publisher
- Thomas Edison invented the radio tube
- The nation's first skyscraper was built in Chicago, totaling 10 stories
- Nationwide 367 hospitals have been established
- U.S. frontiersman W.F. "Buffalo Bill" Cody organized his touring "Wild West Show"
- The first malted milk was produced in Racine, Wisconsin
- The first successful pea-podder machine was installed in Owasco, New York, replacing 600 cannery workers
- American author and feminist Lillie Devereaux Blake published *Women's Place Today*
- The Linotype typesetting machine was patented by Ottmar Mergenthaler, revolutionizing newspaper composing rooms
- More than 80 percent of the petroleum from the United States was marketed by John D. Rockefeller's Standard Oil Trust
- The Waterman pen was invented by New York insurance agent Lewis Edson Waterman
- Montgomery Ward's mail order catalogue offered 10,000 items

THE

GLOBE NAIL

THE BEST

Horse Shoe Nail

EVER MADE.

About ten years ago, The Globe Nail Company, of Boston, put on the market the first pointed, polished, and finished Horse Shoe Nails ready for driving. Previous to that time all Horse Shoe Nails were pointed, and most of them made by the shoers in their own shops.

The Globe Nail was at once found to be much cheaper and better than any then in use. It soon became so popular that all manufacturers of Horse Shoe Nails were compelled to make their Nails to resemble the Globe. For the last ten years it has been the model. Each year the Nail has been greatly improved in quality, and to such a point have we educated the shoers, that now they will hardly use a nail unless it is absolutely perfect.

At the Centennial Exposition in Philadelphia, we were awarded the Medal and the following report, far stronger than that given upon any other Nail:

INTERNATIONAL EXHIBITION, 1876, U. S. CENTENNIAL COMMISSION

[BUREAU OF AWARDS.]

PHILADELPHIA, June 22, 1876.

1883 ECONOMIC PROFILE

Income, Standard Jobs

Bricklayers	$3.23/day/60 hrs. per week
Carpenters and Joiners	$2.57/day/60 hrs. per week
Engineers, Stationary	$2.24/day/64 hrs. per week
Farm Labor	$1.25/day/63 hrs. per week
Firemen	$1.50/day/60 hrs. per week
Glassblowers, Bottle	$4.23/day/51 hrs. per week
Hod Carriers	$1.94/day/60 hrs. per week
Marble Cutters	$2.69/day/60 hrs. per week
Painters	$3.25/day/58 hrs. per week
Plasterers	$2.98/day/59 hrs. per week
Plumbers	$3.50/day/58 hrs. per week
Stonemasons	$3.31/day/60 hrs. per week

Selected Prices

Alfred Peats Wallpaper, per Roll	$0.15
Anti-Skeet Pesticide	$0.10
Baby Educator Crackers, Six to a Box	$0.20
Chromo Business Cards	$0.05
Dental Fee, Silver Filling	$0.50

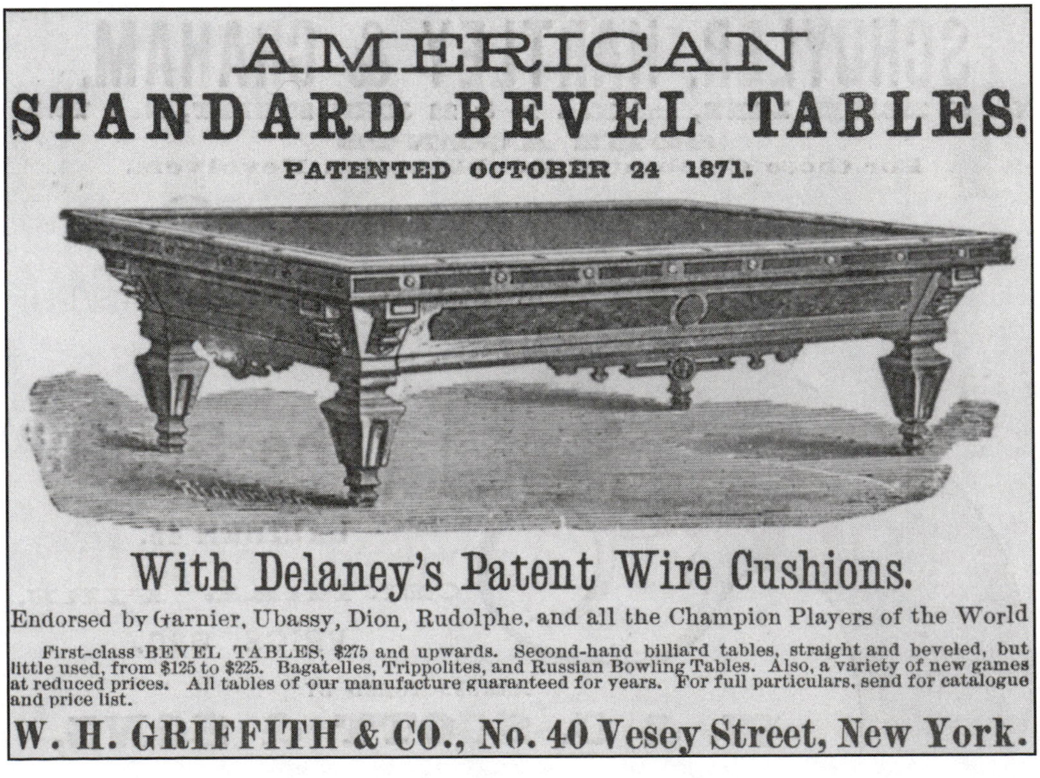

Featherbone Corset $0.18
Hall Typewriter $40.00
Keep's Collar for Men $0.15
Kenton Baking Powder $0.20
Lemonoide Furniture Polish $0.50
Metcalf Writing Paper, 72 Sheets $0.75
Milson's Patent Ozone Disinfectant,
Small $8.00
New Hygeia Bust Form $0.50
Royal Argard Burner and Chimney $1.25
Sun Parasol for Women $0.50
The Great American
Aquarium Ticket, Adult $0.50
Tuition, West Branch
Boarding School, per Year $225.00
Van Camp's Pork & Beans $0.06
Wamsutta Muslin Shirt $1.00
Williams Shaving Soap,
Six Round Cakes $0.40

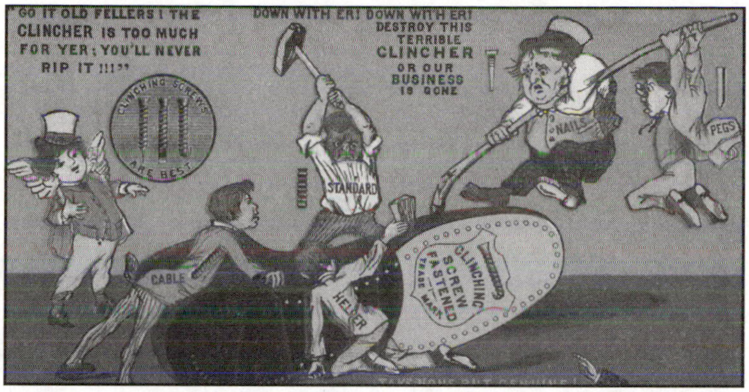

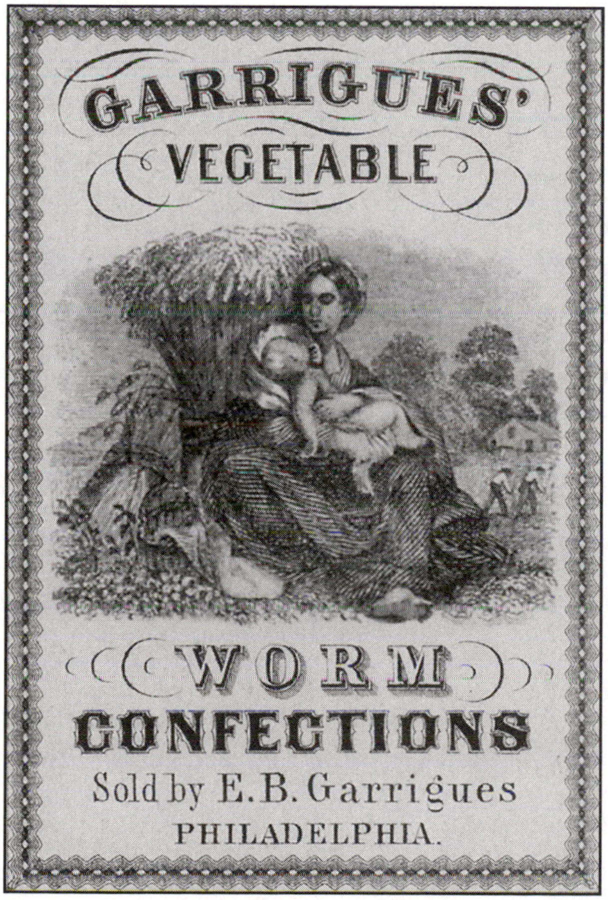

SEASONABLE COSTUMES FOR CHILDREN.

"Mirror Fashions, New Designs for Spring," *Demorest's Monthly Magazine*, 1883:

"Among the features of the new designs for the spring and summer season are neatness and perfect practicability. The novelty is less striking than the beauty and simplicity, which is shown in the elegance of form and the absence of superfluous puffery.

The over-garments for suits exhibit particular evidence of this fact. The first one to which we shall call attention is the 'Helena' polonaise. A very ladylike garment, suited to cashmere, poplin, silk, or any kind of washing goods or grenadine, it is especially becoming in black grenadine, and may be trimmed with fine 'yak' or guipure lace.

The skirt worn with this polonaise may be trimmed with graduated flounces or kilt-plaiting. If the latter, the front breadth should be composed wholly of the plaiting laid lengthwise from the top to the bottom, the sides and back being arranged to form plaited flounces. If gathered flounces are required, as for grenadine, then the flounces upon the front breadth must be extended to the waist."

Railroad Passenger Traffic

- The ability of American railroads to move people in style promoted the nineteenth century development of resort hotels, spas, national parks, and scenic wonderlands.
- The train made it possible for ordinary Americans to take their rest at the seashore, at a cool lake, or in the mountains—far removed from the city.
- Trains also led to the development of bedroom suburbs, allowing workers to live farther and farther from their place of business.
- In 1883, Philadelphia riders could choose among 13 separate passenger railways within the city, operating more than 1,200 cars pulled by over 7,000 horses on 264 miles of track.
- The track mileage was increasing yearly, extending the horsecar lines into the suburban sections and quickening development of rural farmlands.
- Just last year the Union line, inspired by the examples of San Francisco and Chicago, built a cable road on Columbia Avenue from Twenty-Third Street to the east entrance of Philadelphia's famous Fairmount Park.
- After 1880 a pattern of railroad commuting to bedroom suburbs was a fixture of American social life.
- Nearly all cities of any size, especially those in the East, developed railroad commuting.
- Four cities—New York, Boston, Philadelphia, and Chicago—were developing vast and complex networks of commuter rail lines.
- Accommodating commuter traffic provided business, but was not as profitable as freight, which made fewer demands, required less stops, and could be picked up and delivered at remote, less expensive facilities.

Trains led to the development of bedroom communities outside Philadelphia.

"The Greatest Medical Discovery since the Creation of Man, or since the Commencement of the Christian Era," advertisement, 1883:

"There never has been a time when the healing of so many different diseases has been caused by outward application as the present. It is an undisputed fact that over half of the entire population of the globe resorts to the use of ordinary plasters.

Dr. Melvin's Capsicum Porous Plasters are acknowledged by all who have used them to act quicker than any other plaster they ever before tried, and that one of these plasters will do more real service than a hundred of the ordinary kind. All other plasters are slow to action, and require to be worn continually to effect a cure; but with these it is entirely different: the instant one is applied the patient will feel its effect.

Physicians in all ages have thoroughly tested and well know the effect of Capsicum; and it has always been more or less used as a medical agent for an outward application, but it is only of very recent date that its advantages in a porous plaster have been discovered. Being, however, convinced of the wonderful cures effected by Dr. Melvin's Capsicum Porous Plasters and their superiority over all other plasters, they now actually prescribe them, in their practice, for such diseases as rheumatism, pain in the side and back, and all such cases as have required the use of plasters or liniments. After you have tried other plasters or liniments, and they have failed, and you want a certain cure, ask your druggist for Dr. Melvin's Capsicum Porous Plaster, and take no other; or on receipt of $0.25 for one, $1.00 for five, or $2.00 for a dozen, they will be mailed, post paid, to any address in the United States or Canada. Novelty Plaster Works, Lowell, Mass, U.S.A."

1888 Family Profile

Karl Watson and his family of six moved from Union County in upstate South Carolina to San Antonio, Texas, 16 years ago to escape the ravages of poverty and political upheaval that followed the Civil War; they quickly established a cattle ranch that now covers several thousand acres.

Annual Income: Unknown

Annual Budget

The average per capita consumer expenditure in 1888 is not available.

Life at Home

- The Watsons are refugees of the Civil War; similar families are often nicknamed GTTs because of the "Gone to Texas" signs they left behind.
- They originated in Union County, South Carolina, near the North Carolina border where they farmed cotton; the man and one of his sons fought in the War. They owned no slaves prior to the conflict.
- After the war ended, the cost of cotton and vegetable seeds was high, labor was difficult to find, and the federal troops were determined to charge this man with violating the rights of the freed slaves.
- Karl and his family left everything behind and moved west. Although he was not involved in the violence against the former slaves, as a community leader, he was expected to stop it.

Karl Watson moved his family to Texas to escape the turmoil in the south that followed the Civil War.

South Carolina Ku Klux Klan Trials 1871–1872, Federal Intervention and Southern Resistance, by Lou Falkner Williams:

"President Grant determined to do everything in his power to stop the lawlessness in South Carolina despite his sensitivity to the charge he was a military despot. Following the recommendation of (U.S. Attorney General Amos) Akerman and Senator John Scott, chairman of the Joint Congressional Investigation Committee, Grant issued a proclamation on 12 October 1871 which commanded 'all persons composing the unlawful combinations and conspiracies' to turn their weapons and disguises over to a United States marshal and dispense to their homes within five days. Such a proclamation was required by law before the writ of habeas corpus could be suspended. As expected, Klansmen in South Carolina ignored the presidential order. Thus the President issued a second proclamation on 17 November that declared a nine-county area of upcountry South Carolina to be in a state of rebellion. Grant suspended habeas corpus in those counties, an act that was unprecedented in the United States during peacetime—if the Reconstruction era in South Carolina can properly be called a time of peace. The suspension of habeas corpus was tactically important because it enabled federal officials to make mass arrests quickly. Large numbers of Klansmen were arrested and jailed without the usual procedures of due process. . . . Government authorities made large numbers of arrests quickly, most of them in the daytime and with very little resistance. Finding suspects became more and more difficult as the Klansmen took to the mountains. Many of the more affluent Ku Klux members had fled the country as soon as Grant issued his initial proclamation. . . . It is difficult to overestimate the effects of the arrests on the upcountry. . . . virtually every family was affected."

- The small house they first built is now used by the field hands. Their Texas home is a duplication of the house left behind in South Carolina, including a spacious central hallway running the length of the house, high ceilings, and towering square columns on the wraparound porch.
- Although Watson and his sons have prospered in Texas, his wife, Charlotte, is less thrilled; she misses her family, friends, and the opportunity to buy nice things.
- She corresponds regularly with her relatives in South Carolina and misses the beauty of spring. She longs for servants who speak English, finding Spanish to be a very trying language.
- Charlotte hates the weather and the lack of water; when washing clothing, the water is often so dirty, the clothes are no better off for the effort.
- She also wants a more refined life, regularly buying perfumes and scents to make her day smell better, and waiting anxiously for the once-a-week train to get packages she has ordered from Boston, Charleston, and New York.

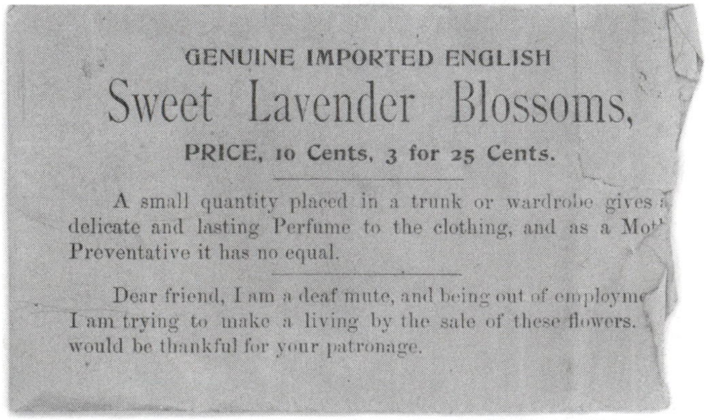
GENUINE IMPORTED ENGLISH
Sweet Lavender Blossoms,
PRICE, 10 Cents, 3 for 25 Cents.
A small quantity placed in a trunk or wardrobe gives a delicate and lasting Perfume to the clothing, and as a Mot Preventative it has no equal.
Dear friend, I am a deaf mute, and being out of employme I am trying to make a living by the sale of these flowers. would be thankful for your patronage.

Charlotte Watson carries a package of Sweet Lavender Blossoms, purchased in Charleston, in her dress pocket to remind her of home and reduce the leather-soaked sweat smell of cowhands.

The ranch includes more than 25,000 head of cattle.

Life at Work

- This family presides over a cattle herd of 25,000 head; last year he sold 5,000 animals and grossed $90,000.
- Karl is using his profits to upgrade the farm, buy additional land, and upgrade his cattle.
- When the family arrived, they had little knowledge of ranching, but he was able to bring sufficient capital to buy quality land and cattle.
- After hiring a few cowhands, he purchased a herd of beef cattle, instructed the hired help to round up wild cattle on the open range, and began acquiring neighboring land.
- The first few years brought high prices for beef; now he plans on doubling the size of the herd by allowing them to graze on public lands.
- Many of his neighbors are now financing their herd expansion with money from foreign investors—primarily Europe—but he doesn't like to have partners, especially partners who only provide money and no labor.
- He also dislikes the claims being made to investors; Walter Baron von Richthofen's recent book, *Cattle Raising on the Plains of North America*, claims "there is not the slightest element of uncertainty in cattle-raising."
- James S. Brisbin claims in *The Beef Bonanza; or How to Get Rich on the Plains*, that $250,000 borrowed at 10 percent and invested in cattle will yield $810,000 in five years.

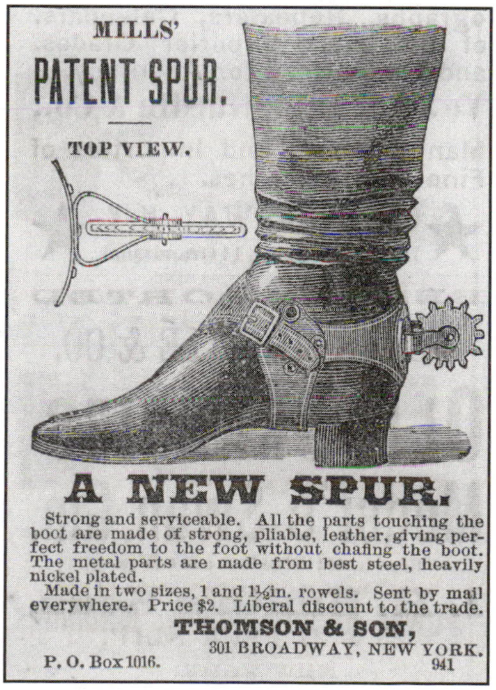

Until the 1850s, pork dominated America's meat supply.

- The cattle industry of the San Antonio area has been growing rapidly for many years; Mexican landowners gave the area its start when they abandoned the land and animals after the Mexican War, turning loose more than 300,000 beef cattle.
- Ranchers from the East and South quickly took advantage of the open lands, wild beef, and established ranches.
- For most of America's history, pork dominated the meat supply of cities; in the 1850s, tastes shifted to beef, driving up demand.
- Chicago, already the "Hog Butcher of the World," emerged from the Civil War as the major meat-packing center of the nation, including beef.

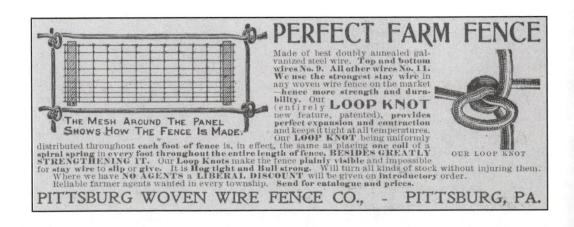

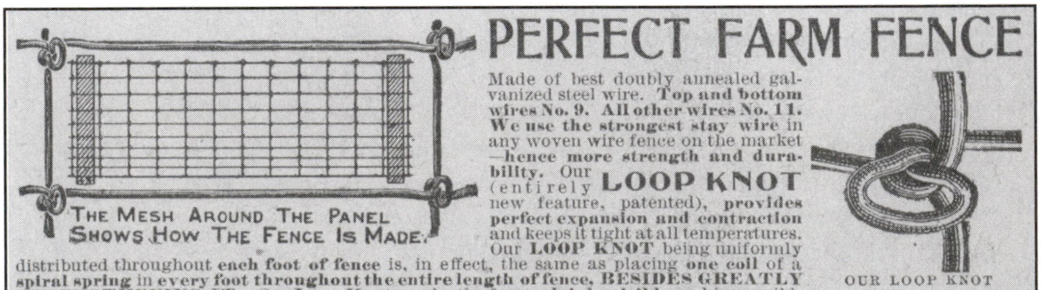

The Log of a Cowboy, by Andy Adams:

"For generations cattle had grazed wild on the plains of the Southwest, too far distant from market to have any value. In 1867 the Kansas Pacific Railroad began to reach out into the Plains, and in that year J.G. McCoy established the first of the cow towns—Abilene, Kansas, from which live cattle could be shipped to the stock markets of the East. Then began the long drive.

The next morning by daybreak the cattle were thrown off the bed ground and started grazing before the sun could dry out what little moisture the grass had absorbed during the night. The heat of the past week had been very oppressive, and in order to avoid it as much as possible, we made late and early drives. Before the wagon passed the herd during the morning drive, what few canteens we had were filled with water for the men. The remuda was kept with the herd, and four changes of mounts were made during the day, in order not to exhaust any one horse. Several times, for an hour or more, the herd was allowed to lie down and rest, but by the middle of the afternoon thirst made them impatient and restless, and the point men were compelled to ride steadily in the lead in order to hold the cattle to a walk. A number of times during the afternoon we attempted to graze them, but not until the twilight of evening was it possible.

We were handling the cattle as humanely as possible under the circumstances. The guards for the night were doubled, six men on the first half and the same on the latter, Bob Blades being detailed to assist Honeyman in night-herding the saddle horse. If any of us got more than an hour's sleep that night, he was lucky. Flood, McCann, and the horse wranglers did not even try to rest. To those of us who could find time to eat, our cook kept open house. Our foreman knew that a well-fed man can stand an incredible amount of hardship and appreciated the fact that on the trail a good cook is a valuable asset. Our outfit, therefore, was cheerful to a man, and jokes and songs helped to while away the weary hours of the night."

- In the 1870s, before refrigeration, most cattle sold in Chicago were shipped East for butchering.
- Using industrialized slaughter techniques developed for hogs, the western expansion of the railroad network, and the development of refrigeration, Chicago brought beef to the tables of America.
- Beef did especially well during the boom times of the early 1870s and the early 1880s; when the economy slumped, the cattle business slowed immediately.
- This man and his sons quickly "learned cow" so they could expand their holdings and get the best breeding stock.
- Properly raised, a $4.00 yearling can turn into a $20.00 steer or heifer in just three years.
- In Texas, generally a single cow needs 10 acres of grass to graze in if the land is good; twice as much if the land is dry.
- Each cow drinks up to 30 gallons a day, so every consideration of cattle ranching revolves around water.
- A small river runs through Karl's property; he wants to control the headwaters so he can expand further. Controlling the lands bordering a stream often includes the exclusive rights to a much larger area of range land lying along the stream.

Each cow drinks up to 30 gallons of water a day.

- The oldest son has been told he can keep the fourth calf born; in just two years he has accumulated 250 head.
- Their focus now is acquiring additional land that includes water. They have learned to locate water by watching swallows: if the birds carry mud for nest building in their mouths, a water hole lies in the direction from which they came.
- They have learned other tricks, including how to recognize different grasses and to judge the freshness of a hoofprint by counting the insect tracks across it.
- The Watson family has begun to maximize its income through specialization; calves survive better in Texas, but fatten faster in the grasslands of Nebraska.
- They are now focusing on breeding stock and shipping cattle north at two years; a steer in Nebraska at age four weighs 1,200 pounds, while the same animal in Texas only grows to 900 pounds.
- Under this system, cattle are often owned by three or four companies before they are led to slaughter in Chicago.
- Specialization also means that if a cattle glut hits the market, similar to the one in 1885, it is the northern ranchers who are most at risk; the cattle ranchers in Texas can hold their cattle until prices go back up.

- Last year was especially worrisome; cattle worth $9.35 per hundred weight in 1882 were only bringing $1.00 for the same weight in 1887.
- He is also concerned about another strike; when the cowboys struck for higher wages in 1883, it required all the cattle ranchers working together to break the strike.
- Currently he employs mostly white cowboys, but has been told that Mexican cowboys will work at half the pay of Anglos.
- On this range, the hands are forbidden to gamble, drink, or carry six-shooters in their off hours; Karl Watson believes that liquor, gambling, and guns are a formula for someone dying.
- After losing hundreds of cattle on the drive north this past year, he is considering shipping his herd by rail; several in the association are also talking about ending the risky and time-consuming cattle drives, although currently rail rates are still very high.
- In addition, the American Humane Society has established a series of rules concerning the shipping of cattle by rail, which may make train travel more trouble than it's worth.
- Between drives, the cowboys on this cattle ranch spend much of their time stringing barbed wire along the property line to control the cattle; the wire controls the cattle, cuts labor costs, and protects the cows from inferior, free roaming bulls.
- In some parts of Texas the smaller cattle ranchers have violently objected to barbed wire fences, believing that the larger rangers were cutting them off from public lands.
- Even President Cleveland has gotten involved, issuing a federal order that he will prosecute illegal fencers who are using barbed wire to control public lands.
- Since the cowboys' strike, Watson and most ranchers in his area belong to a regional cattlemen's organization; working together the association holds round-ups in the spring to gather and brand newborn calves, helps establish registry of brands, and hires detectives to track down cattle thieves.
- Currently the association is fighting to persuade England to drop its embargo on American beef; the ban is designed to prevent pleuropneumonia, a fever prevalent in Texas, from reaching Europe.

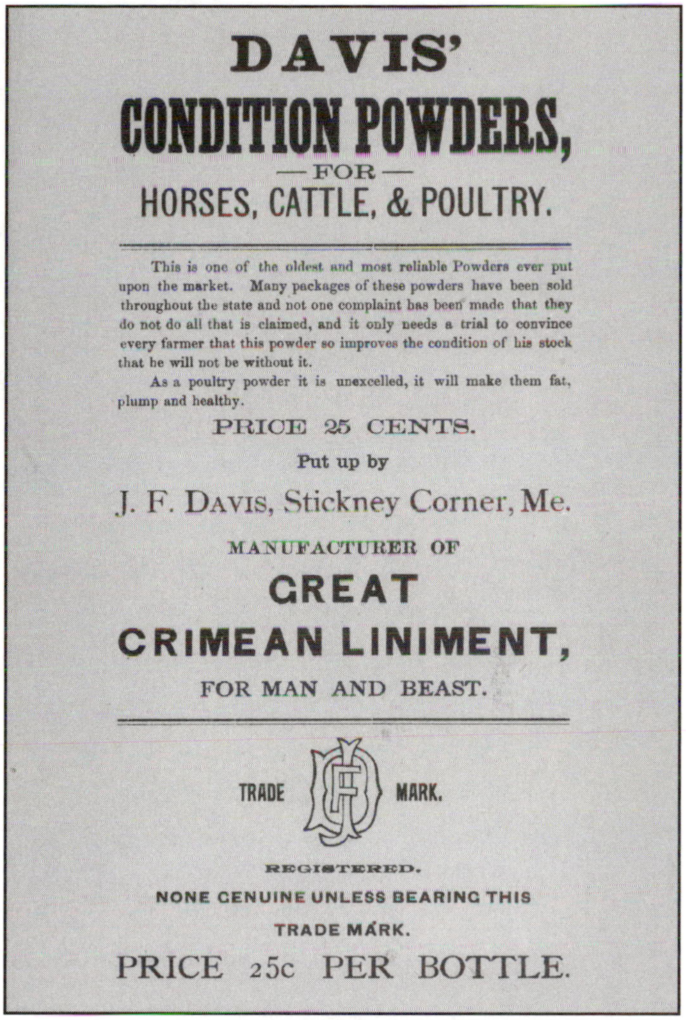

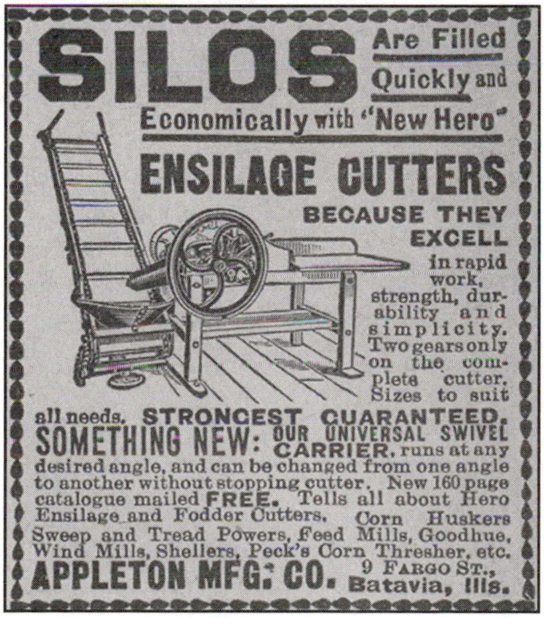

Life in the Community: San Antonio, Texas

- Founded as a Spanish mission in 1700, San Antonio has seen the flags of six countries fly over its city—Spain,

A typical late 1800s street scene by artist A. B. Frost.

Twenty-Five Years of Change in San Antonio, history and guide of 1892:

"Where stood the old adobe huts, magnificent iron, stone, and brick buildings are to be seen. Instead of the yell of the Comanche you hear the scream of the locomotive all round the city. Where the unsightly Mexican cart met the gaze, you see now the beautiful and convenient street cars, with their sleek, fat mules and their jingling bells. In the place of the mesquite thicket, where the coyote held his nightly revels, you see fine, broad avenues, lined on either side with beautiful and stately residences, surrounded with magnificent groves of shade trees and lovely gardens of flowers. Tall spires, piercing the skies, now mark the places where pious people assemble to worship God. The same spot was then occupied by the ravenous wolves that made the night hideous with their weird howls. . . . The cobblestone sidewalks have given place to the beautiful, broad, smooth artificial stone, and the rough cobblestones of the streets have been crushed and filled until they are as smooth as the shell streets of Galveston."

"Clubs for the Coyote Country's Gentry," *American Heritage*:

"No institution better symbolized the rise and power of the cattle barons than the extraordinary Cheyenne Club that Wyoming ranchmen built in 1880 to give themselves the comforts befitting their status. The three-story mansard-roofed, brick-and-wood building had wine vaults, two grand staircases, a smoking room, a reading room, a dining room, hardwood floors, and plush carpets.

Limited by charter to only 200 hand-picked members, the Cheyenne Club claimed, with some reason, to have the finest steward in America. And its deft servants were recruited by founding President Philip Dater in Canada, where, under the British flag, the tradition of genteel service still flourished. 'No wonder they like the club at Cheyenne,' wrote Western buff Owen Wister, who was himself a Philadelphia clubman. 'It's the pearl of the prairies. . .

Inside, members dressed for dinner on gala evenings in white tie and tails, which an old Nebraska member nicknamed 'Herefords' in honor of the white-chested, red-coated cattle. At dinner the members could savor such viands as caviar, pickled eels, French peas, and Roquefort cheese, together with liberal quantities of suitable drink and tobacco. . . Members were strictly accountable for their behavior: they were permitted no profanity, no drunkenness, no cheating at cards, no drinking in the reading room. And when Harry Oelrichs kicked a servant down the stairs the club kicked out Oelrichs. 'Ah, yes,' exclaimed a reminiscing English member, 'cow punching, as seen from the veranda of the Cheyenne Club, was a most attractive proposition.' "

France, Mexico, the Republic of Texas, the Confederate States of America, and the United States.

- The Alamo, where 185 men died in 1836 defending the city against a Spanish army for two weeks, and the Spanish Governor's Palace, are the town's landmarks.
- The economy of San Antonio just after Texas' independence was in ruins.
- Within 10 years, the economy began to improve thanks to large-scale smuggling across the Mexican border and the distribution of finished goods from the Northeast to the newly established ranches and farms of central and south Texas.
- Real prosperity came following the end of the Civil War; mercantile stores, trolley companies, water systems, and breweries all developed quickly, along with a barbed wire manufacturing company.
- By 1881 gas lights, which had flickered in the streets since 1866, were found in the houses of the most prosperous.
- Rail transportation came to San Antonio in the 1870s, connecting the city to Galveston, Texas, on the Gulf, followed in the 1880s by new rail lines running north to ship cattle and south into Mexico.
- As the cattle were shipped out, tourists were shipped in by rail.
- In the 20 years following the Civil War, the city's population increased 208 percent to 37,600.
- By 1882 the telephone exchange boasted 200 subscribers.

Charlotte Watson orders fine objects from Boston, Charleston, and New York.

- By 1888, ranging had become very big business in Texas; in the northern range and Texas alone, no less than 11 million cattle were pastured.
- Unlike many Southern cities, where the aftermath of the Civil War drove wedges between people, San Antonio's German, French, Spanish, and Anglo populations worked together.
- For example, the city's Easiest Street Car Company, organized in 1874, was jointly owned by a number of influential Germans and Anglos.

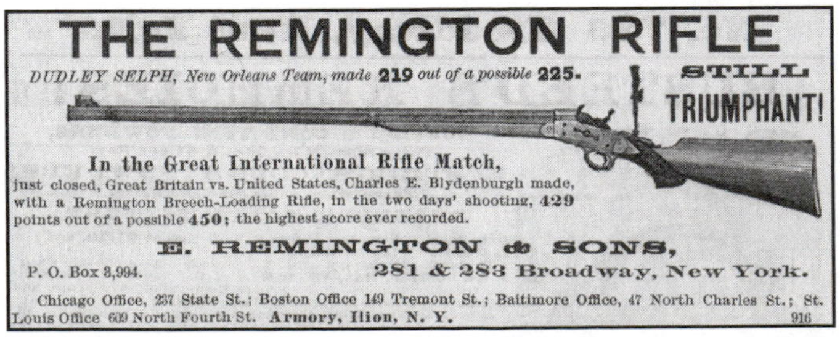

Historical Snapshot: 1888–1889

- The gramophone was invented
- Benjamin Harrison was elected president of the United States
- The alternating-current electric motor was developed
- Anti-Chinese riots erupted in Seattle
- *National Geographic Magazine* began publication
- The first typewriter stencil was introduced
- Parker Pen Company was started in Janesville, Wisconsin
- Tobacco merchant Washington B. Duke produced 744 million cigarettes
- The Ponce de Leon Hotel was opened in St. Augustine, Florida
- The Oklahoma Territory lands, formerly reserved for Indians, were opened to white settlers
- Safety Bicycle was introduced; more than one million would be sold in the next four years
- Electric lights were installed in the White House
- Aunt Jemima pancake flour was invented at St. Joseph, Missouri
- Calumet baking powder was created in Chicago
- "Jack the Ripper" murdered six women in London
- George Eastman perfected the "Kodak" box camera
- J.P. Dunlop invented the pneumatic tire
- Heinrich Hertz and Oliver Lodge independently identified radio waves as belonging to the same family as light waves

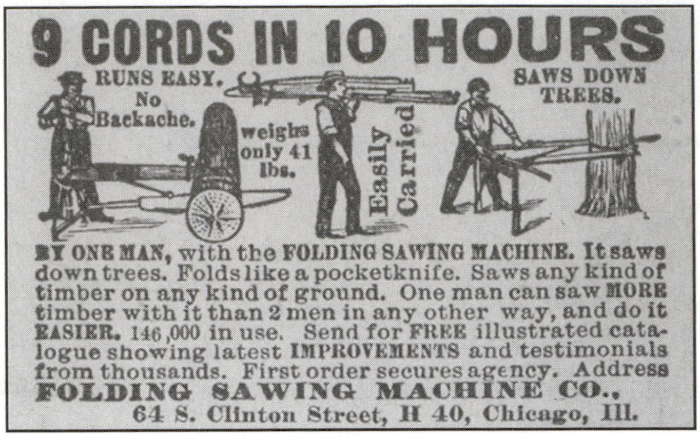

1888 Economic Profile

Income, Standard Jobs

Bricklayers	$3.30/day/56 hrs. per week
Carpenters and Joiners	$2.56/day/54 hrs. per week
Engineers, Stationary	$2.45/day/63 hrs. per week
Farm Labor	$1.40/day/63 hrs. per week
Firemen	$1.43/day/60 hrs. per week
Glassblowers, Bottle	$4.95/day/52 hrs. per week
Hod Carriers	$1.73/day/58 hrs. per week
Marble Cutters	$3.01/day/54 hrs. per week
Painters	$2.59/day/57 hrs. per week
Plasterers	$3.50/day/54 hrs. per week
Plumbers	$3.37/day/54 hrs. per week
Stonemasons	$3.37/day/55 hrs. per week

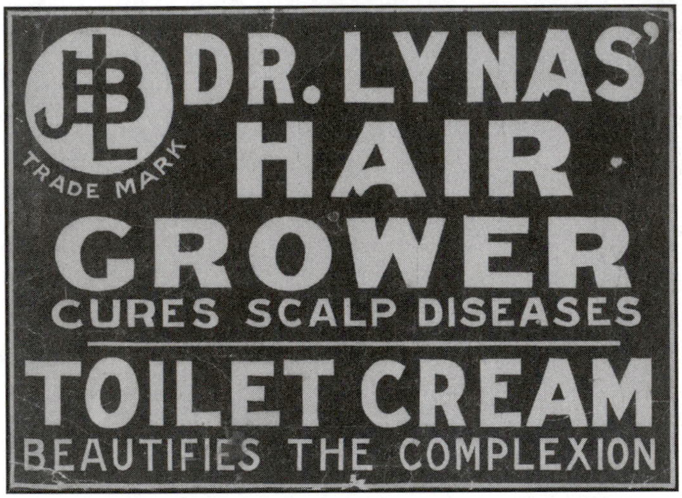

Selected Prices

Ayer's Cherry Pectoral	$1.00
Boraxine Detergent	$0.10
Cassimere Pants	$2.00
Chalmer's Gelatin; Two-Ounce Packets	$1.40/Dozen
Cotton Seeds, Duncan's Mammoth Prolific	$0.10
French China Dinner Set; 149 Pieces	$30.00
Hall Typewriter	$40.00
Hercules Corset	$3.00
Nickel-Plated Hair Curler	$0.50
Nobby Suit	$2.00
Nutmeg Grater	$0.25
Oxidized Silver Cuff Buttons	$0.25/Pair
Paper Dolls	$0.15
Photographs; President and Mrs. Harrison	$0.15
Raisin Grape Vines	$0.35
Royal Argand Burner and Chimney	$1.25
Rubber Roofing	$2.00/100 Square Feet
Silver-Plated Dinner Knives	$3.00/Dozen
Wills Richardson Lactated Food	$1.00
Woman's Evening Suit; All Wool	$6.00

The Disappearing Buffalo

- Early reports of the buffalo population at the time of Lewis and Clark range from 32 million to 75 million.
- Early explorers said that 3,000 buffalo could be seen in a single glance.

Few travelers crossed the great western plains without encountering buffalo herds.

- They were so dense and numerous the Indians said, "The country is one robe."
- Buffalo filled the continent; throughout Texas, they were common.
- Most buffalo cows produced one calf a year, adding 15 million buffalo a year to the population; they typically live 25 to 30 years and remain fertile most of their lives.
- Their numbers and movement frequently created deep, worn paths through pasture land and canebrake bottoms, opening the way for trappers and traders exploring the West.
- Their dried droppings, after about a year, were used for burning and fuel by native Americans and settlers alike.
- Their activities changed the western landscape; buffalo often denuded areas of grassland consuming the same amount as would four deer.
- They also destroyed corn fields, stopped trains, and knocked down tepees.
- The availability of quality meat made living far easier; some settlers found that following the buffalo made for a better living than growing wheat, corn, or barley.
- The presence of buffalo on the Kansas plains slowed the introduction of cattle; the homesteader was able to eat free buffalo and spend his money for plows and seed.
- Few travelers crossed the great western plains without describing the buffalo herds they encountered.
- The Plains Indians measured the world in terms of the buffalo: the Crows measured big trees as one-robe, two-robe, or three-robe trees, depicting the number needed to stretch around the trunk; others spoke of tepees as 12-robe or 15-robe tepees to explain size.

Key Dates in Texas History

1519	Alonso Alvarez de Pineda of Spain mapped Texas coast
1532	Hernando de Soto's expedition explored part of northeast Texas
1541	Francisco Vasquez de Coronado traveled across part of west Texas
1682	Spanish missionaries built two missions in Texas, near present-day El Paso
1685	Robert Cavelier, Sieur de La Salle, founded Fort St. Louis, a French settlement on Texas coast
1718	Spaniards established missions and fort on site of present-day San Antonio
1821	Texas became part of new Empire of Mexico; Americans led by Stephen F. Austin settled in Texas
1835	Texas began revolution against Mexico
1836	Independence from Mexico declared; Mexican forces overwhelmed and defeated American defenders at Alamo; Sam Houston defeated Mexicans in Battle of San Jacinto; Texas won its independence and became Republic of Texas
1845	Texas admitted to Union, becoming 28th state
1861	Texas seceded from Union and joined Confederacy
1870	Texas readmitted to the Union

1896 Family Profile

Seamus Cavanagh manages a salmon cannery cooperative in Alaska, established to streamline the operations of all salmon fisheries and improve profits. Seamus and his wife, Eileen, have four children and divide their time between San Francisco and Sitka, Alaska.

Annual Income: $5,500

Seamus' income includes his salary managing the cannery association ($2,400), stock market income, and a part interest in his father's fishing supply company.

Annual Budget

The average per capita consumer expenditure in 1896 is not available.

Life at Home

- Seamus was born in New Jersey, the son of Irish immigrants.
- His parents brought the family westward in the 1860s to California, one of America's leading fishing states.
- His father has created a company in San Francisco that specializes in fishing supplies; offices have been established in Vancouver, British Columbia, Seattle, and Astoria, Oregon.

One of the Cavanagh's four children.

Christmas cards make the holiday season more joyous; many cards are elaborate and German-made.

- Seamus married the daughter of a Canadian salmon-cannery operator; he met her during his extensive travels throughout the Pacific coast serving as a drummer, or salesman, for his father's fishing supply concern.
- This 46-year old man, his wife, and four children, own a home both in San Francisco and in Sitka, Alaska; the home in Alaska was designed using plans taken from a picture in a magazine.
- During the salmon season he lives in Alaska; seven months out of the year he operates out of San Francisco, where he has many vendor and other business connections.
- Eileen has come to love the social circle of a big city and often dreads the trips into the wilderness each year. Two years ago, her youngest child died of measles and is buried in Sitka; returning to the grave each year is difficult.
- She is involved with charity work at the Salvation Army in San Francisco; the Stevenson Street Women's Shelter and Receiving Home was recently opened, where homeless women can get a bed for a nickel.
- She is currently heading up a shoe-and-stocking fund drive for poor children through the Salvation Army, hoping that a supply of shoes will improve school attendance among the poor.
- The Salvation Army also recently began a fund to help discharged convicts; the wealthy of the city are placing offering boxes on their dining tables so guests can contribute.
- When her husband is on business in Alaska, she enjoys attending lectures. Recently she heard the Rev. Anna Shaw, who "shares with Miss Susan B. Anthony the distinction of leading the female suffrage agitation in this country," according to the *San Francisco Examiner.*
- The Christmas season is special for the Cavanaghs; Eileen makes a great effort to mail fancy, German-made Christmas cards to her childhood friend in British Columbia, Seamus' family in New Jersey, and their friends in San Francisco and Sitka.
- She also enjoys the latest fashions, often hiring a Chinese seamstress to copy the elegant designs that appear in magazines such as *The Delineator.*
- Her husband is closely watching the presidential election, which is pitting Republican William McKinley against Democrat populist William Jennings Bryan.
- Bryan's plans to print silver in a ratio of 16 silver coins to every gold dollar and thus create more money in circulation appears an excellent way of wresting control away from the East by creating inflation; he believes the gold standard has outlived its usefulness.
- Bryan appears to be gaining support throughout the West, building momentum "like a prairie fire."

- Thanks to an invention making the manufacture of political campaign buttons inexpensive, thousands of pictures of both candidates are arriving, even in remote Alaska.
- The boys love anything related to the sea, shipping, and conquering the water; they are currently building a small boat, with their grandfather's help, and imagining a trip across the harbor.

Presidential paraphernalia: McKinley vs. Bryan

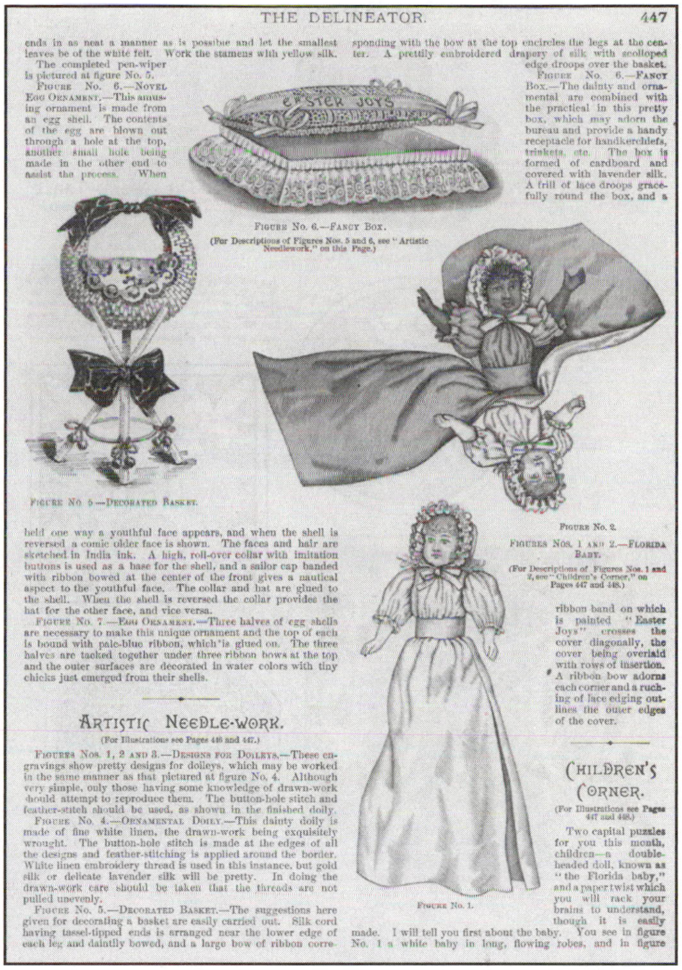

THE DELINEATOR. 447

ends in as neat a manner as is possible and let the smallest leaves be of the white felt. Work the stamens with yellow silk.

The completed pen-wiper is pictured at figure No. 5.

FIGURE No. 6.—NOVEL EGG ORNAMENT.—This amusing ornament is made from an egg shell. The contents of the egg are blown out through a hole at the top, another small hole being made in the other end to assist the process. When held one way a youthful face appears, and when the shell is reversed a comic older face is shown. The faces and hair are sketched in India ink. A high, roll-over collar with imitation buttons is used as a base for the shell, and a sailor cap banded with ribbon bowed at the center of the front gives a nautical aspect to the youthful face. The collar and hat are glued to the shell. When the shell is reversed the collar provides the hat for the other face, and vice versa.

FIGURE No. 7.—EGG ORNAMENT.—Three halves of egg shells are necessary to make this unique ornament and the top of each is bound with pale-blue ribbon, which is glued on. The three halves are tacked together under three ribbon bows at the top and the outer surfaces are decorated in water colors with tiny chicks just emerged from their shells.

FIGURE No. 6.—FANCY BOX.

(For Descriptions of Figures Nos. 5 and 6, see "Artistic Needlework," on this Page.)

FIGURE No 5.—DECORATED BASKET.

FIGURE No. 2.

FIGURES NOS. 1 AND 2.—FLORIDA BABY.

(For Descriptions of Figures Nos. 1 and 2, see "Children's Corner," on Pages 447 and 448.)

FIGURE No. 1.

ARTISTIC NEEDLE-WORK.

(For Illustrations see Pages 446 and 447.)

FIGURES NOS. 1, 2 AND 3.—DESIGNS FOR DOILEYS.—These engravings show pretty designs for doileys, which may be worked in the same manner as that pictured at figure No. 4. Although very simple, only those having some knowledge of drawn-work should attempt to reproduce them. The button-hole stitch and feather-stitch should be used, as shown in the finished doily.

FIGURE No. 4.—ORNAMENTAL DOILY.—This dainty doily is made of fine white linen, the drawn-work being exquisitely wrought. The button-hole stitch is made at the edges of all the designs and feather-stitching is applied around the border. White linen embroidery thread is used in this instance, but gold silk or delicate lavender silk will be pretty. In doing the drawn-work care should be taken that the threads are not pulled unevenly.

FIGURE No. 5.—DECORATED BASKET.—The suggestions here given for decorating a basket are easily carried out. Silk cord having tassel-tipped ends is arranged near the lower edge of each leg and daintily bowed, and a large bow of ribbon corresponding with the bow at the top encircles the legs at the center. A prettily embroidered drapery of silk with scolloped edge droops over the basket.

FIGURE No. 6.—FANCY BOX.—The dainty and ornamental are combined with the practical in this pretty box, which may adorn the bureau and provide a handy receptacle for handkerchiefs, trinkets, etc. The box is formed of cardboard and covered with lavender silk. A frill of lace droops gracefully round the box, and a ribbon band on which is painted "Easter Joys" crosses the cover diagonally, the cover being overlaid with rows of insertion. A ribbon bow adorns each corner and a ruching of lace edging outlines the outer edges of the cover.

CHILDREN'S CORNER.

(For Illustrations see Pages 447 and 448.)

Two capital puzzles for you this month, children—a double-headed doll, known as "the Florida baby," and a paper twist which you will rack your brains to understand, though it is easily made. I will tell you first about the baby. You see in figure No. 1 a white baby in long, flowing robes, and in figure

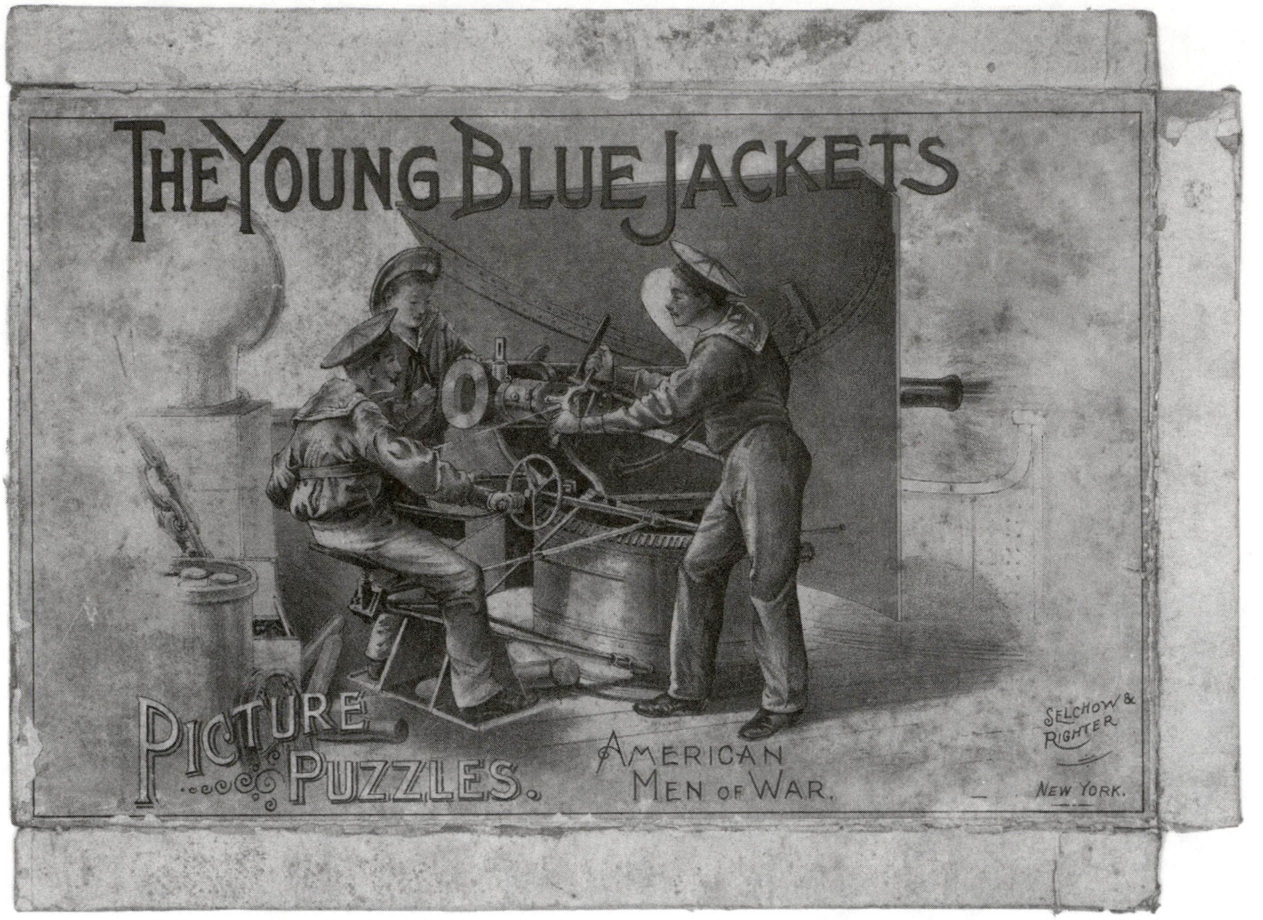

The sea, shipping, and conquering the water are favorite subjects for the Cavanagh boys.

"Tea around the Table: Handkerchiefs," *The Delineator, A Journal of Fashion, Culture and Fine Arts,* published by the Butterick Publishing Company, 1896:

"Take my word for it, my dears, no part of feminine belongings so truly shows the refined gentlewoman as does the handkerchief. Heavy with embroidery or drawn-work it need not be—indeed, any aggressive decoration is in bad taste; but dainty and fine it must be, the finer the better. Who has not seen the toilette of an otherwise well-dressed woman quite spoiled by a coarse, common handkerchief! A *mouchoir* with a colored border may look smart when tucked into a jacket front, but such an extreme better befits Mrs. Dashaway than it does Mme. Juste-Milieu. A frock may be very elegant, but it is the little things that confirm the wearer's claim to being a well-dressed woman. Even if a gown or jacket shows wear, the fresh and well-fitted shoes and gloves, the pretty veil, and fine handkerchief redeem the whole."

The creation of corporations quickly led to specialized and branded salmon marketing.

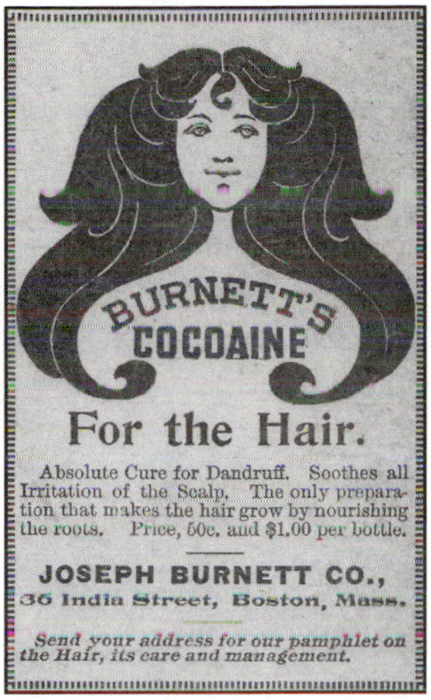

Life at Work

- After several years of running a canning company for his father-in-law, Seamus organized a group of Alaskan canners as a single association.
- This plan is to improve profits for all Alaskan canners in the association by reducing competition among each other; this will allow them to control the price of salmon, even during the peak years.
- The structure he created relies on centralized control and volume buying, abandoning the high-risk, owner-managed cannery for a corporation operated by salaried executives.
- He believes the rapid expansion of the canneries in the early 1890s was creating suicidal competition.
- Many canneries were cutting prices so severely, they could not repay their bank loans or pay for the netting, supplies, and canning materials they needed.
- Following the consolidation, he was asked to manage the 24 canneries that formed the new corporation; each of the former owner-managers is now a director of the association.
- Within this structure, he has reduced the cost of operations; he can also control the quantity and price of raw fish available to each cannery and control the market for canned salmon.
- Most of all, the corporate structure eliminates internal competition for fish and seasonal labor.

The Salmon King of Oregon, Rogue River Salmon, by Gordon Dodds:

"(R.D.) Hume's empire depended on his success in catching the Chinook salmon. If the salmon were taken successfully, he could speculate and develop other enterprises. The fishermen he employed used two techniques for catching salmon. The older of the two was seining. This operation took place as soon as the tide began to recede and, naturally, took place only on the tidelands. When the tide turned, the men waded out on the sand and placed one end of the seine in a large boat; the other end was fastened to a small dory. At a signal, the boat pulling the seine circled around against the current so as to trap the fish heading upstream. The men in the dory hurried to the bar with the shore end of the net, trying to get it in as soon as possible in order to prevent the escape of the salmon around the shore end. After this was done, the outer line was brought in to shore by the seine boat. Up to this point in the process the seining operations were standard on the Sacramento and on the Columbia. Hume, however, patented an invention in 1895 that made use of a windlass. Instead of hauling the seine in from the shore manually, he employed horses to pull the hawser, attached to the seine, around a windlass so that the net could be brought in with greater speed and less labor than under the old method."

- This configuration insures that all salmon canneries will share the profits of the region; when salmon runs are light in one area, they can be supported by heavy runs in another.
- Cooperative buying is also possible; the association has recently cut the cost of canning and netting supplies.
- Currently Alaska's 42 salmon canneries pack 1.5 million cases annually.
- This competition was driving production costs up and increasing the price of the final product.
- This arrangement has allowed the cannery managers to clear their operations of debt and to finance improvements; several are now expanding.
- He has also used his leverage to close less efficient canneries, improving the profits of the collective as a whole.
- To change the corporate structure of the canneries required that bankers raise more than $1 million to finance the merger.
- For his work, this man received a fee of $25,000 in common stock for putting together the deal.
- One area they do not control is the cost of shipping.
- Steamships are the lifeline of coastal Alaska; residents of the territory often pour their wrath in great volumes upon the steamship lines.
- Most residents of Alaska resent their dependence on the water carriers headquartered in Massachusetts.

The family divides their time between San Francisco and Sitka, Alaska.

- They also complain that they are charged exorbitant rates, which have hamstrung the development of Alaska.
- Service quality ranges from poor to indifferent.

Life in the Community: Sitka, Alaska

- Prior to the formation of the salmon canning industry, traders, businessmen, and entrepreneurs had come to Alaska to collect sea otter pelts (early 1800s), hunt whales (1830s), mine gold (1849), and export ice, fur, and coal (1850s).
- Russian Orthodox missions have formed many churches throughout Alaska, especially among the native populations.
- Inspired by the philosophy of "manifest destiny," American leaders debated the acquisition of Alaska as early as the 1840s; Americans had been maritime traders, primarily for furs, for more than 50 years.
- The onset of the Civil War put a temporary halt to American ambitions.
- Following the Civil War, the Russians were willing to negotiate, fearing they could not defend the land if the United States or Britain started a war.

"Progress in Electric Lighting," by S.E. Tillman, *The Cosmopolitan Magazine*, March 1897:

"Both arc and incandescent electric lighting are so well established and so fully developed that any very great or radical improvement can scarcely be expected to come suddenly, yet in both systems, steady, if slow, progress toward perfection is being made.

In arc lighting the 'short arc' with heavy current and low voltage or pressure has been succeeded by the 'long arc' with smaller current and higher voltage. At the same time a larger number of lights have been placed upon the same circuit, and the leading wires diminished in size. Ten years ago 25 lights in one circuit was a large number, whereas now circuits include from 75 to 150; then the total voltage on one circuit amounted to 1,200 or 1,500, and now it runs up to 6,000 or 7,000 volts. Notwithstanding the great increase in pressure employed, the wires have been successfully placed underground; an achievement which the electrical companies in this country were not inclined to admit as economically practicable. The most distinct recent step in arc lighting has been the inclosing [sic] of the carbons in an airtight receptacle, by which they last from 125 to 150 hours without renewal. In these inclosed lights the arc is made longer, the current smaller, and the voltage for a single lamp greater than in any other form. These lamps are giving very satisfactory results and are coming into competition with incandescent lamps for the general illumination of stores, hotel corridors, etc. The standard inclosed arc only requires three or five amperes, and they can run from the ordinary incandescent circuit of 110 volts.

Improvements in the mechanical details of arc lamps have kept pace with the modifications in their principles of construction; indeed, the improved details have made the better lights possible; thus the inclosed lamp only became possible with the production of the refined carbons of the past few years.

In incandescent electric lighting, distinct advantages toward cheaper and better lights have been made. The principal agents tending to this result have been two—first the great reduction in the first cost of the lamps; second the improved efficiency of the lamps. Since incandescent lighting became a success the cost of the lamps has been reduced over one-half, and at the same time the efficiency of the lamps has been nearly doubled. Formerly it required the expenditure of one horsepower of current energy to each seven or eight lamps of 16 candlepower each; now the same amount of energy supplies 15 lamps. It is probable that the efficiency of the lamps will yet be considerably increased, but the limit in cost of production would seem to be nearly reached.

The development of electric lighting has caused greater progress in gas lighting in the past 12 years than had been made in the previous 60. The light-giving power of gas has been trebled and the cost of gas production reduced. The rapid, enormous, and permanent development of incandescent electric lighting is shown by a recent statement in the *Electrical Engineer* that there are now invested in this industry $600 million of capital."

- In the spring of 1867 Russia and the United States agreed on a treaty to transfer Alaska to American control.
- The purchase price was $7.2 million and was often referred to as "Seward's Folly," after William Seward, President Abraham Lincoln's secretary of state, who actively promoted the treaty.

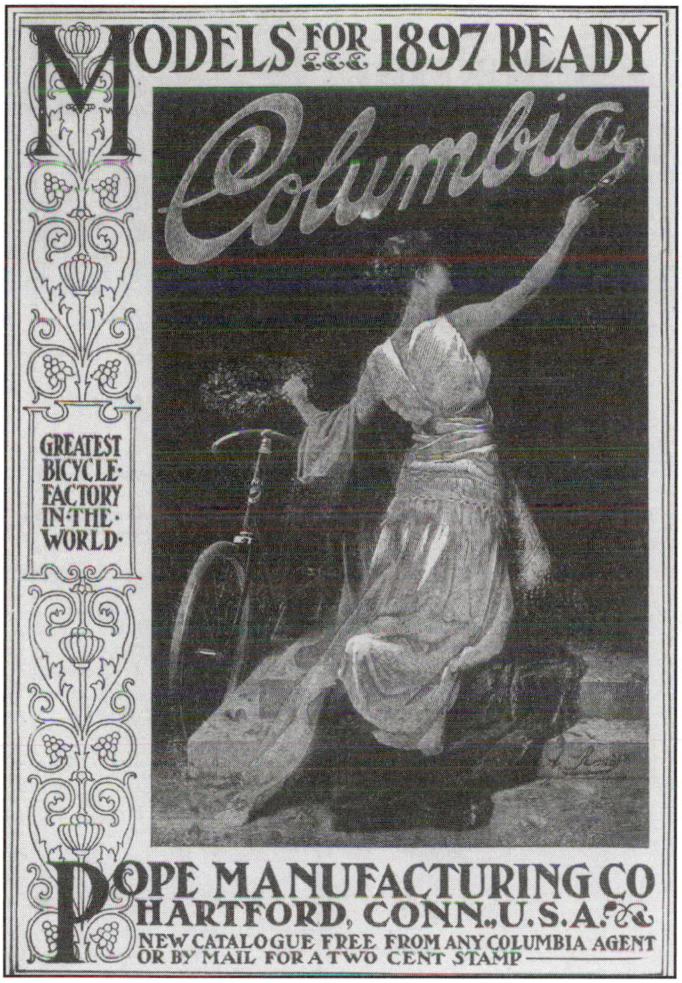

New bicycle models are eagerly awaited.

- When the treaty was taken to the United States Senate, it received a near-unanimous vote; only two senators voted against it.
- On October 18, 1867, Alaska officially became part of the United States.
- By terms of the treaty, the Russian Orthodox church members owned all Russian churches in Alaska and remained an active presence there; Russians had the option of returning to Russia or becoming U.S. citizens.
- The treaty specified that "uncivilized tribes" would be subject to whatever laws the United States adopted toward them.

Historical Snapshot
1896–1897

- The bicycle industry reported sales of $60 million; the average bike sold for $100
- The earliest trading stamps, issued by S&H Green Stamps, were distributed for the first time
- Michelob beer was introduced
- The Klondike gold rush in Bonanza Creek, Canada, began
- The *Boston Cooking School Cook Book* was published, advocating the use of precise measurements to produce identical results
- Radioactivity was discovered in uranium
- William Ramsay discovered helium
- Five annual Nobel prizes were established in the fields of physics, physiology and medicine, chemistry, literature, and peace
- Bituminous coal miners staged a 12-week walkout
- Continental Casualty Company was founded
- Dow Chemical Company was incorporated
- Radio transmission over long distances was achieved by Gugielmo Marconi
- Winton Motor Carriage Company was organized
- The New York City Health Board began enforcing a law regulating women in mercantile establishments
- Mail Pouch tobacco was introduced
- Ronald Ross discovered the malaria bacillus
- Wheat prices rose to $1.09 per bushel
- Jell-O was introduced by Pearl B. Wait
- Boston's H.P. Hill used glass bottles to distribute milk

1896 Economic Profile

Income, Standard Jobs

Bricklayers	$3.87/day/50 hrs. per week
Carpenters and Joiners	$2.04/day/60 hrs. per week
Engineers, Stationary	$2.67/day/63 hrs. per week
Hod Carriers	$2.15/day/49 hrs. per week
Marble Cutters	$2.83/day/54 hrs. per week
Painters	$2.96/day/51 hrs. per week
Plasterers	$3.19/day/49 hrs. per week
Plumbers	$3.49/day/49 hrs. per week
Stonemasons	$3.92/day/49 hrs. per week

Selected Prices

Dominola Card Game	$0.20
Music Box	$15.00
Boy's School Hat	$0.25
Standard Shirt	$1.50
Man's Suit; All Wool	$5.95
Top Coat; English Design	$10.00
Henderson Flexo Girdle	$1.25
Gloves; Kayser Patent Finger-Tipped	$0.50
Singer Sewing Machine	$9.00
Tuition at Columbia Female College	$200/Year
Lowney's Chocolate	$0.60
Pineapple Cheese	$0.40
Smoked Herring	$0.15/Box
Chrysanthemums (Three Each)	$0.10
Cake Tins	$0.35
Carpet	$0.19/Yard
English Decorated Dinner and Tea Set	$7.00
Lemonoide Polish	$0.50
Wallpaper	$0.10/Roll
Autoharp	$7.50

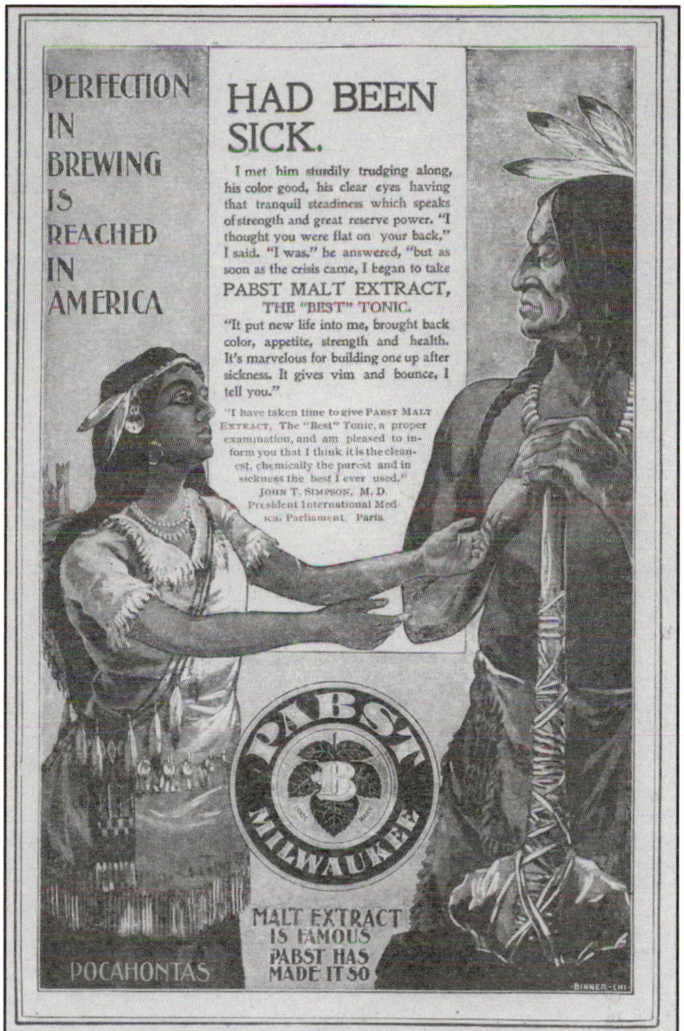

From The Cosmopolitan Press.

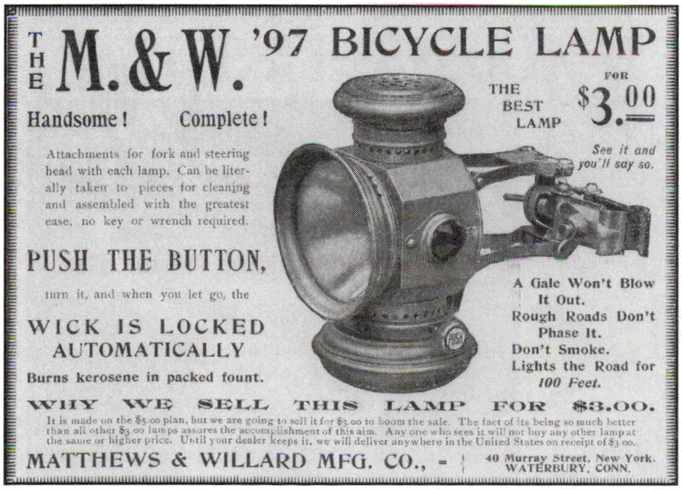

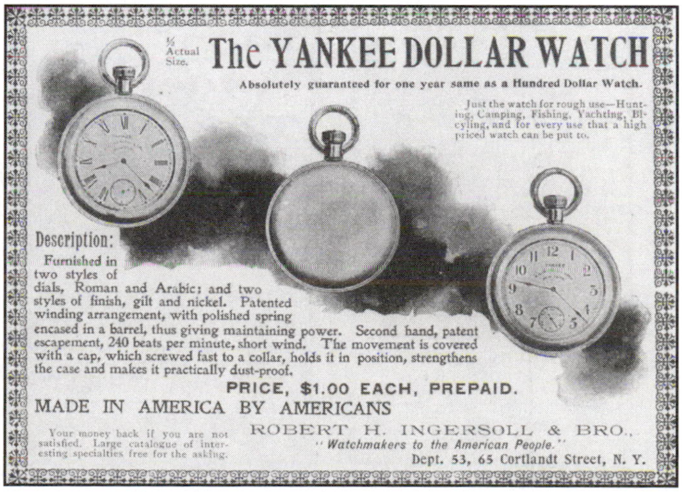

The Alaskan Salmon Industry

- Alaska boasts 20,000 miles of coastline, cut by rivers and streams carrying sediment from the mountains, referred to as glacier milk.
- Every year from late spring until early fall, five species of salmon come back to the rivers where they were born.
- Depending on the species, they are two to seven years old when they return for spawning, after which they die.
- The species often carry Indian names: Chinook (king), sockeye (red), coho (silver), humpbacked (pink), and chum (dog).
- For centuries native fishermen depended on the salmon runs; the Indian, Aleut, and Eskimo consumption of salmon ran 33.5 million pounds a year before the white man arrived.
- The Russians were the first outsiders to attempt to exploit the salmon industry; they shipped the fish to California during the gold rush, but a lack of technology created high spoilage and losses.
- In 1868 a saltery was established on Kodiak Island's Karluk River, a red salmon stream, and others quickly followed.
- In the early days, the fish were stored in brine, 800 pounds to the barrel, and shipped to Europe where salmon was popular; it was considered cheap and nutritious.
- By 1878, placing salmon in tins, a process already in use in California, began to dominate in Alaska.
- Salmon canning factories were established on Prince of Wales Island and Sitka.
- That first year, 8,159 cases of 48 one-pound cans, valued at $50,000 were shipped.
- By 1889 Alaska had 37 operating canneries, whose output totaled 714,000 cases worth $2.8 million.
- A typical cannery, designed to produce 25,000 cases a season, cost $100,000 to $125,000; all materials had to be shipped "stateside" from ports in Seattle, Astoria, or Portland.
- Most were built on pilings over tidewater so the natural ebb of the water would wash away the gully of the operation—the slime, blood, and offal that accumulate when fish are cleaned.

"Millions Shipped East, Gold Coin Sent from California in a Baggage Car," *San Francisco Examiner,* January 1, 1896:

"The gold in the sub-treasury was increased on Tuesday by the arrival of $1 million in $20 pieces from the mint in San Francisco. The rush on the part of some of the financiers at the beginning of the Venezuelan discussion to draw gold from the sub-treasury for foreign shipment caused the authorities to draw on the San Francisco mint, and during the past month $20 million in gold has been shipped East. The last shipment, which included besides the gold almost two tons of silver bullion, left San Francisco in an ordinary baggage car. The car was guarded by two messengers armed with revolvers and rifles, but as it was not generally known that the gold was being shipped, no trouble was expected from outlaws."

- Canning made possible the distribution of salmon on a worldwide basis and contributed to its popularity.
- New Englanders brought canning to California's Sacramento River in the 1860s.
- The industry spread rapidly northward to the Columbia and Fraser Rivers, into Washington's Puget Sound and up the coast into Alaska.
- Alaska became the world base for the industry.
- Salmon migrate from their deep-sea habitat to their native freshwater streams to spawn in definite cycles, ranging from two to six years, depending upon the species.
- Unlike the Atlantic salmon, which spawn many times, Pacific salmon die soon after spawning once, making it highly suited to processing by canning.
- The natural season for any species lasts six to eight weeks and begins later, by several weeks, in the south and the north.
- Gillnetting is the main method for catching sockeye salmon, often done from a small boat.
- There is little incentive for fishermen to consider the future stocks of fish.

"Will Penetrate Wood, A New Light That Is Being Used in Photography," *San Francisco Examiner*, January 8, 1896:

"The noise of war's alarms should not distract attention from a marvelous triumph of science which is reported from Vienna. It is announced Professor Routhen of Wurzburg University has discovered light which, for the purpose of photography, will penetrate wood, flesh, and most other organic substances. The Professor has succeeded in photographing metal weights which were in a closed wooden case, also a man's hand which shows only the bones, the flesh being invisible."

"An Indian Murder; Donald Austin, an Alaska Chief of Police, Killed in a Chinaman's Saloon," *San Francisco Examiner,* December 1895:

"The steamer *City of Topeka,* which arrived from Alaska this morning, brought the news of the brutal murder at Sitka on December 21 of Donald Austin, the Indian Chief of Police. The murder was committed in a saloon run by Chum Long. As a result Herbert Mills, the principal in the tragedy, was held over by Justice Delaney on a charge of murder. Long was held for manslaughter, and two sailors from the revenue cutter *Wolcott* for assault. While they were in the saloon the two sailors assaulted Austin, knocking him down. As soon as he rose, Mills struck him from behind and knocked him down again. Then they pounced on him and pounded his head on the hard floor. Long threw the unconscious Indian into a back room and later, when other Indians began to make inquiries for Austin, Long tossed his lifeless body out into the street, where it was found a few hours later."

- Every harvester knows that if he leaves fish in the water someone else will get it—and the profit—instead.
- Most fishermen believe that the ocean's fish are inexhaustible, and that regulation simply makes no sense.
- They do believe that artificial propagation could increase the number of salmon available and even out the cyclical nature of the runs.
- The first government hatchery was built in 1884.
- Capital from the East coast began the industry, quickly followed by money and marketing agencies from San Francisco.
- An entire year's supply of salmon must be caught during a six- to eight-week season.
- Extremely perishable, it must be preserved within hours of being caught.
- Warm weather and the size of the run often increase the problem of spoilage.
- During the peak of the salmon run, temporary Chinese labor constitutes 40 percent of the total Alaskan work force.
- Increasingly, Japanese fishermen are now taking the place of white and native fishermen supplying the cannery.
- Historically, outsiders have reaped the greatest benefits of the Alaskan wilderness.
- The bowhead whaling industry was largely controlled by businessmen from New England.
- After several financially disastrous years in the 1870s because of wealth and declining numbers of whales, the emphasis shifted to salmon fishing.
- Chinese workers are hired as a gang from Chinese-owned agencies in California.
- The labor agencies also provide a labor boss, or foreman, with the men; they work long hours, sleep in a crowded facility called the China house, and typically make $165 per season, with most of the money being sent home to relatives in China.
- Their tasks include the cutting out and soldering of cans in preparation for the salmon run; an experienced solderer can seam 2,000 cans a day.

- Once the salmon arrive, the pace increases; within two seconds a Chinese worker can butcher a red salmon weighing more than seven pounds, including removal of the head and tail, the fins, and slitting of the belly.
- Native Indian women will then remove the internal organs, allowing them to fall through the fish house floor into the tide.
- Then the fish will be cut crossways to the exact size to fill a one-pound can.
- Once filled, Chinese workers will place and crimp the tops of the cans before sending them on to a solder bath to be sealed.
- The cans are tested for leaks in a vat of boiling water and resoldered, if necessary.

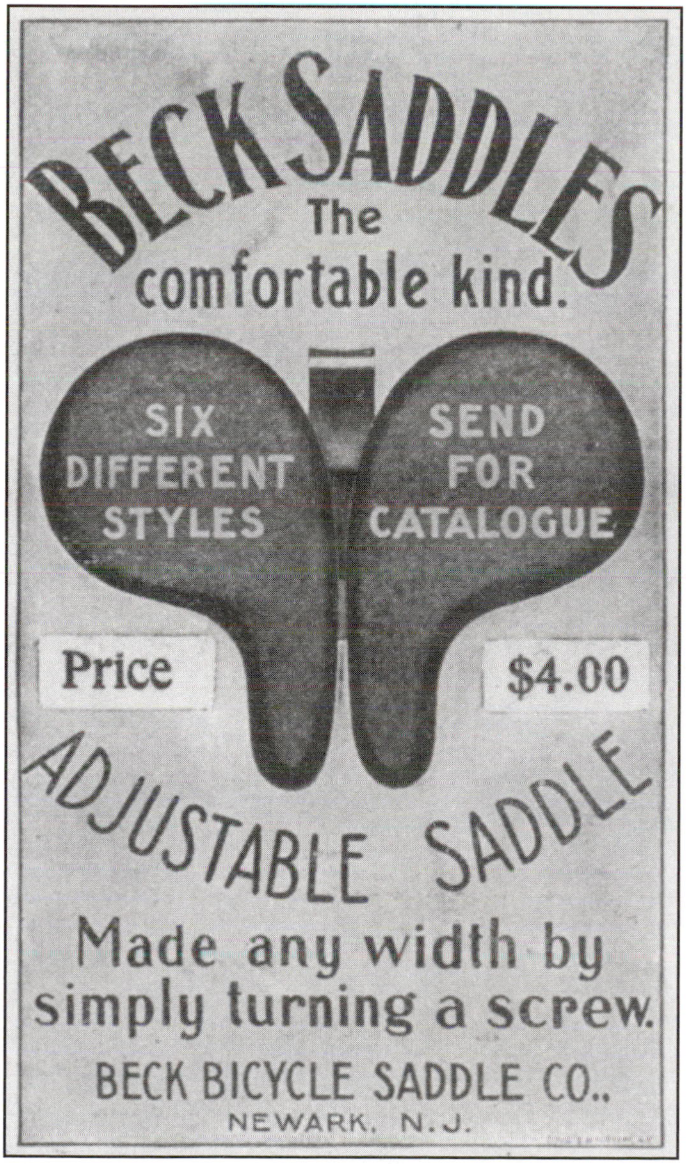

- Once canned, the salmon is cooked twice; first at 212F for 20 minutes, then at 240F for 75 minutes.
- Next, the cans are given a bath of lacquer against rust, labeled, and packed in cases of 48.
- The salmon are caught with purse seines, gill nets, and traps; in 1888 fishermen in Karluk Bay alone caught 2.5 million salmon, enough to fill 200,000 cases.
- By 1889 Congress began limiting the total barricading of salmon streams; in 1892 a small amount of money was provided to enforce the act, though overharvesting continued.
- Labor abuses brought outcries from Alaskans; Governor Swineford said in 1888 that the canneries "are owned and operated by nonresident corporations, who come to the territory in the spring bringing with them all the cheap Chinese and other labor they require, few if any of the employees becoming actual residents, but nearly, if not quite, all returning whence they came in the fall."
- The taxation on the industry is $0.04 a case; one major cannery paid taxes of $5,000 on profits of $250,000.

1896 NEWS PROFILE

"Women in the Professions, Law," by Mrs. Theodore Sutro, *The Delineator, A Journal of Fashion, Culture and Fine Arts*, April 1896:

"Why should women embrace the profession of law as a means of livelihood? For the same reason that men embrace it, for the same reason that has induced women to become physicians, artists, scientists, ministers, educators, financiers, editors, and to engage in almost all pursuits which a few generations ago were considered the exclusive property of men. Because we have arrived at a point in our civilizations when their mental subordination, merely because they are women, has become almost inconceivable.

Why should women *not* study law? This question could be answered far more readily. The reason women have so long been debarred from this particular profession may be partly explained because precedent more than anything else holds sway over the minds of judges and lawyers, and it has become almost a matter of tradition that a woman should not become a lawyer.

It may also be partly explained through a misconception on the part of the public of the character of the profession. Among the laity the lawyer is pictured as a person who must be constantly engaged in the strife and turmoil of the forum, whose stentorian voice must terrorize witnesses and impress juries, and who must move about in all the highways and byways of life like a whirlwind in order to ferret out and discover material which he may use in the trial of a case. No one knows better than members of the profession how remote such an idea is from the facts. The main business of a lawyer, insofar as his time is occupied at all in litigation, is performed in the seclusion of his private office in the careful analysis of the facts of his case and the study of law bearing upon it. Especially in our generation, however, the main portion of his work consists in advising and counselling, [sic] and in performing such labor as rather tends to prevent and avoid litigation than to conduct it when it is unavoidable. Surely in this branch of the profession it is a question of intellect and training solely, and not one of sex, as to whether the person pursuing it is fitted to be successful or not.

Actual experience has proved that in the classes which have now been opened to women for the study of law (as since time immemorial they have been to men) women take as high rank as men, if not higher. There are a hundred avenues in the profession outside of actual court practice in which women, provided they have the necessary qualifications and training, may be equally successful with men.

To succeed in certain legal fields woman is no doubt particularly fitted and adapted by Nature. There is many a subject which a sensitive woman would shrink from revealing to a lawyer of the sterner sex, and therefore, rather bears her cross in silence, which she would only be too glad to confide to a woman lawyer upon whose womanly sympathy, instincts, and comprehension she could rely. Certainly in everything that pertains to office advice and counsel, the preparations for trial and laying out of plans for conducting litigations where the interests of women or young children are involved, woman is especially qualified so far as natural abilities go.

There surely can be no nobler study than that of law. Ages ago Aristotle said: 'Jurisprudence is the principal and most perfect branch of ethics.' Blackstone calls it 'a science which distinguishes the criterions of right and wrong; which tends to establish the one and prevent, punish, or redress the other; which employs in its theory the noblest faculties of the soul, and exercises in its practices the cardinal virtues of the heart; a science which is universal in its use and extent, accommodated to *each* individual, yet comprehending the whole community.'

At all events, women are now *entitled* to admission to the bar in New York as well as in several other states. Paragraph 56 of the Code of Civil Procedure of New York provides that 'Race or sex shall constitute no cause for refusing any person examination or admission to practice.'

The chief drawback to the study of the profession of law by women as compared with men is their greater lack of general educational training, a lack proportionate to the small number of colleges for women in comparison with those open to young men. While exceptional brilliant examples exist of success in almost every profession without ample preliminary general training, there can be no doubt that, as a rule, such training is necessary in law. I would not advise any young woman to undertake the study of law with a view of making a means of livelihood unless she has at least a thorough high school education; properly it should be a college education. The profession being for women as a novelty, many of them are tempted to think they must be adapted for it simply because so many men are engaged in it. These young women, however, forget that while, as Daniel Webster said, 'There is always room in the upper story,' the upper story nevertheless has its limits, and of the thousands of men who undertake to practice law the percentage of those who actually succeed is almost insignificant. Not only does the practice of this profession require thorough preliminary mental training, but also the possession of that peculiar type of intellect known as the 'legal mind.'

Moreover, the exactions of the profession are enormous, and unless able to bear an almost unlimited amount of work and possessing a constitution which can surmount the wear and tear of incessant mental anxiety, no man can succeed in this pursuit; how much less, then, a woman! While I fully believe in throwing open the avenues of every profession to my sex, I think it is also proper to point out to its members the danger of spending years and large sums of money in pursuing a mere fad. Let a young woman pause and well consider whether she has the educational and physical qualifications required for the pursuit of this exacting profession, and, over and above these, whether she has the peculiar mental traits which adapt her to make a success of it. . . .

Up to 1882, 56 women had been admitted to the practice as attorneys-at-law in the United States. There must be at least four times this number at the present time. In New York City there are now probably not more than half a dozen women against about 5,000 men admitted to the bar—a small enough proportion to encourage other women to endeavor to join the ranks of their professional sisters."

Figure No. 1.—Young Ladies' Hat.

Figure No. 8.—Young Ladies' Hat.

Figure No. 2.—Ladies' Round Hat.

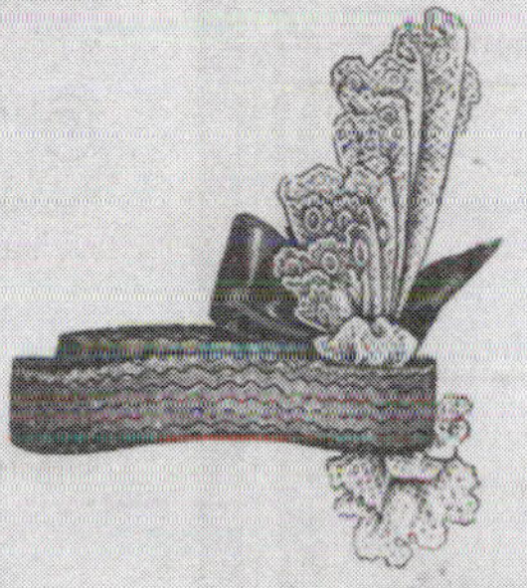

Figure No. 5.—Ladies' Turban.

Figure No. 9.—Ladies' Hat.

Figure No. 6.—Ladies' Hat.

Figure No. 3.—Ladies' Hat.

Figure No. 7.—Ladies' Hat.

Figure No. 4.—Ladies' Large Hat.

Ladies' Spring Hats.

For Descriptions see Page 435.

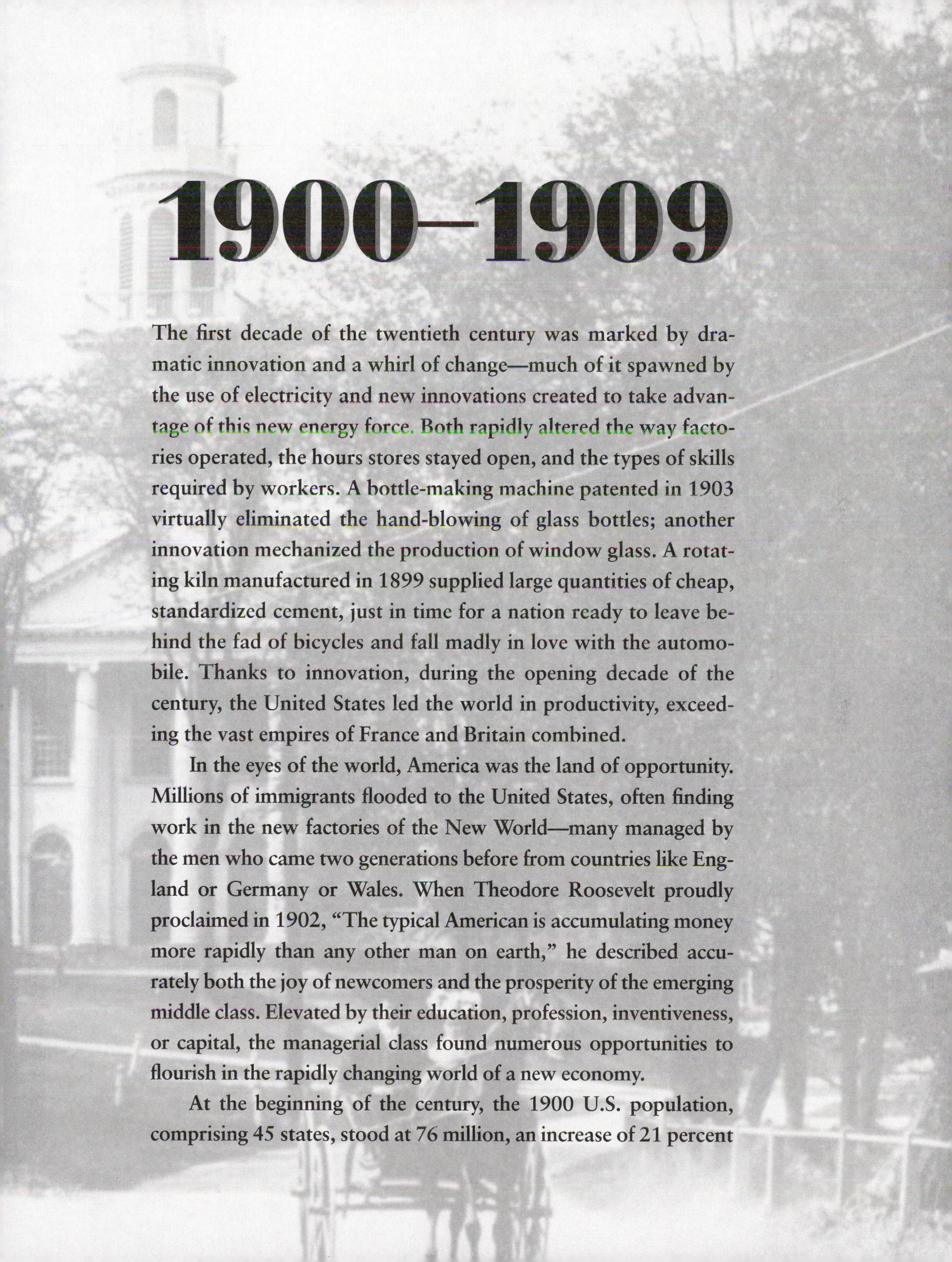

1900–1909

The first decade of the twentieth century was marked by dramatic innovation and a whirl of change—much of it spawned by the use of electricity and new innovations created to take advantage of this new energy force. Both rapidly altered the way factories operated, the hours stores stayed open, and the types of skills required by workers. A bottle-making machine patented in 1903 virtually eliminated the hand-blowing of glass bottles; another innovation mechanized the production of window glass. A rotating kiln manufactured in 1899 supplied large quantities of cheap, standardized cement, just in time for a nation ready to leave behind the fad of bicycles and fall madly in love with the automobile. Thanks to innovation, during the opening decade of the century, the United States led the world in productivity, exceeding the vast empires of France and Britain combined.

In the eyes of the world, America was the land of opportunity. Millions of immigrants flooded to the United States, often finding work in the new factories of the New World—many managed by the men who came two generations before from countries like England or Germany or Wales. When Theodore Roosevelt proudly proclaimed in 1902, "The typical American is accumulating money more rapidly than any other man on earth," he described accurately both the joy of newcomers and the prosperity of the emerging middle class. Elevated by their education, profession, inventiveness, or capital, the managerial class found numerous opportunities to flourish in the rapidly changing world of a new economy.

At the beginning of the century, the 1900 U.S. population, comprising 45 states, stood at 76 million, an increase of 21 percent since 1890; 10.6 million residents were foreign-born and more were coming every day. The number of immigrants in the first decade of the twentieth century was double the number for the previous decade, exceeding one million annually in four of the 10 years, the highest level in U.S. history. Business and industry were convinced that unrestricted immigration was the fuel that drove the growth of American industry. Labor was equally certain that the influx of foreigners continually undermined the economic status of native workers and kept wages low.

The change in productivity and consumerism came with a price: the character of American life. Manufacturing plants drew people from the country into the cities. The traditional farm patterns were disrupted by the lure of urban life. Ministers complained that lifelong churchgoers who moved to the city often found less time and fewer social pressures to attend worship regularly. Between 1900 and 1920, urban population increased by 80 percent compared to just over 12 percent for rural areas. During the same time, the non-farming work force went from 783,000 to 2.2 million. Unlike farmers, these workers drew a regular paycheck, and spent it.

With this movement of people, technology, and ideas, nationalism took on a new meaning in America. Railroad expansion in the middle of the nineteenth century had made it possible to move goods quickly and efficiently throughout the country. As a result, commerce, which had been based largely on local production of goods for local consumption, found new markets. Ambitious merchants expanded their businesses by appealing to broader markets.

In 1900, America claimed 58 businesses with more than one retail outlet called "chain stores"; by 1910, that number had more than tripled, and by 1920, the total had risen to 808. The number of clothing chains alone rose from seven to 125 during the period. Department stores such as R.H. Macy in New York and Marshall Field in Chicago offered vast arrays of merchandise along with free services and the opportunity to "shop" without purchasing. Ready-made clothing drove down prices, but also promoted fashion booms that reduced the class distinctions of dress. In rural America the mail order catalogs of Sears, Roebuck and Company reached deep into the pocket of the common man and made dreaming and consuming more feasible.

All was not well, however. A brew of labor struggles, political unrest, and tragic factory accidents demonstrated the excesses of industrial capitalism so worshipped in the Gilded Age. The labor-reform movements of the 1880s and 1890s culminated in the newly formed American Federation of Labor as the chief labor advocate. By 1904, 18 years after it was founded, the AFL claimed 1.676 million of 2.07 million total union members nationwide. The reforms of the labor movement called for an eight-hour workday, child-labor regulation, and cooperatives of owners and workers. The progressive bent of the times also focused attention on factory safety, tainted food and drugs, political corruption, and unchecked economic monopolies. At the same time, progress was not being made by all. For black Americans, many of the gains of reconstruction were being wiped away by regressive Jim Crow laws, particularly in the South. Cherished voting privileges were being systematically taken away. When President Roosevelt asked renowned black educator Booker T. Washington to dine at the White House, the invitation sparked deadly riots. Although less visible, the systematic repression of the Chinese was well under way on the West Coast.

The decade ushered in the opening of the first movie theater, located in Pittsburgh, in 1905. Vaudeville prospered, traveling circuses seemed to be everywhere, and America was crazy for any type of contest, whether it was "cute baby" judging or hootchy-kootchy belly dancing. The decade marked the first baseball World Series, Scholastic Aptitude Tests, the subway, and Albert Einstein's new theories concerning the cosmos. At the same time, the $1 Brownie Box camera from Eastman Kodak made photography available to the masses.

1903 Family Profile

Edward Caufield works in the manufacturing factory of Holley hand-forged pocketknives in the village of Lakeville, Connecticut.* He was named manager two years ago and is challenged by a declining market for the high quality pocketknives his company sells, severe competition, and the threat of unions.

Annual Income: $1,530

Annual Budget

Families in New England with incomes of more than $1,200 typically experience the following expenditures:

Amusements and Travel for Recreation	$20.13
Clothing	$183.12
Education	$12.50
Fuel and Light	$56.31
Furniture and Household Furnishings	$28.75
Groceries	$355.88
Insurance	$34.40
Meats, Fish, and Ice	$194.25
Milk	$40.24
Newspapers and Periodicals	$11.49
Other	$70.57
Personal Expenses	$88.37
Religion and Charity	$20.38
Rent	$85.12

The family home is within walking distance of the pocketknife factory.

*Until November 2000, the Holley Pocketknife Factory building was home to Grey House Publishing, publisher of this reference work.

Sickness and Funeral Expenses	$45.63
Societies and Unions	$12.85
Travel to and from Work	$12.60
Total	$1,272.59

Life at Home

- Caufield came to the United States as a teenager from Sheffield, England, following in the footsteps of the original team of workers who were hired to start the plant.
- He has worked with Holley Manufacturing his entire life.
- He and his wife, Jane, and one daughter live in a cottage built and owned by the company for upper-level employees.

The beauty of Connecticut attracted many visitors each year. Prior to 1844, however, Lakeville was known as Furnace Village—a treeless, noisy center of iron production.

- The one-story, six-room house is within walking distance of the knife factory.
- The daughter, who is 15 years old, goes to a public school in the area; although dozens of private schools have opened in northwestern Connecticut, they are still outside the budget of this family.
- Jane is active in the community, recently working on the cemetery refurbishing committee; like many women in the village, she is embarrassed that the community has allowed weeds to grow up around the graves.
- Their budget is tight, but since Edward became a manager she can now accompany him on business trips to Boston, where she loves to shop; years of experience at saving money has trained her well to spend money wisely.
- He is thinking that some investments might be appropriate; recently a friend showed him a solicitation for Niagara Light, Heat & Power Company bonds, and he is giving the circular some attention.
- The Water Company's annual charges in the village are set according to the facilities within a home, not actual usage; this family pays $19.50 a year for water service. The Water Company charged $7.50 for having hot and cold water faucets, limited to one faucet each, $2.00 for a wash bowl, $4.00 for having a bathtub, $4.00 for a water closet, and $2.00 for a private stable with one horse.
- If the family wants "private hose service" to water the lawn, it is required to pay $4.00 a year and is limited to one hour's use per day; the hose can only be attached to "ordinary service pipe cocks," only discharged through a quarter-inch nozzle, and used "only when held in hand."

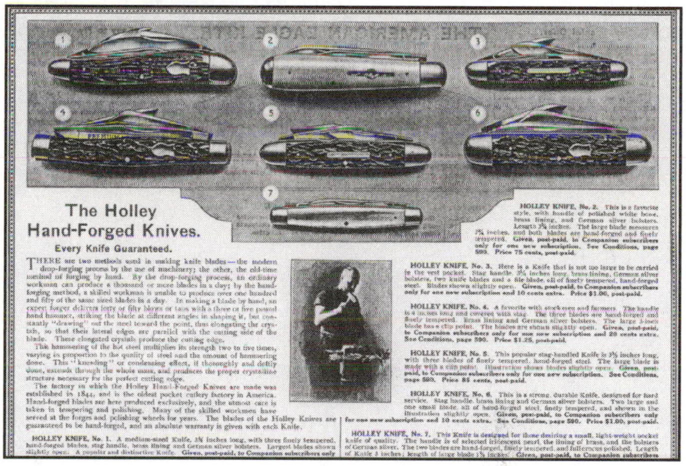

The company catalog emphasizes the man-made nature of the knives.

Life at Work

- This man was named manager two years ago; he is worried because orders are beginning to decline.
- Today's customers are demanding less expensive, machine-made pocketknives; Holley Manufacturing specializes in quality, handmade knives.
- The quality of the steel in Holley products makes it difficult to convert to machine-made knives.
- He is also noticing that orders for large, heavy knives, normally purchased for farm work, are declining, and does not know whether this is caused by his company's prices or the number of men leaving the farms.
- In addition to pocketknives, the company makes pruning, grafting, budding, hunting, and kitchen knives, as well as scissors and razors.
- The pocketknives are handled in horn, bone, ivory, metal, wood, mother of pearl, celluloid (an early plastic) and silvers, usually using brass liners.

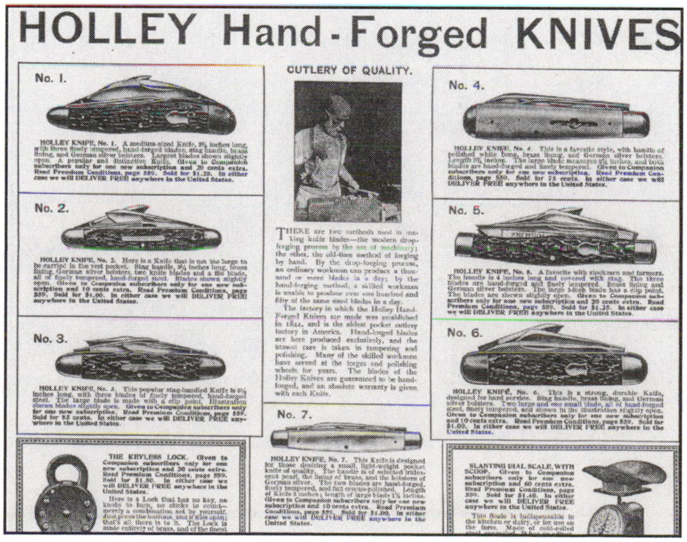

Holley Manufacturing makes 130 different types of knives.

- In all Holley Manufacturing makes more than 130 different lines of knives.
- Currently the company employs 45 men, down from its peak of 65 before the turn of the century.
- This man is worried that he must upgrade all the company's machinery and methods at a time when revenues are going down.
- Competition is increasing; Connecticut alone currently has more than 70 pocketknife manufacturing companies.
- He has been told that the first practical automatic grinding machine has been perfected in New Haven this year, but has not seen it operate.

- To attract sales, the Holley Manufacturing Company is advertising that it will replace any Holley knife that wears out with a brand-new knife of the same model.
- One of this man's innovations two years ago was to set aside each Wednesday morning to allow tours of Holley Manufacturing by anyone interested in the pocketknife manufacturing process; recently he has been forced to stop the tours because "the custom has entailed so great a demand upon the time of the offices of the company that they regretfully take this opportunity to announce the discontinuance of the practice," a notice in the *Lakeville Journal* read.
- He is also worried about keeping his best people. Rental housing in Lakeville is difficult to find; recently Harry Gill, a forger at the factory, moved to Brooklyn because he was unable to locate suitable and affordable rent in either village.

- Holley sells most of its products to wholesalers in Boston and New York; they in turn distribute the pocketknives nationwide.
- The factory operates one shift six days a week, normally eight to 10 hours per day.
- This manager typically works 55 to 60 hours per week, accumulating 10 hours a day Monday through Friday and five to 10 hours on Saturday; he does not work on Sunday.
- During the months of June, July, and August, workers are excused at noon on Saturday "in order that the workmen may enjoy a half-holiday each week during the hot weather."
- Approximately 60 percent of the factory's labor force are British.
- The steel for the knives continues to be imported from Sheffield, England.
- Charcoal is used to heat the steel red-hot; the blades are then beaten into shape on anvils, which are set in the square sockets of limestone blocks.
- The anvils themselves are cushioned on a bed of horse manure to supply resiliency.
- A craftsman then grinds the blade for final shape and sharpness.
- The company's sales catalog lists both lock blade and folding knives for sale; wholesale purchases are always by the dozen.
- The factory includes four buildings—three made of brick, one of wood.
- The manufacturing facility is Lakeville's leading industry; much of the community is built around its workers and spirit.
- Each Christmas Holley Manufacturing creates a series of little knives for the community, known as the Christmas Special.
- Townspeople also come to the plant to gain assistance in sharpening scissors and knives.
- The company was created in 1844, when Alexander Hamilton Holley went to Waterbury, Connecticut, intending to purchase equipment for the manufacture of cotton thread.
- When that deal fell through, he instead purchased all the equipment and talent needed to manufacture "spring cutlery" or folding pocketknives.
- His original plan was to manufacture high-quality knives from Salisbury, Connecticut, iron.
- By 1862, after "hard toil and the acquisition of experience" Holley wrote that the knife factory was "the best single item of my income."
- During the early years, the workers declared a strike and refused to return to work; Holley locked the factory

Holley Manufacturing created a display of all its knives for the 1876 Philadelphia Exposition.

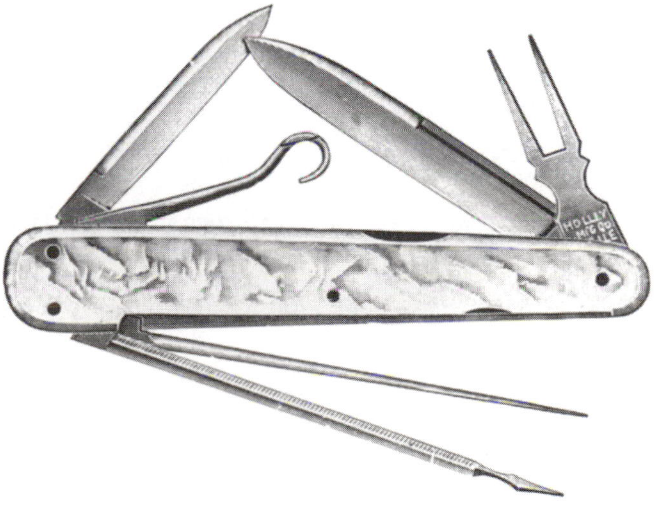

Alexander Hamilton Holley, founder of Holley Manufacturing, said in a speech to ironworkers in 1855:

"This labor must be paid for in this country or in Europe. Who can suppose, then, for a moment, that the laborers, mechanics, farmers, and merchants of this country have no interest in the manufacture of iron? Can a million dollars' worth of labor be paid for in so narrow a limit of country, in the manufacture of one single article, in the midst of our farmers, without their being benefited thereby? It is conceivable that the manufacturer alone derives all the benefit resulting from so much labor? The stale cry that he does derive all the benefit resulting from protection, at least to the extent of that protection, has prejudiced many a laborer against his employer, and led him to vote for a suspension of his own occupation. Rich Manufacturers! Lords of the Loom! Indeed! Are they rich? If so, they are able to go through such a time of depression as this, while thousands of laborers, without this employment, must starve in idleness or abandon their homes in pursuit of work. And if the workmen do this, must they not resort to the primitive occupation of man—the cultivation of the soil? If they do this, do they not come directly in competition with the farmer, instead of remaining consumers of their produce? Gentlemen, these blows aimed at the few destroy the many. In striking down the employer often an [sic] hundred operatives fall with him."

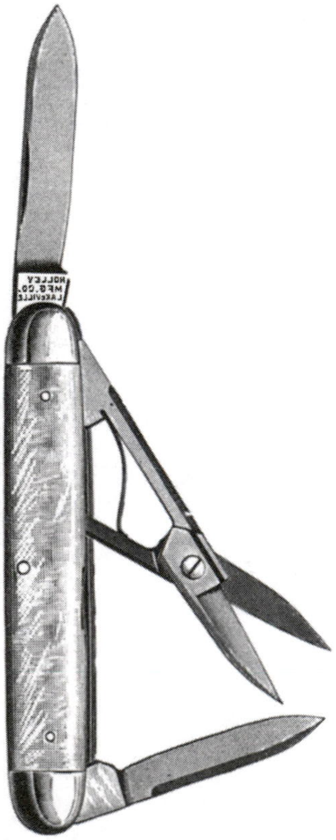

doors, "giving them time to consider whether they were benefiting themselves or their families by these claims." The workers returned a few days later "on the old footings," according to a memorial prepared at Holley's death.

- A critical aspect of gaining profitability was Holley's ability to convince the legislature to allow the level of Lake Wononscopomuc to be raised so that waterpower could be used to operate the factory.
- Holley, a loyal Federalist and devotee of Henry Clay, a Whig, would eventually become first Lt. Governor of Connecticut on the new American Republican ticket, and then Governor in 1857.
- The establishment of the cutlery manufacturing plant required the importing of large numbers of experienced workmen from Sheffield, England.
- When the cutlery factory was established, it was one of the first of its kind in America.
- The manufacturing plant was built on the site where Ethan Allen and neighbors originally operated a blast furnace, starting in 1762.
- The furnace was a leading arsenal for the Continental Army during the Revolutionary War.

Life in the Community: Lakeville, Connecticut

- The Village of Lakeville within Salisbury Township had a population of 3,489 at the turn of the century; little has changed during the past three years.

- Unlike nearby New York, immigration has had little impact on the village; the workers from England who manufacture knives are the largest group of immigrants the town has experienced.
- The year 1903 is marked by a massive, downtown fire; it destroys two-thirds of the business section of Lakeville.
- In all, eight buildings are destroyed, with estimated damage of $32,000.
- In response to the recent fire that destroyed major parts of downtown, the workmen of the knife factory have scheduled a meeting to organize a volunteer fire company.
- In 1900 the Chapinville schoolhouse was erected; it contained two rooms rather than the traditional one. One room was for educational purposes, the second for a winter or bad weather playground; the average salary for a teacher was $35 a month.
- The Board of School Visitors also increased the level of money provided for textbooks and school supplies by $50 for each district; expenditures were not to exceed $450.
- In 1900 the people of Salisbury approved a tax of 11 mills—10 to be used to defray town expenses and one to retire indebtedness.
- The other major employer, in addition to the Holly Knife Company, is the Richardson Barnum Company, which operates three iron ore mines.
- In July 1903, the Salisbury Association stages "Old Home Week"; events during the three-day celebration include music by the Scofield's Orchestra, dinner at the library for $1.50, a game of wicket (restricted to persons 50 and over), an address by the governor, a concert and dance costing $0.50 per person, and boat, tub, and swimming races on Lake Wononscopomuc.
- The village is experiencing a housing shortage that has forced some workers to leave.
- In the 1880s many factories maintained tenement housing for their workers as part of their pay, a practice that is declining statewide by 1903.
- The practice of operating a company store and boarding houses is also in decline.
- Already known for its private academy, a new school, known as Saint Austin's is being built; enrollment is 35 boys, aged 11 to 16. Tuition for one year is $600 with courses of study in Latin, Greek, arithmetic, English, Roman history, and U.S. history.

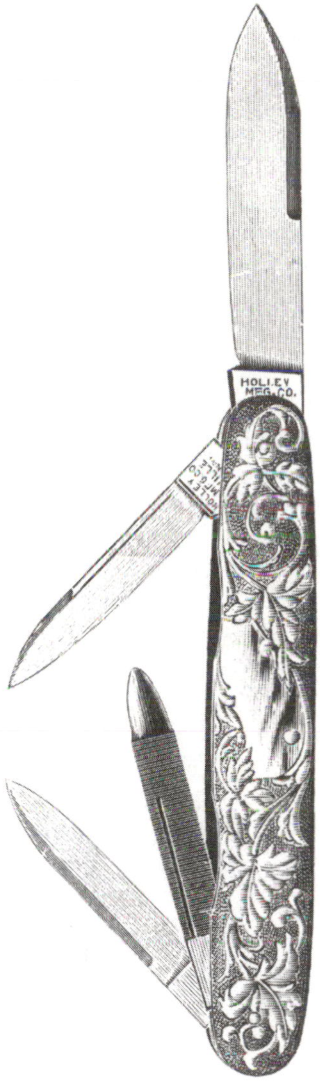

Advertising Letter for Holley Manufacturing Company, Makers of Hand-Forged Pocket Cutlery, February, 15, 1906:

"Every blade we make is forged with hand hammers. We do not operate "drop-forge" blade hammers. We will hand over $5,000 in cash to any man who can disprove these statements, and that is an offer that no other corporation engaged in the manufacture of American pocket cutlery is in a position to make.

Are you wholly satisfied with the pocket cutlery you are selling? Are you buying at first hand, or are you paying middlemen's profits? This is our 'traveler' and he is coming again. In the meantime do us the favor of inspecting the catalog we are sending you, applying 50% and 10% discount to the prices therein. It will do you no harm, it may do us both good."

"Disastrous Fire Visits the Village of Salisbury, Hose from Millerton Saves the East Side of the Street after Eight Buildings Had Gone up," *The Lakeville Journal*, March 3, 1903:

"Probably the most disastrous fire in the history of the town of Salisbury occurred at Salisbury Center at an early hour on Saturday morning, and the greater part of the business section of the village now lays in blackened ruins and probably fully $30,000 have gone up in smoke. At one time almost the entire east side of Main Street seemed to be doomed and everyone made ready to move their effects out as quickly as possible. As it is, the village practically owes it rescue to outside help, a still night, and steady falling rain. But for these agencies many a house would have caught fire and many a family would today have been without a roof to cover them.

As nearly as can be ascertained, the facts are as follows: The village was wrapped in sleep when Professor Charles Warner was aroused and went to the window at about two o'clock. Looking across the street, he was startled to see the interior of Hortie's store and barbershop in flames. He quickly rushed out to summon help. About that time C.F. Wanger, whose store and residence adjoined the burning building, was awakened by noise, smelled smoke, and started for his rear door, only to discover the blaze a few seconds later than Mr. Warner. Both gentlemen immediately started the alarm . . . the cause of the fire cannot be definitely stated but judging from the fact that a window in Hortie's store was found open and the money drawer seen on the counter, the general conclusion is that the fire was the work of an incendiary. Mr. Warner says that when he looked through the window he saw a number of pails containing what might have been kerosene standing about on the floor and near each one was a blaze, so it was evidently intended to make a sure job at firing the building . . . The sight of the fire when entering the village was a grand and awful one. A large number of people from the surrounding country visited the ruins on Saturday and Sunday. Salisbury feels very thankful that Lakeville and Millerton are within calling distance. Only for the help of these villages a still greater calamity would have to be chronicled."

The manufacturing plant sits in the heart of the village.

- The Congregational Church was renovated, acquired a new organ, and began a Girls' Club in 1901.
- Connecticut manufacturers, including companies making cutlery, tools, and saddlery hardware, grossed over $23 million in 1900—an increase of 50 percent over the previous 20 years.
- Of the state's population of 900,000 nearly one-fourth are engaged in manufacturing.
- The number of manufacturing establishments in the state has increased 78 percent from 5,128 in 1870 to 9,128 in 1900.
- During the previous decade, 92 factories have been created, including 31 for the manufacture of fur hats, 17 for hardware, and 16 to manufacture bicycles.

Historical Snapshot
1903–1904

- The Wright Brothers made the first sustained manned flights in a controlled, gasoline-powered aircraft
- The 24-hp Chadwick motorcar was introduced, capable of 60 mph; cost: $4,000
- Massachusetts created the first automobile license plate
- Marie Louise Van Vorst infiltrated factories to expose the problems of child labor
- The Harley-Davidson motorcycle was introduced
- An automatic machine to clean a salmon and cut off its head and tail was devised by A.K. Smith
- Sanka Coffee was introduced by German coffee-importer Ludwig Roselius
- Post Toasties were introduced by the Postum Company
- The St. Louis Fair spawned iced tea and the ice cream cone
- The *Ladies' Home Journal* published an exposé of the U.S. patent medicine business
- Montgomery Ward distributed free catalogues, mailing three million books; Sears, Roebuck distributed a million copies of its spring catalogue
- An outbreak of typhoid fever in New York City was traced to "Typhoid Mary" Mallon, a carrier of the disease who took jobs handling food, often under an assumed name
- The National Women's Trade Union League was formed by middle-class and working women to foster women's education and help women organize unions
- The New York Society for the Suppression of Vice targeted playing cards, roulette, lotto, watches with obscene pictures, and articles of rubber for immoral use
- Florida gained the title to the Everglades swamp and immediately made plans for drainage
- Louis Sherry's on New York City's 5th Avenue opened the New York Riding Club, where members could eat in the saddle
- A Packard Model F went from San Francisco to New York City in 51 days, the first authenticated transcontinental auto trip
- Women's groups led by the wealthy, who were fighting for better conditions for working women, were branded "the mink brigade"
- Horace Fletcher's book *ABC of Nutrition* advocated chewing your food 32 times a bite, sparking a special trend for mastication

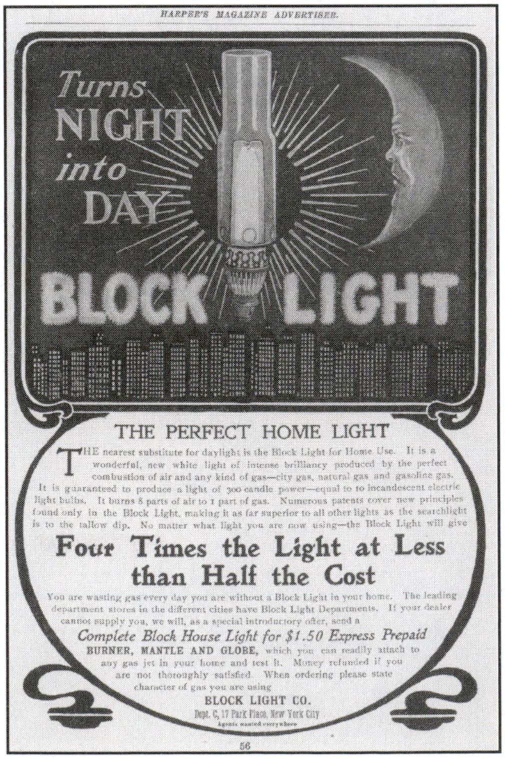

1903 Economic Profile

Income, Standard Jobs

Average of all Industries, Excluding Farm Labor	$543
Average of all Industries, Including Farm Labor	$489
Bituminous Coal Mining	$734
Building Trades, Union Workers	$1,059
Clerical Workers in Manufacturing	$1,037
Domestics	$270
Farm Labor	$277
Federal Civilian	$1,009
Federal Employees, Executive Departments	$1,067
Finance, Insurance, and Real Estate	$1,078
Lower-Skilled Labor	$501
Manufacturing, Payroll	$541
Manufacturing, Union Workers	$989
Medical/Health Services Workers	$275
Ministers	$761
Nonprofit Organization Workers	$679
Postal Employees	$924
Public School Teachers	$358
State and Local Government Workers	$621
Steam Railroads, Wage Earners	$593
Street Railways Workers	$582
Telegraph Industry Workers	$573
Telephone Industry Workers	$379
Wholesale and Retail Trade Workers	$537

Selected Prices

Applewood Pipe	$0.04
Castoria	$0.35
Coffee per Pound	$0.13
Curtains, per Pair	$3.50
Fleece-Lined Undervest	$0.39
Garden Hose, ½", per Foot	$0.10
Hammer, Sears & Roebuck, 1½", One Pound	$0.53
Hotel Room, per Day	$2.00
Man's Suit, Fitzmaurice	$8.50
Palm Reading, Half-Hour	$2.00
Petroleum Jelly	$0.04
Prunes	$0.10
Sheet, 81" x 90"	$0.98
Shotgun	$27.75
Silk Elastic Belt	$0.50
Silver Thimble	$0.15

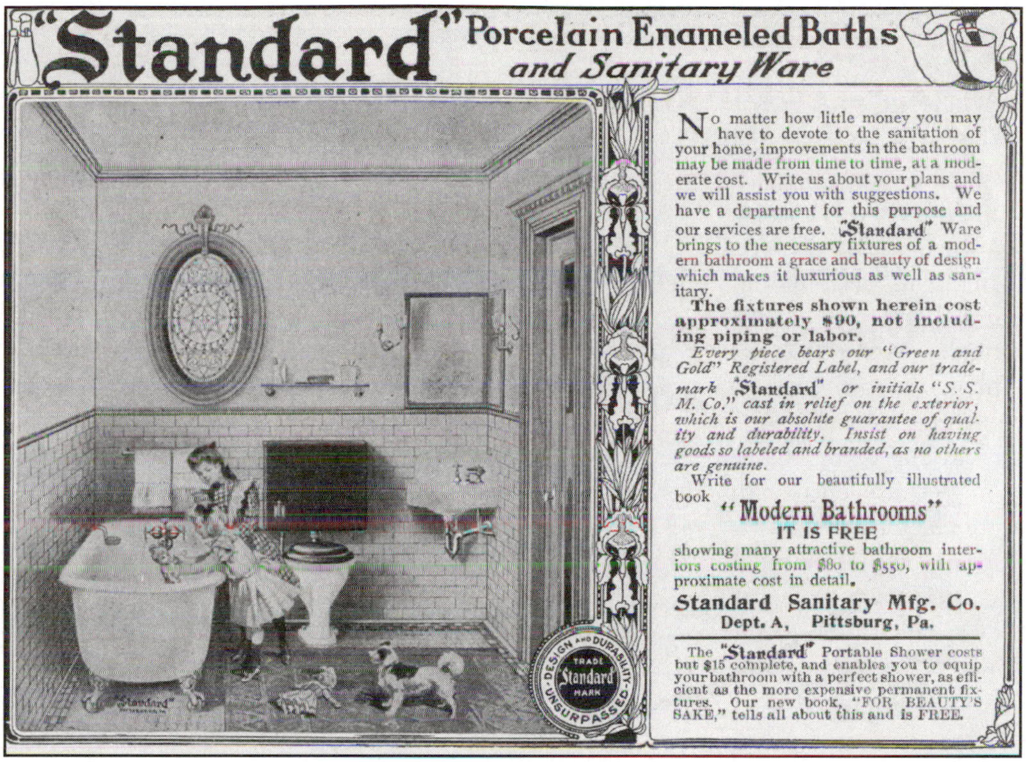

Sweet Pickled Peaches $0.47
Thomas Motor Bicycle $200.00
Yale Touring Car $1,750.00
Zinfandel; 12 Quarts, per Case. $5.00

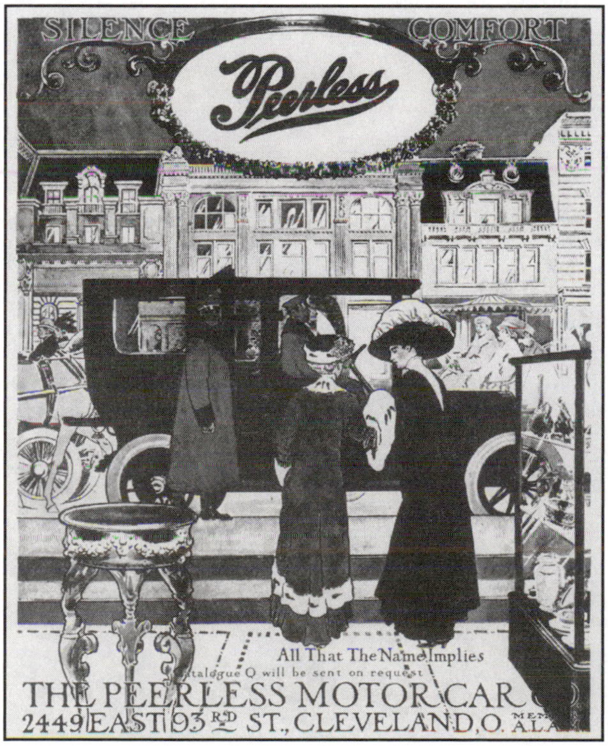

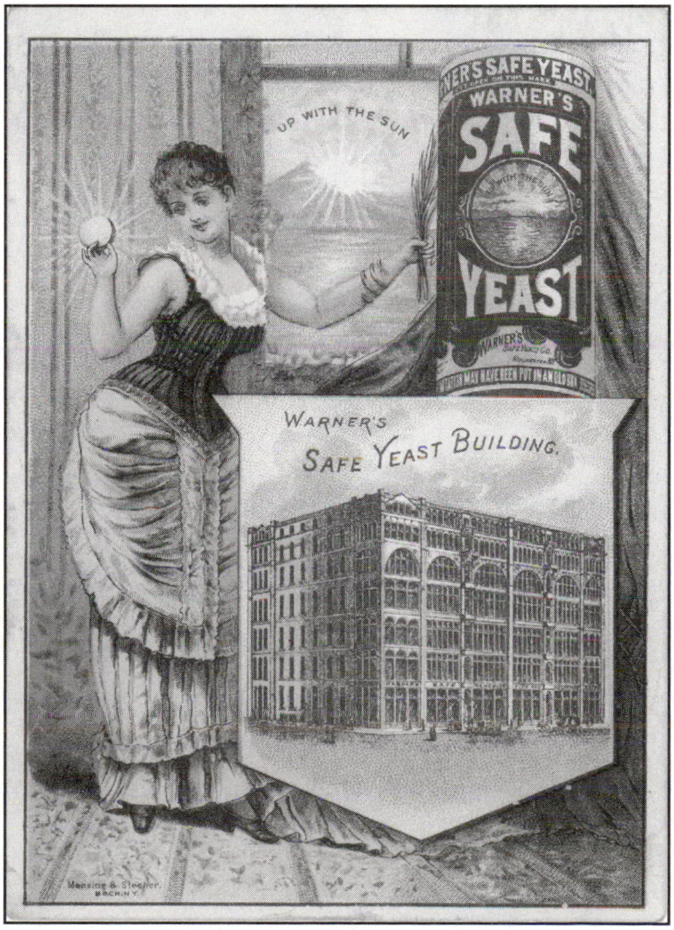

"Lakeville—Its Educational and Commercial Interests," by Edward Bailey Eaton, *The Connecticut Magazine*, December 1903:

"The hill section of Connecticut gives this historic state a claim to distinction for its scenic beauty. Appropriately titled 'The American Switzerland,' the Southern Berkshires and the Litchfield hills have become the Mecca of those who love the wildwood and the lake. The invigorating atmosphere of the mountain heights has given it a wide renown, and the beautiful winding drives under the branches of towering maples are lined with summer homes and educational institutions, its climatic changing having made it the center of some of the best educational institutions in the country. In the center of the village is the quaint country thoroughfare with its mercantile establishments and its hospitable merchantmen.

Though apparently remote from the main lines of travel, Lakeville is easy access from New York and other central points . . . . The run from New York City to Millerton (four miles from Lakeville and Salisbury) occupied about two hours and a quarter, and during the summer season there is through car service between New York and Lakeville. The round trip by this fare is $4.00 . . . In 1844 Alexander H. Holley erected a factory upon the site of the old furnace, and began to manufacture pocket cutlery. In 1846 Nathan W. Merwin was taken into partnership, and Holley and Merwin conducted the business until 1850, when George B. Burrall became a partner and the firm name was changed to Holley & Company In 1854 Holley & Company was merged into the Holley Manufacturing Company, which was incorporated that year. . . . Although this concern has been surpassed in point of size by many of the large manufacturers of recent years, it retains a reputation for the highest quality product, and is recognized locally as one of the chief factors in the prosperity of Lakeville for half a century.

This industry has been the means of introducing a new element into the population in the persons of the Englishmen from Sheffield, the great cutlery center. The usual number of employees is between 40 and 50, and at the present time over 60 percent are of English birth or parentage. The original factory built in 1844 is still occupied, and is beyond question the only building in America which has been used continuously and exclusively for nearly 60 years in the manufacture of pocket knives."

Grocery list for Holley family in Lakeville, Connecticut:

In February 1904, the family made 12 separate shopping trips to the store during the month. Total cost: $12.03

Two Borax	$0.20
11 Butter	$3.84
Six Chimney	$0.60
One Chocolate	$0.40
Three Crackers	$0.25
One Lemon	$0.05
Two Peas	$0.40
Two Macaroni	$0.30
Five Rice	$0.50
12 Soap	$0.50
Three Starch	$0.30
One Stove Polish	$0.10
One Sugar	$1.00
Eight Tomas [sic]	$1.38
Vanilla	$2.15
Three Yeast	$0.06

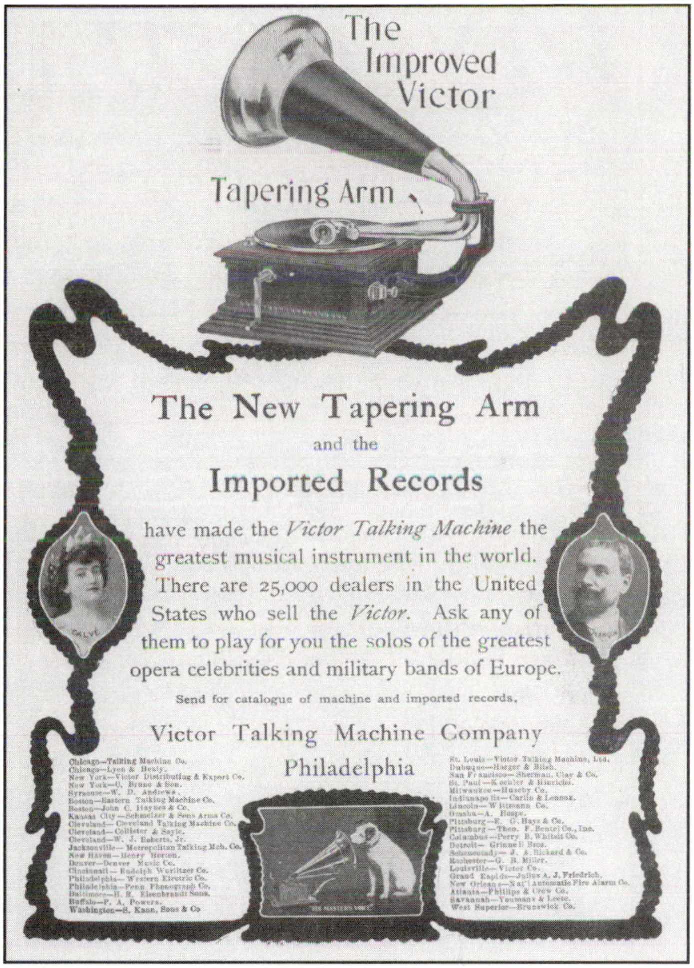

Life in Lakeville, Connecticut, centers around Lake Wononscopomuc.

"Splitting Hairs," by Marlyn Irvin Margulis, *Antique Trader*, January 19, 2000:

"Prior to the Civil War, there weren't many professional hairdressers. Women either cared for their hair themselves or assigned that task to their servants or slaves. Well-to-do women often depended upon the few male hairdressers to give them at-home beauty treatments. By the late nineteenth century, growing numbers of working class women began working as hairdressers, once regarded as a 'vulgarizing calling.'

A new curly style emerged in 1872 when Marcel Grateau, a French hairdresser, invented the Marcel wave, a look that was achieved by using heated tongs on the hair to achieve a look that imitated the hair's natural curl. Beauty industry experts in Europe belittled Grateau's curling iron because they were apprehensive that it would destroy the hair industry. The effect of introducing the Marcel iron in the United States in 1897 was totally different. Hairstylists welcomed the new tool, and their customers enjoyed the soft, wavy results.

The hot-blast hairdryer was introduced by Alexandre F. Godefroy, a Frenchman who emigrated to America in 1879. His dryer did not meet with early success because it was expensive to produce. As salons grew in popularity, the industry added services for beautifying more than the hair. The face steamer was introduced in the late nineteenth century, and salons began offering facials on a regular basis. One chair that featured an attachment for a facial was called the Cleopatra [sic] Portable Vaporizer. An advertisement explained that this product 'enables the customer to sit in the proper upright position for drainage of the waste and impurities that are dissolved by the gently penetrating vapor, and insures reducing of large pores.'

During the 1890s hairdressers were often asked to create the 'Grecian Revival' a popular hairdo of the time. This do included high, pinned hair and some tresses that were curled at the sides and nape of the neck. When illustrator Charles Dana Gibson* introduced what came to be known as Gibson Girl drawings in 1902, thousands of women tried to recreate the look. They used wires or horsehair pads to provide a frame for the romantic pompadour style. Many women used 'hair rats,' pieces of cloth in a cigar or donut-shape with a sponge-like material on the inside and firm netting on the outside. Hairpins could be stuck into the netting."

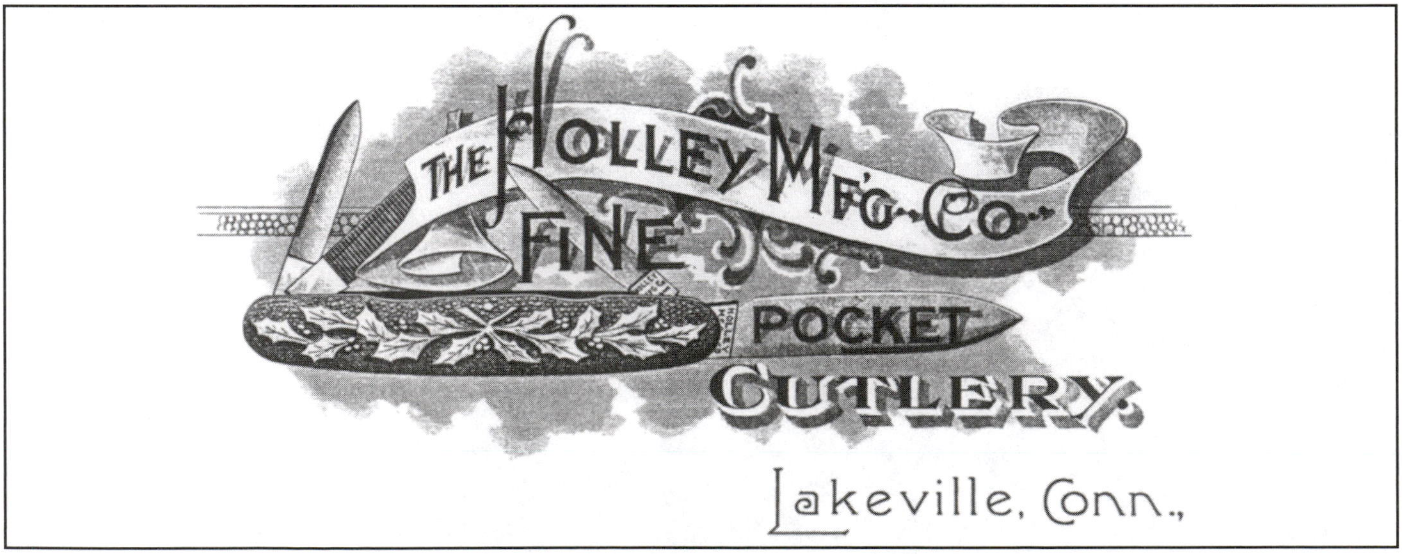

*Gibson's niece, Nancy Tier, of Lakeville, was a model for his Gibson Girl illustrations.

"The Holley Hand-Forged Knives, Every Knife Guaranteed," *The Youth's Companion*, October 1912:

"There are two methods used in making knife blades—the modern drop-forging process by the use of machinery and the other, old-time method of forging by hand. By the drop-forging process, an ordinary workman can produce 1,000 or more blades in a day; by the hand-forging method, a skilled workman is unable to produce over 150 of the same sized blades in a day. In making a blade by hand, an expert forger delivers 40 or 50 blows or taps with a three- or four-pound hand hammer, striking the blade at different angles in shaping it, but constantly 'drawing' out the steel toward the point, thus elongating the crystals, so that their lateral edges are parallel with the cutting side of the blade. These elongated crystals produce the cutting edge.

This hammering of the hot steel multiplies its strength two to five times, varying in proportion to the quality of steel and the amount of hammering done. This 'kneading' or condensing effect, if thoroughly and deftly done, extends through the whole mass, and produces the proper crystalline structure necessary for the perfect cutting edge. The factory in which Holley hand-forged knives are made was established in 1844, and is the oldest pocket cutlery factory in America. Hand-forged blades are here produced exclusively, and the utmost care is taken in tempering and polishing. Many of the skilled workmen have served at the forges and polishing wheels for years. The blades of the Holley knives are guaranteed to be hand-forged, and an absolute warranty is given with each knife."

WE CLAIM

1. That all of our blades are HAND-FORGED.
2. That we use only the best steel and other materials obtainable.
3. That Holley Knives have a deserved and enviable reputation for durability and finish.
4. That we are actuated by the belief that the QUALITY of goods placed upon the market is of the FIRST IMPORTANCE.
5. That Holley Knives are superior to many other makes, and the equal of any, either foreign or domestic.

We do not believe in spurious or inflated advertising, but make only such claims as can be proved by the investigation which they demand.

Please give especial attention to the "IMPORTANT NOTE" on page 111.

The paging of this supplement is continued from our regular catalogue.

All cuts in this supplement are full size.

Prices on application.

THE HOLLEY MANUFACTURING CO.

April 1, 1902.

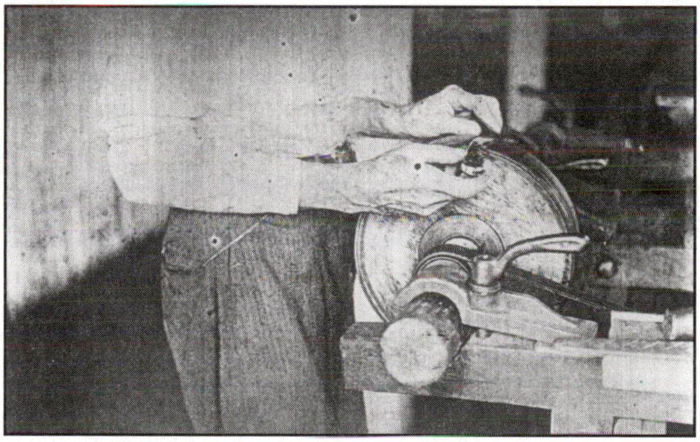

"Labor World," a regular feature of *The Lakeville Journal*, appeared on March 21, 1903:

- Bookbinders have organized in New Haven, Connecticut
- An organization of union carpenters will be formed in Branford, Connecticut
- Efforts are being made at Spokane, Washington, to organize a union of servant girls
- Tacoma, Washington, cigarmakers have asked for a 10 percent advance in wages
- Trouble with the workmen in the iron industries in Montreal, Canada, is now feared
- There are in New York in round numbers 1,000 men teachers and 11,000 women
- In Chicago, Ill., electrical workers will demand an increase of $1.00 a day, beginning April 1. Their scale now is $4.00
- Ten thousand cloak makers have gained advances in wages in New York City. The advances in many instances are from 20 to 40 percent

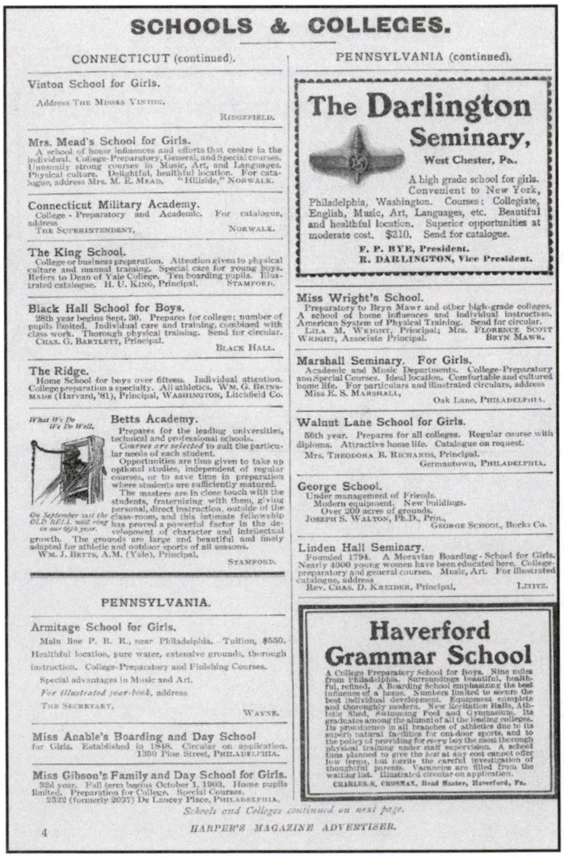

SCHOOLS & COLLEGES.

CONNECTICUT (continued).

Vinton School for Girls.
Address THE MISSES VINTON, RIDGEFIELD.

Mrs. Mead's School for Girls.
A school of home influences and efforts that centre in the individual. College-Preparatory, General, and Special courses. Unusually strong courses in Music, Art, and Languages. Physical culture. Delightful, healthful location. For catalogue, address Mrs. M. E. MEAD, "Hillside," NORWALK.

Connecticut Military Academy.
College - Preparatory and Academic. For catalogue, address THE SUPERINTENDENT, NORWALK.

The King School.
College or business preparation. Attention given to physical culture and manual training. Special care for young boys. Refers to Dean of Yale College. Ten boarding pupils. Illustrated catalogue. H. U. KING, Principal. STAMFORD.

Black Hall School for Boys.
28th year begins Sept. 30. Prepares for college; number of pupils limited. Individual care and training, combined with class work. Thorough physical training. Send for circular. CHAS. G. BARTLETT, Principal. BLACK HALL.

The Ridge.
Home School for boys over fifteen. Individual attention. College preparation a specialty. All athletics. WM. G. BRINSMADE (Harvard, '81), Principal, WASHINGTON, Litchfield Co.

What We Do We Do Well.

Betts Academy.
Prepares for the leading universities, technical and professional schools.
Courses are selected to suit the particular needs of each student.
Opportunities are thus given to take up optional studies, independent of regular courses, or to save time in preparation where students are sufficiently matured.
The masters are in close touch with the students, fraternizing with them, giving personal, direct instruction, outside of the class-room, and this intimate fellowship has proved a powerful factor in the development of character and intellectual growth. The grounds are large and beautiful and finely adapted for athletic and outdoor sports of all seasons.
WM. J. BETTS, A.M. (Yale), Principal. STAMFORD.

On September 21st the OLD BELL will ring in our 65th year.

PENNSYLVANIA.

Armitage School for Girls.
Main line P. R. R., near Philadelphia. Tuition, $550. Healthful location, pure water, extensive grounds, thorough instruction. College-Preparatory and Finishing Courses.
Special advantages in Music and Art.
For illustrated year-book, address
THE SECRETARY, WAYNE.

Miss Anable's Boarding and Day School for Girls. Established in 1848. Circular on application. 1350 Pine Street, PHILADELPHIA.

Miss Gibson's Family and Day School for Girls.
32d year. Fall term begins October 1, 1903. Home pupils limited. Preparation for College. Special Courses.
2322 (formerly 2037) De Lancey Place, PHILADELPHIA.

PENNSYLVANIA (continued).

The Darlington Seminary,
West Chester, Pa.
A high grade school for girls. Convenient to New York, Philadelphia, Washington. Courses: Collegiate, English, Music, Art, Languages, etc. Beautiful and healthful location. Superior opportunities at moderate cost. $210. Send for catalogue.
F. P. BYE, President.
R. DARLINGTON, Vice President.

Miss Wright's School.
Preparatory to Bryn Mawr and other high-grade colleges. A school of home influences and individual instruction. American System of Physical Training. Send for circular.
LILA M. WRIGHT, Principal; MRS. FLORENCE SCOTT WRIGHT, Associate Principal. BRYN MAWR.

Marshall Seminary. For Girls.
Academic and Music Departments. College-Preparatory and Special Courses. Ideal location. Comfortable and cultured home life. For particulars and illustrated circulars, address
Miss E. S. MARSHALL, Oak Lane, PHILADELPHIA.

Walnut Lane School for Girls.
58th year. Prepares for all colleges. Regular course with diploma. Attractive home life. Catalogue on request.
Mrs. THEODORA B. RICHARDS, Principal. Germantown, PHILADELPHIA.

George School.
Under management of Friends.
Modern equipment. New buildings.
Over 200 acres of grounds.
JOSEPH S. WALTON, Ph.D., Prin., GEORGE SCHOOL, Bucks Co.

Linden Hall Seminary.
Founded 1794. A Moravian Boarding-School for Girls. Nearly 4000 young women have been educated here. College-preparatory and general courses. Music, Art. For illustrated catalogue, address
Rev. CHAS. D. KREIDER, Principal, LITITZ.

Haverford Grammar School
A College Preparatory School for Boys. Nine miles from Philadelphia. Surroundings beautiful, healthful, refined. A Boarding School emphasizing the best influence of a home. Numbers limited to secure the best individual development. Equipment complete and thoroughly modern. New Recitation Halls, Athletic Shed, Swimming Pool and Gymnasium. Its graduates among the alumni of all the leading colleges. Its prominence in all branches of athletics due to its superb natural facilities for out-door sports, and to the policy of providing for *every* boy the most thorough physical training under staff supervision. A school thus planned to give the *best* at any cost cannot offer low terms, but merits the careful investigation of thoughtful parents. Vacancies are filled from the waiting list. Illustrated circular on application.
CHARLES S. CROSMAN, Head Master, Haverford, Pa.

Schools and Colleges continued on next page.

4 HARPER'S MAGAZINE ADVERTISER.

HE LADY FROM PHILADELPHIA

"Suppose we ask the Lady from Philadelphia what is best to be done."—The Peterkin Papers.

DRAWINGS BY KATHARINE N. RICHARDSON

What I Am Asked

ve the rules of the
aving each inquirer
ptation according to
rcumstances of her

THE tea service is on the luncheon table except when many guests are present, and the lady of the house makes the tea; the water is supplied from a kettle over an alcohol lamp.

MAID MARIAN. Under the cover of your incognito I may speak the more frankly, especially as you desire the answer published for the benefit of other girls. If a young man insists upon holding your hand when calling upon you, in spite of your protestations, it must be only because he does not believe you to be serious, or else he is a man who should

1904 News Profile

"The Lady from Philadelphia," *The Ladies' Home Journal*, May 1904:

" 'Suppose we ask the Lady from Philadelphia what is best to be done': *The Peterkin Papers*

Many requests have come to me for information on the subject of the conventional setting and serving of the table. I will give the rules of the present usage, leaving each inquirer to make the adaptation according to the means, needs, and circumstances of her household.

The first rule of all is not to attempt more than one can do easily and well. Anything conspicuously out of harmony with one's circumstances is in bad taste. It is, however, quite possible to combine simplicity with a pleasing presentation of food, and the accepted standards have been made with a view to minimizing the difficulties.

For instance, the placing of glasses, spoons, and knives on the right of the plate and the forks at the left is not an arbitrary regulation, but because the forks are used by the left hand and the other things by the right.

That each dish passed around the table by the servant is offered at the left of a person and all plates removed from the right, does not come from any fashionable precedent, but from the greater ease in helping one's self and convenience to the person serving the table, who may thus use the right hand in drawing the plates.

Besides the convenience, the eye is also to be pleased. In setting a table, therefore, the dishes should be placed with careful regularity, the plates at each side opposite each other. The room must be freshly aired, shaded in summer, and every possible sunbeam encouraged to enter in winter.

The modern breakfast table is dainty in appearance, the linen, whatever its quality, immaculate. The dish of fruit or a few growing ferns occupies the centre. The tray with the coffee service, cups—each standing in its saucer if there be room, not piled up—and the plate of the lady of the house is at one end. A teaspoon in each saucer does away with the old-fashioned spoon-holder.

At each place or 'cover' is a plate, dessertspoon, knife, and the forks that will be required, a freshly-filled glass of iced water, but without ice, and a small saltcellar at the left—unless large ones are at the four corners of the table.

If bread-and-butter plates are used they are placed, with small silver knives upon them, at the left of the breakfast plate. Upon this the napkin is laid, simply folded. Napkin-rings are out of fashion. As fruit often forms the first course, sometimes finger bowls are placed at the beginning of the meal—grapefruit or unhulled strawberries make their presence to be desired—otherwise they are used only at its close.

As each soiled plate is removed with one hand a clean one is substituted by the other. When the hot plates have replaced those used for the fruit, the lady of the house will have poured the coffee. A cereal is usually served next, followed perhaps by eggs, fish, kidneys, or mince.

No hot dishes are placed upon the tables of fashionable folk these days; everything is passed around. Those, however, who like old-time ways adhere to the custom of having the principal dishes placed before the master of the house to serve; others wait upon themselves, summoning assistance by a bell when needed. In winter steaming food upon the table has a suggestion of homely comfort, but in warm weather the newer way has its advantages.

Dry toast is hidden in the folds of a napkin to keep it hot, as are also boiled eggs if eggcups are at each cover, or they are passed on a tray in the small eggcups. Dessertspoons are used for grapefruit, berries, and cereals. Smaller napkins are used for breakfast and luncheons.

At luncheons the custom of using a bare table has been revived. Doilies which match the centerpiece are placed under the plates and principal dishes. Many, however, prefer to use a tablecloth over a cover of thick canton flannel.

The tea service is placed on the luncheon table except when many guests are present, and the lady of the house makes the tea; the water is supplied from a kettle over an alcohol lamp.

If the 'good old-fashioned way' be followed, the bread, butter, cake, preserves, or fruit are placed on the table before the summons of the meal is given. A folded doily is interposed between the bread, cake, etc., and the plates containing them. The caster is relegated to the side table, its furnishings being less used than formerly.

As has been said, it is the fashion to have no food on the table, but four small dishes of pretty china, glass, or silver are placed around the formal centerpiece (a foot from it) containing small dainties, as, for instance, cakes or wafers, peppermints, prunes, maple sugar, preserved ginger, almonds, and raisins, etc. Smaller dishes of olives and radishes give a pretty touch to the table.

Though we may prefer the old way when the family is alone, it has been found not only more attractive but also far easier to serve a meal in the newer mode; and when we have guests we welcome all that helps to make the service move smoothly. Each dish is passed around in turn, beginning at the right and left of the hostess alternately, and placed on the side table when not in use. No broken food or half-filled dishes are in sight. That which well-bred people accept today as the most ordinary and commonplace was once an innovation, challenged and demurred at by those who like accustomed ways.

With this fashion has come that of providing little more than just enough—a hint from the frugal French, who deprecate anything that seems wasteful.

A luncheon may begin with fruit and end with some simple sweet, or begin with bouillon (served in cups) and conclude with fruit—the intermediate courses being eggs or fish, one hot meat with a single vegetable, or a cold meat with a salad. The provision of fewer courses is allowable.

Afternoon tea is usually served at five o-clock, but the arrival of callers between the hours of four and six is the signal for offering, whether accepted or not.

Some persons have their tea tables ready, set in their drawing or living rooms, requiring only to have the kettle filled and the cream and cakes or tiny cress, olive, or cucumber sandwiches brought in. Others follow the English custom and have everything brought in on a large tray and deposited upon the tea table.

An informal assemblage of a few congenial spirits asked to meet and chat over a cup of tea is the simplest of feminine functions."

1908 Family Profile

Harold Thompson of Gastonia, North Carolina, is vice president of a local bank, battling a declining economy, unstable cotton prices, and a proliferation of new banks, all backed by stockholders eager to climb on the "bankwagon" of wealth; he and his wife, Eugenia, have two children.

Annual Income: $1,805

Annual Budget

The average per capita consumer expenditure in 1908 is not available. The following is for 1909 for all workers nationwide:

Auto Parts	$0.59
Auto Purchases	$1.85
Clothing	$30.00
Dentists	$0.91
Food	$81.43
Furniture	$3.25
Gas and Oil	$1.36
Health Insurance	NR
Housing	$61.48
Intercity Transport	$2.97
Local Transportation	$5.12
Personal Business	$9.61
Personal Care	$2.88
Physicians	$3.24
Private Education and Research	$4.59

Recreation	$9.49
Religion/Welfare Activities	$9.05
Telephone and Telegraph	$1.00
Tobacco	$6.33
Utilities	$4.00
Average per Capita Consumption	$318.42

Life at Home

- Harold Thompson grew up in the small town of Gastonia, North Carolina, where his father is a prominent farmer and political leader.
- Growing up, he often traveled with his father in a horse-drawn carriage to meetings and political gatherings, where he became skilled in small talk, listening, and joking with other businessmen.
- After two years of college at the University of North Carolina in Chapel Hill, he took his father's suggestion, taking a job assisting the president of the local bank, never returning to school.
- He married, Eugenia, a girl from Charlotte, North Carolina, who finished Williamston College in Greenwood, South Carolina; she has kept all the letters he wrote her while in college.
- She still refers to her husband as Mr. Thompson, never using his first name even in the privacy of their home.
- He controls all the money and pays all of the bills; she sometimes hides the change she receives from the grocery money so she will have "mad money" of her own.
- He enjoys trips to New York once a year with his wife to inspect his bank's investments now that he is the Number Two person in the bank.
- They enjoy everything about the trip, from the long train ride through Washington, D.C., and into New York, the chance to visit Broadway theatres, and eat in nice restaurants.
- On a recent trip she was served a fresh banana and loved the taste.
- They rarely visit live theater in North Carolina.
- Running water is now available at their house through the use of a hand pump; a tub has been installed, the city is talking about gaslights in the streets, and the family recently constructed a new outhouse convenient to the house.
- She is currently a member of the Woman's Missionary Society of the First Baptist Church of Gastonia.
- She is also working to develop the Gastonia Library, which got its start at the Y.M.C.A. and is now operated by the all-volunteer Library Association.

His father is a prominent farmer and political leader.

Life at Work

- He enjoys the gentlemen's world of finance; inside the walls of the bank he is far from large-scale farming, where his father ruled everything and everyone with a stern hand.

- As he has gained experience, he has come to enjoy handling commercial paper and being part of the investment committee decisions that determine how surplus deposits of the bank will be handled.
- Occasionally he has to make a decision between risking the bank's money on a farmer who wants a loan to expand his farm or investing the money in New York, where he can have a secure return on the money.
- He is a natural speaker who enjoys organizing projects, raising money, and promoting his community, although he is unsure he will ever come out from under the shadow of his father.
- His father's reputation for honesty and hard work has assisted this man in his career.
- Harold began as a cashier, then began lending money, helping families in the area finance crop loans, farm expansions, clothing, debt consolidations, and farm equipment.
- Thanks to his years on the farm, he feels comfortable making agricultural loans.
- He feels less comfortable financing unreliable equipment such as automobiles, and is unsure what he'd do with a car if the customer did not pay back the loan and he was forced to repossess the auto.
- Six days a week, he arrives at work at 7 a.m. to meet the mail train from Charlotte; at 7:30 a.m. the officers of the bank go over the previous day's business and any pending loan requests until the bank opens its doors at 9 a.m.

Bank clerks are expected to be ready when the doors open at 9 a.m.

- Most days, he goes home at noon for lunch and a nap, returning at 2 p.m. to make sure all mail and bank documents leave on the 2:30 train; he stays at work until 7 p.m., often discussing local projects with other businessmen over a glass of bourbon.
- When the nationwide Panic of 1908 hits late in the year, he and his bank are able to ride out the economic troubles.
- His bank's deposits are at a high mark because of the recent repayment of farm loans following the harvest; also the demand for money is low and spring planting has not started, allowing his bank to ride the storm.
- Interest rates are currently rising, which will slow down loan demand.
- He knows that several farmers who borrowed heavily last year have experienced a very bad year, largely because of excessive rain; he knows that they will want to borrow more, but is unsure of whether or not he will risk the bank's money.
- If he refuses to loan them more money, they will be forced into bankruptcy, but if he loans them more and they default, he could be risking his future at the bank.
- After a dozen years in banking, he has a credit file on nearly every farmer in the county; about 35 percent of the loans he makes are "character loans," usually made on one signature, without collateral other than a personal note.
- He believes in the "Southern way" of lending; be a gentleman first, a businessman second.
- Men and women in the community whose parents were known to be drinkers, immoral, or lazy sometimes find it difficult getting a loan even with collateral.
- From years of listening, he knows who lives up to their obligations and would be likely to repay a loan; he also knows from experience whose father had cheated his father and might be likely to cheat again: a leopard never changes its spots.
- Early in his career he went to night school to study stenography and bookkeeping, jobs that are now beginning to go to women.

Harold and Eugenia Thompson enjoy the annual Bankers Association Convention, which is often held at resort locations along the coast.

Local business leaders often gather in the evenings to discuss politics over a glass of bourbon.

- For most of his career men have dominated the banking industry; now with the popularity of typewriters and adding machines, more women are entering banking as assistants and secretaries. He does not believe that women will ever be well-suited to making difficult lending decisions.
- He and his wife also enjoy their annual trips to a statewide convention of bankers, where the speeches are lighthearted and the friendships abundant.
- Eugenia occasionally talks about moving to a larger city such as Charlotte or Raleigh, but Harold feels comfortable in Gastonia.
- He knows the people who come from good families, and whom he can trust.
- Every banker makes a few mistakes by lending money to people who will not pay him back, but no banker can afford to make many mistakes if the bank is going to succeed.
- His two favorite banker jokes—when in the company of other bankers—are, "It only takes 10 minutes to teach someone to make a loan; it takes 10 years to teach them how to get it all back," and, always with a wink, "A rolling loan gathers no loss."
- Currently, he is working with an agricultural agent to learn more about growing tobacco and vegetables, because the South's dependence on cotton makes him uneasy.
- Raising cattle, he believes, may offer an excellent way to balance the risk of farming.
- He and the president of the bank have discussed the logistics of purchasing prime breeding stock, which could be leased to farmers.
- The recent formation of the Farmers' Union could bring reforms, he believes, or trouble.
- A spokesman for the Union recently said during a speech, "A flock of sheep girded by ravenous wolves would not be in much worse of a fix than are the farmers of the land, surrounded by predatory trusts," while another declared, "Farmers stand alone as the

Thanks to the textile industry, the city of Gastonia is growing rapidly.

only class of producers who work 15 hours a day in competition with each other and sell their products at auction upon the streets."

Life in the Community: Gastonia, North Carolina

- Gaston County, home of Gastonia, was founded in 1846; the area is part of the original land grant of 1663 when Charles II gave the land to eight Lord Proprietors.
- It stretched from the Atlantic to the Pacific Ocean and included all land between the 30th and 38th north latitude, encompassing all of North and South Carolina.
- The Scotch-Irish, the Germans, commonly called the Pennsylvania Dutch, and the Scotch Highlanders settled the area.
- The region became known for the quality of its farms and distilled liquor, produced in local distilleries.
- The town of Gastonia was incorporated in 1877, with a population of 236 people; its town limits were determined by the location of the railroad lines laid by the Richmond & Atlanta Air Line Railway and the Chester & Lenoir Narrow Gauge Railroad.
- By 1908 the population had swelled to more than 5,000, thanks to the construction of a dozen cotton textile manufacturing plants.
- The construction of the Flint Manufacturing Company in 1906 added 35,700 spindles to the county's output.
- The county's school enrollment in 1898 included 3,324 white children and 1,860 black; a census of school age children indicated that a total of 9,206 children were eligible to attend school.
- The school year lasts 14 weeks.
- By 1900 Gaston County had one telephone exchange and 64 telephones.

"In Memory of Decoration Day Back Home," by Berenice Fearn Young, *The Taylor-Trotwood Magazine*, June 1908:

"Today is Decoration Day back home. Out of sight of the shadowed edges of the lovely Appalachians, remote from the pleasant waters of the Tennessee, today I know that all through the South the evening sun will cast its slanting rays on many a green and peaceful graveyard filled full of the living, bearing armfuls of flowers to place upon that earth that holds the memory of her dead, the shallow, sunken mounds bearing nothing more to mark them than a white board with the letters C.S.A. across their fronts—O multitude of witnesses that once there was a Confederacy...!

Many years ago Talmage drew for the men and women of the North a picture of their returning armies. He told how in the pomp and circumstance of war they came back home, marching with proud and victorious tread, reading their glory in the nation's eyes. This is the day we celebrate another army whose men marched, fought, and fighting, fell, and yet whose memories in all the majesty of death march on reading their glory in the nation's tears.

Further on this day we honor them who came, a saddened remnant of a mighty army, home, its banner furled in defeat and not in victory flung to the air, in pathos, not in pomp and circumstance; from general to drummer boy, each knowing that he would find his house in ruins, his farms devastated, his slaves free, his stock killed, his barns empty, his trade destroyed, his money worthless, his social system swept away, his people without law or legal status, his comrades slain, his very traditions gone, without money, credit, employment, or training....

The South has nothing for which to apologize. She knows that the struggle between the states was war and not rebellion, revolution and not conspiracy. She was overthrown and not suppressed. This it is we teach our children and our children's children, till the end of time. This is the honor and justice that we owe the South, by this we decorate our dead."

- The total of telephones had increased to 200 by 1908.
- Banking in Gastonia began with the organization of the private banking house of Craig and Jenkins in 1887, started with $10,000 in stock.
- This bank began in 1893 as a private banking company before becoming a state bank in 1903.
- Since then five new banks have been formed in the county; many people are eager to own bank stock, convinced that the county's growth will justify more banks.
- At the last census, in 1900, more than 90 percent of the state's 1.9 million residents, mostly farmers, lived in rural areas.
- Many of the state's farms are small and undercapitalized; the average value of an acre of land is $6.24.
- The majority of the farmland owners are white; 41 percent of all farms are operated by tenants or sharecroppers, most of whom are African-American.
- In the years following the Civil War, the only source of capital was the merchant, who also sold farm supplies; to ensure his repayment, the merchant demanded that farmers plant cash crops.
- This dependency on merchant lending resulted in the cotton remaining king, with Southern farms showing little crop diversity in the 50 years following the Civil War.

Sir Oliver Lodge on Internal Combustion Engines, *Scientific American*, 1905:

"For about two hours last December Sir Oliver Lodge interested a large number of members of the Automobile and Cycle Engineers' Institute… Sir Oliver said he would make no distinction between oil engines and gas engines, but take a general survey of the whole subject. From the point of view of combustion, a gaseous mixture was the best. For the purpose of ignition the combustible mixture had first to be raised to a temperature at which combustion took place, and it then spread until it ignited the rest of the gas. Rarefaction, or diminished pressure, would prevent ignition spreading, while a rise in temperature would assist combustion or explosion. The lighter the explosive gas the quicker was the movement of the molecules, and as it had been found, he said that in gas engines the quickest combustible mixture was that in which there was a slight excess of hydrogen, or the lighter material: one would have thought that an excess of either material would be a disadvantage, but that did not appear to be the case, although the excess of the heavier material proved disadvantageous because the atoms forming it were moving more slowly."

- North Carolina produces 460,000 bales of cotton; the high yield is attributed to commercial fertilizer and the freedom from the boll weevil.
- Due to the Panic of 1908, dramatically slashed prices remain unstable.
- The production of tobacco is increasing rapidly, often replacing corn as a farm's cash crop; production currently equals 127,503,000 pounds, valued at more than $8 million.
- Many banks are encouraging farmers to diversify into tobacco and away from cotton.
- North Carolina recently adopted statewide prohibition, effective the next year; although Thompson publicly supported prohibition, privately he enjoys a drink many an evening with business associates.
- He believes that prohibition is good for Gastonia because it reduces absenteeism at the mills, and the community is overwhelmingly supportive of being "dry."
- Much of the community is poor, largely dependent on agriculture and the textile mills for income.
- Often residents borrow small amounts from the bank.
- A survey of nearly 1,000 North Carolina small loan borrowers that year shows that 66 needed money for clothing, 10 for rent, food, and fuel, 52 for automobiles, 10 to pay taxes, four for furniture, 107 for sickness and death, two for attorneys' fees, and the remainder for unspecified living expenses or the refinancing of existing indebtedness.
- Half of the loans are for $10 or less, while 40 percent were for less than $25; only two loans were for more than $50.

Historical Snapshot
1908

- Many U.S. banks closed as economic depression deepened
- President Theodore Roosevelt called a White House Conference on conservation
- Cornelius Vanderbilt's yacht, the *North Star,* was reported to cost $250,000; its yearly maintenance was $20,000
- The 47-story Singer Building in New York became the world's tallest skyscraper
- Both the Muir Woods in California and the Grand Canyon were named national monuments worthy of preservation
- The first transatlantic wireless telegraph stations connected Canada to Ireland; messages could be sent for $0.15 a word
- The AC spark plug, Luger pistol, and oscillating fan all came on the market
- The first Mother's Day was celebrated in Philadelphia, Pennsylvania
- New York City passed the Sullivan Ordinance, prohibiting women from smoking in public places
- Alpha Kappa Alpha, the first sorority for black women, was founded in Washington, D.C.
- Nancy Hale became the *New York Times'* first female reporter
- The U.S. Army bought its first aircraft in 1908, a dirigible; because no one could fly it except its owner, it was never used
- The Olympic Games were played in London; the U.S. was the unofficial winner with 23 gold medals
- Thomas Edison's Amberol cylinders, with more grooves per inch, extended the length of time a single recording would play from two to four minutes
- Israel Zangwill wrote, "America is God's Crucible, the great Melting-Pot where all the races of Europe are melting and reforming."
- More than 80 percent of all immigrants since 1900 came from Central Europe, Italy, and Russia

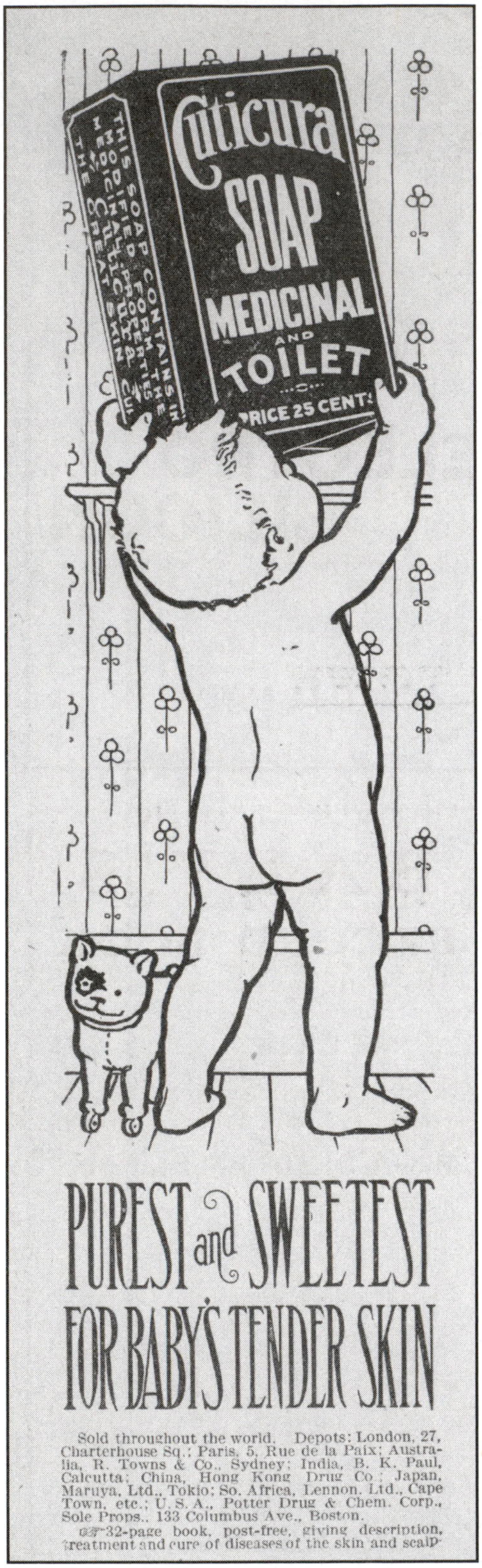

1908 Economic Profile

Income, Standard Jobs

Average of all Industries, Excluding Farm Labor	$564
Average of all Industries, Including Farm Labor	$519
Bituminous Coal Mining	$778
Building Trades, Union Workers	$1,209
Clerical Workers in Manufacturing and Steam Railroads	$1,111
Domestics	$580
Farm Labor	$324
Federal Employees, Executive Departments	$1,102
Finance, Insurance, and Real Estate	$1,218
Gas and Electricity Workers	$595
Lower-Skilled Labor	$496
Manufacturing, Payroll	$563
Manufacturing, Union Workers	$1,022
Medical/Health Services Workers	$313
Ministers	$833
Nonprofit Organization Workers	$743
Postal Employees	$1,023
Public School Teachers	$455
State and Local Government Workers	$695
Steam Railroads, Wage Earners	$667
Street Railways Workers	$650
Telegraph Industry Workers	$639
Telephone Industry Workers	$420
Wholesale and Retail Trade Workers	$609

Selected Prices

Baby Carriage, 16" Steel Wheels with 3/8" Rubber	$4.25
Bed, Brass Post	$28.85
Dental Fillings	$1.00
Furnished Apartment for Rent, per Month	$17.50
Grand Piano	$195.00
Hall Mirror	$3.00
Hat with Ribbon	$6.50
House Paint, per Gallon	$0.98
Iron Stove	$19.50
Man's Glasses, Cable Bow, Gold Filled	$1.98
Oxford Talking Machine	$14.95
Peanuts, Salted, Half-Pound Can	$0.21
Rocking Chair	$2.35
Steel Range	$29.27

Stereoscopic Views, 50 Views
of Sears, Roebuck & Co. $0.35
Strawberries, per Basket $0.15
Tableware, 28 Pieces $4.66
Walking Plow $8.62
Whiskey Flask, Sterling Silver $9.00
Work Shirts $0.46

The Banking Industry

- The National Banking Act of 1863, 1864, and 1865 prohibited private banks from issuing money; national bankers were empowered to issue notes that served as the money supply for the entire nation.
- The national system of money supply lacked central control, especially over credit availability and allocation; its result was that the reserves of banks in agricultural areas were concentrated in New York City, the hub of commercial banking.
- When the demands of farming put strains on the New York banks, the result could be a credit crunch in the South.
- The National Banking Acts disallowed branch banking and the use of first mortgages on real estate as security for loans; it also limited the amount of credit a bank could extend to a borrower to 10 percent of its capital.
- A minimum of $50,000 in capital was required to start new banks; this level was considered so high few banks were chartered across the South.
- Three months into the new century, Congress passed the Currency Act of 1900, designed to strengthen the gold standard and improve the circulation of paper money.
- The legislation also lowered the minimum capital for national banks to $25,000, producing an avalanche of expansion of national banks.
- In 10 years, the number of national banks nearly doubled, from 3,732 to 7,145.

Your Career in Banking,
by Dorcas Campbell, A Horseback Banker:

"A bank doesn't create money, you know, but it can secure deposits from those who have it. Our desire to build deposits and the assurance more would come from the same place became of first-rate importance one day when we acknowledged to ourselves that we weren't getting an appropriate share of deposits, because deposits in our community were shrinking. Business was bad, Main Street reflected this condition, and so did we. We're all dependent on agricultural crops around here, and they seemed to be bringing less and less profit to everyone.

This includes the farmers and their families too. We studied farmers; we read everything we could find, and one old farmer finally gave us a lead. He had hindsight we could respect, for years ago he had had the foresight to personally carry out the program outlined for us. We adopted it as an ideal for every farmer in the community—we dressed it up a little more fancy than he did. That's called merchandising, I understand, but whatever you call it, it focused attention on it. We called it the 'Four Pillars of Income.'

It's been practical; it's brought us results and kept us busy. It kind of had a snowball effect; one thing led to another, so our progress is really the result of a combination of factors. We're just a country bank trying to serve the needs of the people around here."

A popular ditty recited at banking conventions following the Panic of 1907–1908, illustrating how the economy affected both the depositor and the banker:

"The Depositor:
Durn this panic, anyway;
Nuff to make a feller gray.
Got me scared to death, about;
Went and drew my money out.
I been growin' old an' thin
Hidin' it and worryin'.
Guess I'll take it back today;
Durn a panic, anyway.

The Banker:
Durn a panic, anyway;
I've been acting like a jay.
When I heard those Wall Street groans
I just called in all my loans.
Bank is busting full of cash;
Wish I hadn't been so rash.
Loans ain't captured every day;
Durn a panic, anyway."

Christmas cards continue to grow in popularity and sophistication.

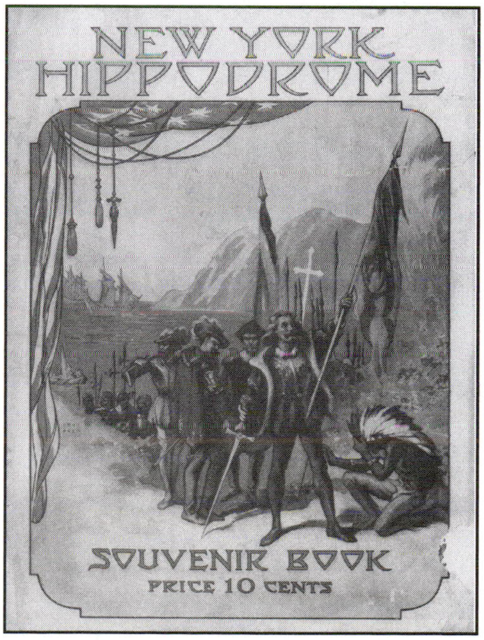

"North Carolina Adopts Statewide Prohibition":

"The best known act of the (Robert B.) Glenn administration was the adoption of statewide prohibition. The temperance forces before 1900 had eliminated the legal sale of liquor from many of the towns by local option elections, and hundreds of rural communities had become 'dry' by obtaining acts of incorporation from the General Assembly. The Democratic-dominated legislature, sensing the popularity of the issue and responsive to the urging of the newly organized North Carolina Anti-Saloon League enacted the Watts Act of 1903. This law prohibited the manufacture and sale of spirituous liquors except in incorporated towns and was calculated 'to get rid of the county distilleries,' which F.M. Simmons called 'Republican recruiting stations.' Two years later the Ward Law, by forbidding the liquor traffic in all communities except incorporated places of at least 1,000 inhabitants, dried up all except 80 of the state's 328 incorporated towns. Sixty-eight of the 98 counties thus had prohibition. The Anti-Saloon League launched an intensive campaign for statewide prohibition in 1907. The following year the General Assembly responded to the urging of Governor Glenn by providing for a statewide referendum on May 26, 1908, to determine whether a statewide prohibition would become effective on July 1, 1909. After a strenuous campaign led by Glenn, who was a powerful and persuasive orator, the people adopted statewide prohibition by a vote of 113,612 to 69,416."

"Cotton Production," *The Ills of the South*, by Charles H. Otken, 1894:

"There is no escape from the argument that the credit monopoly, controlled for 25 years by the merchants, has had much to do with the increase in the cotton crop. Debts and high prices can only be paid by this crop. Considerate merchants who advised farmers to raise corn, grasses, bacon, and stock were almost powerless. If they wanted the farmer's trade they must sell corn, bacon, and mules. But still there is a vast difference between the two merchants; one discouraged his customers from buying corn, bacon, and mules, the other was eager to sell to them whatever they wanted. This eagerness, as rarely freely and frankly expressed, but rather adroitly concealed. The farmer's need was an open book. To make him cringe, and servile in his requests, was the thing wanted. The favor dearly bought was granted. Such men could hardly complain of prices. Such a man was Mr. Easygo. Mr. Windem bought for Mr. Easygo a mule costing $55, and charged him $115; took Mr. Easygo's note drawing 10 percent interest and secured it by lien. He sold him flour for $15—cash price was $8; bacon for $0.15—cash price $0.075; and molasses at $0.75 per gallon. Mr. Easygo was advised to make a big cotton crop. Cotton only can pay for these big prices. All this huckstering business had but one end in view—to get a grip on the man's property and his trade for years to come. The trade was forced by a law of necessity into this merchant's hands. No matter what reasonable and lawful inducement conscientious merchants held out, the farmer's trade had to flow through one and only one channel. More cotton!"

1909 Family Profile

Peter Gargan, a 26-year-old Irish man, is in his fifth year as a department manager of a major department store in Cleveland, Ohio. His salary is excellent; his hours by choice are very long. He is concerned that if he marries his sweetheart, Caroline, his incentive pay will go down because he will be tempted to stay home more.

Annual Income: $11,000
His salary is $4,000 a year; his incentive pay, based on a percentage of sales last year, is $7,000.

Annual Budget
The average per capita consumer expenditure in 1909 of all workers nationwide is:

Auto Parts	$0.59
Auto Purchases	$1.85
Clothing	$30.00
Dentists	$0.91
Food	$81.43
Furniture	$3.25
Gas and Oil	$1.36
Health Insurance	NR
Housing	$61.48
Intercity Transport	$2.97
Local Transportation	$5.12
Personal Business	$9.61
Personal Care	$2.88
Physicians	$3.24
Private Education and Research	$4.59
Recreation	$9.49

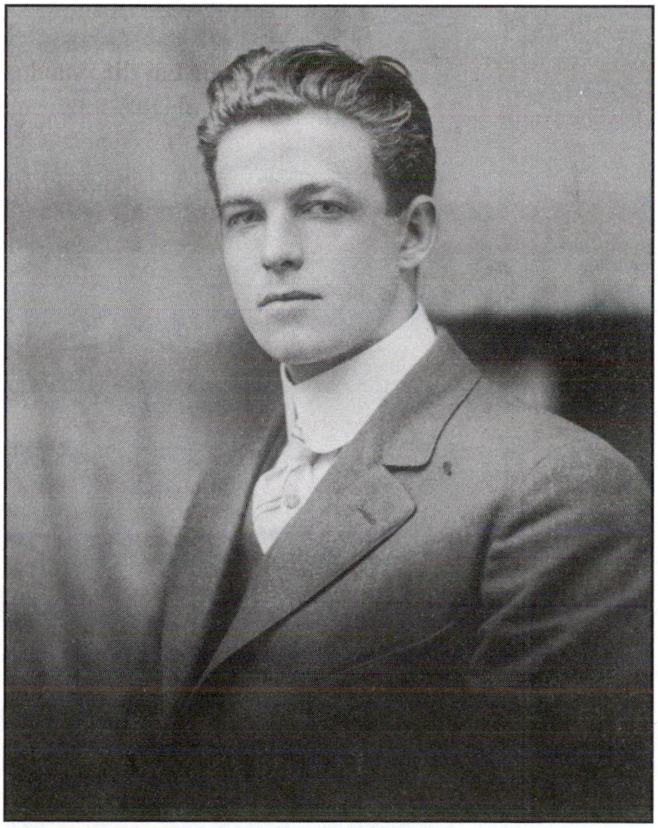

Peter Gargan worries that taking a wife will distract him from his work.

Sundays are often spent in the country with friends.

Religion/Welfare Activities	$9.05
Telephone and Telegraph	$1.00
Tobacco	$6.33
Utilities	$4.00
Average Per Capita Consumption	$318.42

Life at Home

- Born and raised in Chicago, Peter came to Cleveland seven years ago to work for The Mayer-Marks Company, quickly capturing the attention of management for his hard work and excellent sales ability.
- Following high school graduation, he worked for Marshall Fields and Company, gaining valuable experience.
- Like many young men, he read the adventures of Horatio Alger Jr. and dreamed of making his mark on the world.
- He moved to Cleveland believing he could rise faster with Mayer-Marks Co., since Marshall Fields followed strict lines of seniority in selecting department managers.
- Peter lives in a bedroom apartment that includes a parlor, bedroom, kitchen, and tub; the bathroom is down the hall and is shared by three others.
- He rarely buys furniture, preferring to bring home damaged goods or "seconds" from the store, and has never bothered to buy a rug, even though he deals in the finest carpets in the city.
- Buying a house is not a high priority; his money is invested in stocks and bonds.
- His investments include railroad bonds, utilities stocks, and even stock in the new company that manufactures typewriters.
- Twice a year he sends money to his mother, who still lives in Chicago.
- He is thinking about marriage to a 17-year-old girl, who recently completed high school and is now studying music.
- He is concerned about the cost of having a wife and whether he is ready; he is also unsure of how much a new wife would take him away from work.
- Caroline wants a house; she has lived in an apartment her entire life and has dreams of a house with a private tub and access to a yard where she can grow vegetables.
- After marriage she would like to continue taking lessons at the Opera House Dancing Academy.
- He believes hard work is responsible for the store's success and his large income.
- The store is near his home, so he walks to work.
- Peter's one luxury is hiring a buggy on Sundays to take rides in the country with Caroline.

Like many young men, he grew up reading Horatio Alger books and dreamed of being a success.

- A carriage ride in the country is the only time they are alone; when he visits at her home, they must stay in the parlor.
- Even on weekends he wears dark pants, matching jacket, white shirt, and hat.
- He believes that everything he does reflects on his work and has given up smoking in public, concerned that his customers might see him and disapprove.

Life at Work

- His department store is one of the largest in the city, covering nearly a full block and standing four stories.
- Peter is in charge of the carpet, rug, and oilcloth departments, serving as both a buyer for the department and its manager.
- Currently a sale is under way; a Wilton Velvet room-sized rug, measuring 9'x 12', is now selling for $27.50, one-fourth off its normal price of $38.
- His store and especially his department cater to "society people" or carriage trade of Cleveland.
- His aim is to make trading and buying as comfortable as possible.
- The customer is not treated as a potential spender, but a guest in his home.
- He believes that retailers like himself are the purchasing agents for the community, helping to brings goods to the community and set appropriate standards of taste.
- Some women will stay at the store all day with their friends, returning home just in time to greet their husbands coming from work.

Peter Gargan is in charge of the carpet, rug, and oilcloth departments.

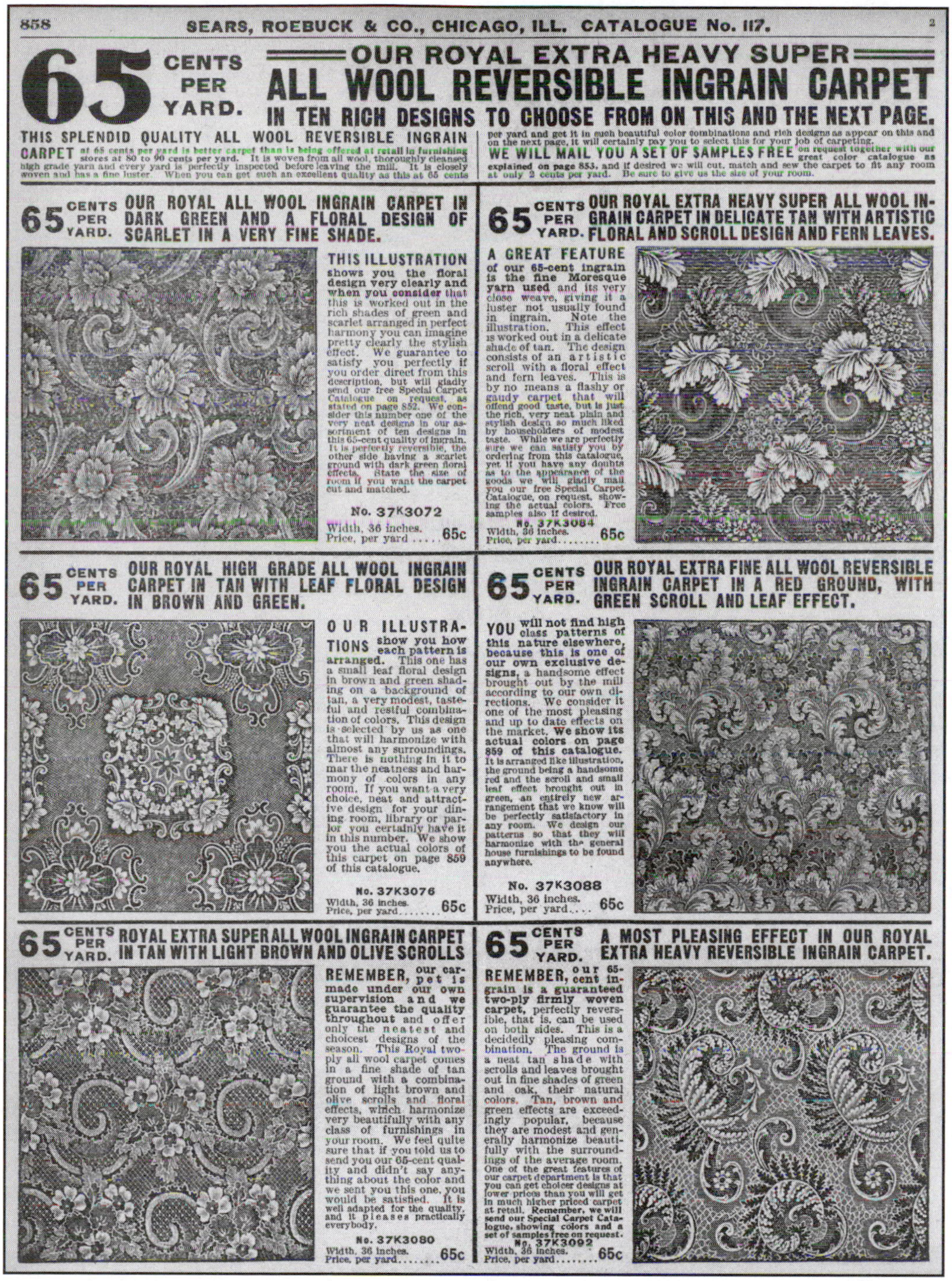

858 SEARS, ROEBUCK & CO., CHICAGO, ILL. CATALOGUE No. 117. 2

65 CENTS PER YARD. OUR ROYAL EXTRA HEAVY SUPER ALL WOOL REVERSIBLE INGRAIN CARPET IN TEN RICH DESIGNS TO CHOOSE FROM ON THIS AND THE NEXT PAGE.

THIS SPLENDID QUALITY ALL WOOL REVERSIBLE INGRAIN CARPET at 65 cents per yard is better carpet than is being offered at retail in furnishing stores at 80 to 90 cents per yard. It is woven from all wool, thoroughly cleansed high grade yarn and every yard is perfectly inspected before leaving the mill. It is closely woven and has a fine luster. When you can get such an excellent quality as this at 65 cents per yard and get it in such beautiful color combinations and rich designs as appear on this and on the next page, it will certainly pay you to select this for your job of carpeting.

WE WILL MAIL YOU A SET OF SAMPLES FREE on request together with our great color catalogue as explained on page 853, and if desired we will cut, match and sew the carpet to fit any room at only 2 cents per yard. Be sure to give us the size of your room.

65 CENTS PER YARD. OUR ROYAL ALL WOOL INGRAIN CARPET IN DARK GREEN AND A FLORAL DESIGN OF SCARLET IN A VERY FINE SHADE.

THIS ILLUSTRATION shows you the floral design very clearly and when you consider that this is worked out in the rich shades of green and scarlet arranged in perfect harmony you can imagine pretty clearly the stylish effect. We guarantee to satisfy you perfectly if you order direct from this description, but will gladly send our free Special Carpet Catalogue on request, as stated on page 852. We consider this number one of the very neat designs in our assortment of ten designs in this 65-cent quality of ingrain. It is perfectly reversible, the other side having a scarlet ground with dark green floral effects. State the size of room if you want the carpet cut and matched.

No. 37K3072
Width, 36 inches.
Price, per yard 65c

65 CENTS PER YARD. OUR ROYAL EXTRA HEAVY SUPER ALL WOOL INGRAIN CARPET IN DELICATE TAN WITH ARTISTIC FLORAL AND SCROLL DESIGN AND FERN LEAVES.

A GREAT FEATURE of our 65-cent ingrain is the fine Moresque yarn used and its very close weave, giving it a luster not usually found in ingrain. Note the illustration. This effect is worked out in a delicate shade of tan. The design consists of an artistic scroll with a floral effect and fern leaves. This is by no means a flashy or gaudy carpet that will offend good taste, but is just the rich, very neat plain and stylish design so much liked by householders of modest taste. While we are perfectly sure we can satisfy you by ordering from this catalogue, yet if you have any doubts as to the appearance of the goods we will gladly mail you our free Special Carpet Catalogue, on request, showing the actual colors. Free samples also if desired.

No. 37K3084
Width, 36 inches.
Price, per yard 65c

65 CENTS PER YARD. OUR ROYAL HIGH GRADE ALL WOOL INGRAIN CARPET IN TAN WITH LEAF FLORAL DESIGN IN BROWN AND GREEN.

OUR ILLUSTRATIONS show you how each pattern is arranged. This one has a small leaf floral design in brown and green shading on a background of tan, a very modest, tasteful and restful combination of colors. This design is selected by us as one that will harmonize with almost any surroundings. There is nothing in it to mar the neatness and harmony of colors in any room. If you want a very choice, neat and attractive design for your dining room, library or parlor you certainly have it in this number. We show you the actual colors of this carpet on page 859 of this catalogue.

No. 37K3076
Width, 36 inches.
Price, per yard 65c

65 CENTS PER YARD. OUR ROYAL EXTRA FINE ALL WOOL REVERSIBLE INGRAIN CARPET IN A RED GROUND, WITH GREEN SCROLL AND LEAF EFFECT.

YOU will not find high class patterns of this nature elsewhere, because this is one of our own exclusive designs, a handsome effect brought out by the mill according to our own directions. We consider it one of the most pleasing and up to date effects on the market. We show its actual colors on page 859 of this catalogue. It is arranged like illustration, the ground being a handsome red and the scroll and small leaf effect brought out in green, an entirely new arrangement that we know will be perfectly satisfactory in any room. We design our patterns so that they will harmonize with the general house furnishings to be found anywhere.

No. 37K3088
Width, 36 inches.
Price, per yard 65c

65 CENTS PER YARD. ROYAL EXTRA SUPER ALL WOOL INGRAIN CARPET IN TAN WITH LIGHT BROWN AND OLIVE SCROLLS

REMEMBER, our carpet is made under our own supervision and we guarantee the quality throughout and offer only the neatest and choicest designs of the season. This Royal two-ply all wool carpet comes in a fine shade of tan ground with a combination of light brown and olive scrolls and floral effects, which harmonize very beautifully with any class of furnishings in your room. We feel quite sure that if you told us to send you our 65-cent quality and didn't say anything about the color and we sent you this one, you would be satisfied. It is well adapted for the quality, and it pleases practically everybody.

No. 37K3080
Width, 36 inches.
Price, per yard 65c

65 CENTS PER YARD. A MOST PLEASING EFFECT IN OUR ROYAL EXTRA HEAVY REVERSIBLE INGRAIN CARPET.

REMEMBER, our 65-cent ingrain is a guaranteed two-ply firmly woven carpet, perfectly reversible, that is, can be used on both sides. This is a decidedly pleasing combination. The ground is a neat tan shade with scrolls and leaves brought out in fine shades of green and oak, their natural colors. Tan, brown and green effects are exceedingly popular, because they are modest and generally harmonize beautifully with the surroundings of the average room. One of the great features of our carpet department is that you can get choicer designs at lower prices than you will get in much higher priced carpet at retail. Remember, we will send our Special Carpet Catalogue, showing colors and a set of samples free on request.

No. 37K3092
Width, 36 inches.
Price, per yard 65c

His customers enjoy looking at the carpets in person, not in catalogues.

- The casualness of his sales approach helps customers understand that consumption is a privilege of the few and should be enjoyed.
- Patterned carpets, for example, which take time to select, are located on the second floor away from the bustle of the first floor crowds, so no one feels rushed.
- Floormen are also available throughout the store to answer questions about the location of goods, call a cab, recommend local theaters, and link customers to a long-distance exchange.

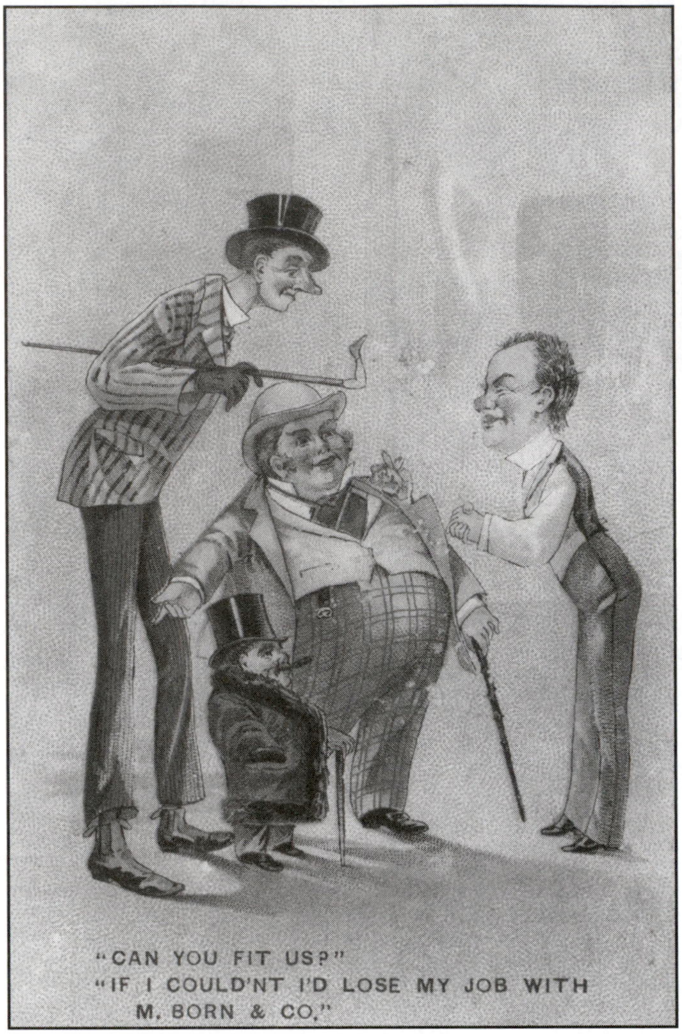
"CAN YOU FIT US?"
"IF I COULD'NT I'D LOSE MY JOB WITH
M. BORN & CO."

Trade cards emphasized dedication to service.

- He has recently shifted the location of a storeroom to create a waiting room for men; he believes women will buy more often if they are not hurried by their impatient husbands.
- His store also provides a money-back guarantee on all merchandise, which he believes allows his customers to buy with confidence and more quickly; only rarely are any of his rugs or oilcloths returned.
- The use of charge accounts is growing more popular, with more than half of all sales in his department involving credit.
- Only recently has his store begun advertising on Sunday; many ads feature items available on Monday, the regular "bargain day" for many department stores.
- He makes a point of greeting every customer, every morning, if possible.
- He fully understands that his store has created a way for women to have a socially acceptable way to enjoy themselves in comfort; in gratitude they spend their family's money on his rugs.
- When he first began working for the company, the store's operating hours ranged from 7:30 a.m. to 6:00 p.m. with one hour allowed for lunch; recently hours were changed to allow the female staff to come in at 8:30 and leave at 5:30 to "provide an atmosphere of protection."
- During July and August, the sales force only works a half-day on Saturdays.
- Holidays include Thanksgiving, Christmas, New Year's Day, Independence Day, and a half-day on Decoration Day, later called Memorial Day.
- The male clerks are asked to dress appropriately, but the women have more rules so as not to offend customers; dresses are to be conspicuous in their neatness and inconspicuous for the color and pattern of the material.
- Employees are expected to act appropriately at all times, even on their own time; employees are warned against frequenting pool halls, dance halls, gambling houses, or any place where intoxicating drinks are served.
- Recently he had to caution a male employee about getting married before he could afford a bride.
- While at work, employees refer to each other as Mister and Miss, never using first names, a style designed to display dignity and courtesy.
- He works hard to make sure that popular items and sizes remain in stock; previously stock was ordered based on the previous year's purchases, not on actual sales; this often caused shortages in the popular sizes and patterns.
- He looks forward to his once-a-year sale in September; the store never has a sale for all merchandise; sales rotate from department to department.
- To move as much merchandise as possible, he hires clowns and jugglers to entertain children while their parents buy rugs. One year he hired a glass blower, at his own expense, who spun glass jewelry for the women; it was a grand success.
- Long ago his store had replaced high shelving and storage cabinets—which were seven feet tall—with shelving five feet high so customers could see the entire store at a glance and have greater access to the goods.

"Editorial Reflections on 1908,"
***The Cleveland Plain Dealer*, March 17, 1909:**

"Much was printed in the closing months of the year to show the encouraging resumption of industry which had been peremptorily checked by the financial panic that occurred something like 14 months ago. The year 1908 opened with business practically paralyzed. Thoughtful men recognized that basic conditions were sound and that the country was in a position to recover rapidly, but confidence is a plant of slow growth and the utmost efforts of the leaders of finance could but little hasten the progress of recovery. The steady resumption of activity was further checked by the oncoming presidential election. The upward trend, slightly hindered by the campaign, was accelerated after the election when trade was stimulated to a marked degree by the renewed confidence of large interests and by the release of a considerable volume of orders that had been delayed or placed contingent on the outcome of the national contest. Conditions at the opening of the new year promise a quick and full restoration of prosperity."

- Small shelving has become particularly important as women replace men as salesclerks.
- When he came to the store, excess merchandise was stacked on the cabinets or floor waiting to be bought; using the knowledge gained at Marshall Fields he made changes.
- All surplus goods are now locked in a storeroom until needed, which reduces congestion and makes the store more visually appealing.
- A recent issue of *The Dry Goods Economic* says the uncluttered, up-to-date designs are "the greatest money-saver, greatest time-saver, and the greatest economizer as well as the greatest attraction to customers that any investment can produce."
- A study team is expected shortly to conduct time studies in selling areas to suggest other improvements.
- In the apparel department, his store is experimenting with coat hangers; currently clothes, including men's suits, are stacked on the counter. He believes the store can save space and sell more suits if they were on hangers.
- Magazine articles for department stores increasingly emphasize "store arrangement as the greatest force in modern merchandising."
- Peter is struggling with jealousy within the sales force; some departments are so competitive they would rather make no sale at all than to lose one to another department. He buys flowers for salespeople who send customers to his floor.
- The constant personnel squabbles make him wonder if he'd rather be just a buyer and no longer a manager, but as much as he dislikes the conflicts, he loves the incentive pay for a high performer.
- The forced-air ventilation system introduced by Macy's and John Wanamaker in the late 1880s is now common and used at The Mayer-Marks store.

He began his career working for Marshall Fields in Chicago.

- When two New York stores, Siegel-Cooper and Simpson, Crawford and Simpson, installed escalators in 1902, they transported as many people in an hour as forty elevators could; the cost of installation prevents many stores from adopting this innovation.
- Department stores are slow to adopt cash registers, preferring to use pneumatic tubes to move money and receipts—a centralized cash system that reduces theft.

Life in the Community: Cleveland, Ohio

- In 1909 Cleveland boasts 560,662 people, making it the sixth largest city in America; it has grown 46.9 percent since 1900, when it was the seventh largest city in the country.
- One-third of the city's population are now foreign-born, many only recently arriving from Poland, Italy, or Bohemia; the Italian population rose from approximately 3,000 in 1900 to nearly 11,000.
- In 1850 rival Ohio city, Cincinnati, was the sixth largest city in America, now it is thirteenth, seven places below Cleveland.
- The principal industries are iron and steel, followed by foundries and machine shops.
- In addition, the city has become well-known for the manufacture of hardware, paints, varnishes, printing presses, druggists' preparations, car wheels, sewing machines, and astronomical instruments.
- The Cleveland Industrial Exposition of 1909 is showing off the city as one of the outstanding manufacturing centers in the world.
- The 1909 census of manufacturers shows the Cleveland metropolitan district has 2,230 manufacturing facilities providing employment to 103,709 persons.
- A hub of the emerging automotive industry, Cleveland produces both steam cars and gasoline cars for national distribution.
- The Haymarket is beginning to feel the influence of the automobile; as the demand for hay declines, many of the spaces set aside for hay wagons are often empty.
- Only New York and Chicago manufacture more women's and children's garments than Cleveland does.
- Cleveland Mayor Tom L. Johnson is a tough-minded entrepreneur-turned-reformer who is championing women's suffrage, municipal ownership of utilities, just taxation, and home rule for Ohio's cities.
- Recently A.B. du Pont, the president of the municipal works in charge of the city's streetcars and engineering, handed in his resignation, leaving a job paying $15,000 a year.
- One of Peter's principal competitors, The Sterling and Welch Company, well-known for its rugs and interior decorating, recently moved to Euclid Avenue into the former home of James J. Tracy.
- The Cleveland Fire Department consists of 30 engine companies, 11 hook-and-ladder, and two hose companies, manned by 515 men.

"Automobiles from Cleveland," *The Birth of Modern Cleveland, 1865-1930:*

"The automobile industry sprang up suddenly in Cleveland. In 1900 the federal manufacturing census did not even include a separate category for automobiles. By 1909 there were 32 automobile factories employing 11,000 persons, and the value of the automobiles being produced ranked it third among Cleveland's industry . . Clevelanders and Cleveland companies were important early developers of the American automobile. Particularly during the first 15 years, when numerous technical problems were still unresolved, innovations in Cleveland were watched closely by other centers of automobile manufacturing. For example, although the gasoline engine seemed to be favored by European builders, Americans did not immediately accept it as the power source of choice. The steam engine traditionally was very strong in the United States, where steam railroad technology had developed to a high degree, and the electric motor seemed to be a reasonable alternative in a nation that had enthusiastically adopted the trolley."

- A group of progressive business and professional men recently organized the Cleveland Athletic Club, which now occupies the space formerly controlled by the Century Club in the New England Building.
- The proposed slogan for the upcoming Cleveland Industrial Exposition, "Onward, Cleveland, Onward," is stirring controversy; one minister denounced it as a parody of "Onward, Christian Soldiers."
- A Community Chest is being formed after a committee of 20 from the Chamber of Commerce investigated complaints from charitable organizations and their supporters regarding incessant appeals to the public for money; a community drive makes more economic sense.
- The streetcar system, which was recently returned to private ownership, is currently in receivership.
- The community is still mourning the loss of 174 people, mostly children, who were killed when the Collinwood School burned; two teachers died in an effort to save the students. All of the doors opened inward, making escape impossible in the panic.
- Because health officials believe that 10 percent of all deaths are due to tuberculosis, an Anti-Tuberculosis League has been formed to develop a preventive program.
- Now that the number of new typhoid fever cases is more than 7,000 yearly, an educational program aimed at getting people to boil drinking water has begun.
- The Red Cross is currently conducting a drive in Cleveland to aid starving Italians whose homes were destroyed in an earthquake; thus far more than $900 has been raised.
- Setting the standards for the nation, Cleveland recently opened a technical high school, based on the manual-training principle; approximately 700 students are enrolled.

Historical Snapshot
1909

- The Lincoln head penny replaced the Indian head, which had been in circulation since 1864
- 127,731 automobiles were produced, twice the number of the previous year; the Ford Model T's production of 20,000 cars was the nation's top seller
- Nationwide 34 states adopted a 25-mile-per-hour speed limit
- The Rockefeller Sanitary Commission led the fight to eradicate the hookworm
- College tuition at Harvard, Columbia, and Princeton was $150 to $250 per year, room and board, $45 to $350; other expenses, including books, amounted to $20 to $75
- The New York play, *The Melting Pot,* examined the disappearance of Jewish tradition when Jews became assimilated into the New World
- The movie industry agreed to use the 35-mm format, introduced by Thomas Edison in 1893, as the standard
- The Niagra Movement joined with white liberals to form a new organization for racial equality; leaders included W.E.B Du Bois, John Dewey, Lincoln Steffens, Clarence Darrow, and Rabbi Stephen Wise
- Chicago's Jane Addams expressed concern about the popularity of movie houses, especially for the poor
- John D. Rockefeller, the world's first billionaire, gave $500 million for medical research
- Westinghouse Electric was placed in receivership
- The Copyright Act of 1909, which significantly extended the rights of authorship, was approved by Congress and became law
- The $17 million Queensboro bridge opened in New York City
- 20,000 members of the Ladies' Waist Makers' Union staged a three-month strike, winning most of their demands
- Wilbur Wright designed an airplane for the U.S. Army that carried two passengers, flew for one hour, and reached a top speed of 49 miles per hour
- Admiral Peary, accompanied by black aid Matthew Henson, planted the U.S. flag at the North Pole; the dogsled journey covered 400 miles
- A bison refuge was created near Boise, Idaho
- Ice cream sales reach 39 million gallons, up from five million 10 years earlier
- The Kewpie doll, gasoline cigarette lighter, and electric toaster all made their first appearance
- The Audubon Society protested the extensive use of bird feathers in fashionable hats

1909 Economic Profile

Income, Standard Jobs

Average of all Industries, Excluding Farm Labor	$594
Average of all Industries, Including Farm Labor	$544
Bituminous Coal Mining	$751
Building Trades, Union Workers	$1,086
Clerical Workers in Manufacturing and Steam Railroads	$1,136
Domestics	$420
Farm Labor	$328
Federal Employees, Executive Departments	$1,106
Finance, Insurance, and Real Estate	$1,263
Gas and Electricity Workers	$618
Lower-Skilled Labor	$443
Manufacturing, Payroll	$469
Manufacturing, Union Workers	$1,020
Medical/Health Services Workers	$326
Ministers	$831
Nonprofit Organization Workers	$741
Postal Employees	$948
Public School Teachers	$476
State and Local Government Workers	$696
Steam Railroads, Wage Earners	$644
Street Railways Workers	$671
Telegraph Industry Workers	$622
Telephone Industry Workers	$430
Wholesale and Retail Trade Workers	$561

Selected Prices

Arnica Jelly Sunburn Remedy, per Tube	$0.25
Baking Powder, Good Luck Brand, per Pound	$0.10
Bed, Iron with Corner Posts Made of Steel Tubing	$1.89
Caster Oil Tablets, per Box	$0.10
Cleaner, Old Dutch, per Can	$0.10
Coca-Cola Drink by Glass	$0.05
Cold Cream, per Tube	$0.10
Corset, High Bust Effect	$1.00
Face Powder, Lablache, per Box	$0.50
Home Lessons In Spanish, French, Italian, German, per Language	$5.00
Mantel Clock, Case Imitates Black Italian Marble	$5.05

"Thinks Concrete Schools Cheaper, Speaker Tells Cement Users Savings of 30 Percent Is Easily Made," *Cleveland Plain Dealer*, January 14, 1909:

"Concrete factories and schools can be erected for 30 percent less cost than other forms of fireproof construction, according to Emil G. Perrot of Philadelphia, who declared last night before the cement users' convention that the lives of thousands of men, women, and children are now endangered through the use of wood in factory and school construction.

'Concrete is now being used extensively for factory buildings,' said Mr. Perrot. 'Factory owners realize the great savings in maintenance, reduction of fire insurance, and the elimination of the great dangers and losses from fire.' "

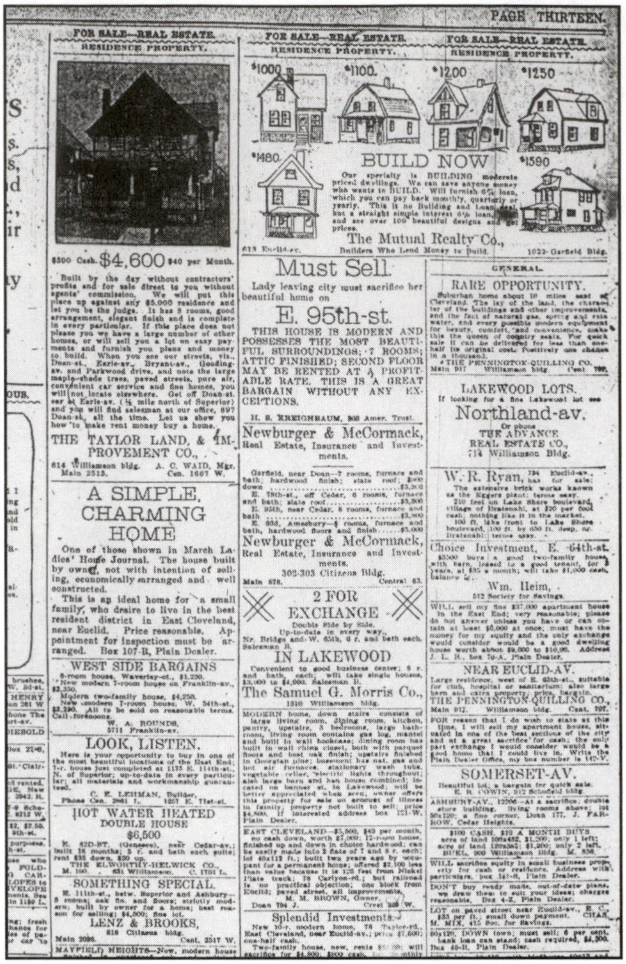

PAGE THIRTEEN.

FOR SALE—REAL ESTATE.
RESIDENCE PROPERTY.

$500 Cash. $4,600 $40 per Month.

Built by the day without contractors' profits and for sale direct to you without agents' commission. We will put this place up against any $5,000 residence and let you be the judge. It has 8 rooms, good arrangement, elegant finish and is complete in every particular. If this place does not please you we have a large number of other homes, or will sell you a lot on easy payments and furnish you plans and money to build. When you see our streets, viz., Doan-st., Earle-av., Bryant-av., Gooding-av. and Parkwood drive, and note the large maple-shade trees, paved streets, pure air, convenient car service and fine homes, you will not locate elsewhere. Get off Doan-st. car at Earle-av. (½ mile north of Superior) and you will find salesman at our office, 897 Doan-st., all the time. Let us show you how to make rent money buy a home.

THE TAYLOR LAND, & IMPROVEMENT CO.,
614 Williamson bldg. A. C. WAID, Mgr.
Main 2515. Cen. 1667 W.

A SIMPLE, CHARMING HOME

One of those shown in March Ladies' Home Journal. The house built by owner, not with intention of selling, economically arranged and well constructed.

This is an ideal home for a small family, who desire to live in the best resident district in East Cleveland, near Euclid. Price reasonable. Appointment for inspection must be arranged. Box 107-R, Plain Dealer.

WEST SIDE BARGAINS

6-room house, Waverley-av., $1,250.
New modern 7-room house on Franklin-av., $3,350.
Modern two-family house, $4,250.
New modern 7-room house, W. 54th-st., $3,250. All to be sold on reasonable terms. Call forenoons.
W. A. ROUNDS,
5711 Franklin-av.

LOOK, LISTEN.

Here is your opportunity to buy in one of the most beautiful locations of the East End; 7-r. house just completed at 1175 E. 114th-st., N. of Superior; up-to-date in every particular; all materials and workmanship guaranteed.
C. F. LEHMAN, Builder,
Phone Cen. 2861 L. 1257 E. 71st-st.

HOT WATER HEATED DOUBLE HOUSE
$6,500
E. 82D-ST. (Genesee), near Cedar-av.; built 18 months; 5 r. and bath each suite; rent $35 down, $30 up.
THE ELWORTHY-HELWICK CO.,
M. 110. 631 Williamson. C. 1701 L.

SOMETHING SPECIAL.

E. 111th-st., betw. Superior and Ashbury—8 rooms; oak fin. and floors; strictly modern; built by owner for a home; best reason for selling; $4,500; fine lot.
LENZ & BROOKS,
818 Citizens bldg.
Main 2036. Cent. 2517 W.

MAYFIELD HEIGHTS—New, modern house

FOR SALE—REAL ESTATE.
RESIDENCE PROPERTY.

$1000 $1100 $1200 $1250 $1480 $1590

BUILD NOW

Our specialty is BUILDING moderate priced dwellings. We can save anyone money who wants to BUILD. Will furnish 6% loan, which you can pay back monthly, quarterly or yearly. This is no Building and Loan deal, but a straight simple interest 6% loan, and see over 100 beautiful designs and get prices.

The Mutual Realty Co.,
613 Euclid-av. Builders Who Lend Money to Build. 1023 Garfield Bldg.

Must Sell.

Lady leaving city must sacrifice her beautiful home on

E. 95th-st.

THIS HOUSE IS MODERN AND POSSESSES THE MOST BEAUTIFUL SURROUNDINGS; 7 ROOMS; ATTIC FINISHED; SECOND FLOOR MAY BE RENTED AT A PROFITABLE RATE. THIS IS A GREAT BARGAIN WITHOUT ANY EXCEPTIONS.

H. S. KREIGHBAUM, 303 Amer. Trust.

Newburger & McCormack,
Real Estate, Insurance and Investments.

Garfield, near Doan—7 rooms, furnace and bath; hardwood finish; slate roof; $500 down $3,300
E. 78th-st., off Cedar, 6 rooms, furnace and bath; slate roof $3,300
E. 85th, near Cedar, 8 rooms, furnace and bath $3,800
E. 93d, Amesbury—8 rooms, furnace and bath, hardwood floors and finish $5,000

Newburger & McCormack,
Real Estate, Insurance and Investments.
302-303 Citizens Bldg.
Main 878. Central 63.

2 FOR EXCHANGE

Double Side by Side.
Up-to-date in every way.
Nr. Bridge and W. 65th, 6 r. and bath each. Salesman B.

IN LAKEWOOD

Convenient to good business center; 8 r. and bath, each; will take single houses, $3,000 to $4,000. Salesman B.

The Samuel G. Morris Co.,
1310 Williamson bldg.

MODERN home, down stairs consists of large living room, dining room, kitchen, pantry, upstairs, 3 bedrooms, large bathroom, living room contains gas log, mantel and built in wall bookcase; dining room has built in wall china closet, both with parquet floors and best oak finish; upstairs finished in Georgian pine; basement has nat. gas and hot air furnace, stationary wash tubs, vegetable cellar, electric lights throughout; also large barn and hen house combined; located on banner st. in Lakewood; will be better appreciated when seen, owner offers this property for sale on account of illness in family; property not built to sell; price $4,800. If interested address box 121-W, Plain Dealer.

EAST CLEVELAND—$5,800, $40 per month, no cash down, worth $7,000; 12-room house, finished up and down in choice hardwood; can be easily made into 2 flats of 7 and 8 r. each; lot 40x112 ft.; built two years ago by occupant for a permanent home; offered $2,100 less than value because it is 125 feet from Nickel Plate track; 78 Carlyon-rd.; but railroad is no practical objection; one block from Euclid; paved street, all improvements.
M. M. BROWN, Owner,
Doan 794 J. Crest 388 W.

Splendid Investments.

New 10-r. modern home, 78 Taylor-rd., East Cleveland, near Euclid-av.; price $7,500; one-half cash.

Two-family house, new, rents $50.00; will sacrifice for $4,800; $800 cash.

GENERAL.

RARE OPPORTUNITY.

Suburban home about 10 miles east of Cleveland. The lay of the land, the character of the buildings and other improvements, and the fact of natural gas, spring and rain water, and every possible modern equipment for beauty, comfort, and convenience, make this the queen of country seats. For quick sale it can be delivered for less than one-half its original cost. Positively one chance in a thousand.
THE PENNINGTON-QUILLING CO.
Main 917 Williamson bldg. Cent. 707.

LAKEWOOD LOTS.

If looking for a fine Lakewood lot see

Northland-av.

Or phone
THE ADVANCE REAL ESTATE CO.,
714 Williamson Bldg.

W. R. Ryan, 734 Euclid-av., has for sale:
The extensive brick works known as the Eggers plant; terms easy.
210 feet on Lake Shore boulevard, village of Bratenahl, at $20 per foot cash; nothing like it in the market.
100 ft. lake front to Lake Shore boulevard, 100 ft. by 650 ft. deep, nr. Bratenahl; terms easy.

Choice Investment, E. 64th-st.
$3500 buys a good two-family house with barn, leased to a good tenant, for 3 years, at $35 a month; will take $1,000 cash, balance &c.
Wm. Heim,
512 Society for Savings.

WILL sell my fine $37,000 apartment house in the East End; very reasonable; please do not answer unless you have or can obtain at least $6,000 at once; must have the money for my equity and the only exchange would consider would be a good dwelling house worth about $9,000 to $10,000. Address J. L. R., box 70-A, Plain Dealer.

NEAR EUCLID-AV.

Large residence, west of E. 65th-st., suitable for club, hospital or sanitarium; also large barn and extra property; price, bargain.
THE PENNINGTON-QUILLING CO.,
Main 917. Williamson bldg. Cent. 707.

FOR reason that I do wish to state at this time, I will sell my apartment house, situated in one of the best sections of the city and at a great sacrifice for cash; the only part exchange I would consider would be a good home that I could live in. Write the Plain Dealer Office, my box number is 142-V.

SOMERSET-AV.

Beautiful lot; a bargain for quick sale.
E. R. COWIN, 312 Schofield bldg.

ASHBURY-AV., 12206—At a sacrifice; double store building, living rooms above; lot 50x120; a fine corner. Doan 177. J. FARROW, Cedar Heights.

$100 CASH, $10 A MONTH BUYS acre of land 100x452, $1,200; only 1 left; acre of land 120x362; $1,200; only 2 left. BUEL, 900 Williamson Bldg. M. 836.

WILL sacrifice equity in small business property for cash or residence. Address with particulars, box 141-S, Plain Dealer.

DON'T buy ready made, out-of-date plans, we draw them to suit your ideas; charges reasonable. Box 4-Z, Plain Dealer.

LOT on paved street near Euclid-av., E. C., $33 per ft.; small down payment. CHAS. M. MIX, 415 Soc. for Savings.

60x120, DOWN town; must sell; 6 per cent. bank loan can stand; cash required, $4,300. Box 40-R, Plain Dealer.

Nestor Cigarettes, Pack of 10,
Imported $0.40
Night Dresses, Handmade $7.25
Records, Wax-Cylinder, Standard Size ... $0.18
Sewing Basket, to Include Scissors, Bodkins, Pen Knife, and Knitting and Crocheting Needles .... $7.50-$35.00
Sewing Machine with Seven Drawers $16.45
Silk Stockings, French, per Pair $4.50
Stereoscopic Views, 100 Views of St. Louis World's Fair $0.85
Washing Machine $5.15
Woman's Coat, for Fall and Winter, Broadcloth $40.00
Woman's Shoes, of Conora Coltskin $1.39

Cleveland, A Concise History, 1796–1996, "The Progressive Years, 1900–1914":

"Under [Cleveland Mayor Tom L.] Johnson's leadership, the city embarked on a host of progressive projects and reforms. 'When he was mayor of Cleveland,' one historian later wrote of Johnson, 'the people for the first time learned that they really owned the parks.' Johnson ordered down all 'Keep off the grass' signs. Mirroring park reform efforts nationwide, he provided playgrounds in the most crowded districts of the city. He built baseball diamonds and basketball and tennis courts, sponsored Sunday band concerts in the parks and ice skating competitions for children, and built public bathhouses in the poorest neighborhoods. He instituted reforms in the city police force and built a model workhouse and reformatory on farmland outside the city. Johnson relentlessly challenged the streetcar monopoly he himself once sought to control."

"Everyday Philosophy," by William J. Burtscher, *The Taylor-Trotwood Magazine*, June 1908:

"If love were not blind some men would never get a wife.

The hotter the cup of coffee, the more steam-ulating it is.

Count what you have, and what you have not count on getting.

Some men are very much like the cedar tree—green all year.

Trust is honesty got into the mouth; honest is truth got into the hands.

Some people blow in their money at the expense of blowing out their morals.

If we hate somebody in any degree, we cannot love anybody in the right degree.

Trouble generally comes to a man without price, but charges heavily for leaving.

Clothes make the man in the end when there is a man in the clothes to begin with.

There are men who write as thoughts come to them, and turn out paragraphs. Others go after thoughts and write volumes.

There are men who worship the dollar and then seem to think that other people ought to worship them for possessing the dollar.

When a lazy man does not know what to do next, he keeps on doing what he has been doing all along, thus preserving his reputation as an idler.

It is possible for an author to borrow so extensively that when he gets his article finished, about all he can claim as absolutely his own is the paper upon which it is written."

"Franklin 1910 automobiles will average 2,500 miles without tire puncture. It is not necessary to carry extra tires," advertisement, 1910:

"Do you realize that only one percent of the roads in this country are macadam, that the rest are ordinary dirt roads?

Do you want an automobile that is comfortable only on macadam roads or on all roads?

Franklins, with their four full-elliptic springs and laminated-wood chassis frame, are always comfortable. And because of their lightweight and easy riding they make better time than automobiles of even greater horsepower.

Franklins are easy on tires. Besides, we use extra large tires—larger than used on water-cooled automobiles of much greater weight. . . The tires are so large in proportion to the weight of the automobile that the usual tire troubles are avoided. It is almost impossible to get stone bruises, as the tires cannot be driven against the rims. With ordinary use they will give 8,000 to 10,000 miles' service."

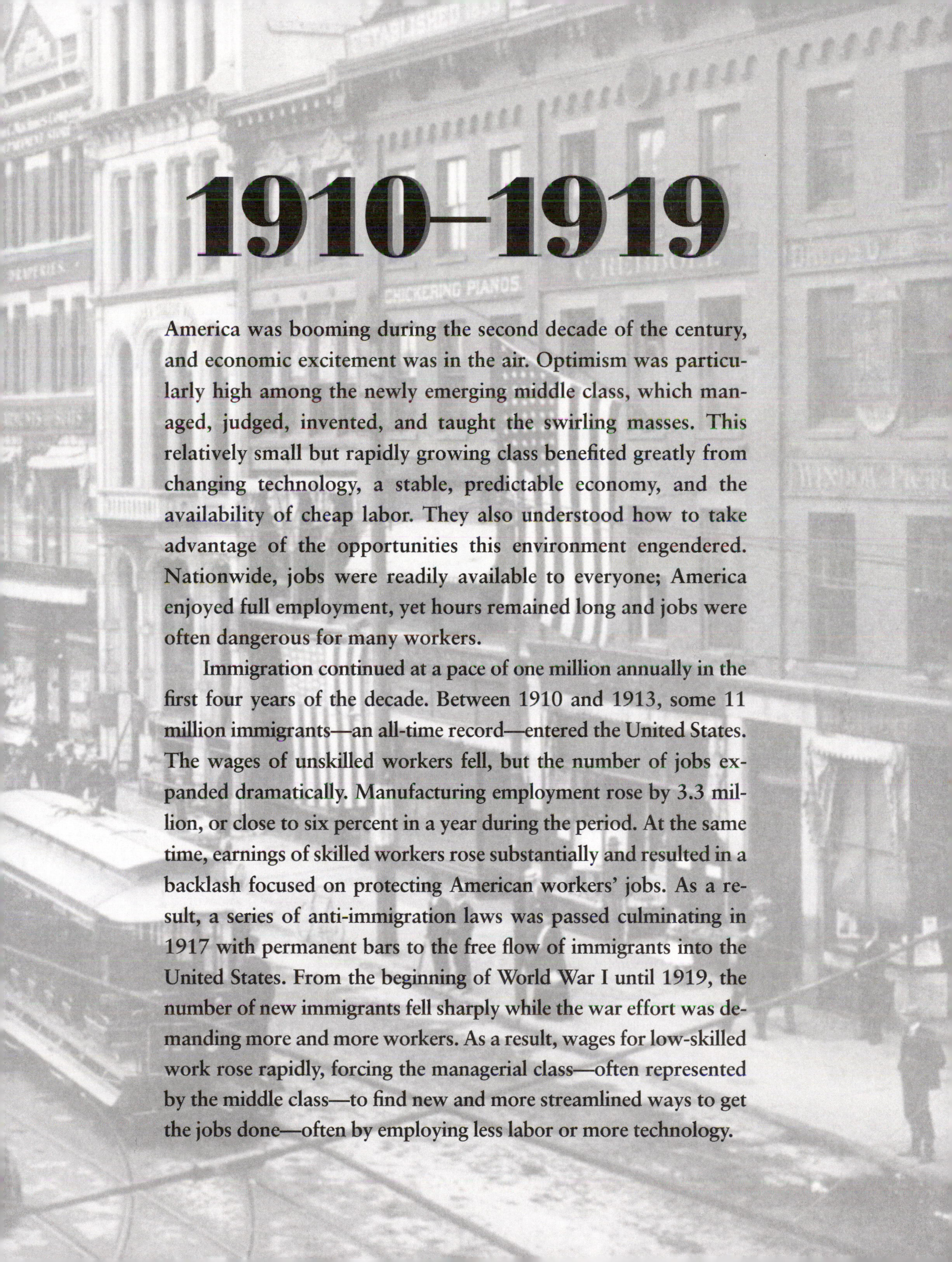

1910–1919

America was booming during the second decade of the century, and economic excitement was in the air. Optimism was particularly high among the newly emerging middle class, which managed, judged, invented, and taught the swirling masses. This relatively small but rapidly growing class benefited greatly from changing technology, a stable, predictable economy, and the availability of cheap labor. They also understood how to take advantage of the opportunities this environment engendered. Nationwide, jobs were readily available to everyone; America enjoyed full employment, yet hours remained long and jobs were often dangerous for many workers.

Immigration continued at a pace of one million annually in the first four years of the decade. Between 1910 and 1913, some 11 million immigrants—an all-time record—entered the United States. The wages of unskilled workers fell, but the number of jobs expanded dramatically. Manufacturing employment rose by 3.3 million, or close to six percent in a year during the period. At the same time, earnings of skilled workers rose substantially and resulted in a backlash focused on protecting American workers' jobs. As a result, a series of anti-immigration laws was passed culminating in 1917 with permanent bars to the free flow of immigrants into the United States. From the beginning of World War I until 1919, the number of new immigrants fell sharply while the war effort was demanding more and more workers. As a result, wages for low-skilled work rose rapidly, forcing the managerial class—often represented by the middle class—to find new and more streamlined ways to get the jobs done—often by employing less labor or more technology.

In the midst of these dynamics, the Progressive Movement, largely a product of the rising middle class, began to shape the decade, raising questions about work safety, the rights of individuals, the need for clean air and fewer work hours. It was a people's movement that grasped the immediate impact of linking the media to its cause. The results were significant and widespread. South Carolina prohibited the employment of children under 12 in mines, factories, and textile mills; Delaware began to frame employer's liability laws; the direct election of U.S. Senators was approved; and nationwide communities argued loudly over the right and ability of women to vote and the need and lawfulness of alcohol consumption.

During the decade, motorized tractors changed the lives of farmers, and electricity extended the day of urban dwellers. Powered trolley cars, vacuum cleaners, hair dryers, and electric ranges moved onto the modern scene. Wireless communications bridged San Francisco to New York and New York to Paris; in 1915, the Bell system alone operated six million telephones, which were considered essential in most middle class homes as the decade drew to a close. As the sale of parlor pianos hit a new high, more than two billion copies of sheet music were sold as ragtime neared its peak. Thousands of Bibles were placed in hotel bedrooms by the Gideon Organization of Christian Commercial Travelers, reflecting both the emerging role of the traveling "drummer" or salesman and the evangelical nature of the Progressive Movement.

Yet in the midst of blazing prosperity, the nation was changing too rapidly for many—demographically, economically, and morally. Divorce was on the rise. One in 12 marriages ended in divorce in 1911, compared with one in 85 only six years earlier. The discovery of a quick treatment for syphilis was hailed as both a miracle and an enticement to sin. As the technology and sophistication of silent movies improved yearly, the Missouri Christian Endeavor Society tried to ban films that included any kissing. At the same time, the rapidly expanding economy, largely without government regulation, began producing marked inequities of wealth—affluence for the few and hardship for the many. The average salary of $750 a year was rising, but not fast enough for many.

But one of the biggest stories was America's unabashed love affair with the automobile. By 1916, the Model T cost less than half its 1908 price, and nearly everyone dreamed of owning a car. Movies were also maturing during the period, growing rapidly as an essential entertainment for the poor. Some 25 percent of the population, including many newly arrived immigrants, went weekly to the nickelodeon to marvel at the exploits of Charlie Chaplin, Mary Pickford, and Douglas Fairbanks, Sr.—each drawing big salaries in the silent days of movies.

The second half of the decade was marked by the Great War, later to be known as the First World War. Worldwide, it cost more than nine million lives and swept away four empires—the German, the Austro-Hungarian, the Russian, and the Ottoman—and with them the traditional aristocratic style of leadership in Europe. It bled the treasuries of Europe dry and brought the United States forward as the richest country in the world.

When the war broke out in Europe, American exports were required to support the Allied war effort, driving the well-oiled American industrial engine into high gear. Then, when America's intervention in 1917 required the drafting of two million men, women were given their first taste of economic independence. Millions stepped forward to produce the materials needed by a nation. As a result, when the men came back from Europe, America was a changed place for both the well-traveled soldier and the newly trained female worker. Each had acquired an expanded view of the world. Yet women possessed full suffrage in only Wyoming, Colorado, Utah, and Idaho.

The war forced Americans to confront one more important transformation. The United States had become a full participant in the world economy; tariffs on imported goods were reduced and exports reached all-time highs in 1919, further stimulating the American economy.

1911 Family Profile

David and Ruth Rosen are at the forefront of the emerging technology of making and distributing short feature films to the thousands of nickelodeons springing up nationwide; it is their dream that Denver, Colorado will become the center of the moviemaking industry in the future. They have two children.

Annual Income: $4,200

Annual Budget

The average per capita consumer expenditure in 1911 is not available. The following is for 1914 for all workers nationwide:

Auto Parts	$1.09
Auto Purchases	$4.21
Clothing	$29.52
Dentists	$0.95
Food	$90.34
Furniture	$3.47
Gas and Oil	$2.35
Health Insurance	NR
Housing	$62.78
Intercity Transport	$3.32
Local Transportation	$6.13
Personal Business	$9.86
Personal Care	$3.08
Physicians	$2.99
Private Education and Research	$4.97
Recreation	$10.06
Religion/Welfare Activities	$8.44

Trains are critical to the commerce and development of Denver.

Telephone and Telegraph	$1.13
Tobacco	$7.39
Utilities	$4.64
Average Per Capita Consumption	$336.95

Life at Home

- This family owns a home in downtown Denver; it includes a photography studio, darkroom, and space to work on David's inventions.
- He was originally from Pennsylvania, leaving home at age 16 to travel to the West.
- He met his future wife, Ruth who was from New York State, in Colorado Springs and they settled in Denver.
- He worked in newspapers and photography before turning to moviemaking in 1902.
- The family owns a four-cylinder Buick, which cost $1,750, a symbol of their prosperity.
- Since Ruth has no desire to learn how to drive the automobile, David always drives, occasionally hiring a driver to take her on trips.
- They have two children, first a son, then a daughter.
- This woman is outspoken on women's rights, and is proud of her record of voting in every election since women in Colorado received the right to vote in 1894.

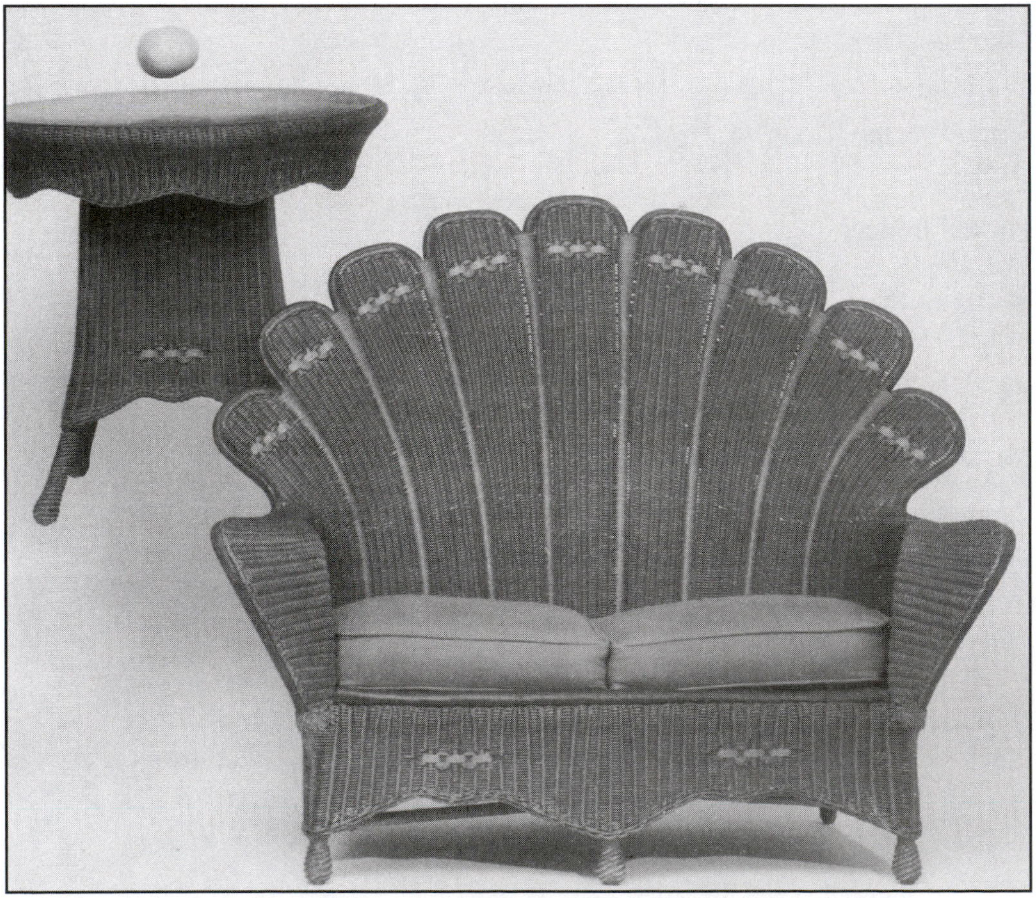

The Rosens collect furniture, particularly wicker, which is growing in popularity.

Sunday dinner at home often includes friends and relatives.

- Much of her free time is spent with associations such as the Eastern Star, affiliated with the Masons.
- He is a member of the Masons, Elks, and the El Jebel Shrine.
- They also collect furniture, particularly wicker, since he first began using wicker as a photography prop and later began bringing it home; the couple now has several pieces including a library table and a Japanese sofa.
- They are intrigued by a recent ocean-to-ocean trip taken by automobile; a Philadelphian named John Guy Monihan guided a group of friends driving Premiers from Atlantic City, New Jersey, to Los Angeles, California, in less than 60 days.

Western travelers often found the roads primitive with few markers to guide their way.

- The travelers reported that when they arrived in the western states they found few roads, no route numbers, and sometimes not even enough telephone poles to help them guide their way.
- If they had come closer to Denver, he could have filmed a portion of the trip.

Life at Work

- He began his training as a still photographer working for newspapers.
- For most of the 1800s, newspaper illustrations were made from engravings, often using a photo as a guide for the engraver.
- In 1894, the *Rocky Mountain News* moved from engravings to halftone photographs, making an investment in equipment and photographers—popularizing the new technique.
- Having gained some experience in newspapers, in 1896 he formed a photographic company to take still pictures of trains and scenes from Colorado.
- He loves promoting Colorado; many say he is the state's unofficial spokesman.
- He also began experimenting with photography innovations such as high-speed shutters to capture objects in motion and panoramic photography to capture the majesty of the West.

- He also manufactured an x-ray tube, experimenting with x-ray photography for a time, and developed a "detectophone," which could be placed in a room to transmit sounds over a telephone line to a listener.
- To meet current demands, he distributed his photographs using the current rage, postcards, which provide lots of ways for friends to exchange greetings without writing extensively.
- By 1902 he turned to the motion picture industry, developed by Thomas Edison and George Eastman.
- His early films feature Colorado's mountainous railroads, spectacular views of the state, and native dances by the Ute Indians on their reservation at Ignacio.
- Like most early films, the movies have little plot; the public is so mesmerized by the action on the screen that no plot is needed.
- His background and experimentation in high-speed still photography make him a natural choice to adopt the new technology.
- Currently, he is intrigued by the chance to be a part of taking movies from the arcades to the big screen, or silver screen, as it is known.
- He has gained financial backing from a pioneer movie producer from Chicago, who believes that the scenery and sunshine of Colorado could make it the movie capital of America.
- The Chicago-based company currently provides national distribution for the short films he produces.
- Typically, a short film is one to three and one-half minutes long and might include clips from a train, a fire, and a mountain range, cut together to create fast action.

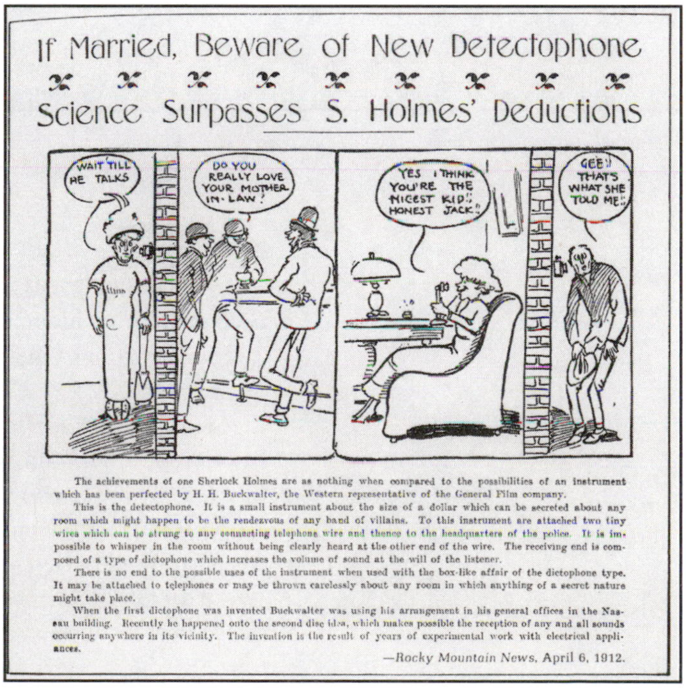

If Married, Beware of New Detectophone

Science Surpasses S. Holmes' Deductions

The achievements of one Sherlock Holmes are as nothing when compared to the possibilities of an instrument which has been perfected by H. H. Buckwalter, the Western representative of the General Film company.

This is the detectophone. It is a small instrument about the size of a dollar which can be secreted about any room which might happen to be the rendezvous of any band of villains. To this instrument are attached two tiny wires which can be strung to any connecting telephone wire and thence to the headquarters of the police. It is impossible to whisper in the room without being clearly heard at the other end of the wire. The receiving end is composed of a type of dictophone which increases the volume of sound at the will of the listener.

There is no end to the possible uses of the instrument when used with the box-like affair of the dictophone type. It may be attached to telephones or may be thrown carelessly about any room in which anything of a secret nature might take place.

When the first dictophone was invented Buckwalter was using his arrangement in his general offices in the Nassau building. Recently he happened onto the second disc idea, which makes possible the reception of any and all sounds occurring anywhere in its vicinity. The invention is the result of years of experimental work with electrical appliances.

—*Rocky Mountain News*, April 6, 1912.

Rosen has developed a "detectophone" to transmit sounds over a phone line.

His work includes making message postcards for sweethearts.

- New York City boasts more than 1,000 movie houses, called the "poor man's grand opera," where short features were displayed.
- To gain acceptance for his movie activity, David contracted with the City of Denver for summertime entertainment; his short movies, shown in the city park, feature girls skipping rope, trains passing deep cliffs, and cowboys riding horses.
- The public response has been so overwhelming, the newspapers carry daily stories concerning upcoming films and the latest films in the making.
- During the first summer they were shown, more than 30,000 people rode the trolley on a single day to see the new moving pictures.
- During the presidential election of 1908, between Howard Taft and William Jennings Bryan, short features were shown to the crowds outside the newspaper office as they waited for election updates to be flashed on a screen.
- As the role of movies developed, he has joined with nine other film producers to control film production and distribution.
- Currently his company is being sued for a violation of antitrust laws.
- One of his latest movie projects almost ended disastrously; while shooting near a river, a cameraman and rider were nearly washed away by a flash flood.
- All filming is done outdoors; when stunts are needed cowboys are hired, and action scenes often include gunfire using live bullets.
- Recently a small movie company was established in Hollywood, California, to produce films; he is worried that they could lure some business away from Colorado.

Life in the Community: Denver, Colorado

- Denver came to life in 1858 when gold was discovered along the South Platte River, located at the foot of the Rocky Mountains, which serves as a 14,000 foot barrier to travel further west.
- It soon became a territorial capital with a reputation as the richest, raciest community between St. Louis and San Francisco.
- In 1869, Dan Castello's Circus left the railroad at Cheyenne and took four days to make the 85 mile trek to Denver; the trip cost the life of the troupe's baby elephant, but the circus performed in Denver.
- Thespian Edwin Booth toured the West presenting Shakespeare's tragedies; this touch of class appealed to the western audiences so much that Booth earned $25,000 a month on tour.
- By 1880 the city's population passed 36,000 and then tripled to 106,000 by 1890; Denver constituted one-third of the state's population.

***Buckwalter, the Colorado Scenes of a Pioneer Photojournalist, 1890–1920*, by William C. and Elizabeth B. Jones:**

"The most colorful of his public relations stunts was based on his determination to dispel the notion held by many Easterners that Denver was a snow-blown wasteland in winter, an idea that kept many conventions away from the city during winter. To prove his contention that Denver had a year-round mild climate, he arranged to stage a filming from the front of a Denver Tramway streetcar running the length of Seventeenth Street on a January day in 1905. The newspaper gave the plan much attention, urging Denverites to cooperate by appearing along the route in short sleeves. The weather was perfect, and the film was made without a hitch. It served its purpose in convincing convention planners to take advantage of Denver year-round. However, the weather had the final say in the matter a few days after the filming when the city was hit by one of the worst spells of winter weather it had had in some time. The newspapers had great fun with the story. *The Denver Post* featured a cartoon of Buckwalter being chased, camera in hand, by Old Man Winter."

- Using the wealth provided by gold and later silver, businessmen quickly built banks and railroads to attract additional businesses and lure the tokens of culture, such as opera, so prized in the East.
- Using locally available natural gas, by 1871 the city was illuminated by gas streetlights.
- Eight years later, the first telephones, called "galvanic muttering machines," were available to the city's elite.
- By 1880 electric lights began to replace gas lighting and attempts were made to install an electric streetcar five years later.
- In 1892 world-trotting journalist Richard Harding Davis called the city "a smaller New York in an encircling range of white-capped mountains."
- The discovery of coal and iron launched a steel industry, turning Denver into an industrial powerhouse and the world's manufacturing center of mining machinery.
- The city's business community displayed its newfound wealth with huge mansions costing more than a quarter of a million dollars, perched on the high ground southeast of the town; David Moffat's four-story house, with white marble columns, included a $25,000 stained-glass window ordered from Tiffany's of London.
- Denver's civic center was recently completed, part of a plan to make Denver, "one of the most beautiful cities of the world."
- In 1911, the city is celebrating the growth of public schools; enrollment has increased by 287 students from the previous year, making a total of 30,059 children attending public schools.
- Currently, Denver is divided over Methodist Bishop H.W. Warren's announcement that Dr. Frederick Vining Young, pastor of the Methodist church at Ogden, Utah, should

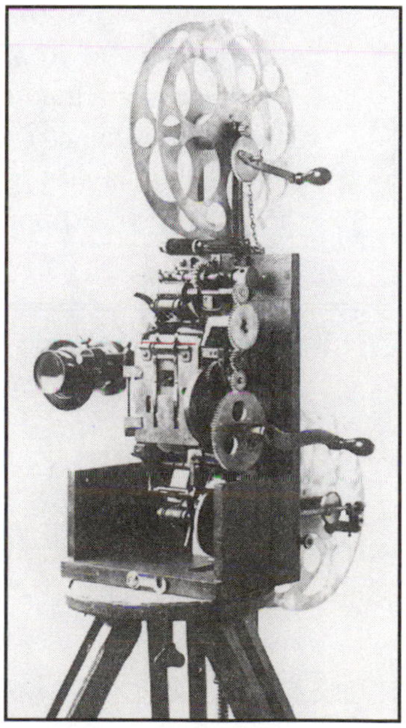

"The Nickel Madness, The amazing spread of a new kind of amusement enterprise which is making fortunes for its projectors," by Barton W. Currie, *Harper's Weekly*, August 24, 1907:

"The very fact that we derive pleasure from certain amusements, wrote Lecky, creates a kind of humiliation. Anthony Comstock and Police-Commissioner Bingham have spoken eloquently on the moral aspect of the five-cent theatre, drawing far more strenuous conclusions than those of the great historian. But both the general and the purity commissioner generalized too freely from particulars. They saw only the harsher aspects of nickel madness, whereas it has many innocent and harmless phrases.

Crusades have been organized against these low-priced moving-picture theatres, and many conservators of the public morals have denounced them as vicious and demoralizing. Yet have they flourished amazingly, and carpenters are busy hammering them up in every big and little community in the country.

The first 'nickelodeon' or 'nickelet,' or whatever it was originally called, was merely an experiment, and the first experience was made a little more than a year ago. There was nothing singularly novel in the idea, only the individualizing of the moving-picture machine. Before, it had served merely as a 'turn' in vaudeville. For a very modest sum the outfit could be housed in a narrow store or in a shack in the rear yard of a tenement, provided there was an available hallway and the space for a 'front.' These shacks and shops are packed with as many chairs as they will hold and the populace welcomed, or rather hailed, by a megaphone-horn and lurid placards. The price of admission and entertainment for from 15 to 20 minutes is a coin of the smallest denomination in circulation west of the Rockies.

In some vaudeville houses you may watch a diversity of performances for four hours for so humble a price as 10 cents, provided you are willing to sit among the rafters. Yet the roof bleachers were never so popular or profitable as the tiny show-places that have fostered nickel madness. Before the dog days set in, licenses were being granted in Manhattan Borough alone at the rate of one a day for these little hurry-up-and-be-amused booths. They were categorized as 'common shows' thanks to the Board of Aldermen. A special ordinance was passed to rate them under this heading. Thereby they were enabled to obtain a license for $25 the first year, and $12.50 for the second year. The City Fathers did this before Anthony Comstock and others rose up and proclaimed against them. A full theatrical license costs $500.

An eloquent plea was made for these humble resorts by many 'friends of the peepul.' They offered harmless diversion for the poor. They were edifying, educational, and amusing. They were broadening. They revealed the universe to the unsophisticated. The variety of the skipping, dancing, flashing, and marching pictures was without limit. For five cents you were admitted to the realms of the prize ring; you might witness

(continued)

resign because of an article he wrote concerning Mormonism which appeared in *Outlook Magazine*; the Bishop says the article appears to be a defense of Mormonism.

- Geologists are predicting that Colorado's coal supply will last 31,000 years at the present production of 12 million tons a year.
- During the 1911 session of the Legislature, proposals before the elected officials include: The Headless Ballot law, which will kill straight ticket voting; a public utility law giving the

the celebration of a Pontifical mass in St. Peter's; Kaiser Wilhelm would prance before you, reviewing his Uhlan. Yes, and even more surprising, you were offered a modern conception of Washington crossing the Delaware 'acted out by a trained group of actors.' Under the persuasive force of such arguments, wit it strange that the Aldermen befriended the nickelodeon man and gave impetus to the craze...?

Already statisticians have been estimating how many men, women, and children in the metropolis are being thrilled daily by them. A conservative figure puts it at 200,000, though if I were to accept the total of the showman the estimate would be nearer half a million. But like all statisticians, who reckon human beings with the same unemotional placidity with which they total beans and potatoes, the statistician I have quoted left out the babies. In a visit to a dozen of these moving-picture hutches I counted an average of 10 babies to each theatre. Of course they were in their mothers' or their nurse-girls' arms. But they were there and you heard them. They did not disturb the show, as there were no counter-sounds, and many of them seemed profoundly absorbed in the moving pictures.

As a matter of fact, some mothers—and all nurse-girls—will tell you that the cinematograph has a peculiarly hypnotic or narcotic effect upon an infant predisposed to disturb the welkin. You will visit few of these places in Harlem where the doorways are not encumbered with go-carts and perambulators. Likewise they are prodigiously popular with the rising generation in frock and knickerbockers. For this reason they have been condemned by the morality crusaders. The chief argument against them was that they corrupted the young. Children of any size who could transport a nickel to the cashier's booth were welcomed. Furthermore, undesirables of many kinds haunted them. Pickpockets found them splendidly convenient, for the lights were always cut off when the picture machine was focused on the canvas. There is no doubt about the fact that many rogues and miscreants obtained licenses and set up these little show-places merely as snares and traps. There were many who thought they had sufficient pull to defy decency in the choice of their slides. Proprietors were said to work hand in glove with lawbreakers. Some were accused of wanton designs to corrupt young girls. Police-Commissioner Bingham denounced the nickel madness as pernicious, demoralizing, and a direct menace to the young.

The popularity of these cheap amusement-places with the new population of New York is not to be wondered at. The newly arrived immigrant from Transylvania can get as much enjoyment out of them as the native does. The imagination is appealed to directly and without any circumlocution. The child whose intelligence has just awakened and the doddering old man seem to be on an equal footing of enjoyment in the stuffy little box-like theatres. The passer-by with an idle quarter of an hour on his hands has an opportunity to kill the time swiftly, if he is not above mingling with the hoi polloi. Likewise the student of sociology may get a few points that he could not obtain in a day's journey through the thronged streets of the East Side."

state the power to regulate all public and quasi-public corporations; an anti-pass law, forbidding railroads from giving, or others from receiving, free transportation; a gun-toting law making it a felony to carry concealed weapons; a law to protect miners in their work.

Historical Snapshot
1911

- Actress Blanche Sweet was one of D.W. Griffith's regulars in the one- and two-reelers that now dominated the movie industry
- David Horsley moved his study from Bayonne, New Jersey, to the Los Angeles suburb of Hollywood to establish a movie studio on Sunset Boulevard
- The Underwood Company attempted to create a noiseless typewriter
- The Triangle Shirtwaist factory fire in New York City aroused nationwide demands for better work conditions; the single exit door had been locked to keep the 146 female workers from stealing thread
- A record 12,000 European immigrants arrived at Ellis Island on a single day, April 17
- During a discussion concerning trade with Canada, a congressional group proposed to annex the neighboring country
- The Self-Mastery Colony in New Jersey and Parting of the Ways home in Chicago were created to help the deserving poor
- An estimated 40 million people attended the religiously based "Chautauquas," which featured inspirational lectures, magicians, American Indians, yodelers, and Hawaiian singers
- California women gained suffrage by constitutional amendment
- F.W. Woolworth was incorporated
- The electric self-starter for the motorcar was perfected and immediately adopted by Cadillac
- Marmon Wasp won the first Indianapolis 500-mile race, averaging 75 miles per hour
- Direct telephone links were opened between New York and Denver
- The use of fingerprinting in crime detection became widespread
- On the fiftieth anniversary of the Battle of Bull Run, Civil War veterans from both the North and South mingled at the battlefield site
- Marie Curie won an unprecedented second Nobel prize, but was refused admission to the French Academy of Science
- 60,000 Bibles were placed in hotel bedrooms by the Gideon Organization of Christian Commercial Travelers
- The socialist-backed magazine, *The Masses,* was founded in Greenwich Village, printing articles concerning "what is too naked for the money-making press."
- The high divorce rate of one in 12 marriages caused concerns; the rate had been one in 85 marriages in 1905

1911 Economic Profile

Income, Standard Jobs

- Average of all Industries, Excluding Farm Labor . . . $629
- Average of all Industries, Including Farm Labor . . . $575
- Bituminous Coal Mining . . . $832
- Building Trades, Union Workers . . . $1,240
- Clerical Workers in Manufacturing . . . $1,213
- Domestics . . . $343
- Farm Labor . . . $338
- Federal Civilian . . . $1,133
- Federal Employees, Executive Departments . . . $1,116
- Finance, Insurance, and Real Estate . . . $1,355
- Gas and Electricity Workers . . . $648
- Lower-Skilled Labor . . . $496
- Manufacturing, Payroll . . . $589
- Manufacturing, Union Workers . . . $1,062
- Medical/Health Services Workers . . . $352
- Ministers . . . $802
- Nonprofit Organization Workers . . . $763
- Postal Employees . . . $1,073
- Public School Teachers . . . $509
- State and Local Government Workers . . . $712
- Steam Railroads, Wage Earners . . . $705
- Street Railways Workers . . . $685
- Telegraph Industry Workers . . . $670
- Telephone Industry Workers . . . $419
- Wholesale and Retail Trade Workers . . . $666

Selected Prices

- Airplane Fare, Sightseeing Flight over Columbia, SC . . . $5.00
- Artistic House . . . $4,750.00
- Chair, Morris, in Quartered White Oak . . $8.75
- Cigarettes, Turkey Red . . . $0.10/Pack
- Egg Incubator and Brooder, 125-Egg Capacity . . . $10.00
- Eureka Vacuum Cleaner . . . $35.00
- Gents Kenwood Bicycle . . . $11.95
- Hair Net . . . $0.15
- Infant's Pants . . . $0.25
- Khaki Trousers . . . $0.98
- *Ladies' Home Journal* Biweekly Magazine . . . $0.10
- Man's Diamond Ring . . . $100.00
- Man's Linen Collar . . . $0.10

The Steinway Pianola
TO those who wish in their homes a musical instrument of unquestionable quality; one that need never be defended to the musically learned—one that may be enjoyed impartially by every member of the family — the Steinway *Pianola* makes an irresistible appeal.
The wonderful technique and capacity for real musical expression that have won for the Pianola the praise and endorsement of every great musician of the present generation—the perfection of piano quality that has made the name of Steinway famous—are at your command in this remarkable instrument.
The Aeolian Company
Aeolian Hall
New York
The Steinway Pianola is obtainable in both Grand and Upright models.

Ministerial Coat	$5.00
Old Dutch Cleanser	$0.10
Old Maid Card Game	$0.19
Sewing Machine, Seven-Drawer	$13.45
Steel Walking Plow	$8.73
Tomato Soup	$0.10
Tuition, Harvard University, per Year	$150.00

U.S. Average Selected Salaries & Savings

	Salary	Savings
Bankers	$7,726	$2,308
Clergymen	$3,150	$369
Lawyers	$4,169	$1,474
Physicians	$3,907	$717
Professors	$2,878	$543
Railroad Officials	$3,441	$628
Steamboat Officials	$2,529	$603

"The Point of View," *Scribner's Magazine*, July 1909:

"The American who claims for his own a certain degree of what Boston women reverently call 'culture' is allowed, all the same, to be a rather impossible person in his dramatic standards. The idea of a play as the vehicle of a 'star' in an emotional or, better yet, a 'character' part, is about as far as he goes in his appreciation of drama. Why then is the newest form dramatic art has taken been left to the office boy and cash-girl and the submerged nine-tenths to enjoy? Enjoy it they, at least, do, and get better value for their money than do the patrons of real theatres. The price is five cents, or at most 10; there is an illustrated song or two, with a real tenor voice on the job; the President's inauguration is shown, and the ex-President's start for Africa via Hoboken—or perhaps some historical scenes (with the Jamestown colony a favorite); finally, some farcical passages and a real comedy—all but the words. Hard on the eyesight, yes, and on the ears, too, when it is accompanied by the piano, but think what you are saving on your entertainment, even as compared with a place at the 'polite vaudeville' theatre around the corner—to say nothing at all of anything so extravagant as attendance at the playhouse where they are giving a dramatized 'bestseller.'

It is only when you tell the Prosperous Person that there are rising 10,000 of moving-picture establishments that he 'takes notice'; it is the figures that talk to him. What all of us should realize is that this new department of the modern dramas is—relatively—a virgin soil. Who knows what crops it may yet raise? And why assume that depravity—gross vulgarity, even—is necessarily bound up in it? In France (it is in France that the evolution has gone furthest) such actors as Le Bargy and Rejane and Bernhardt are not ashamed to pose for the moving-picture camera. . . . This is the age of the machine . . .

The modern evolution of the magic lantern has not only come into its own, but has become a force that can no longer be neglected by social historians. At Suffolk, Virginia, Sam Hardy, the choir singer convicted for the assassination of Tiberius Gracchus Jones, has applied for a new trial on the grounds that an exhibition of moving pictures at the Comedy—a duel in Normandy, a moonshine tragedy in the Kentucky mountains—tended to sway the minds of the jurymen, who went there as one man . . . no longer is the magic lantern a nursery plaything! Men deal with it; it deals with men. Some would have us believe that homes are corrupted thereby, and that children steal in order to raise the price of admission. If it breaks homes, it mends them too. But yesterday we read of brothers brought together through its beneficent agency—brothers separated from childhood. The one recognized the other—the prodigal—as he swung by in a file of sailors parading in San Francisco—all of this, of course, on the screen. 'That's Harry himself!' exclaimed the older brother, whom it is good to know for a prosperous merchant, who will make life easier for the seaman now.

If the moving-picture shows can unite families, what does it matter if they are a bit hard on the eyes, and sometimes almost as vulgar as the contemporary stage itself?"

"Public Shows Are Endorsed by Public Speaker, Professor Libby Approves of People Spending Time and Money for Entertainment," *The Denver Post*, March 11, 1911:

"Man cannot live by bread alone; he needs the moving picture. This is not a literal quotation from the lecture of Prof. M.F. Libby, Chair of Philosophy at the state university, given at the public library last night, but it is an authentic extract from the gist of the professor's remarks.

'It is not a bad sign,' declared Professor Libby, 'when people spend more for amusement than for the necessities of life. Man cannot live by bread alone. We are too much inclined toward Philistinism, (sic) or I may even say we are inclined to be pharisaical about this proposition. Go into the moving picture shows and see for yourself. These people are squandering money on the artistic impulses that are not educating, but what's the difference? Art is the play of grown-ups. . . .' Denver is classed as an intellectual center by Professor Libby, whose investigation shows that one-sixth of the books taken from the Denver public library are the old standards."

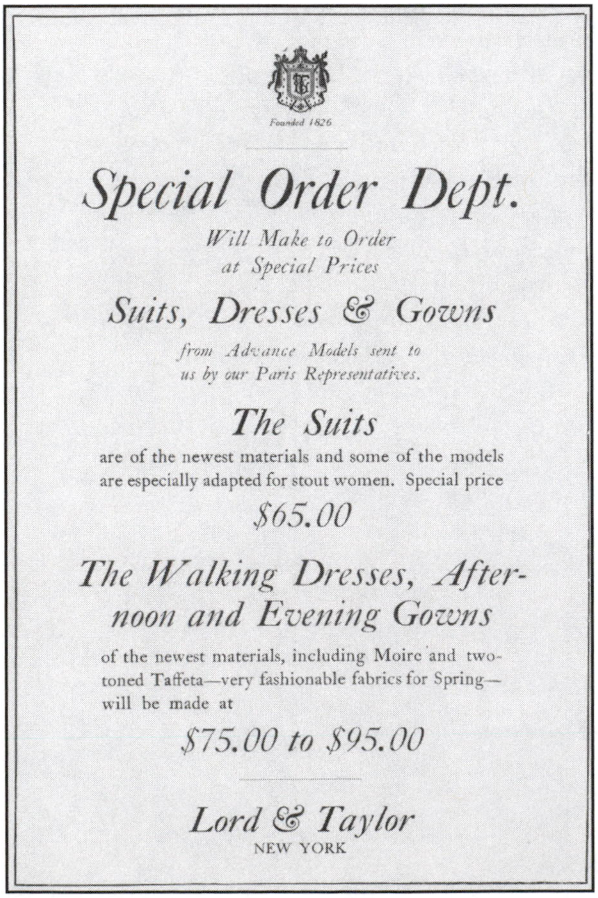

The Socialist magazine, The Masses, *prints articles "too naked for the money-making press."*

"Motion Pictures of Colorado Scenes Now on Screens, First Showing in Denver Brings Cheers from Business Men," *The Denver Post*, September 7, 1911:

"Denver and Colorado in moving pictures, full of action, life, picturesqueness, and beauty will now be shown upon the canvas of the world by the William H. Swanson Film Company. The firm was run off at the Princess Theater yesterday for the first time, bearing the authority of the Denver Chamber of Commerce and viewed by members of that body, together with the Denver press.

It was a success. Hundreds of reproductions will be sent throughout the world for the delectation of the patrons of moving picture theaters. Thursday the film will be on the regular program of the Princess. It will also be released throughout the country.... The pictures open with the great industrial pageant that moved through the streets on July 18. One of the features of the big parade was *The Denver Post* Boys and Girls' Band with 70 pieces. As these young musicians moved through the thoroughfares, which were banked on either side by thousands of spectators, all of whom are shown in the film, they were greeted with enthusiastic applause."

"Colorado Movie Sensation," *Denver Republican*, March 7, 1906:

"Kansas City fire chief George C. Hale has built a little amusement place on the model of a regular coach with a platform, interior, and seats exactly like any railroad car. Then he added a rumbling motion and swinglike curves and put in a motion picture sheet in front of the 'passengers.' The sensation is the most deceptive ever seen. It is just like riding over the actual scenery, and people in Chicago have gone crazy over it. Two of the cars are opposite the Palmer house on State Street and some idea of the business can be gained from the fact that shows are given every hour from nine in the morning until 11 at night, and people are turned away at every show. Lines reaching to the curb are headed toward the ticket office and people stand for a chance to 'buy a ticket to Colorado' for 10 cents. Last week many Colorado motion pictures were shown and they made a hit, over 50,000 persons having registered through the gate. So pronounced is the success that chief Hale has already made contracts for over 350 similar cars to be erected before the first of July."

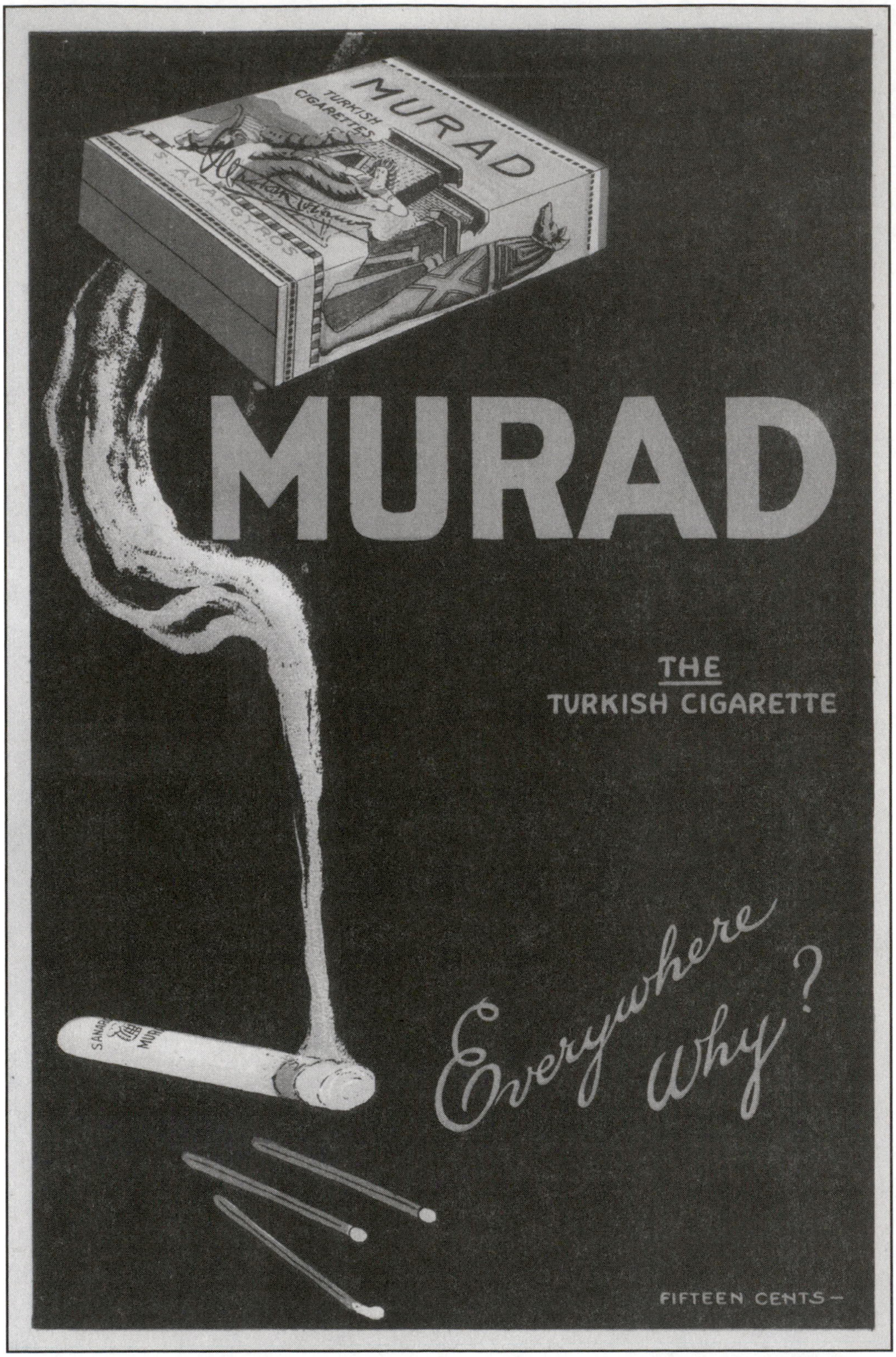
MURAD
TURKISH CIGARETTES
S. ANARGYROS
MURAD
THE
TURKISH CIGARETTE
Everywhere
Why?
FIFTEEN CENTS—

1913 Family Profile

Paul Chéreau works as an engineer of the Amoskeag Manufacturing Company in Manchester, New Hampshire; he started as an office boy, got his education at night with company help, and now supervises plant construction and machinery improvement. He, his wife, Patrice, and their five children live in a house provided by the company.

Paul Chéreau checks the company stock prices every day.

Annual Income: $1,530

Annual Budget

The average per capita expenditure in 1914 for all workers nationwide is:

Auto Parts	$1.09
Auto Purchases	$4.21
Clothing	$29.52
Dentists	$0.95
Food	$90.34
Furniture	$3.47
Gas and Oil	$2.35
Health Insurance	NR
Housing	$62.78
Intercity Transport	$3.32
Local Transportation	$6.13
Personal Business	$9.86
Personal Care	$3.08
Physicians	$2.99
Private Education and Research	$4.97

Patrice believes women should not drive.

Recreation $10.06
Religion/Welfare Activities $8.44
Telephone and Telegraph $1.13
Tobacco $7.39
Utilities. $4.64
Average Per Capita Consumption. $336.95

Life at Home

- The Chéreaus live in a large home built and maintained by Amoskeag for officers of the company.
- They have five children, one of whom is attending college at Yale; the couple is discussing whether they would be willing to pay for college for the two girls.
- They recently purchased a car, which he drives, for trips into the country; she does not believe it is a woman's place to handle machinery.
- Because he views silence as a strength, he rarely shows emotion to his children.
- He also prides himself on his memory and expects his wife and children to remember each of his requests; he does not like to repeat himself.
- He loves dressing well, and many of his clothes are purchased during trips to Boston or ordered from John M. Smyth Company in Chicago.
- In addition to a full work schedule, he is often away from home serving on boards, both governmental and church.
- His grandparents were originally from France; his family, who were Huguenots, lived first in Quebec before moving to Manchester when he was a child.
- His high, consistent wages have allowed him to invest in high-grade bonds, but since he is still cautious of the stock market, the only stock he owns is Amoskeag Manufacturing, some of which he purchased and some of which he was given.
- Paul makes it a practice to check the company stock price every day.
- Amoskeag Manufacturing has experimented with profit sharing and stock option plans, attempting to include all workers; workers have often been suspicious that the company stock program is a way to hold down wages.
- Total wages are important to Amoskeag's financial operation, constituting 35 percent of the total cost of the mill.
- Patrice assists at the annual stockholder's meeting, which is always held in one of the mill buildings in Manchester; last year more than a thousand people attended the meeting and received a free meal.

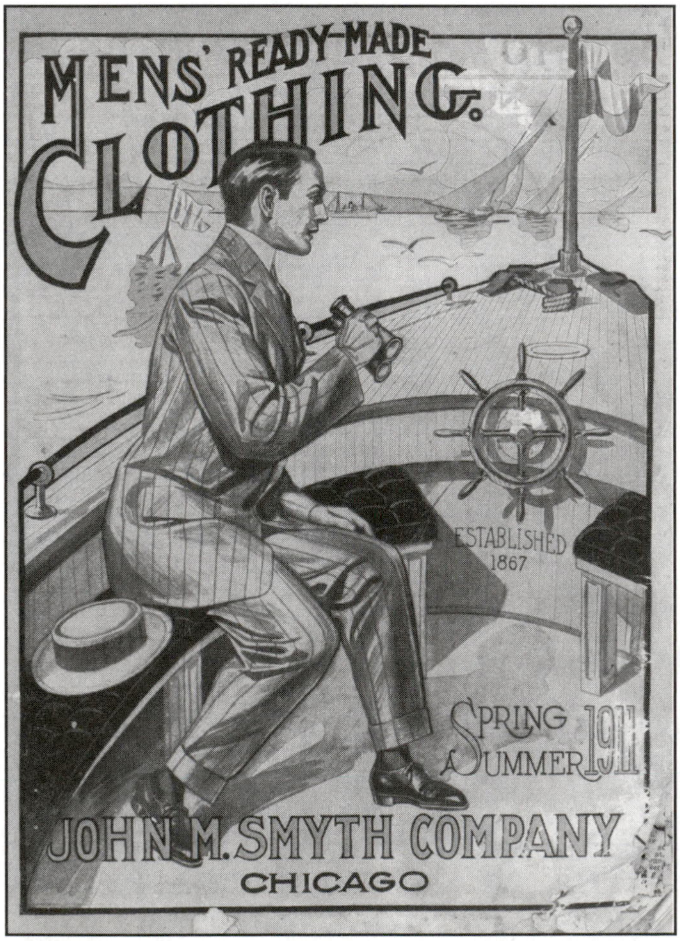

Life at Work

- In 1913 Amoskeag boasts 17,000 workers, making it the largest textile plant in the United States, possibly the world.
- The facility encompasses 30 major mills, each of which is as large as a standard, stand-alone mill elsewhere; the buildings cover eight million square feet.

- The company is totally self-sufficient in its operations, including power generation and construction capabilities.
- Its total operating profit in 1913 is $1.1 million, an increase over 1912; the combined annual production of cotton and worsted cloth is 231.6 million square yards.
- Working first as an office boy and then in payroll while going to school at night, Paul is now an engineer with Amoskeag over textile machinery and new construction.
- Like most managers at the company, he takes great pride in getting the best price for what he buys; Amoskeag is known for making good deals for cotton, supplies, and machinery.
- As an office boy he was expected to arrive at daylight and start coal fires to provide heat; he then swept the office, picked up the mail, and delivered handwritten orders for cotton, wool, machinery, and other items needed in Boston.
- In 1913 he is in charge of installing new textile equipment; the company has a sound reputation for producing excellent yarns with a high count, making them superior goods.
- He loves the precision of quality machines, which produce fewer errors, less waste, and require less supervision.
- Most of the equipment at Amoskeag was manufactured and installed between 1881 and 1900.
- In 1913 the company is replacing most of its own machinery's parts, with 60 men working in the foundry making replacement parts for the aging equipment.
- Weavers want the newest machines; if a weaver's five or six looms are running well, he can walk around, chat with others, and even read, whereas machines in poor repair require more work, more downtime, and often less pay.

Their youngest daughter dreams of going to college.

The giant Amoskeag mill is on the bank of the Merrimack River.

Downtown Manchester is alive with activity.

- Total employment at Amoskeag is 15,000 people, who produce cloth at the rate of 50 miles per hour.
- The facility is so large, he often uses a company taxi to go from his office to the cloth room or to a mill that is experiencing problems.
- Management of the mills operates by a centralized, well-defined hierarchy of authority.
- The company is feeling pressure from cotton goods produced in the South, though Paul believes most of the Southern textile mills produce inferior cloth.
- In addition, last year, management was forced to increase wages because a strike in Lawrence, Massachusetts, was gaining support among workers in Manchester and walkouts were beginning; Amoskeag responded with an overall 10 percent wage increase.
- He is also convinced that if America had not overreacted to immigration, willing workers from Europe would be asking for jobs at any wage right now and the South would not be stealing jobs.
- Further harming profits, many of the fashion changes are coming too quickly, and he does not like the frequent demands from buyers to change patterns, weaves, and styles in order to chase every fad.
- He knows that when styles change frequently, it is often the manufacturer who accumulates too much costly inventory, since manufacturing to order in a changing market can cause wide fluctuations in production and considerable downtime for both workers and machines; it's not good business.

A modern mill requires a large office staff of trained typists.

- He is also puzzled that gingham, Amoskeag's mainstay, is losing popularity; designers say that because of its rigidity in design, gingham is being used less.
- Print cloth, on the other hand, is enjoying wide use because of its flexibility in finishing and styling.
- The solid, red-brick factory walls flank the Merrimack River for more than a mile on one side of the river, and a half-mile on the other.
- The Amoskeag complex is a unique and highly successful attempt at total planning, both of the mill and the city.
- Manchester's arrangement of streets, brick homes, and bridges give it the honor of being "the handsomest manufacturing city in the world."
- It was founded on the nineteenth century belief in providing for the complete life of the new industrial man.
- Amoskeag means "abundance of fish" in Penacook Indian dialect.
- The same waterfall viewed by the Indians as a source of pure water became the engine that drives the operations of the textile machinery.
- The solid wall of the mill facing the cluster of boardinghouses owned by the corporation for the workers was constructed in the style of federal townhouses. The design resembles a walled medieval city.

Workers cross the bridge from the factory into town.

- By 1910, French Canadians comprised 35 percent of the Amoskeag's labor force and 38 percent of the city's population.
- French Canadians are particularly well-suited to textile work because of their large families, which follow them into the mill.
- After the passage of the New Hampshire child labor law of 1911, it is rare to find children younger than 12 working the mill; the law allows children 12 and above to work during school vacations, and at age 14, children can work full-time.
- Recruitment of French Canadians has been made easier because of the railroad route running between Montreal and Boston.
- The French Canadians fill the skilled and semiskilled jobs, while the overseer jobs are filled by native-born Americans, whose origins include English, Scottish, second-generation Irish, Germans, and Swedes.

Amoskeag, Life and Work in an American Factory-City, by Tamara K. Hareven and Randolph Langenbach, an interview with weaver William Moul:

"It seemed like you were locked in when the Amoskeag owned the mills. If you told the boss to go to hell, you might as well move out of the city. The boss had the power to blackball you for the rest of your days. Then the only way you could get a job there again was if you disguised yourself. Some of them did that. They would wear glasses, grow a mustache, change their name. . . . It was either that or starve to death."

Amoskeag employment advertisement in *Le Candado-American*, November 19, 1913, recruiting French Canadians:

"More than 15,000 persons work in these mills that border on both sides of the river. Their wages allow them comfort and ease and all seem to be content with their lot. It is true that the larger company to which they sell their labor treats them as its own children. . . . That is the reason why the Amoskeag Company has never had any trouble with its employees. It treats them not as machines but as human beings; as brothers who have a right not only to wages but also the pleasure of life. . . . Its employees work not only to earn a wage but to please their employers, who know how to treat them well. It has resolved with justice to itself and its workers the problem of the relations between capital and labor."

- Adapting to immigrant workers, supervisors in 1913 have become accustomed to speaking French, whereas the Poles and Greeks often rely on translators hired by the company.
- A paymaster commented that "most of the people who worked in the mill couldn't talk English, but they knew their coinage. They could tell the difference between a silver dollar and a quarter."
- The average weekly pay is $17.50, with employees paid according to the amount of cloth they produce.
- In 1905 Amoskeag opposed the state of New Hampshire's efforts to reduce the workweek from 60 hours to 58.

The mill employs 15,000 workers.

The mill offers training school sessions for immigrant workers.

- To cope with the changing work force, Amoskeag has introduced an employment office designed to centralize the hiring process of all workers and keep a systematic record of all hirings, firings, and reasons for leaving; management is also attempting to control the diversity of the departments by controlling turnover. A centralized system allows management to screen out troublemakers and labor agitators.
- Other reforms include a textile club, a textile school, a cooking school for girls, and a free dental service.
- The curriculum for the textile school includes mechanical drawing, shorthand, typewriting, mathematics, automobile construction, and practical weaving; Paul is very proud that his company has created this opportunity for the workers.
- The company also maintains a small hospital composed of a doctor and nine nurses, who make home visits to employees and families without charge.
- Cloth from the mill is provided to families in need so that clothing can be made.
- The company also provides rental privileges to three- to five-story brick homes located along the streets leading to the center of town.
- Originally designed as boardinghouses for the "mill girls" of the 1840s, the buildings were remodeled for family use; the rent is only $1 per room per month, substantially below the market rate of the rest of the city.
- To qualify for housing, workers must have large families with more than one member employed by the mill.

- The houses are so popular, some families stay on the waiting lists for months, sometimes years.
- The closeness of the houses to the mill allows working women to quickly cross the bridges that divide factory and town to check on their children during breaks.
- By 1913 about 20 percent of the Amoskeag work force lives in corporate housing.
- The company views the workers as its children and expects loyalty in return; association with unions that would disturb this relationship is strongly discouraged.
- The children of workers play on Amoskeag playgrounds, which include a swimming pool, baseball diamond, and a skating rink in the winter; gardening by children and adults is also encouraged.
- In just the past year, nearly $30,000 has been spent to transform these recreational grounds into one of the city's premier attractions.

"The Automobile in 1910," by D.E. Northam, *The World To-Day*, February 1911:

"Estimates obtained from reliable sources show that in this country alone the output for the year 1910 was over 200,000 cars, including both pleasure and commercial cars, and their value will reach beyond the $300 million mark. In order to handle this stupendous 'infant industry,' more than 300,000 employees are kept busy at work and an outlay of capital of approximately $500 million is required. Figures given out by the government statisticians place the value of the cars exported from the United States for 1910 at over $12 million, representing a gain of over 25 percent on the previous year. . . . Prior to 1910 the automobile was considered a luxury rather than a necessity. Now, however, the family touring car, the small-type roadster for getting about in a hurry, and even the limousine, have come to be regarded as not only enjoyable but as positively useful an investment as can be made with the same amount of money. The farmers throughout the country are fast realizing the real value of the car as a time-saver, and in many cases are converting it into a power-producer for farm machinery. It is also esteemed by the farmer in marketing his small produce, and in bringing him in close communication with town in cases where dispatch is wanted. All these things unite in creating the wonderful demand for the smaller type of car by the farmer as well as the city man of average salary, although the number of larger touring cars seen in the country and owned by country residents is surprising. To the doctor the auto has come to be regarded as indispensable, and with the public in general it is safe to say 'once an owner of a car is always to own one.'"

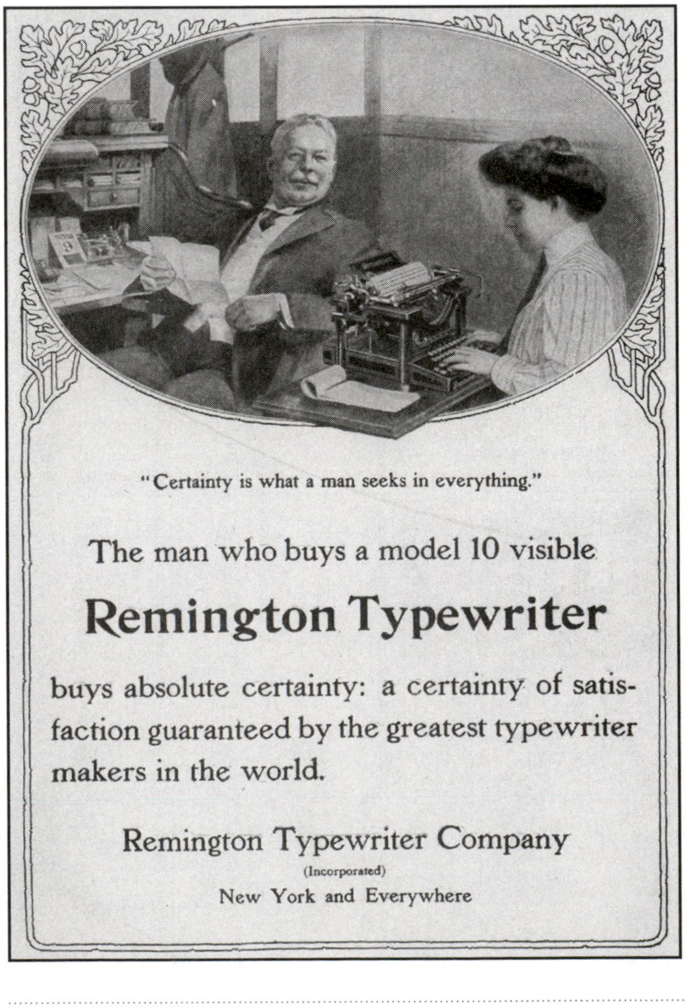

"Certainty is what a man seeks in everything."
The man who buys a model 10 visible
Remington Typewriter
buys absolute certainty: a certainty of satisfaction guaranteed by the greatest typewriter makers in the world.
Remington Typewriter Company
(Incorporated)
New York and Everywhere

Life in the Community: Manchester, New Hampshire

- The Amoskeag Company founded the city of Manchester in 1837 and dominates the economy of the city.
- The city and company were planned and developed by a group of Boston-based entrepreneurs.
- The group purchased the waterpower for the entire length of the Merrimack River, New England's second largest river, and 15,000 acres were set aside across from the Amoskeag Falls as the site for the planned city and mill.
- The community was named after Manchester, England, already famous as the world's largest textile city.
- The developers envisioned a community of young, unmarried women working together in the mills and living together in boardinghouses, mostly from rural New England.
- The company regulated their behavior during work and after hours; the boardinghouses were closed and locked at 10 p.m., church attendance was compulsory, and alcoholic consumption was prohibited.
- To stimulate the development of the city, Amoskeag auctioned off land for stores and homes and gave land to churches and social clubs to encourage their development.
- The sales included deed restrictions that limited the number and size of houses in residential areas—to avoid overcrowding—and dictated the types of materials suitable for construction in the commercial areas.
- After the Civil War, Irish immigrant families willing to work for less than the "mill girls" began dominating the labor force.
- Also, the company began importing skilled gingham weavers recruited in Scotland; the quality of work at Amoskeag was improved by the initial 80 "Scotch girls," who were eventually joined by many of their relatives emigrating from Scotland to work at Amoskeag.
- In 1880 the manufacture of cotton goods was concentrated in New England, comprising 80 percent of the nation's spindles; by 1913 this dominance has eroded to 54 percent.
- Rayon, which would grow in importance, comprised only 0.1 percent of the mill consumption of all fibers in 1913.
- Beginning in the 1880s, the Amoskeag Company annexed and purchased all of the surrounding mills of the city, and by 1905 the company had become the only large textile corporation in the city.
- Workers in Manchester often say, "the Amoskeag is Manchester."
- In 1913 the assessed value of Amoskeag represents slightly less than one-quarter of the total assessed value of all of Manchester, New Hampshire.
- Unlike other textile towns, Amoskeag does not have a company store and in 1913 is a lively city full of private shops, movie houses, and dance halls.

Amoskeag management is active in the civic affairs of Manchester.

- Noted for its clean air and avenue of trees on every street, Manchester is the fifth largest city in New England, boasting a population of more than 70,000.
- In addition to the mill and shops, Manchester has two shoe factories and a cigar industry; most of the cigar workers are Belgian.
- The shoe factory gives the workers economic diversity; many families make sure they have at least one member working there so the family is not too dependent on textile employment.
- The population of Manchester began to change in the early 1900s as large numbers of French-Canadian immigrants, escaping the poverty of the farm, joined the textile company; Quebecois priests established a French parish in the community.
- The Poles also found Manchester appealing; in 1902, 850 Poles founded their first parish.
- The 1910 census recorded that 42 percent of the residents are foreign-born, with French Canadians representing 19.6 percent, followed by the Irish at five percent, Greeks at 1.9 percent, and Poles at 1.5 percent.
- In recognition of the community's importance, President William H. Taft visited the city last year; among the vast crowds that thronged the main streets were 12,000 schoolchildren.

Historical Snapshot
1913

- The Brillo Manufacturing Company was founded
- The 60-story Woolworth building opened in New York
- Peppermint Life Savers were introduced as a summer seller when chocolate sales traditionally declined
- 5,000 suffragists marched down Pennsylvania Avenue in Washington, D.C., where they were heckled and slapped
- Congress strengthened the Pure Food and Drug Law of 1906
- The "Armory Show" introduced Post-Impressionism and Cubism to New York
- Vitamin A was isolated at Yale University
- Zippers, in use since 1891, became popular
- Grand Central Station in New York City was completed
- Henry Ford pioneered new assembly-line techniques in his car factory
- A Chicago company produced the first refrigerator for domestic use
- The first jury of women was drawn in California
- The first federal income tax was imposed on incomes over $3,000; 62,000 of the nation's 92 million people were affected
- U.S. industrial output rose to 40 percent of the world's total production; in 1860 America's proportional output was 20 percent
- Camel, the first modern, blended cigarette, was produced; the package design was inspired by "Old Joe," a dromedary in the Barnum & Bailey circus
- A sheriff in Spartanburg, South Carolina, was tried for preventing a lynching, then acquitted
- Teacher Bridget Peixico was fired after 19 years by the New York Board of Education when she became a mother, but reinstated by the courts, which ruled that "illness…caused by maternity (cannot be) construed as neglect of duty."
- The Schaeffer pen, Quaker Puffed Rice, Chesterfield cigarettes, a dental hygienist's course, and the erector set were all introduced for the first time

1913 Economic Profile

Income, Standard Jobs

Average of all Industries, Excluding Farm Labor	$675
Average of all Industries, Including Farm Labor	$621
Bituminous Coal Mining	$859
Building Trades, Union Workers	$1,307
Clerical Workers in Manufacturing and Steam Railroads	$1,236
Domestics	$357
Farm Labor	$360
Federal Civilian	$1,169
Federal Employees, Executive Departments	$1,136
Finance, Insurance, and Real Estate	$1,349
Gas and Electricity Workers	$661
Lower-Skilled Labor	$536
Manufacturing, Payroll	$642
Manufacturing, Union Workers	$1,100
Medical/Health Services Workers	$357
Ministers	$899
Nonprofit Organization Workers	$802
Postal Employees	$1,123
Public School Teachers	$547
State and Local Government Workers	$779
Steam Railroads, Wage Earners	$760
Street Railways Workers	$704
Telegraph Industry Workers	$717
Telephone Industry Workers	$438
Wholesale and Retail Trade Workers	$685

Selected Prices

Baseball	$0.06
Buttons, Mother of Pearl, per Dozen	$0.10
Cloth, Persian Silk, 19" Wide, per Yard	$1.00
Crayons, Paragon Drawing	$0.04
Girl's Shepherd Checked Dress	$1.65
Hair Barrette, Silvered Filigree, 42 Rhinestones	$0.49
Iron Pot Holder	$0.02
J.F. Oxford Talking Machine	$14.95
Machine Oil, per Three-Ounce Bottle	$0.06
Man's Pajamas	$1.45
Misses' Nightgown	$0.99
Sleigh Bed in Mahogany or Circassian Walnut	$39.50
Steamship Ticket, San Francisco to Los Angeles, Round Trip	$12.00

Steel Cake Turner	$0.02
Suitcase, Lightweight	$4.95
Toupee for Men	$21.65
Umbrella, Genuine Paragon Steel Frames and Silk Taffeta	$2.25
Violin, Student	$3.75
Wedding Ring, Man's, 14-Karat Gold-Filled	$2.59
Wool Scarf	$1.05

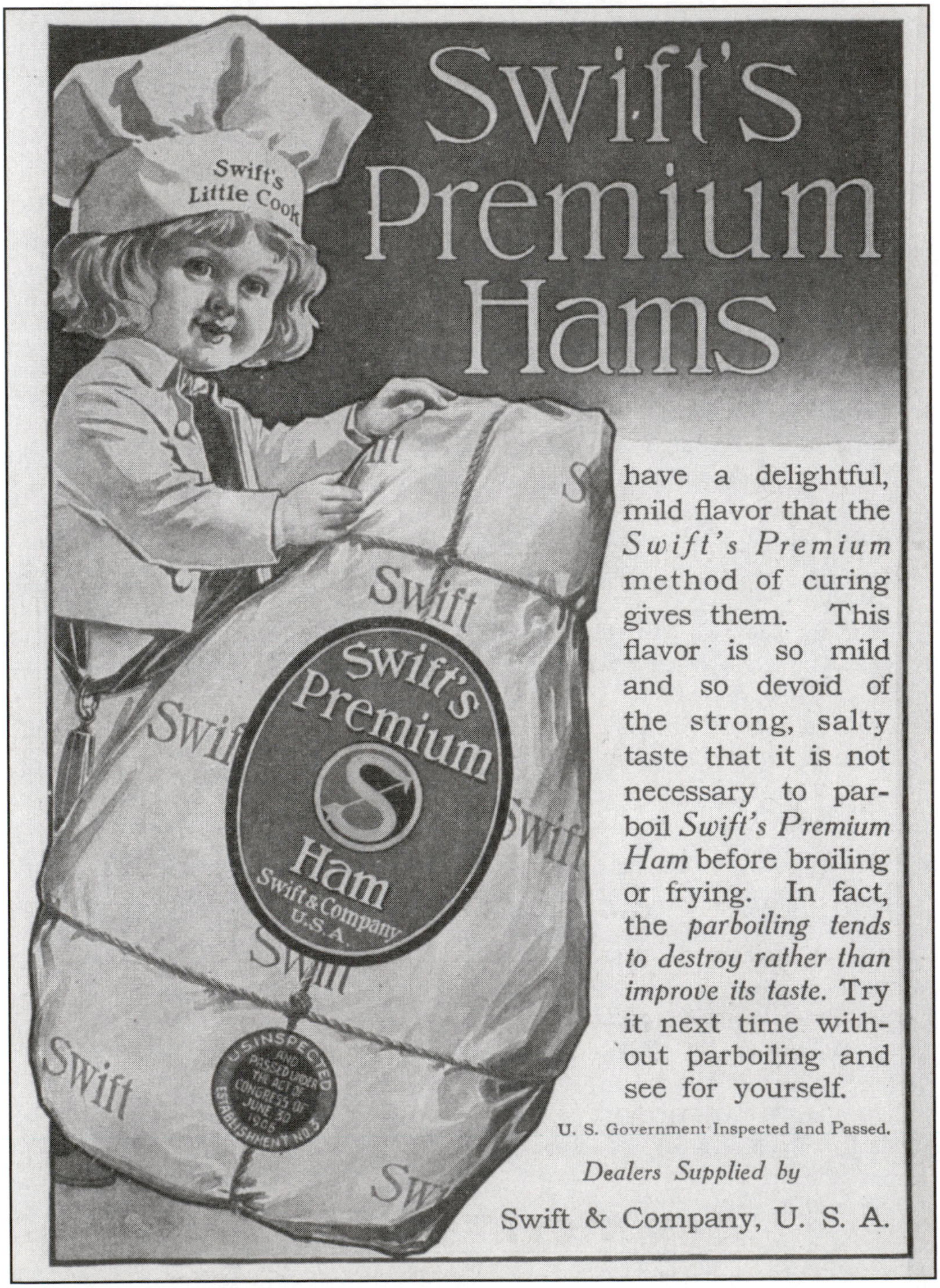

"Making Your Money Do Double Work, How a Shrewd Speculative Investor Made One Security Carry Another," by C.H. Provost, *The Magazine of Wall Street*, June 1913:

"During the early part of May I decided that the market had seen its worst, and as I had been saving up a long while in anticipation of bargains some time this year, I decided to put my money into securities. My available funds amounted to $6,000, and you can imagine how carefully I scanned the list and delved into earnings and other statistics in an effort to secure the greatest obtainable safety and probable profit. Following the teachings of this magazine and bearing in mind Mr. Carnegie's admonition, "put all your eggs into one basket, then watch the basket," I made up my mind that I would pick out the one stock which would be nearest to my personal requirements, and this is how I came to my decision—as near as I can remember my mental processes at the time.

First, I wanted a dividend payer, and second, something that would move. Starting at the top of the list I passed Amalgamated Copper because there were other stocks which would net more on the investment, and with equal chances for improvement in price. American Beet Sugar and American Can were non-dividend payers, so they didn't interest me. Car Foundry with its two-percent dividend didn't yield enough and was too slow a mover. I didn't like any of the industrial preferred stocks, as their varying investment qualities keep them all within a narrow range, and I wanted my principal to grow rapidly as soon as the turn in the market came. American Smelting, I admitted, contained possibilities, but somehow I found it an unsatisfactory stock to deal in. Every time I touch it I promise that it shall be the last. American Sugar Refining is more or less of a bet on the tariff.

American Telephone and Telegraph looked very good to me indeed with its eight-percent dividends and occasional "rights." I reasoned that if it should advance to its former high price, that it would be about 20 points above this level. Twenty points on a stock selling at 120 odd is about a 16 percent increase on the investment, while on a stock selling at 50 it is a 40 percent increase. All other things being equal therefore, I favored a low-priced stock.

This resolution naturally eliminated high-priced issues like American Tobacco, Canadian Pacific, Sears Roebuck, etc., which further narrowed the list. . . . Chesapeake & Ohio were at a stage where doubts as to continuance of dividends appeared frequently in the public press. Other people said the road's credit was poor . . . I threw out Pennsylvania [Railroad], notwithstanding the recent decline, owing to its price being above par, and I decided that I would await a possible chance in Southern Pacific, having in mind the aforesaid idea. This simmered the whole proposition down to two stocks—Chesapeake & Ohio [Railroad] and U.S. Steel common.

Turning over in mind the merits and demerits of Chesapeake & Ohio, I remembered that while its five-percent dividend made it look cheap around 64, there was a possibility that the trouble in placing its bond might make a dividend cut necessary. Hence, I decided that this was a point in favor of Steel, and while it is unknown what effect the tariff will have on the earnings of the steel corporation, orders now on hand are sufficient to carry it well along into the fall with earnings in excess of dividend requirements. . . . To put it another way, it occurred to me that with good crops, which are promised, and the removal of the European war menace, business conditions during the next six months might not be as bad as some of the tariff howlers have predicted, and that Steel was one of the stocks which should respond quickly to any recognition of improved conditions. . . . To sum the whole thing up, I made up my mind to buy 100 Steel common and pay for it. . . . While the stock was being transferred, the thought occurred to me that I wasn't

(continued)

"Making Your Money Do Double Work, . . ." *(continued)*

making my money work hard enough. If my judgment on Steel was correct, then it was time to buy other things—some of these high-grade stocks for instance, which wouldn't decline very much unless everything went to pieces. Accordingly I went back over the list and finally cut out everything but American Telephone and Pennsylvania. . . I turned the whole matter over in my mind and decided to buy Telephone because it was the soundest and yielded the largest return. I then put my 100 shares of Steel up as margin for the purchase of the Telephone, figuring out that if, during the next year, my anticipation of higher prices was realized I would come out, on dividends alone, about as follows:

Dividend on 100 U.S. Steel $500
Dividend on 100 American Telephone . . . $800
$1,300
Carrying charges on $12,800
at five percent $640
Net income from the combined operation . $660

From this I concluded that my net return on the $6,000 investment in U.S. Steel would be 11 percent, even if these two stocks did not move from their present prices during the entire year. . . . So long as there was no reason for me to change my opinion, I would hold this same position, and if everything came out all right there would be an advance from 10 to 15 points on these two stocks, depending on circumstances. Ten points would be $2,000, or a 33 1/3 percent increase on my original capital. Fifteen points in each would amount to 50 percent on my original capital, and that was what I had originally started out to find. Thus I am making my money do double work."

UNCLE SAM, TO CONGRESS: "Toss it aboard—haven't time to stop."—Philadelphia *Record.*

MAY THE NEW DEAL BE A SQUARE DEAL.
—Chicago *Tribune.*

1917 News Profile

First Lieutenant Lemuel Shephard, 55th Company, 5th Marines, 2nd Division, was in college when the war began, dreaming of a career in law or the ministry.

"Virginia Military Institute, over in Lexington, that's where I was when Wilson declared war; I was a senior. I certainly hadn't decided on a military career at this time, not at all. My family would have liked to see me go into medicine or law, maybe even the Episcopal Church, but the war changed all this.

Naturally, after four years in a military college, we were all eager as hell to go once America got in the thing. One of the students, it might have been my roommate, a boy named Robinson, had found out that the Marine Corps would give the VMI boys a shot at the commissions if they would go to Washington for a physical. So right after the declaration about six of us headed for the capital. What a ride! We grabbed the night train, standing up all the way from Lynchburg to Washington. It seemed to me that everyone and his brother was going to the nation's capital that night. Then, of course, we were worried about the physical—it'd be awful if any of us failed. Besides, most of us had borrowed money to make the trip; you know college boys never have any money.

Well, the physical turned out to be a breeze. This old doctor, he just thumped us a few times, checked a few things, and kind of smiled: 'Ever have the clap, Shephard?' he inquired.

This came as somewhat of a shock to me, coming from a proper Virginia family, so I quickly answered, 'No, sir.'

'How about hemorrhoids?'

'No, sir.'

'You'll do, Shephard, you'll do.'

Now that's a little exaggerated, but it really was somewhat of a cursory physical. You see, the marines wanted to get into the war as a major unit, not just some small detachments, and they needed officers badly. . . .

We all went home to await immediate orders. A week or two went by with nothing happening, so I got a hold of Tom Holcomb, the marine personnel officer. Tom was furious, said there must have been a foul-up, as we should have already reported to Parris Island; we all received our orders a day or so after that. Parris Island was a great deal smaller in 1917 than it is now, but it did function even then as an introduction to the Corps. Our stay was short.

They loaded us down with books for study on Marine functions and strategies, then gave us 10 days on the rifle range. None of us was prepared for what happened next when a captain gathered us all together.

'Gentlemen,' he asked, 'are any of you interested in foreign duty? If you are, we can immediately accommodate you.'

Please note: He did not say 'France,' he said 'foreign duty.' I had some buddies who'd gone in the Corps a few months before and were down in Haiti having a great old time. We all volunteered thinking we'd end up in one of those spots in Latin America. That wasn't exactly what they had in mind. We left immediately for Philadelphia to join the 55th Company of the 5th Marines that was getting ready for France. Now the wheels are really turning. They'd been gathering marines from all over as quickly as they could. Some had come up from Cuba, others from navy yards, and a great many from reserve companies in the United States—these lads hadn't even been through Parris Island. They worked us around the clock, issuing all kinds of gear. Then they piled us aboard the USS Hancock—the old handpussy, as the boys called her—and sailed us to New York Harbor. Here we went aboard this brand-new transport called the Henderson and left for France, landing at Saint-Nazaire on June 25. I'll always remember that date because it was the same day my class at VMI graduated—the graduation I'd been told I'd attend.

Of course, we all felt pretty good about the whole thing. This was it. Our convoy was the first contingent of American combat troops to land in France. Along with the Marines, we had 12 or so thousand regular army men who were to go into the 1st Division—I'd say there were about 15,000 in all.

After we landed the question came up: Where the hell are we to go? Well, we had this battalion commander, old Fritz Wise, Frederick M. Wise. And was he ever an old salt, a real 'sundowner.' Whenever he'd address you, it'd be 'damn you, Mr. Shephard,' or whatever your name would be. He gave me the word. 'Shephard, damn you, go lay out a camp.'

So I rounded up a detail and laid out a camp. You can bet your bottom dollar the first thing I did was make sure the old man had a good spot. We had a period at this time when they really didn't know what to do with us. We were there, all right, but certainly in no shape to go into the lines. We'd spent a week drilling the men, trying to get them in shape, but really not doing much of anything.

One of the problems was the language barrier, but the men seemed to learn fast. You could, after all, always talk to the French with gestures. Of course, some of the men were always complaining about the failure of the French to 'talk American.' I can remember one time when we were on a long hike that took us through several villages. They all had their cafés, and there always was a big sign in the window with the word 'bouvette.' Finally, a lad from my company came over to me with a puzzled look on his face.

'Mr. Shephard,' he asked, 'wonder does Mr. Bouvette have any daughters?'

I played straight and asked him why.

'Well hell, Lieutenant, I'd like to meet one. Her old man must own every saloon in France . . . !'

Anyway, in March of '18 the spring started to come to France and with it our first tour of the trenches. It was more or less routine: a certain amount of time in the lines, then a rest while you were held in reserve. But this wasn't going to last long. Toward the end of May our real show was getting ready to start. . . . I'd read a paper a few days before that explained how the Germans had broken through the Chemin des Dames and were moving toward Paris. We were about to find out what the war was all about.

By mid-afternoon we were all ready, full packs, ammunition, everything, so we stacked arms and stood by our gear. You know those damn camions didn't arrive until seven the next morning. We ended up sleeping right there on our packs. When they did arrive, wham, we were hustled right aboard—and they took off as fast as possible. My God, what a ride, crammed into those little trucks, bumping over those roads, and most of us with our overcoats on. Hell, this was the first of June; it was hot. And the dust—we could hardly breathe.

Finally, around four o'clock that afternoon, they stopped and let us off. Then the marching started, if you want to call it that. Here we are trying to move up to the front, while all the French refugees are going the other way. It was pathetic as hell: families with baby carriages, bundles on their heads, children in their arms; old men driving carts pulled by nags, old women trying to walk with canes. It was truly the flotsam of war. . . . Well, they halted us about midnight in this open field. We were so darn tired that no one even bothered to take off his bedroll; we all just collapsed on our packs.

The next morning they turned us to at about seven—no coffee, chow, or anything. We started marching again, this time until about four in the afternoon, when we were stopped at a place called Pyramid Farms, just off the Paris road. The French farmers had all left, so the men started rounding up all these eggs, chickens, and cows—at least we had food. But we sure as hell didn't get any sleep. This battery of French 75s had moved in next door to us. You know that peculiar 'crack, crack' they make? Well, try sleeping through it sometime. The next morning we moved in. Our company took up a position near a placed called Les Mares Farm, not far from the Lucy Torcy road.

By this time we'd gotten the word. The area was called Belleau Wood. If the Germans could break through our division, they could probably go all the way to Paris. Naturally, the French were very concerned. One of their generals had asked Preston Brown, the division chief of staff, if we could hold.

'General,' Brown's supposed to have answered, 'these are American regulars; they haven't been beaten in 150 years!' You never know if things like that are really said, but it made us all feel pretty good.

Our orders were basic: 'Form as skirmishers to withstand attacks.' And that's what we did. We had to spread ourselves pretty thin because we didn't know just where they'd hit us. I'd suggested we put a dozen or so men on this commanding piece of land about two or three hundred yards in front of our lines, with explicit orders to retreat if the pressure got too hot. Just about the time the attack started I'd decided to go out and see how they were doing. . . . Well, after I'd covered about a hundred yards or so, this huge German shell landed about six feet to my right; for one horribly tantalizing instant I saw it coming at me. It covered me with dirt, but that's all. It was a dud. But it sure scared the hell out of me—I can still see it coming down today.

In the meantime, the Germans were attacking, and we're knocking the hell out of them with rifle fire, which was something they obviously didn't expect. The French, you see, were great at the attack with their grenades but not much with the rifle. I guess the Germans didn't realize they were coming against Americans. We could actually hear them yelling about it.

After my dud episode I tried to find a spot where I wouldn't be too exposed but could still see what was going on. I was leaning against this tree when all of a sudden something struck me in the neck and spun me around. Well, I didn't know what the hell had hit me or how bad it was. The first thing I did was spit to see if any blood was coming out that way. When there wasn't any, I knew I'd picked up an ugly wound but it would be nothing fatal. I went back to a field hospital, had it patched up, and returned to my company. . . .

Well, the day after I was hit, they attacked again. Fortunately for my company, I really think they struck with their greatest strength toward the main center of our lines, not at the 55th. Once again they were stopped in most places, and, I think once again it was the rifle fire. It only took one bullet to stop a German if you hit him. And my, how our boys could pick them off!"

National War Savings Day June 28th

That's the day we sign up.

That's the day we tell Uncle Sam just how hard we want to win this war. That's the day our government has officially set for us to purchase War Savings Stamps.

On June 28th every man, woman and child in the United States will be called upon to pledge his or her full quota of War Savings Stamp purchases for 1918.

You will be expected to pledge the full amount that you can afford—no more—but by the same token, no less.

In every state, county, city, town and village the War Savings Committees are preparing for this big patriotic rally of June 28th. Unless you have already bought War Savings Stamps to the $1,000 limit, get busy with paper and pencil and figure out the **utmost** you can do.

Remember this. You take no chances when you go the limit on War Savings Stamps. They are the best and safest investment in the world. They pay you 4% interest compounded quarterly. **They can't** go below par. You can get back every dollar you put into War Savings Stamps **any time you need it.** You can turn them in at the Post Office **any time** for their full value plus interest.

Uncle Sam is asking hundreds of thousands of men to **give** their lives to their country. He is asking you only to **lend** your money.

What are you lending?

National War Savings Committee, Washington.

W.S.S. WAR SAVINGS STAMPS ISSUED BY THE UNITED STATES GOVERNMENT

Contributed through Division of Advertising — United States Gov't. Comm. on Public Information

This space contributed for the Winning of the War by

FRANK V. STRAUSS & CO., Publishers of this Program

1919 Family Profile

Allan Kincaid and his family are feeling particularly prosperous as the First World War draws to an end. As the owner of a dress manufacturing company which sells exclusively to Sears, Roebuck, he has been able to buy a home for his family in fashionable Chicago, acquire a car, and afford a lifestyle that includes trips to the country and "the good life" of America's second largest city. He and his wife, Gladys, have two boys.

The youngest son, age six, loves to dress up like his father.

Annual Income: $13,500

Annual Budget

The average per capita consumer expenditure in 1919 for all workers nationwide is:

Auto Parts	$5.54
Auto Purchases	$12.44
Clothing	$55.52
Dentists	$2.65
Food	$177.53
Furniture	$6.97
Gas and Oil	$11.73
Health Insurance	NR
Housing	$76.98
Intercity Transport	$5.43
Local Transportation	$7.78
Personal Business	$19.83
Personal Care	$5.88
Physicians	$6.87

Private Education and Research	$7.19
Recreation	$20.64
Religion/Welfare Activities	$13.92
Telephone and Telegraph	$1.93
Tobacco	$13.67
Utilities	$6.76
Average Per Capita Consumption	$579.57

Up-to-Date Devices

Tested by Lillian Goldsborough

HOUSEKEEPING MADE EASY

THE housewife who prides herself on the perfection of her preserves, will find great delight in owning a good cherry stoner that removes the pit without injury to the cherry. Such a device is well worth its price of $1.40.

The Enterprise Cherry Stoner is strong and substantial in every part of its construction. The clamp holds it securely on the table, while the crank lifts and lowers the cutting portion. The sweeper brushes the stoned cherry into the pan after the removal of the stone.

A little practise soon develops skill in dropping the cherries, one at a time, into the hopper just as the sweeper has pushed the cherry from the hole, leaving it free for the next instalment. Quarts of stoned cherries will pile themselves up before your surprised eyes in no time if you use this helpful machine.

THIS cherry-stoner removes the pit without injuring the cherry

Rapid Dish Washer

IF all housewives were asked what part of housework is the most trying I am quite sure they would answer "dish washing." A machine, therefore, that relieves women of the drudgery of this work should be of great interest to every home-maker.

At first view, the Rapid Electric Dish Washer appears to be only a beautiful kitchen table with silvery top and spacious lower compartment. Upon lifting the lid, which extends across a portion of the top, one sees a most interesting interior, consisting of removable racks for dishes, so made that there are spaces for all kinds of china and utensils.

All one has to do in order to operate this machine is to scrape the dishes, place them in their proper compartments, pour in eight quarts of boiling water, in which a good washing powder has been mixed, close the lid tight, turn on the current—and go about one's other duties.

In fifteen minutes the dishes are clean, and you may press the lever that allows the water to escape through a drain pipe. Then pour in eight quarts of clear, boiling hot water for rinsing the dishes, and switch on the current again for two or three minutes. The rinse water is drained off, and the result if the water has been hot enough, will be shining, clean dishes that require no wiping with a towel.

One of the great advantages of this machine is that it is adaptable to a small family as well as a large one, and is a special boon for company dinners and when canning multiplies dish-washing. It is self-cleansing, as the process of washing the dishes throws the water at high speed in every direction, cleaning all of the inner spaces and racks at the same time that it washes the dishes. The cost of running it is also inconsiderable, averaging about one cent per hour for the electricity. The electric cord may be attached to any lighting fixture.

If one desires, she may easily connect the drain pipe of the dish washer with the sewerage system, thus disposing of the water without the use of a pail. There may be a hot water connection as well, but this is not advisable unless extremely hot water is available. The price is $40.00.

ALL the articles featured on this page have been thoroughly tested by Mrs. Goldsborough. Write to her if you wish information about tested articles. Enclose a stamp and send your letter in care of Today's Housewife, 461 Fourth Ave., New York.

THERE is no comparison between the crude old-fashioned jelly bag and this modern device

AT first view, the dish washer appears to be only a beautiful kitchen table, but when the lid is lifted one sees how the dishes are washed

Handy-Andy Combination Wrench

HOW often does it happen that the screw cap of a jar or bottle refuses to loosen at a critical moment!

A device (price twenty-five cents) that comes to the rescue, loosening or tightening as need be, will prove most acceptable at those trying times. It is made of a twisted wire loop, and is adjustable to a top of any size. By slipping the wire loop around the lid, pulling it until it fits snugly, then drawing the handles together, the wrench may be turned in the desired direction, and will unscrew or tighten, whichever is necessary. It can be used for tack pulling, removing caps from bottles and cracking nuts.

Knapp Fruit and Jelly Strainer

THERE is no comparison between the crude, old-fashioned, home-made cheesecloth jelly bag, tied with a string and swung from a nail, and this modern device which facilitates the work and leaves both hands free to handle the boiling fruit.

The Knapp Jelly Strainer, priced at 50 cents, serves the purpose admirably. It consists of a wire ring for holding the cloth bag, and has an attachment by means of which it may be adjusted to the back of a square-backed kitchen chair, or by the use of two round-headed screws it may be placed against the wall.

The strainer is held in place by its own weight. It balances safely and may be easily detached. The wire ring may be removed when you wish to wash the bag.

Kerr Self-Sealing Jar Caps

SINCE sealing the jar properly is one of the secrets of successful canning, the Kerr Self-Sealing Lids, adjustable to all Mason jars, is of great service in obtaining good results.

These lids or caps at twenty-five cents a dozen complete, are simply metal discs that fit into a screw band. To adjust, one has only to put the lid on the jar, while the fruit is boiling hot, and screw the band gently until it is tight. To open the jar the band should be unscrewed, and the lid punctured with a knife and lifted up.

The screw bands are usable from season to season, while new lids may be purchased each year at fifteen cents a dozen.

Superior Food-Chopper

ALTHOUGH a food-chopper has come to be an article of almost daily use, its helpful qualities will be of even greater value in the canning and pickling months when food has to be chopped for pickles and relishes. Then it is quite indispensable. In purchasing a chopper it is therefore wise to select a well made machine that will "stand up" under hard and constant usage.

There is an excellent food chopper on the market with knives and plates that are constructed of best quality Swedish steel. It comes in four sizes, ranging in price from $1.90 to $3.65, and is supplied with cutters, cutting discs and grinding discs, each of which may be used for a special purpose, thus insuring the proper coarseness or fineness of the particular food to be chopped.

Good Luck Fruit Jar Rings

IN using the regular Mason or spring top jars, it is essential to have good quality rubber rings that are thick enough to insure air-tight sealing and to be thoroughly durable.

The Good Luck Jar Rings fulfil all that their name promises in the keeping of your fruit. Made of red rubber of high standard, they are firm but elastic and are sufficiently thick to wear well. They may be bought for ten cents per dozen.

Hicks' Aluminum Wash Mitt

THE laundering of dainty things is ever a problem, especially when one is on a journey! It is unsafe and expensive to send delicate materials to the laundry. Yet, it is imperative that the pretty clothes of the moment shall be always fautlessly fresh.

How convenient, then, to have a simple device small and of light weight, and costing but fifty cents, to slip into the traveling bag or trunk. One has only to put the Hicks Wash Mitt over her left hand to be promptly supplied with a miniature washboard.

Life at Home

- This has been a very good year for the Kincaids; the war years have brought prosperity to the nation, particularly retail giant, Sears, Roebuck & Co., for whom he manufactures dresses.
- The family is thinking about a European vacation, but Allan is concerned about inflation eating into their savings; he is also unsure of how long he can leave his business.
- He dresses very conservatively, preferring a hat and coat every day, and the more prosperous he has become, the more conservative his clothing.
- His youngest son, who is now six, loves to dress up like his father.
- Their two-story brick home, which they own, is furnished with antiques he inherited from his mother; most came from her native Germany, and though Gladys loves having nice furniture, she wishes it were not so big and heavy.
- He reads the *Chicago Tribune* avidly, and is astonished at how prices are rising now that the Great War has ended; he hopes it is temporary.
- The cost of living has become a frequent topic of conversation at dinner and at his men's club in downtown Chicago.
- His wife Gladys is unhappy about rising prices, but is pleased that sugar, unavailable during the war, is obtainable again.
- The progress of the Peace Conference makes him uncomfortable; he believes that President Woodrow Wilson is naïve, but he does not wish the Germans to be excluded from future affairs.
- As a second-generation German American he has been careful in his comments during the First World War; he does not believe he has lost any business, but he rarely speaks of the old country anymore.
- Since 1916, orchestras have found it unwise to present German-composed music, including Wagner and Beethoven; financial institutions with German names have been Americanized, and the teaching of the German language has been discontinued in many schools.
- Sauerkraut is now referred to as "liberty cabbage" and hamburgers have become "liberty steak."

- The fashion of 1919 demands that women's skirts, which were tight at the ankles, hang six inches from the ground; Kincaid's spring line—now featured in the Sears, Roebuck catalogs—dares to go slightly higher.
- *Vogue Magazine* is predicting that skirts may soon become even shorter, saying, "not since the days of the Bourbons has the woman of fashion been visible so far above the ankle."
- Gladys always wears stockings, nearly always black, but occasionally tan to match her shoes; stockings are never flesh-colored.
- Her make-up includes powder, but most well-brought-up women still frown on rouge.
- To go shopping, a hat is required, preferably with a veil pinned neatly together behind her head.
- Her bathing suit consists of an outer tunic of silk or cretonne over a tight knitted undergarment, worn, of course with long stockings.
- Fashion still requires her hair be worn long; as short-haired women, like long-haired men, are associated with radicalism and free love.
- Cigarette smoking is increasing in popularity in her circle, including women; the number of cigarettes sold a decade later will double. Fatima cigarettes cost $0.23 for a pack of 20.
- During their monthly dinner and dance at a local hotel, sponsored by the men's club, she has seen several women smoking openly, not caring if anyone saw them, and spoke to her husband about how brazen they were.
- She believes that the First World War, known widely as the Great War, is to blame for ushering in too much change.
- With Prohibition nearing, the realities of the new Constitutional amendment are becoming clear; what liquor is still available is expensive, but shortly it will not be available at all.
- Allan still likes a good drink in the evening and knows that he will miss his evening shot, although Gladys believes that drinking is sinful and is pleased that Prohibition has been approved.
- He is also concerned that Bolshevism is taking over and agrees with an advertisement recently run by Swift and Company that reads, "Everything that falsely encourages unrest also encourages Bolshevism. Misunderstanding of American industrial organization, and its benefits to mankind, leads to unrest, dissatisfaction, and radicalism."
- Even the recent League of Nations Conference staged in Chicago gives him pause, because the delegates included dozens of women and blacks with no head for the complex problems of keeping peace.

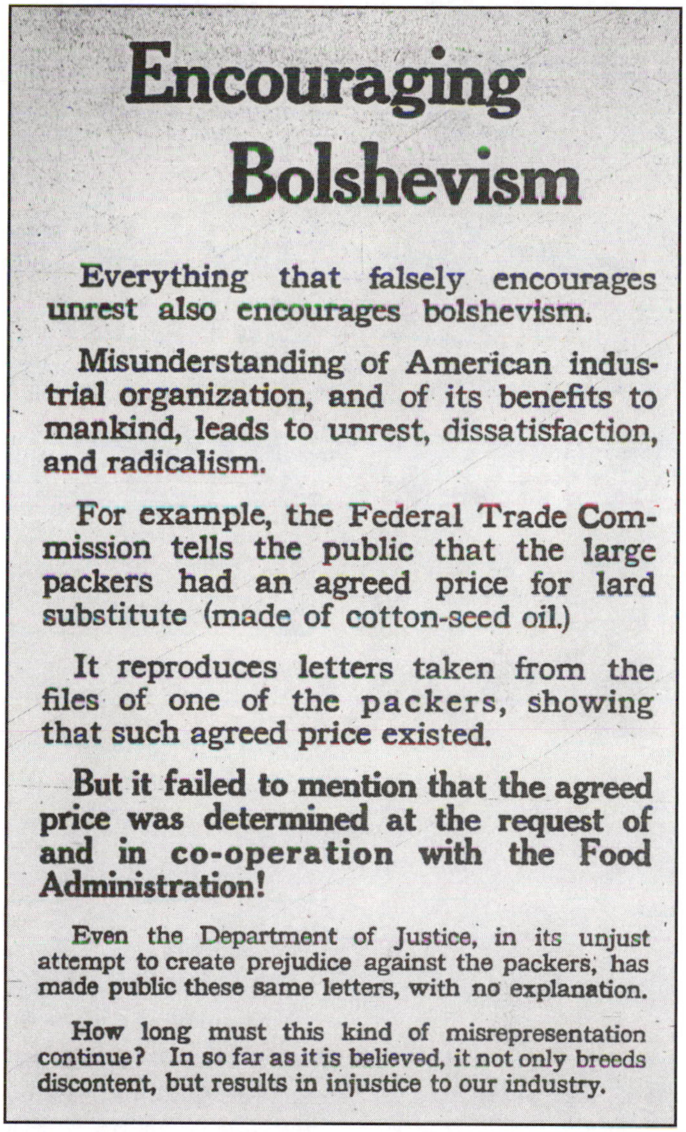
Encouraging Bolshevism
Everything that falsely encourages unrest also encourages bolshevism.
Misunderstanding of American industrial organization, and of its benefits to mankind, leads to unrest, dissatisfaction, and radicalism.
For example, the Federal Trade Commission tells the public that the large packers had an agreed price for lard substitute (made of cotton-seed oil.)
It reproduces letters taken from the files of one of the packers, showing that such agreed price existed.
But it failed to mention that the agreed price was determined at the request of and in co-operation with the Food Administration!
Even the Department of Justice, in its unjust attempt to create prejudice against the packers, has made public these same letters, with no explanation.
How long must this kind of misrepresentation continue? In so far as it is believed, it not only breeds discontent, but results in injustice to our industry.

The recent League of Nations Conference in Chicago includes women and blacks.

- Allan is pleased that the government has relinquished control of the railroads; he never liked purchasing tickets at the United States Railroad Administration Consolidated ticket office.

Life at Work

- World War I has been very good to this company and Sears, Roebuck in general.
- Rising prosperity fuels a desire to own the extras; for many women that means owning additional dresses beyond just the "necessary."
- Women who went to work to support the war are particularly interested in dressing well; many spend the money they earn on themselves for the first time.
- The first signs of the coming recession are building in 1919 as inflation threatens to drive the price of many goods out of the reach of the normal buyer; dress sales, always a luxury, are declining slightly.
- Currently, the economy is confusing; his future is less secure than it was two years ago.
- Since the end of the war, farm prices are plummeting, including the price of cotton used to make many of the dresses he manufactures. Cotton has slumped from a wartime high of $0.35 per pound to $0.16—a problem for farmers but a boon to dressmakers dependent on this raw product.
- At the same time inflation is driving all of his costs higher and the threat of strikes is constant; workers nationwide are desperate to keep up the rapidly rising cost of living, yet thousands of men and women are being thrown out of

Viewing the Future, the American Past:

"While campaigning for U.S. Senate approval of the League of Nations, President Woodrow Wilson said if the League was not approved 'I can predict with absolute certainty that within another generation there will be another world war. What the Germans used (in this war) were toys as compared with what would be used in the next war.' On November 19, 1919, the Senate rejected the League."

Sears, Roebuck, USA, by Gordon L. Weil:

"In 1904, both Sears, Roebuck and Montgomery Ward announced that, in the future, no charges would be made for their catalogs. Richard Sears was not a person to let such a revolutionary change pass without exploiting it. He developed a scheme called "Iowaization" because it was applied on a state-by-state basis with Iowa first. The company wrote to all of its Iowa customers and asked them to distribute 24 catalogs to their friends and neighbors. After each distributor had given the books away, he wrote the company with the list of names of the recipients. The company kept a careful record of the orders submitted by those new customers within the next 30 days. The distributor would receive premiums increasing in value in line with the total volume of the orders submitted by people on his list. This technique turned distributors into salesmen because they had an obvious interest in getting their neighbors to make purchases. At the same time, as satisfied customers of Sears, Roebuck, they could provide living testimonials. Word-of-mouth advertising turned out to be the most effective gimmick ever used by the company because sales in Iowa soon topped those in any other state."

wartime industries as government contracts for war materials—of all kinds—are cancelled.

- With the threat of unions lingering everywhere, all of the 79 women who work for Allan know that he will fire anyone who speaks about unions in his presence.
- Since several chain department stores have asked for his spring dresses, he often wonders whether he should diversify his client base.
- Selling exclusively to Sears has served him well for more than a decade, so he is unsure of the best direction; loyalty counts for something, he believes.
- This spring Sears, anticipating an increase in pregnancies, requests that his dress line include several new maternity dresses; the number of pages devoted to the sale of baby goods has also been increased as more men return from the war in Europe.
- At the same time, Allan believes that some of Sears' top managers have gone soft and seem more interested in their golf game and drinking at the club than selling his dresses.
- From experience, he knows that when mercantile companies fail or slump, the suppliers are the first to get financially hurt; he does not have enough reserves to experience a long downturn.
- Selling directly to Sears has been a successful formula; he makes the dresses and Sears uses its national reach to distribute his goods across the nation.

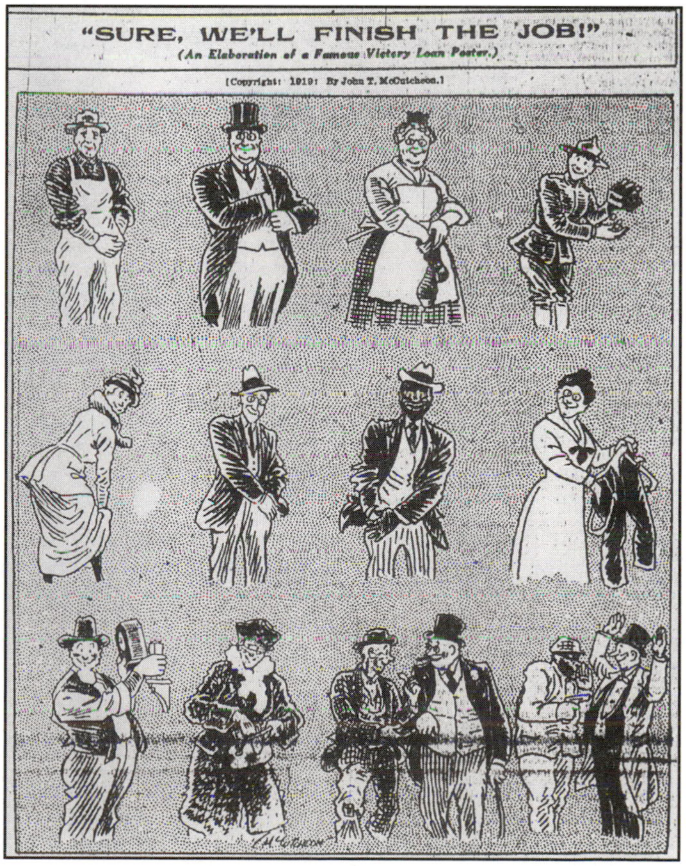
"SURE, WE'LL FINISH THE 'JOB!'"
(An Elaboration of a Famous Victory Loan Poster.)
[Copyright: 1919: By John T. McCutcheon.]

This spring line includes maternity dresses, now that men are returning from war.

- Gladys thinks Allan should modernize his office; currently advertisements for "The Dictaphone" appear regularly in the *Chicago Daily Tribute* claiming "The businessman who says: 'Yes, I should like a Dictaphone demonstration—but some other time' is the very man who needs the demonstration now. He is putting it off because he's busy. And a demonstration shows that The Dictaphone saves hours every day in dictating and transcribing letters."

- He agrees with many of the men at the club, now that the United States has won the war, all socialists and communists should be expelled from the country; their radical ideas are best spoken elsewhere.
- Labor is so out of control that Boston has experienced a police strike, challenging the widely held idea that public servants have no right to strike against the public safety; Allan is concerned that Chicago will experience similar problems if radical ideas are not stopped.
- He especially hates the International Workers of the World or IWW, whose goal, he believes, is to kill capitalism, not raise workers' wages or improve conditions.
- Despite prosperity everywhere he looks, he thinks stock speculation is dangerous. Everyone at the club is talking about getting rich in the market; whereas earlier in the year, the stock market was exchanging 1.5 million shares a day, now it has pushed past two million shares per day.
- Stock speculation has driven the cost of a seat on the New York Stock Exchange to between $60,000 to $110,000.
- Several of his friends at the club have taken up golf—a sport he believes is foolish; why would any grown man spend time knocking a little white ball around the ground, he likes to ask out loud.

Life in the Community: Chicago, Illinois

- Almost a third of Chicago's 2.7 million residents are foreign-born; more than a million are Catholics and another 125,000 are Jews.
- The city is still in turmoil over the recent drowning of an African-American boy who crossed into the white swimming area of Lake Michigan and was stoned by whites. The rioting that followed resulted in the deaths of 23 blacks, 15 whites, and the injury of 537 people, while thousands were left homeless by the fires that raged through the city.
- Immigrant groups consistently and contradictorily band together in Chicago to preserve the Old World cultural patrimony and become Americans; Polish, Greek, German, and Russian neighborhoods are clearly defined.

"Five-Cent Fare for Chicago," *Wall Street Journal*, October 4, 1919:

"Chicago—Decision of Judge Smith in the Sangamon County Court overruling the State Utility Commission which granted seven-cent fares to the Chicago surface lines, means a five-cent fare for these lines, according to a statement by City Corporation Counsel Ettelson. 'There may be some legal difficulties remaining between this decision and restoration of the old fare,' said Mr. Ettelson, 'but my understanding is that the court's action means a five-cent fare within a short time, if not immediately.' "

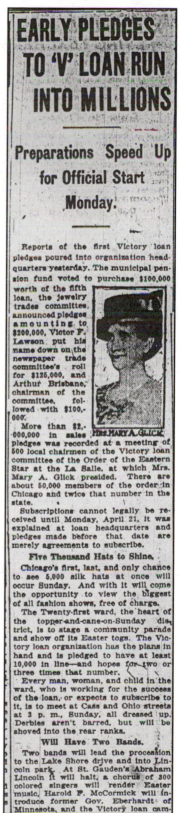

EARLY PLEDGES TO 'V' LOAN RUN INTO MILLIONS

Preparations Speed Up for Official Start Monday.

Reports of the first Victory loan pledges poured into organization headquarters yesterday. The municipal pension fund voted to purchase $100,000 worth of the fifth loan, the jewelry trades committee, announced pledges amounting to $200,000, Victor F. Lawson put his name down on the newspaper trade committee's roll for $125,000, and Arthur Brisbane, chairman of the committee, followed with $100,000.

MRS. MARY A. GLICK

More than $2,000,000 in sales pledges was recorded at a meeting of 500 local chairmen of the Victory loan committee of the Order of the Eastern Star at the La Salle, at which Mrs. Mary A. Glick presided. There are about 50,000 members of the order in Chicago and twice that number in the state.

Subscriptions cannot legally be received until Monday, April 21, it was explained at loan headquarters and pledges made before that date are merely agreements to subscribe.

Five Thousand Hats to Shine.

Chicago's first, last, and only chance to see 5,000 silk hats at once will occur Sunday. And with it will come the opportunity to view the biggest of all fashion shows, free of charge.

The Twenty-first ward, the heart of the topper-and-cane-on-Sunday district, is to stage a community parade and show off its Easter togs. The Victory loan organization has the plans in hand and is pledged to have at least 10,000 in line—and hopes for two or three times that number.

Every man, woman, and child in the ward, who is working for the success of the loan, or expects to subscribe to it, is to meet at Cass and Ohio streets at 3 p. m., Sunday, all dressed up. Derbies aren't barred, but will be shoved into the rear ranks.

Will Have Two Bands.

Two bands will lead the procession to the Lake Shore drive and into Lincoln park. At St. Gauden's Abraham Lincoln it will halt, a chorus of 300 colored singers will render Easter music, Harold F. McCormick will introduce former Gov. Eberhardt of Minnesota, and the Victory loan cam-

Chicago celebrates the end of World War I.

- In Chicago 78,000 work in the downtown area known as "The Loop." Colleges, pressed for cash because of inflation, are beginning to use the money-raising methods learned during the Liberty Loan campaigns.
- The war, which ended on November 11, 1918, lasted 1,563 days, claimed the lives of some 10 million worldwide, and wounded 20 million others.
- When the armistice was declared, people poured into the streets to celebrate, as shopkeepers tacked up signs reading, "Closed for the Kaiser's funeral."
- At that time, more than 3.5 million men were in uniform; two million were in Europe.
- Even the call of patriotism could not stifle labor disputes; during the conflict there were 6,000 strikes, while today, the pace of labor unrest is rising even faster.
- Inflation has driven prices faster than wages, resulting in extensive labor strikes as the high cost of living impacts every household; food, rent, clothing, and taxes are all rising.
- A local joke in Chicago says, "If we coined seven-cent pieces for streetcar fares, in another year we should have to discontinue them and begin to coin 14-cent pieces."
- Milk has jumped from $0.09 to $0.15 a quart in the five wartime years.

Historical Snapshot
1919

- Labor unrest was the most severe since the 1890s, with 2,665 strikes involving four million workers; most were successful in gaining wage benefits and fewer hours
- Unemployment rose to three million
- The Treaty of Versailles assigned Germany sole responsibility for causing the Great War
- 77 percent of newspaper editors favored the ratification of the Peace Treaty, including the provision to create the League of Nations
- The Nineteenth Amendment, granting women suffrage was adopted
- The dial telephone was introduced in Norfolk, Virginia
- The Grand Canyon National Park was established
- Ice cream sales in the United States reached 150 million gallons, up from 30 million in 1909
- Prices were up 79 percent since 1914
- Henry Ford repurchased full control of Ford Motor Company for $105 million
- Seven million cars were registered nationwide
- Conrad Hilton spent $5,000 on the Mobley Hotel in Crisco, Texas
- Seven lynchings occurred in the South, down from 34 in 1917, while the Klan boasted 100,000 members in 27 states
- Attorney General Mitchell Palmer instructed the FBI to round up 249 known communists, who were then deported on the "Soviet Ark" to Finland
- More than 30,000 Jews marched in Baltimore to protest pogroms in Poland and other European countries
- Socialist Eugene Debs went to prison, charged with sedition; he called Lenin and Trotsky the "foremost statesmen of the age"
- The mayor of Seattle set up machine guns in the streets after 45,000 strikers threatened to paralyze the city
- The states finally ratified the Eighteenth Amendment prohibiting the sale of alcohol, to take effect as law in 1920
- A Victory Liberty Loan concert at the Metropolitan Opera raised $7.8 million; Rachmaninoff's encore raised $1.2 million

1919 Economic Profile

Income, Standard Jobs

Average of all Industries, Excluding Farm Labor	$1,272
Average for all Industries Including Farm Labor	$1,201
Bituminous Coal Mining	$930
Building Trades, Union Workers	$1,328
Clerical Workers in Manufacturing	$1,999
Domestics	$539
Farm Labor	$706
Federal Civilian	$971
Federal Employees, Executive Departments	$1,520
Finance, Insurance, and Real Estate	$1,099
Gas and Electricity Workers	$556
Lower-Skilled Labor	$991
Manufacturing, Payroll	$233
Manufacturing, Union Workers	$983
Medical Health Workers	$606
Ministers	$759
Nonprofit Organization Workers	$677
Postal Employees	$948
Public School Teachers	$377
State and Local Government Workers	$640
Steam Railroads, Wage Earners	$600
Street Railways Workers	$610
Telegraph Industry Workers	$601
Telephone Industry Workers	$392
Wholesale and Retail Trade Workers	$508

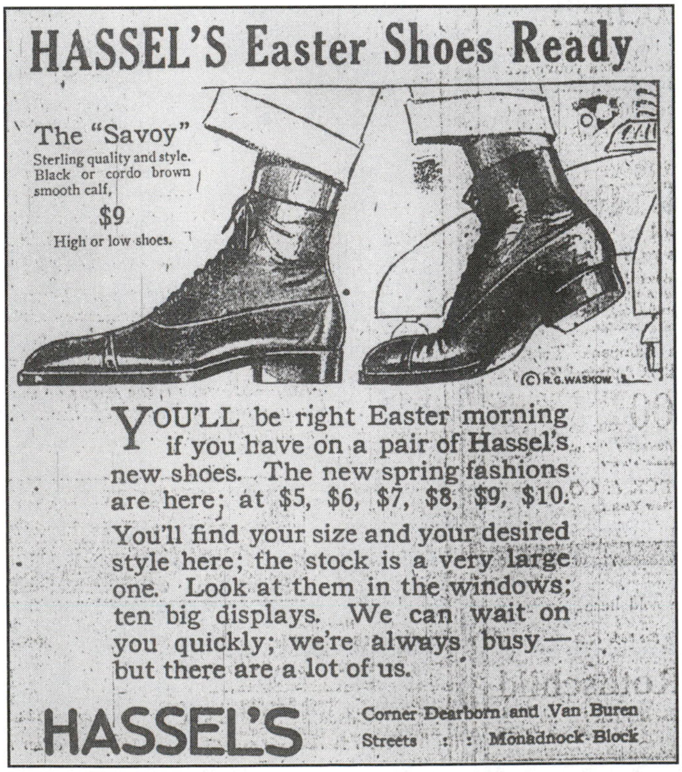

Selected Prices

Bacardi Rum	$3.20/Fifth
Camel Cigarettes, per Pack	$0.18
Cigars	$0.10
Corset Cover	$1.50
Golf Bag	$3.45
Hat, Easter Style	$5.00
Imperial Gin	$2.15/Fifth
Overcoat	$30.00
Phonograph Record	$1.50
Rug, 6'x 9'	$43.50
Single Room for Rent per Week	$4.00
Soap	$0.07
Tobacco, per Package	$0.15
Underwear	$1.25
Washing Machine	$15.75
Work Shirt, Coat Style	$0.75

Selected Advertised Positions in Chicago

Bartender	$25/Week
Die Sinker	$0.85/Hour
Electricians	$0.70/Hour
Elevator Man	$22/Week
Executive Accountant, Loop	$2,700/Year
Lathe Operator, Hand	$0.80/Hour
Manager, Shoe Manufacturing	$10,000/Year
Production Manager, Corset Factory	$3,000/Year
Roofing Salesman	$3,000/Year
Steam Fitter	$0.80/Hour
Watchman	$25/Week

U.S. RAIDS 25 OFFICES; HUNT MILK TRUST

Orders Producers to Present Records to Grand Jury.

Zero hour approached. In twenty-five county seats and thriving farm towns of northern Illinois and Indiana and southern Wisconsin deputy United States marshals waited. On the hour of 10 they stepped into the offices of the Milk Producers' associations and served subpoenas upon the secretaries to take forthwith to the federal grand jury in Chicago all their records and correspondence.

Sixteen thousand milk producers, members of the associations, and several million consumers are interested in this newest federal investigation, which came to light yesterday with the raids on documentary evidence to support suspicions of a price fixing combination to control the milk market of the Chicago district.

See Criminal Violation.

The new milk contract, drawn by former Gov. Charles Deneen for the Milk Producers' association, of which he is counsel, has been held by the department of justice to be a direct violation of the Sherman anti-trust law, and it is claimed that every member of the association is liable to prosecution under the act.

Discussed at several conferences held by United States Attorney Clyne, Assistant to the Attorney General Oliver E. Pagin, and other department of justic heads, the contract was also the topic of an executive session at Washington recently. The subpoenaing of witnesses by the federal grand

Advertisement in the *Chicago Daily Tribune*, October 16, 1919:

"Boys, 14 to 17 years old. Must be grammar school graduate or better. To capable boys we offer positions in our merchandise and mailing departments which prepare them for future advancement. A personal interest is taken in every boy to be sure he develops himself in accordance with his ability. Hours, 8 to 4:45, Saturdays 12 o'clock."

"Five Thousand Hats to Shine," *The Chicago Tribune*, April 18, 1919:

"Chicago's first, last, and only chance to see 5,000 silk hats at once will occur Sunday. And with it will come the opportunity to view the biggest of all fashion shows, free of charge. The Twenty-First Ward, the heart of the topper-and-cane-on-Sunday district, is to stage a community parade and show off its Easter togs. The Victory Loan Organization has the plans in hand, and is pledged to have at least 10,000 in line—and hopes for two or three times that number. Every man, woman, and child in the ward, who is working for the success of the Victory Loan, or expects to subscribe to it, is to meet at Cass and Ohio Streets at 3 p.m. Sunday, all dressed up. Derbies aren't barred, but will be shoved into the rear ranks."

Sears, Roebuck & Company

- For several generations the Sears catalog was the "wish book" for millions, the place to indulge your fantasy for a bicycle or a new dress without a salesman hanging over your shoulder.
- Richard Sears personally wrote the wish book until 1908, when he left the company; he died six years later, leaving an estate of $25 million.
- Sears established its own product-testing laboratory in 1911, phasing out the sale of flamboyant patent medicines two years later.
- After the Illinois State Senate created a special committee to investigate the subject of white slavery in 1913, charging that companies like Sears paid its women employees so poorly they were forced to turn to prostitution, the company became one of the first companies to offer profit-sharing plans to all its employees—a publicity bonanza for Sears, a financial success for employees.
- That same year Sears began to sell tires and published a catalog called the "Baby Book."
- By 1914 the Sears building complex occupied 40 acres, including 501 intercom telephones and an automatic switchboard.
- As hobbies became popular among Americans, Sears adapted, and by 1914 claimed 10,000 subscribers to its publication, *Better Photographs*, a monthly magazine.
- In 1915-16, at the start of the First World War in Europe, farmers especially were flush with cash and willing to buy from their trusted friend, Sears, Roebuck.
- In 1916 Sears experienced a fashion disaster when a line of expensive, upscale dresses flopped—a reminder that the snob appeal of world-famous designers like Lady Duff-Gordon was not important to Sears customers.
- Ten percent of Sears' profits that year came from the sale of the *Encyclopaedia Britannica*.
- During the War years, when people were feeling prosperous, installment buying increased as credit was extended on all goods with a minimum purchase of $20.
- In 1917, Sears CEO Julius Rosenwald contributed $1 million to the Jewish War Relief Fund and created the Julius Rosenwald Fund for charitable giving.
- Sales were strong as the American build-up for the war continued; the catalog offered the Sears Honor Bilt Homes, featuring the Magnolia, a Southern-style mansion with columns, curving staircases, and servant quarters for $5,140 through the mail. The house came complete with wood, nails, paint, and instructions.

***Shaping an American Institution: Robert E. Woods and Sears, Roebuck*, by James C. Worthy described the philosophy of Julius Rosenwald, Chief Executive Officer:**

"1. Sell for less by buying for less. Buy for less through mass buying and cash buying. But maintain the quality.
2. Sell for less by cutting the cost of sales. Reduce to the absolute practical minimum the expense of moving goods from producer to consumer. But maintain the quality.
3. Make less profit on each individual item and increase our aggregate profit by selling more items. But maintain the quality."

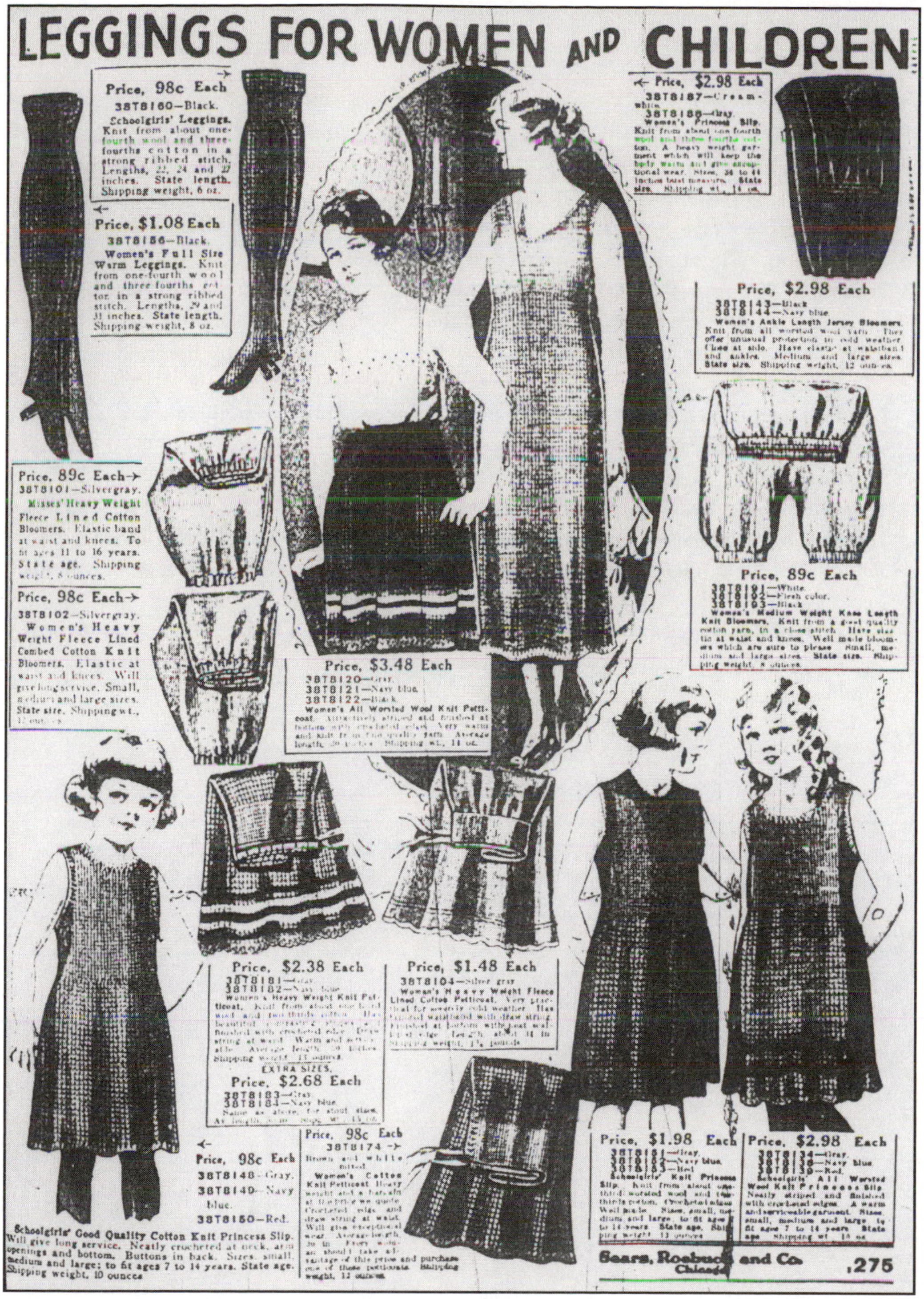

Allan Kincaid sells his dresses exclusively to Sears, Roebuck.

- In 1918, Sears' net sales and dividends on investments were $181.9 million, with an after-tax profit of $23 million, of which $1 million was paid to the Employee's Savings and Profit-Sharing Pension Fund.
- The 1919 Sears Spring Catalog reflected the prosperity of the company; the pictures were big, including an entire page to illustrate a man's work shoe.

- Much of the clothing was shown with models in action; experimentation had shown that school dresses worn by live models sold four times the number of dresses shown without models.
- Sears, Roebuck & Company enjoyed sales in 1919 of $257 million, an increase of $59 million over the previous year, with a net profit of $18.9 million.
- The mail-order business, which was the core of Sears' business, began in 1869 when E.C. Allen of Augusta, Maine, founded the *People's Literary Companion* to sell specialty products from recipes to washing powder to engravings by mail.
- In the second year of publication, its circulation hit 500,000.
- Ten years later, Augusta, Maine, became the direct-mail capital of the United States.
- In 1872 Aaron Montgomery Ward opened the first large concern selling a wide range of goods by mail, using an initial investment of $2,400.
- Montgomery Ward and Company quickly gained success, publishing a catalog of several hundred pages and obtaining the official endorsement of the Grange, the rural organization known as the Patron of Husbandry.
- Ward pioneered the concept of guaranteeing all products, allowing customers to return items they did not want.
- Companies such as Sears, Spiegel, May, and Stern were soon formed to sell goods by mail.
- Established department stores such as R.H. Macy and John Wanamaker also gave mail order a try.
- The advantage of mail-order selling was that companies had little need to lay out money for inventory; they simply purchased and mailed the goods their customers selected in the catalog.

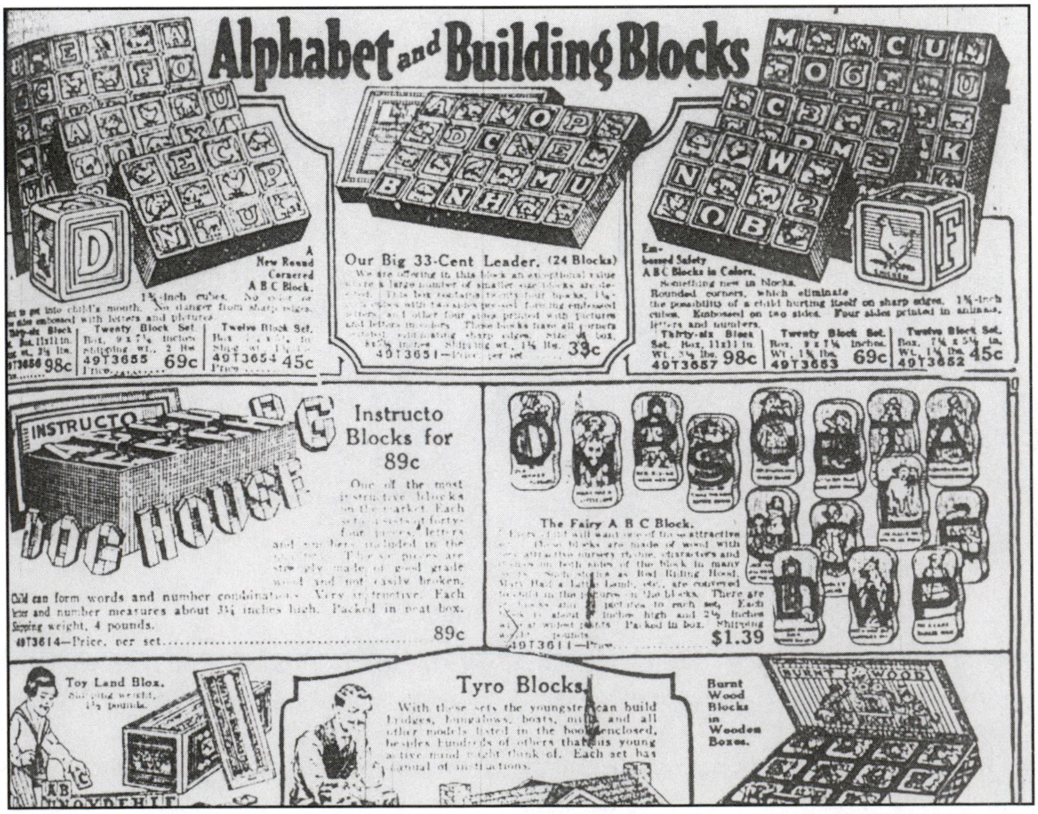

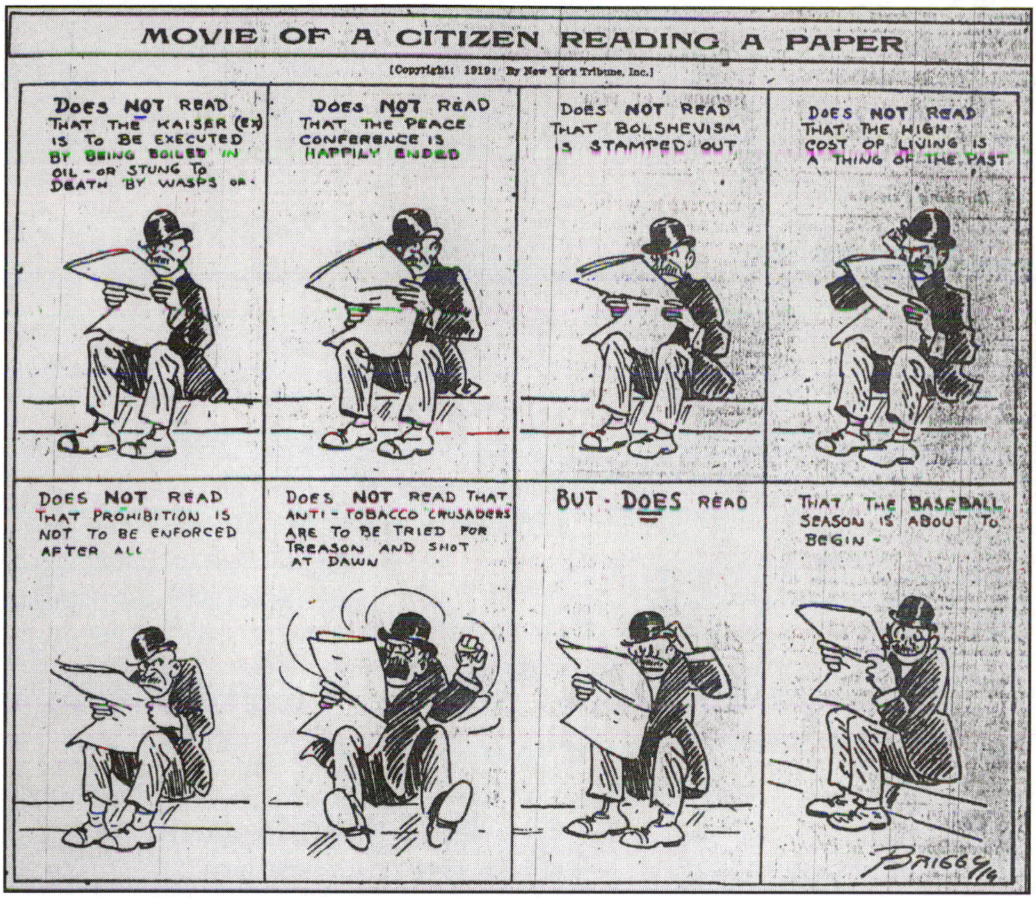

Cartoons in The Chicago Tribune *reflect the spirit of 1919.*

- To fight back, local shopkeepers at the turn of the century gave prizes to the person who could turn in the most catalogs; others simply bought the catalogs for $0.10 each to get them out of their customers' houses.
- Local newspapers, dependent on advertising from shopkeepers, often joined in attacking mail-order selling, often giving wide coverage to catalog book burnings staged by the merchants.
- The opposition of local merchants and the economic pressure they could exert led Sears, Roebuck to mail their orders in plain, unmarked wrappers.
- The golden era for the mail-order business corresponded with the economic resurgence of the farmer during World War I.
- New demands for American agricultural goods, both at home and abroad, brought higher prices, more prosperity, and a desire to enjoy the good life offered by Sears and Montgomery Ward.
- The biggest ally of the mail-order merchants was the United States Post Office.
- To serve the needs of rural people and their desire to read urban newspapers and obtain goods, post offices could be found in 77,000 communities in 1901.
- As important was the classification of catalogs as second-class educational materials, reducing costs.
- Rural Free Delivery (R.F.D.) further aided the mail-order business; for the first time mail was taken to the farmer, saving him a journey to the town post office.

- The creation of parcel post in 1913 meant that large orders could be delivered directly to the buyer, with customers no longer required to go to the freight depot in town to collect their orders.
- By 1914 Sears, Roebuck was the biggest user of parcel post, shipping 20,000 pieces each day.
- Very large items, like the complete homes Sears sold through the mail, were still delivered through the freight depot.

"Foundation of Good Health," *Leslie's Weekly*, January 10, 1920:

"American women are horrified at the mention of Chinese foot-binding through which thousands of Chinese children have been crippled for life. Yet how many of these women calmly accept a fashion which makes a crutch of what should be a foot covering? How many of them force their feet to fit their shoes, rather than fit their shoes to their feet? How many of them prefer style to sense? Children, obeying their instinct, toe straight ahead, and are promptly taught to turn their toes outward. Yet the Indians, doubtless the world's champion walkers, set their feet one before the other, as though following an invisible chalk line . . . 95 percent of our women have foot troubles. We could not build the Woolworth Building standing at an angle of 45 degrees. How can we expect the human body to properly do its work if maintained at such an angle?

Because of incorrect shoes few of our women walk gracefully; they either waddle, hobble, or teeter. The pointed-toed, high-heeled shoe causes not only minor torments such as corns and bunions, but it gives the body only two points of contact with the ground, one at the heel and the other at the bunched-up toes. The health troubles due to improper footwear decrease economic efficiency probably on an average of 25 percent. If horses were not properly shoed they would have foot troubles, and consequently become inefficient. Why should we countenance similar inefficiency in human workers?

The American Museum of Safety claims that 95 percent of the people suffer in one form or another from foot troubles which result in an inefficiency from 10 to 50 percent. The Museum strongly advised manufacturers who have their interests at heart as well as those of their employees to compel employees to wear correct shoes. This has been carried out in the case of nurses and war workers. A well-known obstetrician in the country claims that 40 percent of the instrument childbirths are traceable to injurious footwear.

Very few of our stores or firms employ men who are familiar with the anatomy of the foot to fit or design their shoes. Present-day shoes are made to fit the conventionally trained eye, not the foot. If we had indigestion we should not ask the grocer to prescribe our diet; therefore, why should we ask the shoe clerk, knowing nothing of the anatomy of the foot, to prescribe a shoe to cure our foot ills?"

Forecast for 1920: Dry, with Rising Temperature

"Steelworkers' Wives Want No Strikes," by Peggy Hull, *Leslie's Weekly*, November 15, 1919:

"If the final decision as to strike depended upon the vote of the wives and families of the men involved, there would be no strike. I have reached this conclusion after a visit to the street towns where the wives and daughters of all classes of labor gave me their opinions without restraint. Strikes, like wars, demand many sacrifices from women, and they are apparently becoming more and more unwilling to make them, believing, blindly or not, that the issue can be settled some other way.

The women I interviewed represented almost every race employed in the mills, including Hungarians, Slovaks, Serbians, Russians, Irish, and Americans. I started with the families of the low-paid wage earners and went up the scale to those of the men whose monthly checks run into three figures. In that long and deviating journey, I came upon many interesting and amusing phases of life, and the trip was well worth the doors I had slammed in my face. The first woman I called on was washing. She was big and hard-faced, with a jaw that would make a prize-fighter jealous. I took a convenient seat on an empty box, not too near the washtub.

'Sure, miss, an' Oi'll tell ye pwhat Oi am think' o' this stroike business. Me mon comes home one noight an' he sez, "Katie, Oi don't go to woik tomorrow! And I sez, "Moike, me love, if ye've bin after gittin' yerself fired wid some of o' yer foolishness, ye know pwhat comin' to ye."

"Oh, an' to be sure, me sweet Katie," he sez, blarneying-like, "it's no such misfortune this toime. It's the stroike Oi ben tell' ye was comin'. The strike bosses sez if yez come to this mill tomorrow ye won't be after walkin' back to the place ye come from. Yez'll be goin' in a wagon an' yez won't be arin' much about the bumps in the roads, because ye won't be feelin' 'em. So Katie, me darlint, it's either a widder ye'll be or Oi stay at home."

"Widder me eye," I sez, 'ain't it ever occurrin' to ye that it is sick Oi am of these stroikes an' Oi'm not after standin' it any more? Yer $4.20 a day is keeping us foine, an' if ye don't go to work tomorrow Oi'll be a widder by me own hand."

(continued)

'So Mike went to work?' I asked timidly.

'Sure, an' ye be spakin the truth, miss. 'E went to woik an' I went wid 'im, an' I ain't the only woman pwhat see 'her mon to woik. Maggie Maloney, me friend in the 'ouse two doors from 'ere puts a club on 'er shoulder and she marches along her mon ivery mornin' an' noight, an' not a 'air on 'is 'ead 'as a stroike breaker hurt.'

'Why aren't you in sympathy with the strike, Katie?'

'Whin me an' me mon come to this counthry tin years ago it was woik, woik, woik, all day long—me at tub an Moike doing odd jobs whenever he could get 'em. An some toimes they was far between and me washin' money was all we 'ad. Now Oi've a chance to live like a loidy, wid only me own woik to do, an' I ain't after givin' up me luxury. It's me belief that whin a mon's got a good job he'd better strik to it as long as it'll stick to 'im, an' when me own plazure is at stake me moind is firm on the subject. . .'

I next sought information in the home of a striker. The wife was a little, demure, pale, timid, overworked woman. The daughter, who did the talking, was evidently the dominant member of the family. There could be no doubt about that.

'No, Dad ain't workin',' she replied in answer to my question, 'and I ain't found yet what he's strikin' for. Just last night I told him he'd better come to his senses and go back to work. You see, I know him so well that this strike business is old stuff to me. It's just a chance to get out of work for him—long as I can remember I've never known him to pass one up. And who pays for it? Us kids. I'm waiting tables in a café downtown, and every time I think I've got a few dollars to spend on myself, he pulls something like this. I'm getting mighty sick of it!' . . . I learned later in my investigations that this girl is representative of a class which has sprung up among the unskilled workers within recent years. Girls of this type strive for the same kind of wearing apparel that ultra-smart and wealthy women wear. In order to gratify these new tastes they pool their expenses, live five and six in a little room and eat scanty meals, half-cooked over a gas jet. One mother tearfully complained to me that her daughter had 'gone completely crazy over the movies and fine clothes. She wears silk underwear every day and declares she can't sleep in anything but pink silk crepe. It's so soothing to my nerves, she says.' "

DOWNTOWN
Coming to the
BAND BOX
NEXT SUNDAY
"The Eternal Magdalene"
(FOR ADULTS ONLY)
A powerful film spectacle vibrating with new and brilliant light upon the world's oldest problem.
For your daughter's sake do not fail to see this great film drama. It is
A MASTERPIECE
ZIEGFELD
624 SO. MICH. AV.
—LAST TIMES TODAY—
WOMAN
SEE AMELIA LONG of the Van Vlissingen Studios as
Eve in the Garden of Eden
NORTH
ASCHER'S
CHATEAU
BROADWAY AT GRACE
LET YOUR MEMORY SLIP BACK TO ROMANCE
WHEN KINGS AND QUEENS WERE HIGH IN COURT
LET THE HANDS OF THE CLOCK MOVE FORWARD
TILL THE HOUR OF MIDNIGHT STRIKES
THEN THE SHADOWS OF GRAUSTARK WILL APPEAR
AND HAPPINESS WILL REIGN O'ER ALL
AND—
ANITA STEWART
MOST BELOVED OF ALL FINDS
"A MIDNIGHT ROMANCE"
A STORY SUPREME
TODAY
DON ALBERT AND HIS CONCERT ORCHESTRA
BRYN MAWR
Bryn Mawr, Nr. Broadway, at Bryn Mawr "L" Station—6:45 to 11 P. M.
Last Day
ANITA STEWART
"A Midnight Romance"
—Tomorrow Starts—
BURTON HOLMES TRAVEL CLUB
At This Theater—Win a Prize
BUCKINGHAM
3319 NORTH CLARK STREET
Mat. Daily Cont. 2:30 to 11 P. M.
—PARAMOUNT PICTURE—
ETHEL CLAYTON
In "PETTIGREW'S GIRL"
—ALSO—
CHARLIE CHAPLIN
In "SHANGHAIED"
Soloists' Concert Orchestra
DE LUXE
WILSON AVE. "L" STA.
—MATINEE DAILY—
CHARLES RAY, "The Sheriff's Son"
Hearst Screen Telegram & Vaudeville Movies
DEARBORN
DIVISION ST. AND DEARBORN

STOP & SHOP
The World's Best to Eat
An Interesting Easter Store
Do Your Week End Shopping Here
Don't overlook our Easter Candy Sale—our tempting OWN MAKE BAKERY goods—delicious "tid bits" that are so handy to have in the house—splendid meats, hams, bacons, delicatessen and thousands of good things to eat. Come in today and leave your Easter Dinner Order.
Easter Dinner Specials
Lady Clementine Products
CREAMY SWEET CORN—Put up on the Maine farm, where it grew; per dozen, $2.25; the can 19c
LITTLE MITES OF PEAS—The first pea in the pod, which means the fanciest, tiniest peas we put in a can; regularly 35c—for the week-end, dozen, $3.50; can 30c
RIPE OLIVES—Luscious jumbos—solid and meaty—the quart can 98c
CRAB APPLE JELLY—Delicious with meats or hot rolls; dozen, $4.00; per jar 35c
Delicatessen Section
Try these imported delicacies for appetizers or sandwich spreads—you'll like them.
SARDELLEN BUTTER, BLOATER PASTE, ANCHOVY PASTE Tube, 45c
PUREE OF FOSES GRAS—(goose liver paste) truffled—can 60c
ROYANS A LA BORDELAISE—(sardines in tomato sauce) key opening can 65c
BENGAL CLUB CHUTNEY—Crosse & Blackwell brand, bottle 45c
N. Y. HERKIMER COUNTY CHEESE—Made last June, when the pastures produced the finest grazing; pound 49c
EGGS—24 HOURS OLD
From the White Bear Farm; each egg guaranteed; scientifically produced for table use; dozen 59c
KOLAN KOFFEE
No breakfast or dinner is complete without a cup of our famous Kolan Koffee. Fresh from the roaster daily, and the lowest price in Chicago for coffee of quality; pound 45c
OWN MAKE OVEN PRODUCTS
Delicious bakery goods, made right before your very eyes or while you wait—if you'll wait long enough. For the Week-End:
Hot Cross Buns—full of sugar and spice and everything nice; dozen 25c
Schnecken—just oozing nuts and raisins—individuals, each, 8c; pan dozen 75c
Parker House Rolls—real ones, and light as a feather, dozen 25c
Coffee Cakes—thick with icing, nuts, cin'mun and raisins, each, 30c and 20c
Crisp Rolls—oven fresh, Poppy seed or French, dozen 25c
Home Made Bread—the kind mother used to make—large, fine-grained, white, flaky loaves, each 12c
Special Easter Boxes Assorted Fruit
$1.00 EACH
For Gifts or the Family Dinner Table
Strawberries, Grapes, King Oranges and Tangerines, Apples, Pineapples, Easter Pears, Avocados, Grapefruit.
Telephone Peas, Fancy Florida Tomatoes, Cauliflower, Endive, Cucumbers, Celery, Green and White Asparagus, Mushrooms, Iceberg and Boston Lettuce, Spinach, Egg Plant, String Beans, Rhubarb.
Mail Orders Promptly Filled. Charge Accounts Solicited.
The Tebbetts & Garland Store
16-18 N. Michigan Boulevard Randolph 7000

"Rapid Dish Washer," *Today's Housewife*, June 1917:

"If all housewives were asked what part of housework is the most trying I am quite sure they would answer 'dishwashing.' A machine, therefore, that relieves women of the drudgery of this work should be of great interest to every homemaker.

At first view, the Rapid Electric Dish Washer appears to be only a beautiful kitchen table with silvery top and spacious lower compartment. Upon lifting the lid, which extends across a portion of the top, one sees a most interesting interior, consisting of removable racks for dishes, so made that there are spaces for all kinds of china and utensils. All one has to do in order to operate this machine is to scrape the dishes, place them in their proper compartments, pour in eight quarts of boiling water, in which a good washing powder has been mixed, close the lid tight, turn on the current—and go about one's other duties.

In 15 minutes the dishes are clean, and you can press the lever that allows the water to escape through a drainpipe. Then pour in eight quarts of clear, boiling hot water for rinsing the dishes, and switch on the current again for two or three minutes. The rinse water is drained off, and the result, if the water has been hot enough, will be shining, clean dishes that require no wiping with a towel. One of the great advantages of this machine is that it is adaptable to a small family as well as a large one, and is a special boon for company dinners and when canning multiplies dishwashing. It is self-cleaning, as the process of washing the dishes throws the water at high speed in every direction, cleaning all of the inner spaces and racks at the same time that it washes the dishes. The cost of running it is also inconsiderable, averaging about one cent per hour for the electricity. The electrical cord may be attached to any lighting fixture.

If one desires, she may easily connect the drainpipe of the dishwasher with the sewage system, thus disposing of the water without the use of a pail. There may be a hot water connection as well, but this is not advisable unless extremely hot water is available. The price is $40."

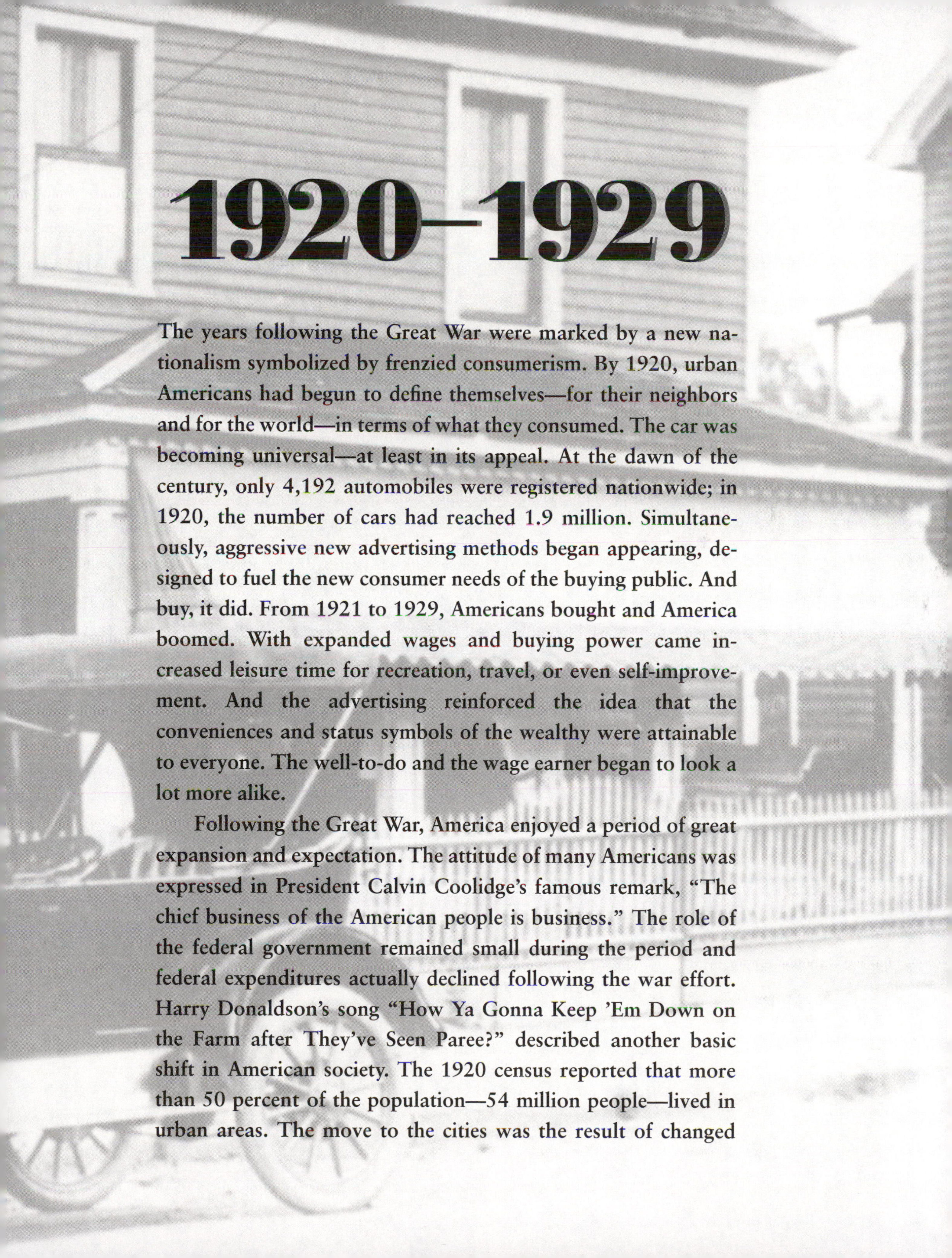

1920–1929

The years following the Great War were marked by a new nationalism symbolized by frenzied consumerism. By 1920, urban Americans had begun to define themselves—for their neighbors and for the world—in terms of what they consumed. The car was becoming universal—at least in its appeal. At the dawn of the century, only 4,192 automobiles were registered nationwide; in 1920, the number of cars had reached 1.9 million. Simultaneously, aggressive new advertising methods began appearing, designed to fuel the new consumer needs of the buying public. And buy, it did. From 1921 to 1929, Americans bought and America boomed. With expanded wages and buying power came increased leisure time for recreation, travel, or even self-improvement. And the advertising reinforced the idea that the conveniences and status symbols of the wealthy were attainable to everyone. The well-to-do and the wage earner began to look a lot more alike.

Following the Great War, America enjoyed a period of great expansion and expectation. The attitude of many Americans was expressed in President Calvin Coolidge's famous remark, "The chief business of the American people is business." The role of the federal government remained small during the period and federal expenditures actually declined following the war effort. Harry Donaldson's song "How Ya Gonna Keep 'Em Down on the Farm after They've Seen Paree?" described another basic shift in American society. The 1920 census reported that more than 50 percent of the population—54 million people—lived in urban areas. The move to the cities was the result of changed expectations, increased industrialization, and the migration of millions of Southern blacks to the urban North.

The availability of electricity expanded the universe of goods that could be manufactured and sold. The expanded use of radios, electric lights, telephones, and powered vacuum cleaners was possible for the first time, and they quickly became essential household items. Construction boomed as—for the first time—half of all Americans now lived in urban areas. Industry, too, benefited from the wider use of electric power. At the turn of the century, electricity ran only five percent of all machinery, and by 1925, 73 percent. Large-scale electric power also made possible electrolytic processes in the rapidly developing heavy chemical industry. With increasing sophistication came higher costs; wages for skilled workers continued to rise during the 1920s, putting further distance between the blue-collar worker and the emerging middle class.

Following the war years, women who had worked men's jobs in the late 'teens usually remained in the work force, although at lower wages. Women, now allowed to vote nationally, were also encouraged to consider college and options other than marriage. Average family earnings increased slightly during the first half of the period, while prices and hours worked actually declined. The 48-hour week became standard, providing more leisure time. At least 40 million people went to the movies each week, and college football became a national obsession.

Unlike previous decades, national prosperity was not fueled by the cheap labor of new immigrants, but by increased factory efficiencies, innovation, and more sophisticated methods of managing time and materials. Starting in the 'teens, the flow of new immigrants began to slow, culminating in the restrictive immigration legislation of 1924 when new workers from Europe were reduced to a trickle. The efforts were largely designed to protect the wages of American workers—many of whom were only one generation from their native land. As a result, wages for unskilled labor remained stable; union membership declined and strikes, on average, decreased. American exports more than doubled during the decade and heavy imports of European goods virtually halted, a reversal of the Progressive Movement's flirtation with free trade.

These national shifts were not without powerful resistance. A bill was proposed in Utah to imprison any woman who wore her skirt higher than three inches above the ankle. Cigarette consumption reached 43 billion annually, despite smoking being illegal in 14 states and the threat of expulsion from college if caught with a cigarette. A film code limiting sexual material in silent films was created to prevent "loose" morals, and the membership of the KKK expanded to repress Catholics, Jews, open immigration, make-up on women, and the prospect of unrelenting change.

The decade ushered in Trojan contraceptives, the Pitney Bowes postage meter, the Baby Ruth candy bar, Wise potato chips, Drano, self-winding watches, State Farm Mutual auto insurance, Kleenex, and the Macy's Thanksgiving Day Parade down Central Park West in New York. Despite a growing middle class, the share of disposable income going to the top five percent of the population continued to increase. Fifty percent of the people, by one estimate, still lived in poverty. Coal and textile workers, Southern farmers, unorganized labor, single women, the elderly, and most blacks were excluded from the economic giddiness of the period.

In 1929, America appeared to be in an era of unending prosperity. U.S. goods and services reached all-time highs. Industrial production rose 50 percent during the decade as the concepts of mass production were refined and broadly applied. The sale of electrical appliances from radios to refrigerators skyrocketed. Consumers were able to purchase newly produced goods through the extended use of credit. Debt accumulated. By 1930, personal debt had increased to one third of personal wealth. The nightmare on Wall Street in October 1929 brought an end to the economic festivities, setting the stage for a more proactive government and an increasingly cautious worker.

1923 News Profile

"Curious discoveries about human nature made by a firm which collects and sells lists of classified names," by E.J. Williams, proprietor and manager of Boyd's City Dispatch, one of the country's biggest classified list agencies, The American Magazine, September 1923:

How Your Name Gets on So Many Mailing Lists

"When you buy a home or an automobile, invest in stocks, join a club, or get married, you become of importance to businessmen in all parts of the country, and they send you letters about the things they think you are interested in—you can often tell from these letters how much people think you are worth.

A man in Des Moines, Iowa, recently inherited fifteen thousand dollars by the will of his brother. A few weeks later he married a girl to whom he had been engaged for two years. He bought a small house, an automobile, and invested two thousand dollars in the shares of a gas and electric company. Presently he noticed that his mail included many communications from persons and firms in various parts of the country that had never been interested in him before.

He received letters from two paint dealers, a wallpaper house, a tree expert, a nurseryman with flowers and shrubs to sell, a portable garage company, a tire manufacturer, a life insurance company, and a house dealing in securities. A jeweler and a mail-order house sent him catalogues, and a manufacturer sent him an announcement about the qualities of a certain baby food.

The man in Des Moines was astonished. In replying to one of the letters he had received, he expressed surprise that the manufacturer knew he was interested in portable garages. 'I have received quite a number of letters recently,' he wrote, 'and they are all about things I am more or less interested in; but I'm curious to know how you or any of the other firms knew about my requirements.'

This letter was forwarded to me by the manufacturer because my company had supplied him with a list of automobile owners, including the man in Des Moines. I wrote the Des

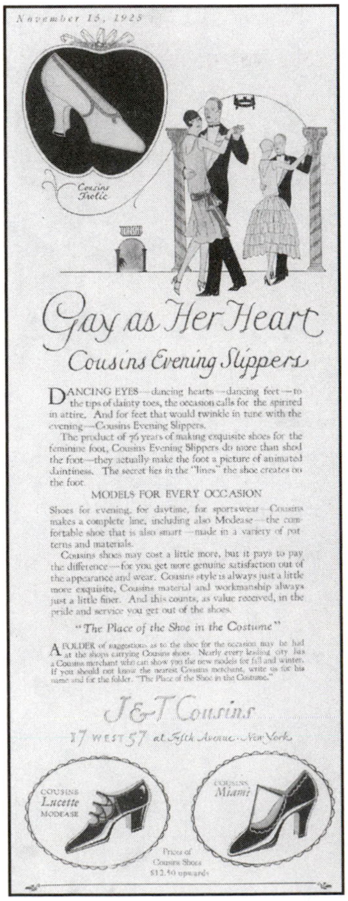

How Your Name Gets on So Many Mailing Lists

When you buy a home or an automobile, invest in stocks, join a club, or get married, you become of importance to business men in all parts of the country, and they send you letters about the things they think you are interested in—You can often tell from these letters how much people think you are worth—Curious discoveries about human nature made by a firm which collects and sells lists of classified names

By E. J. Williams

Proprietor and manager of Boyd's City Dispatch, one of the country's biggest classified list agencies

A MAN in Des Moines, Iowa, recently inherited fifteen thousand dollars by the will of his brother. A few weeks later he married a girl to whom he had been engaged for two years. He bought a small house, an automobile, and invested two thousand dollars in the shares of a gas and electric company. Presently he noticed that his mail included many communications from persons and firms in various parts of the country that had never been interested in him before.

He received letters from two paint dealers, a wall-paper house, a tree expert, a nurseryman with flowers and shrubs to sell, a portable garage company, a tire manufacturer, a life insurance company, and a house dealing in securities. A jeweler and a mail-order house sent him catalogues, and a manufacturer sent him an announcement about the qualities of a certain baby food.

The man in Des Moines was astonished. In replying to one of the letters he had received he expressed surprise that the manufacturer knew he was interested in portable garages. "I have received quite a number of letters recently," he wrote, "and they are all about things I am more or less interested in; but I'm curious to know how you or any of the other firms knew about my requirements."

This letter was forwarded to me by the manufacturer because my company had supplied him with a list of automobile owners, including the man in Des Moines. I wrote the Des Moines man how it happened that his name had been put on quite a number of our lists. What I told him may interest you, for I dare say that ninety-nine out of a hundred persons who read this article are on some one of our lists.

The business of my company is preparing lists of people in all parts of the country who belong in various classifications. Such lists are used by at least one hundred thousand business institutions when sending out circular or personal letters. The number of pieces of mail sent out to persons on such lists totals billions yearly.

When you buy a house your name goes on the tax reports. If you invest in stocks your name goes on a list of stockholders. When you buy an automobile your name goes on the state license records. Your name be may obtained from these or from some one of a great variety of other sources. It is put on the proper list and accordingly you receive mail from business firms, philanthropies, or individuals who think they have something to offer that will interest you, either because you are worth a certain amount of money or because you belong to some particular profession, occupation, or club.

Marriages are generally reported in the newspapers. In any case, the names of newly married people are obtainable from the county clerk's office, as it is a matter of public record. When a man's engagement is announced he becomes of interest at once to life insurance companies and jewelers. After he marries he is likely to receive information from baby food manufacturers and from publishers of books on child education.

We have more than 30,000 classified lists. In size these run from one name to 12,000,000 names. Nearly everybody is on one or more of these lists. Farmers and people who live in towns with a population under 20,000 are on the mail order list. Bill Jones may be on a list simply because he is a voter. Another man may be on twenty different lists because he is worth anywhere from $1,000 to $1,000,000, because he owns a house in town, a country home, an automobile or stocks, and because of his business connections.

A man I know was recently elected president of a golf club, and accordingly his name went on a list of golf club officials. In the course of a few weeks he received letters about golf balls, golf clubs, how to make a perfect swing, lawn mowers, trees and landscape gardening — because these were the things in which he would obviously be interested in view of his position.

Another man I know receives from ten to fifteen circular letters every day. He is a director of several companies, a member of thirteen clubs, president of two clubs, and interested in certain charities.

Bank directors, doctors, and lawyers, whether they live in big cities or small towns, receive more circular letters than any other class of people. The bank director gets notices about investments and banking proposals. He is also usually on the lists that bring him matter intended for well-to-do residents and club members. Doctors often receive notices of new medicines, tonics, shaving soaps, tooth powder and paste. Some of the highest-class manufacturing chemists of the country spend hundreds of thousands of dollars in sending samples to doctors.

Lawyers receive information from investment houses, (*Continued on page 111*)

Where Do You Come In?

"OUR lists show," says Mr. Williams, "that there are in the United States 1,500,000 persons worth over $5,000; 410,000 worth over $50,000; 100,000 worth over $100,000. There are 22,500 persons worth half a million, and there are 8,078 millionaires."

31

Moines man how it happened that his name had been put on quite a number of lists. What I told him may interest you, for I daresay that 99 out of a hundred persons who read this article are on one of our lists.

The business of my company is preparing lists of people in all parts of the country who belong to various classifications. Such lists are used by at least 100,000 business institutions when sending out circular or personal letters. The number of pieces of mail sent out to persons on such lists totals billions yearly.

When you buy a house, your name goes on the tax reports. If you invest in stocks, your name goes on a list of stockholders. When you buy an automobile, your name goes on the state license records. Your name may be obtained from these or from one of a great variety of other sources. It is put on the proper list and accordingly, you receive mail from business firms, philanthropies, or individuals who think they have something to offer that will interest you, either because you are worth a certain amount of money or because you belong to some particular profession, occupation, or club.

Marriages are generally reported in the newspapers. In any case, the names of newly married people are obtainable from the county clerk's office, as it is a matter of public record. When a man's engagement is announced, he becomes of interest at once to life insurance companies and jewelers. After he is married, he is likely to receive information from baby food manufacturers and from publishers of books on child education.

We have more than 30,000 classified lists. In size, these run from one name to 12 million names. Nearly everyone is on one or more of these lists. Farmers and people who live in towns with a population under 20,000 are on the mail-order lists. Bill Jones may be on a list simply because he is a voter. Another man may be on 20 different lists because he is worth anywhere from $1,000 to $1 million, because he owns a house in town, a country home, an automobile or stocks, and because of his business connections.

A man I knew was recently elected president of a golf club, and accordingly, his name went on a list of golf club officials. In the course of a few weeks he received letters about golf balls, golf clubs, how to make a perfect swing, lawn mowers, trees and landscape gardening—because these were the things in which he would obviously be interested in view of his position. . . .

If you are a preacher or a Sunday-school superintendent, you receive letters not only from publishers of books and religious periodicals, but also from manufacturers of paint or church and Sunday school furnishings. If you are a member of the Elks, you hear from manufacturers who have little ivory elk heads to offer. If you are an official of a lodge of either the Elks or Moose organizations, you may receive letters from dealers who sell mounted elk or moose heads. If you are on our list of circus and tent shows, you hear from dealers in wild animals, horses, wagons, and tents—or perhaps from the owner of a sawmill, who will offer to ship you sawdust if you have difficulty in getting your product locally.

From our long experience in preparing lists, we have learned a great many interesting things about people in different parts of the country. We know, for instance, that people in cities are most interested in information about furniture, rugs, cigars, automobiles, insurance, investments, high-class summer or winter resorts, sanitariums, and travel tours. People in the small towns and county districts are most interested in information about seeds,

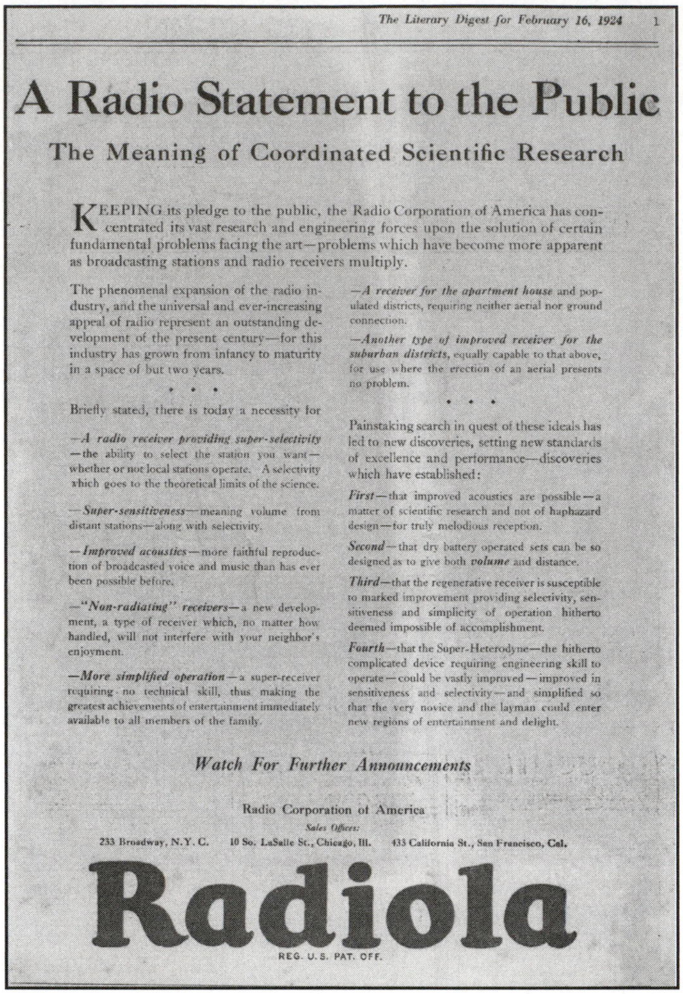

The Literary Digest for February 16, 1924 1

A Radio Statement to the Public

The Meaning of Coordinated Scientific Research

KEEPING its pledge to the public, the Radio Corporation of America has concentrated its vast research and engineering forces upon the solution of certain fundamental problems facing the art—problems which have become more apparent as broadcasting stations and radio receivers multiply.

The phenomenal expansion of the radio industry, and the universal and ever-increasing appeal of radio represent an outstanding development of the present century—for this industry has grown from infancy to maturity in a space of but two years.

* * *

Briefly stated, there is today a necessity for

—*A radio receiver providing super-selectivity* —the ability to select the station you want—whether or not local stations operate. A selectivity which goes to the theoretical limits of the science.

—*Super-sensitiveness*—meaning volume from distant stations—along with selectivity.

—*Improved acoustics*—more faithful reproduction of broadcasted voice and music than has ever been possible before.

—*"Non-radiating" receivers*—a new development, a type of receiver which, no matter how handled, will not interfere with your neighbor's enjoyment.

—*More simplified operation*—a super-receiver requiring no technical skill, thus making the greatest achievements of entertainment immediately available to all members of the family.

—*A receiver for the apartment house* and populated districts, requiring neither aerial nor ground connection.

—*Another type of improved receiver for the suburban districts*, equally capable to that above, for use where the erection of an aerial presents no problem.

* * *

Painstaking search in quest of these ideals has led to new discoveries, setting new standards of excellence and performance—discoveries which have established:

First—that improved acoustics are possible—a matter of scientific research and not of haphazard design—for truly melodious reception.

Second—that dry battery operated sets can be so designed as to give both *volume* and distance.

Third—that the regenerative receiver is susceptible to marked improvement providing selectivity, sensitiveness and simplicity of operation hitherto deemed impossible of accomplishment.

Fourth—that the Super-Heterodyne—the hitherto complicated device requiring engineering skill to operate—could be vastly improved—improved in sensitiveness and selectivity—and simplified so that the very novice and the layman could enter new regions of entertainment and delight.

Watch For Further Announcements

Radio Corporation of America

Sales Offices:

233 Broadway, N.Y.C. 10 So. LaSalle St., Chicago, Ill. 433 California St., San Francisco, Cal.

Radiola

REG. U.S. PAT. OFF.

agricultural implements, fertilizers, farm publications, household and medical books, paint, poultry supplies, phonographs, educational games for children, shoes, clothing, and moderate-priced furniture.

As far as I know, Boyd's City Dispatch is the largest agency in the world dealing in classified lists of names. The firm was founded in 1830, and its business then was delivering letters and special messages. Later on, when the United States Government established mail routes in New York, the private mail delivery business lost its usefulness. Already, however, in connection with our other business we had been employed to furnish special lists of names, and I believed that there was a real future in a country as big as ours for a firm dealing in classified lists.

At that time, however, the business of furnishing lists was so unpromising that I was able to buy a half-interest in the firm for $150. Today, we have 40,000 regular customers buying our lists. During a period of a little over a year, we have sold 150,000 lists containing two million names, at a price for each list ranging from $1.50 to $6,000. . . .

The hardest names to get are those of responsible persons of means. The preparation of any such list as this requires a great deal of expert investigation, covering public records of property holdings and stock lists. Facts that on their surface may indicate that a man is very well-to-do cannot always be relied upon. To some extent, for instance, the kind of automobile a man owns might be accepted as an indication of his worth; but on the other hand, a man may have bought a high-priced car second-hand. . . .

Although we have 30,000 different lists, we are continually being asked to prepare lists of special classifications, such as fat people, bald people, thin people, and sufferers from asthma or liver trouble. In the past few months, we have made up 96 special lists for investors. Some of these investors have wanted the names of financiers who would be interested in buying patents or in financing the development of patents.

One list frequently in demand is that giving the names of the country's wealthiest widows. Sometimes we find that matrimonial agencies seek to buy this list, but we have declined to sell it for that purpose. There are 2,532 widows in the country worth over $50,000. The list is most commonly used by persons or firms wishing to send information regarding real estate, philanthropic enterprises needing contributions, travel tours, and high-class investments.

Our lists show that there are in the United States 2.8 million persons who belong to a selected list of individuals and make good customers, but who have no definite financial rating. There are 1.5 million persons worth over $5,000; 410,000 worth over $50,000, and 100,000 worth over $100,000. There are 22,500 persons worth half a million, and there are 8,078 millionaires."

1924 Family Profile

William Nash, a 34-year-old dentist in Columbia, South Carolina, has been in practice a dozen years. He and his wife, Martha, have just completed a new home on the "country" side of the city. They have two young sons.

Annual Income: $13,800

Annual Budget

The average consumer expenditure in 1924 is not available. The following is a per capita expenditure for 1923 for all workers nationwide:

Auto Parts	$4.97
Auto Purchases	$20.45
Clothing	$64.52
Dentists	$2.72
Food	$128.14
Furniture	$8.78
Gas and Oil	$12.38
Health Insurance	NR
Housing	$94.80
Intercity Transport	$5.22
Personal Business	$22.17
Personal Care	$7.79
Physicians	$7.15
Private Education and Research	$7.26
Recreation	$23.44
Religion/Welfare Activities	$11.57
Telephone and Telegraph	$2.71
Utilities	$8.97

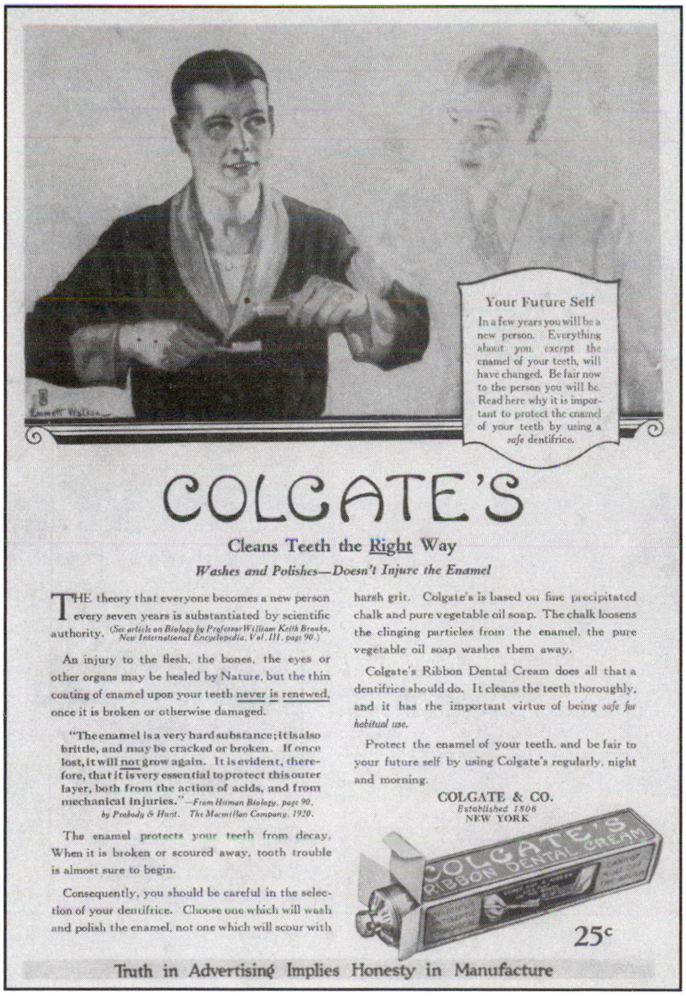

I was glad when they said unto me, Let us go into the house of the Lord
Psa. 122:1
Every pupil in his place!
That is what we want next Sunday - BE THERE!

The Associate Reform Presbyterian Church provides the Nashes with much of their social activity.

Life at Home

- William and Martha met through their church, the Associate Reform Presbyterian Church in Columbia, South Carolina.
- After marriage, their first house in Columbia was located downtown on a small 60-by-80 foot lot—a two-story home with a front porch, living room, and dining room downstairs, and bedrooms upstairs.
- Three years later in 1920, when their second child was born, they moved to a larger home on the "country edge" of the city limits.
- The red-brick home, where the couple stills lives, boasts a wide porch, carport, and garage, as well as a large lot used for growing plants.
- This man has a passion for plants and often drives as far as Charleston to obtain a new azalea bush for his yard; he also enjoys grafting camellia bushes to create different flower combinations.
- This year an early frost has once again burned his English peas; he also has peach trees, cherry trees, and small apple trees in the yard.
- The four-bedroom house has fireplaces in every major room, and since central heat is not available, the back rooms are heated by a coal stove in the kitchen.
- The family spends considerable time in a large breakfast room.
- William loves fresh air and constructed his bedroom so that his bed gets the best ventilation possible.
- The home is not air-conditioned; Columbia heat often reaches the high 90s in the summertime.
- In 1924, the Nashes have to pay extra for their oldest son to go to city schools because the house is on the country side of the city limits.
- Martha does all the cooking and takes great pride in this skill; the family does not employ a maid to clean up or cook.

Their first home was located downtown on a 60 x 80 foot lot.

- She freely calls to her husband by his first name, William; her mother always referred to her husband as Mister and never used his first name.
- They raise chickens behind the house and enjoy fresh eggs and meat; when she buys chickens from the farmer's market, Martha insists on feeding the chickens her way for at least a week before killing and cooking them to make sure they have the right taste.
- Neither he nor his wife drink or smoke; most of their socializing occurs at church.
- When they make large purchases, including an automobile and a house, they avoid going into debt; they do not believe in installment loan debt for cars or appliances, even though the practice is becoming widely accepted.
- Martha wears dresses every day, often changing at midday into "visiting clothes" following her morning cooking and cleaning.

Most social gatherings include singing around the piano.

- During the summertime the children take a bath at lunchtime and change clothes.
- The local dry-cleaning service comes to their home to pick up and deliver clothes; occasionally the dry-cleaner has to come on Saturday night to make sure Martha has the dress she needs for Sunday morning.
- The family is active in church, often attending morning, afternoon, and evening services each Sunday; in between they visit at the homes of friends who belong to the same church.
- Once a year the family entertains the church elders and deacons in their home, providing a full-course meal.
- Most social gatherings also include singing around the piano; the family owns dozens of pages of sheet music, ranging from Irving Berlin's "He's a Devil in His Own Hometown" to "Love's Golden Star."
- The children's actions are strictly controlled on Sunday; they are not allowed to read the Sunday funnies until Monday morning.
- On Sunday, the family meal often consists of chicken or roast beef with rice or macaroni pie, and always includes fresh vegetables; they also enjoy blackberry jam put up by Martha.
- The family's food is cooled in the icebox; the iceman comes to the house three times a week, cutting 25-pound sections from his 300-pound block, carrying the ice to the door, and even setting it into the icebox.
- The house is wired for electric lights.
- Nationwide in 1912, 16 percent of the U.S. population lived in houses with electric lights; in the past dozen years, more than 50 percent of houses have been wired for electric lights.
- The family also has an electric-motor-driven vacuum cleaner, which William purchased to please Martha.
- They regularly take a two-week vacation each year, always in August when Columbia is its hottest.
- This year they are taking a family vacation to Glen Springs, South Carolina, near the North Carolina line, home of a mineral springs resort.
- Guests drink up to 20 glasses of the mineral water in the morning to purge their systems and remove poisons, with more water consumed at lunch; after a treatment, William feels as if he could "eat a cow and a calf."
- The resort furnishes three large meals a day, which are served family-style with large bowls of food passed around to anyone who happens to sit at that table.
- The family also vacations near Asheville in the North Carolina mountains, which William loves to climb; the family often rides horses, which can be rented by the hour.
- He enjoys the independence of an automobile and agrees completely with a recent Chevrolet advertisement that reads, "every owner is in effect a railroad president, operating individually on an elective schedule."
- The Nashes have affection for both automobiles and trains.
- In the 1880s and 1890s, William's father farmed 200 acres near the South Carolina-North Carolina boundary, growing cotton, corn, and vegetables.
- He and his brother, both Irish, had come to the state to farm.

- William was one of eight children—five boys and three girls.
- After his mother died in childbirth when he was five years old, William was raised by his older sisters until his father moved most of the family to Texas to homestead, taking the younger boys with him, including William.
- They later returned, at the insistence of the older daughters, who stayed in South Carolina after the Texas farm failed.
- After they returned to South Carolina, William graduated from high school in Rock Hill.
- The daughters married railroad men—one was a conductor, the other a railroad mechanic.
- Railroad jobs were cherished, since the pay was set, steady, and generally good.
- William's wife Martha, whose grandfather was Irish, was also from South Carolina; her father was associated with the railroad as well.
- Her grandfather maintained a large farm 30 miles from Columbia, where he was considered a community leader; a large bell on his property was rung each day to signal the beginning of the workday, lunch, and end of lunch.

The family owns dozens of pieces of sheet music, most of which can be purchased for a nickel.

Life at Work

- William and his brother opened a joint dental office on Main Street in Columbia in 1912 following their graduation from Atlanta-Southern Dental College.
- They operated from a room on the second floor; a ladies' apparel shop occupied the first floor.
- A year later, they decided that two offices would attract more customers; William then rented a second-floor office near Main Street over Malone's Piano Store.
- He occupies the same office in 1924.
- His wife drives him to work every morning in the family car, a Buick; their cars are always purchased from the same local dealership, Roddy's.
- He begins work every day at 8:45 a.m. and works until 1 p.m., when Martha picks him up and takes him home for the lunch she has prepared; he returns to work at 2:30 p.m., working until 5:45 p.m., when she picks him up again for dinner.
- William lives by the clock; if a customer has an appointment at a specified time, he will meet him or her at that time.
- The waiting room includes magazines such as the *Literary Digest* and publications for women; he does not allow inappropriate literature in his waiting room.

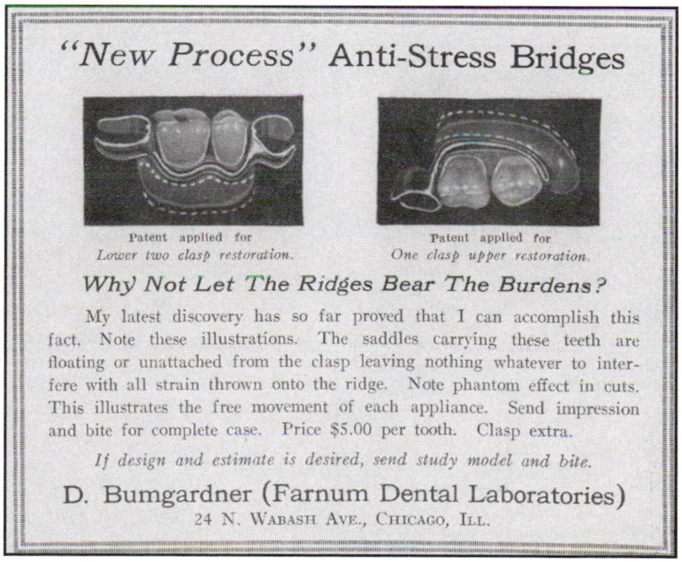

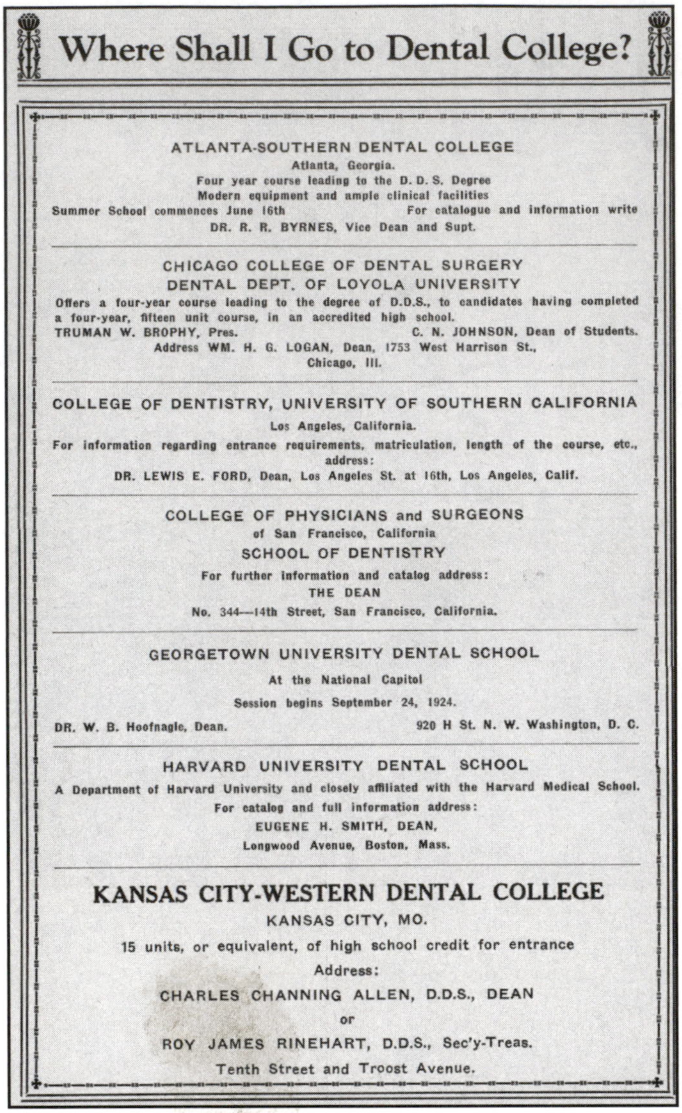

- He typically sees 20 patients a day, and most appointments last no more than 30 minutes.
- He also accepts walk-in customers when time permits, so a few clients never make appointments, always preferring to drop in.
- He proudly carries a gold Waltham train pocket watch, whose highly decorated case shows a steam engine running down the railroad tracks with smoke and steam pouring out of its stacks.
- He does not employ a chairside assistant, bookkeeper, or receptionist to answer the telephone, performing all of these duties himself while serving patients.
- Dentists who do employ assistants train them personally.
- Typically, William charges $0.50 to $1.00 for an extraction; fillings are normally $0.50, depending on size. He occasionally is paid in produce, including live chickens and fresh vegetables.
- He expects payment when the customer gets out of the chair; he does not use credit himself and does not encourage it in others.
- The operatory is furnished with two chairs, both of which face away from the waiting room and toward the windows facing Main Street.
- The afternoon sun comes through the windows; no air-conditioning is available even during the summer months.
- The office also includes a darkroom to develop x-rays, a laboratory for hand washing, and a dental sink.
- He does his own gold-casting work, only occasionally farming out work; sometimes a black man who works for a doctor nearby prepares the gold-casting William cannot handle.
- The office includes an x-ray machine, housed in a brown box. When the machine is turned on, light arcs across the room, and neither the patient nor the dentist has protection.
- The machine is considered the finest invention in dentistry.
- The preferred anesthesia by most dentists is cocaine, although some patients go without a painkiller to avoid using the drug.
- He has a phone at the office and one at home. The residential phone is a two-party line shared with his brother, who lives next door; a local operator connects most callers from a central switchboard. The office telephone number, when dialed at home, is four numbers long, 4591.
- Some businesses are attempting to boost business by using postcard mailers, but he has resisted the trend.
- He works six days a week, caring for patients all day Saturday, and takes off every Friday afternoon, not returning to the office after lunch.
- Often Friday afternoons are spent driving in the country, especially during spring planting and fall harvesting times; he loves the smell and feel of turned soil.
- The afternoon drives often require that the car ford unpredictable creeks; often the trips are rerouted because a stream has become too deep to cross that day.
- He wears a hat and dress suit to work every day. All of his suits are dark, and at Easter, he faithfully wears a square straw hat, like most of the men in his church.

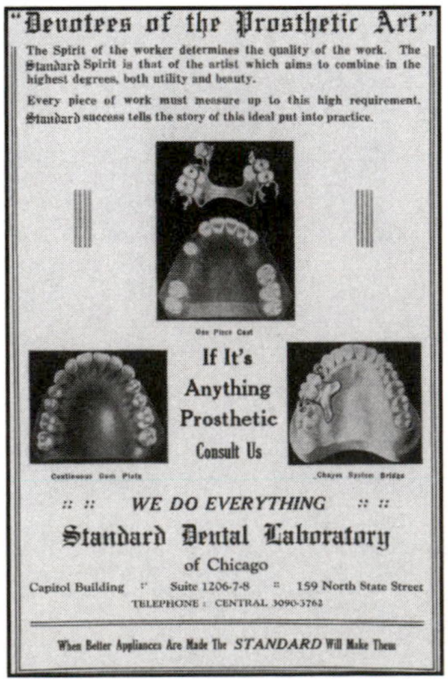

- The F. Scott Fitzgerald look featuring a blue blazer with school badge that was sweeping the nation has not reached the South.
- William became a dentist because of a streetcar accident; while running his normal route, William's Street Car nearly collided with another streetcar doing maintenance. There was considerable debate concerning fault; during the argument, William was cussed by his supervisor, so he quit.
- About the same time, his brother had grown disenchanted with his job at a wholesale grocery store; an accident that involved the dropping of 12 dozen eggs was a contributor to his unhappiness.
- Their sisters agreed to help fund a three-year course in dentistry in Atlanta, Georgia; the school, Atlanta-Southern Dental College, was selected from an advertisement in a magazine.
- Atlanta-Southern was a proprietary school owned by individuals; no governing body had been established to accredit dental schools or establish curricula.
- Atlanta Dental School and Southern Dental School had begun as separate institutions and then merged.
- At that time, most of the dentists in North Carolina, South Carolina, Georgia, and Tennessee were trained in dental schools based in Atlanta.
- At school, they watched seniors work and learned the basics of dentistry, including how to make amalgam fillings composed of silver, tin, zinc, and mercury.
- They also learned how to create and install gold fillings, as little interest was shown in tooth-color fillings.

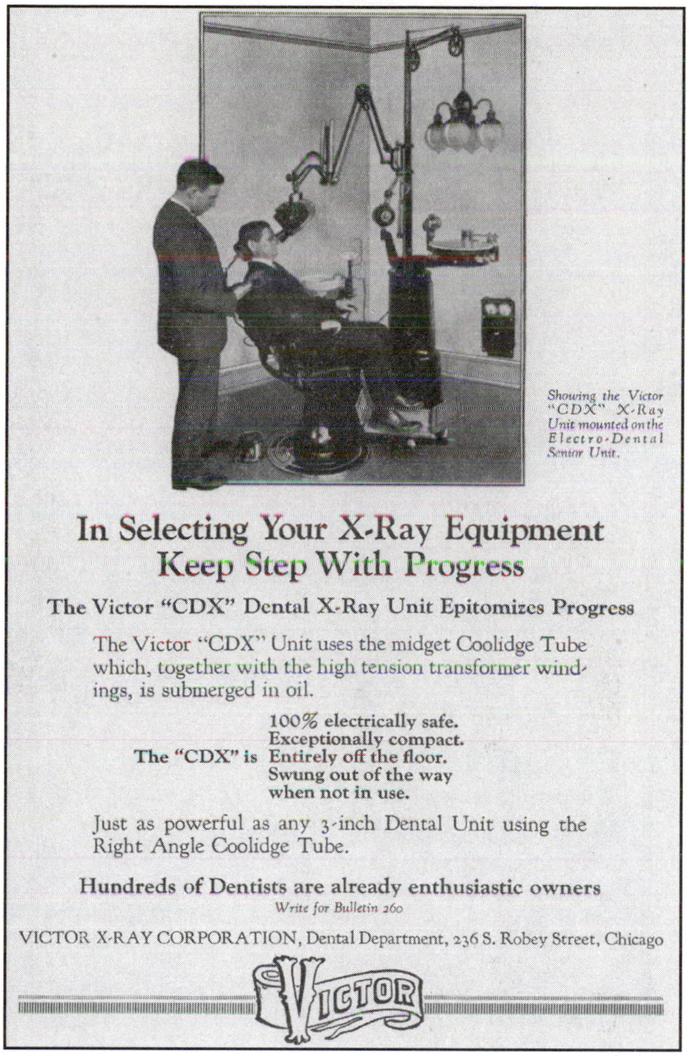

Showing the Victor "CDX" X-Ray Unit mounted on the Electro-Dental Senior Unit.
In Selecting Your X-Ray Equipment Keep Step With Progress
The Victor "CDX" Dental X-Ray Unit Epitomizes Progress
The Victor "CDX" Unit uses the midget Coolidge Tube which, together with the high tension transformer windings, is submerged in oil.
The "CDX" is 100% electrically safe. Exceptionally compact. Entirely off the floor. Swung out of the way when not in use.
Just as powerful as any 3-inch Dental Unit using the Right Angle Coolidge Tube.
Hundreds of Dentists are already enthusiastic owners
Write for Bulletin 260
VICTOR X-RAY CORPORATION, Dental Department, 236 S. Robey Street, Chicago
VICTOR

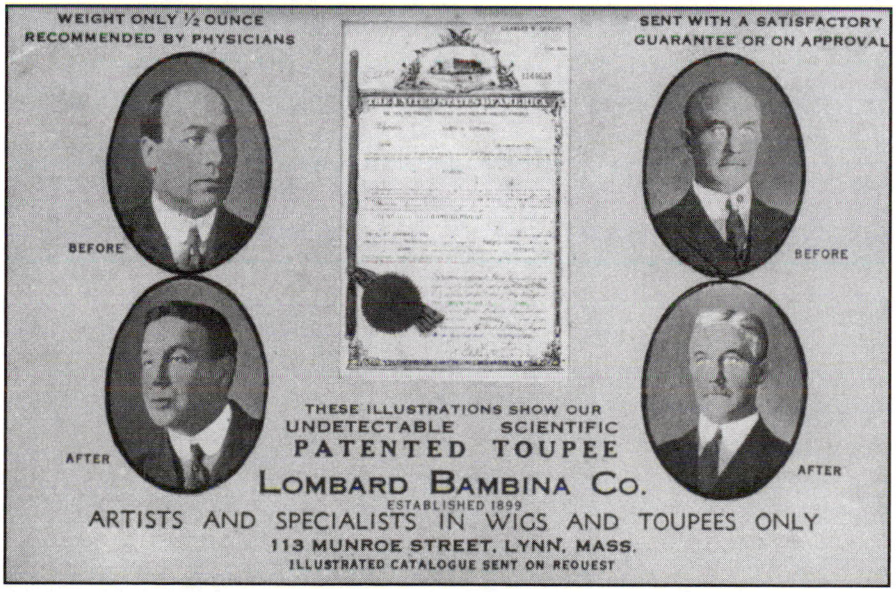

Some businesses are attempting to increase customers by using postcard mailers.

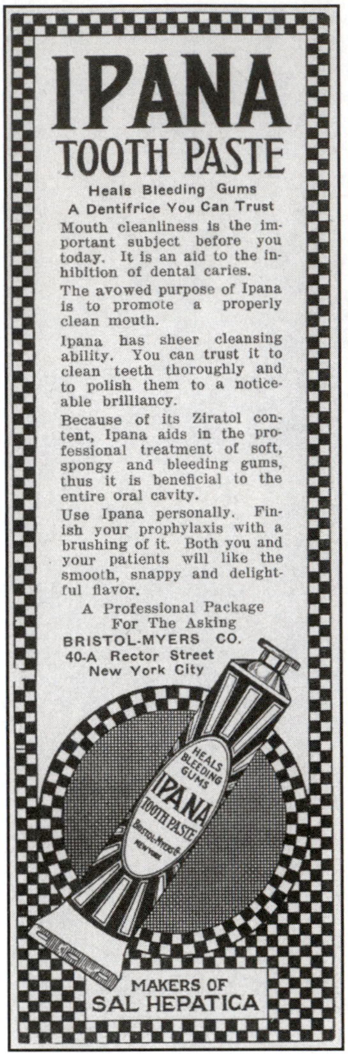

"Development of State Dental Clinics in South Carolina," by E.A. Early, D.D.S., Columbia, South Carolina, *The Journal of the American Dental Association*, September 1924:

"As this article is being written, the State Dental Clinics of South Carolina is on the eve of celebrating its first birthday. The department was authorized at the 1923 session of the South Carolina Legislature as a new feature of state public health work. The appropriation made by the Legislature was for only $2,500. . . . It was too late to get the clinics organized for the spring of 1923, as schools were closing for the summer vacation. . . . It was decided that it would be best to visit every county in the state and every school in each county in which the necessary cooperation could be secured, doing the work for children up to 14 years of age, or through the sixth grade, with a county to be required to give a written guarantee of $600 to establish a clinic in that county. The initial expense of the clinic is $285. Of this amount, $250 goes for the salary of the clinician and $35 toward paying the expenses of the clinic. A fee of $0.50, which is charged for each treatment, is pooled with the $600 and goes out in the payment of the expenses of the clinic. All children not able to pay for the work are treated free of charge, the fee to be taken out of the dental clinic fund. The $600 is raised through the office of the county superintendent of education in most of the counties, but in several counties the parent-teacher associations, the associated charities, mothers' clubs, and improvement associations have helped raise the money. . . . The work was begun in the counties the first of October, 1923. The statistical report below covers the first five months:

Children Examined	26,564
Children Treated	5,972
Amalgam Fillings	10,502
Cement Fillings	1348
Porcelain Fillings	238
Guttapercha (sic) Fillings	57
Pulps Capped	15
Cleanings	4,310
Extractions	2,995
Total Number of Operations	19,465
Amount Collected from Pay (sic) Pupils	$8,514.50
Number of Free Pupils Treated	458
Total Amount Earned	$8,732.50

Of the 26,564 white children examined, 8,321 were above the age limit and were advised to see the local dentist. Of the 18,243 children remaining, 5,972 children accepted the opportunity afforded by the clinic and were treated by the clinician. There have also been 1,200 colored children examined by three colored dentists, who started work January 15, 1924, and of this number 450 took advantage of the clinic."

The open air markets operate in the middle of the city.

Life in the Community: Columbia, South Carolina

- The city of Columbia was a planned city, carved from a plantation in the late 1700s and located in the center of the state at the confluence of three rivers.
- It is known for being the home of the University of South Carolina; tuition is $20 per semester; a dorm room, with roommate, is also $20 per semester. Law school tuition is $32.50.
- Columbia is one of the hottest locations in the state, with temperatures flirting with 100 degrees during the intense summertime.
- South Carolina's capital city is prospering; the combination of "a government town" with its steady government payroll, and the recent construction of dozens of textile plants on the outskirts of the city have created a stable, vibrant economy.
- In addition, now that nine rail lines link the capital with the outside world, Columbia has become a major shopping center for people throughout the state.
- Between 1910 and 1920 the city's population increased 42 percent, from 26,300 to 37,600, with growth continuing in the 1920s at a similar pace.
- The rural economy is doing less well, as falling cotton prices and the destructive boll weevil are forcing thousands of farm bankruptcies; 90 South Carolina banks have failed between 1922 to 1924, including four in Columbia.

From 1910 to 1920 the city's population has increased 42 percent.

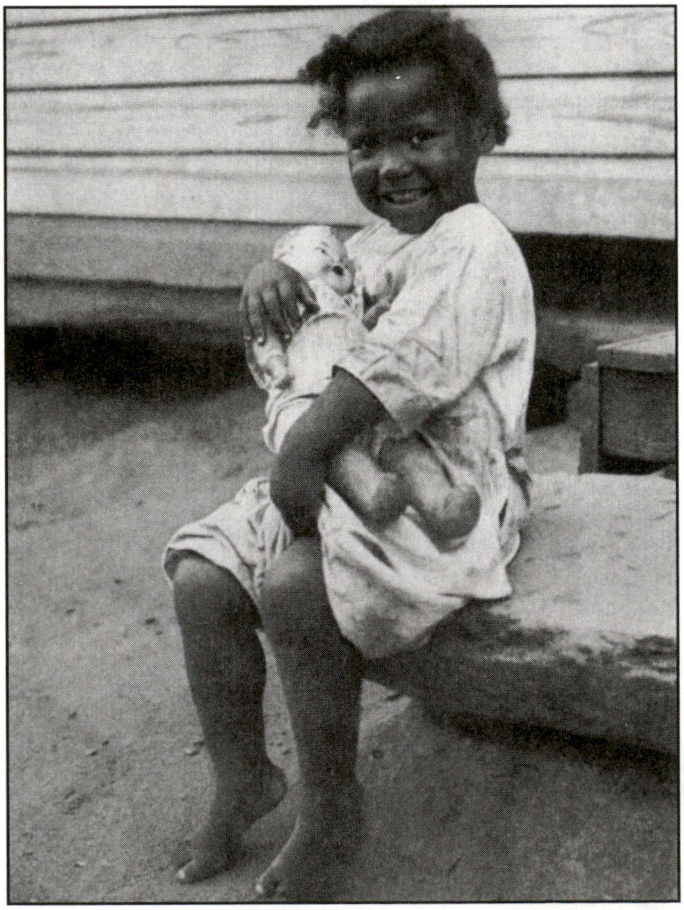

- Public education for white children gained momentum in the years following the First World War. In 1922, a bond issue of $75,000 was approved by the voters to build a new high school; one year later a $300,000 bond issue was approved for general school improvements.
- To improve education, the high school day has been extended with a school closing of 3:00 p.m. instead of 2:00 p.m., while grade school has been lengthened 15 minutes, from 2:00 p.m. to 2:15 p.m.
- A special school for problem and retarded pupils has been organized.
- Currently boasting a membership of approximately 400, the Associate Reformed Presbyterian Church of Columbia is known as the Centennial Church because it was erected as a memorial of the Associate Reformed Synod of the South's hundredth year in existence.
- This couple enjoys going to plays at the historic Town Theatre, which is constructing a new building to meet popular demand.
- The *State Newspaper,* the largest newspaper in the state, is currently crusading against the lynching of blacks, for compulsory education, and for child labor laws.
- Segregation of the races is a largely unquestioned way of life throughout South Carolina and the nation.
- Columbia boasts three motion picture theaters: the Grand and Lyric for white customers, and the Majestic for blacks.

Trolley cars link the city's center with residential areas.

- Many of the men in the community belong to the newly formed Columbia Club, composed of influential members of the state, while many of the women are members of the Assembly, whose fancy balls are designed to maintain a standard of dignity and graciousness in Columbia; the balls are always card dances by custom.
- Martha is an active member of the Century Club, whose object is "to promote social life among our women, to encourage among us diligent literary work, and to foster public spirit among our citizens"; the Club is discussing works by English writers this year.
- The number of streetcar riders nationwide peaked in 1923 at 15.7 billion, but the role of the automobile is growing; General Motors is buying up bankrupt streetcar lines, tearing up the tracks, and installing buses.
- When the first State Highway Commission came into being in 1917, the state claimed 40,000 automobiles; by 1922, the state was levying its first gasoline tax.
- Women's suffrage, which was widely debated nationwide, was not well received in South Carolina; in 1919 the General Assembly refused to ratify the nineteenth amendment giving women the right to vote, which became the law of the land anyway.

Historical Snapshot
1924–1925

- 30 percent of bread was still baked at home, down from 70 percent in 1910
- The first effective chemical pesticides were being introduced to farmers
- *American Mercury* began publication
- James Buchanan "Buck" Duke donated $47 million to Trinity College at Durham, North Carolina; the college changed its name to Duke
- Ford Motor Company produced two million Model T motorcars; the price of a touring car had fallen to $290
- Maxwell Motor Corporation, Ford, and General Motors now manufactured approximately 80 percent of the cars on the road
- Dean Witter and Company was formed
- College football surpassed boxing as a national pastime, largely because of the popularity of "Galloping Ghost" Red Grange
- With prohibition the law of the land, party-goers hid liquor in shoe heels, flasks form-fitted to women's thighs, and perfume bottles
- The Charleston dance, which originated in Charleston, South Carolina, was carried north and incorporated into the all-black show *Shuffle Along*; white dancers immediately adopted the lively dance
- The question of whether women should work was being widely debated
- The U.S. Supreme Court declared unconstitutional an Oregon law that required all grammar school-aged children to attend school
- When Henry Ford paid $2.4 million in income tax, 500,000 people wrote to him begging for money
- The Methodist Episcopal General Conference lifted its ban on theatre attendance and dancing
- Walt Disney began creating cartoons, featuring "Alice's Wonderland"
- Currently, 56 different companies were selling home refrigerators, with an average price of $450
- The permanent wave, contact lenses, IBM, deadbolt locks, and the college-bound notebook all made their first appearance in 1924

1924 Economic Profile

Income, Standard Jobs

Average of All Industries,
Excluding Farm Labor $1,402
Average of All Industries,
Including Farm Labor $1,303
Bituminous Coal Mining. $1,955
Building Trades, Union Workers. $2,391
Clerical Workers in Manufacturing $2,196
Domestics $732
Farm Labor. $571
Federal Civilian $1,747
Federal Employees,
Executive Departments $1,708
Finance, Insurance, and Real Estate $1,944

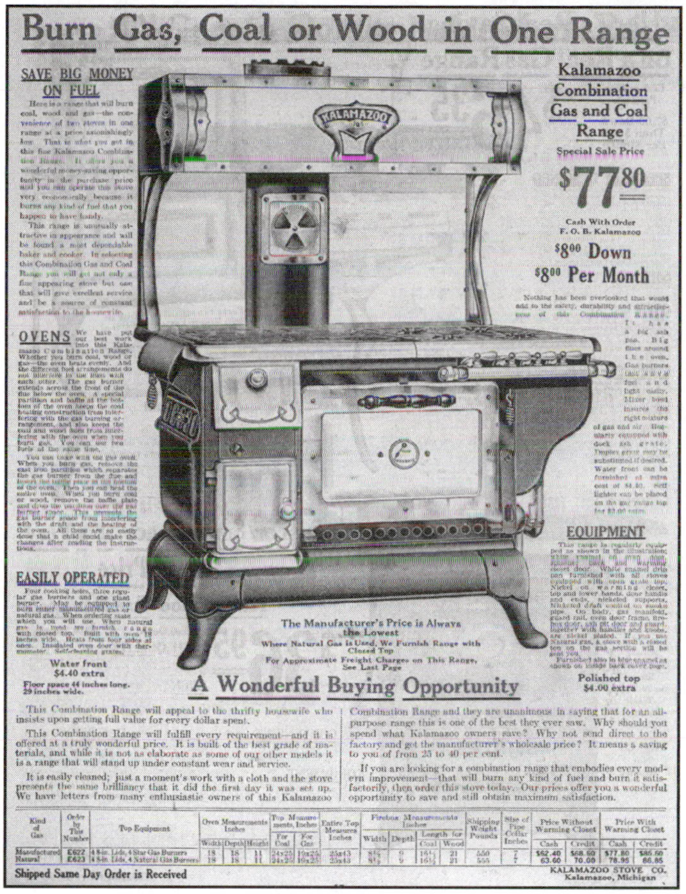

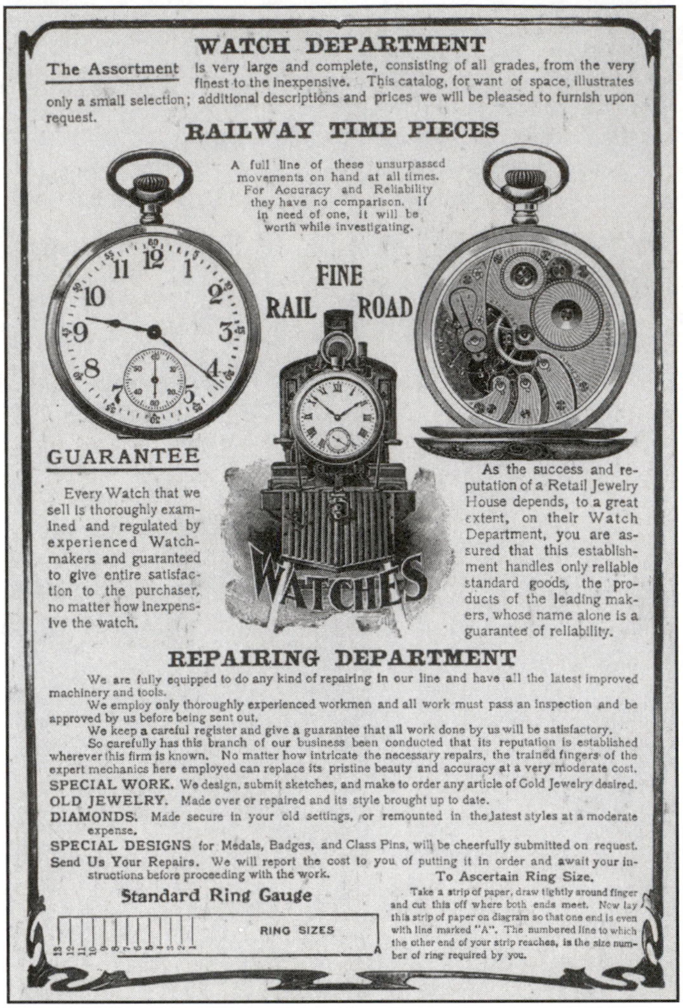

Gas and Electricity Workers	$1,417
Lower-Skilled Labor	$1,128
Manufacturing, Payroll	$1,558
Manufacturing, Union Workers	$2,325
Medical/Health Services Workers	$845
Ministers	$1,678
Nonprofit Organization Workers	$1,507
Postal Employees	$1,847
Public School Teachers	$1,269
State and Local Government Workers	$1,346
Steam Railroads, Wage Earners	$1,570
Street Railways Workers	$1,544
Telegraph Industry Workers	$1,150
Telephone Industry Workers	$1,104
Wholesale and Retail Trade Workers	$1,314

Selected Prices

Aladdin Mail-Order House, Seven Rooms	$975.00
American Kampkook Gas Grill	$15.00
Baseball Outfit for Boys	$1.79

Buffdentco Electric Heating Oven $55.00
BVD Union Suit. $1.50
Chrysler Six Phaeton Automobile . . . $1,395.00
Colgate's Dental Cream $0.25
Condo Typocraft Typewriter
Ribbon, per Dozen $3.00
Elliott Nursery Daffodils,
60-Bulb Collection $4.00
Fancy Knit Fiber Silk Tie. $0.39
Forhan's for the Gums Mouthwash $0.60
Hat Box, Circular-Shaped. $5.00
Jackson's Regulating Dental
Appliances, Gold-Plated $7.00
Licecil Insecticide, per Bottle. $1.00
Milk of Magnesia Laxative. $0.39
Pepsodent Co. Toothbrush $0.50
Remington Typewriter $60.00
Sani-Flush Toilet Cleaner $0.25
Victrola Talking Machine $125.00
Wahl Eversharp Mechanical Pencil. $3.00

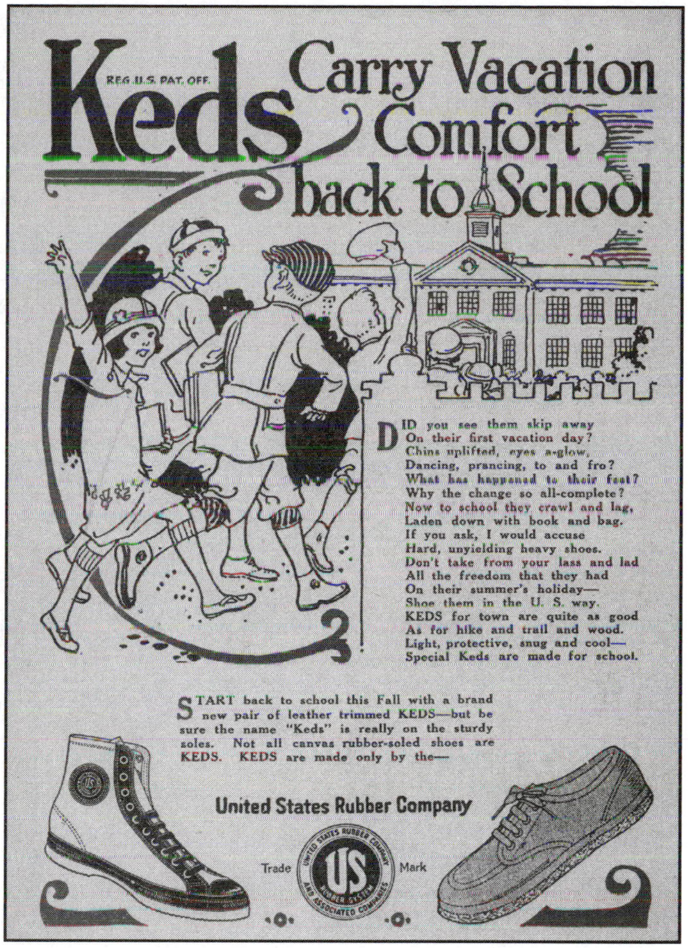

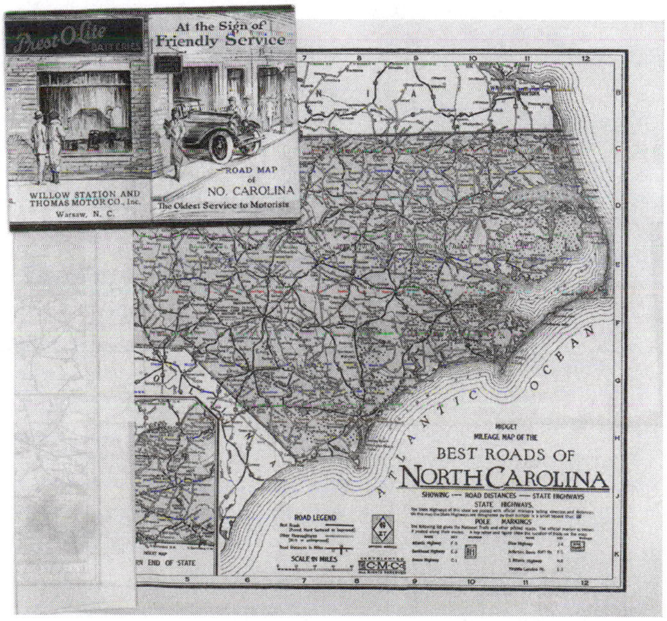

President Harding is popular throughout post-war America.

"Legislative Outlook," *Members of the General Federation of Women's Clubs*, February 1924:

"Department of Education: The President's recommendation along this line was: 'I consider it a fundamental requirement of national activity which, accompanied by allied subjects of welfare, is worthy of a separate department and a place in the Cabinet.' This does not go quite far enough to suit the National Education Association, nor the General Federation, who think the Department of Education in the Cabinet should not be coupled with 'allied subjects of welfare.'

Federal Industrial Institutions for Women: This bill, providing for the segregation of women who are committed for federal offenses, has already passed the Senate. It really opens negotiations by the appointment of a committee to select a site for such farm or institution. No definite plans could be made until it was known whether the site selected would make use of existing buildings, or require new equipment."

Advertisement of the Association of Railway Executives, *Leslie's Weekly*, 1923:

"The old-time pack-bearer could carry 100 pounds 10 miles a day. The railroad is the modern pack-bearer. For every employee, it carries 2,000 times as much. Back of each railroad worker there is a $10,000 investment in tracks and trains and terminals, with steam and electricity harnessed like a great beast of burden.

Without this mighty transportation machine, the railroad worker could do no more than the old-time packer could. But with it he is enabled to earn the highest railroad wages paid in the world, while the country gains the lowest-cost transportation in the world. The modern railroad does as much work for half a cent as the pack-bearer could do for a full day's pay. The investment of capital in transportation and other industries increases production, spreads prosperity, and advances civilization.

To enlarge our railroads so that they may keep pace with the nation's increasing production—to improve them so that freight may be hauled with less and less human effort—a constant stream of new capital needs to be attracted. Under wise public regulation, the growth of railroads will be stimulated, the country will be adequately and economically served, labor will receive its full share of the fruits of good management, and investors will be fairly rewarded."

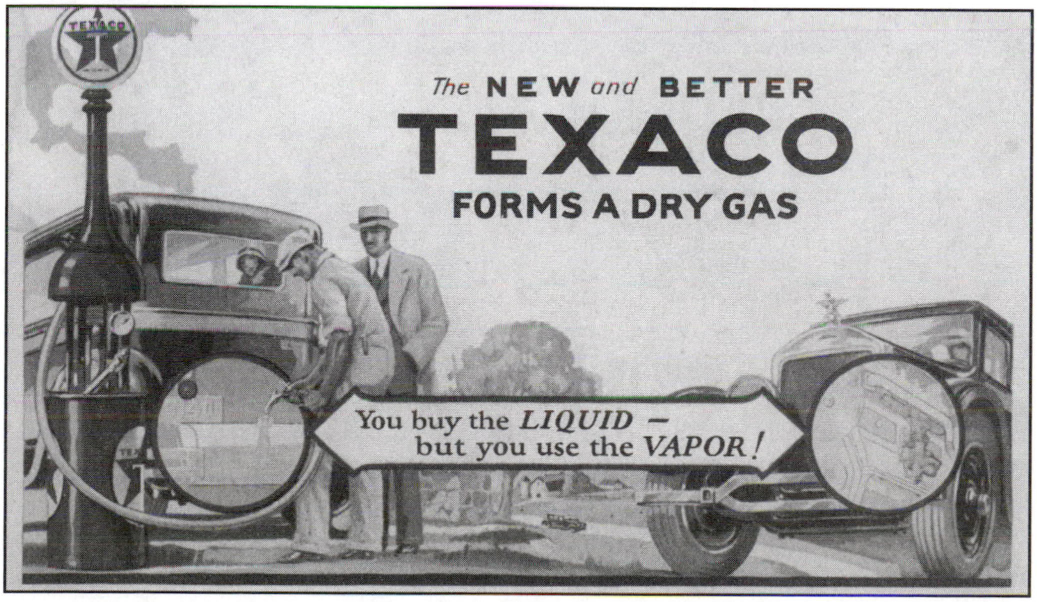

Kuppenheimer
GOOD CLOTHES
THIS SEASON Kuppenheimer Good Clothes give you everything—fine style, perfect fit, excellent fabrics at prices one-third less than last year. A real investment in good appearance.
The HOUSE of KUPPENHEIMER · Chicago
© B. K. & Co.

1926 Family Profile

This ambitious, 28-year-old Jewish cartoonist named Saul Bloomfield works for a newspaper in San Francisco, drawing editorial, sports, and event cartoons on demand. Newly married, he is wondering whether he should be living in New York, the center of the cartoon industry.

American cartoonists are commanding more space in America's newspapers.

Annual Income: $8,500

He makes $4,500 a year as a cartoonist and $4,000 a year as his share of the jewelry business he started, which is now run by his brother.

Annual Budget

The average consumer expenditure in 1926 is not available. The following is a per capita expenditure for 1925 for all workers nationwide:

Auto Parts	$6.96
Auto Purchases	$20.82
Clothing	$62.04
Dentists	$3.26
Food	$160.59
Furniture	$9.49
Gas and Oil	$15.70
Health Insurance	NR
Housing	$98.89
Intercity Transport	$4.95
Local Transport	$9.13
Personal Business	$27.33
Personal Care	$7.79

Women are less reluctant to drive automobiles.

Physicians	$7.68
Private Education and Research	$7.72
Recreation	$24.52
Religion/Welfare Activities	$11.31
Telephone and Telegraph	$5.88
Tobacco	$13.13
Utilities	$9.82
Per Capita Consumption	$619.45

Life at Home

- Saul grew up in Chicago and was an errand boy for a wholesale jewelry concern, becoming a salesman at an early age.
- He dropped out of school to sell jewelry and make money.
- His job allowed him to travel extensively throughout the West, peddling a line of watches and jewelry.
- He earned so much in commissions, he started his own business.
- Back in Chicago, he became friends with many of the city's best-known writers and artists, often meeting them in the bars after work.
- They loved his jokes and ideas so much that the established cartoonists encouraged him to begin drawing and cartooning.
- Saul first began by collaborating with an artist who drew Saul's ideas for him; now he does his own artwork.
- His father is convinced he is crazy, and cannot believe that anyone would give up a good-paying job selling jewelry to be a cartoonist.
- Thanks to hard work and the prosperity of the 1920s, many of Saul's friends, mostly the children of Jewish immigrants, are entering law, medicine, dentistry, and teaching.
- The rapid rise of Jews into professional jobs is creating controversy; Harvard University recently debated the use of a quota system for Jewish students to "preserve the representative character" of the school.
- Saul's father believes that his son will lag behind his peers, since drawing pictures for newspapers is not "a respectable living."
- Saul has experienced less discrimination than his Jewish friends have who entered medicine; newspaper cartooning is an open field.
- He laughs at his father's suggestion that he "at least work for a Jewish paper."
- Across the United States, the Jewish press consists of 111 periodicals, including nine dailies and 68 weeklies; 44 are in New York, where he longs to live, and 12 are in Chicago, where he grew up.
- One Jewish newspaper exists in San Francisco with a circulation only a fraction the size of the San Francisco paper where his work is displayed.
- Currently, San Francisco has a Jewish population of 35,000 across 13 congregations; seven have their own rabbi.
- His new wife, Heddy, is from San Francisco, and dreams of going to New York to shop in person at B. Altman and Company.

- Despite a pledge to "save every dime," they recently went to Mexico to see first-hand the Mayan forms and Pre-Columbian art that are having such a big influence on the art scene.

Life at Work

- Currently, cartoons are showing up throughout the newspapers, appearing on the front page, editorial page, sports page, the classified section, and, of course, on the funny pages.
- Most of Saul's days are spent at sporting events getting ideas for boxing cartoons that his sports editor demands.
- Once he gets an idea, he makes a rough sketch, normally in a matter of minutes, then spends several hours creating the final cartoon.
- Frequently, an editor is standing over his shoulder telling him to hurry up.
- He is known for his sharp ideas and speed, while his shading and perspective are getting more praise.
- As the drawing is getting easier, coming up with great ideas is getting harder.
- The competition is intense; within the city alone, six other cartoonists are producing cartoon drawings for newspapers.
- The demand is high for cartoons, and wages are excellent even for beginning artists.

Heddy dreams of shopping in New York City for the latest fashions.

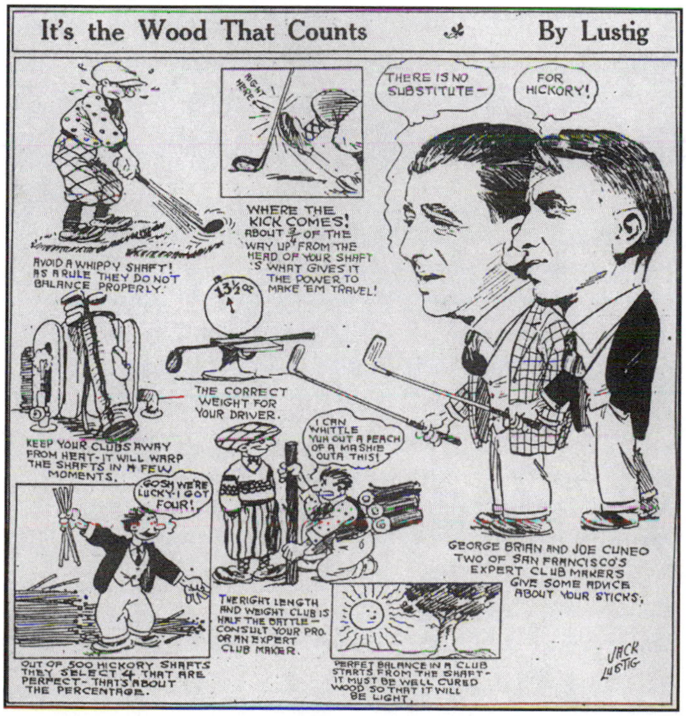

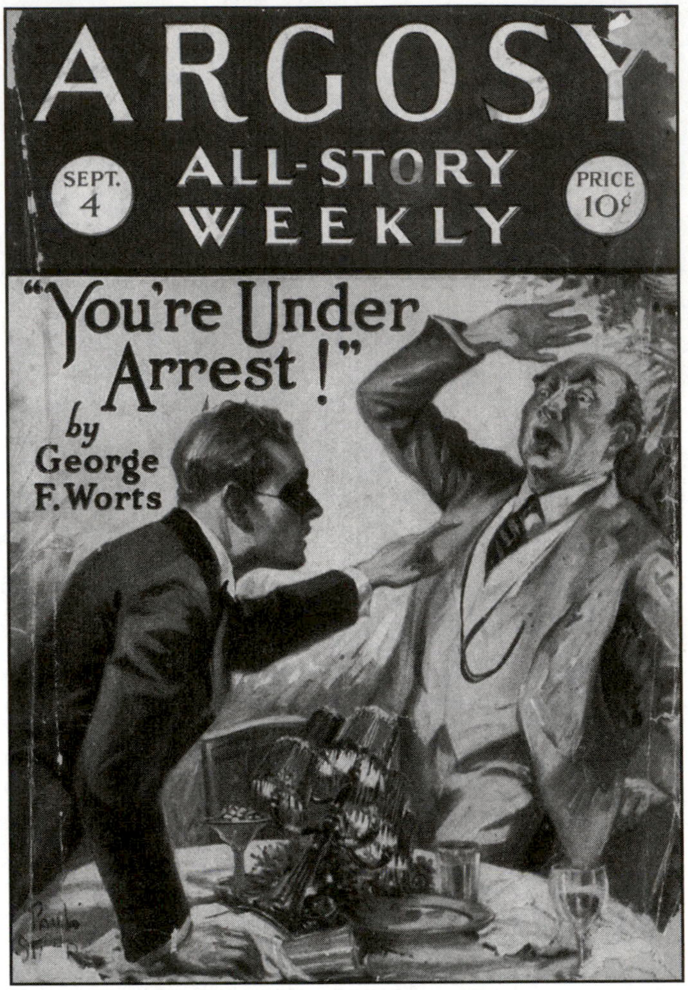

Saul submitted his work to Argosy *for consideration.*

- Veteran cartoonist Sidney Smith, creator of the *Gumps* cartoon strip, recently signed a $100,000-a-year contract.
- The national demand for new cartoon characters is also high; Saul is currently talking with Bell Newspaper Syndicate for a regular strip, but nothing has developed.
- Using his well-established skills selling jewelry, he has proposed that he be allowed to market his new strip directly to newspapers across the country.
- At the urging of his friends, he has submitted his work to *Argosy*, the all-story weekly; he believes that a cover illustration in *Argosy* is the break he needs.
- He has kept his jewelry business, allowing his brother to manage sales.
- He used his Western contacts and his Chicago friends to land a job doing editorial, sports, and banquet cartoons for a newspaper in San Francisco.
- When his work is particularly good, the entire sports page is built around his drawings.
- He is also called upon to do editorial cartoons and events-of-the-day drawings, but his first love is sports.
- Nationwide, 2,001 daily newspapers exist, with a total circulation of 36 million; Sunday circulation nationwide is 24 million.

The Sporting Life, Murray Olderman

"When I was growing up in the 1930s in a little hamlet northeast of New York City on the western side of the Hudson River, my father used to take the Rockland bus home from his Manhattan sweatshop job. On his trip home, he'd gather up all the New York newspapers left behind by the other commuters and bring them home for me. The city was then home to 12 dailies, and it seemed that every one of them—with the exception of the august *Times* and the almost-august *Herald-Tribune*—had a sports cartoonist whose work was showcased on the front page of the sports section, and I began turning there before anything else. I became familiar with the dramatic realism of Burris Jenkins Jr.'s fluid drawings in the *Journal American*; the little lion that cavorted in the work of Leo O'Mealia in the *Daily News*; the brush strokes of John Pierotti in the *Post*; the precise portraits surrounded by goonies in the work of Tom Paprocki (who signed his work "Pap") in the *Sun*; and Willard Mullin's rangy figures sprawling across the columns of the *World-Telegraph*. Even the local *Nyack Journal-News* featured syndicated sports panels by Alan Maver of the *Central Press*. It was a heady time for sports cartoonists."

The combination of San Francisco architecture with natural settings is attractive to Saul.

Life in the Community: San Francisco, California

- To satisfy the incredible demand for sporting events, President Harrison has a stable of wooden horses that run races on the sun deck, with a pair of dice to indicate each steed's speed.

"31 Countries Inquire for U.S. Goods," *San Francisco Examiner*, March 1, 1926:

"An expanding stream of American factory and farm products is entering the arteries of world commerce and finding ready reception in the marts and bazaars throughout the world.

Corned beef, fat back, lemon squeezers, broom handles, shoe polish, playground equipment, bathroom fixtures, and radio sets are among the articles being sought by foreign merchants, according to a list of foreign sales opportunities made public by the Department of Commerce. Machinery for the establishment of new industries and the reorganization of old ones, together with the everyday requirements of foreign peoples, are included in the list of opportunities."

City Up to Date; Has Own Still

Idle Incinerator Is Rum Plant

They were inspecting—of all things!—the city's various garbage disposal plants.

As the official car, bearing City Engineer M. M. O'Shaughnessy, Clyde E. Healy and E. P. Jones, assistants, drew near the abandoned incinerator at Kansas and Army streets, the air wafted an odor which seemed inappropriate to the place. An odor, in fact, of mash.

"I can't be wrong," said Jones, who is in official charge of the city's garbage disposal system. "My nose knows."

He led the party to the massive iron door which, theoretically, has protected the place from intruders since the plant was abandoned 10 years ago. A look, a sniff, and the truth dawned.

"A still," exclaimed Jones, "and upon city property. This should either make or break us, politically."

As they discussed their discovery an indignant citizen dashed across the street toward them, shouting lustily.

"Hey, get out of there!" he yelled.

"Get out yourself," said Jones, pointing his finger at the indignant citizen. "You are under arrest."

Jones and Healy thereupon knocked the man down and sat on him until Patrolmen John Collins and Jeremiah Cowhig and a squad of Federal prohibition agents arrived. The man gave his name as Tony List, 607 Texas street, and he was booked on a charge of manufacturing and possessing liquor.

Closer inspection of the interior of the plant revealed a 300-gallon still and a 200-gallon still, both warm from recent use, several gallons of moonshine liquor, a large vat of mash, and lumber for the construction of more vats.

Saul is often asked to draw cartoons about humorous events.

- M. Friedman and Company is offering Jacquard velour furniture on sale, payable in easy monthly payments; their armchair is $65, the Cogswell occasional chair to match is $55, and the Chesterfield is $115.
- Advertisements are everywhere, many promoting ways the product can make people more successful.
- The days of simply describing a product are largely gone; toothpaste, breakfast food, and automobiles are promoted as important ingredients to achieving middle-class success.
- An army of personal advisors has been created from Betty Crocker to Mary Hale Martin for Libby, Ruth Miller for Odo-ro-no, Dorothy Dix for Lux Soap, and Mary Pauline Callender for Kotex.
- Many provide cures for newly defined diseases such as halitosis (bad breath), bromodosis (smelly feet), homotosis (bad taste in furniture), and acidosis (sour stomach).
- In 1914, American firms spent $682 million on advertising; by 1926 the total is nearly $3 billion.

"Bug-a-Boos," by Bugs Baer, *San Francisco Examiner,* March 2, 1926:

"A girl used to be very careful about her feet. In fact, a small foot and a trim ankle were considered the hallmarks of society. Not that society got its marks in halls, although some struggles have occurred there. The old-time flapperette used to wear dancing shoes two sizes too small so that her feet would look normal. But the girl of today, and last night, doesn't care what she puts on her feet. It is O.K. provided it doesn't fit. She wears oversized slippers, twin galoshes, and Russian boots. Those Russian boots are the last word in small bungalows. A flapper rattles around in them like a doughnut on a cane.

Of course, if it is fashionable to be silly, then 'tis folly to be on a diet. Take any girl with bobbed hair, hoot-owl glasses, a paper hat, short skirts, bowlegs, and Russian boots. Add them all together. And you will find that so far as her future is concerned, she might as well have been with Custer. She might win a beauty prize from Punch and Judy. But otherwise, she looks like a Christmas tree in an alley. They must be getting their fashions out of the retail hardware catalogue. But a young man, who is anxious to meet a nice girl and get married, can't be annoyed by carrying a mouse around in his watch pocket.

It's about time to go back to the fashions of our ancestors. Not too far back, or we will once again be in the year when leaves were full dress and pie plates were hats."

- Saul regularly uses the trolley cars to get to work and sporting events; nearly everyone he knows uses the streetcars, as few use cars simply to drive to work.
- However, automobile traffic is increasing; recently Chief of Police Daniel J. O'Brien ordered that on Sundays and holidays, traffic controls will be stationed on Market Street from First to Sixth Streets to control the situation.
- Residents along Pacific Avenue from Van Ness to Fillmore are organizing a protest; they believe the area is losing its scenic beauty because of too many telephone wires, which they want installed underground.
- Recently, San Francisco's City Engineer began inspecting the city's garbage disposal plants looking for the smell of illegal stills hidden among the garbage.
- The city is excited that the inventor of phonographs and motion picture machines has recently designed a new radio; "I reproduce every sound from the broadcasting station twice with a double loud-speaking unit"; he delays the second sound 1/75 of a second to increase the volume and enrich the quality of the tone.
- The San Francisco Port is reporting a total of 505 ships in April, with a tonnage of 1.3 million—an increase of 452 tons over the same month in 1925.

HISTORICAL SNAPSHOT
1926

- Congress reduced the taxes on incomes of more than $1 million, from 66 percent to 20 percent
- The Book-of-the-Month Club was founded
- To fight the depression in the automobile industry, Henry Ford introduced the eight-hour day and five-day work week
- With prohibition under way, the Supreme Court upheld a law limiting the medical prescription of whiskey to one pint every 10 days
- 2,000 people died of poisoned liquor; the illegal liquor trade netted $3.5 billion a year, with the price for bootleg Scotch at $48 a case
- Machine-made ice production exceeded 56 million pounds, up from 1.5 million in 1894
- The movies became America's favorite entertainment, with more than 14,500 movie houses showing 400 movies a year
- The United States sesquicentennial was celebrated
- *True Story Magazine* reached a circulation of two million with stories such as "The Diamond Bracelet She Thought Her Husband Didn't Know About"
- Ham in a can was introduced by Hormel
- Flues with slide fasteners were introduced by H.D. Lee Company
- Synthetic rubber was pioneered by B.F. Goodrich Rubber Company chemist Waldo Lonsbury Sermon
- Philadelphia's Warwick Hotel and the Hotel Carlyle in New York were opened
- Currently, 40 percent of all first-generation immigrants owned their own homes, while 29 percent of all second-generation immigrants were homeowners
- Kodak introduced 16 mm film
- Sinclair Lewis refused to accept the Pulitzer Prize because it "makes the writer safe, polite, obedient, and sterile"
- Martha Graham debuted in New York as a choreographer and dancer in *Three Gopi Maidens*
- *The Jazz Singer,* the first talking film, made its debut
- Women's skirts, the shortest of the decade, now stopped just below the knee with flounces, pleats, and circular gores that extended from the hip
- Ethel Lackie of the Illinois Athletic Club broke the world's record for the 40-yard freestyle swim with a time of 21.4 seconds

1926 Economic Profile

The Crystal Palace Market in San Francisco offered the following grocery specials:

Australian Brown Onions, Eight Pounds	$0.15
Bohemian Brand Butter, Two Pounds	$0.95
Del Monte Tomatoes, Solid Pack	$0.15
Loin Pork Chops, per Pound	$0.35
M&M Tall Milk, Three	$0.25
Macaronis Solid, Two Pounds	$0.15
Rivers Potatoes, Eight Pounds	$0.25
Roquefort Cheese, One Pound	$0.39
Strictly Fresh Ranch Medium Eggs, Three Dozen	$0.80
Sugar Mill, Pure Cane Sugar, 18 Pounds	$0.40

"Four of a Kind" Wins at Meeting

Here are four boosters who seek for a greater promotion of commerce on the Pacific slope and are attending the Foreign Trade Convention in San Francisco. Left to right: Marshall Dana, E. P. Kemmer, William Piggott and Robert Bentley.

Income, Standard Jobs

Average of All Industries, Excluding Farm Labor	$1,473
Average of All Industries, Including Farm Labor	$1,473
Bituminous Coal Mining	$1,446
Building Trades, Union Workers	$1,708
Clerical Workers in Manufacturing and Steam Railroads	$2,310
Domestics	$748
Farm Labor	$386
Federal Civilian	$1,888
Federal Employees, Executive Departments	$1,809
Finance, Insurance, and Real Estate	$2,008
Gas and Electricity Workers	$1,571
Lower-Skilled Labor	NR
Manufacturing, Payroll	$1,502
Manufacturing, Union Workers	$2,411
Medical/Health Services Workers	$857
Ministers	$1,769
Nonprofit Organization Workers	$1,607
Postal Employees	NR
Public School Teachers	$1,342
State and Local Government Workers	$1,422
Steam Railroads, Wage Earners	$1,613
Street Railways Workers	$1,566
Telegraph Industry Workers	$1,215
Telephone Industry Workers	$1,117
Wholesale and Retail Trade Workers	$1,480

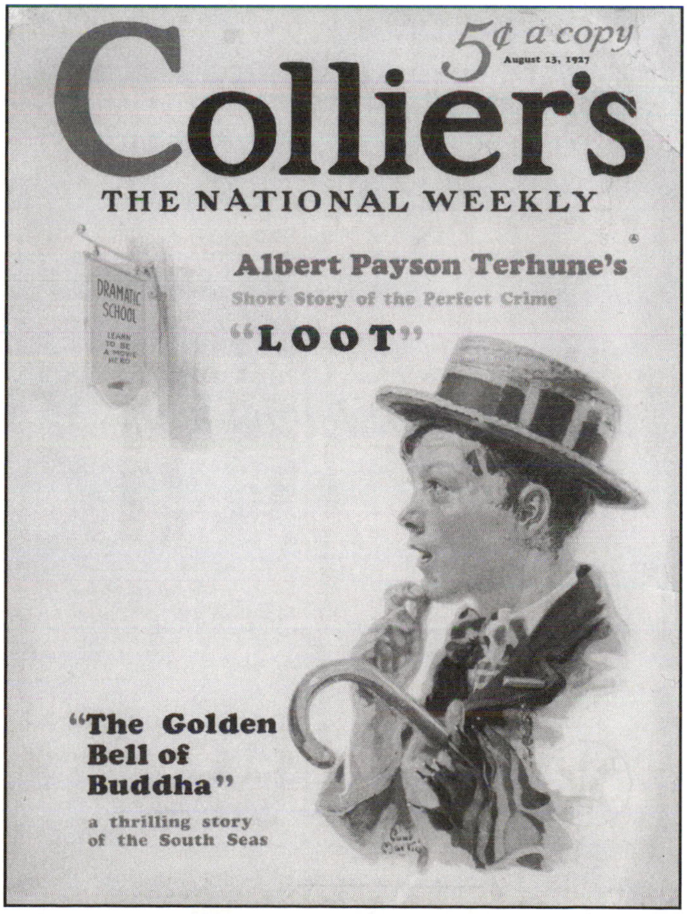
5¢ a copy
August 13, 1927
Collier's
THE NATIONAL WEEKLY
Albert Payson Terhune's
Short Story of the Perfect Crime
"LOOT"
DRAMATIC SCHOOL
"The Golden Bell of Buddha"
a thrilling story of the South Seas

Selected Prices

Amgerg Newborn Baskit Babe Doll $1.00
Bayer Aspirin Tablets $0.98
Bildmor Blox Lumber $3.50
Carlin Comforter with Wool Filling $21.00
G.C. Alexander Baseball Glove. $3.39
Graves Saw $10.00
Hershey's Milk Chocolate Bars, Box of 24 . . . . $0.97
Hohner Harmonica $0.50
Ivory Soap, 12 Cakes. $0.49
Junior Art-Kraft Stencils $1.50
Ouija Board Game $0.98
Pitch-Em Horseshoes. $0.89
Roly Poly Fleeced Diapers, 30 x 30, per Half-Dozen $1.12
Rubens Crayola Crayons, Box of 24 . . . . $0.30
Seroco Exterior Paint, per Gallon $2.45
Toastmaster Automatic $12.50
Vaseline Petroleum Jelly, Four Ounces . . . $0.13
Winchester Model 94 Gun $31.98
Winnie the Pooh Book $2.00
Wrigley's Spearmint Gum $0.39

The Nebbs *focuses on the everyday issues of raising a family.*

The Development of Comics

- Around 1880, the United States lagged far behind Europe in the field of illustrated literature and cartoons.
- This changed rapidly with the appearance of humor magazines in the 1880s, notably *Puck*, *Judge*, and *Life*, which published cartoons by artists such as Richard Outcault, James Swinnerton, and Frederick Burr Opper.
- In 1894, a large cartoon by R.F. Outcault featuring a bald-headed, nightshirted kid appeared in the humor magazine, *Truth*.

Adventure comics are gaining popularity.

- In 1896, Outcault introduced the *Yellow Kid* as part of his series about the antics of his many characters in a New York slum.
- By the turn of the century, the new cultural form was well-established.
- With the creation of Rudolph Dirks' *Katzenjammer Kids*, the comic strip rapidly grew in popularity.

Mutt and Jeff *was the first successful daily newspaper strip.*

- By 1902, Outcault created *Buster Brown* and James Swinnerton created *Mr. Jack*, and in 1904, *Little Jimmy*.
- By 1907, the first successful daily newspaper comic strip appeared in the *San Francisco Examiner,* Bud Fisher's *A. Mutt*, which later became *Mutt and Jeff*.
- George McManus' *Bringing up Father* stirred nearly everyone's imagination by featuring Jiggs as an Irish bricklayer who became a millionaire.
- One of the favorites of the decade was Sidney Smith's *The Gumps*.
- Begun in 1917 for the *Chicago Tribune*, *The Gumps* comic strip depicted the soap opera lives of Andy, his long-suffering Win, their overbearing housekeeper Tilda, and the rich Uncle Bim, characters that were followed by millions.

- The hapless adventures of *Mutt and Jeff* brought Bud Fisher great popularity throughout the 1920s.
- By 1920, the Chicago Tribune-New York News Syndicate was created.
- *Tillie the Toiler, Minutes Movies,* and *Our Boarding House* all debuted in 1921.
- In 1924, Harold Gray introduced *Little Orphan Annie*.
- Cartoons and cartoonists were an obsession; many cartoon characters were depicted in advertising and used just to boost circulation of their newspapers.

***Communal Organization for Palestine Work*, by Harry S. Linfield, 1930:**

"The Jewish community of the United States has shown much interest in the rehabilitation and development of Palestine. Numerous organizations exist whose purpose is to promote various directions of the progress of the new settlement in Palestine, ushered in by the Balfour Declaration and the entrustment of the Mandate over Palestine to Great Britain by the League of Nations.

In 1927, there was a total of 1,227 such organizations joined in 10 national federations. There were, in addition: 1) a central agency for the collection of funds; 2) two semi-philanthropic corporations engaged in special activities; 3) three organizations for the advancement of the interests of the Hebrew University in Jerusalem; and 4) two central offices, which collected funds for the support of a number of educational societies and institutions in Palestine for the care of dependents.

The local societies and their federations, commonly called Zionist organizations, engaged primarily in fostering the ideal of the restoration of Palestine along the lines laid down in the Mandate and expressed in the Joint Resolution adopted by the Congress of the United States on May 2, 1922, and in furthering the collection of funds for work in Palestine. There were in 1927 a total of 10 national Zionist societies with 1,227 local branches and an aggregate membership of 107,182. Of the latter number, 93,677, or 87.40 percent, were adults and 13,505, or 12.60 percent, were youths, including an organization of 1,500 college students."

Abie the Agent, Classic Comics and Their Creators:

"Shortly after the turn of the century, an excited picture editor rushed into the art department of the *Chicago Daily News*. It seems that some famous building in Rome had collapsed. He brought in several photographs of other old Italian buildings, passed them around to the various artists, and requested they do a hurry-up retouching job. Fifteen minutes later he returned, gathered up the pictures, and looked them over. He stopped and stared at one.

'Good Lord!' he yelled. 'Who in the world worked on this picture?' He held up a photograph of a tall tower.

'I did,' one of the artists replied.

'Do you know what you have done?'

'Sure,' the artist continued. 'That photograph was off so I squared it.'

'Why, you sap!' raged the picture editor. 'You've pulled the biggest boner in the business. This is the Leaning Tower of Pisa and you tried to straighten it.'

And the young man was fired—temporarily. Today that artist is Harry Hershfield, creator of *Abie the Agent*, the eighth-oldest comic strip in existence and one of the few old strips that has always been drawn by its original creator. . . . Then came the famous Leaning Tower incident in 1907, which cost young Hershfield his job. Later he heeded Horace Greeley's advice, went West, and began to draw cartoons for the *San Francisco Chronicle*. The beloved Tad's (Thomas Aloysius Dorgan) cartoons were being syndicated to the *Chronicle* from New York. Slow train service caused them to appear one week after the sports events occurred. Hershfield, of course, was on the spot with his drawings, making Tad's appear out of date."

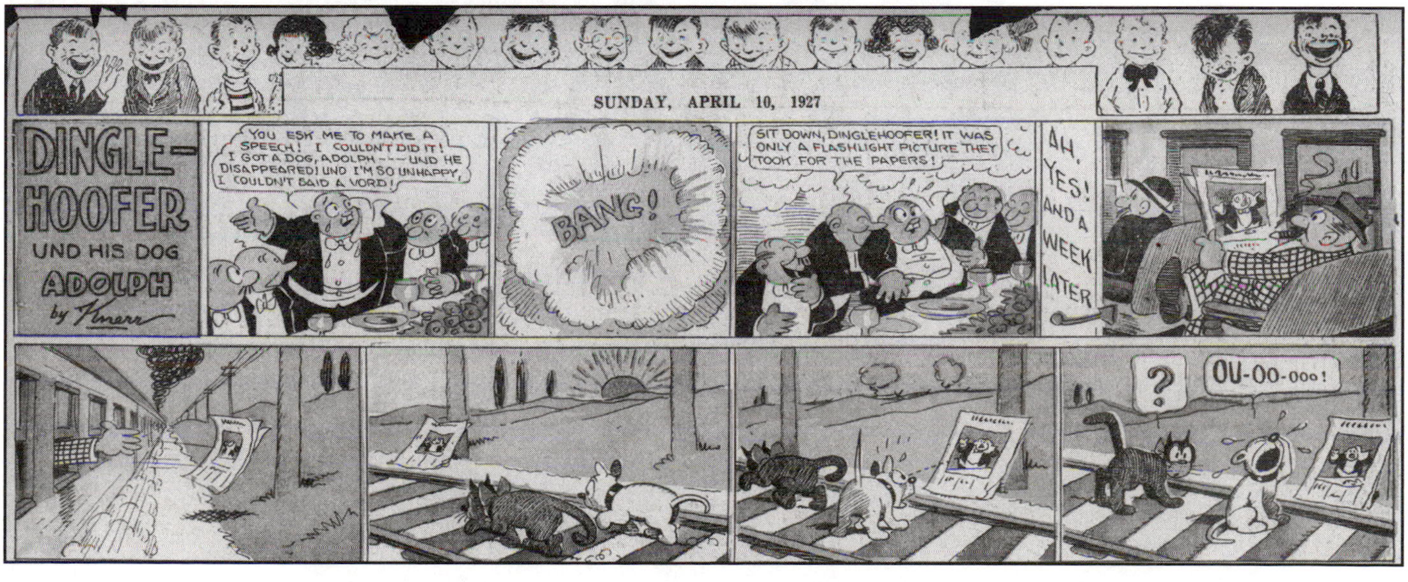

Bloomfield is fascinated by the architecture of San Francisco.

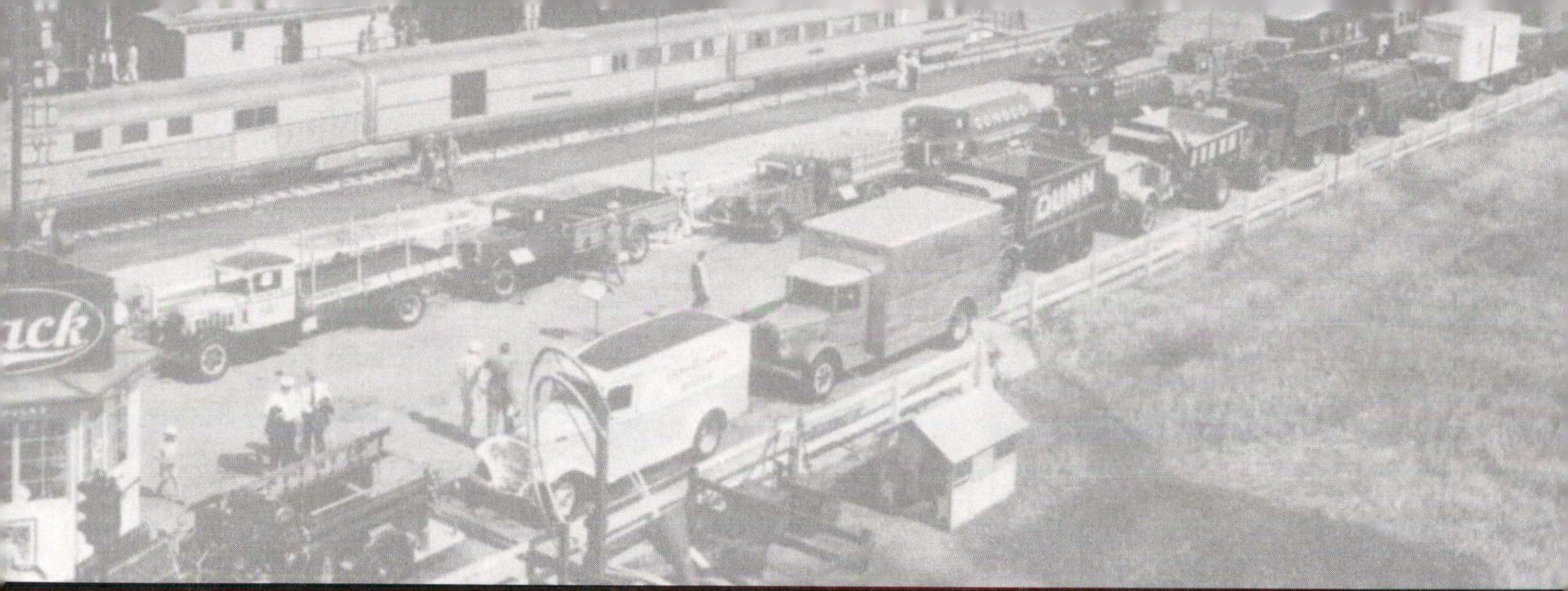

1929 Family Profile

Susan Burdick, a native of New York, has worked in the engineering department of Mack Trucks for the past 11 years. She was hired to fill the place of men going to the First World War; suffrage and prohibition have been part of her entire adult life. She is unmarried and happily dating a co-worker.

Annual Income: $1,970

Annual Budget

The national consumer expenditures in 1929 per capita are:

Auto Parts	$4.92
Auto Purchases	$21.35
Clothing	$63.24
Dentists	$3.26
Food	$160.14
Furniture	$9.49
Gas and Oil	$14.78
Health Insurance	$0.82
Housing	$96.08
Intercity Transport	$4.11
Local Transport	$9.03
Personal Business	$32.85
Personal Care	$9.03
Physicians	$8.21
Private Education and Research	$5.75
Recreation	$35.31
Religion/Welfare Activities	$9.85
Telephone and Telegraph	$4.93

Susan was hired to help replace the men going to war.

Tobacco. $13.96
Utilities $24.64
Per Capita Consumption . . $634.82

Life at Home

- Susan was born and raised on Sixtieth Street in New York City; her grandfather was a successful florist.
- After graduation from high school, she studied interior decorating at the School of Applied Design in New York City.
- A class in architecture captured her attention and she migrated away from interior decorating.
- After the death of her father, she was able to travel to France, Switzerland, and Germany.
- When the First World War erupted, she returned to the United States and began doing animated cartooning for the International Film Company.
- There she was made a supervisor of other women.
- Mack Trucks was looking for women to replace the men going to war; she answered an advertisement and was hired.
- She has been at Mack 11 years.
- Both at home and at work, she prides herself on being patient, and skillful with details; she is not considered talkative.
- The new taste sensation is sauerkraut juice, which she thinks is silly, but she is pleased that broccoli is making a comeback.
- Her boyfriend, in keeping with the current airplane craze, gave her a delightful valentine card showing a passenger airplane circling the Capitol, surrounded by a heart.

Her boyfriend, in keeping with the airplane craze, gave her a valentine card with a plane motif.

- Susan loves to cook and enjoys all the new gadgets; her home includes an electric mixer and an electric vacuum cleaner. She has looked at the new electric ranges, but is not convinced she wants one if she ever owns her own home.
- Most of her clothes are cleaned at the commercial laundry; if she has the time, she likes to use the wet wash, in which she picks up the clothes wet and takes them home to dry and iron. She does not like the way the laundry folds her clothes.
- She likes to do her own ironing; her electric iron is so much easier to operate than the cast-iron, stovetop instrument her mother continues to use.

Life at Work: Mack Trucks

- Susan got her job by answering a newspaper advertisement from Mack Trucks seeking women with training in technical drawing.
- The flood of men going to Europe to fight in the First World War had reduced the number of available draftsmen, and Mack purposely sought out women.
- Encouraged by her success at Mack, she began studying engineering at night.
- While still working at Mack, she went to Cooper Union, becoming the first woman admitted to engineering classes; her course work took three years.
- Her artistic skills and love of mathematics helped her in her studies.
- Regularly, she read "unladylike," technically-based papers such as "Springs and Shock Insulators" in preparation for her degree.
- She graduated with honors and was admitted into the Society of Automotive Engineers, the first woman to earn that honor.
- At first, she was asked to work on the interior look of the Mack Truck, a traditional role for women, but she said little and did her work.

Mack

The assembly line of Mack Trucks includes a variety of makes and models.

- Then, help was needed to design the drive train of an engine.
- Now she has been assigned to design brake piping for air brakes; she is proud that she is allowed to design unladylike parts.

CHIPPING of ice to cool drinks is inconvenient, wasteful and insanitary. This discourages the drinking of sufficient water

- Recently, the company's internal publication, the *Mack Bulldog*, did a story about the "girl designer."
- Few middle-class women work outside the home, as few professional jobs are open to women except teaching, social work, and nursing.
- At the college ranks, few women are invited to be professors.
- The only woman in the 20-person design department, she is careful of how she dresses; most days she wears a silk dress and light smock.
- The men dress in dark business suits and ties every day; currently, most are wearing a double-breasted suit with wide lapels and padded shoulders.
- This cut allows the businessman to appear more athletic and aggressive—both are important features for success.
- Few display facial hair, and all wear hats to work, but never inside a building or in the presence of a woman.
- Everyone understands how important it is to "fit in" if you wish to be successful in a "modern world."
- She loves eating candy, especially Baby Ruth and "It" candy bars, which she can carry in her purse.
- The company recently began a safety program, focusing on drinking clean, cool water provided by Frigidaire.
- Her office has fully adopted the scientific management methods of specialization; consultant Frederick Taylor believes that efficiency is enhanced if employees do only one job, such as opening mail, accounting, or sales.

- This philosophical shift has led to the elimination of roll top desks with dozens of drawers to more efficient desks with three drawers, backed by filing cabinets.
- Desktop neatness is paramount, as too many papers can distract workers.
- At Mack, all clerks are told to use the same nib on dipping pens, which are tied to the desks; middle-management executives, such as this woman, are allowed to use fountain pens.
- Susan believes that for Mack to be successful, appearances should matter down to the tiniest detail; she likes scientific management and she loves designing trucks.
- Trucks were part of America's love affair with the automobile; in 1920, Secretary of the Interior Franklin K. Lane reported that the United States had more automobiles than did all the nations of the world combined.
- By 1929, the nation's automobiles had increased by four times.
- A 1923 sociological study of Muncie, Indiana, showed that of 123 working-class families, 60 had cars; of this group, 23 lived in "very shabby houses" and had no bathtub.
- Trucks began to appear in 1904, but were not numerous until the early 1920s.
- Most trucks were local carriers, with few engaged in interstate commerce.
- By 1910, only 10,000 trucks had been produced, and by 1915, the annual output was 75,000 trucks.
- By 1925, half a million trucks a year were being built; by 1929, they were beginning to challenge the railroads for freight business.
- Jack Mack was inspired to build a large commercial motor vehicle in 1901 after riding in a neighbor's new two-cylinder Winton automobile.
- The first Mack Brothers sightseeing bus used a four-cylinder, 24-horsepower engine capable of going up to 20 miles per hour.
- Aided by the economic uplift provided by the European war, Mack introduced the model AC, with its highly distinctive hood and the nickname Bulldog; the 74-horsepower vehicle helped the company launch the slogan, "Built Like a Mack Truck."
- Many of America's first modern highways were built by Mack equipment, which was used to spray a hot, bituminous binder on crushed rock to form a solid road surface.
- Up until 1916, solid tires were standard on all trucks of one ton or more, which allowed a maximum speed of 20 mph on good roads, 15 mph on country roads; pneumatic tires were introduced in 1919, speeding delivery.

Trucks are beginning to challenge the railroads for freight business.

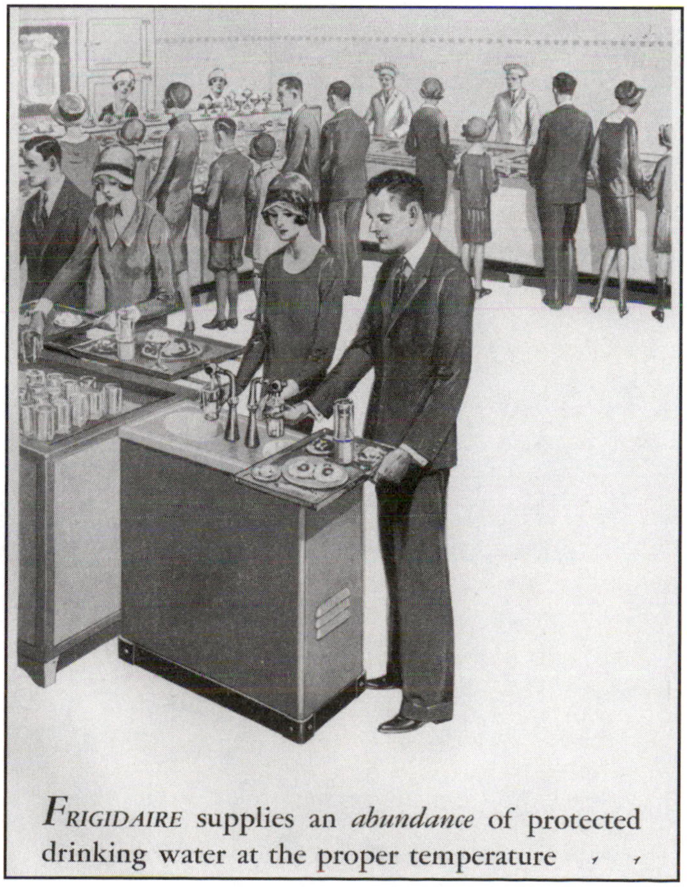
FRIGIDAIRE supplies an *abundance* of protected drinking water at the proper temperature

Total Mack Truck chassis output increased from 5,000 to 8,000 during the 1920s.

- More than 4,000 Mack AC trucks were ordered for the American armed forces in World War I; the trucks were so successful the American Expeditionary Forces (AEF) declared the "Bulldog" to be their only standard truck in capacities of five tons or more.
- The name of the company was changed from the International Motor Truck Company to Mack Trucks, Incorporated, in 1922, because they wanted to avoid confusion with a competitor, the International Harvester Company.
- In 1926 and 1927, Mack introduced a complete line of high-speed, six-cylinder Mack trucks, featuring four-speed transmission, dual-reduction rear axle, and four-wheel brakes.
- Mack is preparing to introduce a light delivery truck of one-ton nominal capacity—the first one-ton truck built by Mack since 1918.
- Mack products now include a line of truck equipment, such as winches, dump bodies, full trailers, and an aluminum container unit used with less-than-carload railroad freight.
- Total Mack chassis output has gone from 5,000 units in 1919 to 8,000 units in 1929.
- Profits in 1919 reached $1.9 million on $22 million in sales; in 1928, the profits topped $5.8 million on $55 million in sales.

Life in the Community: Plainville, New Jersey

- For most of the decade, the economy in New Jersey and much of America has been booming.
- Nationwide, the number of gainfully employed people increased from 41.6 million to 48.8 million between 1920 and 1930.
- The number of manufacturing jobs remained at 11 million during most of the period; the number of middle-class occupations increased from 11.5 million to 16.7 million.
- Office machines such as typewriters, addressing machines, mechanical accounting machines, and dictating machines are in widespread use.
- Even though the telephone has now become accepted as a business standard, more Americans own cars than rent telephones.
- Mack began its operations in Allentown, Pennsylvania, through a merger in 1912 with Saurer Motor Company, which expanded the company into Plainville, New Jersey.
- The "Good Roads" Movement is gaining momentum nationwide; heavy-duty Mack trucks are needed to haul crushed rock and asphalt in highway construction.

Telephone service, a public trust
An Advertisement of the
American Telephone and Telegraph Company
The widespread ownership of the Bell Telephone System places an obligation on its management to guard the savings of its hundreds of thousands of stockholders.
Its responsibility for so large a part of the country's telephone service imposes an obligation that the service shall always be adequate, dependable and satisfactory to the user.
The only sound policy that will meet these obligations is to continue to furnish the best possible service at the lowest cost consistent with financial safety.
There is then in the Bell System no incentive to earn speculative or large profits. Earnings must be sufficient to assure the best possible service and the financial integrity of the business. Anything in excess of these requirements goes toward extending the service or keeping down the rates.
This is fundamental in the policy of the company.
The Bell System's ideal is the same as that of the public it serves—the most telephone service and the best, at the least cost to the user. It accepts its responsibility for a nation-wide telephone service as a public trust.

AT&T advertises a variety of ways to promote the use of the telephone.

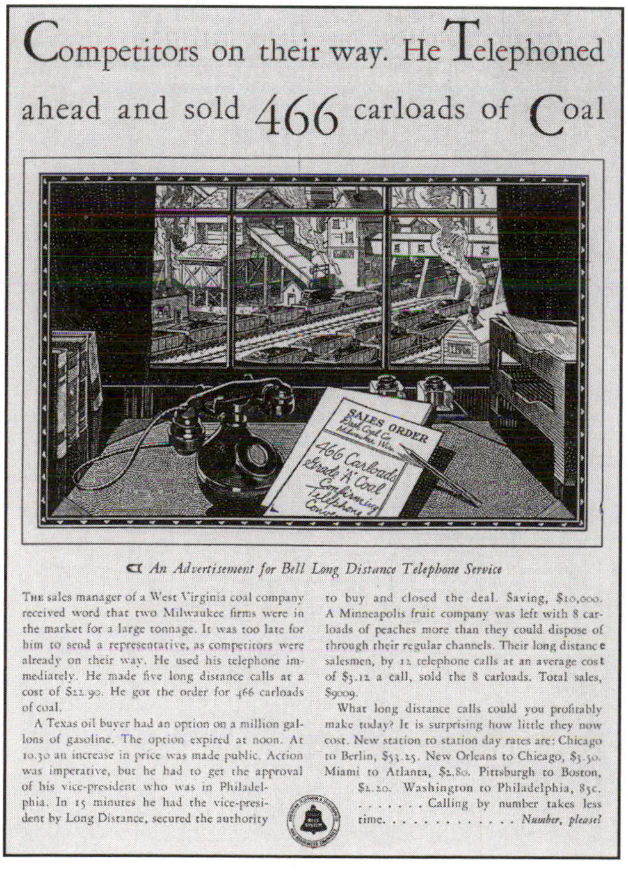

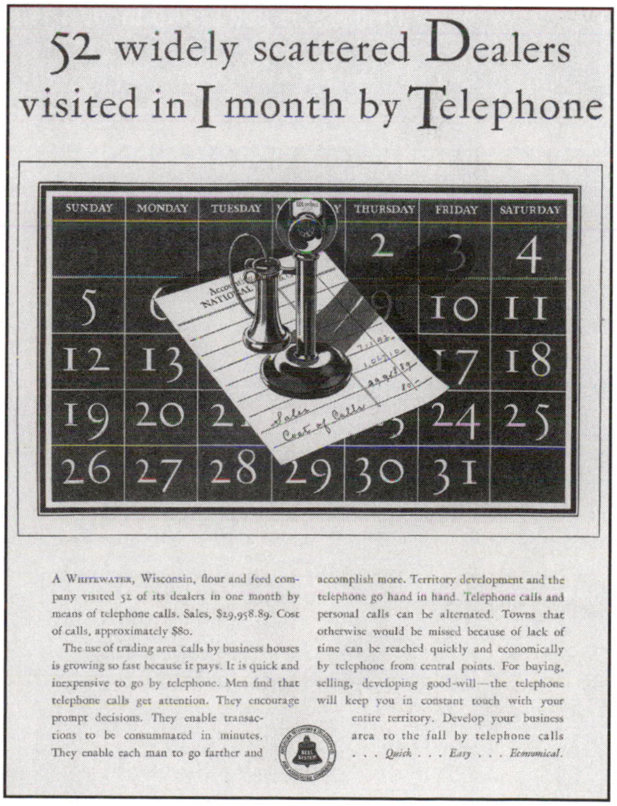

Competitors on their way. He Telephoned ahead and sold 466 carloads of Coal

The sales manager of a West Virginia coal company received word that two Milwaukee firms were in the market for a large tonnage. It was too late for him to send a representative, as competitors were already on their way. He used his telephone immediately. He made five long distance calls at a cost of $22.90. He got the order for 466 carloads of coal.
A Texas oil buyer had an option on a million gallons of gasoline. The option expired at noon. At 10.30 an increase in price was made public. Action was imperative, but he had to get the approval of his vice-president who was in Philadelphia. In 15 minutes he had the vice-president by Long Distance, secured the authority to buy and closed the deal. Saving, $10,000. A Minneapolis fruit company was left with 8 carloads of peaches more than they could dispose of through their regular channels. Their long distance salesmen, by 12 telephone calls at an average cost of $3.12 a call, sold the 8 carloads. Total sales, $9009.
What long distance calls could you profitably make today? It is surprising how little they now cost. New station to station day rates are: Chicago to Berlin, $53.25. New Orleans to Chicago, $3.50. Miami to Atlanta, $2.80. Pittsburgh to Boston, $2.20. Washington to Philadelphia, 85c. . . . . . . Calling by number takes less time. . . . . Number, please?

52 widely scattered Dealers visited in 1 month by Telephone

A Whitewater, Wisconsin, flour and feed company visited 52 of its dealers in one month by means of telephone calls. Sales, $29,958.89. Cost of calls, approximately $80.
The use of trading area calls by business houses is growing so fast because it pays. It is quick and inexpensive to go by telephone. Men find that telephone calls get attention. They encourage prompt decisions. They enable transactions to be consummated in minutes. They enable each man to go farther and accomplish more. Territory development and the telephone go hand in hand. Telephone calls and personal calls can be alternated. Towns that otherwise would be missed because of lack of time can be reached quickly and economically by telephone from central points. For buying, selling, developing good-will—the telephone will keep you in constant touch with your entire territory. Develop your business area to the full by telephone calls . . . Quick . . . Easy . . . Economical.

Historical Snapshot
1929

- A Baltimore survey discovered rickets in 30 percent of the children
- For the first time in history, a U.S. inaugural proceeding, this one for President Herbert Hoover, was carried worldwide by radio
- German Kurt Barthel set up the first American nudist colony in New Jersey, which began with three married couples
- Of the 20,500 movie theaters nationwide, 9,000 installed sound during the year to adapt to "talkies"
- Calvin Coolidge was elected director of the New York Life Insurance Company
- The "Age of the Car" was apparent everywhere; one-way streets, traffic lights, stop signs, and parking regulations were hot topics
- At least 32,000 speakeasies thrived in New York City; the Midwest had similar institutions named "beer flats," "Blind Pigs," and "shock houses"
- On September 3, the stock market peaked; on November 13, it reached bottom, with U.S. securities losing $26 billion in value
- Within a few weeks of "Black Tuesday," unemployment rose from 700,000 to 3.1 million nationwide
- The number of stockbrokers had risen from 26,600 in 1920 to 70,950
- Following the stock market crash, New York Mayor Jimmy Walker urged movie houses to show cheerful movies
- Coast-to-coast commercial travel required 48 hours through a combination of airplanes and overnight trains
- Lt. James Doolight piloted an airplane solely using instruments
- Commander Richard E. Byrd planted a U.S. flag on the South Pole
- W.A. Morrison introduced quartz-crystal clocks for precise timekeeping
- Ford introduced a station wagon with boxed wood panels
- Radio program *Amos 'n' Andy* was so popular that Atlantic City resorts broadcast the show over loudspeakers
- Admission to New York theaters ranged from $0.35 to $2.50
- On St. Valentine's Day, six notorious Chicago gangsters were machine-gunned to death by a rival gang
- American manufacturers began to make aluminum furniture, especially chairs
- The cartoon *Popeye*, the Oscar Meyer wiener trademark, 7-Up, front-wheel-drive cars, and *Business Week* magazine all made their first appearances

1929 Economic Profile

Income, Standard Jobs

Average of All Industries, Excluding Farm Labor	$1,534
Average of All Industries, Including Farm Labor	$1,425
Bituminous Coal Mining	$1,816
Building Trades, Union Workers	$2,808
Clerical Workers in Manufacturing and Steam Railroads	NR
Domestics	$731
Farm Labor	$378
Federal Civilian	$1,916
Federal Employees, Executive Departments	NR
Finance, Insurance, and Real Estate	$2,062
Gas and Electricity Workers	$1,589
Lower-Skilled Labor	$1,065
Manufacturing, Payroll	$1,330
Manufacturing, Union Workers	NR
Medical/Health Services Workers	$925
Ministers	NR
Nonprofit Organization Workers	$1,712
Postal Employees	$2,062
Public School Teachers	$1,445
State and Local Government Workers	$1,549
Steam Railroads, Wage Earners	$1,749
Street Railways Workers	$1,598
Telegraph Industry Workers	NR
Telephone Industry Workers	NR
Wholesale and Retail Trade Workers	$1,359

Selected Prices

Brill Brothers Chauffeur's Outfit	$78.00
Cahill Fireplace Grate	$10.00
Campbell Automatic Electric Fireless Cooking Range	$25.50
Confederate Grave Marker	$1.50
Cushion Truck Tire	$16.45
Daisy Ironing Table	$2.35
Gillette Razor Blade	$0.50
Hunter Ceiling Fan	$52.00
Louisville Slugger Baseball Bat	$2.00
Luxeberry Interior Wood Varnish	$1.45
Official Boy Scout Ax	$1.65
Oliver One-Horse Plow	$8.25
Polar Cub Electric Hair Dryer	$4.95

Famed Newspaper Cartoonist Ralph Barton, 1929:

"Americans are crazy people. They drink too much, do everything too much. They like something for 15 minutes, then turn about and like something else. They are faddists. They idolize some hero of the hour beyond all sensibility, then leave him flat for someone else."

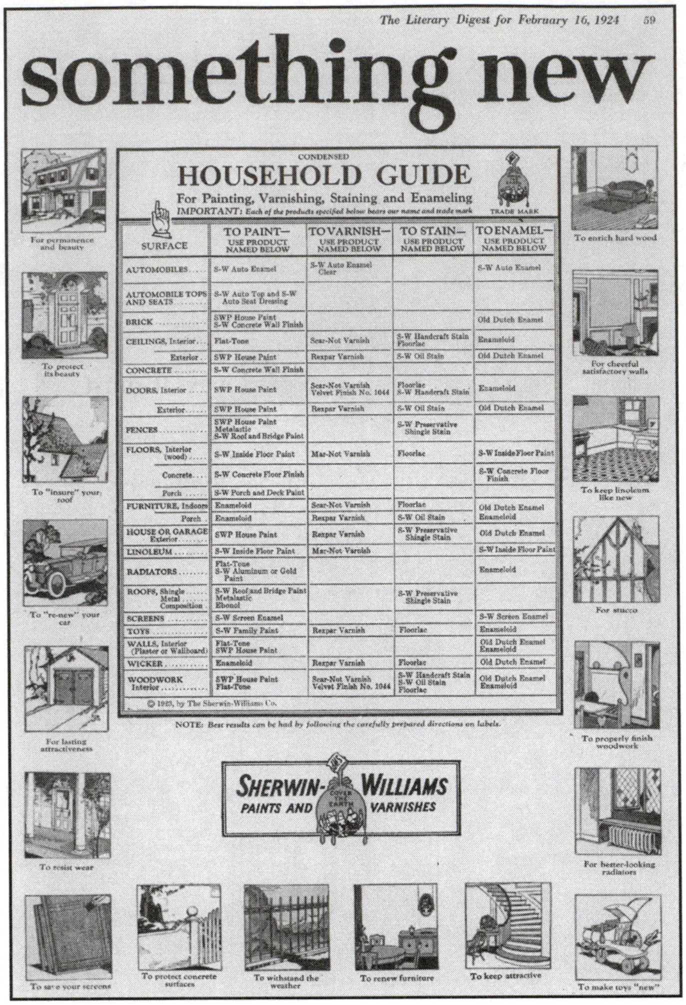

Read Head Hunting Coat $3.50
Remington Pocket Knife $3.50
Universal Fuse Plug $1.20
Universal Waffle Iron $9.75
Wall Street Journal Annual
Subscription $15.00
Westclox Big Ben Alarm Clock $3.25
White Delivery Truck $1,545.00

America's Candy Bar Obsession

- The success of the candy business in America exploded with the invention of the commercially available candy bar.
- Confectioner Milton Snavely Hershey had built a successful business in caramels when he saw a German chocolate-making machine at the 1893 Chicago World's Fair.
- In 1894, Hershey created the Hershey Bar, made in Lancaster, Pennsylvania.
- Sold for $0.02, the candy bar was an immediate success.
- By 1911, his company had sales of $5 million a year; by 1921, sales had reached $20 million.
- In 1896, Leonard Hirschfield, a candy maker with a daughter named Tootsie, introduced the first paper-wrapped candy, known as the Tootsie Roll.
- The convenience of a candy that could be carried in a pocket or purse made it immensely popular and quickly copied.
- Perley G. Gerrish of Cambridge, Massachusetts, brought out the first peanut bar, Squirrel Brand, in 1905.
- The first combination bar, with multiple ingredients, was the Goo Goo Cluster, concocted in a copper kettle in Nashville, Tennessee, in 1912; the candy bar combined marshmallow, peanuts, coconut, and milk chocolate.
- Candy bars were so popular, some 30,000 different brands appeared prior to World War I, though most sold regionally, not nationally.
- During World War I, the Army Quartermaster Corps, recognizing that chocolate boosted energy and morale, got chocolate companies to contribute to the war effort by supplying chocolate in 25-pound blocks; after the war, thousands of soldiers returned home with a sweet tooth.
- Some brands, including Legion's Buddy, were created especially for the returning troops.
- By 1921, many candy drops, sticks, and bars were on the market when New Haven, Connecticut, confectioner Peter Paul Halijian manufactured a bittersweet chocolate and coconut bar called Mounds, which sold for a nickel.
- That same year, the Baby Ruth bar hit the market, named for the daughter of former President Grover Cleveland—not the Yankee Slugger, Babe Ruth.
- Two years later, the inventor of the Baby Ruth, Otto Schnering, produced another success with his Butterfinger bar.
- The Milky Way bar, blending sweet milk chocolate, corn syrup, milk, sugar, cocoa, malt, butter, and frothy egg whites soon followed, producing sales of $800,000 in its second year of production.

"The Stock Market Is NOT America; 1930 Should Be a Good Year," by Ray W. Sherman, January 1930, *Motor Magazine*:

"There are millions of people in America who are bored with newspaper headlines telling about the latest 'market news.' It meant nothing to them in the first place. Like the two well-known comedians, they would rather 'hear nothing more about it.' They would much prefer to read about a 'good murder.'

The most overrated 'catastrophe' in the industrial history of America was the 'great market smash.' It is true that the 'smash' caused losses, but with the majority of the great common people who may have been involved, the losses were of surplus assets. The fundamental structure of the people has been little affected.

The 'New York mind,' which is that of a few major cities, is responsible for much of the foreboding with which industry enters this new year of 1930. Were it not for that, the 'smash' and fears that followed it would have been practically forgotten.

During the weeks following the 'smash,' editors of *Motor* visited cities remote from New York and contacted hundreds of American people. Most of them had not been 'in the market,' most of them were still working at the jobs which had kept them busy during past years, and none of them could see any reason why 1930 should not be a good year. They were working, they still are working, and they expect to keep working. And as they work they earn—and spend.

An almost amusing aspect of the event of a few months back is that while the market was in a turmoil and stock prices were falling, the industries behind the stocks were all moving along in their usual way, the workmen were all busy at their machines, goods were being made and shipped, and the workers were going home to supper every night in the same old way. It must have looked funny to those of them who had a real knowledge of what was happening. The papers said the value of the company that employed them had been cut in half, or thirds, or less. But when they got up in the morning there still stood the same old plant and at the whistle they all went back to work and created more dividends.

They are still working, these citizens of America, except for a few industries which have had normal declines. Even those will resume. In the turmoil we rather lost sight of these people, but if we ring the doorbells of any average hometown street in America tonight, these folks will be found living in the same way—the most substantial foundation on which any nation was ever built.

And they will continue to buy automobiles. They have been doing it for a quarter-century with no letdowns of consequence. They won't walk. They don't like old cars—and they aren't broke. Business executives may be a bit pessimistic because THEY 'lost in the market.' It would do most of them good if they would take a day off and talk to the great common people. They would learn that the stock market is NOT America and that the 'hometown folks' are ready to make 1930 a good year."

- Otto Schnering's company was called the Curtis Candy Company, after his mother's family; he was concerned a company named after his German ancestry would be a liability.
- Candy bar magnate Frank Mars made it big with a soft, fluffy, nougat center that was discovered by accident in the Pendergast Candy Company in Minneapolis; in 1923, he copied the error for his Milky Way bar, which was followed quickly by Snickers and the Mars bar.
- Andy bars were also created for movie stars and presidential campaigns; in 1928, the manufacturer of Oh Henrys made the Big Hearted Al bar for democratic candidate Al Smith.

- From Hollywood the It bar appeared to promote silent-movie actress Clara Bow as the "It Girl," a Jazz Age symbol of beauty and sexual freedom.

Truck Development Milestones

1920

- Postwar prosperity and enthusiasm ushered in an era of one-ton speed truck development, giving rise to a trend toward lighter models.
- Fourteen manufacturers offered four-wheel-drive trucks.
- Nearly two-thirds of new models now used the worm-driven rear axle.
- Automatic tire pumps were introduced.
- A gasoline shortage scare swept the nation; the Pacific Coast feared that prices would reach $0.40 per gallon, although inefficient distribution of gasoline—not an inadequate supply—was the problem.
- The Motor Truck Association of America was formed to distribute information and prevent laws that limited motor truck operations.
- Crowley-Milner department store in Detroit built a 150-truck parking facility exclusively for its delivery trucks.

1921

- Truck manufacturers reduced truck prices as more models became available.
- Metal-type wheels began to appear, though wood wheels still dominated.
- A rash of highway banditry between New York and Philadelphia resulted in the use of armed guards and convoy travel.
- The Federal Highway Act of 1921 provided for state and federal governments to create a nationwide road system, with Washington paying half the cost on designated federal-aid roads.
- America had 3.2 million miles of highways, with only 14 percent surfaced.
- Mack replaced spring shackles with rubber-shock insulating blocks on its new bus model; other features were a gasoline tank on the rear of the chassis and an exhaust pipe and muffler extended to the rear of the vehicle.

1922

- The National Highway Traffic Association pushed for uniform highway signs, state boundaries on highways, and uniform highway weights, speeds, and loads.
- The Fay Motor Bus Service of Rockford, Illinois, provided shopping service reached by the bus line for county patrons; after receiving an order, a shopper made the purchase and sent it back on the bus' return trip, paying a small fee for the service.
- When modern trucks were introduced into rural Alabama for use as school buses, attendance increased 45 percent.

- The Mayo Clinic used a special bus on the Mack chassis to transport patients to its clinic.
- A unique refrigerator plant for transporting perishables was devised by R.H. Hatch of San Francisco using a Mack truck.
- To curb motor vehicle thefts, a bill was introduced in the United States House of Representatives calling for federal regulation of all motor vehicles.
- Motor-driven snow removal equipment opened 27,096 miles of snow-covered highways from the East Coast through the Midwest.

1923

- By 1923, 25 states had passed a gasoline tax; eight others were considering it.
- Titan Truck introduced a special counter-balanced crankshaft to eliminate four-cylinder engine vibration and provide exceptional smoothness and power.
- A special van body on a Mack chassis was introduced with bulletproof steel cab and safety glass, bulletproof windshield to protect drivers from a rash of truck robberies.
- Ford Motor Company announced that its truck chassis and tractor production had attained a new high of 193,294 units, and had reached record heights for its total vehicle production.

1924

- White Motor Company shipped 60 buses to Yellowstone National Park for tourist transportation, with the park fleet numbering 279 White buses.
- The National Automobile Chamber of Commerce urged preservation of national scenery and called for curbs on outdoor advertising.
- Bethlehem Motors introduced four-wheel brakes as optional on its large models.
- The U.S. Bureau of Standards introduced vehicle brakes testing to regulate braking in motorcars.
- The motor bus market grew, with more than three billion passengers carried by buses in 1924, and 75 bus companies serving the public with 60,000 buses.

1925

- Approximately 20,000 buses were owned by rural schools for transporting children.
- The U.S. Supreme Court ruled that no state could interfere with interstate commerce and that interstate highways must be open.
- Balloon tires grew in popularity.
- The United States now had 500,000 miles of surfaced roads.
- More than 150 electric railway systems now operated at least part of their network using motor buses.
- United States truck and bus exports for the year totaled 56,624 units, more than double the exports of 1924; the total value was nearly $38 million.

1926

- Trucks adopted passenger car features such as six-cylinder engines with their quicker acceleration and smoother power.
- Driver comforts were added to trucks, such as closed cabs, low-pressure tires, windshield wipers, and air cleaners.
- White introduced a heavy-duty dump truck featuring an auxiliary transmission for increased pulling power.
- Six-Wheel Company offered air brakes as standard equipment on its motor coaches.
- The use of pneumatic tires surpassed solid rubber tires, improving the ride and saving taxpayers millions of dollars in road surface repairs.

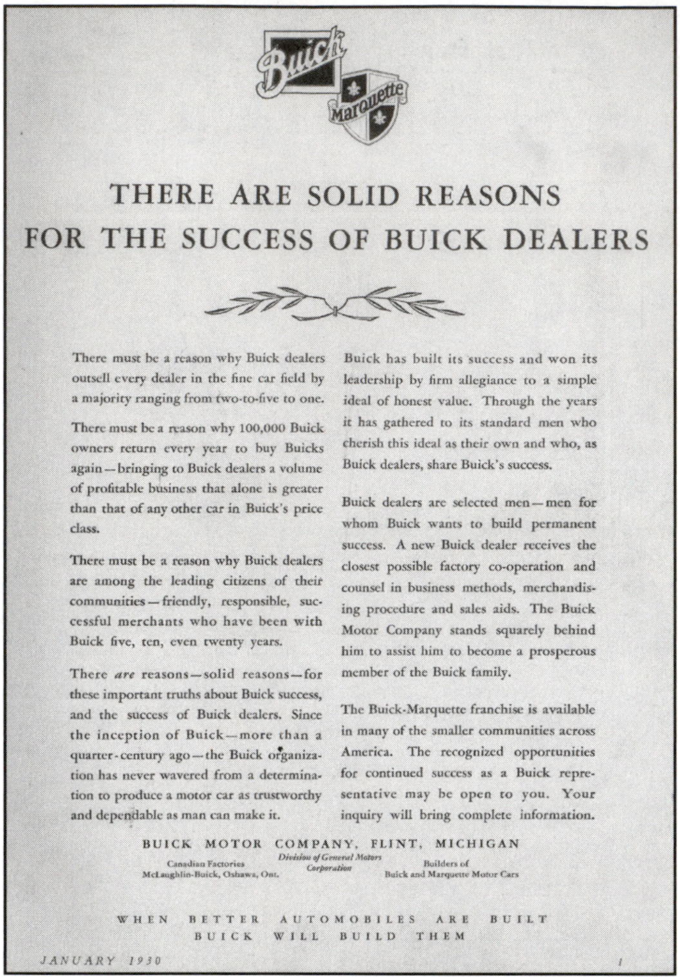

Buick
Marquette
THERE ARE SOLID REASONS
FOR THE SUCCESS OF BUICK DEALERS
There must be a reason why Buick dealers outsell every dealer in the fine car field by a majority ranging from two-to-five to one.
There must be a reason why 100,000 Buick owners return every year to buy Buicks again—bringing to Buick dealers a volume of profitable business that alone is greater than that of any other car in Buick's price class.
There must be a reason why Buick dealers are among the leading citizens of their communities—friendly, responsible, successful merchants who have been with Buick five, ten, even twenty years.
There are reasons—solid reasons—for these important truths about Buick success, and the success of Buick dealers. Since the inception of Buick—more than a quarter-century ago—the Buick organization has never wavered from a determination to produce a motor car as trustworthy and dependable as man can make it.
Buick has built its success and won its leadership by firm allegiance to a simple ideal of honest value. Through the years it has gathered to its standard men who cherish this ideal as their own and who, as Buick dealers, share Buick's success.
Buick dealers are selected men—men for whom Buick wants to build permanent success. A new Buick dealer receives the closest possible factory co-operation and counsel in business methods, merchandising procedure and sales aids. The Buick Motor Company stands squarely behind him to assist him to become a prosperous member of the Buick family.
The Buick-Marquette franchise is available in many of the smaller communities across America. The recognized opportunities for continued success as a Buick representative may be open to you. Your inquiry will bring complete information.
BUICK MOTOR COMPANY, FLINT, MICHIGAN
Canadian Factories McLaughlin-Buick, Oshawa, Ont.
Division of General Motors Corporation
Builders of Buick and Marquette Motor Cars
WHEN BETTER AUTOMOBILES ARE BUILT BUICK WILL BUILD THEM
JANUARY 1930

1927

- The use of power brakes accelerated, stimulated by increased traffic and demands for safety.
- Approximately 80,000 buses were in service nationwide; 30,000 were owned by schools.
- Ford introduced a one-ton model with a 40-horsepower, four-cylinder engine, multiple-disc clutch, three-speed transmission, and four-wheel brakes; the price was $460.
- AC Spark Plug Company introduced a mechanically operated fuel pump consisting of a diaphragm pump operated by a lever driven from the push rods on either side of the camshaft.
- All windows on the Murray Duralumin coach were fitted with Protex safety glass; the windshield was Triplex glass.

1928

- Demand for high-speed vehicles with pneumatic tires was very strong.
- The first highway interchange was built in New Jersey.
- Many manufacturers increased the cooling capacity of their models; the use of thermostats in cylinder heads increased.
- World Motors Company introduced an eight-cylinder model truck.
- Mack introduced a hypoid bevel gear, with a single-reduction rear axle on its Model BB; the change allowed quieter, simpler, more efficient operation than did the double-reduction drive.

Costs

The book *Recent Social Trends* listed many of the changes in the first 20 years of the new century, saying these are "a few of the many happenings which have marked one of the most eventful periods in our history." The "epoch-making events" listed included the Great War, mass immigration, race riots, rapid urbanization, the rise of giant industrial combines like U.S. Steel, Ford, and General Motors, and new technologies like electrical power, automobiles, radios, and motion pictures. Novel social experiments mentioned were prohibition, daring campaigns for birth control, a new frankness about sex, women's suffrage, the advent of mass-market advertising, and consumer financing (freedom from fear).

- All 48 states had imposed a gasoline tax ranging from $0.02 to $0.05 per gallon.
- Texaco became the first company to market gasoline in all 48 states.

1929

- Door-to-door delivery trucks doomed horse-drawn vehicle delivery businesses, which had maintained that the horse remained viable because "he knows the route."
- Aluminum use in trucks increased, giving trucks greater load capacity.
- Adjustable steering columns, sun visors, and four-wheel brakes were offered on many truck models.
- The use of dry ice in refrigerated truck bodies was replacing the old water-ice method.

"The Economic Condition of the World Seems on the Verge of a Great Forward Movement," interview with Bernard Baruch, *American Magazine*, 1929:

"For the first time in history, we have sound reason for hope for a long period of peace. For the first time, the businessmen of all nations are supplied with statistical information, together with some understanding of the laws of economics. For the first time, we have sound, centralized banking systems in the countries and close cooperation between those systems internationally. Because all these factors are favorable, and because of the universal stirring of desire and ambition . . . I believe in the 'industrial renaissance.' We are already seeing something of it in the United States."

"I Learned to Drive and So Can You, Over 50 and a Grandmother," by Georginna Conkling, *Motor*, January 1930:

"I was tired of waiting for crowded streetcars. If I wanted to visit my old home, I was obligated to travel three hours by train and boat, while if I had a car I could drive over in an hour, and take along my friends and all the bundles we pleased.

It was most embarrassing to have persons put themselves out to give me a lift. My friends felt that when they asked me to their homes they must also call for me and take me back. I would always insist upon having a taxi, but often it was late or lost the way.

I had expected to drive a car someday, and after a particularly trying experience when I needed one very much, I decided that because I was born in the nineteenth century there was no reason why I should not join the great American procession. That was one of the happiest and wisest decisions of my life.

I remember the day when an automobile was a 'horseless' vehicle, a terror to the countryside, and a doubtful experiment. Consequently, I have more respect for the motorcar than has the flapper, whose first thought is to go fast as possible or at least faster than the next car.

I wonder now how I could have ridden in automobiles for years and shown so little curiosity as to how they were managed. For that reason I had to begin with the first principles. I decided to take plenty of time to learn, fearing that if I attempted to drive alone before I was thoroughly familiar with the technique, I would lose my nerve and perhaps never drive.

It was my good fortune to find as a teacher a young college man who was firm, but sympathetic with my stupidity. He had the patience of Job. As soon as I learned to go a few feet, fearing all the time that the car with all that feel of power might get away from me, I insisted upon knowing how to stop. Then we made proper turnings and signals. I live in a region of hills and winding roads, a trying combination to master. We haunted real estate developments, going around and around the canna-planted, irregularly shaped islands at street intersections.

My teacher insisted upon everything being properly done. How particular he was about taking curves slowly and being on the right side of the road! I did one thing over and over until, fearing I was tired, he proposed a different problem. I was the only pupil he ever had who did not give the poor engine enough gas. That was the conservatism of age.

When we came to backing the car, it was like meeting the irregular verbs in French. I felt that we were going right across the country, and in my nervousness, stalled the engine.

After a while, we went daily up the faithful hill where the tests for licenses were given. My teacher made me stop the car and turn around. The road was highly crowded. Some days I did it perfectly, and then the next hit the curb and backed up too many times.

Then came the day to take the state test. No flapper could ever be as excited over that as I. She could not appreciate how big a thing I thought I was doing. went with the officer not to the high, crowded, steep hill, but luckily to an easier one a block away. While we were turning, I remembered my teacher and gave right of way to an old vegetable truck coming down. On a curved street where a white line marked the center, I kept carefully to the right of the mark, even though a parked car made this a little difficult. . . . All that happened a year ago. I had a new but low-priced car to learn with. It was but a short time before I wanted a bigger engine, one that would purr when I stepped on the gas. Now I have that car and bless the day I decided to drive it."

10,000 Miles and Not an Accident!

By
Georgianna Conkling

Over 50
and a
Grandmother

I Learned to DRIVE *and so can* YOU

"I don't have to wait for trolley cars now. And when I go to see friends or relatives I can have company on the way and take all the bundles I want."

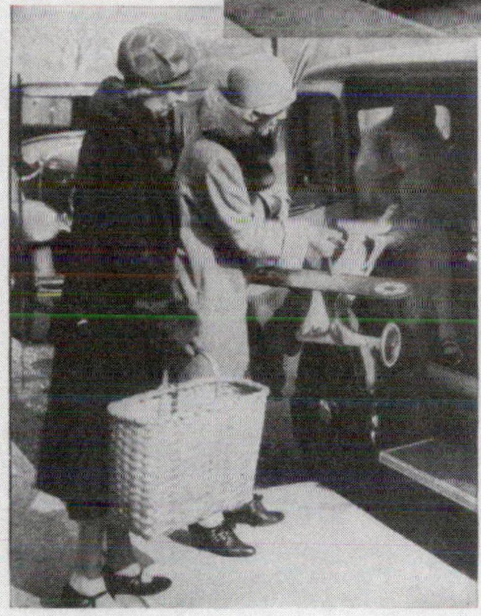

I WAS tired of waiting for crowded street cars. If I wanted to visit my old home, I was obliged to travel three hours by train and boat, while if I had a car I could drive over in an hour, and take along my friends and all the bundles we pleased.

It was most embarrassing to have persons put themselves out to give me a lift. My friends felt that when they asked me to their homes they must also call for me and take me back. I would always insist upon having a taxi, but often it was late or lost the way.

I had expected to drive a car some day, and after a particularly trying experience when I needed one very much, I decided that because I was born in the nineteenth century there was no reason why I should not join the great American procession. That was one of the happiest and wisest decisions of my life.

I remember the day when an automobile was a "horseless" vehicle, a terror to the countryside, and a doubtful experiment. Consequently I have more respect for the motor car than has the flapper, whose first thought is to go as fast as possible or at least faster than the next car.

I wonder now how I could have ridden in automobiles for years and shown so little curiosity as to how they were managed. For that reason I had to begin with the first principles.

I decided to take plenty of time to learn, fearing that if I attempted to drive alone before I was thoroughly familiar with the technique I would lose my nerve and perhaps never drive.

It was my good fortune to find as a teacher a young college man who was firm, but sympathetic with my stupidity. He had the patience of Job. As soon as I learned to go a few feet, fearing all the time that the car with all that feel of power might get away from me, I insisted upon knowing how to stop. That gave me confidence. Then we made proper turnings and signals. I live in a region of hills and winding roads, a trying combination to master. We haunted real estate developments, going around and around the canna planted, irregular shaped islands at street intersections.

MY teacher insisted upon everything being properly done. How particular he was about taking curves slowly and being on the right side of the road! I did one thing over and over until, fearing I was tired, he proposed a different problem. I was the only pupil he ever had who did not give the poor engine enough gas. That was the conservatism of age.

When we came to backing that car it was like meeting the irregular verbs in French. I felt that we were going right across the county, and in my nervousness, stalled the engine.

After a while we went daily up the faithful hill where the tests for licenses are given. My teacher made me stop the car and turn around. The road was highly crowned. Some days I did it perfectly, and then the next hit the curb and backed too many times.

THEN came the day to take the state test. No flapper could ever be as excited over that as I. She could not appreciate how big a thing I thought I was doing. I went with the officer, not to the high crowned steep hill, but luckily to an easier one a block away.

While we were turning I remembered my teacher and gave right of way to an old vegetable truck coming down. On a curved street where a white line marked the center I kept carefully to the right of the mark, even though a parked car made this a little difficult. At a right turn I slowed down and hugged the curb when we turned left I made a slow, wide swing. Perhaps the officer realized that grandma was not nervous and that was why he gave me my license the next day. But grandma would have been nervous had she not taken four weeks to practise with the agreeable young man.

All that happened a year ago. I had a new but low priced car to learn with. It was but a short time before I wanted a bigger engine, one that would purr when I stepped on the gas. Now I have that car and bless the day I decided to drive it.

I UNDERSTAND Lindbergh's "We," for my car and I have been alone over some of New England's famous trails and "we" are faithful friends. I do not think we are a nuisance on the road, or drive too slowly, though we rarely exceed 40 miles an hour, because we wish to enjoy the country. The sunset hour and moonlight inspire us, and we also enjoy coming home through lighted streets after spending the evening out. I am no longer dependent upon street cars, buses, or the taxi man, or a burden to my friends.

There must be many women who miss the thrill of sitting behind the wheel because they are afraid to try. It is easy to learn to drive provided one masters one operation after another, slowly but surely, and is determined not to be nervous. So I say to all women who think they would like to learn to drive:

Get a patient teacher and go ahead. Don't let your family talk you out of it. They may say you are too nervous or that you can never understand machinery. I know women who jump into their cars and drive out into the country to quiet nerves that have become ragged with home cares and problems. And as for machinery, who needs to know more than the mere rudiments of motor car construction to drive nowadays, with operating made so simple and with service stations at almost every corner, so it seems, to take care of maintenance?

There is thrill, there is independence in driving a car. I hope the women who read these words won't wait as long as I did before trying. And if you have waited, don't put it off any longer. The woman of today drives an automobile. Don't go on living in "yesterday."

And now, a final suggestion: You will want good company on your trips, but until you are very sure of yourself take along no "back seat drivers."

92 MOTOR for JANUARY 1930 93

1930–1939

Few workers escaped the devastating impact of America's longest, most severe depression in the nation's history. Banks failed, railways became insolvent, unemployment rose, factories closed, and foreign trade declined. Economic paralysis gripped the nation. By 1932, one in four Americans was jobless. One in every four farms was sold for taxes. Five thousand banks closed their doors, wiping out the lifetime savings of millions of average Americans. In urban areas, apple sellers appeared on street corners. Bread lines, as well as soup kitchens with lines snaking down the block, became common sights. People slept on park benches. The homeless wandered from city to city seeking work, only to rediscover the pervasive nature of the economic collapse. In some circles the American Depression was viewed as the fulfillment of Marxist prophecy—the inevitable demise of capitalism.

President Franklin D. Roosevelt thought otherwise. Backed by his New Deal promises and a focus on the "forgotten man," the president produced a swirl of government programs designed to lift the country out of its paralytic gloom.

Roosevelt's early social experiments were characterized by relief, recovery, and reform. Believing that the expansion of the United States economy was temporarily over, Roosevelt paid attention to better distribution of resources and planned production. The Civilian Conservation Corps (CCC), for example, put 250,000 jobless young men to work in the forests for $1.00 a day. By 1935, government deficit spending was spurring economic change. By 1937, total manufacturing output exceeded that of 1929; unfortunately, prices and wages rose too quickly and the economy dipped again in 1937, driven by inflation fears and restrictions on bank lending. Nonetheless, many roads, bridges, public buildings, dams, and trees became part of the landscape thanks to federally employed workers. The Federal Theatre Project, for example, employed 1,300 people during the period, reaching 25 million attendees with more than 1,200 productions. Despite progress, 10 million workers were still unemployed in 1938 and farm prices lagged behind manufacturing progress. Full recovery would not occur until the United States mobilized for World War II.

While the nation suffered from economic blows, the West was being whipped by nature. Gigantic billowing clouds of dust up to 10,000 feet high swept across the parched Western Plains throughout the 'thirties. Sometimes the blows came with lightning and booming thunder, but often they were described as being "eerily slight, blackening everything in their path." All human activity halted. Planes were grounded. Buses and trains stalled, unable to race clouds that could move at speeds of more than 100 miles per hour. On the morning of May 9, 1934, the wind began to blow up the topsoil of Montana and Wyoming, and soon some 350 million tons were sweeping eastward. By late afternoon, 12 million tons had been deposited in Chicago. By noon the next day, Buffalo, New York, was dark with dust. Even the Atlantic Ocean was no barrier. Ships 300 miles out to sea found dust on their decks. During the remainder of 1935, there were more than 40 dust storms that reduced visibility to less than one mile. There were 68 more storms in 1936, 72 in 1937, and 61 in 1938. On the High Plains, 10,000 houses were simply abandoned, and nine million acres of farm turned back to nature. Banks offered mortgaged properties for as little as $25 for 160 acres and found no takers.

The people of the 1930s excelled in escape. Radio matured as a mass medium, creating stars such as Jack Benny, Bob Hope, and Fibber McGee and Molly. For a time it seemed that every child was copying the catch phrase of radio's Walter Winchell, "Good evening, Mr. and Mrs. America, and all the ships at sea," or pretending to be Jack Benny when shouting, "Now, cut that out!" Soap operas captured large followings and sales of magazines like *Screenland* and *True Story* skyrocketed. Each edition of *True Confessions* sold 7.5 million copies. Nationwide, movie theaters prospered as 90 million Americans attended the "talkies" every week, finding comfort in the uplifting excitement of movies and movie stars. Big bands made swing the king of the decade, while jazz came into its own. And the social experiment known as Prohibition died in December 1933, when the Twenty-first Amendment swept away the restrictions against alcohol ushered in more than a decade earlier.

Attendance at professional athletic events declined during the decade, but softball became more popular than ever and golf began its drive to become a national passion as private courses went public. Millions listened to boxing on radio, especially the exploits of the "Brown Bomber," Joe Louis. As average people coped with the difficult times, they married later, had fewer children, and divorced less. Extended families often lived under one roof; opportunities for women and minorities were particularly limited. Survival, not affluence, was often the practical goal of the family. A disillusioned nation, which had worshipped the power of business, looked instead toward a more caring government.

During the decade, United Airlines hired its first airline stewardess to allay passengers' fears of flying. The circulation of *Reader's Digest* climbed from 250,000 to eight million before the decade ended and *Esquire*, the first magazine for men, was launched. The early days of the decade gave birth to Hostess Twinkies, Bird's Eye frozen vegetables, windshield wipers, photoflash bulbs, and pinball machines. By the time the Depression and the 1930s drew to a close, Zippo lighters, Frito's corn chips, talking books for the blind, beer in cans, and the Richter scale for measuring earthquakes had all been introduced. Despite the ever-increasing role of the automobile in the mid-1930s, Americans still spent $1,000 a day on buggy whips.

1931 Family Profile

The Beltran family lives in Camden, New Jersey, where Kenneth Beltran is working in secret on the development of television for RCA-Victor Company. Many believe that television will replace radio in the next few years. Kenneth and his wife, Celeste, have no children.

Annual Income: $6,600

Annual Budget

The average per capita consumer expenditures in 1931 for all workers nationwide are:

Auto Parts	$3.22
Auto Usage	$24.01
Clothing	$32.01
Dentists	$3.22
Furniture	$6.44
Gas and Oil	$12.08
Health Insurance	$0.81
Housing	$84.58
Intercity Transport	$2.42
Local Transport	$7.25
New Auto Purchase	$8.86
Personal Business	$25.78
Personal Care	$8.05
Physicians	$6.44
Private Education and Research	$5.64
Recreation	$26.58
Religion/Welfare Activities	$5.64
Telephone and Telegraph	$4.83

Kenneth Beltran is working with Dr. Vladimir Zworykin.

Several companies, and inventors, are competing to control the patents on television.

Tobacco	$12.08
Utilities	$22.55
Per Capita Consumption	$487.73

Life at Home

- The family lives in Camden, New Jersey, where Kenneth works for RCA-Victor Company on developing television.
- Quiet by nature, he does not discuss his work; Celeste believes he is still involved in improving the sound transmission of radio.
- He has been working on his current assignment for two years, and has been told never to discuss what he is doing.
- RCA wants to delay the introduction of television to the public until it has perfected the receiver and controls the patents.
- For the past two years, RCA has been declaring publicly "television, as it stands today, cannot by the wildest stretch of the imagination be declared a public service for the benefit of the vast audience which radio broadcasting has won."
- Currently, individual inventors and innovators outside RCA are pushing for faster introduction, as the public is demanding television.
- For the first time, RCA is beginning to acknowledge the potential commercial benefit of television.
- This couple lives in a cottage home with two bedrooms; they have discussed children but he insists he is too busy right now.
- He has little interest in yard work, baseball, fishing, or taking rides in the country; "Work is my recreation," he loves to say.
- Active in her church, Celeste recently sponsored a tea at her home for Margaret Winslett, a missionary from China who is home on furlough.
- She also serves on the membership committee of the Junior Service League, whose work is focused on helping the children of men who are temporarily out of work due to the current economic downturn.
- Recently, she has been buying clams, which sell for $0.25 a peck, from unemployed factory workers who are now digging clams to support their families.
- She has noticed that many of the unemployed, along with their families, spend considerable time at the newly introduced double feature movies, and wonders if they are lazy or simply trying to escape.
- Many of the new films feature gangsters and monsters, hardly the type of entertainment suitable for children.

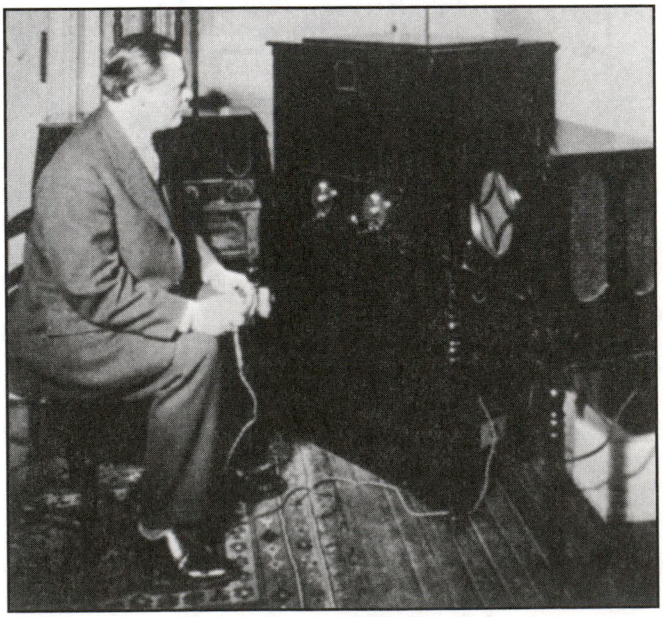

There is intense pressure to be the first to develop working television.

Life at Work

- Kenneth is working with Dr. Vladimir Zworykin to perfect the cathode ray tube system of scanning for RCA-Victor Company.
- If the new technology can be created, the patent rights will be worth millions to RCA-Victor.
- Currently, many independent inventors are working on similar projects; a 24-year-old youth named Philo Farnsworth from Los Angeles is working on similar technology.
- The pressure to be first is intense; secrecy is paramount while RCA works on a plan to create a 400-line screen that will provide better detail.
- Currently, television stations are broadcasting either a 45-line screen or 60-line screen.
- The more advanced 60-line screen is composed of 3,600 little dots of varying light and shadow intensity; even with enhanced illumination, the 60-line screen leaves much detail on the screen to the imagination.
- Another inventor, 25-year-old U.A. Sanabria, recently demonstrated a projection method that provides 6' x 6' images.
- Instead of employing 60 to 75 impulses to each stripe, Sanabria varies the light up to 400 times, but the exact details are being kept secret; the Shortwave Corporation, with whom Sanabria is consulting, has insured his life for $2 million.

Image projection allows for a larger picture.

- The majority of television receivers show an image from 3" x 5" to 8" x 8".
- With the use of a projector, it is possible to increase the image to 2' x 2'.
- Projection causes a loss in definition and illumination; some engineers believe the larger size makes up for a lack of sharpness.
- A new light cell, which makes possible a black-and-white picture rather than a pinkish hue on the screen, was recently introduced by Dr. Alexanderson of the General Electric Company.
- A key element of many experiments is the cathode ray, a form of electrical discharge that can be produced in a thin, pencil-like stream; unfortunately, the life of the tube is short, rarely lasting longer than 200 hours.
- All of the television equipment manufacturers are now preparing to sell stock, raise capital for expansion, and capture the current TV craze.
- Many believe the future of television will be defined by RCA when it brings out its long-awaited television set in 1932.
- Television sets currently on the market, made by Shortwave and Television Corporation of Boston, the Jenkins Television Corporation of Passaic, New Jersey, and the Western Television Corporation of Chicago, sell for $125 to $300.
- Teams of engineers are employed on the project; already, more than $500,000 has been spent to develop television experimental broadcasting and receiving units.
- RCA and affiliates currently hold experimental licenses to 11 of the 29 proposals.
- Lawsuits are also in vogue; currently, competitors have filed damage suits against RCA—which dominates the radio field—totaling $48 million charging unfair competition.

Dr. C.B. Jolliffe, chief engineer of the Federal Radio Commission, 1931:

"In the opinion of the engineers, television is still in an experimental stage. Every time you see anything about television in the papers today, something is bound to be said about 'great progress,' or 'revolutionary invention.' The greatest progress I have noticed in the past few months has been in publicity. The basic principles of present-day television were laid down several years ago, but progress seems faster now because engineers are making refinements to those basic principles. The progress of television is steady and normal, with nothing unusual about it, not even the statement that recognition (by the Federal Radio Commission) is just around the corner."

"Television, Is It Getting Anywhere?" by George Tichenor, *The Forum*, October 1931:

"A variety of programs are regularly broadcast, with sound accompaniment. There have been Helen Morgan, Vera Hurst, George Gershwin, Sigmund Spaeth, and others in individual appearances. Jimmy McLaunin, boxer, and Ray Steele, wrestler, were interviewed. A fashion show was staged by W2XCR, with six models parading before the camera. Boxing bouts, fencing, golf lessons, and even piano lessons have been scheduled. From its Passaic station, W2XCD, the DeForest Company conducted the first band concert by remote control. The concert was given by the police band at their headquarters. The Commissioner of Public Safety led the movements before the transmitter in the studio. His Lieutenant in the concert hall followed the directions as he viewed them in the receiver, and a sound radio hook-up brought the music back to the studio so the Commissioner could take up his lead.

The Jenkins studio once broadcast pictures that were received on the *Ile de France*, but the Shortwave and Television Corporation of Boston outshowmanshipped its rival by sending to the *Leviathan*, which is, of course, a larger boat. The Chicago Daily News station, W9XAP, claims to have broadcast the first sight and sound play, with WMAW as a sound outlet. The air talk was presented in movie style: close-ups, without a break in the dialogue. Station W2XCW, of Schenectady, New York, on 20,000 watts, has sent out images received in Germany."

- Radio, in its early days, passed through a similar phase.
- General James G. Harbord, chairman of the board of RCA, says television will play a role in business: "A great corporation whose directorate is scattered across the continent suddenly needs a meeting of its board of directors. Buzzers buzz, wires hum, and bells ring in a dozen distant cities. The call goes out. The hour is named. Switches are thrown and at the appointed time, say perhaps an hour after the call was issued, a quorum is assembled by electricity and called to order by the chairman."
- Under Harbord's vision, a television meeting would require a television set in each man's office, and each could see and hear all of the other members of the group just as though all were present in the same room.
- Harbord believes that businessmen at the meeting will be able to affix their signatures and facsimiles could be flashed back to the chairman before the board meeting adjourned.
- Another use of television will be purchasing; at a designated time, "great stores" can display their wares over the television and using telephones, companies can order what they need instantly.
- This innovation will eliminate salesmen's travel time and expense; some believe actors will become important to the television sales process.

"Says Big Business Threatens Society, Prof. Wormser Likens Nation to a Frankenstein Facing Its Own Destruction," *New York Times*, October 24, 1931:

"'Modern American Society is a Frankenstein which has built new and mighty monsters in the shape of a corporation of unrestrained power, which now threatens to destroy its creator,' I. Maurice Wormser, professor of law at Fordham University and editor of the *New York Law Journals*, declares in his book, *Frankenstein Incorporated*. It is a study of the corporate wills of the United States and suggested remedies for them. . . . Professor Wormser wants immediate steps taken to prevent the 'overpowering' of American society by big business. He says there should be created by the federal government a board of five highly paid members invested with the power to approve or disapprove trade agreements and mergers and with the right to subsequent scrutiny and supervision of the operation for the public good. This agency, he goes on to say, would clear the way for health business mergers of public benefit and would clarify the Sherman and Clayton antitrust laws in their application to business agreements and mergers."

Life in the Community: Camden, New Jersey

- Camden, like much of New Jersey, is connected to water; it is located on the Delaware River, across from Philadelphia, Pennsylvania.
- The smallest of the Mid-Atlantic states, New Jersey's history has been shaped by heavy manufacturing and by its proximity to New York City and Philadelphia.
- The first tunnel under the Hudson River was constructed between Jersey City and New York, and was opened by the Hudson and Manhattan Railroad Company in 1908.
- In 1921, the world's second radio station, WJZ, was founded in Newark, New Jersey.
- Recently, advertisements began appearing concerning the occupancy of the new Continental Bank building at 30 Broad Street, opposite the N.Y. Stock Exchange buildings; the advertisements state "the prestige of tenancy will be accorded only to those who through position and standing are suitable as neighbors for this important institution."
- In West Orange, New Jersey, efforts are under way to complete the last great experiments of Thomas A. Edison, who recently died; his son has announced that in the last month of Edison's life, Goldenrod yielded a product that could be vulcanized into rubber.
- New Jersey trade groups are fighting the planned increase of intrastate freight rates, which will be based on rate groupings within the state instead of on a straight mileage basis.
- The effects of the economic depression are hitting all aspects of society, even college football; promised athletic scholarships across the nation are being withdrawn.
- American hero Charles Lindbergh built a house commonly dubbed a "Nest for the Lone Eagle," in a secluded area of New Jersey.

Historical Snapshot
1931

- As the full effect of the depression took hold, the national income dropped 33 percent in two years; payrolls were off 40 percent
- Unemployment reached eight million, or 15.9 percent, inflation was at -4.4 percent, and the gross national product at -16 percent
- For the first time, emigration exceeded immigration; John Reed Clubs, named after the American communist who died in Moscow, formed in many cities
- Car sales collapsed as one million auto workers were laid off; Ford Motor Company halted production of the Model A
- 2,294 banks closed
- As the sale of glass jars for canning increased, sales of canned goods declined
- The rate of admissions to state mental hospitals tripled in 1930-1931 over the 1922-1930 period
- More than 75 percent of all cities banned the employment of wives
- To produce more jobs and reduce unemployment, the National Forty-Hour Work Week League formed, calling for an eight-hour workday
- Major James Doolittle flew from Ottawa to Mexico City in a record 11 hours and 45 minutes; as recently as 1927, Charles Lindbergh had astonished the nation with his 27-hour flight from Washington to Mexico City.
- Pope Pius XI posed for the first telephoto picture to be transmitted from the Vatican; the transmission of the picture from Rome to Paris took 10 minutes
- To generate income, Nevada legalized both gambling and the six-month divorce
- Nearly 6,000 cases of infantile paralysis struck New York; many cities experienced partial quarantines
- Farmers attempted to stop hordes of invading grasshoppers with electrified fences; 160,000 miles of America's finest farmlands were destroyed by the insect invaders
- Alka-Seltzer was introduced by Miles Laboratories
- Chicago gangster Al Capone was convicted of evading $231,000 in federal taxes
- Clairol hair products were introduced by U.S. chemists
- New York's Waldorf-Astoria Hotel was opened
- Silent film extra Clark Gable appeared in the movie *A Free Soul*, gaining instant stardom, while Universal studios recruited Bette Davis

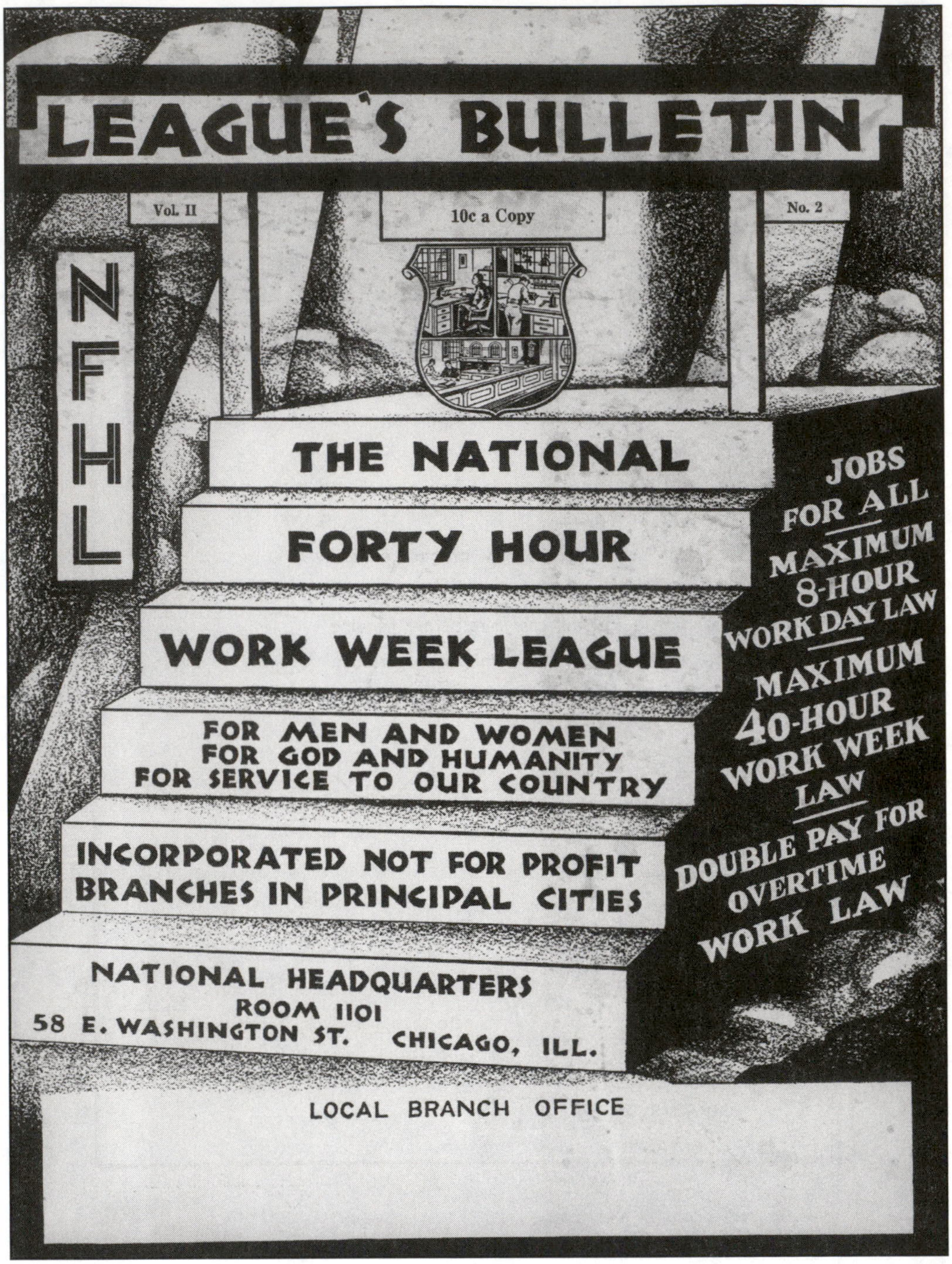

1931 Economic Profile

Income, Standard Jobs

Average of All Industries, Excluding Farm Labor $1,406

Average of All Industries, Including Farm Labor $1,298

Bituminous Coal Mining $723
Building Trades. $907
Domestics $584
Farm Labor. $355
Federal Civilian $1,895
Federal Employees,
Executive Departments $1,549
Federal Military. $1,164
Finance, Insurance, and Real Estate $1,858
Gas and Electricity Workers $1,600
Manufacturing, Durable Goods $1,127
Manufacturing, Nondurable Goods. . . . $1,352
Medical/Health Services Workers $919
Miscellaneous Manufacturing $1,230
Motion Picture Services. $2,175
Nonprofit Organization Workers $1,653
Passenger Transportation
Workers, Local and Highway $1,500
Personal Services $1,136
Public School Teachers $1,463
Radio Broadcasting. $2,732
Railroads $1,661
State and Local Government Workers . . $1,497
Telephone and Telegraph Workers $1,436
Wholesale and Retail Trade Workers . . . $1,495

Selected Prices

Ames 3-Star Shovels, per Dozen $25.00
Aristo Golf Balls $0.59
Brown and Sharpe Hair Clippers $3.87
Croquet Set $3.98
Fargo, 20 Double Early Tulips $1.10
Galvanized Fire Pails, per Dozen $8.55
Jonathan Apples, 100 per Box $3.25
King Fisher Black Wonder
Fishing Line $1.35
Line-O-Graph Highway Traffic &
Safety Zone Marks $150.00
Mary T. Goldman Hair
Color Treatment $1.29
Pacquin's Hand Cream $0.74
Patapar Cookery Parchment. $0.10
Rogers Bros. Silver-Plate
Flatware, 26 Pieces $28.45
Spear-Cap Bottle Opener
and Resealer $0.10
Stanley Atha Plain Face
Adze Eye Hammer. $1.50
Starrett Wrenches, Complete Set. $15.00

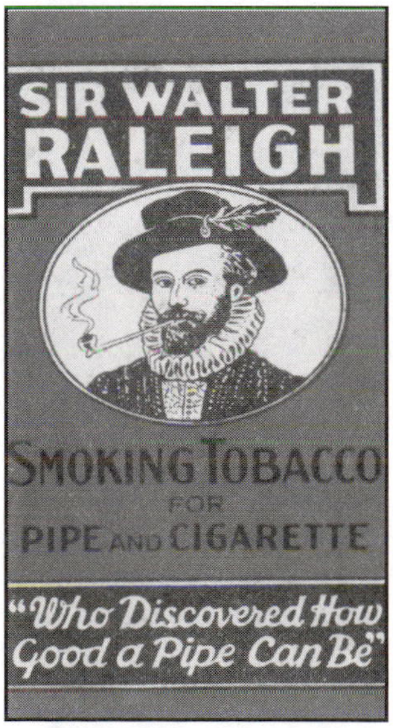

Steel Highway Flare Torches, per Dozen $24.00
Tobrin Machinist's Screwdriver, per Dozen $10.00
Viscol Dressing Leather Treatment, per Dozen $2.23
Windsor Seminole Five-Burner Kerosene Range $28.95

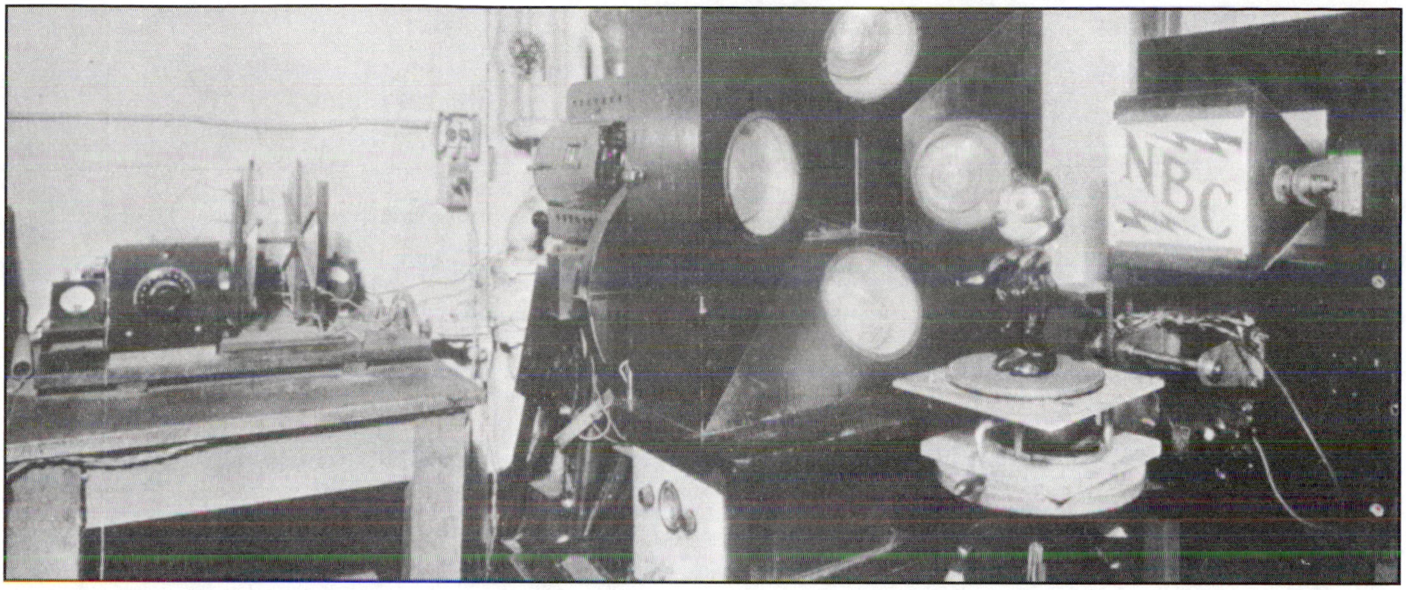

Television in 1931

- Currently, 15,000 television receivers operated nationwide; *Forbes Magazine* predicted the number would be 100,000 by 1932.
- In the public's mind, television was vaguely the process of seeing things with a radio set.
- Television stations in New York, Chicago, Boston, and Washington were offering synchronized audio-visual broadcasting on a regular schedule.
- License applications for experimental stations were "flooding" the Federal Radio Commission, according to news reports; only temporary licenses were being issued until a commercially practical television network could be demonstrated.
- Three manufacturers were marketing reliable receiving sets; a dozen more companies were now being formed.
- Applicants for a license to operate an experimental television station were asked to appear in person before the Federal Radio Commission to prove they were bona fide experimenters and had a program that would lead to the improvement of "radio art," a laboratory capable of transmitting visual images, and the financial backing to make it all work.
- Currently, 29 experimental licenses were in effect, mostly stations affiliated with the Radio Corporation of America and the National Broadcasting Company.
- Of the 150 patents covering television, Charles Jenkins of the Jenkins Corporation controlled 58; the Jenkins Corporation was controlled by the DeForest Radio Corporation.
- The Commission assigned four channels for television, between 2,000 and 3,000 kilocycles.
- The visual broadcast and reception of a television were comparable with the early crystal set days of radio a decade earlier.
- Talking pictures made up the main part of the programming in most cities.
- When live entertainment was shown, it was by necessity short; the intense lighting necessary for television prohibited artists from being in the heat glare for long periods.
- David Sarnoff, president of the Radio Corporation of America (RCA), said television "is still in the laboratory stage; National Broadcasting Company does not plan to market a television unit until 1932."

"Television Draws 1,700 to Theatre, Images Generally Clear," *New York Times*, October 23, 1931:

"More than 1,700 persons visited the Broadway Theatre yesterday morning to see on a large screen television images flashed by wire lines from an improvised stage in the lobby of the Theatre Guild Playerhouse, a few hundred yards' distance. The audience displayed a keen interest in the demonstration. Except for bursts of spontaneous applause at the ends of the feature presentations, the spectators were completely absorbed in the mysteries of the new science of seeing by electrical means. For the most part, the images were clear enough to afford recognition of a well-known face.

Only once was it necessary to interrupt the show; the operator turned off the mechanism for a few minutes to allow the glow tube in the receiver to cool. During the lull in the scheduled program, Carveth Wells, who served as master of ceremonies, told about the television mechanism. He made it clear that while television is still in a process of development, the Broadway management desired to place on record its conviction that the new art has reached the point where it can command recognition from the theatres.

One feature presented was part of a scene from a current Broadway production. The players were Margaret Barker and Franchot Tone. The images flashed on a screen 10 feet square simultaneously with the sound of their voices reproduced by loudspeakers. Emily Day, formerly soprano of the National Grand Opera of Mexico, Carl Paul Ican, Indian baritone of the Philadelphia Grand Opera Company, and Ruth Burns, New York actress, did the singing. . . . The system used was that developed by Ulisses A. Sanabria, chief engineer of Sanabria Television of Chicago."

- Currently, National Broadcasting Company (NBC) and Columbia Broadcasting System (CBS) were considered the most likely companies to dominate television hook-ups in the future.
- Competitors Western Television Corporation and the Shortwave and Television Corporation both believed television had arrived, and that they would be players.
- Carl H. Henrikson, research assistant at Chicago University, recently said that he thinks television will be used to broadcast stock market quotes.
- Others believed that the broadcasting of major news events would be the most important role of television in the future.
- Some were discussing the ways that television broadcasts could be captured on a record at home and played back when the viewer had more time.
- The inspiration for television came in 1873 when an Atlantic cable operator named Willoughby Smith noticed his instruments acting in a peculiar manner.
- He traced the cause to his selenium insulators.
- Selenium was used as a high resistance to electricity at that time, and the operator noticed that when the sun shone onto the selenium, the needle on the instrument moved.
- The discovery gave science its first clue to the photocell, which is the heart of visual transmission; selenium became the first electric eye.
- In 1884, a Russian conceived the idea of television and invented the scanning disk, which broke up the picture into component parts of varying light and shadow.

"You Are Invited to Join the *G-E Circle*," by Grace Ellis:

"A new and different General Electric radio program, sponsored by Grace Ellis, a graceful new radio personality, is based on the idea of bringing to American women a new appreciation of the advantages and conveniences which they enjoy through our American Standard of Living. Emphasizing the importance of the conveniences that the electrical industry has made to the convenience and comfort of modern life, the program also is designed to bring definite, practical help and inspiration for the woman who is working at the job of homemaking.

The program is called the *G-E Circle* and is built around a definite club idea, with Grace Ellis as the director of the *G-E Circle*. Thousands of letters already received attest to the quick response which women have made to this helpful program. Every weekday except Saturday, at noon, Eastern Standard Time, the *G-E Circle* goes on the air over the NBC coast-to-coast network of 54 stations.

And every Sunday evening at the *Twilight Hour* Grace Ellis again assembles the *G-E Circle* for the benefit of the whole family. This Sunday evening meeting of the *G-E Circle* brings a new program of outstanding entertainment value—the great stars of the Metropolitan Opera singing those simple melodies whose beauty and sentiment have made them dear to all of us. Just think of the privilege that this Sunday program is bringing—the finest voices in the world singing the favorite songs of the world. The home sets the tone of the family life. And it is the homemaker who sets the tone of the home. General Electric hopes, through the *G-E Circle*, to give homemakers a new enthusiasm for their great profession."

- In 1925, C. Francis Jenkins, the father of the television and pioneer of the movie projector, demonstrated his innovation in Washington, D.C.
- Two years later, the Bell Laboratories and AT&T successfully demonstrated one-way television by wire and radio from Washington and Whippany, New Jersey, to New York.
- By April 1930, they had perfected two-way television.
- With the perfection of the television receiver in 1931, it was expected that two-way long-distance television would be part of the regular telephone service in the near future.
- For technical reasons, television broadcasts through private telephone wires currently were not possible, but under discussion.

The 1930 U.S. Census listed the following occupations under "Professional Persons"; nationwide, this category constituted six percent of all jobs.

	Male	Female
Actors and Showmen	54,411	20,785
Architects	21,621	379
Artists, Sculptors, and Teachers of Art	35,621	21,644
Authors, Editors, and Reporters	46,922	17,371
Chemists, Assayers, and Metallurgists	45,163	1,905
Chiropractors	9,203	2,713
Clergymen	145,572	3,276
College Presidents and Professors	41,774	20,131
Dentists	69,768	1287
Designers, Draftsmen, and Inventors	93,518	9,212
Healers	7,866	9,774
Lawyers, Judges, and Justices	157,220	3,385
Musicians and Teachers of Music	85,517	79,611
Osteopaths	4,554	1,563
Photographers	31,163	8,366
Physicians and Surgeons	146,978	6,825
Religious Workers	11,339	19,951
Teachers	202,337	860,287
Technical Engineers	226,136	113
Trained Nurses	5,452	288,737
Veterinary Surgeons	11,852	11

"World Ills Laid to Machine by Einstein in Berlin Speech," *New York Times*, October 22, 1931:

"Discussing the effects of national science on man's life, Professor Albert Einstein in a lecture tonight deplored the fact that the industrial technique, which was meant to serve the world's progress by liberating mankind from the slavery of labor, was now about to overwhelm its creators. He characterized the great distress of the present times as the result of domination by man-made machines, but blamed technique not as much as lack of organization in economic and social life, the stabilization of which is one of the chief tasks of the present time."

Social-Economic Status of Gainful Workers, 1930, U.S. Department of Commerce, Bureau of the Census:

"During the 20-year period from 1910 to 1930, some significant changes were taking place in the social-economic distribution of gainful workers. The professional class increased rapidly—from 4.3 percent of the total workers in 1910 to six percent in 1930. Farmers decreased strikingly from 16.1 to 12.3 percent of the total. The clerical group increased more rapidly than any other social-economic group—from 10 percent of the total workers in 1919 to 16.3 percent in 1930. The relative importance of skilled workers and foremen increased somewhat between 1910 and 1920, and then decreased between 1920 and 1930. Between 1910 and 1930, the proportion of the total male workers in the semiskilled group increased from 11.1 percent to 14.3 percent, but the proportion of the total female workers in this group decreased from 27.1 to 23.5 percent. . . . These statistics show striking differences among the several states, and also among cities, in the distribution of the workers by social-economic groups. For example, they show that the proportions which male professional persons formed of all male workers ranged from 1.9 percent in Mississippi to 5.7 percent in California and 9.6 percent in the District of Columbia; they ranged from four percent in Cleveland, Ohio, to 8.5 percent in Los Angeles, California. . . The proportion of the total female workers engaged in professional pursuits in 1930 was over twice as high for native whites as for foreign-born whites, and over five times as high for native whites as Negroes."

But He's Getting Over It

The Elephant and the Mouse

Famous Wardway DeLuxe Gyrator
TRADE MARK
at the LOWEST PRICE in History!
1930 PRICE $86.50
1931 PRICE $69.95
OUR 60th ANNIVERSARY PRICE
$57.95
Cash Price
3-FIN AGITATOR
The secret of Wardway's greater efficiency. Combines back-and-forth and lift-and-drop motions. The most thorough washing action known. Eliminates center post. Does not tangle clothes.
Tested and Approved by Good Housekeeping Institute
GOOD HOUSEKEEPING MAGAZINE
Try It in YOUR Home!
Big 60th Anniversary Sale Special!
Greatest Washer Value in America!
Never before has a Washer of this quality been sold at anywhere near this low price! It's the genuine Wardway DeLuxe—exactly the same machine sold in 1931 for $69.95—in 1930 for $86.50. Now Ward's brings the price down to meet today's lower incomes. Unequalled in beauty—unequalled in performance! Twice winner of the National "Whiteness Tests" against 5 other nationally known machines selling for $90 to $165! An extraordinary value! Try it for 30 days in your own home. If it is not all we claim—send it back and your money will be refunded including all transportation charges.
Has the Features of $165 Washers
The famous 3-Fin Agitator: Because of reasons listed above, puts more surge into the water and whips up heavier suds, washing quicker and whiter. The Extra-Large Tub, 21 inches across and 17 inches deep, holds 6 to 8 large sheets. Your choice of ivory porcelain enamel fused on Armco iron or solid polished copper, nickel-plated inside. Both models are easy to keep clean and are so easy to operate. Lovell Wringer locking in 6 positions has no superior. Balloon rolls 12 inches long and full 2¼-inch diameter. Instantaneous safety release. ¼ H.P. splash-proof motor is strong, dependable, and easily accessible. Operates washer and wringer at same time. Drive Shaft has leak-proof housing, runs for months without oiling. V-Belt Drive gives full power. All working parts enclosed. Leak-proof Marine Gland insures against water leaking into motor. Self-adjusting Extra large swivel casters; big oversize faucet; heavy water-tight cover.
Remember the Wardway De Luxe is the product of one of America's finest factories whose product is nationally advertised and sold at much higher prices. The Wardway has been tested by Good Housekeeping Institute and bears their official approval shown above at left.
Choice of Copper or Porcelain Tub
Either model comes equipped with regular motor for 105 to 120-volt, 60-cycle A C. Special motor for any other voltage or current $4 extra. When ordering give full information on your meter or state make and voltage of Farm Lighting Plant. Shipped Not Prepaid from our stock or factory in Cleveland, Ohio, whichever is nearer you. Ship. wt. 185 lbs. Estimated freight charges: 150 miles $1.20; 300 miles $1.42; 500 miles $2.22; 750 miles $3.24; 1000 miles $4.13.
186 U 2990—With PORCELAIN TUB.
Cash Sale Price $57.95
Easy Payment Price: $5 with order and $6.50 a month 63.45
186 U 2992—With Solid COPPER TUB.
Cash Sale Price $59.95
Easy Payment Price: $5 with order and $6.50 a month 65.45
$5 DOWN ... 30-DAY TRIAL!

1937 Family Profile

After more than a dozen moves to various parishes around the state, the Merriwether family has settled in Huntington, West Virginia, where James Merriwether is a district superintendent for the Methodist Church. He and his wife, Edie, have four children.

Annual Income: $1,800

Annual Budget

The average per capita consumer expenditures in 1937 for all workers nationwide are:

Auto Parts	$3.10
Auto Usage	$41.87
Clothing	$42.65
Dentists	$3.10
Furniture	$6.98
Gas and Oil	$16.28
Health Insurance	$0.78
Housing	$68.24
Intercity Transport	$3.10
Local Transport	$6.98
New Auto Purchase	$15.51
Personal Business	$25.59
Personal Care	$7.75
Physicians	$6.16
Private Education	$4.65
Recreation	$26.36
Religion/Welfare Activities	$6.98
Telephone and Telegraph	$3.88
Tobacco	$13.18
Utilities	$23.26
Per Capita Consumption	$517.21

The Merriwethers' house is a parsonage provided by the Church.

While working for a newspaper, he received the call to the ministry.

Life at Home

- Born on January 1, 1873, the second of four children, James Merriwether grew up near Washington Crossing, New Jersey.
- He quit school in the third grade because of his father's financial misfortune, and was sent to live and work on a neighboring farm.
- After the farm failed, his father began to manage the estate of the Cadwalders, a wealthy family.
- As a teenager, James left the farm and went to Trenton, New Jersey, where he worked in a brickyard and later as a typesetter for the newspaper.
- When he was in his early twenties, he took a job writing for the Trenton newspaper, eventually becoming its city editor.
- While at the newspaper, he received "the call" and decided to attend seminary.
- He enrolled in Princeton University and bought a grocery store to support himself; to pay for college, his brother ran the store, which was later sold to the Redfronts chain.
- James's wife, Edie, was born in 1880; one of five children, she grew up working in the small grocery store her family owned.

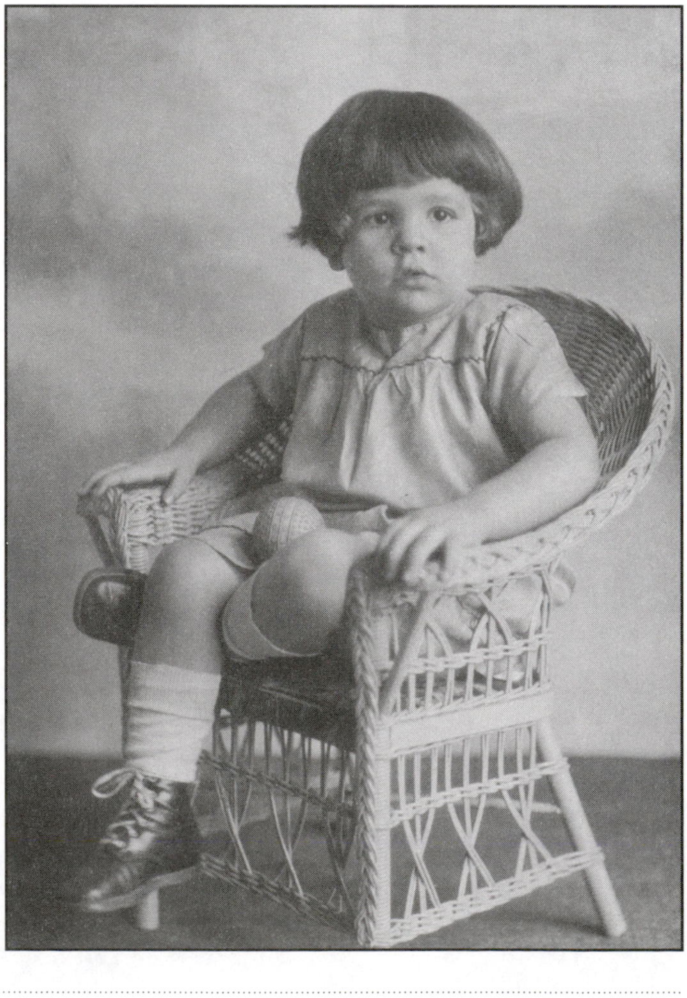

- As a child, she suffered from scarlet fever, then brain fever; as a result she lost all her hair and suffered a hearing loss for most of her life.
- This couple met at church; as a teenager, Edie decided she was going to marry James, even though he was eight years older.
- After he graduated from Princeton, the bishop of the Methodist Church in New Jersey asked him to go to West Virginia to minister to the men working in the coal mines.
- In 1899, he moved to Mingo County, home of the famous Hatfields and the McCoys.
- He made $125 his first year.
- The couple became engaged before he left for West Virginia and were married on December 25, 1901.
- Shortly after their marriage, they moved to Monongalia County, West Virginia; a child was born in 1903 when he was 30 and she was 23.
- By 1937, James has served in 11 churches and is now district superintendent for the West Virginia Methodist Church.
- The Methodist church is the largest denomination in West Virginia.
- Often away from home traveling for the church, James sometimes wakes up the entire family when he returns home to fix French toast and celebrate his return.
- Ever clever with words, before a meal he will often tell the children, "I don't know how I'm going to get outside of this"; after a meal he might remark, "I feel of fullness."
- Edie is the disciplinarian in the family; at mealtimes she uses a stick to whack the children if they misbehave—the same stick she uses to keep order when they go for a ride in the car.
- Their house, a parsonage provided by the church, is a two-story cottage with three bedrooms upstairs and a living room, dining room, kitchen, and back porch downstairs.
- The living room is furnished with a piano, a couch called a divan, a rocking chair, and an overstuffed chair.
- Family sing-alongs around the piano are a standard entertainment; songs include both religious ballads and popular secular songs.
- To assist Edie, a woman has been hired to help with the cleaning; they work together.
- Mondays are reserved for washing, using one tub to wash and one to rinse; Tuesdays are for ironing—they still rely on heated irons; Thursday is baking day and Saturday is for cleaning the house, including taking the rugs out and beating them.
- On Wednesday nights, the family attends prayer meetings; they attend church twice on Sundays.

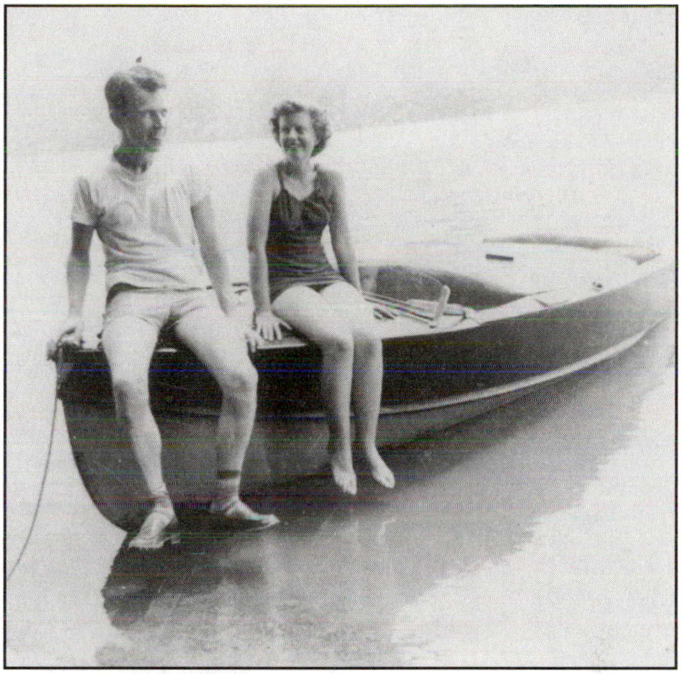

The Merriwethers enjoy spending time swimming at Ritter Park.

Mickey Mouse helps sell ice cream.

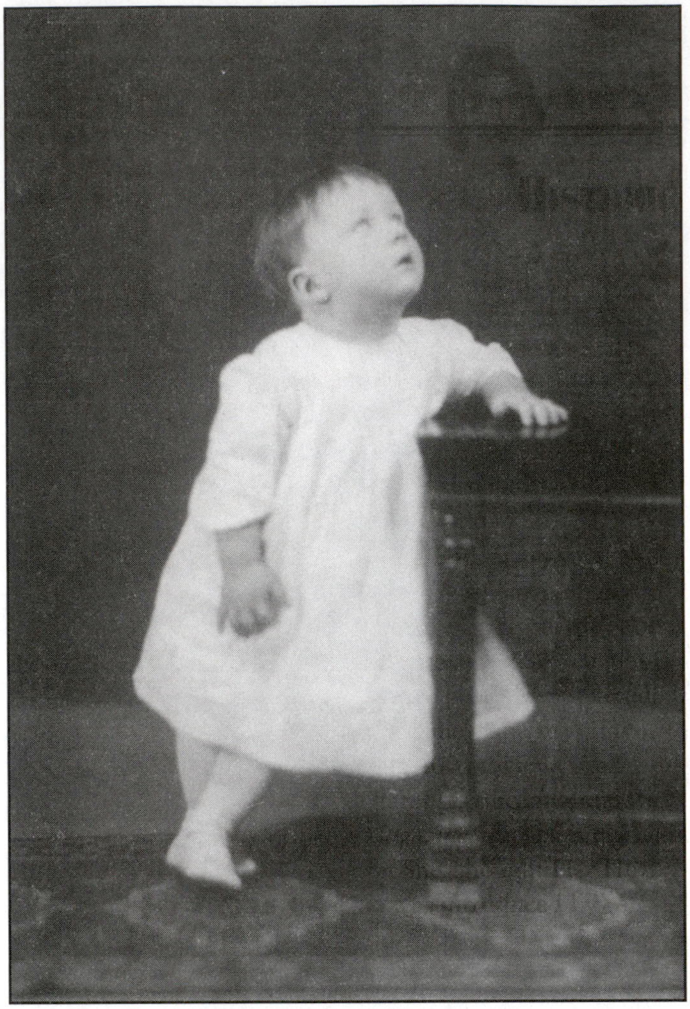

James was the second of four children.

Games are popular in the Merriwether house.

- Since no work is done on Sundays, the afternoon meal is prepared on Saturday; the children do not play cards, and Edie does not use any electrical equipment, such as a vacuum cleaner, on that day.
- The family gets little of its food from the store, though the children relish getting "store-bought bread."
- Edie and the girls make their own clothing, from the cotton shirtwaist tops they often wear, to three-piece suits.
- The boys wear three-piece suits to church; the man is always dressed in a black suit with a dark Fedora hat.
- Going to the Anderson-Newcomb department store is a special treat for the family.
- The girls enjoy collecting paper doll figures and dresses from the Sunday newspaper; they now have dozens of dolls and doll dresses.
- The boys love to play a game called the "Flying Puzzle," based on an airplane trip from New York to Paris—two cities they have never seen.
- The constant presence of railroad cars in Huntington also brings hobos; the family often feeds the hungry that appear at their doorstep.
- When the family can afford a movie, they attend the Keith-Albee theater, considered a movie palace, where Will Rogers movies always draw big crowds.
- Much of the family's free time is spent at Ritter Park, which offers tennis courts, a baseball diamond, a skating rink, and swimming.

Life at Work

- After many years of "rescuing" troubled churches, James has been named the district superintendent for eight counties in West Virginia.
- As district superintendent, he often travels to different churches to preach, meet with ministers, and deal with administrative matters of the church.
- Often he will be gone for four or five days at a time as he attempts to cover all the churches in his district.
- He travels in a Model A Ford.
- A typical work weekend might include preaching on Sunday morning in Parkerburg, a conference with preachers in Clarksburg that afternoon, preaching an evening service in Charleston, and then an all-night drive to Cleveland to begin meetings there the next morning; his teenage son often helps with the driving.
- He is known for his forceful presentation, often leaving the pulpit to walk around while he talks.
- Because he is also known for his ability to "raise troubled churches," the bishop assigned him to several churches

that needed to increase enrollment, raise additional funds, or gain a more stable foundation.

- During some parts of his career, he and the family moved annually to assist churches.
- The congregations love his deep, powerful voice.
- Although known as a dynamic speaker, around his family he is often silent; when his son drives him to appointments across the state, they rarely speak during the trip.
- During trips, he often stops at church members' homes where he has been invited to eat.
- Most of his church members are coal miners or connected to the mine.
- Services often include preaching and "witnessing," during which the men and women of the church will tell everyone "what the Lord has done for them that week."
- Music in the church often includes old favorites such as "Rock of Ages" and "Amazing Grace," all sung from the *Cokesburg Hymn Book*.
- A typical Methodist church in his district has 100 members; a large congregation reaches 250 members, with the largest churches typically boasting a brick building with a steeple.
- As district superintendent, he is also responsible for coordinating the annual meeting, when pastors in his area gather to discuss changes in membership, giving, conversions, baptisms, and other church administrative matters.
- Many of the pastors within his district are circuit riders, traveling from one church to another on a typical weekend.

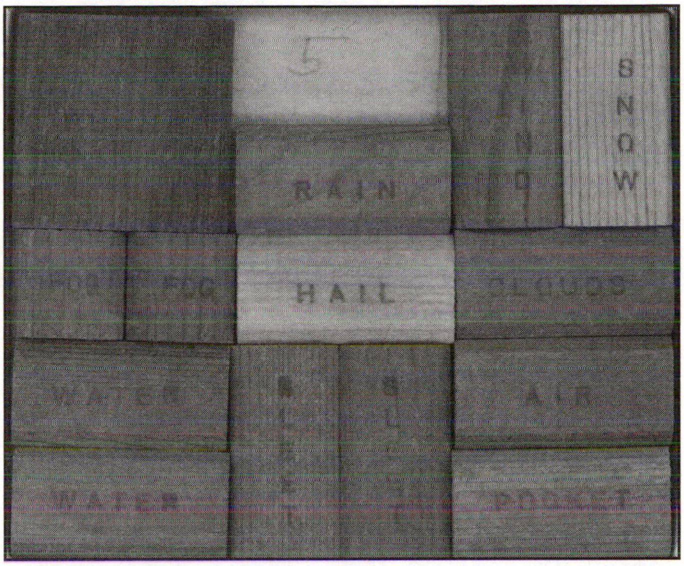

The solutuion to this puzzle requires 59 moves.

Help me in all the work I do,
To ever be sincere and true
And know that all I'd do for
you
Must need be done for—others.

And when my work on earth is
done,
And my new work in heav'n's
won,
While thinking still of—others.

Others, Lord, Yes, Others!
Let this my motta be,
Help me to live for others,
That I may live like thee."

"If I had but one year to live:
One year to help; one year to give;
One year to love; one year to bless;
One year the better things to stress;
One year to sing; one year to smile;
To brighten earth a little while;
One year to sing my Maker's praise;
One year to fill with work my days;
One year to serve for a reward,
When I should stand before my Lord;
I think I would spend each day
In just the very self-same way
That I do now: For from afar
The call may come to cross the bar
At any time, and I must be
Prepared to meet eternity.
So if I have a year to live—
Or just one day in which to give
A pleasant smile, a helping hand,
A mind that tries to understand
A fellow-creature when in need—
'Tis one with me—I take no heed,
But try to live each day He sends
To serve my gracious Master's ends."

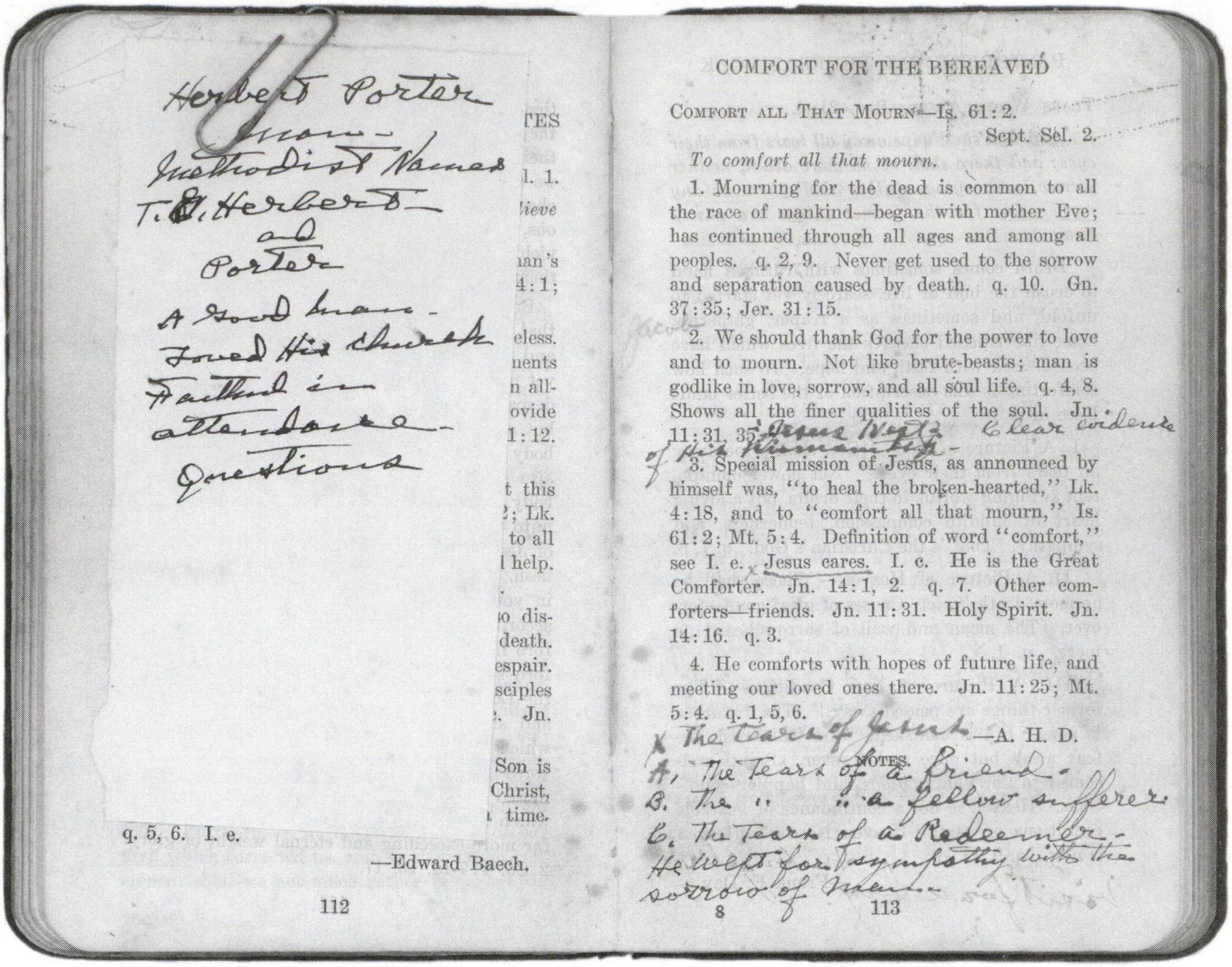

COMFORT FOR THE BEREAVED

Comfort all That Mourn—Is. 61:2.
Sept. Sel. 2.

To comfort all that mourn.

1. Mourning for the dead is common to all the race of mankind—began with mother Eve; has continued through all ages and among all peoples. q. 2, 9. Never get used to the sorrow and separation caused by death. q. 10. Gn. 37:35; Jer. 31:15.

2. We should thank God for the power to love and to mourn. Not like brute-beasts; man is godlike in love, sorrow, and all soul life. q. 4, 8. Shows all the finer qualities of the soul. Jn. 11:31, 35.

3. Special mission of Jesus, as announced by himself was, "to heal the broken-hearted," Lk. 4:18, and to "comfort all that mourn," Is. 61:2; Mt. 5:4. Definition of word "comfort," see I. e. Jesus cares. I. c. He is the Great Comforter. Jn. 14:1, 2. q. 7. Other comforters—friends. Jn. 11:31. Holy Spirit. Jn. 14:16. q. 3.

4. He comforts with hopes of future life, and meeting our loved ones there. Jn. 11:25; Mt. 5:4. q. 1, 5, 6.

—A. H. D.

q. 5, 6. I. e.

—Edward Baech.

112 113

- Currently, James is working to establish a pension fund; traditionally ministers have retired without any means of support, often having to live their final years on the sometimes unpredictable generosity of congregations.
- The telephone perplexes him; when answering the phone he yells, "Well, how's that?"
- He is also known for his brief letters, often written on paper with the bottom torn off; while on one of his frequent trips, he recently wrote Edie, "I met two ladies today. One of them smiled."
- Edie often attends church conferences with James; she is also a leader in the Ladies' Aid, Women's Home Mission, Women's Foreign Mission, and the Temperance Union.
- He likes to tell people, "I have everything but money."
- When congregations make special gifts to him for preaching or marrying a couple, he gives it away to church missions funds.
- Congregations often give him food, including corn and chickens, and even dress clothing in appreciation for his work.
- Many congregations have little to give, as the entire economy in 1937, especially mining, is in its deepest depression since 1933.

- The character of his congregations often changes based on the prosperity of the company; many miners move every two to three years to search for better jobs.
- He believes that people should balance their lives; "Show me a good church worker," he often says, "and I will show you a neglected family."
- He also believes in humor; around the kitchen table, the family loves to tell and retell stories about people they have met or adventures they have enjoyed.

COPR & PRINTED BY PROV. LITHO. CO., U.S.A.

TWO MIRACLES OF POWER

Golden Text: What manner of man is this, that even the wind and the sea obey him? Mark 4:41.

MR. C. H. HESSE

Funeral Services Will Be Held Sunday Afternoon

Funeral services for Mr. Christian Henry Hesse, of 76 Rutledge avenue, whose death in his 81st year occurred Friday night at his residence, will be conducted at four o'clock Sunday afternoon at St. Andrew's Lutheran church with the Rev. Clarence K. Derrick, assisted by the Rev. Dermon Sox, officiating.

Mr. Hesse, who formerly conducted a grocery store at a corner of Wentworth street and Rutledge avenue for a number of years and who was a native of Walhalla, was the son of C. Henry and Henrietta Damann Hesse of Germany.

He is survived by three daughters, Mrs. W. H. A. Halsall of Charleston, Mrs. E. A. Cain of Bluefield, West Virginia; Mrs. W. C. Quack of Long Beach, Cal.; and by four sons, Ernest and George Hesse of Charleston; William Hesse of Albany, N. Y. and Louis Hesse of Canton, O. Pallbearers will be: Messrs. Robert McCarrell, Leroy Beckmann, W. R. Zobel, C. W. Parham, E. C. DuPuis and Edward Albers.

Interment will be at Bethany cemetery. J. Henry Stuhr, Inc. is in charge of arrangements.

Life in the Community: Huntington, West Virginia

- The economy of Huntington revolves around the Chesapeake and Ohio Railroad and the transportation of coal.
- Tons of coal pass through the city either by barge or the Chesapeake and Ohio Railroad.
- Jobs with the railroads are cherished positions, offering good—but also steady—pay.
- International Nickel Company and West Virginia Steel are also critical to the economy of the area.
- Marshall College, now 100 years old, has a reputation for providing a quality education to the men and women of West Virginia; efforts are under way to shift its image from that of "primarily a teacher's college."
- The current president of Marshall, James E. Allen, believes in the value of a liberal education; he idealizes the "universal man" as exemplified in the Italian Renaissance.
- The 1937, the college and community are struggling to recover from a flood caused by the rampaging waters of the Ohio River; property losses are severe.
- The county high school, the only one in the area, is currently operating on double shifts, since the county has too many students, too few buildings, and no ability to raise taxes during the depression.
- One group of students attends from 8 a.m. to noon, while the second shift runs from 1 p.m. to 4 p.m.
- A highlight of the year is the annual band festival, when up to 50 high school bands come to Marshall College in Huntington to compete.
- Huntington is known as a "City of Churches," with most grouped downtown.

The college and community are still struggling to recover from a flood.

Marshall College serves as a gathering place for the community.

- City leaders are concerned about creeping immorality; some of the recent movies have shown kissing, and one newsstand now sells a magazine called *Sexology, The Magazine of Sex Science* from under the counter; articles include "Sexual Mismating," "What Shall a Single Man Do?" and "Do Schools Create Perversion?"
- Huntington also suffers severely, thanks to the depression; many of the industries that came to the city prior to World War I have closed their doors.
- Skiing and Ping-Pong are rising in popularity throughout the East Coast; miniature golf—the rage of the mid-depression years—is dying out.

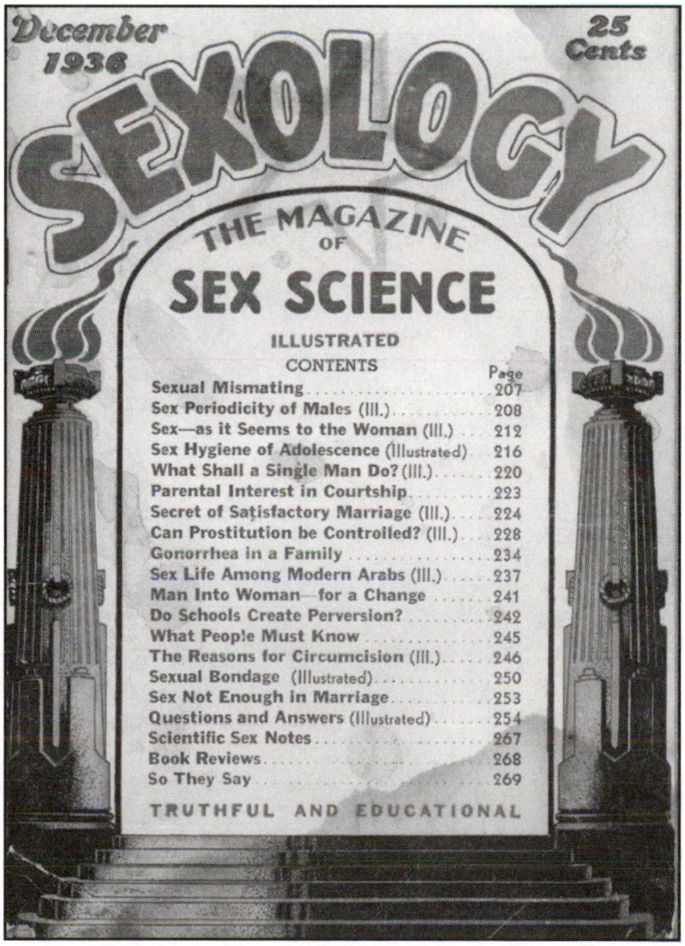

"Sex Not Enough in Marriage," *Sexology, The Magazine of Sex Science*, December 1936:

"Romantic youth has been educated to the idea that love conquers everything; true love triumphs over every obstacle, and so forth, and so forth. It is disquieting, therefore, to discover in later life that love alone is no guarantee of a happy marriage. It is, of course, a help where men and women understand the cultivation of love through day-by-day mutual adjustments and modifications of individual habits and tastes to provide opportunity for the maximum growth of two personalities. But, even in the narrow field of sexual relations, love alone is inadequate. Knowledge of technique is perhaps the first requisite and this, very frequently, is lacking. Premarital experience of the man does not, as a rule, furnish the requisite knowledge. Indeed, quite the contrary can be the case, for such experience has usually been with prostitutes, in which case the responsibility of facilitating relations rests with the woman, whereas in marriage it rests with the man, in the beginning at least. French prostitutes during the war commented on the lack of finesse in approach exhibited by the American soldiers, contrasting them in this respect with the French. It would appear from this that possibly the untaught youth of America has less artistry in such matters than the more sophisticated youth of Europe. In this country, the Puritan tradition has exalted romantic love, while condemning all consideration of the more intimate details of this expression. The result is men, however capable of romantic love they may be, often enter marriage and even go through life in most appalling ignorance of the physiological and psychological nature of their partners. The Puritan tradition has created an altogether false and extremely restricted view of the wife's possible participation in sexual pleasure, in regard to both its possibility and its seemliness. The result is, often, complete lack of cooperation between partners in any attempt to arrive at a beautiful and mutually satisfactory sex expression. There are very frequent cases of men seeking outside of marriage those satisfactions which should be found within marriage. As long as such conduct is limited to prostitutes, since there is no competition in the field of love, the wife often condones it because of her own mistaken idea of the scope of marriage relationships. The motive for marriage should be what natural law makes it, the desire for personal satisfaction, complete sexual and psychological development, and a more abundant emotional life. We are not preparing our youth for marriage until we teach them to attain first all of these fundamentals."

Historical Snapshot
1937

- The U.S. economy plunged back into a deep recession; unemployment climbed to 14.3 percent
- A Gallup poll showed that 80 percent of Americans approved of relief through public work, as opposed to the dole
- Hugo L. Black's appointment to the U.S. Supreme Court raised controversy because of Black's youthful membership in the KKK
- A *Fortune* poll reported that 50 percent of all college men and 25 percent of all college women had had premarital sexual relations; two-thirds of the women reported they "would for true love"
- The principle of the minimum wage for women was upheld by the U.S. Supreme Court
- *Popular Photography* magazine began publication
- Spam was introduced by George A. Hormel & Company
- Icemen continued regular deliveries to more than 50 percent of middle-class households
- Despite high unemployment and severe poverty, show business salaries were soaring; Louis B. Mayer of Metro-Goldwyn-Mayer made $1.16 million, while Major Edward Bowes of the *Amateur Hour* on radio made $427,817
- An estimated 500,000 American students took part in a student strike against war, united in a pledge never to support any war declared by the United States
- General Motors introduced the automatic transmission
- Parkard Motor Car Company sold a record 109,000 cars; Pierce-Arrow autos went out of business
- United Auto Workers was recognized by General Motors as the sole bargaining agent for its workers; Henry Ford declared he'd never recognize the UAW or any union
- Spinach growers erected a statue of Popeye the Sailor Man in Wisconsin
- Of the great silent movie comedians, only Charlie Chaplin made a successful transition to talkies
- Americans reportedly spent 4.5 hours daily listening to the radio
- The restoration of Colonial Williamsburg, Virginia, was completed
- John D. Rockefeller, who died at 98, left an estate estimated at $1 billion
- Several thousand Americans joined the Abraham Lincoln Brigade to fight with the Loyalists against the fascist-supported Franco forces; about 50 percent died in battle
- United States Steel agreed to terms with John L. Lewis without a strike, enhancing Lewis's prestige and bargaining power
- From September 1, 1936, to June 1, 1937, 484,711 workers were involved in sit-down strikes
- The trampoline, skywriting at night, Pepperidge Farm, the shopping cart, and the Lincoln Tunnel all made their first appearances in 1937

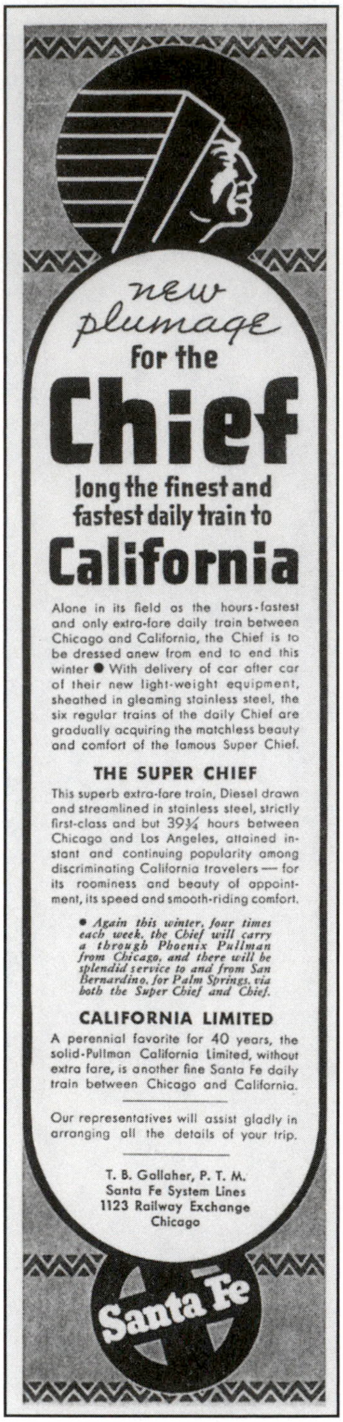

1937 Economic Profile

Income, Standard Jobs

Average of All Industries, Excluding Farm Labor	$1,341
Average of All Industries, Including Farm Labor	$1,259
Bituminous Coal Mining	$1,170
Building Trades	$1,278
Domestics	$588
Farm Labor	$407
Federal Civilian	$1,797
Federal Employees, Executive Departments	$1,188
Federal Military	$1,132
Finance, Insurance, and Real Estate	$1,788
Gas and Electricity Workers	$1,705
Manufacturing, Durable Goods	$1,491
Manufacturing, Nondurable Goods	$1,267
Medical/Health Services Workers	$876
Miscellaneous Manufacturing	$1,359
Motion Picture Services	$1,972
Nonprofit Organization Workers	$1,497
Passenger Transportation Workers, Local and Highway	$1,505
Personal Services	$978
Public School Teachers	$1,367
Radio Broadcasting	$2,361
Railroads	$1,774
State and Local Government Workers	$1,505
Telephone and Telegraph Workers	$1,481
Wholesale and Retail Trade Workers	$1,352

Selected Prices

Chesterfield Pipe, 5" Size	$0.39
Cold Wave Fan, Oscillating	$5.50
Eileen Drury Women's Frock	$1.98
Florsheim Men's Shoes	$8.75
Goodyear Double Eagle Car Battery	$16.95
Goodyear Wings Deluxe-8 Radio	$38.50
Hercules Pitchfork	$1.35
J.C. Higgins Basketball	$3.59
Kenmore Deluxe Vacuum Cleaner	$31.45
Kodak Bantam Camera	$22.50

Lifetime Steel Bed, Complete $16.50
Lysol Disinfectant, Large Size $0.83
Maternity Corset $2.98
Merit Ax $0.98
Morninglow Bath Towels, Four $0.79
Nestle's Baby Hair Treatment $0.83
Polar Air Refrigerator $22.98
Sir Walter Raleigh Smoking Tobacco $0.15
Supertone Gene Autry Guitar $8.45
Velflor Rug, 9' x 12' $8.75
Wildroot Hair Tonic $0.47
Windex Window Cleaner $0.39

GENERAL ELECTRIC
FULL RANGE RADIO
SPECIFICATIONS

THE POPULAR CONSOLE

Nine-tube, screen-grid superheterodyne. Tone control. Improved automatic volume control. Exclusive G-E Tone Equalizer eliminates ill effects of cabinet resonance. Brown walnut cabinet, grille cloth of antique woven damask.

THE DE LUXE LOWBOY

Ten-tube, screen-grid superheterodyne. Tone control. Improved automatic volume control. Chassis doubly shielded. Brown walnut cabinet, Renaissance design.

THE DE LUXE AUTOMATIC COMBINATION

For chassis features, see DeLuxe Lowboy. Automatic phonograph plays ten 10-inch records for thirty minutes before repeating. Will reproduce new long-playing records. Will record and reproduce both 6- and 10-inch home recording records. New improved type microphone.

—16—

SPECIFICATIONS

THE MODERN LONGFELLOW GRANDFATHER CLOCK-RADIO

Ten-tube, screen-grid superheterodyne with two Pentode tubes. Tone control. Improved automatic volume control. Remote control available at additional cost. General Electric Clock. Genuine mahogany case, authentic early American design. Controls concealed behind door.

THE GEORGIAN GRANDFATHER CLOCK-RADIO

Nine-tube, screen-grid superheterodyne. Tone control. Improved automatic volume control. General Electric Clock. Genuine mahogany case, authentic Georgian design. Controls concealed behind door.

THE BATTERY CONSOLE

Eight-tube, screen-grid superheterodyne. One complete unit, totally shielded. New type dynamic speaker has permanent magnet field. Uses new "air cell" "A" battery which operates approximately one year without renewal.

—17—

Coal mining drives the economy of the state.

The Coal Mines

- West Virginia was one of the nation's largest suppliers of coal.
- Coal was not only plentiful; it was of very high quality.
- However, the coal seams in West Virginia were far from population centers, as 80 percent of West Virginia's miners lived in company-owned houses.
- Most were finished outside with weatherboard, usually nailed directly to the frame, with only paper for sheeting; only 38 percent were plastered, only 2.4 percent had tubs or showers, three percent had inside flush toilets, and 14 percent had running water.
- To maintain maximum control, most mines required their workers to rent company houses; those who chose to live outside the miners' camps were often the first to be laid off during the slow season.
- The company often owned everything in the camp; a popular saying was "The only thing the company don't own is God."
- Irregular employment, insecurity of job, lack of home ownership, frequent moving, payment in scrip, and high prices at the company store were considered part of the life of being a coal miner.
- Prices in the company-controlled stores were often two to three times higher than the prices charged by chain stores in town.
- The children of miners were often undernourished and many had pellagra and rickets; for many, milk was a special treat.
- Coal production peaked in 1918 at 523 million net tons, driven by war demands.
- Despite declining demand after World War I, West Virginia and Kentucky coal production continued to expand.

The Plight of the Bituminous Coal Miner, by Homer Lawrence Morris, Ph.D.:

"I ain't had a regular job for four years and I've only been able to pick up odd jobs on the road. I've only had 11 days' work, and that on the road, during the past year. I own a four-room house and lot but I gotta pay $9.00 taxes on it and I ain't got the money to pay it. When a man has been out of work as long as I have, he loses his heart to do anything." West Virginia Coal Miner, 1934

- Railroad profits were closely linked to coal production; in 1930, a quarter of railroad revenues were derived from coal transportation.
- Since the early 1920s, the West Virginia miners had been joining unions, often in large groups, to reduce the chance of company retaliation.
- Several major strikes were extremely bloody; newly unionized miners were murdered as a threat to other miners.
- By the late 1930s, many were discouraged; often the miners got fired by the company and received less support from the National Miner's Union than they had expected.

"Social Security Betrayed," by Abraham Epstein, *The Nation*, October 10, 1936:

"Far from being a rational social measure, the New Deal Social Security Act is the most reactionary social-insurance plan in existence. Its major features are neither social nor conducive to security. In a world ruled by slogans, it is not surprising, however, to find American liberals ensnared into unquestioning acceptance of the act. The promise of security is most alluring. The slogan of 'social security' encompasses all fond hopes and pious wishes. Even enemies of social legislation insist they favor the idea of social security.

The vast range and complexity of the act has served to obscure its social limitations and sinister implications. The combination of 10 different insurance and relief programs, based on three different philosophies of governmental operation, has made understanding well-nigh impossible. The embodiment of good, bad, and indifferent plans in one measure has impeded critical discussion of the socially questionable features.

Sooner or later, the American people are bound to realize that, despite its glittering title, the act does not solve the problems of insecurity. The law does not even attempt to meet the major ills of present-day society. The great modern hazards afflicting millions of wage and salaried earners are sickness and invalidity, unemployment, old-age dependency, industrial accidents, death, widowhood, and orphanage. Although illness is one of the major causes of economic insecurity, threatening workers in good times as in bad and accounting for nearly half of all dependency in normal times, the act completely ignores this problem. It does not touch upon accident compensation, which is still non-existent in two states and extremely inadequate in most others, nor does it make burial provisions. Except for the destitute blind, it fails to provide for the invalid. Its chief concern is with unemployment and old-age dependency."

"Twenty Years When Nothing Stood Still," *Forbes Magazine*, December 15, 1937:

"Twenty years ago—remember back to 1917?

People used shoe buttons then, and buckles, and the zipper was a new kind of haircut.

Detroit and Cleveland went on daylight-saving time in the summer, and farmers fanatically opposed the idea elsewhere.

Stainless steels, small diesel engines, radio broadcasting—thousands of things we now take for granted were unborn in 1917.

We yelled "sissy" at anyone who wanted too much comfort. Now we demand comfort in offices, factories, homes, cabs of motor trucks, airplanes—everywhere.

The first beauty shop was yet to be born. First, permanent waves cost $60 each. Now 65,000 beauty shops do over a $200 million business each year, spend over $60 million for wages, and support 85 exclusive manufacturers. And there is an additional beauty bill of $125 million for lipsticks and other supplies the girls use themselves.

The men aren't so choosy.

They go to any old barbershop, so there are twice as many shops to serve them, but the income per average shop is less. The girls buy from their shops fifteen cents' worth of supplies for every $1.00 in service; the men seldom buy supplies from barbers.

But the safety razor has zoomed to almost universal use since 1917. Now it is challenged by electric shavers. Shaving soap- and cream-makers watch with bated breath, but they are developing beard stiffeners to make the electrics work better. The art of shaving is now the subject of industrial research—with the Mellon Institute spending five years to study it.

We admired blind believing then. Now we get the facts on everything. Statistics are gathered by the government, colleges and universities, and the National Industrial Conference Board, thousands of trade associations, labor unions, and so many 'foundations' that it takes a thick book to catalog them.

Foreign nations had holds on our machinery, dyes, ball bearings, and lots of others. Now we lead in this production.

We have become 'clothes conscious.' Rayon consumption is up 3,500 percent since 1920, but cotton is up also. We wear more of more kinds of clothes specially designed for individual activities.

The war brought the vogue for streamlined figures. Waistlines and skirt lengths have gone up and down amazingly.

We eat drugstore lunches, and our national dietary habits have changed. The California Fruit Growers' Exchange had been going strong on orange juice for 10 years by 1917. Now vitamins have come in. Tomato juice, sauerkraut juice, and others have joined the parade. Baby diets have changed so much for the better that dentists and doctors are doomed to less work per thousand of population.

Mazda lamps were then just replacing carbon arcs in silent movie projectors. Now three-dimensional pictures in full colors with sounds are just around the corner.

Fountain pens with iridium-tipped gold points were cheap at $5. Now electric welding makes stainless steel iridium-tipped points in good pens for $0.50 or less.

Screwdrivers have safe plastic handles. They can be hammered on like chisels, do not conduct electricity, and at last the tips are nonskid. Shoelace tips are of plastic instead of metal.

And drugs have improved. The morphine habit was the terror of all who needed drugs for pain. Now, synthetic drugs—at one-thirtieth of the price—are non-habit-forming.

Three-day drying periods for Portland cement were taken for granted. Now a day is enough for some kinds.

Night photography was largely by flash powder. There were some floodlights, but they were not as good as the present ones. Now we have developed photo floodlights, flash powders which

(continued)

"Twenty Years . . ." *(continued)*

are not fire hazards nor dangerous to the eyes—and even flash bulbs which do not burn out with one exposure.

More than 1,500 industrial laboratories spend $300 million per year to develop new things—a major industry all by itself—with over 40,000 research men employed.

Technical improvements are legion. The cotton mill work week was 66 hours. Now it's 40 hours, with two shifts. The result: Mills then needed five spindles in place for each bale of cotton used. Now they need only three and one-half. Modernization has helped.

Cigarettes dropped on rugs were hotel keepers' horror. Now rugs are fireproofed. Moths did heartbreaking damage. Now fabrics are mothproofed. Even wood is fireproofed.

Book pages were reduced to postage-stamp size and projected on screens for reading. A library used to be a space-consuming luxury, but now a five-foot shelf can contain thousands of volumes. Books may even become talking affairs which are read aloud to listeners.

In radio, talking pictures, and even in ordinary business, voice training is now as important as appropriate dress was in 1917."

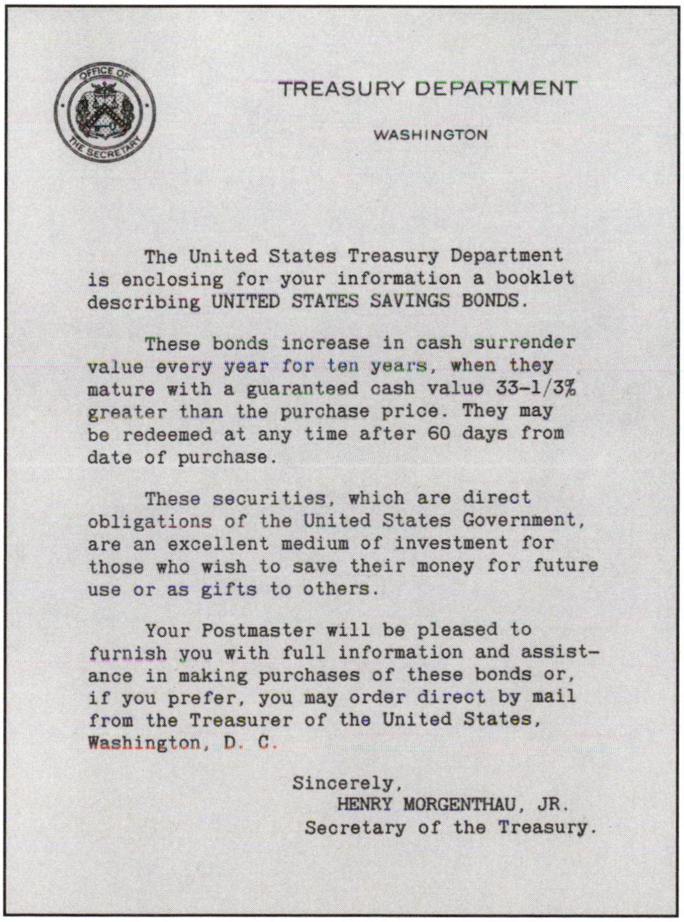
TREASURY DEPARTMENT

WASHINGTON

The United States Treasury Department is enclosing for your information a booklet describing UNITED STATES SAVINGS BONDS.

These bonds increase in cash surrender value every year for ten years, when they mature with a guaranteed cash value 33-1/3% greater than the purchase price. They may be redeemed at any time after 60 days from date of purchase.

These securities, which are direct obligations of the United States Government, are an excellent medium of investment for those who wish to save their money for future use or as gifts to others.

Your Postmaster will be pleased to furnish you with full information and assistance in making purchases of these bonds or, if you prefer, you may order direct by mail from the Treasurer of the United States, Washington, D. C.

Sincerely,
HENRY MORGENTHAU, JR.
Secretary of the Treasury.

WOMAN'S WORLD
HOME EDITION
ONIONS
MARCH • 1939
10 CENTS A COPY
"I SHALL COME BACK"—A Story by EARL REED SILVERS

B. F. STURTEVANT COMPANY, HYDE PARK, BOSTON, MASS.

Sturtevant

REG. U. S. PAT. OFF.

Puts Air to Work

1937 News Profile

"Air Conditioning Nears Its Goal," *Forbes Magazine*, November 15, 1937:

"Air conditioning is approaching its goal: Yesterday it was considered an expensive luxury; today it is rapidly becoming a necessity.

Public acceptance is increasing, production is rising and sales are booming. Buyers of air-conditioning equipment spent $74,036,822 during the first nine months of 1937, 48 percent more than in all of 1936, and nearly twice as much as during the corresponding period of that year. Markets are rapidly expanding, and the industry is moving into the $100 million class.

But it is not yet a major industry. Today it approximates in size such industries as lighting equipment and aircraft parts. Born with aviation after the turn of the century, the industry suffered during war and depression, and only since 1934 has it made impressive strides to hit its present all-time high.

With rapid growth, air conditioning is feeling the 'growing pains' common to other expanding industries. It also faces totally new difficulties which require new and ingenious solutions.

The public does not appreciate the complexity of these problems, and as a result is sometimes impatient with deficiencies and delays. Air conditioning is not, and for a long time to come will not be, a standardized industry. It involves installation under physical conditions of infinite variety, requiring the use of parts of widely differing sizes and types, and involving technical engineering skill of a high order.

Some of the problems which face the industry, as disclosed by the manufacturers, are the following: 'Lack of trained men' is a universal complaint. 'We need more men who can make the equipment, more men who can sell it, more men who can install it, and more men who can operate it and service it to the satisfaction of the buyer.'

This scarcity of trained personnel is incident to the development of a new science. Knowledge of heating and ventilating does not necessarily mean a knowledge of air control in the fullest sense of 'air conditioning.' The industry, therefore, has need of men trained in the engineering of this science.

This need is not so acute in the field of production. Air-conditioning equipment involves no new technical devices that require specially trained labor. It is simply a reorganization of

the old units—filters, washers, fans, coils, and so on—assembled to produce a new result. But in the channels of distribution, men of special training are an absolute necessity.

A salesman contacts a prospective customer and engages his interest. The salesman is asked to estimate the job. This involves a problem of engineering which the salesman without special training is not qualified to solve, and the services of an engineer are needed. Some companies send out both a salesman and an engineer to engage the prospective buyers. A majority of the manufacturers, however, in order to meet the problem, are following one of two courses: Either they provide the salesmen with training in the fundamentals of engineering, or they train air-conditioning engineers in salesmanship.

But after the installation has been contracted for, the problem is to no means solved. Installation and subsequent service by trained men are absolutely necessary for full performance of the contract. The equipment must be made to work under the particular, often peculiar, physical circumstances of the case.

Confronted by this paucity of trained men in the rapidly growing industry, the manufacturers are taking steps to meet the situation. They are now active in promoting schools in the factory and practical training in the field. The length of training courses ranges from six weeks to two years, depending on the experience of the student and the amount of ground to be covered.

In the plant instruction, distributors, dealers, and salesmen study equipment in the factory, learn how to estimate a job and how to install the equipment in the field, and the field instruction supplements the study in the plant. . . . Along with the scarcity of trained men, there is the problem of the lack of uniformity in the industry.

While manufacturers recognize the diversity in air conditioning and urge the importance of suiting the equipment to the particular job, at the same time they realize the advantages of setting uniform engineering standards whenever possible. In their attempt to make uniform the methods of estimating the equipment required for a particular job, for example, many producers of air-conditioning equipment supply charts and checklists for calculations."

1939 Family Profile

Forty-year-old Richard Hastings is a bond trader in New York City, working for the prestigious Manufacturer's Trust; he and his wife, Helen, live in the suburbs of New York and have three children.

Richard Hastings works in New York City and commutes to his home in the suburbs.

Annual Income: $7,500

Annual Budget

The average per capita consumer expenditures in 1939 for all workers nationwide are:

Auto Parts	$3.82
Auto Usage	$39.69
Clothing	$45.03
Dentists	$3.05
Furniture	$6.87
Gas and Oil	$16.79
Health Insurance	$1.53
Housing	$71.74
Intercity Transport	$3.05
Local Transport	$6.87
New Auto Purchase	$12.21
Personal Business	$24.42
Personal Care	$13.74
Physicians	$6.87
Private Education and Research	$4.58
Recreation	$26.71
Religion/Welfare Activities	$7.63
Telephone and Telegraph	$4.58

Richard and Helen married in 1929. She was an assistant reseracher for The American Museum of Natural History for six years.

Tobacco	$13.74
Utilities	$23.66
Per Capita Consumption	$511.34

Life at Home

- This family lives in Mamaraneck, New York, within commuting distance by train to New York City, where Richard works.
- Despite his work schedule, Richard enjoys the physical work of maintaining the house; the yard is cut with a push mower.
- He memorizes very well and loves to quote poetry, freely quoting poems or lines from Shakespeare he has only read once or twice.
- The couple has compromised on religion; Helen was raised Catholic, while Richard was raised Presbyterian. They now go to the Episcopal Church.
- They currently drive a 1938 Dodge, having just traded in the car they bought in 1932 shortly before he lost his job.
- The family vacation this year is a week-long summer trip to a Vermont farm owned by a friend.
- Since the car averages about 30 miles per hour because of road conditions, it takes all day to make the trip.
- Richard's father had been a steel-plate engraver who traveled the world doing engravings for the American Bank Note Company.
- A heavy smoker, his father died from a perforated ulcer at the age of 41, leaving his estate to his oldest son, Richard's brother.
- Richard's older brother went to Columbia University, studied economics, and began work on Wall Street, strictly forbidding Richard from majoring in engineering.
- Richard majored in economics at Columbia University, as dictated by his brother.
- After college, when Richard worked for a general contractor instead of going into banking, as his brother wished, resentment between the brothers grew.
- Richard and Helen married in 1929; their first child was born the following year.
- Helen is a graduate of Barnard and was an assistant researcher for the American Museum of Natural History for six years.
- Her work resulted in the publication of an article in the October 1928 edition of *The Scientific Monthly*, entitled, "Survey of the Life of Louis Agassiz, the Centenary of the Glacial Theory."
- After leaving the museum, but before she married, she toured Europe to visit relatives.
- As she grew up, her father was influential in local education issues, while her mother, an Irish Catholic, was known for her fire; when the local newspaper published an article critical of her husband, and which she considered "scurrilous," she confronted the editor, saying, "You will retract this article or I will horsewhip you." The article was retracted.

"Survey of the Life of Louis Agassiz, The Centenary of the Glacial Theory," by Helen Ann Warren, Assistant in the Osborn Research Room, American Museum of Natural History, *Scientific Monthly*, October 1928:

"During the sixteenth century, science was still an avocation of the man of wealth and leisure who could afford to dabble in peculiar phenomena, and of the man with an inborn love of puzzling out the secrets of nature, who was fortunate enough to interest some rich patron or publisher of his investigations. Physics and chemistry, astronomy, mathematics, and medicine enjoyed a restricted vogue; the natural sciences, zoology, botany, geology, and mineralogy, were less considered. Aristotle had supposedly defined their scope once for all and, though occasional men like Leonardo da Vinci were interested in the animal and vegetable life amid which they lived, most men dismissed it from the speculations.

The discovery of America insensibly changed this attitude. Here were adventure, romance, fabulous wealth, strange beasts. Men eagerly sought for details of this Eldorado, and tales spread from learned men and courtiers to the illiterate laborers swapping stories in country inns. Shakespeare, painting the passing show in England, remarked in *The Tempest*:

'Were I but in England now, (as once I was), and had but this fish painted, not a holiday fool there would give a piece of silver; there would this monster make a man; when they will not give a doit to relieve a lame beggar, they will lay out ten to see a dead Indian.' "

- By 1931, the impact of the economic crash was so pervasive, Richard lost his job; Helen was pregnant with their second child.
- He spent a year looking for work while they lived off their savings and her inheritance.
- Nationwide, unemployment reached 13 million persons, or a quarter of America's work force; it stabilized at 17 percent, leaving 9.5 million people out of work.
- Currently, they live in her parents' house, which she inherited, in Mamaraneck, a suburb of New York City.
- The two-story house includes a living room, dining room, and kitchen on the first floor, with a master bedroom, three other bedrooms, and a bath on the second floor; the house also features a basement for storage.
- An experienced contractor, Richard spent considerable time working on his home, painting, repairing, and fixing up, while looking for work.
- One of his major projects was replacing all of the lighting fixtures in the house to give the house a more contemporary look.
- He obtained his job in banking in 1932 when his mother-in-law ordered his older brother to find Richard a job.

Helen with one of the couple's children.

- He went to work for Manufacturer's Trust, a well-respected Wall Street firm, as a bond trader.
- He takes the train into the city each morning; when traveling on business, he frequently shaves himself with a set of straight razors on the train; he has a different razor for each day. He returns home on the train at 7:30 p.m.
- They are saving their money, unsure of the future; if they must replace the furnace, for example, they want to use cash, not credit.
- John Wanamaker stores are offering a "young modern" line of furniture complete with revolving credit that "gives you all the comfort of a regular charge account plus four months to pay and no carrying charge."
- He loves to sail and continues his passion of doing things with his hands; he is currently building a flat-bottom, straight-sided canoe called the *Damnation*.

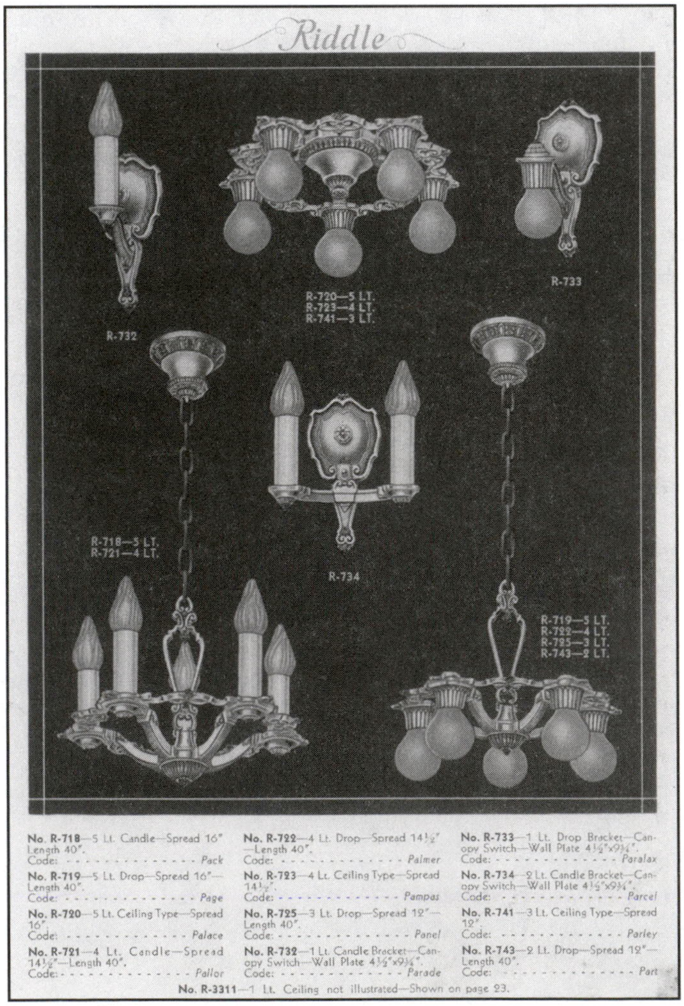

- He often sails with his best friend, a local judge.
- Once a week, he attends a luncheon meeting of the Kiwanis Club, forever amazed that so many men can sing so badly, so consistently.
- The biggest meal of the week is served at 4:30 each Sunday, and is centered around roast beef, pork or lamp chops, and lots of fresh vegetables.
- Most nights, he plays the piano for half an hour, largely classical pieces.
- They often invite friends over to listen to the radio as couples, especially to hear the *Chase and Sanborn Hour*, featuring an invisible ventriloquist and his irreverent puppet, Charlie McCarthy.

Life at Work

- His position at Manufacturer's Trust primarily involves investing bonds for hospitals, schools, and colleges.
- He loves the research required by the job—understanding the cash flows, predicting problems, and calculating risk; he likes to make money for others.

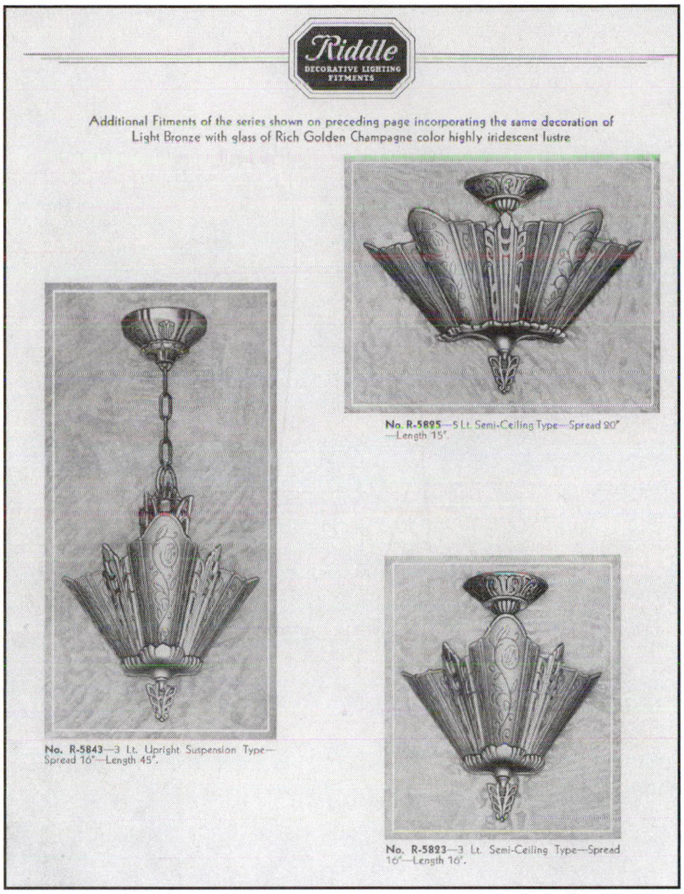

He occasionally attends large dinners with fellow bond traders and bankers.

New Yorkers believe that the city is at its zenith.

Richard's father did steel-plate engraving for the American Bank Note Company.

- He especially enjoys the ever-changing risks within his business; one minor change in Europe can have a major impact on the United States bond market.
- Currently, business is booming as, despite the recession in 1938, the war in Europe is driving the economy; the need for capital expansion is very high, and businessmen are feeling optimistic.
- The war is also causing gold to flow into the United States from Europe—more than $3 billion in 1939 alone, up 80 percent from the previous year.
- This surplus of funds into the United States, and particularly into New York banks, has driven interest rates down.
- The average bank rate on short-term loans in New York City is 1.8 percent; the average rate in 11 Southern and Western cities is 2.5 percent.
- Pundits are declaring "the old stock market is dead; the new stock market is emerging"; a seat on the New York Stock Exchange costs approximately $80,000, while the Dow Jones Industrial Average hovers around 150.
- The fluctuating economy has Richard cautious; business failures are running 70 per 10,000 business concerns, the highest since 1933.

Life in the Community: New York City

- New York and New Yorkers believe the city is at its zenith.
- The towering shaft of the RCA Building, the starkness of the new George Washington Bridge, the vivid colors of Radio City Music Hall, all make New York City a magic place.
- Mayor Fiorello La Guardia is making the city work; his theme is "to the victor belongs the responsibility for good government."
- Reflecting the diversity of New York, La Guardia, who is half Jewish, campaigns in English, Italian, and Yiddish.
- *Harper's Magazine* recently said, "New York City happens to be one of the communities in the United States where good government is measured by getting a great deal for your money."
- New York boasts the tallest building in the country, also the second, third, fourth, fifth, and sixth largest.
- The city claims three major baseball teams and eight major daily newspapers; the largest newspaper, the *Daily News*, claims to have twice the circulation of the second largest paper in the U.S.
- The World's Fair, created in 1935 to chase away the recession, epitomizes late-thirties New York—big, bold, and thrilling.

The World's Fair opened in New York in 1935.

- Built on a former garbage dump, the Fair covers 1,200 acres and is nearly three miles long.
- New York reflects the old and the new; only blocks from the imposing Chrysler Building, herds of cattle stand on the sidewalk waiting to be butchered in one of the slaughterhouses along "Blood Alley."
- Italian hand organs can be heard on the streets near Yiddish-language movie houses as New York hosts the World's Fair.
- *Gone with the Wind* takes New York by storm; it is one of 530 feature films to appear in 1939.
- The New York World's Fair Music Festival is featuring Beethoven's *Ninth Symphony,* with tickets ranging from $1 to $2.50; the Brooklyn Academy of Music is featuring Martha Graham and Company in *American Document*.
- In a city that prides itself on its diversity, the census shows that 73 percent of New York's nearly one million people are of foreign white stock, while its black population totals 250,000.
- New York is the nation's leader in manufacturing and service industries, and the center of the national communications industry.

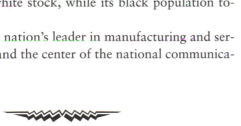

Historical Snapshot
1939

- World War II began in Europe with the Germans invading Poland in September and the Russians invading Finland in November
- The Birth Control Federation of America began its "Negro Project" designed to control the population of people it deemed less fit to rear children
- The Social Security Act was amended to allow extended benefits to the aged, widows, minors, and parents of a deceased person
- A poll reported that 50 percent believed radio was the most reliable news media; 17 percent voted for newspapers
- After the Daughters of the American Revolution (DAR) denied her the chance to sing at Constitution Hall because of her race, Marian Anderson sang at the Lincoln Memorial in Washington, D.C., before a crowd of 75,000
- *Reader's Digest* reached a circulation of eight million, up from 250,000 10 years earlier
- Despite the depression, the sale of radios continued to rise from 1929 to 1939; 27.5 million families now owned 45 million radio sets
- The Federal Theatre Project was disbanded after accusations of communist influence
- Movie box-office receipts reached an all-time high; 85 million Americans, or 65 percent of the total U.S. population, went to the movies at least once a week
- A Gallup poll showed that 58 percent of Americans believed the U.S. would be drawn into the war, while 65 percent favored boycotting Germany
- Hollywood production code restrictions were lifted to enable Clark Gable in *Gone with the Wind* to say, "Frankly, my dear, I don't give a damn."
- 60,000 German immigrants had arrived since 1933
- Newly emigrated Enrico Fermi and John R. Dunning of Columbia University used the cyclotron to split uranium and obtain a massive energy release; Fermi suggested the idea of a "chain reaction"
- Paul Miller developed the insecticide DDT
- Because of the war, the Finns ceased shipping cheese to the United States; Swiss production took its place
- Gangster Louis Lepke surrendered to popular newspaper and radio columnist Walter Winchell, who handed him over to J. Edgar Hoover
- The U.S. Supreme Court ruled that sit-down strikes were illegal
- The federal budget topped $9 billion, supported by only four million taxpayers; America had 1.13 million federal civilian employees
- The first baseball game was televised
- The New York World's Fair, whose theme was, "The World of Tomorrow," was attracting thousands to the city
- General Motors controlled 42 percent of the United States market in cars and trucks; its 220,000 employees made an average of $1,500 annually
- Transatlantic airmail service, the marketing of nylon stockings, the use of fluorescent lighting, and Packard's air-conditioned automobile were all introduced
- The Sears, Roebuck catalogue still featured horse-drawn farm wagons, washing machines run by gasoline, and refrigerators designed to cool with a block of ice
- Zippers on men's trousers became standard equipment

1939 Economic Profile

Income, Standard Jobs

Average of All Industries, Excluding Farm Labor	$1,346
Average of All Industries, Including Farm Labor	$1,266
Bituminous Coal Mining	$1,197
Building Trades	$1,268
Domestics	$544
Farm Labor	$436
Federal Civilian	$1,843
Federal Employees, Executive Departments	$1,137
Federal Military	$1,134
Finance, Insurance, and Real Estate	$1,729
Gas and Electricity Workers	$1,766
Manufacturing, Durable Goods	$1,479
Manufacturing, Nondurable Goods	$1,263
Medical/Health Services Workers	$908
Miscellaneous Manufacturing	$1,337
Motion Picture Services	$1,971
Nonprofit Organization Workers	$1,546
Passenger Transportation Workers, Local and Highway	$1,569
Personal Services	$1,034
Public School Teachers	$1,403
Radio Broadcasting	$2,427
Railroads	$1,877
State and Local Government Workers	$1,569
Telephone and Telegraph Workers	$1,600
Wholesale and Retail Trade Workers	$1,360

Selected Prices

Carbon Arc Sunlamp	$6.75
Challenge Flashlight	$0.55
Cold Wave Oscillating Fan	$5.50
Copley Plaza Luxury Hotel Room, per Night	$4.00
Ex-Lax Laxative	$0.19
Giralda Farms English Cocker Spaniel Pups	$50.00
Hammacher Schlemmer Dining Table	$10.50
Hammacher Schlemmer Wrought Iron Table	$56.00
Hercules Pitchfork	$1.35
Ingraham Regulator Wall Clock	$6.98
Kodak Bantam Camera	$22.50

Kook-Kwick Pressure Cooker	$7.45
Listerine Mouthwash, 14 Ounces	$0.59
Lombard & Co. English Sandstone Birdbath	$50.00
Milk of Magnesia	$0.08
Prima Milker	$42.50
Same Sex Life, by H.W. Long, M.D.	$1.85
Simmons Beautyrest Box Spring and Mattress	$345.00
Sta-Sharp Pocketknife	$0.95
Velflor Rug, 9' x 12'	$8.75

The Risks and Rewards of 1939—A Financial Review of the Year, Federal Reserve Bank of New York:

"January to April

In the first few weeks of the year, the inflow of capital from abroad, which had diminished considerably following the Munich Agreement in September 1938, remained at a relatively low level. The inward movement increased in March, when a new crisis was precipitated by German demands on Czechoslovakia, and continued in heavy volume for several weeks after the occupation and dismemberment of that country by Germany. As a result of the increased transfers of capital into this country, together with payments due on the continued excess of merchant exports over imports to the United States, heavy pressure was put on European exchanges, especially sterling. At the same time, large transfers of funds in United States paper currency were demanded for shipment to Europe, presumably for hoarding. In March and April, shipments of U.S. currency to Europe reached record levels; total shipments topped $73 million during the two months.

The influence of European demands tended to check requirements for bank credit by industrial and commercial concerns; the U.S. Treasury found it unnecessary to borrow on the usual Treasury financing date. In the absence of these opportunities or the possibility of employing its funds, New York City banks added to their holdings of outstanding government bonds. Prices of high-grade securities rose, and yields declined further.

Despite the accentuation of easy money conditions, there was no evidence of a stimulating effect on business activity.

May to July

As the disquieting effects of the dismemberment of Czechoslovakia subsided, there was a temporary respite from disturbances in Europe. The movement of capital from Europe to America ceased; the foreign demand for United States currency subsided. Gold imports continued in large volume during May and were sizable during June and July. Only a part of the gold was sold to obtain dollars; the remainder was earmarked for foreign central banks; this reflected a tendency of European countries to transfer part of their gold reserves to the United States for safekeeping. At the end of July the total amount of gold held under earmark for foreign accounts at the Federal Reserve Bank of New York reached the unprecedented figure of $1.3 billion. The accumulation of idle funds continued to have a stimulating effect on prices of high-grade securities and a depressing influence on money rates. Prices on government and other prime bonds reached new high levels, and bond yields corresponding declined to new low levels. New security flotations increased considerably, most for refunding purposes. Business activity remained at a relatively low level in May and there was little demand for business loans or for loans to finance security trading. In June, there was an abrupt increase in business activity, reflecting the temporary relief from disturbing developments in Europe.

August and September

The lull between the crises in Europe proved to be of short duration. An increasingly critical situation in the relations between Germany and Poland led in August to the third major European crisis within a year. Germany invaded Poland on September 1; shortly thereafter, England and France declared war against Germany. This resulted in an accelerated flow of capital from Europe to the United States, chiefly by way of London; this produced heavy pressure against the sterling exchange and required the British authorities to provide support to maintain the value of the sterling against the dollar.

The decision of the British authorities to suspend official support of sterling on August 25 resulted in a sharp drop in the pound from $4.68 to $4.12; this action abruptly checked the flow of capital to the United States."

"Town of Tomorrow," by Dorothy Ducas and Elizabeth Gordon, *The New York Herald Tribune* World's Fair Section, April 30, 1939:

"The 15 demonstration houses which make up the Town of Tomorrow at the New York World's Fair bear a marked resemblance to the Town of Today. This is no accident. Housing prophets at the Fair apparently believe there is nothing very startling in the immediate future of home building, nothing to dazzle the eye and confound the mind. If these 15 houses are an indication, good houses, compact and well-made and containing all the conveniences and comforts of present-day living, will be the order of a New Day, probably at a lower cost than all these things have been possible before.

Making no attempt to present 'trick' houses, created to wrest 'ohs' and 'ahs' from a newly house-conscious public, World's Fair architects have given us 15 houses such as everyone yearns to own today. There are houses done in the modern style, of course—six of them, five with attractively arranged flat roofs—but traditional Colonial, Georgian, Swedish, and Rural French, too. There is an increased use of glass, in sliding wall panels and glass/brick sections of walls. There is one new-fangled entrance to a home through the garage, which is wallpapered and windowed so it merits the name 'motor room.' And utility rooms galore, to house heating equipment, replacing traditional basements. But none of these things is exactly unheralded, as a look at a new building in any up-and-coming city will convince you. . . .

In general, they are small houses, ranging in price from $2,500 to $35,000, depending upon where they would be built and how much special equipment you put into them. . . . They show definite trends, such as the elimination of dining rooms, increased attention to fire safety, more garden space, lots of built-in shelving and cabinet work, definite recreation space, outdoor decks and terraces. And here's an interesting detail: only two houses eliminate fireplaces. The future, like the present, will preserve a sentimental attachment to the family hearth."

"Cabarets to Pay City Sales Tax by the Month,"
***New York Herald Tribune*, April 30, 1939:**

"Because many fly-by-night cabarets have swindled the city of the sales tax they collected from patrons by closing up after only a few weeks' existence, Comptroller Joseph D. McGoldrick issued a new rule yesterday requiring all-night clubs and cabarets to pay the sales tax monthly instead of quarterly. . . 'Numerous fly-by-night cabarets have been able to avoid any sales tax whatsoever by the simple process of going out of business,' said Mr. McGoldrick. 'Despite the fact that the patrons have paid the tax to the clubs, the city has never received it.'"

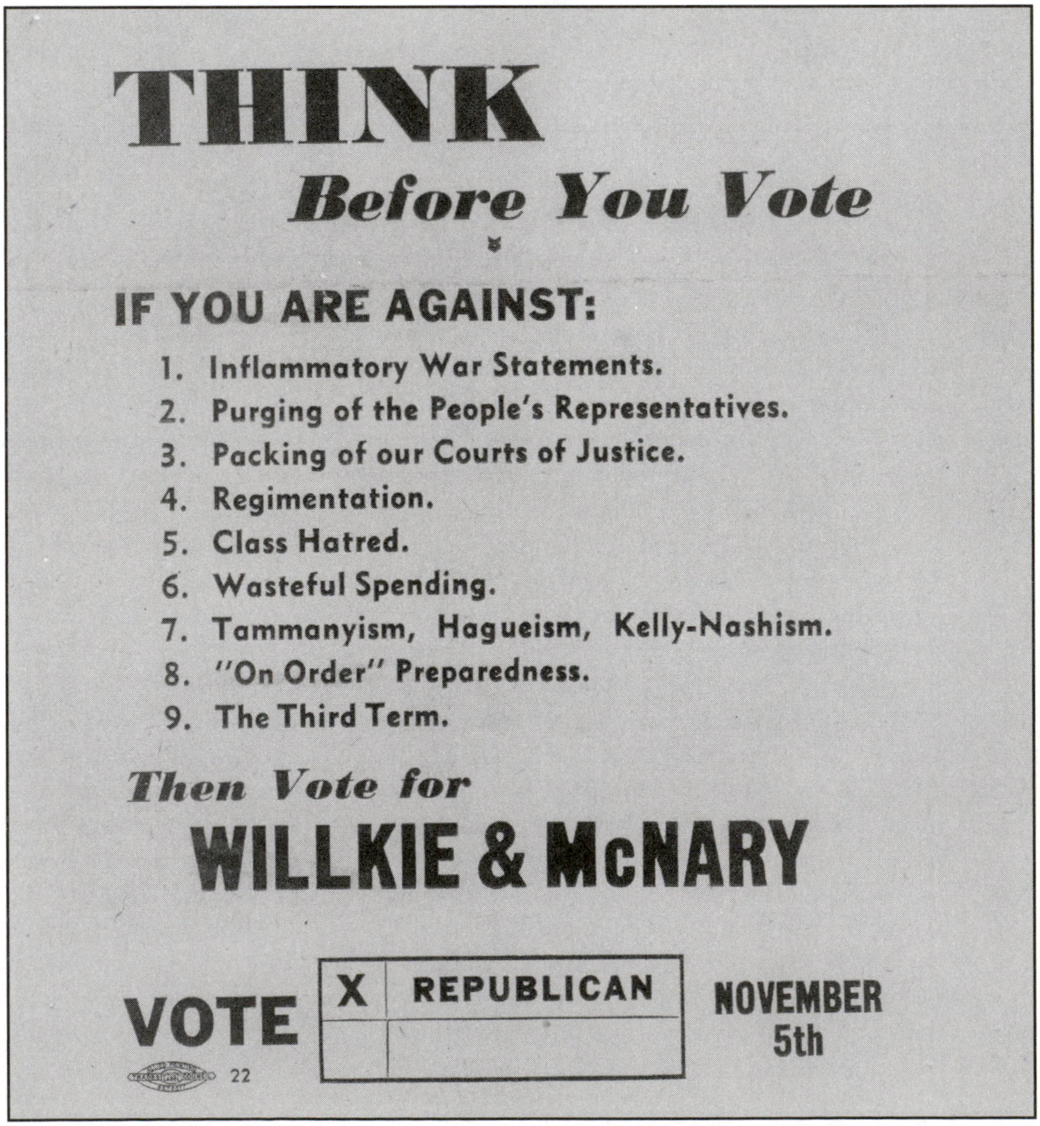

THINK
Before You Vote
IF YOU ARE AGAINST:
1. Inflammatory War Statements.
2. Purging of the People's Representatives.
3. Packing of our Courts of Justice.
4. Regimentation.
5. Class Hatred.
6. Wasteful Spending.
7. Tammanyism, Hagueism, Kelly-Nashism.
8. "On Order" Preparedness.
9. The Third Term.
Then Vote for
WILLKIE & McNARY
VOTE
X REPUBLICAN
NOVEMBER 5th
22

COME IN AND SAVE MONEY!
Make driving happier, safer, smoother—save money, too. Don't pass up a single page of the thrift ideas and suggestions inside.
1937
SPRING AND SUMMER CATALOG .
GOOD YEAR

The Great Leap, Before and After, **by John Brooks:**

"A nationwide survey of 1,400 husbands and wives made by the American Association of University Women resulted in the conclusion that children of middle-class families were more apt to suffer from their mothers' over-conscientiousness than from neglect. The same survey showed that among the educated couples under consideration, 92 percent handled their money jointly, 80 percent took joint responsibility for the upbringing of their children, 60 percent of the husbands regularly took a hand in the cooking. Incidentally, two-thirds of the husbands in the survey earned under $5,000 a year, and almost one-third of the families—presumably the other third—had full-time domestic help."

GATE 2
GATE 2
Prison is Better Than Army Jimcrow Service
WE DEMA
OUTLAWING
Military Segreg
MOVIETONE NEWS

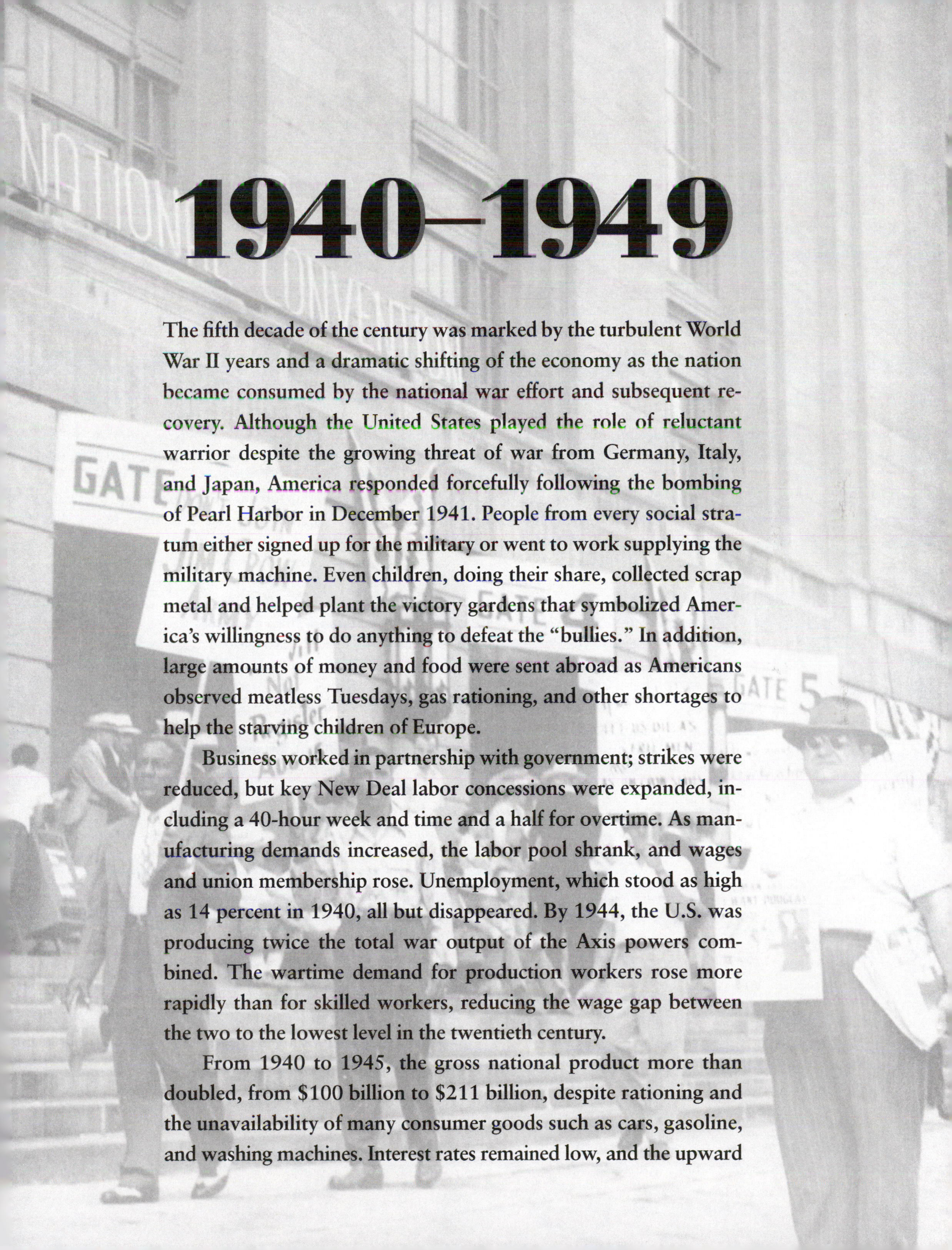

1940–1949

The fifth decade of the century was marked by the turbulent World War II years and a dramatic shifting of the economy as the nation became consumed by the national war effort and subsequent recovery. Although the United States played the role of reluctant warrior despite the growing threat of war from Germany, Italy, and Japan, America responded forcefully following the bombing of Pearl Harbor in December 1941. People from every social stratum either signed up for the military or went to work supplying the military machine. Even children, doing their share, collected scrap metal and helped plant the victory gardens that symbolized America's willingness to do anything to defeat the "bullies." In addition, large amounts of money and food were sent abroad as Americans observed meatless Tuesdays, gas rationing, and other shortages to help the starving children of Europe.

Business worked in partnership with government; strikes were reduced, but key New Deal labor concessions were expanded, including a 40-hour week and time and a half for overtime. As manufacturing demands increased, the labor pool shrank, and wages and union membership rose. Unemployment, which stood as high as 14 percent in 1940, all but disappeared. By 1944, the U.S. was producing twice the total war output of the Axis powers combined. The wartime demand for production workers rose more rapidly than for skilled workers, reducing the wage gap between the two to the lowest level in the twentieth century.

From 1940 to 1945, the gross national product more than doubled, from $100 billion to $211 billion, despite rationing and the unavailability of many consumer goods such as cars, gasoline, and washing machines. Interest rates remained low, and the upward pressure on prices remained high, yet from 1943 to the end of the war, the cost of living rose less than 1.5 percent. Following the war, as controls were removed, inflation peaked in 1948; union demands for high wages accelerated. Between 1945 and 1952, confident Americans—and their growing families—increased consumer credit by 800 percent.

To fight inflation, government agencies regulated wages, prices, and the kind of jobs people could take. The Office of Price Administration was entrusted with the complicated task of setting price ceilings for almost all consumer goods and distributing ration books for items in short supply. The Selective Service and the War Manpower Commission largely determined who would serve in the military, whose work was vital to the war effort, and when a worker could transfer from one job to another. When the war ended and regulations were lifted, workers demanded higher wages; the relations between labor and management became strained. Massive strikes and inflation followed in the closing days of the decade and many consumer goods were easier to find on the black market than on the store shelves until America retooled for a peacetime economy.

The decade of the 1940s made America a world power and Americans more worldly. Millions served overseas; millions more listened to broadcasts concerning the war in London, Rome, and Tokyo. Newsreels brought the war home to moviegoers, who numbered in the millions. The war effort also redistributed the population and the demand for labor; the Pacific Coast gained wealth and power, and the South was able to supply its people with much-needed war jobs and provide blacks with opportunities previously closed to them. Women entered the work force in unprecedented numbers, reaching 18 million. The net cash income of the American farmer soared 400 percent.

But the Second World War extracted a price. Those who experienced combat entered a nightmarish world. Both sides possessed far greater firepower than ever before, and within those units actually fighting the enemy, the incidence of death was high, sometimes one in three. In all, the United States lost 405,000 men and women to combat deaths; many suffered in the war's final year, when the American army spearheaded the assault against Germany and Japan. The cost in dollars was $350 billion. But the cost was not only in American lives. Following Germany's unconditional surrender on May 4, 1945, Japan continued fighting. To prevent the loss of thousands of American lives defeating the Japanese, President Truman dropped atomic bombs on the Japanese cities of Hiroshima and Nagasaki, ending the war and ushering in the threat of "the bomb" as a key element of the Cold War during the 1950s and 1960s.

Throughout the war, soldiers from all corners of the nation fought side by side and refined nationalism and what it meant to America through this government-imposed mixing process. This newfound identity of American GIs was further cemented by the vivid descriptions of war correspondent Ernie Pyle, who spent a considerable time talking and living with the average soldier to present a "worm's eye view" of war. Yet, despite the closeness many men and women developed toward their fellow soldiers, spawning a wider view of the world, discrimination continued. African-American servicemen were excluded from the marines, the Coast Guard, and the Army Corps. The regular army accepted blacks into the military—700,000 in all—only on a segregated basis. Only in the closing years of the decade would President Harry Truman lead the way toward a more integrated America by integrating the military.

Sports attendance in the 1940s soared beyond the record levels of the 1920s; in football the T-formation moved in prominence; Joe DiMaggio, Ted Williams, and Stan Musial dominated baseball before and after the war, and Jackie Robinson became the first black in organized baseball. In 1946, Dr. Benjamin Spock's work, *Common Sense Baby and Child Care,* was published to guide newcomers in the booming business of raising babies. The decade also discovered the joys of fully air-conditioned stores for the first time, cellophane wrap, Morton salt, daylight-saving time, Dannon yogurt, Everglades National Park, the Cannes Film Festival, Michelin radial tires, Dial soap, and Nikon 35mm film.

1944 Family Profile

Rosemary Charrette, a 1941 graduate of Wellesley College, is working in Chicago as a securities analyst. Her major in economics helped her land the job just as men were leaving for the war. Currently, she is packing to leave for New York to be with her sister, whose husband has been declared missing in action.

Annual Income: $2,100

Annual Budget

The average per capita consumer expenditures in 1944 for all workers nationwide are:

Auto Parts	$2.89
Auto Usage	$21.68
Clothing	$83.82
Dentists	$4.34
Food	$265.18
Furniture	$9.39
Gas and Oil	$10.12
Health Insurance	$2.17
Housing	$88.87
Intercity Transport	$7.95
Local Transport	$12.02
New Auto Purchase	$0.72
Personal Business	$28.18
Personal Care	$13.01
Physicians	$9.39
Private Education and Research	$7.23
Recreation	$39.02

Her economics degree helps her secure a job.

Religion/Welfare Activities	$12.28
Telephone and Telegraph	$7.95
Tobacco	$18.71
Utilities	$30.35
Per Capita Consumption	$781.81

Life at Home

- Following her graduation from Wellesley College, Rosemary took a job at the telegraph company, but eagerly joined Harris Trust and Savings in 1942 as a securities analyst.
- She does not know typing or shorthand and sees no reason to learn.
- She has worked with Harris Trust and Savings for two years and is preparing to move to New York; her sister's husband has been reported missing in action and her father has asked her to support her sister at this time.
- She plans to work for Banker's Trust, a correspondent bank of Harris Trust and Savings.
- For the past two years, she has lived with a friend in a large house on Aster Street that has been divided into a guest house; she lives in the master bedroom of his elegant home, which includes a bathroom featuring smooth marble and beautiful tile.
- The house is one block off Lake Shore Drive.

Following graduation from Wellesley College, she joined Harris Trust and Savings as a securities analyst.

Rosemary's apartment is one block off Lake Shore Drive.

- As part of her rent agreement, she turns her ration book over to the man who owns the house; he fixes breakfast and dinner.
- Even with the ration books of all the tenants in his building, the landlord is rarely able to buy eggs or certain types of meat.
- Chicken, fish, and organ meat can be purchased, but beef is only available on special occasions.
- Rosemary has developed a love for beef tongue, classified as organ meat, which is not rationed and therefore is more readily available.
- In the late afternoons, she loves walking along Michigan Avenue and seeing the sailboats dotted across Lake Michigan.
- Her rent includes dinner at the guest house at 6 p.m. each evening; often by the time she arrives home, her roommate has gotten home, changed, and had a chance to begin sipping a glass of port before dinner.
- Most evenings are spent writing letters; her only dates are with her current boss, a nice man who has a severe stutter.
- Because of the war, few men are available or have time for dating.
- She also spends time doing her laundry by hand, as few washing machines are available and many of those need parts; she also spends time reading romance novels, which are rapidly gaining in popularity.
- She checks out the romance novels from the library during her trips home to South Bend, Indiana.
- Once a week, she volunteers with the Red Cross at the hospital as a nurse's aid; her father had told her, "You will be sorry if you don't do something during the war."
- As a nurse's aid, she dresses open wounds, cares for the critically ill, and handles emergencies, since nurses are scarce.
- Often when she gets off her volunteer duty after 10 p.m., her boss meets the streetcar and walks her home; recently, some women have been attacked, even in respectable neighborhoods.
- She takes the Clark Street car to work each morning, often with the man she works with at Harris Trust.

She enjoys watching sailboats race across Lake Michigan.

- Her father is an advertising executive from South Bend, Indiana, with clients primarily in the northern part of Indiana and southern section of Michigan.
- He has a B-ration card that allows him to travel, but his trips must be planned very carefully to stretch his wartime gasoline allotment.
- Americans now believe in the power of advertising and are eager to promote their products, but careful about new ideas.
- Her work schedule demands that she work two Saturdays a month.
- On the weekends she does not work, she generally takes the interurban train to her parents' home in South Bend.
- During weekends, she often sees the "90-Day Wonders"—soldiers with a minimum of training—being pushed through Notre Dame; colleges nationwide are being used to process soldiers for war.
- Newly minted soldiers are sometimes invited to Sunday dinner at her parents' house; many people in the community make it their job to ease the soldiers' transition by inviting them for a meal.
- As she was growing up, her parents were affluent, capable of affording two maids to assist in the care and cleaning of the house.
- Although her brothers and sisters all went to prep schools prior to college, she attended public school because the depression had depleted the family's resources.

"The Corset Question,"
Vogue Magazine

"The Corset Question has been one of this war's small but persistent problems. American women know that the rubber went out of corsets in an overwhelmingly worthy cause—but they can't help feeling some secret longing for it. Since 1942, the corset manufacturers have done very well with the materials on hand. . . . But women still ask wistfully when the real prewar stuff will be back."

Chicago celebrates as the war draws to a close.

- She selected Wellesley to attend because a friend of her sister attended the college, and it sounded romantic.
- When she went to college, 1,000 miles away, it was the farthest she had ever traveled from home.
- She was horribly homesick, rarely eating for four months and dreaming of returning home, but eventually she adjusted.

Life at Work

- Rosemary works for Harris Trust and Savings, one of Chicago's oldest financial firms.
- Even though she has only been at the firm for two years, she shares her company's loathing for its principal competitor, Northern Trust.

- The securities research department is divided into groups; her section follows the publishing, printing, and real estate industries for the Trust Department of Harris Trust and Savings.
- Her office is on the mezzanine of Harris Trust, with the credit department on the same floor in the back; her hours are 9 a.m. to 5 p.m.
- She works in research during the week, but every other Saturday she assists on the bond-trading desk, even though she is unsure of her skills.
- During the week, the first duty of the day is to read the *New York Times, Wall Street Journal,* and *Chicago Journal,* then mark them for clipping; any article that pertains to publishing, printing, or real estate is then circulated and filed.
- She also spends considerable time answering letters pertaining to the holdings of the company's customers, especially in real estate.
- With regularity, elderly women totter up the stairs to inquire about the value and viability of a bond they own.
- Often, because of the depression throughout the 1930s, many of the real estate bonds have little or no value, and she must tell these people, mostly women, that their bonds are worthless.
- She sits out front and sees all customers first; customarily, her male boss would greet customers, but because of his speech impediment, she has been asked to handle all visitors.
- Often she escorts them to different departments to get their issues and problems handled.
- After work, she often window-shops at Carson Pirie and Marshall Fields, although she rarely buys.
- When she does spend money it is for something to wear to work.
- She wears suits to work; her favorite suit is an ivory and tan suit of wool tweed with a box-pleated skirt.
- As a result of rationing, during the war she particularly misses having nylon stockings, since the cotton stocking substitutes are not worth wearing.
- Eligible to vote for the first time, she is carefully following the presidential race between Franklin D. Roosevelt and Thomas Dewey; the *Chicago Tribune* is rabidly against a fourth term for Roosevelt and regularly editorializes against the President.
- Two years after the United States entered the war, the unemployment rate has dropped from 14 percent to zero, and both the government and the media are affirming the importance of working women.
- Prior to the war, women's avenues were severely restricted; married women who worked outside the home, particularly during the depression, were perceived as taking jobs away from men.
- At the height of war production, 3.5 million women worked on assembly lines alongside six million men.
- A survey found that 57 percent of American women and 63 percent of men believe that if the man of the house could support his family, his wife should not be allowed to work, regardless of her wishes.

Life in the Community: Chicago, Illinois

- World War II unleashed the greatest economic boom in American history.
- From 1940 to 1945, federal expenditures soared from $9 billion to $98.4 billion; nationally, per capita income has doubled during the war.
- The labor force has expanded by nine million workers.
- War rationing impacts everyone, whether their need is for tires, shoes, or steaks.
- Despite the rationing of meat, meat consumption has risen to 128.9 pounds per person, per year.
- Because all metal winds up in military hardware, new toasters, refrigerators, washing machines, or automobiles are unavailable—at virtually any price.
- Approximately 30 percent of all cigarette production is set aside for the armed forces; smokers in Chicago stand in lines up to a mile long to get a pack.
- The military personnel are also consuming 40 percent of all cheese and 46 percent of canned milk.
- American war expenditures from mid-1940 to V-E Day top $276 billion, or $104 billion more than the government had spent in its entire history.
- The Servicemen's Readjustment Act, known as the GI Bill of Rights, which provides 12 months of educational training, encourages eight million men to further their education.
- Sixty percent of veterans had not completed high school prior to going to war.

Historical Snapshot
1944

- On D-Day, June 6, the Normandy invasion was mounted by 6,939 naval vessels, 15,040 aircraft, and 156,000 troops; casualties numbered 16,434, 76,535 were wounded, and 19,704 were missing
- The War Refugee Board revealed the first details of the mass murder at Birkenau and Auschwitz, estimating that 1.7 million were killed
- Nearly half the steel, tin, and paper needed for the war was provided by people salvaging goods
- Jell-O became a popular dessert substitute for canned fruit; baking powder sales fell as women continued to join the work force
- Horse racing was banned because of the war
- Paper shortages stimulated publishers to experiment with soft-cover books
- A New York judge found the book *Lady Chatterley's Lover* obscene and ordered publisher Dial Press to trial
- Bill Mauldin's cartoon *Willie & Joe,* originally in *Yank* and *Stars and Stripes,* was picked up by the domestic press and achieved great acclaim
- More than 81,000 GIs were killed, wounded, or captured in the Battle of the Bulge, Germany's last big offensive of the war
- Because of a shortage of cheese and tomato sauce, the sale of pasta fell dramatically
- Gen. Douglas MacArthur returned to the Philippines; his American army annihilated the troops commanded by Gen. Tomoyuki Yamashita, the Tiger of Malaya; 50,000 Japanese were killed, and fewer than 400 were captured
- Nationwide, 372,000 German POWs were being held in the United States
- The Dow Jones reached a high of 152, a low of 135; unemployment stood at 1.2 percent
- Victory bonds became an obsession, with actress Hedy Lamarr offering to kiss any man who bought $25,000 worth; Jack Benny auctioned his $75 violin—*Old Love in Bloom*—for a million dollars' worth of bonds
- "Kilroy was here" became the graffiti symbol of valor for GIs everywhere
- Herr Adolf Hitler was among the citizens of enemy nations whose assets were frozen during the war; $22,666 from the sale of *Mein Kampf* was later used to pay Americans' claims against enemy nationals
- Chiquita brand bananas were introduced
- Expenditures for spectator sports hit record levels, topping 80 million; the nation had 409 golf courses and 910,000 bowlers
- Seven laboratories refined and improved DDT, used to reduce typhus and malaria; 350,000 pounds a month were sent to the military for spraying

1944 Economic Profile

Income, Standard Jobs

Average of All Industries, Excluding Farm Labor	$2,360
Average of All Industries, Including Farm Labor	$2,292
Bituminous Coal Mining	$2,535
Building Trades	$2,602
Domestics	$1,140
Farm Labor	$1,189
Federal Civilian	$2,677
Federal Employees, Executive Departments	$1,929
Federal Military	$1,763
Finance, Insurance, and Real Estate	$2,191
Gas and Electricity Workers	$2,467
Manufacturing, Durable Goods	$2,774
Manufacturing, Nondurable Goods	$2,081
Medical/Health Services Workers	$1,262
Miscellaneous Manufacturing	$2,176
Motion Picture Services	$2,379
Nonprofit Organization Workers	$1,795
Passenger Transportation Workers, Local and Highway	$2,458
Personal Services	$1,575
Public School Teachers	$1,730
Radio Broadcasting and Television Workers	$3,333
Railroad Workers	$2,714
State and Local Government Workers	$1,797
Telephone and Telegraph Workers	$2,035
Wholesale and Retail Trade Workers	$1,946

Selected Prices

Carmen Jones Theater Ticket	$3.00
Thom McAnn Shoes	$4.20
Webb Coffee, per Pound	$0.33
Armour's Peanut Butter, 24-Ounce Jar	$0.41
Early American Four-Piece Bedroom Set	$49.50
Dulux Paint, per Quart	$2.00
Norcross Valentine Greeting Card	$1.00
Enoz Moth Spray, per Quart	$1.29
Jesse W. Miller Wallpaper, per Roll	$0.65

As the war drew to a close, labor unrest increased.

Baldwin Six-Room Cottage	$6,950
Bayer Aspirin	$0.59
Iron Jack Plane	$3.98
Overhead Garage Door, 8' x 7'	$7.98
Johnson Paste Wax, One-Pound Can	$1.90
Tufcote Varnish, per Quart	$1.43
James Bones Wright, Jr., Glazed Chintz Draperies, per Yard	$4.00
Edgewood Handbag	$5.00
Kayser Leatherette Gloves	$2.50
Lace Handkerchief	$0.25

Chicago Social Highlights:

- 1900—Theodore Dreiser's *Sister Carrie* was published in an edition of only 1,000 copies; until its publication in England seven years later, it was a failure. It is widely regarded as the novel that brought American fiction into the twentieth century.
- 1900—A small Chicago house agreed to print a much-rejected story written by L. Frank Baum, *The Wonderful Wizard of Oz;* by 1902, five million copies had been sold.
- 1902—Muckraking novelist Frank Norris published *The Pit,* the first exposé of life in the Board of Trade floor.
- 1905—Robert S. Abbott founded the *Chicago Defender,* which became the national voice of black people; his publication helped propel the migration of black workers from the rural South to cities like Chicago.
- 1906—*The Jungle,* Upton Sinclair's exposé of the Chicago stockyards, was published; his tale of worker exploitation resulted in national outrage over filthy conditions in the slaughterhouses, initiating enhanced food inspection laws.
- 1906—Carl Laemmle used $2,000 to open the White Front Theatre to produce motion pictures; by 1915, he opened his 230-acre studio called Universal City in Hollywood, California.
- 1909—Scott, Foresman & Company began publishing schoolbook readers, leading to the creation of *Dick and Jane* readers.
- 1913—Ringer Lardner began writing a sports column for the *Chicago Tribune* and built a national reputation by writing the way people talk.
- 1914—Right-wing eccentric Robert McCormick inherited control of the *Chicago Tribune.*
- 1915—Edgar Lee Master's *Spoon River Anthology* was published, becoming the most widely read book of poetry in the country; his law partner was Clarence Darrow, lawyer for Eugene Debs after the Pullman Strike, defender of murderers Nathan Leopold and Richard Leob, and lead attorney for Tennessee schoolteacher, John Scopes, in the famous "Monkey Trial."
- 1916—"Chicago" by Carl Sandburg, widely regarded as the most famous paean to the Windy City, was published.
- 1919—*Gasoline Alley,* the longest-running comic strip in American history, began.
- 1921—Lee De Forest brought a vacuum tube into the offices of Western Electric Company; Chicago would become the world's largest manufacturer of radios and television sets.
- 1921—Henry Windsor started a magazine for fellow do-it-yourselfers called *Popular Mechanics.*
- 1921—Chicago's first radio station began to broadcast; its call letters were KYW.
- 1923—The publishing and printing industry employed 35,000 people.

(continued)

Chicago Social Highlights: *(continued)*

- 1926—Radio station WCFL, owned by the Chicago Federation of Labor, began operation.
- 1927—Sears Roebuck & Company brought the *Encyclopaedia Britannica* to Chicago, underwriting the $2.5 million cost of printing the fourteenth edition, which contained 38 million words from 3,500 contributors.
- 1928—Freeman Gosden and Charles Correll began the *Amos 'n Andy* show.
- 1929—Jack L. Cooper became the country's first African-American radio personality with his show, the *All-Negro Hour* on WSBC.
- 1931—The comic strip *Dick Tracy* was created for the *Chicago Tribune* by Chester Gould.
- 1933—The first issue of Arnold Gingrich's *Esquire* was published; one of the magazine's editors in its early days was Hugh Hefner.
- 1937—One-third of all radios produced in the United States were made in Chicago; eight companies produced radios for RCA.
- 1941—Marshall Field, III, debuted a new Chicago newspaper, the *Chicago Sun,* on December 7, Pearl Harbor Day.
- 1944—Saul Bellow, Chicago's most famous late-twentieth-century writer, published his first novel, *Dangling Man.*

"The Navy's Battling Builders," by A.D. Rathbone, IV, *The American Legion Magazine*, February 1943:

"When the Japs attacked Wake Island, they unwittingly set in motion a brand-new force that is destined to play a major role in wrecking the little monkey men, and in the smashing of Japan's Axis partners. The bombs, the shells, and the machine-gun bullets that rained down on that tiny Pacific outpost for 17 days and nights took their harsh toll, not only of marines, but also among a crew of civilian engineers and construction men, whose business at Wake was that of building and improving naval installations. From the scant available facts concerning the amazing defense of that four-and-one-half-mile-long atoll, it is known that those civilian workers—many of them World War I veterans—grabbed whatever would shoot and fought alongside the marines, a prophetic promise of the new force to come.

The echoes of that Jap bombardment rolled across the Pacific, reverberated over the Rocky Mountains, rumbled on to Washington, and culminated in a navy directive in December 1941, authorizing the recruiting of one Construction Regiment of approximately 3,300 officers and men. Thus began a new arm of the navy—that force unintentionally motivated by the Japs—an arm now grown to a strength of more than 210,000 men."

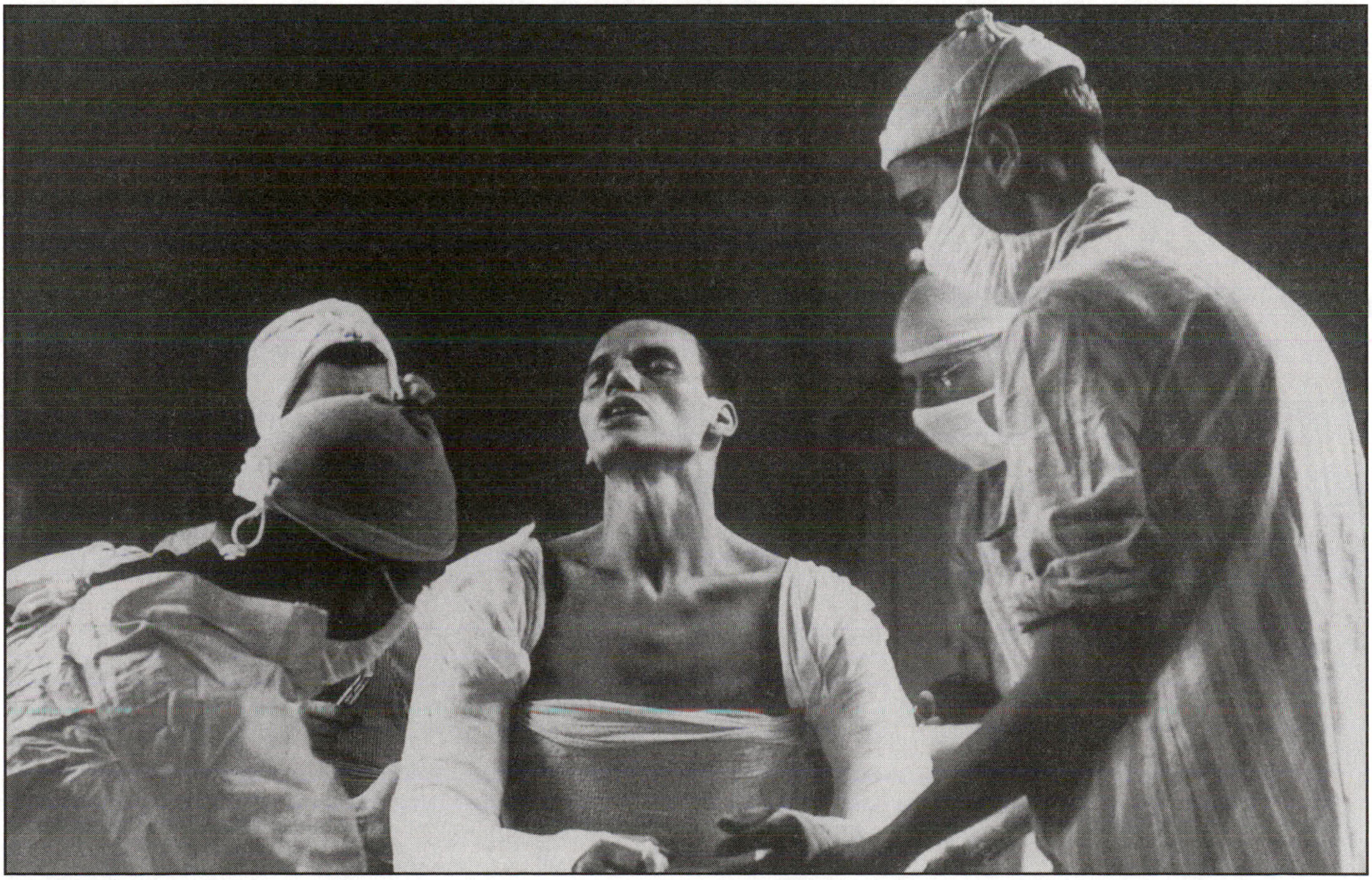

Soldiers come home badly wounded from the war.

Advertisement, Joe Kindig, Jr., *Antiques*, July 1945:

"Twenty or more years ago, along one of the Virginia rivers, John Williar of Baltimore located, bought, and sold this Chippendale corner cupboard. Later he always referred to it as the finest antique he ever owned. Completely original with a fine old finish, this cupboard which I recently acquired is probably the most unusual American Chippendale corner cupboard that has been found.

Now dead these many years, John Williar was one of the pioneer Southern antique dealers. Through his shop passed many of the finest antiques then found in the Chesapeake Bay county. Remembering many interesting deals negotiated in his shop on North Howard Street, I illustrate this old photograph with sincere pleasure. Mr. Williar, his shop in the background, stands beside the Chippendale cupboard of which he was so justly proud."

"Advertising in Wartime," by Henry C. Flower, Jr., *Forbes Magazine*, 1942:

"Prior to the war, most advertising had virtually a single, unqualified objective—direct selling. Today there are many objectives.

Many advertisers no longer have any products to sell—except Uncle Sam. Many others have little need of advertising to help them move restricted stocks. Still others may offer their wares or services only under the rigid moral restrictions imposed by the total war effort.

For all these advertisers, direct sale is no longer an objective at all. They realize, however, that advertising is still a potent influence for both the present welfare and future development of their organizations. They also realize that advertising must be aimed at a series of new objectives.

The present-day situation of the advertiser may be compared with that of the field artillery commander on new and unfamiliar terrain. His first duty is to determine his own position.

Similarly, the advertiser must determine his own relationship to the public, the government, his status in relation to his competitors, and the new, unfamiliar conditions that surround him. At this point it must be noted that we are now experiencing a new kind of war, totally different from World War I or any other war, in disruptive effects on the national economy.

The artillery commander's second duty is to select his target—the one, among many perhaps, that seems most to call for attention and offers the greatest promise of desired results. The advertiser, too, must select an objective so that his advertising may be pointed to an effective accomplishment.

Finally, the officer decides upon the means best suited to reduce the enemy's strong points. He sets the range, the orientation, and fuse, and fixes the amount of the powder charge. For the advertiser there must be a selection of media, of copy to be used, space sizes, and frequency of insertion. In determining the objective of an advertiser, it may be discovered as the relatively simple one of keeping the name of the product before the people, reminding them what it looks like, and protecting the goodwill built up through advertising in the past.

It may be that advertising will be called on to justify the very existence of the product under total war economy . . .

As a matter of fact, the war period may offer certain businesses unusual opportunities to build up defenses against future demagogues by creating consumer and governmental goodwill through performing meritorious actions and then publicizing these facts through advertising. Finally, the objective of the advertising might still be simply to sell the product on a competitive basis, almost (but never quite) as if no war were going on."

"Birth of the Atomic Age, December 2, 1942," *Chicago Days, 150 Defining Moments in the Life of a Great City*, by Stevenson Swanson:

"After months of preliminary work, the scientists at the University of Chicago's new Metallurgical Laboratory were ready to run their first experiment on this date. The experiment did not involve metallurgy. In fact, there were no metallurgists in the Metallurgical Laboratory. The name was a screen to disguise a key part of America's vast effort to beat Nazi Germany in the race to build an atomic bomb.

An early hurdle in that race was to prove that a nuclear chain reaction could be turned on and off, something that had never been done before. That was the dangerous job of the 43 physicists who crowded into a freezing squash court beneath the stands of Stagg Field, where the first nuclear reactor had been built.

Considering the sophisticated science involved and the risk of conducting such an experiment in a city neighborhood, the materials that the scientists used in building 'Chicago Pile No. 1' were laughable. Spheres of a uranium compound were placed between layers of solid granite bricks, which were held together by a wooden frame. The chief researcher, Italian refugee and Nobel Prize-winner Enrico Fermi, relied upon a six-inch slide rule. Most incredible of all, three young physicists stood by at the top of the pile. In case the reaction started to run out of control, they were to pour a cadmium solution over the pile and hope for the best.

Throughout the day, a control rod was withdrawn from the reactor a few inches at a time. Shortly after 3:30 p.m., a measuring device finally traced a steep line on a piece of graph paper. 'The pile has gone critical,' Fermi said, signifying that the reaction had figuratively caught fire. With that laconic announcement, the Atomic Age was born.

From that beginning grew not only the atomic bombs that destroyed Hiroshima and Nagasaki, but also peaceful uses of nuclear power, such as nuclear medicine. The early reactor work at the University of Chicago led to the establishment of the Argonne National Laboratory in a forest preserve southwest of the city. Fermi, who died of cancer in 1954, was commemorated in the 1960s when another national laboratory, Fermilab, was built in the Chicago area. In 1995, Fermilab scientists announced they had discovered what is believed to be the last remaining piece of the subatomic jigsaw puzzle, the long-elusive 'top quark.'"

Chicago plays a key role in the building of atomic bombs.

During the war, Chicago directed all its energy into defeating the enemy.

AIR FORCE
THE OFFICIAL SERVICE JOURNAL OF THE U. S. ARMY AIR FORCES ☆ OCTOBER 1944
FLIGHT NURSE PAGE 28

1946 Family Profile

Meredith Dempsey, a 33-year-old reporter, works for the *Pittsburgh Courier,* the largest Black newspaper in the nation. He is rapidly building a reputation for insightful writing. After eight years with the paper, including four years reporting the Second World War, he is unsure whether he has the energy to continue in newspapers. He and his wife, Jeanine, have one small child.

Meredith Demsey has a reputation for tough, insightful writing.

Annual Income: $1,600

Annual Budget

The average per capita consumer expenditures in 1946 for all workers nationwide are:

Auto Parts	$9.90
Auto Usage	$67.19
Clothing	$106.79
Dentists	$5.66
Food	$334.54
Furniture	$15.56
Gas and Oil	$24.05
Health Insurance	$2.83
Housing	$100.43
Intercity Transport	$7.07
Local Transport	$13.44
New Auto Purchase	$14.15
Personal Business	$33.29
Personal Care	$14.85
Physicians	$12.73
Private Education and Research	$7.78

Recreation	$60.12
Religion/Welfare Activities	$14.85
Telephone and Telegraph	$9.19
Tobacco	$24.05
Utilities	$35.36
Per Capita Consumption	$1,017.76

Life at Home

- The Dempseys are enjoying the birth of their first child, but are shocked by the cost of everything from baby food to diapers.
- Their baby was born in a hospital, the first child on either side of the family not to be born at home; the Urban League has played a key role in linking improved medical care to new arrivals.
- Until she got pregnant, Jeanine worked as a nurse's aid in the same hospital where her baby was born.
- To hold down inflation but allow prices to rise to competitive levels, the government has been gradually lifting the wartime controls; recently, because the Office of Price Administration approved a two-percent increase in the price of cotton fabrics and yarns, Jeanine knows the price of cloth diapers is bound to go up.
- According to the newspapers, the average price of goods has risen 18.5 percent in a year; her budget tells her the government's report is low.
- The retail price of chocolate bars, cooking chocolate, and cocoa recently jumped 27 percent.

- Until recently, she was thinking about supplying a local market with baked goods to supplement their income, but now she is unsure if she can turn a profit.
- Before the baby arrived, she had grown tired of the long hours Meredith devoted to his job; now she wants him to leave the newspaper business and find a job with more regular hours.
- He loves being a reporter so much she is afraid to tell him her thoughts.

Life at Work

- When covering a story, Meredith is expected to defend the Negro position, and to seek civil rights at every turn.
- Although the *Chicago Defender* defined the role of the Black press during World War I and the Black great migration period of the 1920s and 1930s, his paper, the *Pittsburgh Courier,* is emerging as the national voice of blacks during World War II.
- The *Pittsburgh Courier* is the largest Black newspaper in the country; its circulation exceeds 280,000.
- Because the *Courier* is often passed from apartment to apartment, many believe its influence is four times greater than its circulation numbers.

The war leads to aggressive campaigns to end segregation in America.

The Double V campaign is demonstrated in a variety of ways.

- One of its readers is the FBI; several times, agents have come to visit the newspaper following the publication of an article.
- The FBI is concerned that the newspaper is "holding America up to ridicule"; they also want to know whether any outside forces are trying to influence the paper.
- In the past, the army has stated publicly that the Japanese and communists are using the Negro press to influence Americans.
- The *Courier* replied to the charges of disloyalty, saying, "The Japanese, Germans, Italians, and their Axis stooges know that it is futile to seek spies, saboteurs, or Fifth Columnists among American Negroes. Every attempt in that direction has been a miserable failure."
- Meredith knows several of his contacts are linked to the Communist party; they will occasionally call him to write a story that will help a family whose father has been lynched or simply is in desperate need.
- He believes the *Courier* has given a voice to African-Americans.
- He is especially proud that the *Courier* launched the famous Double V campaign, thanks to a letter to the editor from a factory worker in Kansas.
- The Double V campaign calls for victory abroad and victory at home, meaning an end to Jim Crow, and has become a national symbol for blacks.
- Some of his stories recently dealt with a rising tide of anger now that the war has ended; he believes the paper serves as a safety valve within the community, and that without the Black press there would be more riots, not fewer.
- His stories are frank and clear, just what his editors demand; writing politely is for the White press, he has been told repeatedly.
- Since labor disputes are rampant now that the war has ended, he has spent much of the year covering strikes.
- Strikes in Pittsburgh alone have involved bellhops, waitresses, the Independent Union of Duquesne Light Company, steelworkers, state and county workers, and textile workers.
- A recent story he wrote focused on who was to blame for an act of sabotage during the strike against Duquesne Light Company; a rope thrown over a 22,000-volt line caused it to burn out and pitch the city into darkness for 15 minutes.

- The strike at the power company has also forced more than 100 large steel-fabricating factories to close; their output ranges from straight pins to steel for houses, autos, refrigerators and multi-ton heavy machinery.
- In sympathy, the city's 2,700 streetcar motormen have also staged a work stoppage, virtually closing the city down.
- The pressure for a settlement is intense and tempers are short.
- Covering strikes can be exhausting since neither side trusts a reporter, and management will rarely even meet with a reporter from the Black press, especially the *Pittsburgh Courier.*
- In an attempt to keep up with breaking events, Meredith has a cot set up near the presses at the newspaper office; some days he does not go home.
- The paper now has 10 regular columnists, and although he has enjoyed reporting, he thinks he now wants to leave "beat" work and write a column.
- Many of the columns are written by professors, businessmen, and labor leaders; columnists for the *Courier* currently include two non-blacks—a Chinese man and an Indian woman.
- He is also desperate for money and thinks a columnist job will both pay better and allow him to make money on the side.
- The *Courier* began in 1907 when Edwin Nathaniel Harleston, a security guard at the H.J. Heinz food packing plant, decided to put his love for poetry to use and started a newspaper, *A Toiler's Life;* sales were slow.

As more blacks are drafted, children take up the cause.

The Negro in the United States, Franklin Frazier:

"The Negro reporter is a fighting partisan. The people who read his newspaper . . . expect him to put up a good fight for them. They don't like him tame. They want him to have an arsenal well-stocked with atomic adjectives and nouns. They expect him to invent similes and metaphors that lay open the foe's weaknesses and to employ cutting irony, sarcasm, and ridicule to confound and embarrass our opponents. The Negro reader is often a spectator at a fight. The reporter is attacking the reader's enemy and the reader has a vicarious relish for a fight well fought."

The city has smog so heavy that it sometimes turns day into night.

Buildings once thought to be black, due to the constant smog, are being scrubbed white.

- By January 15, 1910, the four-page newspaper had a new name, the *Courier,* new partners, and a press run of 500.
- Within five years, the paper was a social force for neighborhood issues and was calling for Southern blacks to "come North."
- To meet the demand of the newly arrived rural blacks from the South, the *Courier* wrote extensively about the need for housing, health, and education reform.
- During World War I, the paper advised blacks who had gained employment to "save your money and prepare for the day when white soldiers return from war and reclaim their old jobs."
- In 1925, the *Courier* sent George Schuyler on a nine-month tour of the South, during which he visited every city with more than 5,000 African-Americans.
- Also in 1925, Florida was given the "pennant in the Lynching League of America" because eight blacks were lynched in the Sunshine state that year; seven were lynched in Texas, four in Mississippi, three in South Carolina, two in Arkansas, and one person each was lynched in Georgia, Kansas, New Mexico, and Tennessee.
- Emboldened by its successes, the paper then battled White government, complacent Black churches, Marcus Garvey's Back to Africa Movement, and the "do-nothing" NAACP.
- By 1936, the *Courier* boasted a circulation of 174,000.
- The *Courier,* like most Black newspapers, attracts few regular advertisers, while the few that do appear are for skin creams and lucky charms; most of its income results from subscriptions.
- By the start of the war, the *Courier* was calling for mass meetings and rallies to protest the exclusion of blacks from the military and the industrial defense program.

Pittsburgh's steel mills work around the clock to meet war demands.

Life in the Community: Pittsburgh, Pennsylvania

- Since the start of the war, Pittsburgh's steel industry had been working around the clock to supply tools and weapons to defeat the enemy.
- Since Pearl Harbor Day, Pittsburgh has produced 95 million tons of ingot steel, and is proud of its contribution to the war effort.
- Unfortunately, Pittsburgh's long association with steel has given it the nickname, "The Smoky City," even though industry has made strides to reduce pollution.
- For decades, the city has accepted smog so heavy it turns day into night.
- The battle to control smoke in the 1940s has been led by Edward T. Leech, editor of the *Pittsburgh Press,* and several other prominent citizens.
- The impact on the city has been dramatic; buildings once thought to be black have been scrubbed white.
- Beginning in 1916, the Black population of Pittsburgh began to swell as part of the great migration of blacks from the South.
- They moved North between 1910 and 1930 for the same reason that eastern European immigrants came to America in the preceding decades—jobs in the iron and steel mills.
- Between 1910 and 1930, the Black population of Pittsburgh grew 115 percent—from 25,623 to 54,983; the number of black iron and steel workers in Pittsburgh jumped 326 percent from 786 to 2,853.
- In 1917, a survey of black immigrants showed that half were in their prime work years—18 to 30, most resided in

"Should I Sacrifice to Live 'Half-American'?" Letter to the Editor, *Pittsburgh Courier*, from James G. Thompson, cafeteria worker, Cessna Aircraft Plant, Kansas, January 31, 1942:

"Being an American of dark complexion and some 26 years, these questions flash through my mind: Should I sacrifice my life to live half-American? Will things be better for the next generation in the peace to follow? Would it be demanding too much to demand full citizenship rights in exchange for the sacrificing of my life? Is the kind of America I know worth defending . . . ? Will colored Americans suffer still the indignities that have been heaped upon them in the past?

The V for victory sign is being displayed prominently in all so-called democratic countries that are fighting for victory over aggression, slavery, and tyranny. Yet we colored Americans adopt the double VV for double victory. The first V for victory over our enemies from without, the second V for victory over our enemies from within."

boardinghouses for unmarried men, and more than two-thirds had been in the city for less than six months.

- In 1920, the average black family—including two wage earners—brought home $3.60 per day; rents were generally $10 per month.

Church is an important gathering place for black families.

- The migration continued in the 1920s; the ravages of the boll weevil drove many black families off the Southern farms, while restrictive immigration policies designed to close the door to eastern Europeans created new job opportunities.
- During World War II, some jobs opened to black workers in Pennsylvania, thanks to the Committee on Fair Employment Practices.
- President Franklin D. Roosevelt created the committee to investigate complaints of job discrimination, while an order was issued to prevent black leader A. Philip Randolph from leading a march on Washington.
- Several labor strikes have taken place because black workers were added to the work force.
- As labor shortages grew during the war, many blacks were hired to platform jobs at the Pittsburgh Railroad, or as welders at the Sun Shipbuilding Company.

Historical Snapshot
1946

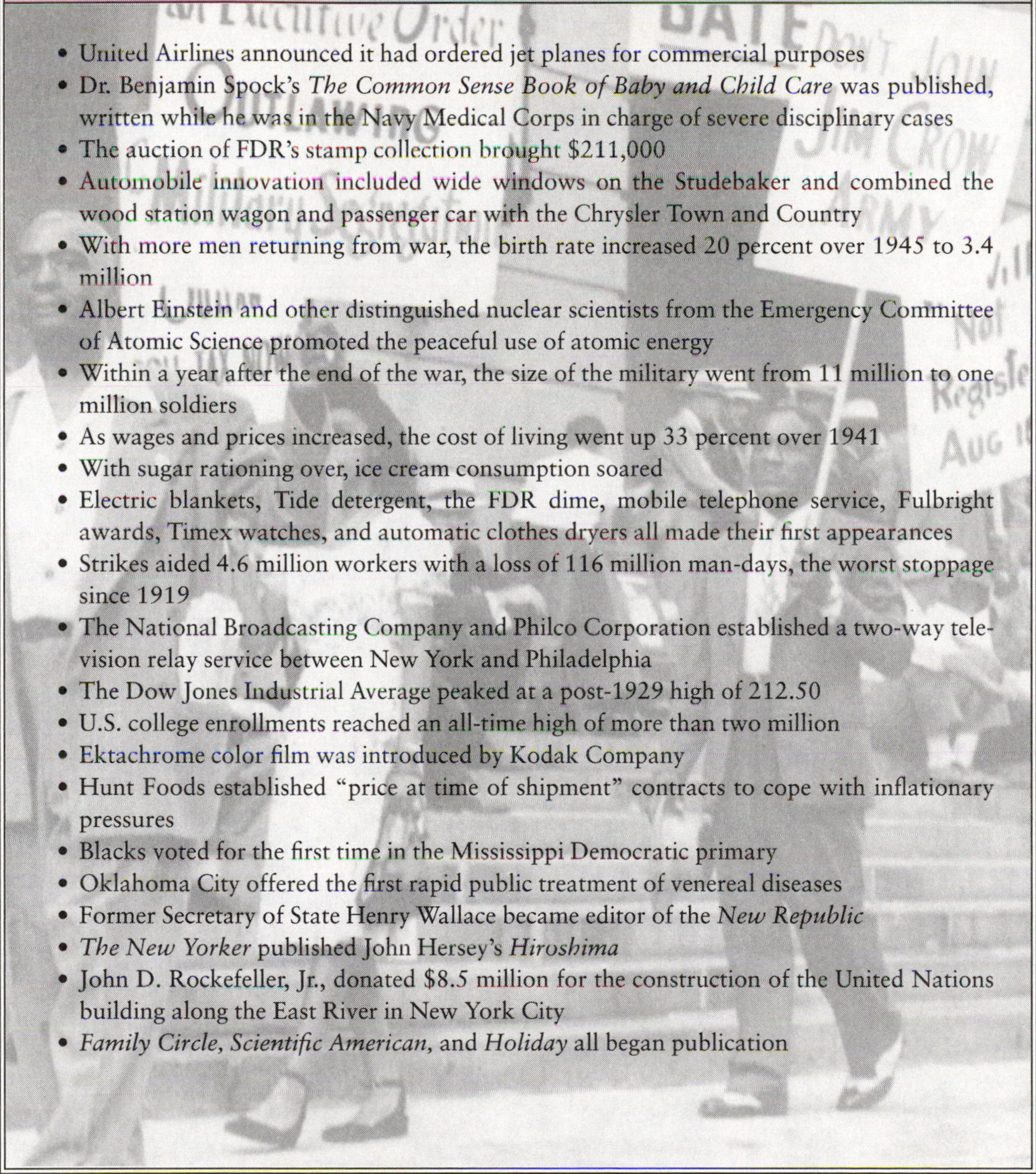

- United Airlines announced it had ordered jet planes for commercial purposes
- Dr. Benjamin Spock's *The Common Sense Book of Baby and Child Care* was published, written while he was in the Navy Medical Corps in charge of severe disciplinary cases
- The auction of FDR's stamp collection brought $211,000
- Automobile innovation included wide windows on the Studebaker and combined the wood station wagon and passenger car with the Chrysler Town and Country
- With more men returning from war, the birth rate increased 20 percent over 1945 to 3.4 million
- Albert Einstein and other distinguished nuclear scientists from the Emergency Committee of Atomic Science promoted the peaceful use of atomic energy
- Within a year after the end of the war, the size of the military went from 11 million to one million soldiers
- As wages and prices increased, the cost of living went up 33 percent over 1941
- With sugar rationing over, ice cream consumption soared
- Electric blankets, Tide detergent, the FDR dime, mobile telephone service, Fulbright awards, Timex watches, and automatic clothes dryers all made their first appearances
- Strikes aided 4.6 million workers with a loss of 116 million man-days, the worst stoppage since 1919
- The National Broadcasting Company and Philco Corporation established a two-way television relay service between New York and Philadelphia
- The Dow Jones Industrial Average peaked at a post-1929 high of 212.50
- U.S. college enrollments reached an all-time high of more than two million
- Ektachrome color film was introduced by Kodak Company
- Hunt Foods established "price at time of shipment" contracts to cope with inflationary pressures
- Blacks voted for the first time in the Mississippi Democratic primary
- Oklahoma City offered the first rapid public treatment of venereal diseases
- Former Secretary of State Henry Wallace became editor of the *New Republic*
- *The New Yorker* published John Hersey's *Hiroshima*
- John D. Rockefeller, Jr., donated $8.5 million for the construction of the United Nations building along the East River in New York City
- *Family Circle, Scientific American,* and *Holiday* all began publication

1946 Economic Profile

Income, Standard Jobs

Average of All Industries, Excluding Farm Labor	$2,529
Average of All Industries, Including Farm Labor	$2,473
Bituminous Coal Mining	$2,724
Building Trades	$2,537
Domestics	$1,411
Farm Labor	$1,394
Federal Civilian	$2,904
Federal Employees, Executive Departments	$2,490

Thousands of Southern blacks migrate to the tenement housing of Pittsburgh, seeking jobs.

"Pittsburgh Help Quits 8 Hotels, Bellhops, Waitresses, Maids Strike in Wage Dispute after Voting 4 to 1," October 1, 1946:

"Employees of eight major hotels in Pittsburgh went on strike at 12:01 a.m. today after voting a few hours earlier for a work stoppage in a wage dispute. . . The union is asking for a 40-hour week at the same wages as for the present 48 hours, with time and a half for the additional eight hours. The hotels say they have offered an increase of $15.25 a month for women and $16.64 a month for men who do not receive tips, and half that for those who receive tips."

Federal Military	$2,279
Finance, Insurance, and Real Estate	$2,570
Gas and Electricity Workers	$2,697
Manufacturing, Durable Goods	$2,615
Manufacturing, Nondurable Goods	$2,404
Medical/Health Services Workers	$1,605
Miscellaneous Manufacturing	$2,442
Motion Picture Services	$2,978
Nonprofit Organization Workers	$2,070
Passenger Transportation Workers, Local and Highway	$2,886
Personal Services	$1,881
Public School Teachers	$2,025
Radio Broadcasting and Television Workers	$3,972
Railroad Workers	$3,055
State and Local Government Workers	$2,093
Telephone and Telegraph Workers	$2,413
Wholesale and Retail Trade Workers	$2,378

Selected Prices

Dixie Belle Gin per Fifth	$3.12
Ouija Board Game	$1.59
Silvertone Commentator Radio	$11.75
Steel-Frame Baby Swing	$1.85
Biltwell Baby Shoes	$1.79
Illinois Clothing Manufacturing Suit	$27.00
Kerrybrooke Purse	$4.69
Harmony House Box Springs	$21.98

Craftsman Broad Hatchet	$1.69
Rose Bushes	$1.15
Craftsman Hammer	$1.39
Harmony House Mirror	$5.31
Tablevogue by Rosemary Tablecloth, 54" x 54"	$1.69
Walgreen's Mineral Oil, per Pint	$0.05
Brewer's Yeast Tablets	$0.27
Allstate Seat Covers	$3.33
Silvertone Harmonica	$1.79
Toni Home Permanent Kit	$2.00
Flower Grower Magazine Subscription for Two Years	$4.00

The Black Press

- When Franklin D. Roosevelt entered office in 1933, there were 150 Black newspapers with a combined circulation of 600,000, but by 1943, the Black press had more than doubled its weekly circulation to 1.6 million; in 1946, the combined total was 1.8 million copies weekly.
- Only five newspapers had a circulation of more than 50,000; nationwide, the 1940 census showed a Black population of 13 million.
- The Black, or Negro, press became known as a "fighting press" or "crusading press"; it always kept its eyes on the United States Government and its policy toward blacks.
- To create a more united front on confronting racial issues, the National Negro Publishing Association was created in 1940.
- The issues included the U.S. Navy's recruitment policy that virtually excluded blacks, the rampant use of employment discrimination, concerns over possible governmental charges of sedition and disloyalty during the war, and the need to balance the timidity of advertisers with the desire for militancy.
- The Black press and the traditional federal government did not always see eye to eye.
- When the Black press began pushing in 1939 for more Negroes in the army, particularly the officer corps, the White House declared "the policy of the War Department is not to intermingle colored and white enlisted personnel in the same regimental organizations."

"Race Bias Charged in Hospitals Here," *New York Times*, October 1, 1946:

"While 'whole sections of hospitals' are being closed because of the serious nursing shortages, 'discriminatory polices still reign even in our municipal hospitals as to the number of Negro doctors and nurses that gain employment in these tax-supported institutions,' it was declared last night at the first fall meeting of the Physicians Forum at the New York Academy of Medicine, by Dr. Ernest P. Boas, chairman of the Forum."

Editorial, by Perival Prattis, Editor, *Pittsburgh Courier,* 1942, following a meeting with the Federal Office of Facts and Figures:

"The hysteria of Washington officialdom over Negro morale is at once an astonishing, amusing, and shameful spectacle.

It is astonishing to find supposedly informed persons in high positions so unfamiliar with the thought and feeling of one-tenth of the population. One would imagine they had been on another planet, and yet every last one of them insists that he 'knows the Negro.'

It is amusing to see these people so panicky over a situation which they have caused and which governmental policies maintain.

It is shameful that the only 'remedy' they are now able to put forward is Jim Crowism on a larger scale and the suppression of the Negro newspapers, i.e., further departure from the principles of democracy. . . .

If the Washington gentry are eager to see Negro morale take an upturn, they have only to abolish Jim Crowism and lower the color bar in every field and phase of American life.

Squelching the Negro newspapers will not make the Negro masses love insult, discrimination, exploitation, and ostracism. It will only further depress their morale."

Labor strikes following the war are the worst since 1919.

- When 13 Negro seamen aboard the *U.S.S. Philadelphia* wrote to the *Pittsburgh Courier* to voice their discontent with the navy's racial policy, the sailors were jailed and scheduled to be court-martialed.
- The editorial work of the *Courier* resulted in the soldiers' release without trial or court-martial; the sailors were sent back to the United States and released with bad conduct discharges.
- Later in 1941, during the attack on Pearl Harbor, the *Courier* made the world aware of a black navy mess attendant, Dorie Miller, who dragged his captain to safety, then manned a machine gun until it ran out of ammunition; although the paper called for the Congressional Medal of Honor, Miller received the Navy Cross.
- Taking the lead of the *Pittsburgh Courier*, Black newspapers nationwide began promoting the Double V: "victories over totalitarian forces overseas and those at home who are denying equality to Negroes."
- Nationwide, the Double V campaign improved circulation for all papers; the *Courier* boosted circulation to 270,000, *The Afro-American* in Baltimore reached 229,000, followed by the *Chicago Defender* with 161,000, and the *Journal and Guide* in Norfolk, Virginia.
- The increased circulation allowed the Negro press to become more aggressive.
- The government wanted the Black press to give up its demands for full black rights until the end of the war, having made the same demand during World War I.

"Child Care Urged to Aid Middle-Aged," *New York Times*, October 1, 1946:

"Philadelphia—Lack of medical care for the mental difficulties of childhood causes many chronic diseases for the middle-aged persons, delegates to the forty-eighth annual convention of the American Hospital Association were informed today by Dr. Ester L. Richards, Assistant Professor of Psychiatry at Johns Hopkins University's School of Medicine. The public concentrates with alarm on cancer and infantile paralysis, but has little knowledge of ever-increasing chronic diseases of middle-aged persons, she said.

'Statistics show that every other person over 50 dies of cardio-renal disease,' she asserted, 'and that hypertension is the greatest problem of middle life, not excepting cancer.'

Declaring that it 'is an undisputed fact' that such diseases can be traced to the 'emotional factors' of childhood, Dr. Richards said the 'relationship between pediatrics and psychiatry must grow from that of an occasional luxury to the status of necessity if we are to go forward in public and private hospital objectives toward better understanding of child care.'"

1949 Family Profile

Louis Wallace is a harbor pilot in Tampa, Florida. He maintains two homes—one in Tampa where his extended family lives, and the other on Egmont Key at the mouth of Tampa Bay. He and his wife, Nora, have two children.

Annual Income: $22,000
His income includes his payment for piloting ships into the harbor as a harbor pilot, rent from two apartments, loans to friends, and his ownership of several tugboats in the area.

Captain Wallace enjoys a trip out West.

Annual Budget

The average per capita consumer expenditures in 1949 for all workers nationwide are:

Auto Parts	$8.04
Auto Usage	$126.69
Clothing	$107.25
Dentists	$6.03
Food	$351.90
Furniture	$18.09
Gas and Oil	$35.53
Health Insurance	$5.36
Housing	$131.38
Intercity Transport	$6.03
Local Transport	$13.41
New Auto Purchase	$51.61
Personal Business	$39.55
Personal Care	$15.42
Physicians	$16.76

His grandchildren look forward to trips to the country.

Private Education and Research	$11.39
Recreation	$67.03
Religion/Welfare Activities	$15.42
Telephone and Telegraph	$11.39
Tobacco	$27.48
Utilities	$43.57
Per Capita Consumption	$1,119.51

Life at Home

- Born in 1887, he was the last child of a family that emigrated to the wilderness of Bradenton, Florida, from Indiana.
- The family took the railroad as far as it went in Florida, then sailed aboard a schooner to Tampa Bay.
- As a boy, Louis worked at his uncle's drugstore, beginning work at 5:30 a.m. by sweeping the store and making ice cream.
- The only phone in town was at the drugstore; part of Louis's job was to answer the phone, ask who the party wanted to speak with, and then ride his bicycle until he found the person and bring him or her to the drugstore to answer the call.
- Growing up, he realized that in the new frontier of Florida, he had a choice of going to sea or raising oranges to make his fortune.
- He went to sea at age 17, beginning as a deck hand.
- His brother and mother-in-law had been the captain of several boats operated by the Plant Line, the *Plant,* the *Favorite,* and the *Manatee.*
- Nora's family came to Florida from Texas wishing to start over, disillusioned by the Civil War and its lasting impact.
- Prior to moving to Florida, her father had been a surgeon in the Civil War, later becoming Superintendent of Education for Manatee County.
- Her mother died of an infection when her foot caught on a nail in a boardwalk; when the toe became infected, the foot was amputated, but eventually she died of gangrene.
- In 1910, Nora and Louis married, having delayed the wedding until he became a boat captain; they moved to Tampa and lived on Nebraska Avenue.
- Their first child, a girl, was born in 1911, the second, also a girl, in 1914.
- Early in their marriage, Nora took in boarders to fill up the house; as a ship captain, Louis was often away from the family for long stretches.
- In 1919, he was an officer on an ocean-going ship, doing "blue water sailing," taking cargo from Norfolk, Virginia, to Chile.
- While in Norfolk, he was appointed to the bar in Tampa and elected to the job of harbor pilot.
- He returned to Tampa to take the job and settled into a home on fashionable South Dakota Avenue in Hyde Park.
- In 1923, he built a house off Bay Shore in Hyde Park, where he still lives in 1949.
- The house has a wide front porch, large enough for six rocking chairs and a porch swing.

Their home, built in 1923, houses an extended family of children and grandchildren.

- The first floor includes a large living room, kitchen, breakfast room, dining room, half-bath, and back porch; the second floor has three bedrooms, a library, a bathroom, and a sleeping porch.
- Scottish by background and nature, he pays for everything in cash; he has a strong savings ethic and believes in saving before spending.
- He does not trust the stock market, particularly after the losses suffered by so many during the depression.
- He will lend money to others, though, and is currently holding the mortgage for the home of a man who owns a haberdashery and for a fellow harbor pilot.
- During vacations away from the harbor, he loves to travel on the water; before the Second World War, they went to Cuba and the Panama Canal, where he enjoyed watching the locks work as he passed from the Atlantic Ocean to the Pacific.
- Since the war, he has traveled little outside the United States.
- Immediately after the attack on Pearl Harbor, the Coast Guard took control of the shipping there; he has been a Lt. Commander in the Coast Guard for the past several years.
- German submarines and U-boats, taking advantage of U.S. intelligence blunders early in the war, sank 24 ships off Florida's east and gulf coasts.
- Residents watched in horror as tankers burned and thick oil coated the white sands; hundreds of lives and millions of dollars in cargo were lost.
- During the war, he wore the military uniform of a Lt. Commander rather than the black, three-piece suit and tie that were standard among pilots prior to the war.
- Only recently has he been decommissioned and allowed to return to civilian status.
- Currently, five adults and one child are living at his home; his oldest daughter and his granddaughter have moved "back home," as have his second daughter and her husband.
- His oldest daughter went to college for two years, but left to get married.

- She works at MacDill Air Field military base as an ordnance secretary, keeping track of airplane parts.
- German POWs were housed at MacDill Air Field during the war.
- After the war, a woman's average weekly pay fell from $50 to $37, a decline of 26 percent.
- When her husband returned from fighting overseas, she asked for a divorce.
- Now that gas is no longer rationed, the family takes long rides in Louis's four-door, bright blue 1948 Packard.
- The family has property at Land-O-Lakes, approximately 45 minutes away by car; recently, they improved the house, adding running water and electricity.
- Other items rationed during the war included rubber tires, tobacco, shoes, sugar, and electrical appliances.

- During the war, Louis refused to buy butter, steak, and gasoline on the black market and did not permit anyone in his home to circumvent the rationing regulations.
- Pamphlets, along with booklets of ration stamps, handed out to consumers said, "Fuel-oil rationing is making it much tougher on Hitler and Hirohito than anyone here."
- Like his ship, his car and home are immaculate.
- The captain's word is law on the ship and at home; he is a man of few words, but those are to be obeyed.
- The family eats a full breakfast, dining in shifts; Louis, Nora, and one daughter eat first, the second daughter and her husband second, joined by the grandchild.
- He rarely goes visiting and never stays long when he does; "Always leave before they wish you would," is his rule.
- He keeps a parrot, a gift from a ship's captain, having attempted a few years ago to keep a monkey, but after it tossed a dozen eggs onto the floor, the primate was ousted.
- He is actually going deaf from the constant sound of machinery, but hides this fact to protect his business.
- He is always on time and expects everyone in the house to do the same.
- He does not drink alcohol, does not tolerate drinking in his presence, and has no patience with those who do choose to drink.
- He does not discuss religion, money, or politics; it is impolite for anyone to bring up these three topics.
- He considers himself extremely fortunate to have succeeded without a formal education; during the depression when many men lost their jobs, ships continued to dock in Tampa and he continued to be paid, which allowed him to make investments when others had no money.
- During the dark days of the depression, a relative lost his job as a banker, and his home, when his bank failed; his brother-in-law committed suicide when his lumber business failed so his wife could collect the insurance.

- He believes it is his job to protect the women in his life, and though he does not want them exposed to the rigors of the working world, he paid for his daughters to attend school.
- However, he does allow his wife to rent out the two apartments above the six-car garage behind their house, since a woman needs a little "pin money" of her own to spend on luxuries.
- When home, he spends considerable time with his wife and even takes her shopping; he also enjoys tending to the fruit trees which include oranges, grapefruits, persimmons, tangerines, and lemons.
- When in Tampa, he keeps a low profile, belonging only to the Shriner's Club, and is careful not to call attention to himself or to his rapidly increasing wealth.
- While in Tampa, much of his spare time is spent tending to his tugboat business.
- The church is Nora's social outlet; she is especially interested in the care of orphans and is planning a trip to the Thornwell Orphanage in Clinton, South Carolina.

Large ships entering the Bay usually have a harbor pilot aboard.

Life at Work

- Currently, Tampa Bay supports eight harbor pilots to bring seagoing ships in and out of the ever-changing and often treacherous waters of the harbor.
- Harbor pilot is a highly prized, well-paying position, with only the best ship's captains selected for the job; mistakes by harbor pilots can result in huge ships running aground, costing thousands in ship repairs, delayed orders, and blockage of the harbor for others.
- Every harbor pilot must have a master's license and be ships' captains in their own right.
- To be selected as a harbor pilot, a man must be well-respected by his peers and above reproach in integrity.
- The pilots guide boats into the harbor and back out by actually taking the place of the captain and steering them in and out of port.
- When guiding out, the harbor captains may be asked to board the ships at one of three ports; when guiding in, they board the boats when they near shallow water, often near Egmont Key, an island between Tampa Bay and the Gulf of Mexico that serves as the temporary home of harbor pilots.
- The Coast Guard also maintains a station at the end of Egmont Key, which includes a fort built during the Spanish American War; otherwise, no one else lives on the island except rattlesnakes and gophers.
- Large ships entering the bay are required to have a harbor pilot aboard to pilot and dock the huge ships.
- Until they reach the gulf, ships leaving Tampa Bay require a harbor pilot, who then boards a smaller boat that takes him to Egmont Key.
- The profession can be extremely dangerous; several pilots have been killed or maimed when transferring from one ship to another—especially at night or in a storm.
- Everyone in Louis's family is aware of the dangers and anxious on cold, windy nights when he is working.

Egmont Key serves as the temporary home of harbor pilots.

- On one occasion, while jumping from the ship to the transfer boat, a wave pushed the boat away, and though Louis didn't go into the water, he did suffer severe rope burns on his hands.
- The pilots are paid by the shipping lines based on the tonnage being carried; a large ship drawing lots of water requires more expertise and means more money.
- The pilots employ an accountant, working out of the First National Bank building in Tampa, to establish schedules, collect from the shipping lines, and make payments to the pilots.

Harbor pilots must understand the problems of deep-drafting boats.

- He takes great pride in his ability to dock any ship at any facility in Tampa—without using a tugboat.
- On Egmont Key, the harbor pilots have individual cottages, but gather at a communal kitchen and at a reading room where maps and logs are kept; no one except harbor pilots is allowed in the reading room.
- A blackboard in the reading room records the coming and going of ships.
- The pilots spend considerable time discussing the fine points of the ever-shifting currents, the effect of seasonal tides, recent dredging projects, and other changes that might impact their ability to guide a huge ship.
- Because Tampa Bay harbor requires constant maintenance, staying up to date is critical to the pilots, but impossible for ships' captains who only use the harbor a few times a year.
- To do their job, harbor pilots must know how much water a ship requires and understand the problems caused by deep-drafting ships.
- When questions arise, the captain of the ship usually defers to the harbor pilot.
- In case of an accident, harbor pilots are liable and must carry insurance; boats are their business.
- Occasionally a ship's captain will request a particular harbor pilot; many friendships develop over the years among these professionals.
- Louis speaks a few words of a lot of languages, needing to understand enough to bring the ship in, since many of the crews bringing materials into Tampa Bay do not speak English.
- Nations represented in Tampa shipping include China, Japan, Norway, England, Greece, France, The Netherlands, Chile, Argentina, the Caribbean islands, and Cuba.
- One of the most frequent cargoes is guano, for fertilizer manufacture, from South America; other ships bring in phosphate, grain, oil, and bananas.
- He also pilots passenger ships carrying tourists to and from Cuba.
- Ships do not like to dock long, as time in port is lost money.
- Despite his reserved nature, he actively keeps up his political contacts; habor pilots want quality appointments; any mistake by a single pilot could be a liability for all.

Electricity for the cottages on Egmont Key is supplied by a generator.

- Louis's nickname is "Bub," although most people simply call him "Captain."
- Religiously, he takes a "grip," or leather suitcase, to work with him, which includes field glasses, Hershey Bars, extra clothing, a raincoat, and money.
- Occasionally, the weather is so treacherous he cannot climb down the rope ladder from one ship to another and must stay on board until its next port; he must always be prepared.
- On Egmont Key, the pilots employ a cook to prepare meals for them at any one time.
- Water on the island is collected in cisterns made of cypress.
- Once a year, the cisterns are drained and cleaned, ready to be refilled by the rain.
- A boat carrying supplies, groceries, and ice comes from Pass-A-Grille once a week.
- Electricity is provided by a generator; lights go out on the island at 10 p.m. except during an emergency.
- Louis loves to walk around the island, which is three miles long and one and one-half miles wide.
- On nighttime jaunts during the summer, he can watch the loggerhead turtles lay their eggs; he loves to watch the huge turtles come ashore and enjoys collecting a few of the eggs to eat—considering them a delicacy.
- He also has a fascination with the night sky, watching the stars and their movements whenever possible; early in his training, he was taught to sail solely by the position of the stars.
- He adores his family and enjoys his time in Tampa, but he lives for the solitude of the island, near the water.

Life in the Community: Tampa, Florida

- Tampa is booming and wants to grow even faster in the days following the Second World War; selling to soldiers, sailors, and airmen is a big business.
- In 1933, Floridians earned $424 million in income, and by 1943, they earned $2 billion.
- War contracts revived the state's agricultural and manufacturing sectors and surprisingly, tourism thrived during the war.
- Defense contracts breathed life into Tampa in particular; reeling from the near collapse of the cigar industry, the construction of MacDill Air Field in 1939 and the rejuvenation of shipbuilding brought jobs to the area.
- The Tampa Shipbuilding Company employed 9,000 workers by 1942, and by 1944, defense workers averaged $1.08 per hour with unlimited overtime.
- During the 1940s, more than two million men and women were trained in military bases in Florida; the federal government opened major military bases throughout the state to meet the needs of the navy and the air force in particular.
- The arrival of service personnel not only pumped economic life into cities from Miami to Jacksonville, but also provided millions in federal funds to build modern transportation facilities to speed travel and connect cities.
- Farm prices bounced back; cotton prices, depressed since World War I, rose from $0.10 to $0.22 a pound between 1939 and 1945.
- During the war, Florida's citrus harvest surpassed California's for the first time just in time to provide soldiers with a dehydrated citrus concentrate that could be shipped overseas.
- "Food will win the war and write the peace," promises a popular poster in many agricultural communities of Florida.
- A two-bedroom house on South Bayshore Drive in Tampa is advertised to veterans "for nothing down" and includes a seven-cubic-foot deluxe electric refrigerator, an electric range with deep well cooker, and an electric water heater; the price is "Veteran's Administration Appraised Value."
- Nationwide, the unions are demanding high wages; most salaries were frozen during the war years, and people everywhere are concerned about inflation.

"$7,500 Homes Planned for 'Average' Family," *Tampa Tribune*, April 17, 1949:

"San Diego—A plan has been started here to build homes for the 'average-income family' with take-home pay of approximately $50 a week. The homes would sell for $7,500.

An advisory committee of representatives of builders, architects, labor, lending agencies, and city and county officials has been organized. 'Anyone can build a house for $10,000; what we've got to do and do fast is build houses for $7,500,' said Earle Peterson, president of the San Diego chapter, Building Contractors' Association.

'Everyone will have to do his part,' Peterson said. 'The contractor will have to shave his profit to the bone, the city must stop insisting on $5,000 worth of payments on each 50-foot lot, and labor will have to quit asking for pay raises.' "

LIFE-SIZE television
There'll be wonderful television fare this season— welcome it into your home on the largest direct-view screen made. Du Mont's new sensitivity and freedom from interference give a picture unsurpassed in clarity and brilliance—opening whole new areas to fine television reception.
THE DU MONT BRADFORD—Life-size direct-view screen. 203 square inches on a 19-inch Du Mont tube. FM radio. Record player for the new 45 RPM records. Cabinet of fine mahogany veneers.
DUMONT First with the finest in Television
Your Du Mont Dealer invites you to see the Morey Amsterdam Show on the Du Mont Television Network.
Copyright 1949, Allen B. Du Mont Laboratories, Inc.
Allen B. Du Mont Laboratories, Inc., General Television Sales Offices and The Du Mont Television Network, 515 Madison Avenue, New York 22, N.Y. Home Offices and Plants, Passaic, N.J.

- A box of 50 locally made Tampa Beauties cigars is selling for $4.19, Lucky Strike cigarettes are $0.21 a pack or $1.99 a carton, 10 pounds of flour costs $0.81, and a fifth of Marker's Mark 90 is $5.99.
- The *St. Petersburg Times* is editorializing about the need for continued economic planning: "When nations are at war, no one questions the absolute necessity of providing the soldier with arms, ammunition, clothing, housing, transportation, fuel. Comes peace, though, and the 'planner' suddenly becomes a subversive sort of socialistic person."

HISTORICAL SNAPSHOT
1949

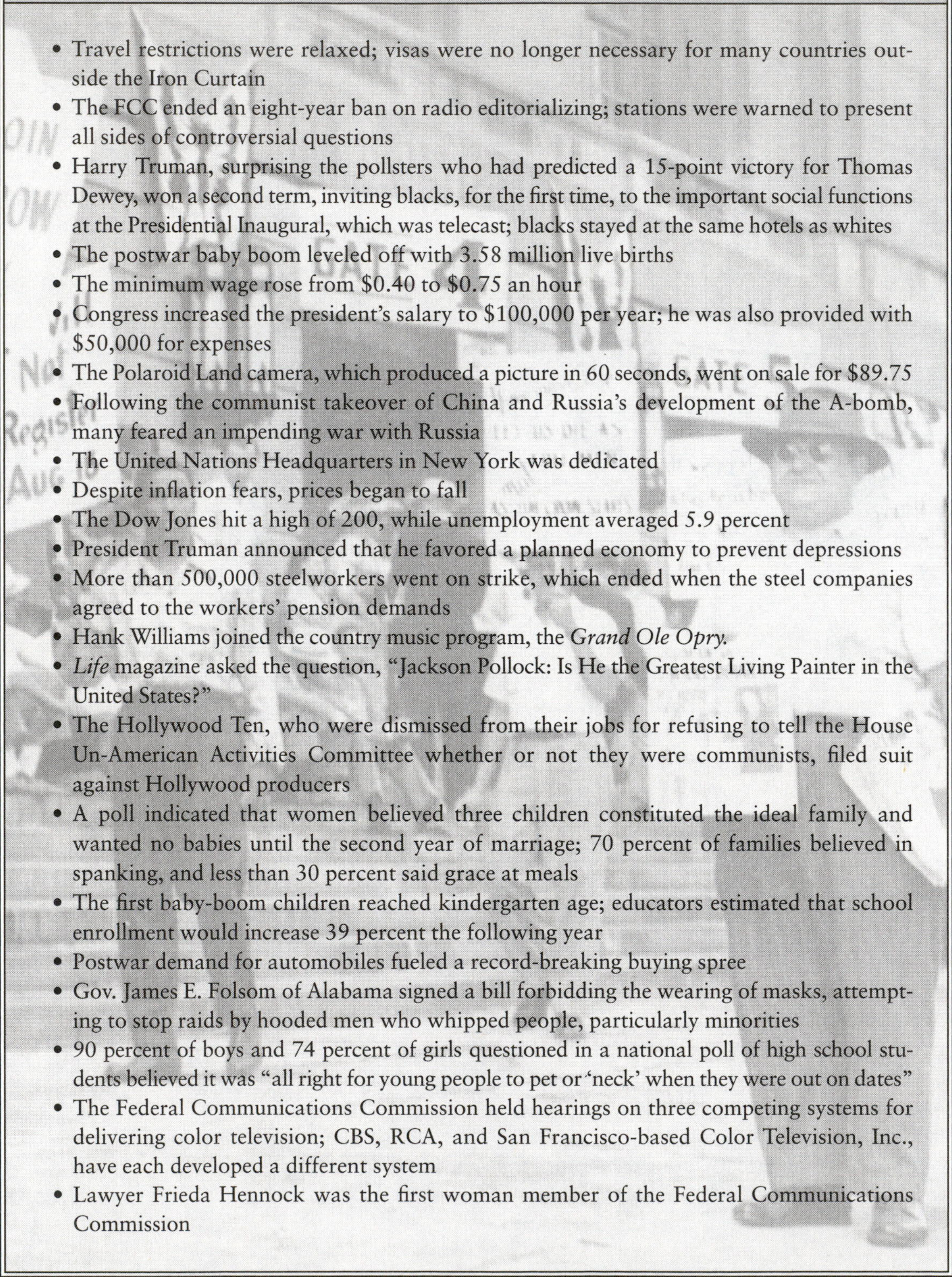

- Travel restrictions were relaxed; visas were no longer necessary for many countries outside the Iron Curtain
- The FCC ended an eight-year ban on radio editorializing; stations were warned to present all sides of controversial questions
- Harry Truman, surprising the pollsters who had predicted a 15-point victory for Thomas Dewey, won a second term, inviting blacks, for the first time, to the important social functions at the Presidential Inaugural, which was telecast; blacks stayed at the same hotels as whites
- The postwar baby boom leveled off with 3.58 million live births
- The minimum wage rose from $0.40 to $0.75 an hour
- Congress increased the president's salary to $100,000 per year; he was also provided with $50,000 for expenses
- The Polaroid Land camera, which produced a picture in 60 seconds, went on sale for $89.75
- Following the communist takeover of China and Russia's development of the A-bomb, many feared an impending war with Russia
- The United Nations Headquarters in New York was dedicated
- Despite inflation fears, prices began to fall
- The Dow Jones hit a high of 200, while unemployment averaged 5.9 percent
- President Truman announced that he favored a planned economy to prevent depressions
- More than 500,000 steelworkers went on strike, which ended when the steel companies agreed to the workers' pension demands
- Hank Williams joined the country music program, the *Grand Ole Opry.*
- *Life* magazine asked the question, "Jackson Pollock: Is He the Greatest Living Painter in the United States?"
- The Hollywood Ten, who were dismissed from their jobs for refusing to tell the House Un-American Activities Committee whether or not they were communists, filed suit against Hollywood producers
- A poll indicated that women believed three children constituted the ideal family and wanted no babies until the second year of marriage; 70 percent of families believed in spanking, and less than 30 percent said grace at meals
- The first baby-boom children reached kindergarten age; educators estimated that school enrollment would increase 39 percent the following year
- Postwar demand for automobiles fueled a record-breaking buying spree
- Gov. James E. Folsom of Alabama signed a bill forbidding the wearing of masks, attempting to stop raids by hooded men who whipped people, particularly minorities
- 90 percent of boys and 74 percent of girls questioned in a national poll of high school students believed it was "all right for young people to pet or 'neck' when they were out on dates"
- The Federal Communications Commission held hearings on three competing systems for delivering color television; CBS, RCA, and San Francisco-based Color Television, Inc., have each developed a different system
- Lawyer Frieda Hennock was the first woman member of the Federal Communications Commission

1949 Economic Profile

Income, Standard Jobs

Average of All Industries, Excluding Farm Labor	$3,075
Average of All Industries, Including Farm Labor	$3,000
Bituminous Coal Mining	$2,922
Building Trades	$3,229
Domestics	$1,498
Farm Labor	$1,501
Federal Civilian	$3,481
Federal Employees, Executive Departments	$2,995
Federal Military	$2,599
Finance, Insurance, and Real Estate	$3,034
Gas and Electricity Workers	$3,383
Manufacturing, Durable Goods	$3,240
Manufacturing, Nondurable Goods	$2,961
Medical/Health Services Workers	$1,995
Miscellaneous Manufacturing	$2,856
Motion Picture Services	$3,028
Nonprofit Organization Workers	$2,465
Passenger Transportation Workers, Local and Highway	$3,164
Personal Services	$2,189
Public School Teachers	$2,671
Radio Broadcasting and Television Workers	$4,380
Railroad Workers	$3,706
State and Local Government Workers	$2,670
Telephone and Telegraph Workers	$2,920
Wholesale and Retail Trade Workers	$2,899

Selected Prices

General Electric Model 65 Clock Radio	$36.95
Gorham Chantilly Sterling Silver Flatware, Six-Piece Place Settings	$23.00
Canasta Playing Cards	$1.59
General Electric Tidy Vacuum Cleaner	$39.95
RCA Victor Record Player	$12.95
General Electric Television, 61-Square-Inch Screen	$189.95
Hammond Organ	$1,300.00
Kenmore-A Washer	$119.95
Novel Crib Exerciser	$1.89
Hearthside Loom	$99.50

The Alligator Co. Rainwear $10.75
Miss Swank Slip $1.95
Sealtest Butterscotch Eclairs,
Box of Four $0.59
Troy Glider $59.50
Flowering Pink Dogwood $2.85
Eclipse Packhound Lawn Mower $127.50
Two Dozen Long Red Roses in Vase. $5.00
Baby Chenille Bedspread,
Full or Twin, ... $3.99
Wedgwood Woodstock China,
20 Pieces $75.60

Early Development of Florida

- Florida's past, including the development of Tampa, was a patchwork of opportunists, crooked deals, and big dreams.
- When admitted to the Union in 1845, Florida's population was only 69,000 residents; even as late as the 1920s, Florida was the last great frontier in the eastern United States.
- In 1864, the *New York Herald* said, "I am confident no sane man who knows what Florida is would give . . . a thousand dollars to gain possession of all the territory beyond the St. Johns. No decent man would think of living in the state outside of two or three points on the St. Johns and the Gulf."
- In 1881, desperate to make a $1 million bond payment on $14 million in debt, the state of Florida sold four million acres—at $0.25 an acre—to Hamilton Disston of Philadelphia.

- It was the largest amount of land ever bought by a private individual in the history of the United States; Disston provided the government with an I.O.U., repaying the debt by selling much of the land to others.
- He attempted to develop the state, including the areas near Tampa on the west coast of Florida, using steamboat transportation and the lure of rich farming lands that "grew two crops a year."
- Connecticut native Henry Plant, on the other hand, invested in railroads and hotels to develop Florida; when Plant was born in 1819, only three miles of railroad track existed in the nation, and when he died in 1899, he controlled 2,139 miles of railroads and owned seven coastal shipping lines.
- His trains and shipping lines brought Tampa to life and helped transform the city from a fever-ridden village to a prosperous shipping port; he also helped establish the city as the

"Railroads," *Fortune Magazine*, October 1949:

"For some 950,000 U.S. railroad workers, September 1 was a red-letter day. For on that date the nation's railroads, in compliance with an arbitration-board award, reduced the work week for non-operating personnel (about two-thirds of the payroll) from 48 to 40 hours. Since hourly wages had just been hiked, weekly wages were cut only slightly ($0.56); the industry figured the added annual cost at $450 million. Said Frank Hopkins, terminal superintendent of the Texas & New Orleans Railroad Co., 'Our problem is maintaining a seven-day service with a five-day staff.' "

self-proclaimed "Cigar Capital of the World" with the relocation of the cigar industry from Cuba.

- Port Tampa went into full operation in June 1888, anchored by the Tampa Bay Hotel, built in its Arabic-Moorish-Turkish-Colonial American style.
- Every one of the 511 rooms in the hotel, covering six acres, had electricity, gaining Tampa a national reputation.
- Florida is marked by both the enormous distances between centers of population and the difficulty of travel; the distance from Key West in the south and Pensacola in the north is the approximately the same distance as from Pensacola to Chicago.
- During the early twentieth century, Florida's southern region was more closely linked to the Caribbean than to Tallahassee, the capital.
- D.P. Davis set the pattern for Florida land speculation in October 1924, when he sold to land speculators hundreds of lots that were still under water in Tampa Bay.

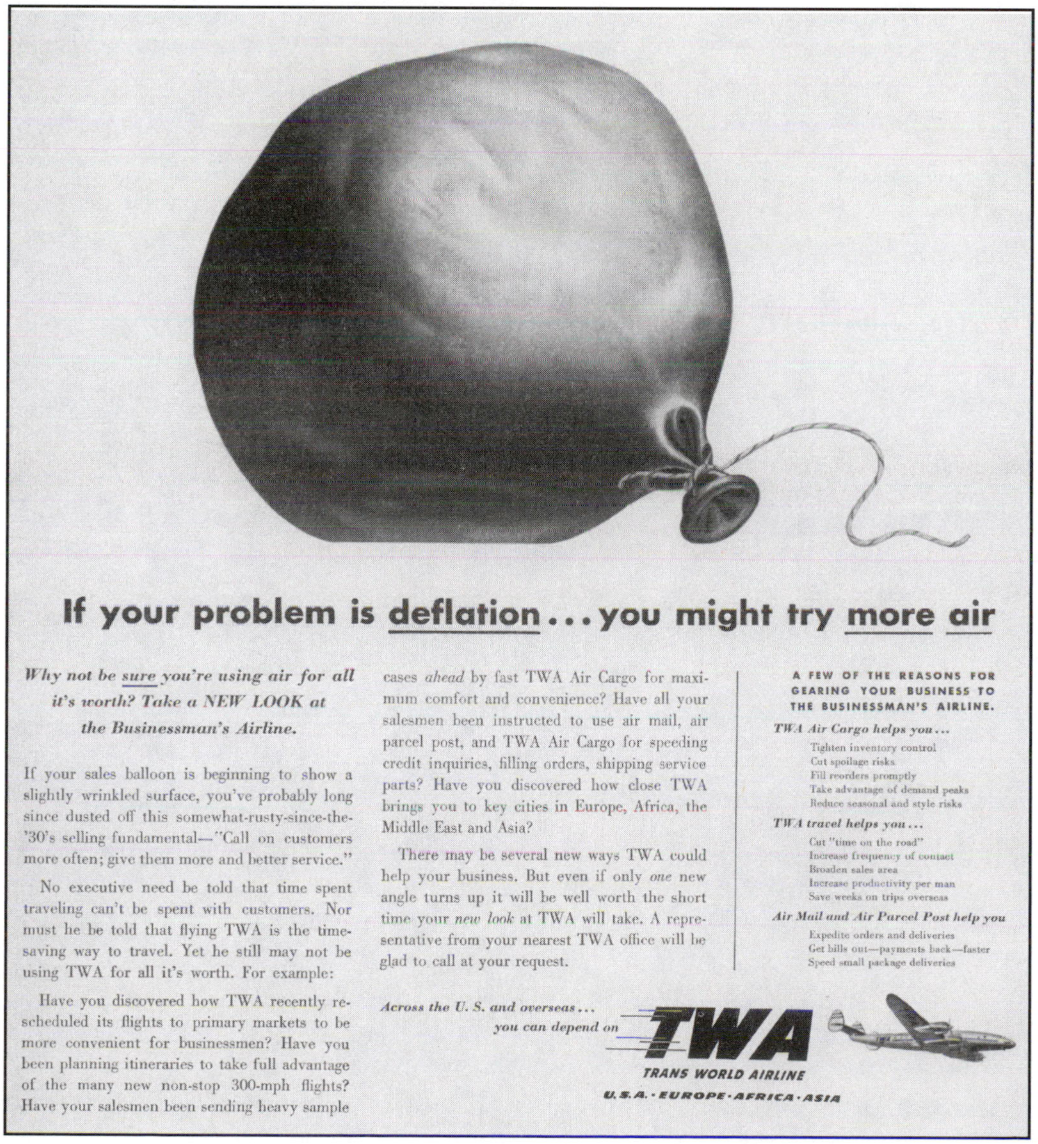

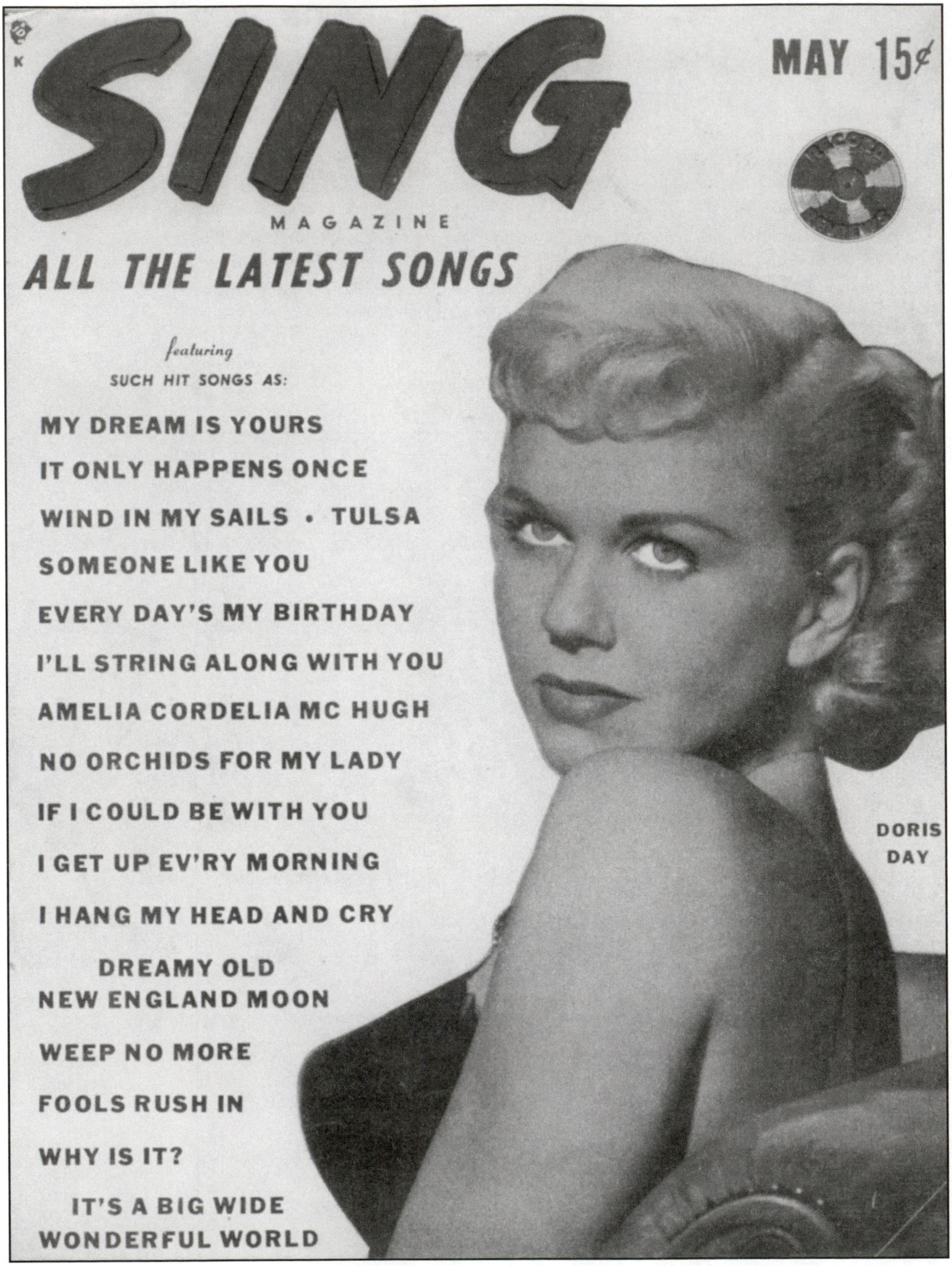
SING
MAGAZINE
MAY 15¢
ALL THE LATEST SONGS
featuring
SUCH HIT SONGS AS:
MY DREAM IS YOURS
IT ONLY HAPPENS ONCE
WIND IN MY SAILS • TULSA
SOMEONE LIKE YOU
EVERY DAY'S MY BIRTHDAY
I'LL STRING ALONG WITH YOU
AMELIA CORDELIA MC HUGH
NO ORCHIDS FOR MY LADY
IF I COULD BE WITH YOU
I GET UP EV'RY MORNING
I HANG MY HEAD AND CRY
DREAMY OLD
NEW ENGLAND MOON
WEEP NO MORE
FOOLS RUSH IN
WHY IS IT?
IT'S A BIG WIDE
WONDERFUL WORLD
DORIS
DAY

1949 News Profile

" 'You'll Never Get Rich,' but He Did,"
by Marion Hargrove, *Life Magazine*, December 12, 1949:

"To all appearances, Sgt. First Class John Ross is the typical old army man. His face is broad and rather leathery, his eyes a trifle shrewd. His belt hangs contentedly across his solid front at a point arbitrarily chosen to represent a waistline. His uniform has the peculiar old army look, as if the wearer had been fitted to the uniform rather than the uniform to the wearer. And he has about him that air of solidity and well-being that comes of long years in the service. But Johnnie Ross, except for his appearance, is by no means a typical old soldier. He is not allergic to work and he has not acquired the sour temper that characterizes many an Old Sarge. A further distinction is that he has demolished the myth best expressed in the old song, 'You'll never get rich, you . . . , you're in the army now.'

Sergeant Ross retired late last month at half pay after 22 years of service to devote himself exclusively to his sporting, agricultural, and business interests. At the age of 44, still in good health and spirits, he can look back on one good life and begin another. His wife is still young and pretty, his six children have turned out remarkably well, and he himself is a pillar in his community. His material blessings include his farm, a fine pack of foxhounds, a filling station which he built himself and which does a daily business ranging from $45 to $110, and the rents from three nearby houses and a store. Ross says without blushing that he made all his acquisitions honestly and without neglecting his military duties. This appears to be so. He lays his success in life to thrift, good management, and running an occasional crap game for the officers.

Ross succumbed to a recruiting sergeant's spiel in Meridian, Mississippi. In 1927, he was sent to Fort Bragg, North Carolina, where he found himself in the old 5th Field Artillery, learning the squads-right drill and the names of his army superiors from his first sergeant to Calvin Coolidge. Within a few months he acquired a first-class gunner's rating that added $5 a month to his pay. Then he went to work after hours in the barber-and-tailor shop, for which he got another $10 a month and free pressing for all his uniforms. A private's pay at the time was $21, minus $1.75 for laundry. Most soldiers were always broke except for a few fleeting moments on payday. The seventh of the month was 'canteen check day,' when a private could draw credit for $5 at the post exchange, $2 at the barber's, and $1.40 (10 tickets) at the theater. Most men drew their limit, sold the checks at cut rates, or used them in the day's big poker game. Ross found that he could buy a $5 canteen book from somebody for $3 cash and save 40 percent on such PX items as gasoline, tires, and shoes. In no time at all he was lending money to master sergeants.

By the end of Ross's first year in the army, he had become chief projectionist at the post theater, risen to the high rank of private first class, married a nice Fayetteville girl named Mary Bolton, and settled down. The pertinent question—how a man in such a ridiculously low income bracket could hope to keep a wife and family—had occurred to many people, among them a battery commander to whom Ross once applied for permission to turn in his last year's Chevrolet and get the new model. Ross's pay as a private first class was $30 a month and his rations allowance was $12 to $14. His rent was $20 a month, his food bill, even at the low commissary prices, was $35 and (disregarding his other expenses) the payments on his car were $36. 'Well,' said the captain, 'if Al Capone could have a car, I suppose you can, too.' One reason Ross could make ends meet was that Mary made all her own and the children's clothes, but the chief reason was that Ross himself was gifted with a magnetic attraction for every stray dollar in his vicinity.

In addition to pay, Ross usually drew $18 a month at the theater, plus an average of $10 a month for setting up the ring for boxing matches, plus $5 from each of the road shows that played Bragg every month or so. He not only played in the barracks poker games, but supplied the peanuts and his wife's sandwiches at them. He had a troop of small boys hawking these wares all over the post. He carried candy on marches and retailed it to his hiking comrades at a profit of $0.40 a box. He sometimes rented out his car at $5 a night or took parties to Wilmington and Charlotte and Raleigh at $5 per round trip per man. . . .

The army's expansion in the two years after Pearl Harbor did not at first work out too well for Ross. He had been a private first class, with a second-class specialist rating and the extra pay that went along with it. Suddenly, he was 'promoted' to sergeant, without the specialist rating. This added two more stripes to his uniform and subtracted $12 from his pay. He was still brooding about this when Congress instituted family allotments. The army was to dock every married soldier's pay $22 a month, giving him in return $50 for the support of his wife, $30 for his first child, and $20 each for the others. The Rosses, blessed with six chil-

"Keep The Carrot Dangling," by Peter Drucker, *Fortune Magazine*, October 1949:

"How high tax rates encourage inequality can be quickly demonstrated. To most people it is gross income before taxes that counts. Net income, to be sure, determines purchasing power. But income before taxes is at once the measure of a man's responsibility, his worth to society, and the symbol of his social standing. In defending the present tax policy, Dean Erwin N. Griswold of the Harvard Law School asked: 'Are financial incentives the only ones worth talking about, the only ones that induce men to action?' They aren't, of course. But differences in gross income are, in a sense, non-financial incentives. Two vice presidents in the same big company, what with different family exemptions, etc., may have the same net income after taxes. But if one has a gross income before taxes of $40,000 and the other a gross income before taxes of $50,000, their position, standing, and authority within the company are markedly different. The one who gets the lower gross income will break his neck to get his salary raised to the higher figure even if little of this increase reaches his pocket. Since each higher step is distinguished by a higher salary, the differences between the salary of the top and that of the lower hierarchy can be enormous.

The only alternatives to money as a symbol of status—however sordid they may be—are uniforms, titles, medals, in other words, crass symbols of position and power. But not even the Russians, for all their penchant for uniforms and medals, have substituted power symbols for money rewards for their managerial group. The difference between the gross pay of the Russian manager and the pay of the Russian worker is several times greater than the difference between that of the American manager and worker—and there is practically no income tax in Russia.

What happens, therefore, is this: so long as taxes take away from high earned incomes, the pressure to raise incomes inexorably increases. A medium-sized paper company needed a financial vice president. The man it wanted was willing to change; all he demanded was a moderate increase in real income. In order to give him a modest net increase of $3,000, the paper company had to pay him a salary $12,000 higher."

dren, put the extra money to good use. The family bank account went into a down payment on the purchase of their home, three neighboring houses, and a store building. Since then the allotment checks have paid for all his real estate, $2,000 worth of improvements for the Ross home, and an extra nine acres of surrounding land. . . .

Once when Ross, who has been accused of burying his money, applied to his battery commander for a seven-day furlough, the captain asked him what he wanted it for. 'I'd like to spade up my money and turn it over,' Ross told him. 'It's getting moldy on one side.' The captain was delighted by the explanation. 'Take 10 days,' he said, 'and do the job right.' In the community to which Ross is retiring, a mile or so from Fayetteville on the Murchison Road, he is respected as a hard worker and an upright man. He and Mrs. Ross are known for their easygoing ways and their unflagging devotion to their children. . . . Neither Ross nor his wife worries much about the danger of his having too much time on his hands in retirement. He has already cleared 12 acres behind the house for truck farming and another 10 acres are on the agenda. Eight more are being considered for a swimming pool and fish pond. There is no indication that the new civilian will differ greatly from the old sergeant. As he sits on his front porch, gazing off at his gas station and the empty lot across from it, a look of dreaming speculation comes into his eyes. 'You know,' he says, 'if I was to buy my gasoline by the tank-carload, I could possibly save considerable money that way.' "

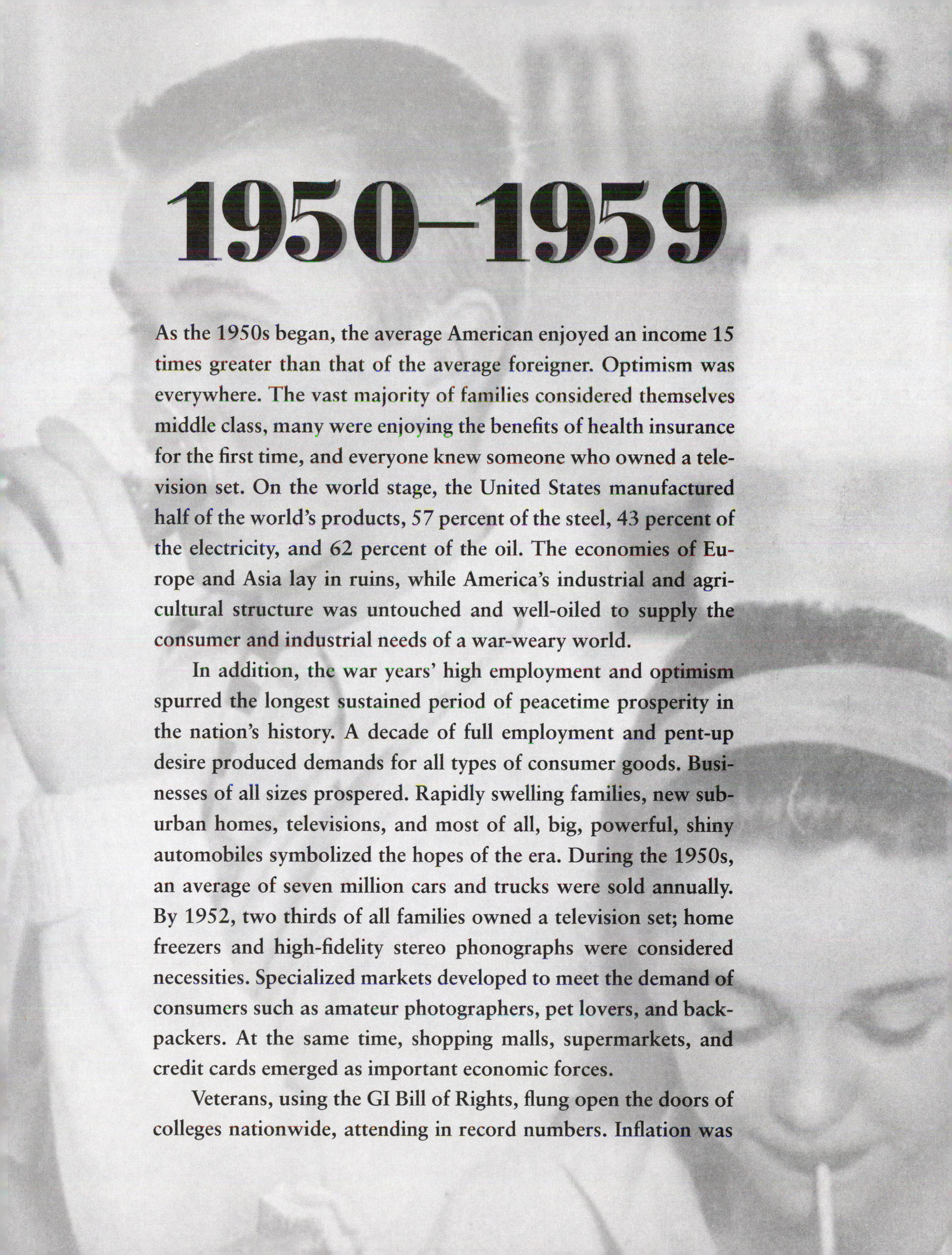

1950–1959

As the 1950s began, the average American enjoyed an income 15 times greater than that of the average foreigner. Optimism was everywhere. The vast majority of families considered themselves middle class, many were enjoying the benefits of health insurance for the first time, and everyone knew someone who owned a television set. On the world stage, the United States manufactured half of the world's products, 57 percent of the steel, 43 percent of the electricity, and 62 percent of the oil. The economies of Europe and Asia lay in ruins, while America's industrial and agricultural structure was untouched and well-oiled to supply the consumer and industrial needs of a war-weary world.

In addition, the war years' high employment and optimism spurred the longest sustained period of peacetime prosperity in the nation's history. A decade of full employment and pent-up desire produced demands for all types of consumer goods. Businesses of all sizes prospered. Rapidly swelling families, new suburban homes, televisions, and most of all, big, powerful, shiny automobiles symbolized the hopes of the era. During the 1950s, an average of seven million cars and trucks were sold annually. By 1952, two thirds of all families owned a television set; home freezers and high-fidelity stereo phonographs were considered necessities. Specialized markets developed to meet the demand of consumers such as amateur photographers, pet lovers, and backpackers. At the same time, shopping malls, supermarkets, and credit cards emerged as important economic forces.

Veterans, using the GI Bill of Rights, flung open the doors of colleges nationwide, attending in record numbers. Inflation was the only pressing economic issue, fueled in large part by the Korean War (in which 54,000 American lives were lost) and the federal expenditures for Cold War defense. As the decade opened, federal spending represented 15.6 percent of the nation's gross national product. Thanks largely to the Cold War, by 1957, defense consumed half of the federal government's $165 billion budget.

This economic prosperity also ushered in conservative politics and social conformity. Tidy lawns, bedrooms that were "neat and trim," and suburban homes that were "proper" were certainly "in" throughout the decade as Americans adjusted to the post-war years. Properly buttoned-down attitudes concerning sexual mores brought stern undergarments for women like bonded girdles and stiff, pointed, or padded bras to confine the body. The planned community of Levittown, New York, mandated that grass be cut at least once a week and laundry washed on specific days. A virtual revival of Victorian respectability and domesticity reigned; divorce rates and female college attendance fell while birth rates and the sale of Bibles rose. Corporate America promoted the benefits of respectable men in gray flannel suits whose wives remained at home to tend house and raise children. Suburban life included ladies' club memberships, chauffeuring children to piano and ballet classes, and lots of a newly marketed product known as tranquilizers, whose sales were astounding.

The average wage earner benefited more from the booming industrial system than at any time in American history. The 40-hour work week became standard in manufacturing. In offices many workers were becoming accustomed to a 35-hour week. Health benefits for workers became more common and paid vacations were standard in most industries. In 1950, 25 percent of American wives worked outside the home; by the end of the decade the number had risen to 40 percent. Communications technology, expanding roads, inexpensive airline tickets, and a spirit of unboundedness meant that people and commerce were no longer prisoners of distance. Unfortunately, up to one third of the population lived below the government's poverty level, largely overlooked in the midst of prosperity.

The Civil Rights movement was propelled by two momentous events in the 1950s. The first was a decree on May 17, 1954, by the U.S. Supreme Court which ruled "that in the field of public education the doctrine of 'separate but equal' has no place. Separate educational facilities are inherently unequal." The message was electric but the pace was slow. Few schools would be integrated for another decade. The second event established the place of the Civil Rights movement. On December 1, 1955, African-American activist Rosa Parks declined to vacate the White-only front section of the Montgomery, Alabama, bus, leading to her arrest and a citywide bus boycott by blacks. Their spokesman became Martin Luther King, Jr., the 26-year-old pastor of the Dexter Avenue Baptist Church. The year-long boycott was the first step toward the passage of the Civil Rights Act of 1964.

America's youths were enchanted by the TV adventures of "Leave It to Beaver," westerns, and "Father Knows Best," allowing them to accumulate more time watching television during the week (at least 27 hours) than attending school. TV dinners were invented; pink ties and felt skirts with sequined poodle appliqués were worn; Elvis Presley was worshipped and the new phenomena of *Playboy* and Mickey Spillane fiction were created only to be read behind closed doors. The ever-glowing eye of television killed the "March of Time" newsreels after 16 years at the movies. Sexual jargon such as "first base" and "home run" entered the language. Learned-When-Sleeping machines appeared, along with Smokey the Bear, Sony tape recorders, adjustable shower heads, *Mad Comics*, newspaper vending machines, Levi's faded blue denims, pocket-size transistor radios, and transparent plastic bags for clothing. Ultimately, the real stars of the era were the Salk and Sabin vaccines, which vanquished the siege of polio.

1950 News Profile

Spending of Middle-Income Families

Incomes and Expenditures of Salaried Workers in the San Francisco Bay Area in 1950

Money Income

These families had an average money income before taxes of $6,637. The lowest family income before taxes was $4,917, the highest was $9,304, and the median was $6,588. Clearly these families belonged to an upper income group in the population, since the U.S. Census reported that in 1949 only 33 percent of the families in the San Francisco-Oakland urbanized area had incomes of $5,000 or more, and the median income of all families was $3,958.

Average Receipts and Disbursements
All Families

Total receipts	$9,991.98	Total disbursements	$10,202.32
Money income before taxes	$6,637.10	Total expenditures	$7,227.99
Consumption	$5,957.25	Non-consumption	$1,270.63
Other money receipts	$323.90	Increase in assets and/or decrease in liabilities	$2,974.44
Decrease in assets and/or increase in liabilities	$3,030.98		

Balancing Difference –$210.34

Families with Incomes under $6,000

Total receipts	$8,668.03	Total disbursements	$8,888.80
Money income before taxes	$5,788.20	Total expenditures	$6,512.69
Other money receipts	$315.80	Consumption	$5,424.23
		Non-consumption	$1,088.46

Decrease in assets and/or increase in liabilities $2,564.03	Increase in assets and/or decrease in liabilities $2,376.11

Balancing Difference –$220.77

Families with Incomes $6,000 and over

Total receipts $11,204.25	Total disbursements $11,405.07
Money income before taxes. $7,414.40	Total expenditures. $7,882.76
Consumption. $6,445.32	Non-consumption $1,437.44
Other money receipts $331.31	Increase in assets and/or decrease in liabilities $3,522.31
Decrease in assets and/or increase in liabilities $3,458.54	

Balancing Difference –$200.82

Ninety-one percent of the income before taxes of these families came from the earnings of the head of the family; although most families had some other sources of income, the average additional sum was only $592. When income taxes were deducted, the average spendable income from regular sources was $6,077, and nearly three-quarters of the families had incomes between $5,000 and $7,000.

Expenditures for Current Consumption

These families reported average total expenditures of $7,228, of which $5,957, or 82 percent, was for consumption items. The sums spent for the various consumption categories varied widely: in order of size the largest was of course food, which was followed by trans-

portation, housing, and clothing. These four categories combined accounted for 65 percent of all consumption expenditures. Families spent between $350 and approximately $450 for house operation, house furnishings, medical care, and recreation, and a little more than $100 for personal care. For no other current consumption category was the average expenditure as much as $100.

Food and alcoholic beverages—The average expenditure for food was $1,622, or 27.2 percent of the amount spent for all current consumption items. Sixty-two percent of the families spent between $1,500 and $2,686; 82 percent spent from one-fifth to 35 percent of their total consumption expenditures for food; and about one-eighth spent 35 to 43 percent. Families with incomes over $6,000 spent more money for food than did those in the lower income brackets, but the two income groups spent almost the same proportion of their total consumption expenditures for food: 27.8 percent and 26.8 percent, respectively.

Eighty-nine percent of the families bought some beer, wine, or liquor. The average expense for the entire group of families was $91, or 1.5 percent of total consumption expenditures. The average sums spent by families in both the income group under $6,000 and the higher bracket were very similar: $97 and $106, respectively.

Transportation—Second in order of size were transportation expenditures, which averaged $924, or 15.5 percent of total consumption expenditures. Since all but eight of these families owned cars, it is not surprising to find that $822 of the $924 was spent for automobile transportation. Unlike the situation in most categories of expenditure, the families with incomes less than $6,000 not only spent more money on total transportation than did the higher income group, but these expenses represented a larger proportion of all their current consumption expenditures: 17.8 in contrast with 13.7 percent. Since both income groups spent almost identical sums for non-automobile transportation, the difference in their total expenditures came solely from their car expenses and reflected the greater necessity of replacing old cars, which the lower-income families faced in 1950.

Overall automobile costs were, of course, higher for those who purchased cars; 27 percent of the families spent $1,000 or more for automobile transportation, and most of this group bought cars in 1950. All families spent an average of $458 for car purchase and $364 for operation and upkeep. For those who actually bought cars, the average cost was $1,323 after the trade-in allowance. Fifty-two percent of these cars were purchased new, and the average expenditure for new cars was $1,839, whereas used cars cost the buyers an average of $720. Forty-seven percent of the families who bought cars paid cash for them, another 22 percent made these purchases on installment, and 31 percent borrowed money that was probably used to buy a car. Only 44 percent of the buyers with incomes of $6,000 or more used any credit in making car purchases, in contrast with 59 percent of those in the lower income group.

In the main these were one-car families, and most of the automobiles they owned were in the low- or moderate-priced classes. The average price before trade-in of all the cars purchased in 1950 was $1,660, including any financing charge and all extras bought at the time of purchase; the average price of new cars was $2,347, and second-hand cars, $922.

Clearly the families in this study used automobiles as their chief mode of transportation, since they spent an average of only $101 for all other transportation. Only three families spent more than $300, and these expenses were largely for vacation travel.

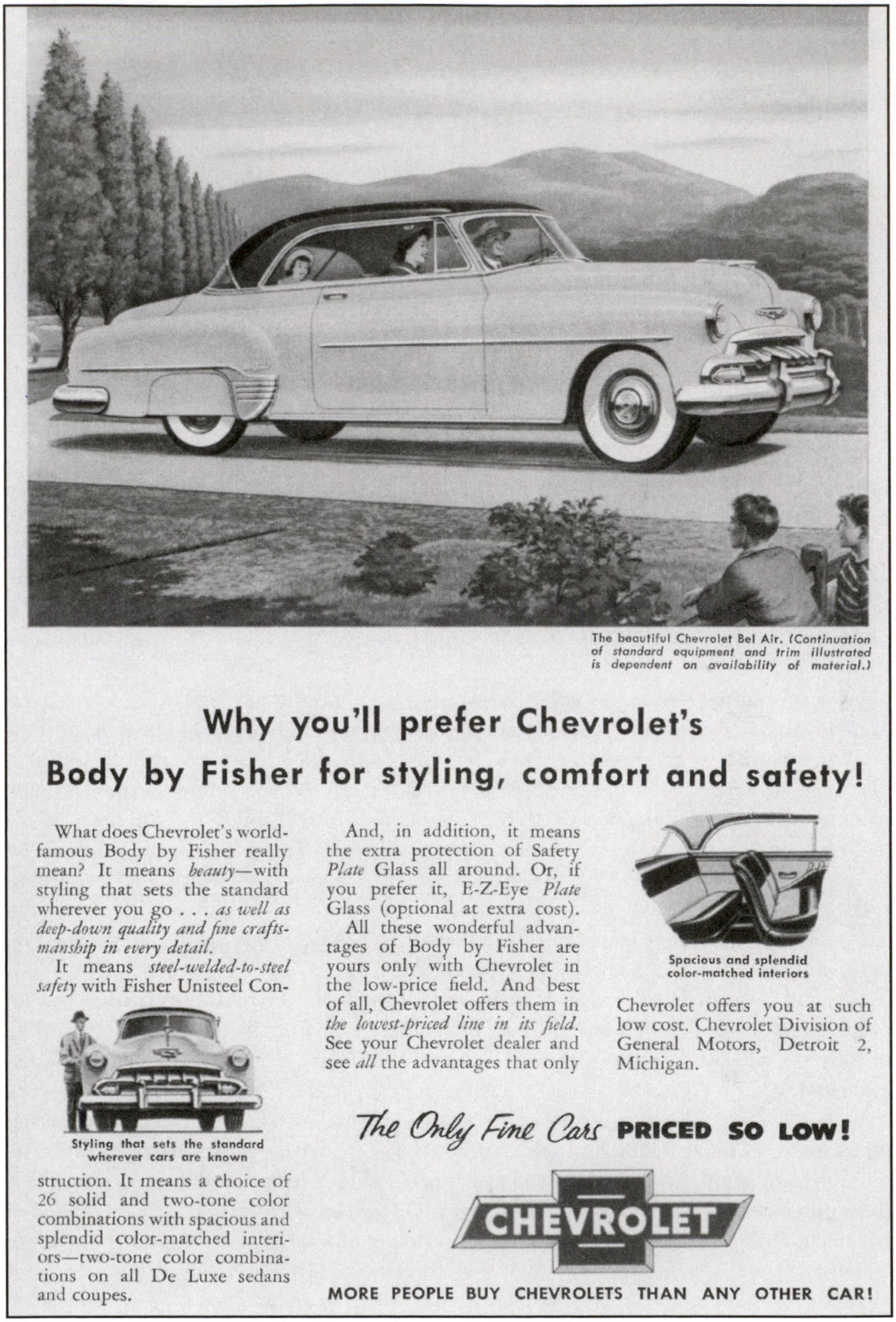

Housing—Housing expenditures averaged $711 per family, which was 11.9 percent of total consumption expenditures. Of this sum, $676 was spent for the family home, and the remainder chiefly for vacation housing. Families with incomes under $6,000 spent $582 for all their housing, whereas those in the higher income brackets spent $829. These expenditures for the two income groups represented 10.7 and 12.9 percent, respectively, of their total consumption expenditures.

Sixty-nine percent of the families lived in owned homes, and not quite one-quarter lived in rented homes, during all of 1950. The owners usually lived in five- to seven-room houses, and the renters in four- to five-room houses or apartments; the full-year owners' average cash expenditure for the family home was $568, whereas the renters spent $774. However, if the net value of occupancy (N.V.O., the difference between the estimated rental value of an owned home and the actual cash expense for that home) had been added to the cash outlay, the family home would have cost the full-year owners an average of $1,338.

Clothing—Clothing expenditures were very moderate; the average family expense for clothing and clothing services combined was $623, or 10.5 percent of the average of all expenditures for current consumption. Families with incomes less than $6,000 spent an average of $542, or 10 percent of all consumption expenditures, whereas the higher income group spent $697, which was 10.8 percent of their consumption expenses.

Clothing purchases averaged $549 per family. Wives spent an average of $194, while their husbands spent $162, for boys more than two years, $89 was spent, and for girls in the same age bracket, $117; the average cost of infants' clothing was $47. In general, the higher-income families spent more for clothing purchases than did those in the lower-income group. Clothing upkeep and repair cost an average of $74 per family, and expenditures for these services varied little with income.

Household operation—The average expenditure for all household operation was $459, or 7.7 percent of total consumption expenditures. Families with incomes less than $6,000 spent an average of $391, which was 7.2 percent of consumption expenses, whereas those with higher incomes spent $521, or 8.1 percent. Since fuel, light, refrigeration, and water took very similar amounts from both income groups, the difference in their expenditures is largely attributable to all other expenses for house operation.

Fuel, light, refrigeration, and water accounted for 30 percent of all household operation expenses and cost all families an average of $135; of this amount, gas took 40 percent, electricity one-third, and water nearly one-quarter. The main factor governing the size of expenditures for gas and electricity appeared to be the size of the dwelling units.

Among the innumerable other household expenses, the largest were for telephone and telegraph service and for wages, which averaged about $70 each and together accounted for 43 percent of these miscellaneous household operation costs. Laundry sent out, plus laundry and cleaning supplies, accounted for almost another quarter of these costs. For all household operation except fuel, light, refrigeration, and water, all families spent an average of $324; families with incomes below $6,000 spent $262, whereas the higher income brackets spent $380.

House furnishings—Expenditures for house furnishings represented 7.5 percent of the average cost of all current consumption items. The average cash outlay was $445; families with incomes less than $6,000 spent $385, and the higher-income families spent $500. For the lower group, this represented 7.1 percent of all consumption expenditures; for the upper bracket it was 7.8 percent.

Since the size and nature of house furnishings purchases varied so widely, it is impossible to describe the typical family expenditure pattern. Full-year homeowners spent an average of $397, whereas those who rented all year spent $395; however, the 13 families that were both renters and owners during the year spent $984.

Kitchen, cleaning, and laundry equipment accounted for one-third of the total cost of house furnishings; furniture took just over one-fourth of the money, and floor coverings and textiles together represented almost another fourth of the house furnishings dollar.

The majority of families bought their house furnishings for cash, but 29 percent of the sample reported purchasing some furnishings on installment—26 families purchased one item, and 20 bought two or more items with this type of credit. The two families with the largest installment expenditures became homeowners during the study year.

Medical and dental care—Medical and dental care cost the families in this study an average of $375, or 6.3 percent of all their consumption expenditures. Of the total, $270 went for medical care, and dentistry took $101. There was no consistent relationship between the size of the bills for total health care and family income, although families with incomes of less than $6,000 spent an average of $339, and those with higher incomes spent $407, large and small bills appeared in both income groups. The proportions of total consumption expenditures were virtually identical in the two groups (6.2 and 6.3 percent).

An average of $199 was spent by all families for all medical care except the cost of prepayment plans. Fifty-five percent of this amount went for physicians' bills, drugs and medicines accounted for another 26 percent, laboratory tests and x-rays took seven percent, and eye care took six percent of the total. Ninety-four percent of the individuals in the study reported receiving some kind of medical care, at an average cost of $54. The average cost for those persons whose expenses could be allocated to family members was $66. The expenditures of the family heads averaged $46, their wives spent $124, and the children under 18 years, $45.

Ninety-three percent of the families reported that at least 1 family member belonged to some kind of a prepaid medical care plan during 1950, and more than three-quarters of the memberships covered the entire family for a full year. There was little difference in the proportions of husbands, wives, and children who were members of prepayment plans, but memberships were somewhat more frequent among the husbands.

The average premium paid for prepayment plans by all families in the study was $74, which represented slightly more than one-fourth of the average total medical care expenditure. The average cost of full-year family coverage for those families reporting such coverage was $77. Almost three-quarters of the families who reported full-year coverage belonged to plans that provided hospital, surgical, and medical care; 24 percent had plans that gave hospital and surgical care, and two percent belonged to plans providing only hospital care. However, within each of these three broad types of coverage, the extent of care provided by the various policies varied considerably.

Of the total of 412 individuals who reported receiving some medical care and who were full-year members of a prepayment plan, 159, or 39 percent, received some service from their prepayment plans. Those who used their prepayment plans when hospitalized received substantial assistance in paying their hospital bills, and a large majority of the prepayment plan members who received services from their plans for non-hospitalized illnesses had relatively small bills. However, there were some prepayment plan members who had high hospital or non-hospital bills in addition to what was paid by the prepayment plans.

Ten families had no expenditures for dental care in 1950. The average family expenditure for dentistry for the entire sample was $101. Families with incomes under $6,000 spent an average of $86, whereas those in the higher brackets spent $116, but there were both large and small bills at every income level. The average cost of dentistry for all individuals in the sample was $26. Dental service was reported by 65 percent of the husbands, 77 percent of the wives, 79 percent of the children six to 17, and by slightly more than one-fourth of the children under six. The average dental cost for those individuals who received care was $40; the wives spent $6 more than this, and the average for children under six was $18.

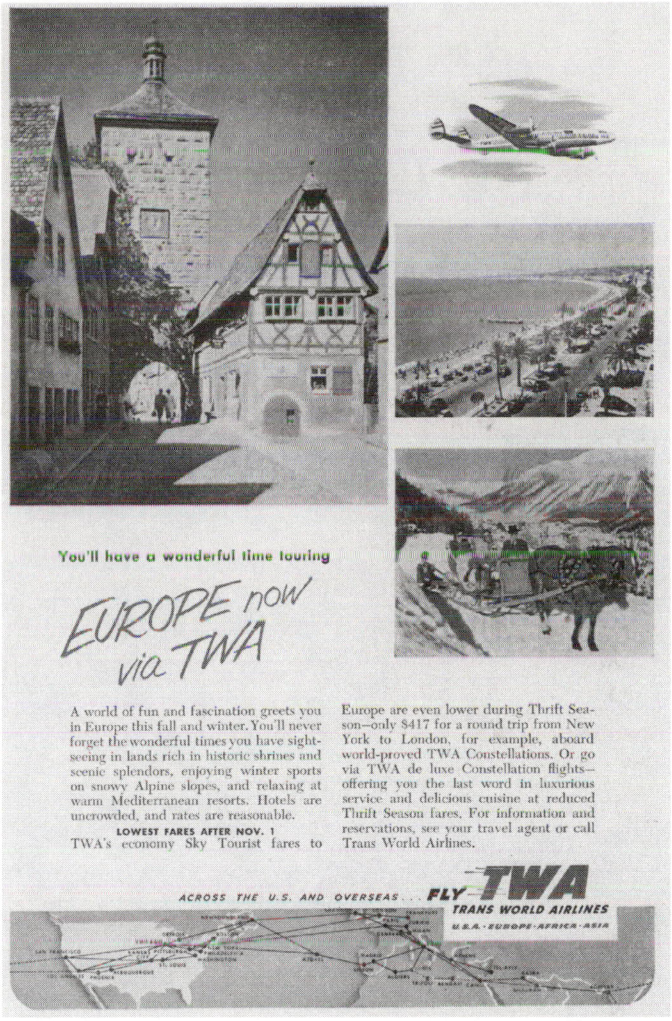

Recreation—Every family spent something for recreation, and the average outlay was $355, or six percent of all consumption expenditures. Those families with incomes below $6,000 spent considerably less than the higher income brackets—$290 in contrast with $415. The proportions of total consumption expenditures were also relatively far apart: 5.3 and 6.4 percent, respectively.

The largest expenditures were for the purchase and repair of television sets, radios, and musical instruments, which as a group absorbed 43 percent of the average recreation expenditure for all families in the sample. Those who reported expenditures in this category spent an average of $240 per family, and almost half of all the money spent went for television sets. The only recreation items bought on installment were in this category. Installment credit was used in the purchase of 38 percent of the television sets and 42 percent of the radio phonographs, as well as to buy three of the seven pianos, an organ, and an accordion.

The money spent for all other types of recreation purchased a wide variety of items. The average expenditures for any of these categories were never large—ranging from $13 to $42—and the vast majority of purchases in any category was less than $50.

Personal care—All families reported expenditures for personal care, spending an average of $111, almost equally divided between services and supplies. Expenditures did not vary consistently with income, and in families with incomes either under or over $6,000, the per capita expenditure was $28. The lower-income families spent two percent of all current consumption expenditures for personal care, whereas the upper bracket spent 1.8 percent.

Two families managed to spend nothing for personal services by having home haircuts, shampoos, etc. The average expenditure for these services among the other 157 families was $55. Husbands spent 45 percent of all the money going for services, with an average expenditure of $25. Wives accounted for slightly less than one-third of the total spent, and the average for that spending was $20. Services for the children averaged $12 a family among all families and $16 for those families that reported expenditures. Seventy-two percent of all the boys spent something for personal services, at an average cost of $13. Only 41 percent of the girls had any expenditures, and their average expense was $6.

Every family bought some personal care supplies, spending an average of $56. In contrast to the situation in personal services, it seems likely that more of the supplies dollar was allocated to the women than to the men.

Education, reading, tobacco, and miscellaneous expenditures—The average expenditure of all families for each of these categories amounted to 1.2 percent, or less of the average cost of all consumption items.

About three-quarters of the sample had some expenses for education, and these expenses averaged $66 for all families, and $88 for those with expenses. Such expenses were generally for tuition, or for music, dancing, or other private lessons.

Every family spent something for reading material; the average was $49, and most families spent only enough to have a daily paper, one or two magazine subscriptions, and perhaps an occasional book.

Seventy-two percent of the families bought tobacco, at an average cost of $57 for all families, and $80 for those who reported purchases.

Among the miscellaneous expenses, the most numerous or largest were for real estate other than occupied homes, interest on loans, bank service charges, and safe deposit box rental. For the combined items in this heterogeneous category, the average expense for all families was $71; those families who actually had expenses reported an average of $76.

Non-consumption Expenditures

In addition to current consumption expenditures, all families reported outlays for personal insurance, gifts and contributions, and personal taxes. The combined average expenditure for these items was $1,271, or 18 percent of their total expenditures. Forty-two percent of these non-consumption expenditures went for personal insurance, 14 percent for gifts and contributions, and 44 percent for taxes.

The average cost of personal insurance was $533, or 7.4 percent of the average of all consumption and non-consumption expenditures. Families with incomes under $6,000 spent seven percent of all their expenditures, or $457, and those with higher incomes spent 7.7 percent, or $603. Slightly more than half of the average paid for all personal insurance was spent on commercial insurance, which averaged $278 for the entire sample. The remaining insurance payments went to state, federal, or company retirement or disability plans.

The average family expense for gifts and contributions was $177, or 2.4 percent of the total of all consumption and non-consumption items. Those with incomes less than $6,000 spent 2.6 percent of their total expenditures on gifts and contributions, whereas the higher-income brackets spent 2.3 percent. Church contributions and gifts of cash or goods to persons outside the economic family were the chief expenditures. Support of persons outside the economic family also took relatively large sums from one-quarter of the families who had such responsibilities.

Personal taxes cost this group of families an average of $561, or 7.8 percent of all consumption and non-consumption expenditures. Ninety-seven percent of this expense was for federal income taxes, which averaged $546, in contrast to an average state income tax of $14 for those reporting. Families with incomes under $6,000 paid an average for all taxes of $463, or 7.1 percent of all their expenditures, whereas the upper bracket families paid $650, which was 8.2 percent of their total expenditures.

Categories of Consumption

	Average Expenditures	Total Expenditures (percent)	Consumption Expenditures (percent)
Total expenditures	$7,227.88	100.0	...
Current consumption expenditures, total	$5,957.25	82.4	100.0
Food	$1,622.28	22.4	27.2
Alcoholic beverages	$90.66	1.3	1.5
Housing	$711.21	9.8	11.9
House operation, total	$459.09	6.4	7.7
Fuel, light, refrigeration, water	$135.41	1.9	2.3
Miscellaneous	$323.68	4.5	5.4
House furnishings and equipment, total	$444.85	6.2	7.5
Household textiles	$49.69	.7	.8
Furniture	$115.38	1.6	1.9
Floor covering	$57.40	.8	1.0
Kitchen, cleaning, and laundry equipment	$145.72	2.0	2.4
All other	$76.66	1.1	1.3
Clothing, total	$622.98	8.6	10.5
Purchase, total	$548.70	7.6	9.2
Women and girls	$295.48	4.1	5.0
Men and boys	$243.09	3.4	4.1
Children under two years	$10.14	.1	.2
Services, total	$74.27	1.0	1.2
Transportation, total	$923.52	12.8	15.5
Automobile	$822.04	11.4	13.8
Other	$101.48	1.4	1.7
Medical care	$374.63	5.2	6.3

Categories of Consumption

	Average Expenditures	Total Expenditures (percent)	Consumption Expenditures (percent)
Personal care	$110.57	1.5	1.9
Recreation	$355.35	4.9	6.0
Tobacco	$57.30	.8	1.0
Reading	$48.63	.7	.8
Education	$65.62	.9	1.1
Miscellaneous	$70.56	1.0	1.2
Non-consumption expenditures, total	$1.270.63	17.6	...
Insurance and retirement	$533.27	7.4	...
Gifts and contributions	$176.79	2.4	...
Personal taxes	$560.57	7.8	...
Money income after taxes	$6,076.53		
Other money receipts	$323.90		
Net decrease in assets and/or increase in liabilities	$56.54		
Balancing difference	–$210.34		
Total families in sample	159		
Average family size	3.9		

1953 Family Profile

Jeffrey Connor, a captain in the Air Force, is assigned to the Strategic Air Command and is currently stationed in Wichita, Kansas. Married with two children, he recently returned from the Korean War.

Annual Income: $2,800

Annual Budget

The average per capita consumer expenditures in 1953 for all workers nationwide are:

Auto Parts	$9.40
Auto Usage	$164.19
Clothing	$117.19
Dentists	$7.52
Food	$409.86
Furniture	$23.19
Gas and Oil	$46.38
Health Insurance	$8.15
Housing	$187.38
Intercity Transport	$6.89
Local Transport	$12.53
New Auto Purchase	$69.56
Personal Business	$50.76
Personal Care	$19.43
Physicians	$20.68
Private Education and Research	$13.79
Recreation	$81.47

Jeffrey Connor recently returned from the Korean War.

Base housing reminds Karen of a mill village in the South.

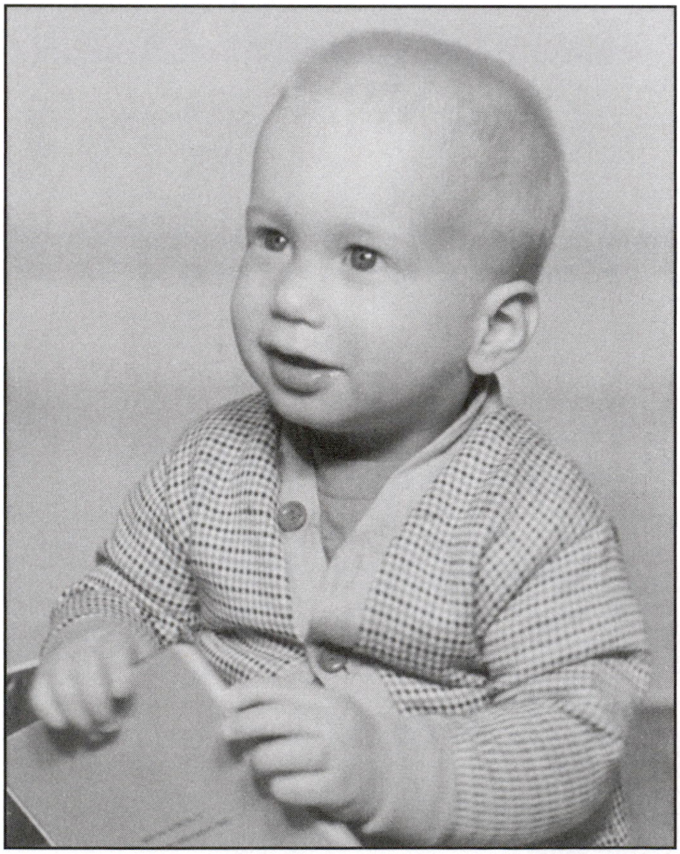

The couple has an 18-month-old son.

Religion/Welfare Activities	$19.43
Telephone and Telegraph	$16.92
Tobacco	$31.96
Utilities	$54.52
Per Capita Consumption	$1,457.71

Life at Home

- In many ways, it doesn't matter where they are living; all Air Force bases begin to look alike.
- The Connor family has been moved by the military five times in the past three years. Jeffrey's wife, Karen, insists on hanging all the pictures they own on the first day; it is her way of creating a home environment in an ever-changing world.
- The new house, provided for by the government, reminds Karen of mill village housing in the South—1,200 square feet with three small bedrooms, a living room, dining room, and kitchen.
- They are currently in Wichita, Kansas, where the sunshine, wind, and bugs all come in large quantities.
- Even though they are always conservative with their money, Jeffrey recently bought the "new, easy, miracle way to rid their home of flies . . . bugs, Bug-Kil" to reduce the insect population.
- The couple has an 18-month-old son and a five-year-old daughter who is attending school for the first time.
- The girl likes base school; the teacher allows her to read all the "Sally" parts of the *Dick and Jane Reader* because that is her first name.
- The school recently sponsored a Dress Up Day for Dogs and Sally took her English Bulldog to school wearing her dad's pajamas.
- She has learned that on windy Kansas days she has to walk home from school backwards to keep the wind and sand from stinging her face.
- Recently, her mother has made her and her brother take naps every afternoon; it is believed that keeping children indoors during the heat of the day will reduce the chance of catching infantile polio—currently a serious problem.
- For recreation, the couple bowls weekly; he has been bowling for years, while she took up the sport after marriage. Every military base where they have lived has a movie theater and a bowling alley.
- He also makes it a point to play catch with his daughter for one half-hour each day he is home; it is her time with her dad. He also takes time to read with his son, who is still too young to play sports.
- Karen plays bridge twice a month with a group composed entirely of military wives, mostly the wives of pilots.

- Because their husbands tell them little about their assignments, the bridge games often help the wives understand their husbands' duties and how they are feeling.
- For people like Karen, who move constantly, the military is their only family.
- Scrabble is currently the rage, and some bridge clubs are experimenting with one table of Scrabble; she thinks it is a dumb idea, but has been hesitant to say so.
- The children know that if the phone rings in the middle of the night, their dad gets dressed, takes his pistol from the top of the closet, and goes out to the street to wait on the carpool to the flight line; he is going on alert and will be away for a while.
- They rarely ask any questions about where he has gone.
- Karen normally sleeps poorly when he is away and compulsively cleans the house until he returns.
- The children are instructed to put up all toys at night and she completely cleans the house by 9:00 each morning in case anyone drops by to visit, invited or not.
- Even though money is a constant worry, she keeps a full pantry at all times so she can entertain guests or feed her husband's crew if they return home from an assignment sooner than expected.
- From the pantry she can put a meal on the table in 30 minutes; reflecting her experience in Hawaii early in their marriage, she enjoys preparing Asian foods.
- A mild-mannered man by nature, Jeff enjoys the structure of the military and believes the Air Force has been good to him and his family.
- Karen gets to see her mother every other year; on even years they use their two-week vacation to drive to Michigan to see his parents; on odd years they drive to South Carolina so her mother can see the grandchildren.
- A native of Zeeland, Michigan, he joined the army on his eighteenth birthday in January 1942.
- With the war raging, older men in the community had been asking him why he wasn't already in the military; he hated for anyone to think he was a slackard.
- Although only a high school graduate, he was selected for officer candidate's school in the newly forming Army Air Corps.
- He was sent to Winthrop College in Rock Hill, South Carolina; before the war the small teacher's college was exclusively for women.
- Under the military's assignment system, the training at Winthrop included all candidates whose names started with "C."
- The group that followed all carried a surname starting with "D."
- While at Winthrop, he met Karen.

Sally likes base school because she is allowed to read the "Sally" parts of the Dick and Jane Reader.

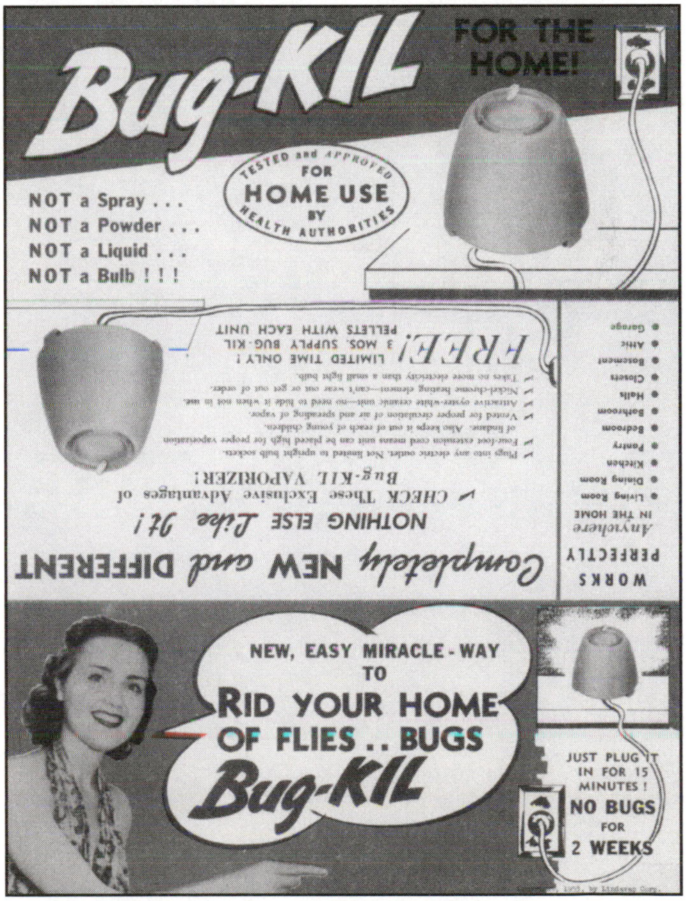

The Connors are waging a losing battle against the bugs in Kansas.

Every other year Karen visits her mother during their two-week vacation.

- After one year of training, he transferred to pilot school and later to communications and electronics school.
- He is now into his eleventh year in the military and considering whether to leave and become a civilian or go for 20 years; he has been told military retirement is excellent.

Life at Work

- He has recently returned from Korea, where he flew the new B-29; stationed at McConnell Air Force Base and assigned to the Strategic Air Command, he is now piloting the new B-47s.
- Although heavier than the B-29, its size is disguised by slender lines and the novelty of a fighter-type cockpit.
- A B-47 crew includes a pilot, co-pilot, and navigator hidden in the nose of the plane.
- Its shoulder-mounted wings, which are razor-edged and remarkably thin, sweep back at a startling angle of 35 degrees.

When their father leaves in the middle of the night, the children rarely ask where he has gone.

His first overseas assignment was to Wheeler Field, Hawaii.

He is currently assigned to the Strategic Air Command.

- To retain the aerodynamic advantages of thin airfoils, the practice of housing the engines, fuel, and wheels in the wings has been abandoned.
- Korea is Jeff's third overseas assignment.
- His first was to Wheeler Field, Hawaii, in 1946, where the military was still rebuilding the war-torn territory.
- The second was in support of the Berlin Airlift in 1948 to supply a city of two million people with everything needed for survival by air.
- The airlift required 4,500 tons of food, fuel, and medicine a day to keep Berlin alive.
- The airlift was necessitated by the Russians' attempt to blockade the divided city of Berlin and force the allied forces out of West Berlin.
- Under various pretexts, the Russians closed all highway traffic to the city and stopped all trains.
- As part of Operation Vittles, under the command of Gen. Curtis LeMay, Jeff flew C-47 transports into the city.
- He sometimes flew two or three flights each day to bring supplies into the embattled city.
- By late 1950, he was in Korea, supporting the newly declared war against North Korea.
- North Korea, divided from South Korea following World War II, was controlled by Red China; under communist direction, North Korea attacked the Republic of Korea in June 1950.

F-86 Sabre Jet
designed and built by
NORTH AMERICAN AVIATION, INC.
NORTH AMERICAN HAS BUILT MORE AIRPLANES THAN ANY OTHER COMPANY IN THE WORLD

Following World War II, bases were strategically placed across Europe.

- At first, the North Koreans overwhelmed the small garrisons of the Republic of Korea, quickly capturing its capital of Seoul.
- Captain Connor flew B-29s in support of the United States while United Nations forces rushed to the area; the bombers struck industrial targets and occasionally flew in support of ground troops.
- The Air Force played a critical role in Korea, demonstrating America's ability to use superior technology to attack an invading force.
- One of Jeff's missions was to hit North Korea's giant hydroelectric plants, knocking out 90 percent of the country's electric power.
- A second wave of pilots flying jet aircraft struck the Toksan and Chasan irrigation dams, flooding important road and rail communications.
- Of the 839 Korean MIG fighters shot down over Korea, 792 were brought down by American F-86 Sabrejets.
- During the conflict, 78 U.S. Sabrejets were lost.
- Since returning from Korea, he has been part of the Strategic Air Command, known as SAC.

"Operation Pullback," *Time Magazine*, November 10, 1952:

"Between the Baltic Sea and the Bavarian Alps, the U.S., Britain, and France have a string of air bases equal to any in the world. Inherited from the Nazis, the accommodations at this base reflect the care that Hermann Göring lavished on his pet, the Luftwaffe. Runways (extended by the jet-flying allies) are long and smooth, operations buildings snugly efficient, living quarters furnished down to the last monogrammed china dinner service. Only snag about the old German system of air bases: they face the wrong way. The best of the fields, i.e., those in the Reich's rear areas, have two irremediable defects: 1. They are uncomfortably close to the Iron Curtain—many of them less than 10 minutes by jet, and 2. Their supply lines run back eastward toward Soviet Germany. 'The U.S. Air Force in Germany,' cracked a U.S. staff officer after the fields had been taken over, 'is ideally deployed to fight France.'

The only solution was to pull back from Göring's finest bases to safer territory on the west bank of the Rhine, far enough away from the Iron Curtain to give allied planes a chance to get into the air before being overrun by Russian Panzers. Slowly, painfully slowly, NATO began building a brand-new air frontier, 100 to 250 miles farther back, in France and the Low Countries.

To pay for the new bases, NATO has already put up $750 million (the U.S. share: about 40 percent) and laid down plans for 'standard bases, designed to suit the operational requirements of all participating air forces. Specifications for the standard fields: 8,000-foot runways (a compromise between the U.S.A.F.'s demand for 9,000 feet and the R.A.F.'s insistence that 6,000 feet is plenty) and standardized lighting, storage, and fueling facilities. Beyond these bare essentials, each air force building has its own barracks, canteens, and bowling alleys—at its own expense. To get a standard airfield ready for occupation by Americans, the U.S. shells out an extra $12 to $18 million. . . . Within a week or two, the first U.S. F-86 Sabrejets will be landed in Europe to replace F-84 Thunderjets. A Canadian wing stationed in France is already flying Sabrejets. With F-86s, battle-tested in Korea and equipped to deliver tactical A-bombs, U.S. fighter pilots will at last feel able to cope with the Russian MIGs, if they have to."

- If an unknown aircraft enters the fly zone, bombers must not be caught on the ground and are immediately sent into the area before an enemy can strike.
- He is required to be in full combat uniform while on duty.
- More than 40 SAC bases in the United States can launch their planes in minutes; SAC is considered the greatest deterrent to Soviet aggression.
- If deployed, he and his fellow pilots can fly nonstop around the world to deliver bombs; this threat is designed to keep the peace.
- Often on an alert they are not told where they are going until after they have left the ground.
- Recently, an airplane crashed during an alert about the time Jeff was taking off.
- Karen made her children stay inside the house, refused to answer the phone, and did not answer the door when military officers knocked.
- Fortunately for this family, the plane that crashed was behind Jeff's and he was not aware of the tragedy until later; the military men who died are all friends in a community which by necessity is small and tight.

LeMay's Air Force, American Eagles, A History of the United States Air Force, by Ron Dick:

"If any command exemplified the face of the new Air Force, transformed by technological advances and determined leadership, it was Strategic Air Command (SAC). In 1950, SAC had 71,490 personnel and 868 aircraft. The backbone of its striking force consisted of 390 B-29s. Five years later, the personnel strength was 196,000, and there were 3,068 aircraft including well over 1,000 B-47s backed by a tanker fleet of more than 700. At the same time, standards of performance rose dramatically, driven by the implacable (General Curtis) LeMay. Besides the impact of his steely personality, he brought fresh ideas to encourage his command to new heights. The SAC bombing and navigation competitions were established as annual events, and he introduced a system of spot promotions to reward outstanding performance. …

SAC's first Boeing B-47s were delivered in October 1951. This was a force which had inherited practices learned the hard way in WWII, when heavily armed piston-engined bombers with large crews operated in formation, preferably with a fighter escort. The B-47 brought with it revolutionary changes in operational doctrine and in aircrew attitudes to the bombing mission. It was an extraordinary technical achievement, bearing almost no resemblance to its predecessors and pointing the way to the future for large aircraft in both military and civil aviation."

The Connor family has found the landscape of Kansas both vast and exceedingly plain.

Kansas, "the plainest of the plains states" is extremely hot in the summer and very cold and windy in the winter.

Life in the Community: Wichita, Kansas

- Kansas has been described as the plainest of the Plains states, a quip the Connors agree with.
- Outside McConnell Air Force Base, the countryside appears to be little more than an endless ocean of grains and grasses.
- Kansas is America's one wheat producer.

Historically, agriculture has played a critical role in the economy of the state.

- The state is also the aircraft capital of the world, with Wichita producing nearly 60 percent of all the airplanes made in the United States, including Beechcraft, Cessna, and Lear.
- The Mid-Continent Airport, a major international port of call, is now nearly completed.
- Kansas is also one of the windiest inland areas in the nation; Karen is used to coping with heat that touches 100 degrees, but has difficulty with the cold and wind during the winters.
- Largely because of the need for railroad-building labor following the Civil War, the state is mostly populated by the laborers recruited for that work, including Russians, Germans, Bohemians, and Scandinavians.

Historical Snapshot
1953

- The Screen Actors Guild adopted by-laws banning communists from membership
- For the first time, a link was made between coronary heart disease and diets high in animal fats
- New York subway fares rose from $0.05 to $0.15.
- Nationwide, 30 million attended performances of classical music and 15 million attended major league baseball, while 7.2 million children took music lessons
- The Dow Jones Industrial Average showed a high of 293 and a low of 255
- Per capita state taxes averaged $68.04
- An airmail stamp cost $0.07 per ounce; a postcard, $0.02
- All-black military units had largely disappeared; 90 percent were now integrated into white military units
- Leland Kirdel wrote in *Coronet* magazine, "The smart woman will keep herself desirable. It is her duty to be feminine and desirable at all times in the eyes of the opposite sex."
- In the wave of McCarthyism, libraries were ordered to remove books by "communists, fellow travelers, and the like"
- Lucille Ball and Desi Arnaz signed an $8 million contract to continue "I Love Lucy" for 30 months
- Optimistic about peace with Korea, new president Dwight D. Eisenhower restored the traditional Easter egg roll for children on the White House lawn
- *TV Guide* and *Playboy* both began publication
- The number of comic books exploded, comprising 650 titles
- Nationwide, 25 percent of young Americans were now attending college, thanks to the GI Bill—an increase of 65 percent from before the Second World War
- President Eisenhower pledged rigid economy in government, a lifting of controls, and an effort toward a more balanced budget
- During his inaugural address, the new president called on Americans to make whatever sacrifices may be necessary to meet the threat of Soviet aggression; he defined the contest now as being a matter of freedom against slavery
- Charlie Chaplin said it was "virtually impossible" to continue work in the United States because of "vicious propaganda" by powerful reactionary groups
- General Motors introduced the Chevrolet Corvette, the first plastic-laminated, fiberglass sportscar; the cost was $3,250
- Elvis Presley paid $4.00 to cut "My Happiness" in Memphis for his mother's birthday
- Russia's Joseph Stalin died in May; the coronation of England's Queen Elizabeth occurred in June
- New York's Seeman Brothers introduced the first instant ice tea
- Nearly half of U.S. farms now had tractors
- 17 million homes had television sets
- Four out of five men's shirts sold in America were white
- The DC-7 propeller plane, Sugar Smacks, 3-D cartoons and movies, and Irish Coffee all made their first appearance

1953 Economic Profile

Income, Standard Jobs

Average of All Industries, Excluding Farm Labor	$3,927
Average of All Industries, Including Farm Labor	$3,852
Bituminous Coal Mining	$4,061
Building Trades	$4,354
Domestics	$1,805
Farm Labor	$1,464
Federal Civilian	$4,411
Federal Employees, Executive Departments	$3,410
Federal Military	$2,927
Finance, Insurance, and Real Estate	$3,663
Gas and Electricity Workers	$4,404
Manufacturing, Durable Goods	$4,383
Manufacturing, Nondurable Goods	$3,784
Medical/Health Services Workers	$2,365
Miscellaneous Manufacturing	$3,560
Motion Picture Services	$3,326
Nonprofit Organization Workers	$3,041
Passenger Transportation Workers, Local and Highway	$3,809
Personal Services	$2,573

Public School Teachers $3,314
Radio Broadcasting and
  Television Workers $5,734
Railroad Workers $4,418
State and Local Government
  Workers. $3,140
Telephone and Telegraph
  Workers. $3,720
Wholesale and Retail Trade
  Workers. $3,446

Selected Prices

Ann Barton Hair Dryer. $21.50
Automobile Chassis Lubrication. $1.25
Axminster Rug, All Wool $93.50
Bayer Aspirin, 30 Tablets $0.30

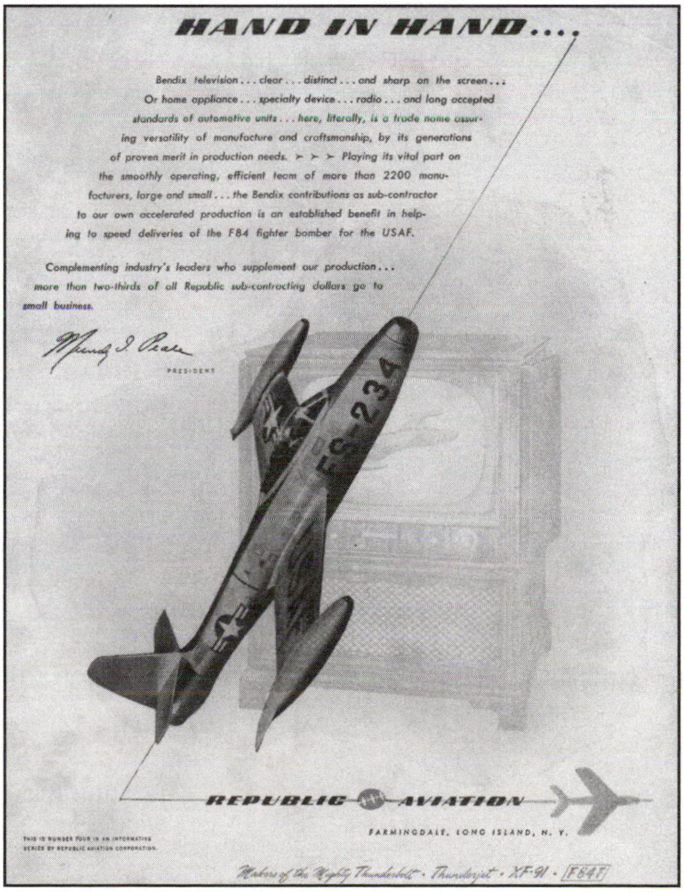

Smoke Rings Flavored with LICORICE!
Most American cigarettes—in fact nearly all tobacco products—contain licorice in varying amounts. The quantity in a cigarette, cigar or pipeful of tobacco is relatively small, but industry-wide the use of MacAndrews & Forbes pure licorice extract adds up to a yearly total of nearly 20 million pounds!
The ancient "sweet root," whose fabled virtues are imperishably inscribed in stone and whose lore has filtered through the centuries, still holds its own in company with other irreplaceable natural products. In pharmaceuticals, licorice is used chiefly to mask the taste of bitter medicines. In candy and confections it has long been a unique and dominant flavoring ingredient. In tobacco it is used to add a subtly sweet flavor, enhance mellowness, and serve as a moisture-retaining agent. And several licorice root by-products, such as Foamite Firefoam, have won worldwide recognition in their own right.
MacAndrews & Forbes Company is the principal importer and largest processor of licorice root in the United States. This carries with it a responsibility we guard through scrupulous manufacturing and marketing standards and by pursuing a program of continuous research into new and improved uses for licorice and the residual products of the spent root.
To Business Executives: Perhaps you can use licorice or one of its by-products in your business. Write for a free copy of "The Story of Licorice." It offers additional information that may spark a profitable idea. Or, for specific information on any point, consult our Research Department.
MacAndrews & Forbes Company
Licorice and Licorice Products • Since 1870
200 Fifth Avenue New York 10, N.Y.
Plant: Camden, New Jersey
Time, November 10, 1952
79

Betty Crocker Cake Mix, 20-Ounce Package	$0.35
Cotton Jacquard Bedspread	$6.35
Dan River Sheet, Bordered	$10.50
Gas Water Heater, 30 Gallons	$151.90
Goldberger Doll, in Party Dress	$3.98
Hammond Chord Organ	$975.00
Hollob's Supreme Peanut Butter, 12 Ounces	$0.33
Kerrybrooke Wallet	$3.50
Motor Oil, Quart	$0.32
Nylon Hose, per Pair	$0.95
Reardon Laboratories Mouse Seed	$0.25
Table Model Radio	$21.70
Toilet Tissue, per Roll	$0.09
Tooth Extraction	$5.50
Upright Vacuum Cleaner	$86.70
Waring Products Blender	$44.50
Zippo Lighter Fluid	$0.25

Advertisement: "What would you have done?" asks George Fehlman, Executive Vice President, Belnap & Thompson, Inc., Chicago—merchandise prize incentive programs.

Recently, we had to deliver prize material to client sales meetings, scheduled all over the country for the same day. We were forbidden to ship early—and we must not be late! What would you have done?

We called Air Express.

Within 24 hours, almost 1,000 shipments were dispatched. All arrived on schedule. Not a single call or wire inquiring about a shipment was received! We've become accustomed to that kind of service from Air Express. What's more—on practically every shipment we make, the Air Express rate is the lowest in the field. These rate differences often save several hundred dollars in one day's shipping!"

Advertisement by the General Aniline & Film Corporation:

"Blue . . . for the Reds

Paris, June 18, UP . . . The French government today announced new measures to enforce its vigorous campaign against Communism.

Minister of Interior Charles Brune said legislation is being drafted which will bar Reds from key posts in all government and defense establishments.

Police, he said, have been ordered to spray participants in any future demonstrations with a penetrating blue dye, which they will find almost impossible to wash off.

Police also will make extensive use of photographs of street fights to identify Red leaders and hoodlums.

The French have a sound idea. It is not copyrighted. Others countries might care to follow suit.

As a contribution to freedom, liberty, and a better world, General Aniline & Film Corporation will donate 10 pounds of our Victoria Blue dye, which will make 25 gallons of indelible solution available . . . to the government of any United Nations member which will follow the example of the French. And for taking documentary photographs, we recommend the Ansco cameras and film.

General Aniline & Film, as the largest U.S. maker of high-quality dyestuffs and the second largest producer of cameras and photographic films and papers . . . hopes for eventual days of universal peace, better world understanding, and amity and friendship among free peoples . . . when dyestuffs and cameras can be used normally in every nation . . . to make the world a better, brighter, happier place to live for all people everywhere."

The Korean War

The Toll of the War—Casualty Totals

United Nations Forces:
United States: 36,913 dead, 103,248 wounded, 8,142 missing
South Korea: 58,127 dead, 175,743 wounded, 166,297 missing
Other nations: 3,194 dead, 11,297 wounded, 2,769 missing

Communist Forces:
North Korea: 214,899 dead, 303,685 wounded, 101,680 missing
China: 401,401 dead, 486,995 wounded, 21,211 missing

Civilians:
An estimated two to 2.6 million dead, wounded, and missing

Key Dates of the Conflict

1950

June 25:	North Korea invaded South Korea.
June 27:	The United Nations sought aid for South Korea. President Harry Truman said the U.S. would intervene.

June 28–29:	The North Koreans captured South Korean capital, Seoul.
July 1:	U.S. troops arrived in Korea.
July 7:	U.S. Gen. Douglas MacArthur was named head of the United Nations Command.
August 4:	U.S. troops established the defensive Pusan Perimeter in southeast Korea.
September 15:	MacArthur masterminded Inchon landings behind North Korean lines.
October 9:	U.N. forces began the invasion of North Korea.
October 13–14:	Chinese troops entered the war.
November 27 to December 9:	Chinese troops encircled U.S. troops at the Battle of the Changjin (Chosin) Reservoir. Marines and others fought southward for evacuation.

1951

February 1:	The United Nations called for an end to the Korean conflict.
April 11:	MacArthur was fired by President Truman.
July 10:	Truce talks started.

1952

December 5-8:	President-elect Dwight Eisenhower secretly informed the North Koreans and Chinese that he was prepared to use nuclear weapons and carry the war to China if a peace agreement was not reached.

1953

July 27:	A cease-fire was signed.

1955 Family Profile

Conrad Davis, a 45-year-old physician, lives with his family in South Carolina in one of Charleston's oldest "single houses," built in 1722. He loves being a doctor and is known for his ability to hunt and fish the areas around this historic city. He and his wife, Sylvia, who is from Virginia, have just had their fourth child, a son.

Annual Income: $29,000

Annual Budget

The average per capita consumer expenditures in 1955 for all workers nationwide are:

Auto Parts	$9.68
Auto Usage	$193.01
Clothing	$118.59
Dentists	$9.08
Food	$414.46
Furniture	$26.62
Gas and Oil	$52.03
Health Insurance	$8.47
Housing	$208.14
Intercity Transport	$6.66
Local Transport	$11.49
New Auto Purchase	$83.49
Personal Business	$58.69
Personal Care	$22.39
Physicians	$22.99
Private Education and Research	$15.13
Recreation	$87.73

The couple has just had their fourth child, a son.

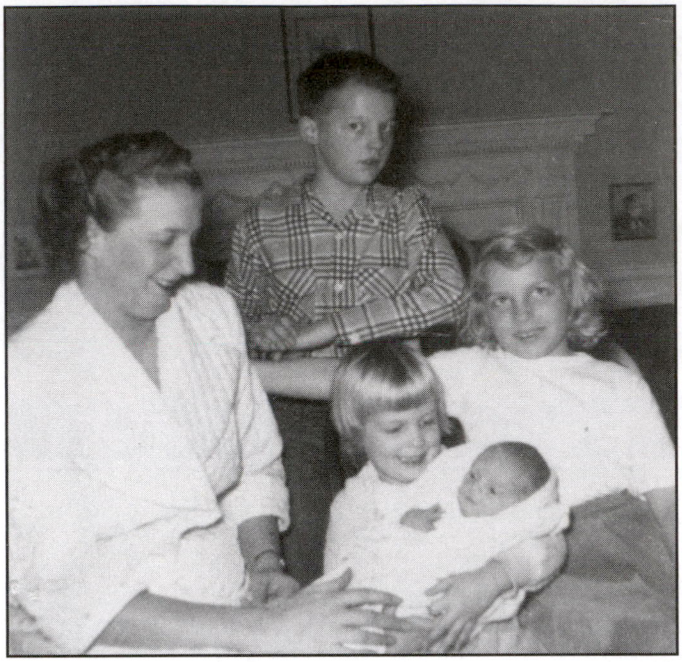

The children range from newborn to 12 years.

Religion/Welfare Activities	$21.18
Telephone and Telegraph	$18.76
Tobacco	$30.86
Utilities	$61.72
Per Capita Consumption	$1,560.43

Life at Home

- Born in 1910, Dr. Davis has spent his entire life in Charleston, except for a stint at schools in Atlanta, New Jersey, and New York City for his residency.
- He graduated from the College of Charleston and the Medical College of South Carolina, located in Charleston, in 1935.
- He served his internships at Grady Hospital in Atlanta and at Burlington County Hospital in New Jersey.
- When he married in 1939, he was associated with the Home for Incurables in New York City; he and Sylvia met in New York.
- Their home, built in 1722, is believed to be the oldest single house in the city.
- Purchased for $14,100 at an executor's sale in 1943, the lot is 39 feet wide by 220 feet long.
- The three-story brick house has handsome marble quoins on either side, a shaped brick cornice, and a tile roof.
- It exemplifies the floor plan peculiar to the city's houses, which are one room wide.
- The house is turned sideways on the lot, with its length running perpendicular to the front property line and its side, or gabled end, facing the street.

Their home, built in 1722, is located on historic Church Street in Charleston (second building).

The residence is one room deep with two rooms to a floor.

- The residence is one room deep with two rooms to a floor; the entrance is located in the center of the house midway along the piazza, which is approached from the street through a formal doorway.
- The second floor includes the formal living room for entertaining.

The second floor includes the formal living room for entertaining.

Charleston is well known for its decorative iron gates.

- Sylvia's mother, who lives with the family, spends much of her time seeing friends or simply crocheting; Conrad's mother also crochets and is making a tablecloth for each of her seven grandchildren.
- The third floor has four bedrooms, with porches extending from every floor.

- Conrad's roots go deeply into the state; his forebearer was an Episcopal priest who helped start Trinity Church in Columbia, South Carolina, in 1814.
- The family attends St. Philip's Episcopal Church, which was completed in 1838 to replace the building destroyed by fire in 1835.
- They are also part of the most important social clubs in the city, including the exclusive St. Cecilia Society and the Yacht Club.
- The annual St. Cecilia Society Ball, a card dance, is much anticipated; this couple traditionally exchanges dance partners with friends they have known for many years.
- In his free time, Davis heads to the nearby waters of the Atlantic Ocean or the creeks of Wadmalaw Island.
- Charleston is seven miles from the open ocean; the channel is 40 feet deep at low water and 47 feet deep at high tide.
- While fishing off the old ferry wharf, he hauled in a 25-pound sea bream, a fish more common to Florida than to Charleston.

The spire of St. Michael's Episcopal Church pierces the skyline of Charleston.

While fishing off the old ferry wharf, he caught a 25-pound sea bream.

The Davis family attends St. Philip's Episcopal Church, which was completed in 1838.

- In 1953, he was licensed by the U.S. Coast Guard to "carry passengers for hire," and last year passed the examination to join the United States Power Squadrons.
- He recently indulged a dream and purchased a 40-foot, ocean-going boat for fishing and travelling the intercoastal waterway.
- The boat is large enough for two couples to sleep aboard on long trips—if the mosquitoes can be kept at bay.
- When at home, he indulges his passion for genealogy, constructing elaborate charts of the lineage of his relatives and friends and writing dozens of letters to track down the most obscure details.
- Sylvia is five years younger than Conrad; their four children—two boys and two girls—now range in age from newborn to 12 years.
- The family has just purchased its first television set; the boys love the Westerns, while the six-year-old girl is a fan of Disney cartoons.
- The two middle children are currently taking piano lessons, and the oldest boy is focused on hunting and fishing with his dad.
- On Thanksgiving day, he will be allowed to take part in a deer-drive at Middleton Plantation; in a tradition dating back to Colonial days, the deer will be driven by dogs and handlers toward the hunters.

The daily tides influence the rhythm of this coastal city.

- With four children, Sylvia often feels stress because of her hectic schedule carpooling the children, managing the house, and attending social functions with her gregarious husband.
- She has just ended her term as president of the Junior League, which is establishing a speech correction school in the city.

Life at Work

- Dr. Davis starts work early most days, leaving the house by seven so he can begin surgery at the hospital by 8 a.m.; a full schedule of patients at his downtown office starts at 10 a.m.
- He drives a 1953 Oldsmobile to the hospital across town and then returns downtown for appointments at his office located on Bull Street a dozen or so blocks from his home.

> "Recognition of the Supreme Being is the first, the most basic, expression of Americanism. Without God, there could be no American form of government, nor American way of life."
> President Dwight D. Eisenhower

- He returns home at 2 p.m. for a midday meal—the main meal of the day.
- The meal always includes rice, fresh vegetables and, frequently, shrimp or fish purchased either from the local market or from the "shrimp man," who pushes a cart filled with fresh shrimp through the downtown neighborhoods each morning.
- The children run out of the house when they hear him holler out, "Shrimp man, shrimp man"; he puts the shrimp in a rice steamer or pot brought by the children and is always paid on the spot.
- The family dinner, prepared by a cook who has worked for the family for many years, also includes ample portions of okra and tomatoes.
- She comes in each morning from one of the barrier islands surrounding Charleston where she lives; the trip normally takes 30 minutes each way.
- Following the meal, Davis takes a 30-minute nap in his upstairs bedroom, then sees patients for the remainder of the afternoon.
- Following work, he socializes at the Yacht Club before going home.
- He is a member of a poker club that meets every two weeks in one of the members' homes.

"Vaccines, Salk and Otherwise," *Worcester Massachusetts Medical News*, May 1955:

"There are a lot of long-buried doctors, scientists, and intellects whirling in their graves at this moment as they hear of the mass acceptance of polio vaccination.

The opposition of the people to all mass vaccinations in the past is reminiscent of the attacks of the anti-vivisection groups today. Where are the anti-polio-vaccination groups? Has the masterful publicity associated with the Salk vaccine results driven them into their fanatic holes?

However much we deplore publicity, we must doff our hats and expose our crew cuts or scalps in admiration for a publicity stunt that outdid the unveiling of the Model A Ford. It did many things:

It aroused the country. It made us forget what a small percentage of the money collected by the March of Dimes was unnecessary to effect this wonderful result. It made us overlook the high administrative expense prevalent for years in the March of Dimes. It made us forget that this was the last step in many steps to this perfection. It reminded us that a lot of money and a lot of brilliance exhibited by Jonas Salk proved the value of the anti-polio vaccine several years before it would ultimately be proved. . . .

We must keep our feet off the ground and on our desks. The ground trembles with great noises and appropriations. Some of us in many specialties are swelling our chests and making plans. Give Salk his due and his glory and get our feet off this trembling ground. Treat this disease with what is available to us in our usual manner just as we do with typhoid and smallpox: with as little fanfare.

Let us not contribute to the hysteria of discovery. Let the publicists, like the lay executives of all fundraising organizations, have their today; but let us try to control their tomorrow.

We have read in our own Medical Library the writing of our predecessors about preceding vaccines and their efforts to have them accepted. It is a much different story today. Theirs were voices crying for converts and advocates. The historians will find us crying for restraints and orderliness."

Medical College Hospital Dedication Exercises, Dr. Kenneth M. Lynch, President of the Medical University of South Carolina, May 10, 1955:

"In the social progress of man, as civilization has produced the modern community—now grown in advanced countries to densely populated societies of hundreds, thousands, and even millions of individuals—more and more group activities have become required. Among the first community-supported protective services were police and fire departments. Another was the health department. Without this service to develop and apply knowledge of how to protect against the many health hazards, practically nothing that we enjoy today would have become possible. In fact, until we learned enough to establish effective community health service, threats of devastation of lawlessness or war were minor as compared to the constant threat of disease—disease that repeatedly depopulated cities and doubtlessly destroyed whole civilizations—disease about which we are entirely unconcerned today.

Having brought the great destroyers of previous ages under control by concerted effort, local, state, and national, we have arrived at the next phase of action against other types of health hazards. Although we believe that the personalized service of a physician to his patient is of such nature that it must remain under the system of direct responsibility and professional control, it is obvious that it is beyond the opportunity and means of any individual to secure by himself the medical care that he may need at any moment—that only through the means of the community support can he have at hand at all times the services that have become available to save him from loss of health and life.

Thus, we no longer question the right and the responsibility of a community to provide the facilities that would make it possible for each citizen to receive the medical care that the medical profession is prepared to give. In this development, South Carolina is at the forefront."

- The city has a long history of medical excellence; the Medical Society of South Carolina was founded in 1789, and in 1824, the state's first medical school was opened, attended in the 1830s by James Marion Sims, the father of American gynecology.
- By 1840, the Medical College opened a College Hospital for "furnishing instruction at the bedside of the sick" for medical students; it became one of the first teaching hospitals in America.
- The South Carolina Training School for Nurses was established in 1883 and by 1894, women were first admitted to train at the Medical College, the same year a College of Pharmacy was permanently added to the school.
- Recently, the cost of care for the city's indigent ill was shifted from the city to the Medical College of South Carolina, which through federal grants is enjoying tremendous growth.
- Statewide physicians are attempting to organize the Salk vaccine program to eradicate polio, trying to determine who will provide the shots, who will pay, and how the administration will be handled.
- The current president of the Medical University of South Carolina, Dr. Kenneth Lynch, was a pioneer in the investigation of industrial dust diseases; his 91 papers and two books have helped reduce health hazards in industry.
- Since 1946, when the Hospital Survey and Construction Program was begun, 2,500 hospitals and health facilities have been approved for federal aid in construction nationwide, with 1,700 completed so far.

- Despite new construction, the nation's hospitals are short 800,000 beds, including hospitals serving the general populations, as well as facilities for mental, tuberculosis, and chronic care.
- Dr. Davis recently joined with the Medical Association to defeat two pieces of legislation in South Carolina; one bill could lead to "socialized medicine" and the second would help "rid the state of the Naturopathic cult."
- Currently, 1,134 physicians, or 90 percent of the practicing physicians in the state, are participating members of the Blue Cross-Blue Shield insurance program provided by the Medical Association.
- Dr. Davis is serving on the four-member Committee on Medical and Hospital Insurance Contracts.

Life in the Community: Charleston, South Carolina

- Charleston was founded in 1670 by 93 passengers arriving aboard the ship *Carolina*.
- A few of the first settlers were rich, but most were poor; they had been at sea seven months, having left England in three ships loaded with 15 tons of beer and 30 gallons of brandy, 59 bushels of flour, 12 suits of armor, 100 beds and pillows, 1,200 grubbing hoes, 100,000 four-penny nails, 756 fishing hooks, 240 pounds of glass beads, 288 scissors, garden seeds, and a set of surgical instruments.
- In all, the founders of the city included 29 men of property and 63 indentured white servants.
- By the eighteenth century, the principal cities of British North America were Boston, New York, Philadelphia, and Charleston.
- Of these four, Charleston abounded in glamour.

Charleston's Church Street at the turn of the twentieth century.

Many homes boast secret gardens down hidden alleyways.

- Today, the city continues to boost tourism; the Azalea Festival, dormant for several years, has recently been revived.
- Davis is currently working with the city council to approve a new traffic plan that creates more one-way streets, and he is encouraging the city to make further efforts to identify streets and house numbers "to facilitate finding patients."

- Charleston is a city of contrasts; inside many of the nation's great architectural treasures live the poor in an area which has one of the highest infant mortality rates in the nation, where the life expectancy of a black male is 55 years, and half the county's population has less than eight years' education.
- The *Charleston News and Courier*, owned by an associate of Dr. Davis, is vehemently opposed to the integration of the schools and in favor of the purging of unqualified black voters from the polls.
- As pressure for integration grows, the *News and Courier* has been excoriating the NAACP and its liberal friends who perpetuate the "utterly false contention that Southern colored people have not been well treated," maintaining, rather, that Southern Negroes have been "generously treated since they were brought to North America out of savagery and slavery in Africa."
- With racial tensions high, attacking the NAACP in the South is politically analogous to assaulting the Communist Party in the rest of the nation.
- When the U.S. Supreme Court made its unanimous ruling in Brown v. the Board of Education of Topeka, Kansas, calling for the end of "separate but equal" segregated schools last year, the *News and Courier* assailed the decision: "It can be carried out only by an army, dispatched into South Carolina from the outside."
- Other revolutionary winds are blowing in Charleston; in 1951, inexpensive and efficient window air-conditioning units came on the market, and in June 1953, Charleston's first television station, WCSC-TV, broadcast its first program.
- During that broadcast, Charlestonian Cotesworth Pinckney Means served as master of ceremonies for the program, which included the Society for the Preservation of Spirituals; some of the same persons had hosted the show when WCSC-Radio first went on the air 23 years earlier.
- The growing influence of Congressman Mendel Rivers was confirmed in April of this year by the dedication of a $3 million Electric-Electronics building at the Naval Shipyard, the first major construction project there since 1945.
- The state's economy is still dominated by the textile industry; 133,555 people, or 69 percent of all industrial wage earners, are in textiles.
- Per capita personal income, which has been improving since the 1940s, is now 60 percent of the national average.

Historical Snapshot
1955

- HEW Secretary Oveta Culp Hobby opposed the free distribution of the Salk vaccine to poor children as "socialized medicine by the back door"
- Disneyland in Anaheim, California, opened
- The minimum wage went from $0.75 to $1.00 per hour
- The first television press conference occurred, featuring President Dwight Eisenhower
- Smog and poisoned air became a public concern
- *Confidential Magazine* had a circulation of 4.5 million readers
- President Eisenhower suffered a heart attack; the stock market plunged $14 billion
- The population explosion created a shortage of 120,000 teachers and 300,000 schoolrooms
- Weekly church attendance comprised 49 million adults—half the total adult population
- Construction of suburban shopping centers and motels jumped dramatically, with 1,800 built nationwide
- Jacqueline Cochran became the first woman to fly faster than the speed of sound
- Nationwide, the U.S. had 214,000 physicians, 95,000 dentists, and 1,604,000 hospital beds
- The Chase Manhattan Bank, Sperry Rand, H&R Block, and the Dreyfus Fund all made their first appearance
- Racial segregation on interstate buses and trains was ordered to end
- President Eisenhower submitted a 10-year, $101 billion highway construction program to Congress
- The AFL and CIO merged, with George Meany as president
- The Dow Jones Industrial Average hit a high of 488, and a low of 391
- The *National Review* and *Village Voice* both began publication
- Special K breakfast food was introduced by the Kellogg Company; Crest, featuring stannous fluoride, was introduced by Procter and Gamble
- The Ford Foundation gave $500 million to colleges and universities nationwide
- Whirlpool Corporation merged with Seeger Refrigerator Company and began producing refrigerators, air conditioners, and cooking ranges

1955 ECONOMIC PROFILE

Income, Standard Jobs

Average of All Industries, Excluding Farm Labor	$4,224
Average of All Industries, Including Farm Labor	$4,128
Bituminous Coal Mining	$4,470
Building Trades	$4,607
Domestics	$1,874
Farm Labor	$1,498
Federal Civilian	$4,801
Federal Employees, Executive Departments	$3,774
Federal Military	$3,237
Finance, Insurance, and Real Estate	$4,005
Gas and Electricity Workers	$4,757
Manufacturing, Durable Goods	$4,737
Manufacturing, Nondurable Goods	$4,134
Medical/Health Services Workers	$2,488
Miscellaneous Manufacturing	$3,789
Motion Picture Services	$4,330
Nonprofit Organization Workers	$3,291
Passenger Transportation Workers, Local and Highway	$4,142
Personal Services	$2,766
Public School Teachers	$3,608
Radio Broadcasting and Television Workers	$6,250
Railroad Workers	$4,701
State and Local Government Workers	$3,447
Telephone and Telegraph Workers	$4,153
Wholesale and Retail Trade Workers	$4,616

Selected Prices

Boy Scout Uniform	$8.97
Brach's Chocolate Covered Cherries, 13-Ounce Box	$0.55
Capri Roto-Broil 400 Grill	$79.95
Clearasil Lotion	$0.59
Eureka Super Roto-Matic Vacuum Cleaner	$69.95
Gerber Baby Doll	$2.00
Gerber's Baby Food, Four Three-Ounce Jars	$0.87

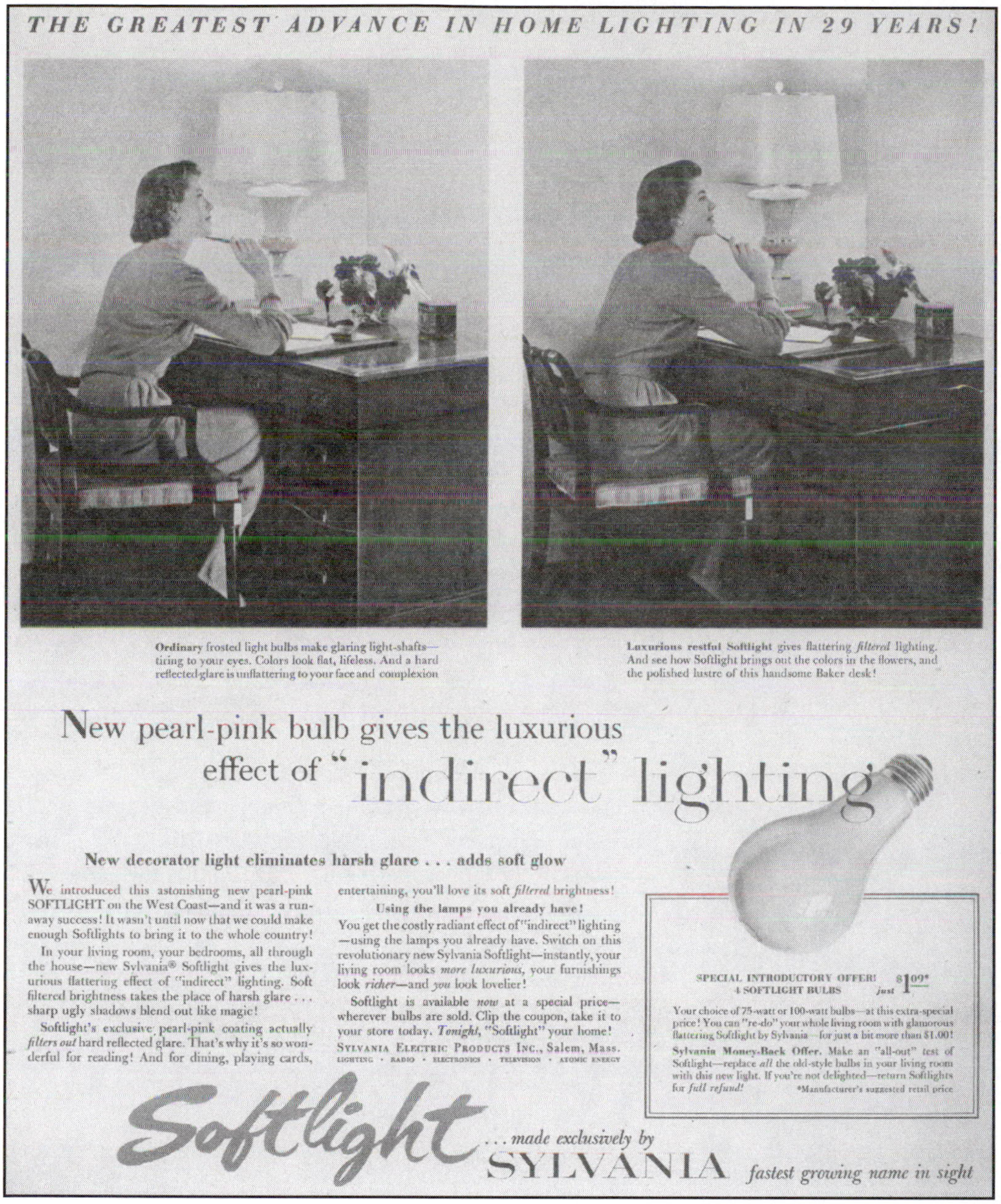
THE GREATEST ADVANCE IN HOME LIGHTING IN 29 YEARS!
Ordinary frosted light bulbs make glaring light-shafts—tiring to your eyes. Colors look flat, lifeless. And a hard reflected glare is unflattering to your face and complexion
Luxurious restful Softlight gives flattering filtered lighting. And see how Softlight brings out the colors in the flowers, and the polished lustre of this handsome Baker desk!
New pearl-pink bulb gives the luxurious effect of "indirect" lighting
New decorator light eliminates harsh glare . . . adds soft glow
We introduced this astonishing new pearl-pink SOFTLIGHT on the West Coast—and it was a run-away success! It wasn't until now that we could make enough Softlights to bring it to the whole country!
In your living room, your bedrooms, all through the house—new Sylvania® Softlight gives the luxurious flattering effect of "indirect" lighting. Soft filtered brightness takes the place of harsh glare . . . sharp ugly shadows blend out like magic!
Softlight's exclusive pearl-pink coating actually filters out hard reflected glare. That's why it's so wonderful for reading! And for dining, playing cards, entertaining, you'll love its soft filtered brightness!
Using the lamps you already have!
You get the costly radiant effect of "indirect" lighting—using the lamps you already have. Switch on this revolutionary new Sylvania Softlight—instantly, your living room looks more luxurious, your furnishings look richer—and you look lovelier!
Softlight is available now at a special price—wherever bulbs are sold. Clip the coupon, take it to your store today. Tonight, "Softlight" your home!
SYLVANIA ELECTRIC PRODUCTS INC., Salem, Mass.
LIGHTING · RADIO · ELECTRONICS · TELEVISION · ATOMIC ENERGY
SPECIAL INTRODUCTORY OFFER! 4 SOFTLIGHT BULBS just $1.09*
Your choice of 75-watt or 100-watt bulbs—at this extra-special price! You can "re-do" your whole living room with glamorous flattering Softlight by Sylvania—for just a bit more than $1.00!
Sylvania Money-Back Offer. Make an "all-out" test of Softlight—replace all the old-style bulbs in your living room with this new light. If you're not delighted—return Softlights for full refund!
*Manufacturer's suggested retail price
Softlight . . . made exclusively by SYLVANIA fastest growing name in sight

Glamorene Wool Rug Cleaner,
Half-Gallon $2.29
Gordon's Gin, per Fifth $4.47
Kotex Miracle Brand Nylons $1.00
Maybelline Eyelash Curler $1.00
Playtex Brassiere $3.95
Puss 'n' Boots Cat Food $0.39
Rit Dye $0.25
Seagram's Whiskey, per Fifth $4.89
Sherwin-Williams Kem-Tone,
per Gallon $5.59

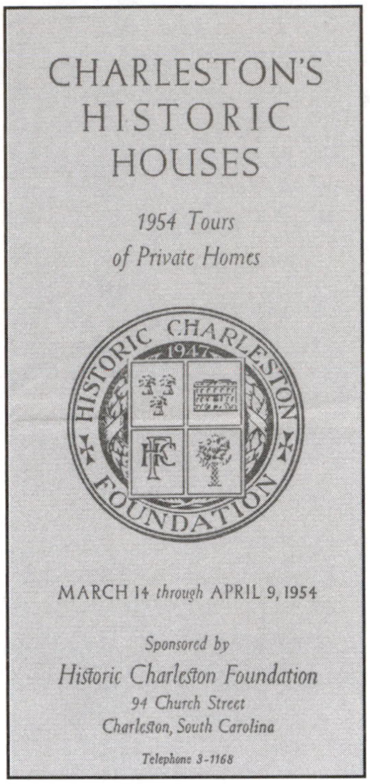

Tam o' Shanter Beau Brummel
Shirt, Three-Piece Set $4.98
Timex Boy Scout Watch $9.95
Tootsie Roll $0.05
Van Camp's Pork and Beans $0.25
Warner's LeGant Girdle $4.95

Key Events in Charleston

- 1901: The South Carolina Interstate and West Indian Exposition opened; this "world's fair" drew 375,000 visitors during its six-month run.
- 1902: President Theodore Roosevelt toured Ft. Sumter and the site of the new 1,189-acre Navy Yard.
- 1905: The Gibbes Museum of Art opened on Meeting Street.
- 1920: Concern for the destruction of historical buildings inspired the forming of the Society for Preservation of Old Dwelling Houses, later renamed the Preservation Society.
- 1929: The first Cooper River Bridge opened, spanning 2.7 miles, the fifth longest bridge in the world at that time; to defray the $6 million construction cost, a $0.50 toll was charged.
- 1931: Dorothy Legge purchased 99 and 101 East Bay, beginning the restoration of the area known as Rainbow row.
- 1931: Charleston adopted the first Historical Zoning Ordinance in the United States.
- 1935: The American folk opera *Porgy and Bess* opened in Boston and New York; George Gershwin spent three months in the city gathering material, launching songs such as "Summertime," "I Got Plenty of Nuttin," and "It Ain't Necessarily So."
- 1947: Charlestonians established the Historic Charleston Foundation to help preserve the city's architectural heritage; to raise money for this work, the Foundation began its "Festival of Houses" tour of private homes.

"Don't Let Censorship Destroy Us," by Alexander P. de Seversky. *Chicago Daily News*, September 17, 1955:

"Question: Today's question comes from Mary Alice Applegater of Glendale, California, and is in two parts:

First: Major de Seversky, do you think the American people are being given a true picture of the relative strength of U.S. and Soviet air power?

Second: Does talking about our defense weaknesses make us stronger or weaker? Does it help us see how we can protect ourselves, or does it give valuable information to potential enemies?

Answer: As to the first question, I am sorry to say the answer is an emphatic 'No.' The true facts of our military position are being hidden from the American people. Whether by accident, thoughtlessness, or design, we are being misled. As the enemy forges ahead with superior weapons, we witness an all-too-human tendency on the part of our officialdom to clamp down the lid of censorship, and divert public attention to other, pleasanter subjects.

For example, on July 7, at the height of the national consternation over the sudden revelation of Russia's recent leap to air superiority, a month-old confidential statement of Secretary of State Dulles before a Congressional committee was released to the press. The headlines on that day read, 'Dulles Says Red System on Point of Collapse.' It worked. America relaxed. Who's afraid of the big Red planes?

Such tactics are often rationalized in official circles as a safeguard to protect public morale. This is nonsense! The morale of the American people is at its height in the face of adversity. At such times, they are spurred to united and vigorous action, provided they know the facts and understand the predicament. What, then, are the facts?

The grim truth is that the recent development of Russia's air might has qualitatively pushed America back to the position of a third-rate air-power nation. In size, too, our Air Force is trailing Russia's. We have now lost our once-vaulted capacity for 'massive retaliation' by atomic air offensive. As this was the one and only bar to Soviet aggression, our country now lies prostrate and vulnerable to enemy attack.

I realize that these are frightening statements. But they are facts which no one should dare to hide from the American people."

DON'T LET CENSORSHIP DESTROY US!

Has Russia's air force outstripped ours? If so, can our people be trusted with the truth? Here a noted airman presents his challenging views on these crucial questions

by Alexander P. de Seversky

MAJOR ALEXANDER P. de SEVERSKY, combat pilot, inventor, aeronautical engineer, has predicted many notable air-war developments. His books are texts in most military colleges

This Week

QUESTION: *Today's question comes from Mary Alice Applegate, of Glendale, Calif., and is in two parts:*

First: *"Major de Seversky, do you think the American people are being given a true picture of the relative strength of U.S. and Soviet air power?"*

Second: *"Does talking about our defense weaknesses make us stronger or weaker? Does it help us see how we can protect ourselves, or does it give valuable information to potential enemies?"*

ANSWER: As to the first question, I am sorry to say the answer is an emphatic "No."

The true facts of our military position are being hidden from the American people. Whether by accident, thoughtlessness or design, we are being misled. As the enemy forges ahead with superior weapons, we witness an all-too-human tendency on the part of our officialdom to clamp down the lid of censorship, and divert public atten-

For example, on July 7, at the height of the national consternation over the sudden revelation of Russia's recent leap to air superiority, a month-old confidential statement of Secretary of State Dulles before a Congressional committee was resurrected and adroitly released to the press. The headlines on that day read, "Dulles Says Red System on Point of Collapse." It worked. America relaxed. Who's afraid of the big Red planes?

Grim Truth

Such tactics are often rationalized in official circles as a safeguard to protect public morale. *This is nonsense!* The morale of the American people is at its height in the face of adversity. At such times, they are spurred to united and vigorous action, provided they know the facts and understand the predicament.

What, then, are the facts?

The grim truth is that the recent development of Russia's air might has, qualita-

of a third-rate air-power nation. In size, too, our Air Force is trailing Russia's. We have now lost our once-vaunted capacity for "massive retaliation" by atomic air offensive. As this was the one and only bar to Soviet aggression, our country now lies prostrate and vulnerable to enemy attack.

I realize that these are frightening state-

should dare to hide from the American people. Here is some of the evidence on which they are based.

1. Intercontinental Bombers. Most dramatic of the Soviet revelations at the recent Moscow air show was the new T-37 intercontinental jet bomber, the "Bison."

"Problems of Prepaid Sickness Insurance," J. Decherd Guess, M.D., Medical Director, South Carolina Hospital Service and Medical Care Plans, Greenville, South Carolina, *Journal of the South Carolina Medical Association*:

"The basic problems of prepaid sickness insurance arise from unnecessary and wasteful utilization of hospital facilities by insured persons. This statement applies to both Blue Cross and Blue Shield nonprofit insurance plans and commercial insurance carriers. Already over-utilization has forced costs of sickness insurance up so high that such insurance is out of reach of at least 25 percent of American families. That is bad, but what is even worse is that, in spite of successive rate increases and some restrictions in benefits, most Blue Cross and some Blue Shield plans are experiencing financial difficulties. It is said that some commercial companies are compensating for losses from sickness insurance contracts by profits from life insurance coverage. These commercial companies are able to restrict their losses to a considerable extent by the device of providing only cash indemnities with definite limitations.

The basic and unique principle of Blue Cross is to insure against all necessary hospital costs of covered illnesses. Insofar as it deviates from the principle, it approaches the type of coverage offered by commercial companies. Blue Shield attempts to provide similar service benefits to low- and medium-income groups, and in that way to take care of the doctor's entire bill. Perhaps the fear of the unpredictability of the amount of the costs of illness is greater than the fear of illness expense itself. When a Blue Cross member knows that he, by simply presenting his identification card, can be admitted to a member hospital without making an advance payment and with no expectation of a bill for extras, he enjoys a marvelous peace of mind which has therapeutic value. There is no fear of embarrassment or insolvency. . . . By a method of trial and error . . . restrictions for eligibility for membership in Blue Cross have been reduced, so that almost anyone not already sick and under 65 years of age may join a Blue Cross plan.

Coincidental with this broadening of eligibility for Blue Cross membership, the spiral of increasing hospital costs began. There soon followed the building of many new hospitals. With all hospital charges covered by Blue Cross, it became both more convenient and cheaper to be sick in hospital than at home. It became also more worthwhile to join a plan in contemplation of operations and other illness, and to demand either that the doctor fake the history or for the patient to change doctors. Utilization began to climb and is still climbing.

There have arisen several other factors tending to increase hospital utilization. Doctors, busy as they are, more scientific in their approach to diagnosis, and more impatient for results, prefer hospital patients rather than home patients. They advise hospitalization for minor illness.

Furthermore, once the patient is in the hospital, it is so easy to order x-ray examinations, repeated laboratory examinations, EKGs, BMRs, etc., that such examinations are ordered frequently without very well-thought-through indications. Furthermore, because of half-knowledge gotten from parlor conversations, patients are asking for these tests—especially when they have insurance."

1958 Family Profile

As the national sales manager for Welch's Grape Juice for the past nine years, Gordon Young has made a significant mark on the company by improving distribution, brand recognition, and overall sales. Currently, the company is undergoing a corporate ownership transition. He and his wife, Donna, have three grown children.

Annual Income: $44,500
His income includes $32,000 in salary, plus a bonus of $12,500 based on the previous year's sales.

Annual Budget
The average per capita consumer expenditures in 1958 for all workers nationwide are:

Auto Parts	$10.91
Auto Usage	$183.76
Clothing	$118.87
Dentists	$10.91
Food	$447.34
Furniture	$29.29
Gas and Oil	$60.87
Health Insurance	$8.61
Housing	$241.18
Intercity Transport	$6.32
Local Transport	$10.91
New Auto Purchase	$55.70
Personal Business	$70.06
Personal Care	$28.14
Physicians	$29.29
Private Education and Research	$19.54
Recreation	$93.03

Religion/Welfare Activities	$25.27
Telephone and Telegraph	$22.39
Tobacco	$34.45
Utilities	$70.63
Per Capita Consumption	$1,691.73

Life at Home

- The Youngs live in the former home of Paul Welch, one of the sons of the founder of Welch's Grape Juice.
- The house is located on East Main Street in Westfield, New York; considerable effort has been put into converting the yard into an elaborate English garden.
- When they first moved to Westfield, the townspeople were polite but standoffish, and little has changed.
- Westfield townspeople are suspicious of change and outsiders, especially those who come from New York City.
- A private man by nature, Gordon enjoys having few social obligations when at home.
- Since he spends so much time on the road, when home, he and Donna can focus on each other.
- He is very close to his wife; he has few other close friends, and is cautious about forming close relations at work.
- All three of their children attended good Eastern colleges and are now married; Gordon and Donna have three grandchildren.
- When Gordon is away on business trips, Donna sometimes visits the grandchildren, most of whom live in "the city" where they were raised.
- While on a recent trip, she, her daughter, and granddaughter all watched *Old Yeller* and cried together at the end.
- In Westfield, she attended a Tupperware party at a friend's house, advertised as the "answer to the Housewife's demand for efficiency-economy . . . the woman's demand for beauty."

Recently, Donna Young and her grandchild watched the movie Old Yeller.

- A dapper dresser, Gordon is proud of his trim figure, high position, and knowledge, taking care to be cordial to all.
- An optic problem causes him to wipe his eyes frequently with a carefully laundered handkerchief.
- Rarely does he show emotion at work or at home; a temper is the sign of low-class people unable to control themselves.
- He loves his big, black cigars, which he smokes with tremendous flair.
- His personal reward for a great year is the sexy 1957 Corvette parked in his driveway, purchased in cash, as he likes to say.

A Tupperware party at a friend's house was advertised as the "answer to the Housewife's demand for efficiency-economy."

Life at Work

- He spends much of his time on the road nationally overseeing brokers and promoting Welch's products.
- He is known for his ability to get the job done his way; at this stage in his career, he does not want or welcome a lot of unsolicited advice.
- Currently, Welch's has more than 70 percent of the national grape juice and frozen grape juice concentrate market.
- The sales of Welch's Grape Juice have nearly tripled.

To reward himself for a great year, he bought his dream car, a 1957 Corvette.

Welch's Grape Juice founder Dr. Charles E. Welch was devoted to the temperance movement.

- This year, the net sales reached $40 million, $4 million more than last year; gross profits topped $10.8 million, up $2 million over the previous year.
- Most of the competition comes from private label and regional brands that lack the history or sales expertise of Welch's.
- Welch's also sells grape spreads, cranberry cocktail, and tomato juice, placing them in direct competition with Smucker's, Kraft, Ocean Spray, and Libby's.
- Welch's was recently acquired through a planned buyout program, shifting control from Jack Kaplan, who bought the company in 1945, to a cooperative of grape growers who supply the Concord grapes critical to the quality of the product.
- The sale was engineered through an ingenious plan: Welch's Company would accept the growers' Concord grapes, process the fruit, manufacture and sell the products, and give the farmers the full net proceeds that would accrue for five years—allowing them to buy the company without paying any cash from their own pockets.
- The five-year plan helped Welch's by guaranteeing a flow of quality grapes sufficient to the meet the demands of a growing company and demonstrate the mutual profitability of associating with Welch's.
- The National Grape Cooperative Association took control of Welch's in 1956; Gordon's duties have changed little in the transition.
- Changes in the food industry have forced him to pay more attention to marketing, demographic changes, and other modern sales approaches, though he has been reluctant to rely on "marketing gimmicks."
- He keeps Welch's product line limited and simple to make sales and distribution easy.

Welch's was recently acquired through a planned buyout program from Jack Kaplan, who bought the company in 1945.

- Few do their homework more thoroughly; his focus does not waiver from selling quality products as promised and demanding a quality price, and he is cautious that frequent sales promotions will erode the profitability of Welch's Grape Juice.
- He is under considerable pressure to promote additional grape-related products; a few years ago, Welch's introduced "Fruit-of-the-Vine," a preserve of whole Concord grapes that gained rapid acceptance.
- One of his recent decisions was to move his advertising dollars from the popular *Howdy-Doody* television show to Walt Disney's *Mickey Mouse Club*.

Welch's
"The lips that touch Welch's are all that touch mine"

From the company's earliest days, Welch believed in a strong advertising program.

- He also agreed to establish a grape juice concession in the Disneyland Amusement Center at Anaheim, California.
- Under his direction, Welch's spends a smaller average percentage of its budget for research and development than do other food companies.
- Competitors are amazed that he can create the image in the consumer's mind that Welch's is a national brand without spending vast amounts of money on advertising.
- Instead of marketing with big advertising, Gordon moves in and out of different mediums, keeping people convinced that Welch's is a consistently advertised brand.
- He worked for Standard Brands, a major food company, for 25 years before joining the Welch's family in 1949.
- His first job with Welch's was as vice president in charge of sales and advertising, and his first assignment was to take a month and travel the United States, making a study of Welch's sales techniques.
- His compensation includes salary, plus a performance bonus based on sales.
- In 1949, he directed sales from his office in New York City; since 1953, he has lived in Westfield, New York.
- That same year, he was named an executive president in the company, reporting only to the president, Jack Kaplan.
- He has believed he should be the president of the company, and was very disappointed that he was not named so when the cooperative was created.
- The new president does not take an active part in day-to-day operations.
- When making a decision, he deliberately and cautiously gathers information from all sides, then renders an opinion, always assuming the final decision is his to make.
- The growers, who now own the company, respect his cautious, deliberate process, believing sales are in good hands.
- Despite his strengths as a decision maker, he finds it very difficult to fire employees and often relegates the duty to others.
- At Welch's, he has created a strong sales team who believe they are responsible for the product's success.
- Often, though, when the sales staff acts independently without consulting others, conflicts result.
- Sales and production are currently blaming each other for a sales-designed Welch's promotion that was so successful, the company could not provide all the products ordered.

Life in the Community: Westfield, New York

- The small farming community of Westfield is located on the western edge of New York state near Lake Erie.

- Westfield's largely white, homogeneous population of Methodists is known for its clannish, suspicious, hardworking ways, and change is not always a welcome sight in this community dominated by grape growers and the Welch's Grape Juice Company.
- At the turn of the century, viticulture, or the growing of grapes, was limited to 12 states, including California, New York, Ohio, and Pennsylvania.
- In New York, grape growing was concentrated in four districts: Chautauqua, the Finger Lakes, the Hudson, and Niagara.
- Nationwide, good grape soils are numerous, though the perfect grape climate is rare, but the Chautauqua-Erie area, where Westfield is located, is nearly perfect.
- In the spring, the waters of Lake Erie are cool, which holds back blooming until the threat of winter frost has passed, while in the fall, the warm waters of the lake extend the growing season.
- In 1898, the *Westfield Republican* advertised the community as being the "largest grape producing town in the grape belt"; flanked by two railroads, the town boasted municipal electric lights, a gravity water system, and an efficient fire department.
- Today, less than four percent of the state's population is engaged in farming, and much of that percentage is concentrated in the Chautauqua-Erie area.
- Only the sprawling state of California grows more grapes than does New York.

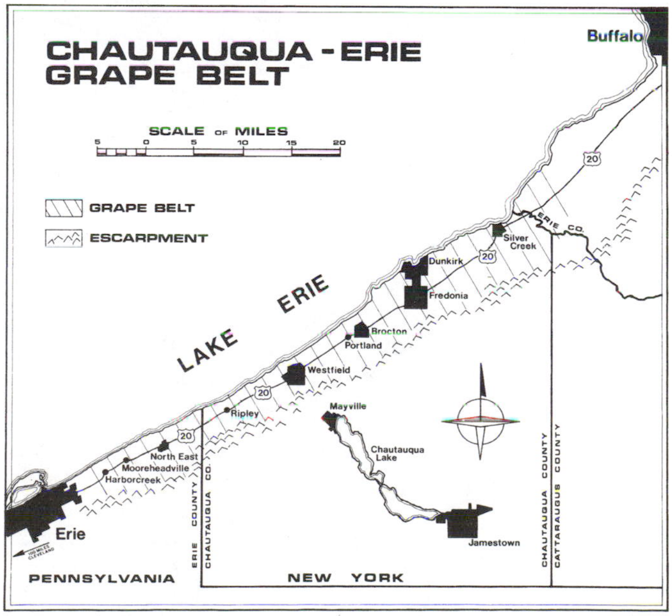

Historical Snapshot
1958

- *Life Magazine*'s series, "Crisis in Education," focused on major U.S. educational problems, including poor curricula, overcrowding of classrooms, and poorly paid teachers
- The Pizza Hut chain began in Kansas City
- Paul Robeson, denied a passport for eight years because of his Leftist comments, was allowed to tour overseas
- Forty percent of college students admitted to cheating, many with no regrets
- The cost of college had doubled from 1940 to 1958; the average cost was now $1,300 a year
- The construction of a nuclear power plant at Bodega Head, California, was stopped by a court action of environmental groups
- Gasoline cost 30.4 cents per gallon
- The paperback edition of *Lolita* sold a million copies
- The BankAmericard credit card was introduced
- Elvis Presley was inducted into the army as No. 53310761
- For the eleventh year, Eleanor Roosevelt was first on the "Most Admired Women" list; Queen Elizabeth was second
- SANE (Scientists Against Nuclear Energy) was formed with 25,000 members
- The terms beatnik, DNA, news satellite, sex kitten, and sick joke entered the language
- The nation was shocked when a number of television quiz shows were exposed for providing contestants with the answers beforehand
- Ford Motor Company introduced the Edsel
- The cost of 100,000 computerized multiplication computations fell from $1.26 in 1952 to $0.26
- Unemployment reached a postwar high of 6.8 percent
- The United States' standing army included 2.6 million men and women
- Kansas and Colorado were invaded by grasshoppers
- John Kenneth Galbraith's book *The Affluent Society* contended that materialism and conformity characterized the United States; he argued for a redistribution of income to end poverty
- The sale of television sets topped 41 million
- First-class postal rates climbed to $0.04 per ounce
- Sixty-four percent of American households now had incomes above $4,000 a year
- More than 250,000 people attended the Jehovah's Witness Convention at Yankee Stadium
- The Grammy award, John Birch Society, Chevrolet Impala, Sweet 'n' Low, Cocoa Krispies, American Express, and Green Giant canned beans all made their first appearance

1958 Economic Profile

Income, Standard Jobs

Average of All Industries, Excluding Farm Labor	$4,818
Average of All Industries, Including Farm Labor	$4,707
Bituminous Coal Mining	$4,809
Building Trades	$5,305
Domestics	$2,131
Farm Labor	$1,690
Federal Civilian	$5,781
Federal Employees, Executive Departments	$4,462
Federal Military	$3,697
Finance, Insurance, and Real Estate	$4,523
Gas and Electricity Workers	$5,543
Manufacturing, Durable Goods	$5,478
Manufacturing, Nondurable Goods	$4,725
Medical/Health Services Workers	$2,751
Miscellaneous Manufacturing	$4,408
Motion Picture Services	$4,940
Nonprofit Organization Workers	$3,672
Passenger Transportation Workers, Local and Highway	$4,571
Personal Services	$3,140
Public School Teachers	$4,343
Radio Broadcasting and Television Workers	$7,051
Railroad Workers	$5,836
State and Local Government Workers	$3,958
Telephone and Telegraph Workers	$4,707
Wholesale and Retail Trade Workers	$5,294

Selected Prices

Acoustic Research AR-2 Loudspeakers, per Pair	$89.00
Ballerina Raincoat	$5.74
Chrysler Simca DeLuxe Automobile	$1,698.00
Cory Coffee Maker	$39.95
Craftsman Home Barber Set	$14.95
Goose Down Pillows, Extra Large	$14.97
Harbor View Hotel Single Room, per Night	$6.00
Hercules Snap-Front Model Shirt	$2.34
Home Riding Exercise Bike	$71.50

Kerrybroke Soft Leather Shoes $3.77
Life Magazine, Weekly $0.25
Milk, per Quart $0.60
Orange Juice, per Glass $0.40
Roy Garter Top Hosiery $0.97
Royal Facial Treatment $5.50
Serta Perfect Sleeper Mattress $79.50
Smith-Corona Portable Electric
Typewriter $164.50
Sunbeam Rain King Automatic
Lawn Sprinkler $9.95
Troutman's Cough Syrup $0.49
Zippo Chrome Finish Lighter $4.75

Welch's Grape Juice

- Welch's Grape Juice founder Dr. Charles E. Welch was driven by a religious zeal to serve mankind.
- Disappointed at himself for not joining the missionary movement to Africa, he turned his energy into creating a grape juice devoid of alcohol.
- His grape juice company satisfied his need to serve his Methodist temperance devotion while creating a profitable business that allowed him to make large donations to Methodist-oriented causes.
- Dr. Welch moved to Westfield, New York, in 1897 and established his company.
- As a result, Welch's Grape Juice became one of the nation's first national brands with distribution outlets nationwide before the First World War.
- A want ad in 1911 reflected his beliefs: "Office Help, Young Man. No Tobacco. Methodist preferred, with business acumen, experience in dictating letters or similar work, with or without stenography; may find it of interest to write Dr. C.E. Welch, Westfield, New York."
- Dr. Welch's success was built on high-grade fruit for processing grape juice, a national network of selling through brokers, involvement in the international market, and a strong advertising program.
- At the turn of the century, a typical day began at seven in the morning and ended at six in the evening; the 11-hour schedule was typical of contemporary factory operations.
- Even when the factory was overloaded with ripe, perishable grapes during the pressing season, the company never operated on Sunday.
- To court the grape farmers, Dr. Welch sponsored Grower's Dinners, gave tours of the processing plant, and invented uniform "Welch's crates" that were stackable, portable, and reusable for delivering grapes.
- The area farmers tended to be loyal and Welch had a reputation for paying well for quality; in 1904, the average price paid to farmers was $22 per ton, and in 1913, the average price was $52 per ton.
- Early advertisements promoted temperance through drinking Dr. Welch's Unfermented Wine.
- A master promoter, Welch invented many ways to introduce Welch's Grape Juice to the public.

- During the Pan-American Exposition in 1901, cards were distributed reading, "good for a glass of Grape Juice."
- He also offered $10.00 in gold to anyone who could produce 1,366 words from the phrase "Welch's Grape Juice."
- Welch also promoted his product to churches with an offer of free Welch's Unfermented Wine for their next communion service along with an essay written by his father entitled, "What Wine Shall We Use at the Lord's Supper"; the article offered nine objections to using intoxicating wine in church.
- Sales were promoted when teetotaler Secretary of State William Jennings Bryan refused to serve wine during state dinners; the decision, which received generous press, came to be called Bryan's "grape juice diplomacy."
- Welch and his product received further publicity when Secretary of the Navy Josephus Daniels issued a "No Alcohol aboard Naval Vessels" order; parodies were published reading, "Josephus Daniels is a goose/If he thinks he can induce/us to drink his damn grape juice."
- Dr. Welch's campaign to substitute grape juice for alcohol coincides with the popular groundswell for prohibition that culminated in the passage of the Eighteenth Amendment.
- The advertising budgets for Welch's Grape Juice Company averaged $575,000 a year from 1912 to 1926; Charles E. Welch promoted his produce at state fairs, county fairs, medical conventions, and expositions.

Inventor Charles E. Welch was a master promoter.

Teetotaler Secretary of State William Jennings Bryan (right) refused to serve wine during state dinners, causing considerable publicity for Welch's.

- In 1924, $102,000 was spent on ads in magazines with national circulation such as *Ladies Home Journal*, *Woman's Home Companion*, *Good Housekeeping*, *Literary Digest*, *Harpers*, *Scribners*, and *Atlantic Monthly*.
- As a result, he created the only nationally known name in grape juice.
- In the 1920s, the company shifted from using pine boxes to ship its produce to cardboard boxes; the resulting savings allowed Welch's to double its dividend from $1.00 to $2.00 a share.
- To help create the feeling of a big, happy family, Charles Welch held annual picnics for the employees at his camp overlooking Chautauqua Lake.
- Salesmen for the company were known as Welch's Associates.
- Following Dr. Charles Welch's death in 1926, his sons sold The Welch's Grape Juice Company to the American National Company, a syndicate from Nashville, Tennessee.
- The syndicate's plan was to get control of the company and sell out rapidly for a quick profit.
- As part of the sale, the sons distributed 5,000 shares of Welch's Grape Juice stock to employees valued at $400,000; the average gift per employee in 1928 was $1,400.
- The syndicate continued many of the practices begun by Welch and operated the company until 1945.
- One of the few changes was the new medium of radio, which captured half of the advertising dollars of the company.
- The focus of advertising in the 1930s was away from temperance themes and toward controlling your weight, and Welch's Grape Juice was widely advertised as a "get thin" drink.

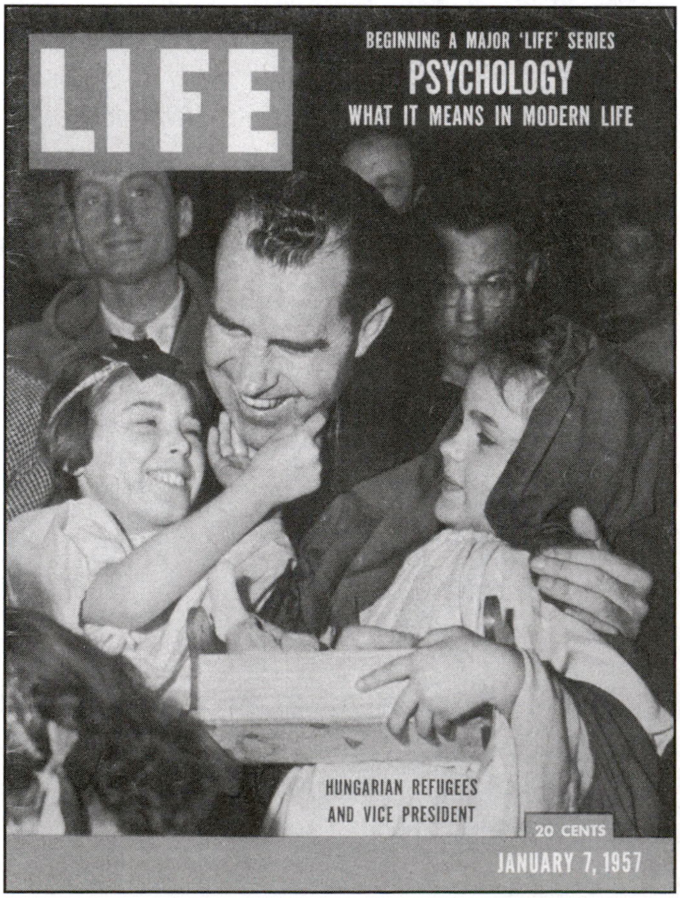

- By the 1940s, the company was producing grape juice, tomato juice, grapeade, plus six kinds of preserves and eight types of jellies.
- Within the Chautauqua-Erie Grape Belt, the dependence on Welch's was nearly complete; in 1941, 98 percent of the grapes grown in the area were used for grape juice, up from 33 percent in 1916.
- By 1945, the syndicate had earned substantial profits, invested little in plant upkeep, and decided to sell.
- That year, Welch's sales hit $10.1 million, over three times more than competitor National Grape Company, which purchased Welch's.
- New York-based, Jewish businessman Jack Kaplan merged Welch's and the National Grape Company to create a national powerhouse.
- Sales from 1945 to 1956 jumped from $10 million to $36 million; while the average annual net income under the Nashville syndicate had been $216,000, under Kaplan, it was $1 million.

"Marketing: Big Appetite for Gourmet Foods," *Business Week*, August 23, 1958:

"Next week, the National Fancy Food & Confection Show will hold its fourth annual exhibit for buyers in New York. They expect at least 20 percent more than last year's 14,000. Four years ago only 7,000 buyers showed.

A clue to the trend was the entry of General Foods, giant in the mass distribution food field, into the market just a year ago. The fancy food industry doesn't ever expect to be a billion-dollar industry. But the fact that a company of the size of General Foods is sticking its toe into this relatively small pool epitomizes what is happening. The mass market that itches for something new and better has reached far beyond its old economic and social boundaries. To a man, the industry agrees the recession has passed them by.

To be sure, General Foods is a special case. Its prime concern is to keep customers hungry for its mass-distribution foods. In setting up Gourmet Foods, it had a sharp eye on the potential prestige value of such a line to the staple lines that are its mainstay.

Old-timers in the fancy food field have no such double objective. They have flourished simply by catering to today's more demanding palates.

'This is a small industry, but a growth industry,' says Harry Lesser, president of Cresca Co. Inc., conceded to be one of the biggest companies in the field. The National Association for the Specialty Food Trade estimates wholesale volume has jumped from $39 million in 1931 to $70 million this year. Specialty food outlets have doubled since 1950, to 6,000 today. Add in the other outlets that carry some specialty foods and the total is around 15,000, Lesser figures. He estimates 1958's wholesale volume at around $100 million. . . .

How to account for surging appetites for Danish ham, pickled water chestnuts, wild boar, Euphrates bread, innumerable cheese concoctions, marinated mushrooms—not to mention the 'spooky foods' such as chocolate-covered ants and fried grasshoppers?

Economic Factors—The pervading uptrend of income explains much, of course. Another economic factor, says Harold Roth, head of the agent-importer firm of Roth & Liebmann, Inc., and now trade association president, is that the rising cost of food staples is narrowing the gap between them and fancy foods. Some 65 to 70 percent of fancy foods are imported. Inflation has hit many foreign countries less severely than the U.S. and the growing volume of imports tends to bring prices down, too.

But economics isn't the whole story. Travel has given the industry a tremendous push. Whether consumers go to Europe or the Orient or to a new section of the U.S., they come back home with appetites whetted for new tastes.

Home Entertainment—The home-centered trend of postwar decades puts new stress on home entertaining. Even the humblest hostess wants at least one special goody for such occasions. The recession, which makes dining out costly, may have built up this trend. John G. Martin, president of Heublein, Inc., has some ideas for consumer tastes. His company's No. 1 product by far is Smirnoff Vodka, but it also imports gourmet foods and makes specialty foods.

Tired Palates—Martin is convinced that the U.S. consumer—at any economic level—finds the foods on his table rather dull. This partly explains the small, steady growth of such Heublein gourmet items such as Edouard Artzner Paté de Foie Gras, Grey Poupon Mustard, James Robertson & Sons Preserves, and Huntley & Palmer Biscuits."

"Don't Smash the Profit Machinery," by Malcolm S. Forbes, *Forbes*, May 14, 1959:

"At the turn of the eighteenth century in Great Britain, the social upheaval we now call 'technological unemployment' raised an exceedingly ugly head. Cartwright's and Arkwright's new steam-driven spinning looms could turn out cloth far faster than the old hand-operated looms. The result was that tens of thousands of people were thrown out of jobs.

The workers' reply was a senseless and violent movement known as Luddism. Masked men would raid Midland textile mills in the dead of night, smash the frames, and sometimes burn the very buildings, acting in the name of a probably mythical 'General Ludd.' They thought they were protecting their jobs against the dreaded machines.

Luddism did the workers themselves no good and certainly helped not at all the cause of human progress. It is merely a footnote to history. But there is a moral in all this which Mr. David McDonald, Mr. Walter Reuther and some like-minded labor leaders would do well to ponder at this time. Once again we are facing technological unemployment. Currently, our Gross National Product is running nine percent ahead of a year ago, but unemployment is up only 2.4 percent. Unemployment is shrinking, but at 4.3 million it is still far higher than we would like to see it at a time when the GNP is at a record level.

Part of this is due to the growth of the labor force. But in part, it is technological unemployment, pure and simple, caused by the tremendous strides of automation. Five years ago U.S. manufacturing plants had 17.2 million workers; today we produce more goods with only 15.4 million workers.

What do some of our labor leaders suggest we do about it? 'The U.S. Government,' says, Walter Reuther. 'should take measures to raise consumer buying power. There should be a progressive reduction of the work week. . . . The government should also create new jobs.' On other occasions, Mr. Reuther has suggested that the trouble was profits were claiming too large a portion of what the industry produced. In his preliminary broadside for the forthcoming steel industry talks, United Steel Workers' President David J. McDonald has said much the same thing. He made it very clear that he thinks the steel industry can and should pay higher wages without raising prices.

The only way it can do so, of course, is by dipping into profits. I am afraid these two labor leaders do not quite realize what they are proposing. Mr. McDonald and Mr. Reuther are making the same mistakes the Luddites made. They misunderstand the nature of technological unemployment. For if one man can operate a machine where two men toiled. then the way to give the misplaced man a job is to build another machine for him to produce with.

This, of course, means that we have to find someone willing and able to pay for the machine. For this we must have profits. Profits supply today much of the savings with which we build new capital equipment. They also provide the incentive without which no one will invest his dollars and cents in machinery and plants."

"Washington Outlook," *Business Week*, August 23, 1958:

"**Eisenhower is much worried about inflation,** according to associates. The result may be a cut in spending plans during the winter and spring months. The summer step-up in defense and public works spending can't be slowed quickly. . . .

Spending will be sharply up—In January, President Eisenhower thought the cash outlay would approach $74 billion, or about $2 billion more than was spent in the year ended June 30. Prospects now are that spending will be near $79 billion. Part of this is for defense—the race with Russia in outer space. Part is for recession cures—[spending on] public works.

Agriculture Secy. Benson's farm victory will be costly—Benson forced Congress to come around to his position—less control of acreage and lower government price props. Nearly everyone agrees this was a major victory, in the economic sense. But it does have its drawbacks. The GOP, thinned out in the Midwest farm belt in 1954 and 1956, will be pressed harder than ever to hold on to House and Senate seats. And there will be no relief for the taxpayer. With fewer price controls, plantings will rise. And given good weather, Benson's policy may produce the biggest farm glut ever next year. That's when politics may take over again, with a return to high price supports at a heavy cost to taxpayers.

School integration will influence the fall voting—The issue isn't confined to the Southern and border states, where it has been dramatized in the past two years. Racial tensions will be high in all major cities, often centering around schools. Eisenhower has threatened to put troops back in Little Rock [Arkansas]. And across the Potomac from the White House, there's the threat in Virginia to close the public schools, rather than accept court-ordered integration.

Eisenhower's role in the fall campaign is still uncertain—The President will make at least one major swing, perhaps two, before the Congressional elections in November. The President is dissatisfied with his party. He has never backed it across the board. Many party workers feel that's the chief reason Eisenhower, since his first landslide in 1952, has had a Democratic Congress since 1954. Local bosses consider their party as permanent and Eisenhower as temporary. This has made cooperation, based on compromise, difficult."

"French Car of the Future Needs No Gasoline Tank," *Popular Mechanics*, June 1958:

"Tomorrow's car will be driven by electricity and will need no gasoline tank, if the dreams of French designers materialize. The dream car, called the Arbel, generates its own electricity with an engine mounted in the rear. Four separate electric motors, one at each wheel, do the driving and eliminate the need for a transmission or differential. The chassis is made of rugged tubing which, being hollow, is used as the fuel tank. Still only a dream, the car is said to be easily adaptable to nuclear power."

1960–1969

The 1960s were tumultuous. Following the placid era of the 1950s, the seventh decade of the twentieth century contained tragic assassinations, momentous social movements, remarkable space achievements, and the longest war in American history. Civil Rights leader Martin Luther King, Jr., would deliver his "I have a dream" speech in 1963, the same year President John F. Kennedy was killed. Five years later in 1968, King, along with John Kennedy's influential brother Bobby, would be shot. And violent protests against American involvement in Vietnam would be led and heavily supported by the educated middle class, which had grown and prospered enormously in the American economy.

From 1960 to 1964, the economy expanded; unemployment was low. The gross national product and total federal spending increased by nearly 25 percent as inflation was held in check. Internationally, the power of the United States was immense. Congress gave the young President John F. Kennedy the defense and space-related programs he wanted, but few of the welfare programs he proposed. Then inflation arrived, along with the Vietnam War. From an annual average of less than two percent inflation between 1950 and 1965, suddenly inflation soared, ranging from six percent to 14 percent a year, and averaging a budget-popping 9.5 percent. Investors, once content with the consistency and stability of banks, sought better rates of returns in the stock market or real estate.

The Cold War became hotter during conflicts over Cuba and Berlin in the early 1960s. Fears over the international spread of communism led to America's intervention in a foreign conflict that would become a defining event of the decade: Vietnam. Military involvement in this small Asian country grew from advisory status to full-scale war. By 1968, Vietnam had become a national obsession leading to President Lyndon Johnson's decision not to run for another term and fueling not only debate over our role in Vietnam, but more inflation and division nationally. The antiwar movement grew rapidly. Antiwar marches, which had drawn but a few thousand in 1965, grew in size until millions of marchers filled the streets of New York, San Francisco, and Washington, DC, only a few years later. By spring 1970, students on 448 college campuses made ROTC voluntary or abolished it.

The struggle to bring economic equality to blacks during the period produced massive spending for school integration. By 1963, the peaceful phase of the Civil Rights movement was ending; street violence, assassinations, and bombings defined the period. In 1967, 41 cities experienced major disturbances. At the same time, charismatic labor organizer Cesar Chavez's United Farm Workers led a Civil Rights-style movement for Mexican-Americans, gaining national support which challenged the growers of the West with a five-year agricultural strike.

As a sign of increasing affluence and changing times, American consumers bought 73 percent fewer potatoes and 25 percent more fish, poultry, and meat and 50 percent more citrus products and tomatoes than in 1940. California passed New York as the most populous state. Factory workers earned more than $100 a week, their highest wages in history. From 1960 to 1965, the amount of money spent for prescription drugs to lose weight doubled, while the per capita consumption of processed potato chips rose from 6.3 pounds in 1958 to 14.2 pounds eight years later. In 1960, approximately 40 percent of American adult women had paying jobs; 30 years later, the number would grow to 57.5 percent. Their emergence into the work force would transform marriage, child rearing, and the economy. In 1960, women were also liberated by the FDA's approval of the birth-control pill, giving both women and men a degree of control over their bodies that had never existed before.

During the decade, anti-establishment sentiments grew: men's hair was longer and wilder, beards and mustaches became popular, women's skirts rose to mid-thigh, and bras were discarded. Hippies advocated alternative lifestyles, drug use increased, especially marijuana and LSD; the Beatles, the Rolling Stones, Jimi Hendrix, and Janis Joplin became popular music figures; college campuses became major sites for demonstrations against the war and for Civil Rights. The Supreme Court prohibited school prayer, assured legal counsel to the poor, limited censorship of sexual material, and increased the rights of the accused.

Extraordinary space achievements also marked the decade. Ten years after President Kennedy announced he would place a man on the moon, 600 million people around the world watched as Neil Armstrong gingerly lowered his left foot into the soft dust of the moon's surface. In a tumultuous time of division and conflict, the landing was one of America's greatest triumphs and an exhilarating demonstration of American genius. Its cost was $25 billion and set the stage for 10 other men to walk on the surface of the moon during the next three years.

The 1960s saw the birth of Enovid 10, the first oral contraceptive (cost $0.55 each), the start of Berry Gordy's Motown Records, felt-tip pens, Diet-Rite cola, Polaroid color film, Weight Watchers, and Automated Teller Machines. It's the decade when lyrics began appearing on record albums, Jackie and Aristotle Onassis reportedly spent $20 million during their first year together, and the Gay Liberation Front participated in the Hiroshima Day March—the first homosexual participation as a separate constituency in a peace march.

1961 Family Profile

Twenty-eight-year-old Steve Brewster is involved in programming decisions at ABC, the upstart television network still struggling to compete with CBS and NBC. He works long hours and is often separated from his 21-year-old wife Gretchen, a struggling movie and TV commercial actress. Both live in Los Angeles and have no children.

Annual Income: $28,000
This income includes the $23,000 earned by Steve, plus the $5,000 in fees from Gretchen, all of whose income is from soap commercials and modeling.

Annual Budget
The average per capita consumer expenditures in 1961 for all workers nationwide are:

Auto Parts	$14.15
Auto Usage	$207.41
Clothing	$125.21
Dentists	$11.43
Food	$462.19
Furniture	$26.13
Gas and Oil	$65.33
Health Insurance	$10.89
Housing	$278.73
Intercity Transport	$7.62
Local Transport	$10.89
New Auto Purchase	$65.87
Personal Business	$65.87
Personal Care	$33.21
Physicians	$32.12
Private Education and Research	$22.32

Recreation	$103.98
Religion/Welfare Activities	$29.94
Telephone and Telegraph	$26.13
Tobacco	$38.65
Utilities	$76.21
Per Capita Consumption	$1,856.92

Life at Home

- Steve and Gretchen are rarely home together, often meeting on weekends.
- Their apartment is completely furnished so they will be prepared to entertain on short notice, but they rarely have time.
- The walls are white, and most of the furniture is modern; they avoid putting pictures and other objects on tables to avoid a cluttered look.
- Steve works a 12-hour day, often six days a week, while Gretchen often travels for movie shoots in remote locations, mostly for minor roles.
- She has cut several TV commercials, which have brought her financial rewards, but fears she will not be cast in movies if she appears in too many commercials.
- For the right person, Los Angeles is the land of opportunity, but competition is intense.
- Gretchen really wants a baby, but is afraid of what childbirth will do to her figure and career; Steve keeps saying they'll have children once he "makes it."
- Wages on a television or movie set are strictly controlled and regulated by contracts.
- In a TV western, an extra earns a minimum of $25.47 for eight hours, during which he or she might spend two or three hours just waiting for something to happen.

FALL 1961 SCHEDULE

Day	Network	7:00	7:30	8:00	8:30	9:00	9:30	10:00	10:30
MONDAY	ABC	Expedition	Cheyenne		The Rifleman	Surfside Six		BEN CASEY	
MONDAY	CBS	local	To Tell The Truth	Pete And Gladys	WINDOW ON MAIN STREET	Danny Thomas Show	Andy Griffith Show	Hennessey	I've Got A Secret
MONDAY	NBC	local		National Velvet	The Price Is Right	87TH PRECINCT		Thriller	
TUESDAY	ABC	local	Bugs Bunny Show	Bachelor Father	CALVIN AND THE COLONEL	THE NEW BREED		ALCOA PREMIERE	Bell And Howell Close-Up
TUESDAY	CBS	local	Marshal Dillon	DICK VAN DYKE SHOW	The Many Loves Of Dobie Gillis	Red Skelton Show	ICHABOD AND ME	Garry Moore Show	
TUESDAY	NBC	local	Laramie		Alfred Hitchcock Presents	DICK POWELL SHOW		CAIN'S HUNDRED	
WEDNESDAY	ABC	local	STEVE ALLEN SHOW		TOP CAT	Hawaiian Eye		Naked City	
WEDNESDAY	CBS	local	THE ALVIN SHOW	Father Knows Best	Checkmate		MRS. G GOES TO COLLEGE	U.S. Steel Hour / Armstrong Circle Theater	
WEDNESDAY	NBC	local	Wagon Train		JOEY BISHOP SHOW	Perry Como's Kraft Music Hall		BOB NEWHART SHOW	DAVID BRINKLEY'S JOURNAL
THURSDAY	ABC	local	The Adventures Of Ozzie And Harriet	Donna Reed Show	The Real McCoys	My Three Sons	MARGIE	The Untouchables	
THURSDAY	CBS	local	FRONTIER CIRCUS		NEW BOB CUMMINGS SHOW	THE INVESTIGATORS		CBS Reports	
THURSDAY	NBC	local	The Outlaws		DR. KILDARE		HAZEL	Sing Along With Mitch	
FRIDAY	ABC	local	STRAIGHTAWAY	THE HATHAWAYS	The Flintstones	77 Sunset Strip		TARGET: THE CORRUPTORS	
FRIDAY	CBS	local	Rawhide		Route 66		FATHER OF THE BRIDE	The Twilight Zone	Eyewitness
FRIDAY	NBC	local	INTERNATIONAL SHOWTIME		Robert Taylor's Detectives		Bell Telephone Hour / Dinah Shore Show		FRANK McGEE'S HERE AND NOW
SATURDAY	ABC	Matty's Funday Funnies	The Roaring Twenties		Leave It To Beaver	Lawrence Welk Show		Fight Of The Week	Make That Spare
SATURDAY	CBS	local	Perry Mason		THE DEFENDERS		Have Gun, Will Travel	Gunsmoke	
SATURDAY	NBC	local	Tales Of Wells Fargo		The Tall Man	NBC SATURDAY NIGHT AT THE MOVIES			
SUNDAY	ABC	Maverick [from 6:30]	FOLLOW THE SUN		Lawman	BUS STOP			
SUNDAY	CBS	Lassie	Dennis The Menace	Ed Sullivan Show		General Electric Theater	Jack Benny Program	Candid Camera	What's My Line
SUNDAY	NBC	The Bullwinkle Show	Walt Disney's Wonderful World Of Color		CAR 54, WHERE ARE YOU?	Bonanza		DuPont Show Of The Week	

- Actors earn $5.00 more if they do not mind getting wet, and $8.07 more if they ride a horse; driving a team of four horses adds an extra $20.50 to their paycheck.

Life at Work

- For the past seven years, after merging with United Paramount Theaters, the ABC television network has been battling for ratings respectability with the other two networks.
- This was accomplished in 1960-61 with a line-up heavily composed of the action-adventure format; news, public affairs, sports, and daytime programming are virtually non-existent.
- Steve is focused on broadening the appeal of the ABC network, since too much of its line-up is based on the type of action-adventure shows which can lose favor overnight.
- Currently, *77 Sunset Strip* and *The Untouchables* are doing well, but many of the new action-adventure clones are getting poor ratings; *Klondike*, featuring Ralph Taeger and James Coburn, has already been slated for cancellation.
- Some other shows are showing weakness, and Steve has been asked to develop new strategies for ABC.
- One of his peers, and a competitor for advancement at the network, has launched the first adult cartoon show, *The Flintstones*.
- Placed in the 8:30 p.m. time slot when children are in bed, and sponsored by Winston cigarettes, *The Flintstones* is getting a mixed reception.
- Nearly everything else is bombing, including the re-appearance of comedian Jackie Gleason in a quiz show format so insipid, the program was pulled after one week.
- The only apparent hit of the season is *My Three Sons*; CBS appears to be striking gold with *The Andy Griffith Show*—a show whose appeal is completely lost on Steve.
- Steve is betting on sports, and though ABC has already stubbed its toe on sports, he thinks that spending heavily for sporting events will give the network revenues and respectability, and allow him to be promoted.
- In 1959, to deepen its reach and gain leverage for the summer Olympic games, ABC paid $167,000 for the exclusive television rights to the 1960 Olympics in Squaw Valley, California.
- When ABC failed to also get the rights to the summer games, the network canceled plans for covering the winter games entirely; CBS picked up the rights for both.
- Unfortunately for ABC, the ratings for the winter games were high, which boosted excitement for the summer games, during which CBS extensively employed videotape to provide same-day coverage of the games from Rome, dramatically increasing the immediacy and ratings of the Olympics.
- CBS emerged a winner, with ABC the clear loser.

ABC aired two of the four presidential debates, which contributed to the election of John F. Kennedy.

- Many at ABC, including Steve, are furious that the network was not willing to show the Winter Olympics—even if commercial sponsorships were scarce—to establish itself as a solid network player.
- Currently, ABC's only major, long-running sporting event is boxing, which is considered a joke; both NBC and CBS long ago abandoned coverage of weekly boxing matches, a staple of the early 1950s.
- Steve is now promoting ABC's involvement with the brand-new American Football League; linking ABC and the upstart AFL will help both, he believes.
- Also, plans are under way for the creation of a Saturday afternoon program called *Wide World of Sports*, hosted by former CBS sportscaster Jim McKay.
- Based on the idea that lots of different sports can be featured during a single show, *Wide World of Sports* is getting heavy promotion.
- The format is modeled after the Olympic coverage pioneered by CBS—live or pre-taped segments that bring together action highlights from various venues.
- No one is sure whether it will work, but Steve is excited that ABC will be trying something new.
- Gaining respectability through sports has an immediate appeal, since upgrading ABC's news and public affairs programming, everyone believes, will take more time.
- Because of the intense pressure to challenge CBS and NBC, Steve does not believe that ABC will have patience with any programming that develops slowly; ABC needs hits.
- ABC's history of supporting news broadcasts is weak; the network was the last of the three to create a nightly news show, settling in the early 1950s for a weekly commentary program by former radio analysts Paul Harvey and Walter Winchell.
- Even when news was added in 1953, featuring CBS refugee John Daly, most of the ABC affiliates refused to carry the 15-minute news program.
- To strengthen its news position and control distribution, ABC moved its news programming into prime time, which it controlled, in 1958–59, using the 10:30–10:45 p.m. time slot.
- News at ABC is still considered a lost cause; Steve believes daytime soap operas and sports are the ticket to ratings respectability.
- ABC's most recent attempt at producing documentaries under the title of *Bell and Howell Closeup*, was heavily panned, and Steve's fellow programmer was fired.
- The revamped *Bell and Howell Closeup* series, headed by Time-Life, is gaining respectable reviews for its interviews with Fidel Castro on the verge of announcing he is a communist, and "Walk in My Shoes" concerning the defiant attitude of American blacks.
- Last fall, during the presidential campaign, Steve was unsure of the wisdom of his network producing two of the four presidential debates.
- Privately he wondered how many "eggheads," who could be watching a sitcom, would be willing to tune in to see John Kennedy and Richard Nixon discuss the issues.
- He was surprised and delighted when the presidential debates produced a windfall of good publicity for television and its ability to allow millions of people across the entire country to share in an important and historic event.
- He was less pleased by the comments of FCC Commissioner Newton Minow, who called television "a vast wasteland."

Speech: Newly appointed FCC Chairman Newton Minow, March 9, 1961, at the National Association of Broadcasters:

"I invite you to sit in front of your television set when your station (or network) goes on the air and stay there without a book, magazine, newspaper, profit-and-loss sheet, or ratings book to distract you—and keep your eyes glued to that set until the station signs off. I can assure you that you will observe a vast wasteland. You will see a procession of game shows, violence, audience participation shows, formula comedies about totally unbelievable families, blood and thunder, mayhem, violence, sadism, murder, Western bad men, Western good men, private eyes, gangsters, more violence, cartoons, and—endlessly—commercials, many screaming, cajoling, and offending, and most of all, boredom. True, you will see a few things you enjoy, but they will be very, very, few, and if you think I exaggerate, try it. Is there one person in this room who claims that broadcasting can't do better? Is there one network president in this room who claims he can't do better? Why is so much of television bad? We need imagination in programming, not sterility; creativity, not imitation; experimentation, not conformity; excellence, not mediocrity."

Life in the Community: Los Angeles, California

- In the 1940s, Los Angeles was the film center of the world; 90 percent of all motion pictures made in America were made here.
- During that time, Hollywood studios were producing up to 400 movies a year for the American audience.
- Los Angeles' cherished position as entertainment capital of America was challenged in the 1950s by a dramatic decline in movie attendance from its wartime peak and by live television productions from New York.
- With the advent of taped programming, Hollywood talent and studios are both in vogue for television production, and many shows are produced in the facilities once used for movies.
- While movies get the glamour, aerospace—housed south of the L.A. International Airport—is the main intellectual center of missile design and fabrication in the non-Communist world.
- California Institute of Technology, located in suburban Pasadena and referred to reverently as "a young MIT," plays a key role in the scientific development of aviation and rocketry.
- In Greater L.A., the RAND Corporation, a nonprofit, strategic think tank created and largely funded by the Air Force, attracts to the area physicists, chemists, mathematicians, astronomers, social scientists, and other scholars for research.

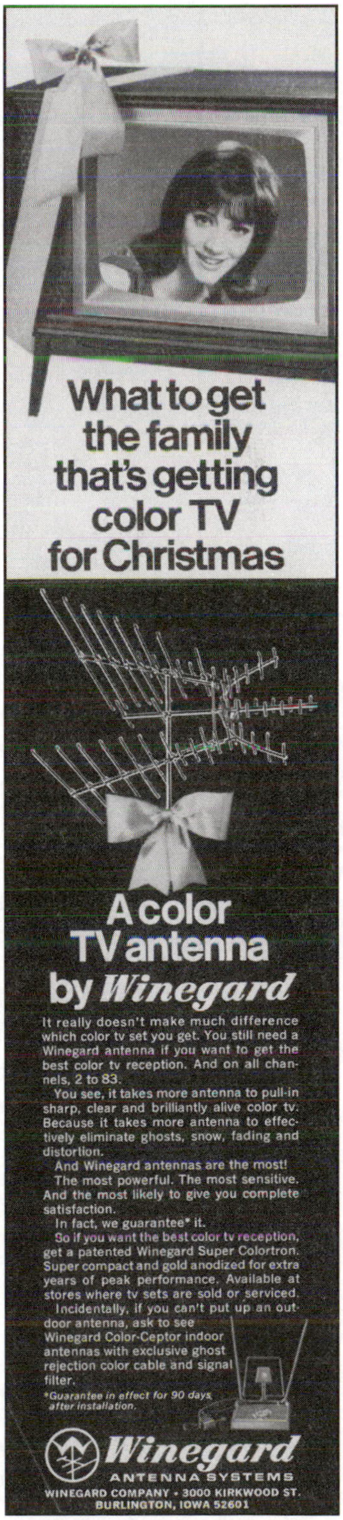

What to get the family that's getting color TV for Christmas
A color TV antenna by Winegard
It really doesn't make much difference which color tv set you get. You still need a Winegard antenna if you want to get the best color tv reception. And on all channels, 2 to 83.
You see, it takes more antenna to pull-in sharp, clear and brilliantly alive color tv. Because it takes more antenna to effectively eliminate ghosts, snow, fading and distortion.
And Winegard antennas are the most!
The most powerful. The most sensitive. And the most likely to give you complete satisfaction.
In fact, we guarantee* it.
So if you want the best color tv reception, get a patented Winegard Super Colortron. Super compact and gold anodized for extra years of peak performance. Available at stores where tv sets are sold or serviced.
Incidentally, if you can't put up an outdoor antenna, ask to see Winegard Color-Ceptor indoor antennas with exclusive ghost rejection color cable and signal filter.
*Guarantee in effect for 90 days after installation.
Winegard
ANTENNA SYSTEMS
WINEGARD COMPANY • 3000 KIRKWOOD ST.
BURLINGTON, IOWA 52601

Historical Snapshot
1961

- President Kennedy launched an exercise campaign urging all Americans to be more fit
- The Interstate Commerce Commission banned segregation on all interstate facilities
- CORE organized Freedom Rides to integrate buses, trains, and terminals throughout the South
- The Civil War Centennial celebration began
- The minimum wage rose from $1.00 to $1.25
- Civil Defense officials distributed 22 million copies of the pamphlet *Family Fallout Shelter*
- FCC Chairman Newton Minow called television "a vast wasteland" during a speech at the National Association of Broadcasters
- President Kennedy appointed a committee to study the status of women
- The DNA genetic code was broken
- A university poll reported that 72 percent of elementary and high school teachers approved of corporal punishment as a disciplinary measure
- Clark Gable died at the conclusion of filming *The Misfits*
- Robert Zimmerman, known as Bob Dylan, began singing in Greenwich Village nightclubs; his first recording opportunity was as a backup harmonica player
- Ray Kroc borrowed $2.7 million to buy out the McDonald Brothers and began the McDonald's empire
- New York's First National Bank offered fixed-term certificates of deposit for the first time
- The IBM Selectric typewriter was introduced
- Four thousand servicemen were sent to Vietnam as advisors
- The words Peace Corps, high rise, New Frontier, soul, zonked, and new wave all entered the language
- A Gallup poll indicated that 74 percent of the teens interviewed believed in God; 58 percent planned to go to college
- A poll of 16- to 21-year-old girls indicated that almost all expected to be married by age 22 and most wanted four children
- Cigarette makers spent $115 million on television advertising
- Canned pet food was among the three top-selling categories in grocery stores
- The electric toothbrush, Coffee-mate, Country corn flakes, and self-wringing mops all made their first appearance

1961 Economic Profile

Income, Standard Jobs

Average of All Industries, Excluding Farm Labor	NR
Average of All Industries, Including Farm Labor	$4,961.00
Bituminous Coal Mining	$5,357.00
Building Trades	$5,938.00
Domestics	$2,356.00
Farm Labor	$1,929.00
Federal Civilian	$6,451.00
Federal Employees, Executive Departments	$4,812.00
Federal Military	$3,813.00
Finance, Insurance, and Real Estate	$5,203.00
Gas and Electricity Workers	$6,390.00
Manufacturing, Durable Goods	$6,048.00
Manufacturing, Nondurable Goods	$5,250.00
Medical/Health Services Workers	$3,636.00
Miscellaneous Manufacturing	$4,753.00
Motion Picture Services	$5,871.00
Nonprofit Organization Workers	$3,684.00
Passenger Transportation Workers, Local and Highway	$4,966.00
Personal Services	$3,810.00

Bob Dylan began his career singing in Greenwich Village nightclubs.

The Civil Defense distributed millions of pamphlets concerning nuclear fallout.

Public School Teachers	$4,991.00
Radio Broadcasting and Television Workers	$7,384.00
Railroad Workers	$6,440.00
State and Local Government Workers	$4,721.00
Telephone and Telegraph Workers	$5,793.00
Wholesale and Retail Trade Workers	$5,932.00

Selected Prices

American Flag Set, 3' x 5' Flag and Pole	$3.95
Bluebrook Margarine, per Pound	$0.15
Boy's Life Magazine, Monthly	$0.25

Consumer Expenditures and Income, Urban Places in the Western Region, 1960–61, Bureau of Labor Statistics:

"Urban families in the Western region spent an average of $5,971 for current annual living expenses in 1960–61. In addition, they made gifts and contributions averaging $324, put $334 into various types of life insurance and retirement funds, paid $844 in income and other personal taxes, and showed savings of $157, on the average, through a net increase in assets over liabilities. . . Families enjoyed a substantial rise in incomes, both before and after taxes, between 1950, when the Bureau conducted its previous nationwide survey, and 1960–61. Annual income after taxes rose by about 62 percent to an average of $6,324. Consumer units increased their spending for current consumption by only 52 percent, however. With this widened margin between their incomes and expenditures, families were able to increase their gifts and contributions, as well as personal insurance, and to set aside more for savings than in 1950. The amount classified as going into personal insurance was almost equally divided between various types of life insurance and social security and other public and private retirement funds.

Dollar expenditures were higher in 1960–61 than in 1950 in all major categories of family expenses, but there were significant shifts in the proportion of total current living expenses going for different purposes. The relative importance of expenditures for food and beverages declined from 30.0 percent in 1950 to 25.6 percent in 1960–61. The declines continued trends shown by the Bureau's surveys since the early 1900s. Spending for shelter, fuel, light, etc., by homeowners and renters moved in the opposite direction, increasing from 14.9 percent of total consumption expenditures in 1950 to 17.8 percent in 1960–61. However, the combined share for the three basic categories of family expense—food, clothing, and shelter—decreased over the decade between surveys from 56 to 53 percent. Expenditures for the purchase and operation of automobiles were almost unchanged over the period, although the proportion of families owning cars rose from 70 percent in 1950 to 80 percent in 1960–61."

Chap-et Lip Balm $0.35
Chrysler Newport Automobile $2,964.00
Daisey BB Gun $12.98
Ethan Allen Desk, Four-Drawer $85.60
Flintstones Child's Feeding Set $1.99
Kelvinator Air Conditioner.......... $169.00
Kodak Brownie Super 27 Camera $22.00
Kraft Miracle Whip Salad
Dressing, Quart.................... $0.43
Little Star Dress for Teens............. $5.00
Magnavox Broadway
Stereo Theater.................. $495.00
Magna-Lite Shop Light................ $6.95
McGregor Meteor Slacks $10.00
Pakula Necklace $3.00
Pioneer Ebonetts Kitchen Gloves $0.98
RCA Victor Tape Recorder,
Reel-to-Reel..................... $99.95
Scott Tissues, Two Packages of 400 ..... $0.39
Scripto Goldenglo Lighter............. $5.00
Smarteens Blouse for Girls, Cotton...... $3.00
Tums Antacid, per Roll............... $0.12
Ultra-Sheer Seamless Stockings,
Box of Six $5.28
Young Men's Caumet Shoes $9.99

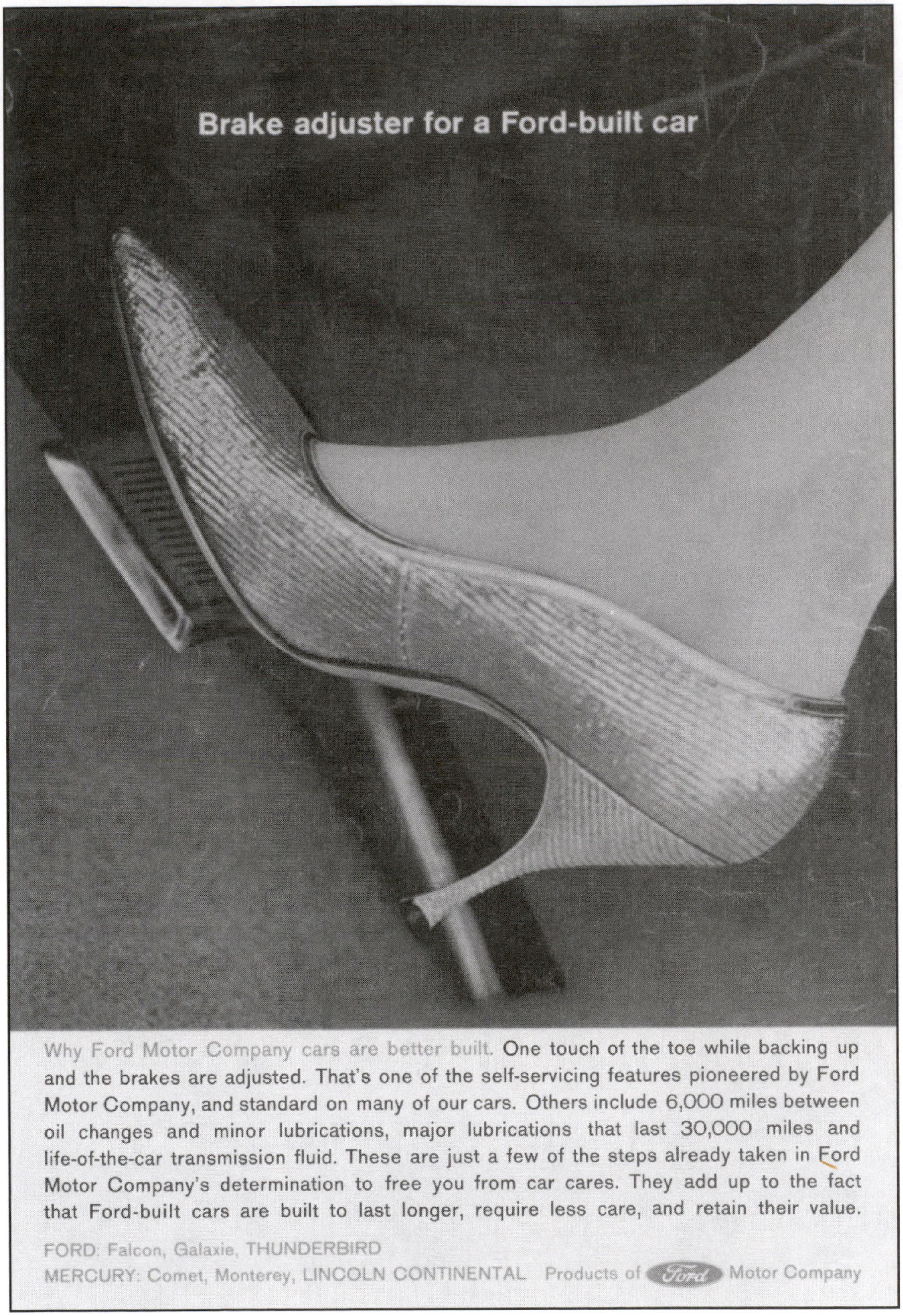
Brake adjuster for a Ford-built car
Why Ford Motor Company cars are better built. One touch of the toe while backing up and the brakes are adjusted. That's one of the self-servicing features pioneered by Ford Motor Company, and standard on many of our cars. Others include 6,000 miles between oil changes and minor lubrications, major lubrications that last 30,000 miles and life-of-the-car transmission fluid. These are just a few of the steps already taken in Ford Motor Company's determination to free you from car cares. They add up to the fact that Ford-built cars are built to last longer, require less care, and retain their value.
FORD: Falcon, Galaxie, THUNDERBIRD
MERCURY: Comet, Monterey, LINCOLN CONTINENTAL Products of Ford Motor Company

Lucille Ball filed for divorce from Desi Arnaz in 1960; their TV program, I Love Lucy, *had been a cornerstone of television culture.*

Television in 1961

January: *The Avengers*. Britain's ABC network presented the spy duo of Dr. David Keel (Ian Hendry) and a mysterious character referred to simply as Steed (Patrick MacNee).

March: Newton Minow was sworn in as chairman of the Federal Communications Commission.

April: Death of *Omnibus*. Age: Nine years. In its final season, the show was relegated to a Sunday afternoon slot once a month on NBC.

April: *ABC Final Report* (ABC). The first network attempt at late-night news each weeknight. At first, the program was only carried by ABC's owned and operated stations, but in October it expanded to the entire network.

June: Worthington Miner's syndicated theater presentation, *Play of the Week*, was canceled.

June: *PM East/PM West.* Westinghouse entered late-night television, syndicating 90 minutes of talk and variety five nights a week. One half of the program came from New York (with Mike Wallace), while the other half originated from San Francisco (with Terry O'Flaherty). In February 1962, the West portion was dumped.

July: John Chancellor took over NBC's *Today* from Dave Garroway.

September: *DuPont Show of the Week* (NBC), after four years as a series of floating dramatic specials for CBS, switched to NBC, changing formats as well. The weekly series now included drama, documentary, and variety presentations ranging from "The Wonderful World of Christmas" (with Carol Burnett and Harpo Marx) to "Hemingway" (narrated by Chet Huntley).

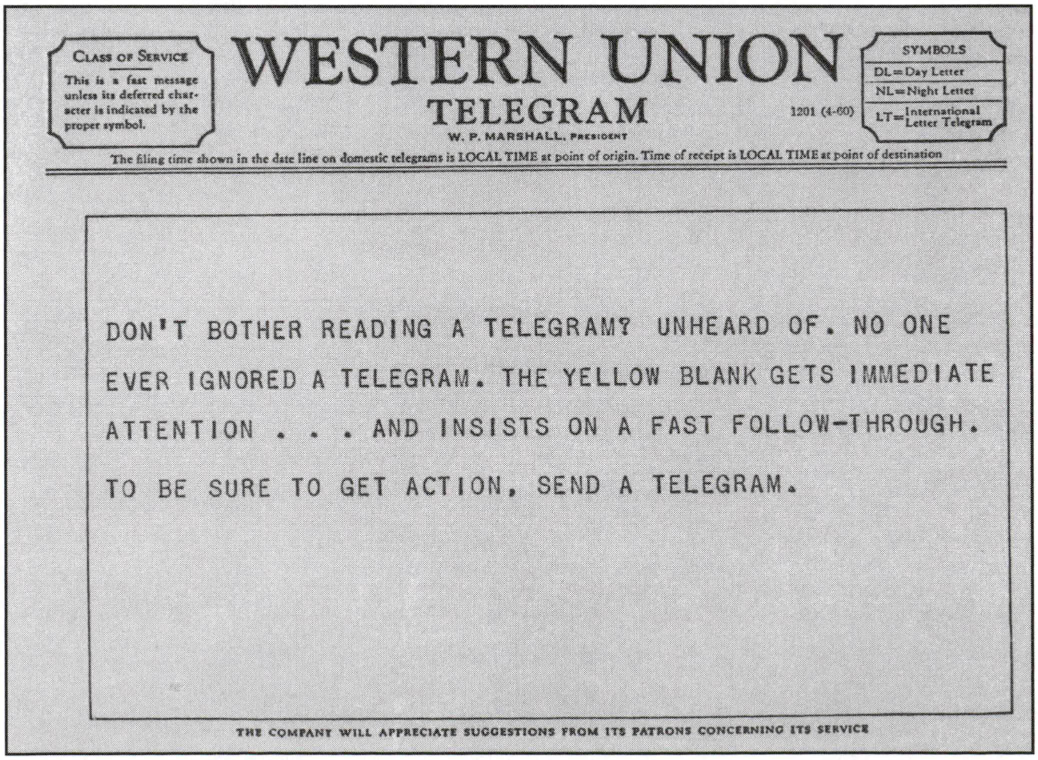

CLASS OF SERVICE
This is a fast message unless its deferred character is indicated by the proper symbol.

WESTERN UNION
TELEGRAM
W. P. MARSHALL, PRESIDENT

1201 (4-60)

SYMBOLS
DL=Day Letter
NL=Night Letter
LT=International Letter Telegram

The filing time shown in the date line on domestic telegrams is LOCAL TIME at point of origin. Time of receipt is LOCAL TIME at point of destination

DON'T BOTHER READING A TELEGRAM? UNHEARD OF. NO ONE EVER IGNORED A TELEGRAM. THE YELLOW BLANK GETS IMMEDIATE ATTENTION . . . AND INSISTS ON A FAST FOLLOW-THROUGH. TO BE SURE TO GET ACTION, SEND A TELEGRAM.

THE COMPANY WILL APPRECIATE SUGGESTIONS FROM ITS PATRONS CONCERNING ITS SERVICE

"The 1959–60 Season," *Watching TV, Four Decades of American Television*, by Harry Castleman and Walter J. Podrazik:

"This decade, which gained such an identifiable (if not always accurate) character in retrospect, didn't end in December 1959. The moods, trends, and attitudes of the Fifties petered out over the next four years, during the administration of President John F. Kennedy. Nevertheless, three events took place in the 1959–60 season that seemed to symbolically mark a turning point in television culture and its passage into a new decade.

In 1959, George Reeves, who had appeared as the Man of Steel in all 104 episodes of the six-year-old syndicated classic, *The Adventures of Superman*, killed himself. In writing his obituary, many felt that Reeves had chosen suicide out of frustration at being unable to escape his Superman image and that his epitaph might be that he died of typecasting. To millions of youngsters who heard the news, it brought a sobering realization that television was not reality and that even Superman could die. In March 1960, Lucille Ball filed for divorce from Desi Arnaz. Lucy and Desi had been seen together only in monthly specials for the past few seasons, but their breakup officially ended, in reality and forever, a marriage whose fictionalized portrayal had been the cornerstone of television culture throughout the decade. Finally, on September 24, 1960, NBC presented the 2,343rd (and final) episode of *Howdy Doody*. Howdy had been there when TV began and kids who watched the earliest episodes had children of their own who watched the last. It was a graceful farewell that rang down the curtain on one of the last remnants of television's infancy. Perhaps there was never a more poignant moment on television than the last moment of that last show when Clarabell the clown, silent through all 13 years of the program, looked into the camera and quietly spoke, 'Goodbye, kids.' "

September: Walt Disney's *Wonderful World of Color* (NBC). Robert Kinter, who had signed Disney to television when he was with ABC, brought the popular family program with him to NBC. For the first time, the show aired in color (which ABC had always shied away from), beginning with the premier episode, "Mathmagic Land," featuring Donald Duck and a new animated character, Professor Ludwig Von Drake.

September: *Gunsmoke* expanded to 60 minutes, while the cream of six years of the half-hour shows was rerun on Tuesday nights under the title *Marshal Dillon*.

October: *Calendar* (CBS). Harry Reasoner hosted a 30-minute morning show combining hard news and soft features. Reasoner's wry essays, co-written with Andrew Rooney, were a high point of the program.

December: *The Mike Douglas Show*. The former band singer started a 90-minute afternoon talk show on Westinghouse's KYW in Cleveland. By October 1963, the show was syndicated nationally.

"Making the Tax Mess Worse," Editorial, *Life Magazine*, March 3, 1961:

"President Kennedy's program for federal aid to schools and colleges ($5.6 billion in five years) reminds us of nothing so much as the need for federal tax reform. We are really not trying to change the subject; there's a connection. For, once the federal tax structure is reformed, states and municipalities can have more ample tax sources of their own, and the chief excuse for massive federal school aid would vanish.

In contrast with 20 years ago, when the ratio was about 50-50, the federal government now collects about twice as much in taxes as all state and local governments together. It does this through a patchwork tax system that has become hopelessly complex and inequitable and requires drastic rewriting. This system has also pre-empted or crowded all tax sources except real estate, not virtually the sole source of local school taxes.

Despite their cramped resources, states and localities (as well as private institutions) have done a heroic job of keeping abreast of the need for more and better schools. Total expenditures on U.S. education have more than doubled since 1952. This was done with practically no federal aid or stimulus. After *Sputnik*, the people of the U.S. did not need to be told by Washington that their educational system was in trouble.

The unceasing strain on local money and the need for still further school improvement in the decade ahead have steamed up the lobbies for massive federal aid. More steam came from the unevenness of our recent progress—that the fact that Alabama, for example, is spending only $217 per pupil in public schooling, while New York spends $585. This gross inequity of educational opportunity is undemocratic and there is plenty of precedent for steps by the federal government to correct it. The simple way would be such a formula as the Committee for Economic Development proposed last year which confines federal aid to the poorer states. But the Kennedy plan subsidizes everybody—$30 extra per child in Alabama, but $15 extra in New York, and California, too.

By moving massively into education, however, the federal government would compound the very problem—i.e., federal taxes—that keeps the chief and proper sources of school funds under such strain. The school Boards would become increasingly dependent on federal aid, as have the farmers, veterans, and aged, etc., before them. This is too bad, because if Kennedy would shift his legislative priorities, the traditional supports of American education could still prove strong enough to meet all foreseeable requirements. His administration is studded with experts who realize that the basic reform of our tax laws is an absolute must for the health of the whole U.S. economy. This reform is on Kennedy's agenda, but not for this year. His immediate "musts" are some 16 other bills, including school aid, most of which cost money and therefore tend to make the tax mess even worse. If tax reform came first, the problems behind these bills would be a lot easier to handle."

"The Presidency, A Damned Good Job," *Time*, March 3, 1961:

"The wail of a child broke up a television taping session in the White House broadcasting room. Jumping to his feet, the President of the U.S. raced through the door, shouting, 'Who's crying in this house?' A moment later, he returned carrying his sniffling, snowsuited daughter. He handed her the first object that came to hand, a plastic Red Cross that he was using in the taping. 'Here, Caroline,' he soothed, 'want a nice red cross? You've got that cap pistol in one hand, you might want this for the other.' Caroline Kennedy's tears quickly evaporated, and she scampered off, all smiles, to rejoin her nurse. 'Have a nice walk,' her father called after her, as he turned back to the cameras. Another small domestic crisis solved. Life at 1600 Pennsylvania Avenue was like that. Nothing was too trivial for Jack Kennedy to give it at least momentary attention. He could discuss affairs of state with Canada's visiting Prime Minister Diefenbaker or Australia's Prime Minister Robert Menzies, and then reflect on the future of Dwight Eisenhower's putting green on the White House lawn ('I plan to use it. You forget I'm a pretty good golfer, too.')"

FOREIGN NEWS

UNITED NATIONS

New Orders

The news crashed into the Security Council chamber like a thunderclap. There had been more killings in the Congo. This time six Lumumbaists had been summarily executed by little Albert Kalonji, boss of the Mining State of South Kasai. In the corridors, Africans, already convinced that the murdered Premier Patrice Lumumba was a victim of white men's machinations, gathered in angry clusters, and in the chamber, African delegates took the floor to demand U.N. action.

Soviet Delegate Valerian Zorin seized the chance to press for his blunt resolution calling for Secretary-General Dag Hammarskjold's ouster, and for the U.N.'s exit from the Congo within a month. He was defeated before he started, but plowed doggedly on. Brandishing a magazine showing Hammarskjold and Katanga's Belgium-backed Moise Tshombe together in the same photo (taken as Hammarskjold led the first U.N. troops into Katanga last August), Zorin suggested that it proved that Dag was "allied" with "a Belgian puppet"; this brought weary grins from everyone at the horseshoe table, including Hammarskjold. When it was time to vote, not a hand rose in Zorin's support.

The Loophole. But on the impetus of their outrage, the Africans were ready to rush through a new proposal produced by Liberia, Ceylon and the U.A.R. It called for the reconvening of the Congolese Parliament under U.N. protection, urged that Congolese army units (of all factions) be "reorganized" (*i.e.*, disarmed), and pressed for the withdrawal from the Congo of Belgian and other foreign troops and political advisers. Most important, the U.N. was authorized to use force "if necessary" to block the Congo's threatened civil war.

Terrence Spencer

KATANGA'S TSHOMBE INSPECTS BELGIANS SERVING IN KATANGA ARMY

Divided Congo

TIME Map by J. Donovan

U.S. Delegate Adlai Stevenson detected a dangerous loophole. The resolution said nothing about banning foreign arms shipments into the Congo, nor did it authorize Hammarskjold's forces to search arriving planes or trucks for such contraband. Since the U.A.R. itself had been busily sneaking arms and equipment to Congo Rebel (and Russia's chosen puppet) Antoine Gizenga in Stanleyville, Stevenson suspected the omission was deliberate, at least as far as the U.A.R. was concerned. Under pressure from the aroused Africans, who were in no mood to change their proposal, Stevenson finally had to vote for the measure, figuring that opposition would cost the U.S. heavily in disillusion among its African friends.

The Manpower Problem. The resolution did achieve the U.S.'s main goal—backing for Hammarskjold and strengthening of his mandate. He now had authority to get tough in pushing the squabbling, killing, Congolese factions apart.

Applying his new authority might be more difficult. From Katanga came ominous rumblings from Moise Tshombe who threatened a "bloodbath" if the 2,500 U.N. troops stationed in his area tried to disarm his 5,000-man army. Premier Joseph Ileo in Léopoldville and Rebel Chief Antoine Gizenga in Stanleyville roared their own defiance. To face these threats, the U.N. needed more manpower; the Congo combat force was already down to 17,500, would drop to 13,800 by mid-March if the Indonesian and Moroccan troop units pulled out and went home as planned. Needed was a minimum total of 20,000 men. On the day after the big debate, Dag Hammarskjold began recruiting among the Indians, Pakistanis, Iraqis and other Afro-Asian delegates.

Proof quickly came that Stevenson's fears were well grounded. In Cairo, Gamal Abdel Nasser defiantly announced that the U.A.R. would continue to give arms and aid to Gizenga as the "legitimate government."* And in a letter to India's

Terrence Spencer

BELGIAN INSTRUCTS KATANGA MACHINE GUNNERS (NEAR BUKAMA)
But who would run the power stations?

* Gizenga was Lumumba's vice premier, the legal governor of the nation, and its recognized chief of state, is President Kasavubu.

TWENTY-FIVE CENTS
MARCH 24, 1961
HEYDAY OF THE HAGGLE
The Buyers' Market in Cars
TIME
THE WEEKLY NEWSMAGAZINE
FORD DEALER
JIM MORAN
VOL. LXXVII NO. 13

1965 News Profile

"Inside the Twentieth Century," by John Gunther, *Look*, January 12, 1965:
"Sixty-five years ago, when this most turbulent, unpredictable, and fruitful century began, nobody had ever flown in an airplane, read a Geiger counter, or argued about the welfare state. Nobody in 1900 listened to radio, looked at a newsreel, read a tabloid, stayed in a motel, watched a striptease, rode in the New York subway (which wasn't built until 1904), washed with hard-water soap, or traversed the Panama Canal (opened in 1914).

Things that we take utterly for granted today were unknown when this, our century, began—things like frozen foods, the theory of the self-determination of nations, nylon, the organization of man, national public-opinion polls, and penicillin. The diesel engine was three years old in 1900, the Kodak camera, 12, and the fountain pen, 16, but still to come were the permanent wave and air conditioning. Nobody had ever heard of radar, the urbanization of suburbs, plastics, or automation. Newspaper headlines in 1900 dealt with the Galveston flood, the Boxer Revolution in Peking, and Carrie Nation, the prohibitionist zealot who broke saloon windows with an axe. And, of course, there was a presidential election in which William McKinley and Theodore Roosevelt were the winning Republican candidates against William Jennings Bryan and Adlai E. Stevenson, Democrats.

Nineteen hundred was the birth year of today's Adlai E. Stevenson, who is thus a true child of the century. It was also the birth year of the first rigid airship known as the Zeppelin, and of cellophane, invented by a Swiss. Sam Goldwyn was 18 in 1900. Walter Lippmann and Mao Tse-tung, seven. Unknown were LBJ, DDT, Harold Wilson, urban renewal, Garbo, and the federal income-tax amendment. . . .

Enormous quadrants of the earth's surface belonged to the German, Dutch, French, Spanish, Belgian, and above all, British empires, as if by divine right. The anti-colonial revolution, like several other cataclysmic revolutions of our time, was still to come. Negroes were mostly serfs in the American South or the lowest-class labor in our Northern towns. Women did not have the vote in national elections. . . .

Troubles afflicted the world in the early 1900s, yes, but they were troubles limited, shallow, and capable of being circumscribed or covered up. By and large, both America and Europe basked in rosy optimism, based on the rationalist ideas of the nineteenth century. The ruling classes were prosperous and packed with privilege, and the poor were dealt with by charity, if at all. Capitalist society and the established order seemed unshakable, and revolutionists were generally dismissed as long-haired cranks. . . .

The twentieth century does not remotely resemble the nineteenth or any other century. There have been more changes in the past 65 years than in all other centuries put together. No longer do most people believe in the orderly progression of cause and effect; no longer do they believe in the natural goodness of man and the inevitability of progress. Stability is gone. This is an era of quibble, doubt, and qualm. Science, technology, art, architecture, music, literature have all acquired new values, and revolutionary conflicts rage.

Here, in 1965, are some other distinguishing and more specific characteristics of our century:

1. It is an age of big government, big business, and, a more novel factor, big labor. In 1901, the giant hands of J.P. Morgan put together the U.S. Steel Corporation, the first billion-dollar corporation in history. The CIO was founded by John L. Lewis in 1935, and merged with the older AFL in 1955. Prolonged strikes attended labor's rise to a successful bargaining position. Good pay 50 years ago was $0.29 an hour for 10 hours' work a day. Think what your plumber or carpenter would say today if you followed his scale and offered him $17.40 a week.
2. It is also the age of the Common Man. This was symbolized after World War I, when various governments erected monuments not merely to heroes, but to an 'unknown' soldier. The common man, the average man, the little man is probably the outstanding hero of the century. He thrives today because of the spread of education, social legislation, greater economic opportunity, and the redistribution of wealth through taxation. Nor will we tolerate being pushed around. Exploitation of man by man is on the way out.
3. This is an age of managed economies and the welfare state, if only because the old laissez-faire system has broken down. Governments today prop up the economy, go in for vast exercises in paternalism and deficit spending, regulate industry, support agriculture, administer scientific research, sponsor education and housing, and exercise wide regulatory powers over banking, the stock exchanges, transportation, power, and communications.
4. This is an age of almost limitless abundance and economic well-being, but a disgraceful amount of poverty remains. Our Gross National Product has risen from $102 billion in 1929 to $554.9 billion in 1962, but between 40 and 50 million Americans are still classified as 'poor'. . . . There are more than 79 million cars and trucks on the roads in the United States today, but a substantial segment of the nation is still inadequately housed, clothed, and fed. The national budget stands at nearly $100 billion (half of it for defense), but a lot of us still have trouble paying the grocery bill. Also, there have come tremendous changes in industrial management and production, including the new role of computers, a fantastic growth in sales, and the influence of Madison Avenue merchandising—something unknown in 1900. Roughly 4,000 passenger automobiles were sold in the United States in 1900, and almost seven million in 1962. Then, too, women play a role in the national economy overwhelmingly greater than before.
5. This era has been distinguished also by the most formidable educational advance in history, partly because rank-and-file people almost everywhere demand education as a natural right. It is no longer doled out or reserved for the privileged.
6. This is the century in which the Negro problem has become the most gravid, difficult, and cancerous in the nation, one that can only be solved by full civil rights for our Negro population.
7. This is the age in which colonialism (except in a few isolated areas) disappeared. Thirteen Asian countries have become free since World War II, including such giants as

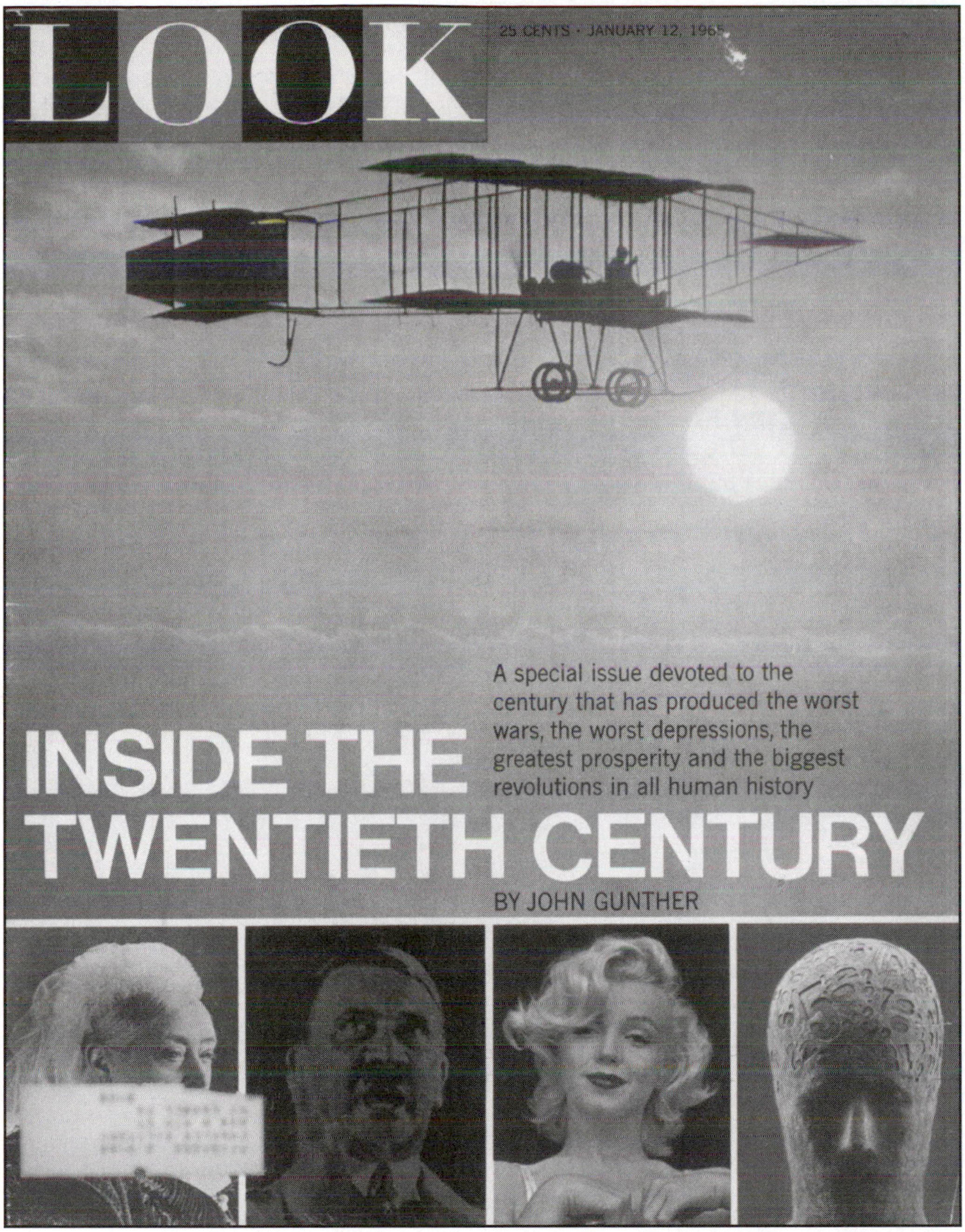
LOOK
25 CENTS · JANUARY 12, 1965
A special issue devoted to the century that has produced the worst wars, the worst depressions, the greatest prosperity and the biggest revolutions in all human history
INSIDE THE TWENTIETH CENTURY
BY JOHN GUNTHER

India, Indonesia, and Pakistan (respectively, the second, fifth, and sixth biggest nations in the world in population), and no fewer than 33 nations in Africa. . . .

8. The principal imponderable in today's political picture is the position of Communist China, with its 684.4 million people—particularly since 1964 when it exploded its first nuclear device. China has attacked India and still threatens it. Much in the general international field will depend on future developments between China and the Soviet Union, which are in a puzzling flux. Meanwhile, relations between the U.S. and U.S.S.R., pivotal to everything, have eased a bit, but they may not stay eased for long. . . .

9. This is the era in which, atop everything, above everything, is poised dangerously the supreme question of peace or war. A paradox brings hope. It is that the nuclear stalemate prevailing today makes full-scale war impossible (except for egregious blunder or accident), if only because no nation can reasonably hope to win. Absolute military power did not come with the bomb, but went out."

1966 Family Profile

Luther Henderson, a 22-year-old African-American rookie baseball player, is being hailed as the next Ted Williams based on his talent, power, and hustle. He plays first base for the Washington Senators.

Annual Income: $75,000

Annual Budget

The average per capita consumer expenditures in 1966 for all workers nationwide are:

Auto Parts	$19.33
Auto Usage	$294.06
Clothing	$158.73
Dentists	$15.26
Food	$555.05
Furniture	$35.61
Gas and Oil	$81.40
Health Insurance	$15.26
Housing	$353.58
Intercity Transport	$11.70
Local Transport	$10.68
New Auto Purchase	$106.84
Personal Care	$117.52
Physicians	$46.29
Private Education	$39.68
Recreation	$156.69
Religion/Welfare Activities	$43.24
Telephone and Telegraph	$35.61

Tobacco	$43.24
Utilities	$93.10
Per Capita Consumption	$2,450.14

Life at Home

- Luther is living in an apartment outside Washington, DC, which the Senators helped him locate; though he wants a house, his teammates have told him to go slow with his money because "rookie money" can disappear.
- During the season, he travels with the team three to four days a week; he is excited about being in the majors, but finds the size of Washington, DC, intimidating.
- Because he is afraid to drive in the city, he takes cabs to work.

- He has also learned that city women are more aggressive; when he was in the minor leagues, he found it difficult to meet women, but as a Washington Senator, he is approached by women for dates.
- At age nine, he began picking cotton 12 hours a day in Mississippi alongside his mother; to forget the bleeding sores on his hands, he dreamed of becoming a major league baseball player.
- From an early age, it was his dream to help his mother escape the poverty of picking cotton, which paid $2.50 for every hundred pounds.
- At age 14, he left sharecropping with his family and moved into the city.
- His mother did housework for others, making approximately $20 a week.
- To support his mother, he dropped out of high school during his sophomore year; the principal worked out a special arrangement that allowed Luther to work in a dry-cleaning plant and still attend classes on a rearranged schedule.
- Eventually he was able to play baseball, basketball, and football in high school; Southern California offered him a football scholarship, while Oklahoma wanted him to play basketball; he selected professional baseball because he knew a contract would bring immediate cash to his family.
- He signed at the earliest possible moment, midnight of the day he graduated from high school.
- When he got the signing bonus of $10,000, he went home, asked his mother to sit at the kitchen table, and put a pile of money in front of her, telling her she would never have to work again.
- Now that he is in the majors, he plans to build his mother a home.
- His only real interest is baseball, which he loves to talk about morning, noon, and night—on trains, buses, and in hotel lobbies.
- His tastes run to brightly colored clothes; now that he has money for the first time, he enjoys spending it.
- While on a road trip, he bought himself a Sunbeam electric toothbrush for $14.99, and he found for his mother an electric knife with twin reciprocating blades for $16.99 in the same store.

Life at Work

- Luther is a rookie baseball player with the Washington Senators, called up from the minor leagues after the season began.
- At 6'2" and 220 pounds, he is considered a big professional athlete, though he moves with the grace of a smaller man.

Henderson waited four years to reach the major leagues.

- He signed a professional contract at age 18, immediately following his high school graduation night in Greenville, Mississippi.
- Considering the potential he has shown, his signing bonus of $10,000 was low, probably due to his lack of exposure in Mississippi.
- The scout who found Luther was the first Negro scout ever employed by the team.
- Traditionally, the scout would write a letter to the director of the minor league system when he found a promising prospect, but when he saw Luther play in high school, he raced to a telephone.
- Luther has played in the minor league system for the past four years, hoping for a shot at the major leagues.
- To gain additional experience, he played winter baseball in Nicaragua, gaining confidence in his ability to play at the highest level of his sport.
- In high school and in the minor leagues he played third base; with the Senators he is playing first base.
- This season, he has improved his batting average by taking the advice from veteran players, who told him to use a heavier bat; he now swings a 36-inch bat, which results in more control and fewer strikeouts.
- His teammates enjoy telling stories about his power, including game-winning home runs off the scoreboard in center field.
- His biggest weakness is chasing bad pitches just outside the strike zone, though he is learning to be more patient at the plate.
- Competing managers are predicting he will hit .340 to .350 once he learns the strike zone and understands how to read major league pitchers.
- He is currently batting sixth in the line-up with a .289 average; the Senators are given little chance of winning the pennant.
- The Senators have never enjoyed the popularity of the National Football League's Washington Redskins, for whose games tickets are often as hard to get as a White House invitation.

Life in the Community: Washington, DC

- Washington is a town of amazing diversity and contrasts, ranging from the posh Georgetown section to the poverty of the inner city.
- Washington has two major products: government and tourism.
- Approximately 35,000 civil servants drive into town every day from the Virginia and Maryland suburbs; the Washington metropolitan area comprises approximately three million people.
- Approximately 20 million people enjoy the city's tourist attractions each year.
- Demonstrators, whose causes and concerns are numerous, are also attracted to the city in large numbers.
- Civil Rights activists known as the Free DC Movement are currently picketing and boycotting Washington retail businesses that are not supporting a move toward home rule for the city.
- The federal city's total land area is only 61 square miles, with a population of approximately 700,000; 70 percent are black.

Editorial, "Self-Protection," *Washington Post*, May 2, 1966:

"Are the people of Washington adequately armed for their own protection? There are no more than 65,000 handguns registered in the District of Columbia. The local populace is not, of course, as completely helpless as this pathetic figure would suggest. District police are able to register only such handguns as are purchased inside the District from licensed District dealers. Thanks to the complete ineffectuality of existing federal firearms legislation, anyone at all—from the first grader to the high-school dropout, from a despondent housewife to a rejected suitor, from the graduate of the District Jail to the graduate of St. Elizabeth's—can get a pistol by mail order from any of a number of flourishing commercial enterprises. And, as everyone knows, he can still arm himself in the suburbs without having his purchase registered in the District, although this now entails, under the terms of recently adopted legislation, an annoying and frustrating delay to those who may be in a hurry to dispatch a spouse or settle some altercation with a neighbor.

So the solution is not as bad as one might think from the bare figures. There is an ample supply of weapons for those who want to hold up liquor stores, gas stations, groceries, or foreign embassies in Washington. There are still many citizens, however, who have no pistols with which to protect themselves from citizens who do have pistols. Would it not be sensible, therefore, to encourage the sale of pistols through street corner vending machines? Surely the ingenuity that can perfect a device capable of delivering a Tootsie Roll in response to the deposit of a dime could work out a way of delivering instantly a Colt .45 or a Smith and Wesson .38 in order to put self-protection within the easy reach of everyone."

"Congressmen Tap Outside Sources to Bolster Their $30,000 Salaries," by Richard Harwood, *The Washington Post*, May 1, 1966:

"A week ago in Thomas Corcoran's capacious backyard in Woodley Park, a sparse crowd of lawyers, lobbyists, and politicians gathered to celebrate the twenty-fifth wedding anniversary of Senator and Mrs. Thomas McIntyre of New Hampshire.

It was not a celebration in the traditional mold. The price of admission was $100. The party was not the idea of the host—a lawyer-lobbyist whose clients include the Tennessee Gas Transmission Company of Houston—but of a Chevy Chase housewife, Mrs. Esther Coopersmith, who has made a hobby of raising money for 'fine Democratic candidates.'

The turnout of about 150 people was smaller than expected. Not all the guests paid. The 'candidate'—Senator McIntyre—is not officially a candidate for anything, though his Senate term expires this year. And the proceeds from the affair will be used, the Senator has said, not for a political campaign, but to underwrite McIntyre's entertainment and office expenses during the next few months.

This pleasant gathering on a Sunday afternoon symbolized the ethic dilemmas and the financial problems confronting public men of every description in Washington today. They are reaching out into the private society in increasing numbers for financial help to subsidize the political way of life.

Rep. Morris Udall (D-Arizona) recently accepted a $30,000 testimonial dinner gift to underwrite various office expenses and his extensive travels back home.

Rep. Paul J. Krebs (D-New Jersey) has set up the Paul J. Krebs Civic Association to collect funds for political purposes, including the purchase of tickets for 'political, social, and charitable affairs.'

Rep. William D. Hathaway (D-Maine) has created a Hathaway Newsletter and Public Information Committee to underwrite his publicity activities.

The DC Western Development Committee was created to subsidize the travels of Sen. Quentin Burdick (D-North Dakota).

Indiana's six Democratic Congressmen and two Democratic Senators received subsidies averaging $1,500 last year from the Indiana State Democratic Committee. The Committee's main sources of revenue are (1) a two-percent levy on the salaries of 14,000 Indiana state employees, and (2) a $0.04 tribute collected on every automobile license plate sold in the state. . . .

These practices raise serious questions for the public and for the public men who benefit from them. Should Congressmen be subsidized by lobbyists, special interest groups, and other contributors whose careers often depend on their ability to influence public policy? Is the Washington lifestyle so lavish that a Senator or Congressman is unable to live on a $30,000 salary? Are his office allowances so niggardly he must seek charity to meet his obligations?

Precisely these questions are at the heart of the current controversy over Sen. Thomas J. Dodd's financial practices. The senatorial way of life, his associates have said, is so costly that Dodd was forced to accept somewhere between $100,000 and $200,000 in 'testimonial gifts' from constituents, political allies, and lobbyists.

'It is well known,' Dodd's friends have said, 'that a Senator's salary is inadequate and that for most men in Washington the "break-even" point on expenses is about $50,000 a year. Unless a Senator has outside income he is in financial difficulty. . . . Testimonial dinners enable a poor man to remain in office. They are part of the American way of life.' "

"The Ku Klux Klan Is Moving Boldly into the Open in a Last-Ditch Fight against Integration; 'We Got Nothing to Hide,'" by Harold H. Martin and Kenneth Fairly, *The Saturday Evening Post*, January 30, 1965:

"One starlit evening not long ago, in a tobacco patch near the little town of Hemingway, South Carolina, 29 robed and hooded men and women gathered in a circle around a 50-foot black-gum cross which had been wrapped in burlap and soaked in crankcase oil. Solemnly they set the towering shaft ablaze and marched around it singing, as a record player hitched up to a loud-speaker boomed into the darkness the opening strains of the 'The Old Rugged Cross.' Suddenly the needle stuck, and over the dark woods surrounding the little field, the speaker repeated over and over the phrase that ends the first line of the song, '. . . and shame'—'and shame'—'and shame.'

If the Klansmen who set the cross aflame felt any shame at this use of the symbol of Christian brotherhood to publicize an organization which thrives on racial hatred, they gave no sign of it. There was nothing clandestine about the meeting in the Masonic Hall in Hemingway; ladies of the Klan sold barbecue, slaw, cake, and soda pop, and passed out literature extolling the noble purposes of the order. At the rally itself, on a flatbed truck decorated with Confederate and American flags, the assembled Dragons, Titans, and Exalted Cyclopses of the two Carolinas sat proudly in their emerald, white, and crimson robes, waiting for 'his Lordship,' one Robert Shelton of Tuscaloosa, Alabama, Imperial Wizard of the United Klans of America Knights.

None wore a mask. 'We want you to see our faces,' bellowed Robert Scoggins, the Grand Dragon of South Carolina, to the crowd of 800 men, women, and barefoot children who stood before the speakers' platform in the glare of the burning cross. 'We want you to know who we are and what we are doing. We got nothing to hide.'

Passage of the Civil Rights Bill in June of 1964 brought the Klan boldly into the open. All over the South crosses blazed at public rallies. Fierce-eyed preachers, most of them self-ordained, began to shout in public the twisted doctrine they had proclaimed in the secrecy of the Klaverns—that Jesus Christ was not a Jew, that the Pope of Rome was anti-Christ, that the Negro was a beast who must be destroyed. 'Oh, God,' prayed one, 'please put grace and grit into the white race and let us wipe out this black-ape race before it is too late.'

The Saturday Evening Post January 30 1965 25¢
POST
HOW WE'LL REBUILD THE G.O.P.
BY DWIGHT D. EISENHOWER
THE GIRL WHO WROTE
'SEX AND THE SINGLE GIRL'
THE KU KLUX KLAN:
"We got nothing to hide"
GERM WARFARE
THE FAKE DOCTOR
KANGAROO STEW

"My Dear Old Friend! The Last Time We Met Socially, I Tried To Help You Along With A Cattle Prod"

The Voting Rights Act is changing politics in Washington and across the South.

- The city's bedroom counties—Fairfax in Virginia and Montgomery in Maryland, have the highest median income level of any in the nation.
- Lawyers make up the largest single group of professionals in the city; there are close to 20,000 attorneys in Washington, half of whom work for the government.
- Until Brasilia became the capital of Brazil, Washington was the only capital city in the world that was planned before it was built.
- Currently, the area's 3,500 carpenters are on strike, affecting many heavy construction projects in the DC area.
- Congress recently approved $2.9 billion over three years to help build college classrooms.
- The state of Virginia, home of many of Washington's workers, turned back to the federal government $12 million of the $30 million in school aid allocated to the state.
- Howard University has announced a plan to train 45 poor high-school dropouts as teacher's aids in Washington's elementary schools.
- Three African-Americans ran for two Council seats in the nearby town of Seat Pleasant, the first time a black has been on the ballot in the town of 6,800 across the District of Columbia line in Prince George's County; one black candidate won.

Lily-white underwear was your mother's idea.
Here's ours.
Since you're leading a more colorful life now, Paris is making underwear to match.
For a modest $4 each, you can own our zig-zag boxer or tapered shorts and athletic shirts in this less-than-modest color combination:
Or, if you prefer straighter stripes in tapered or boxer shorts, the dynamic duo on the right is available for $4 each in these unrestrained colors:
We also make briefs in both patterns for $3.50. They're comfortable because they're nylon knit, easy to care for, and every color stays as fresh and bright as it looks right here. It's just too bad everybody won't get to see them on you.
Paris
2150 FRONTAGE ROAD, DES PLAINES, ILLINOIS
KR
Another fine product of Kayser-Roth

Historical Snapshot
1966

- The term "Black Power" was introduced into the Civil Rights movement
- The exquisite playing of Jimi Hendrix helped popularize the electric guitar
- The President's Commission on Food Marketing reported that consumers pay 29 percent more for nationally advertised brands than for high-quality local brands
- The per capita consumption of processed potato chips rose from 6.3 pounds a year in 1958 to 14.2 pounds
- Blanket student military deferments were abolished; the draft demand for the Vietnam War was 50,000 young men a month
- Jackie Robinson, the man who broke the color barrier in major league baseball, became the general manager of the Brooklyn Dodgers of the Continental Football League
- The International Days of Protest against the war in Vietnam took place in seven American and seven foreign cities
- The Fillmore Theater in San Francisco popularized strobe lights, liquid color blobs, glow paint, and psychedelic posters
- Boxing Heavyweight Champion Cassius Clay became a Muslim and changed his name to Muhammad Ali
- Civil Rights activist James Meredith was shot during a march from Memphis, Tennessee, to Jackson, Mississippi
- The National Organization for Women (NOW) was formed
- 2,377 corporate mergers took place
- Tape cartridges, stereo cassette decks, lyrics on record albums, and the Rare and Endangered Species List all made their first appearance
- Haynes Johnson of the *Washington Star* won the Pulitzer for his coverage of the Selma, Alabama, Civil Rights conflict; the *Los Angeles Times* staff won the Pulitzer in the local reporting category for its coverage of the racially charged Watts riots
- Frank Robinson became the first baseball player to win a Most Valuable Player award in each league
- Los Angeles Dodger pitcher Sandy Koufax won his third Cy Young Award and retired
- The terms LSD, miniskirt, and Third World came into popular use

1966 ECONOMIC PROFILE

Income, Standard Jobs

Bituminous Coal Mining	$7,398.00
Building Trades	$7,363.00
Domestic Industries	$6,062.00
Domestics	$2,780.00
Farm Labor	$2,923.00
Federal Civilian	$8,170.00

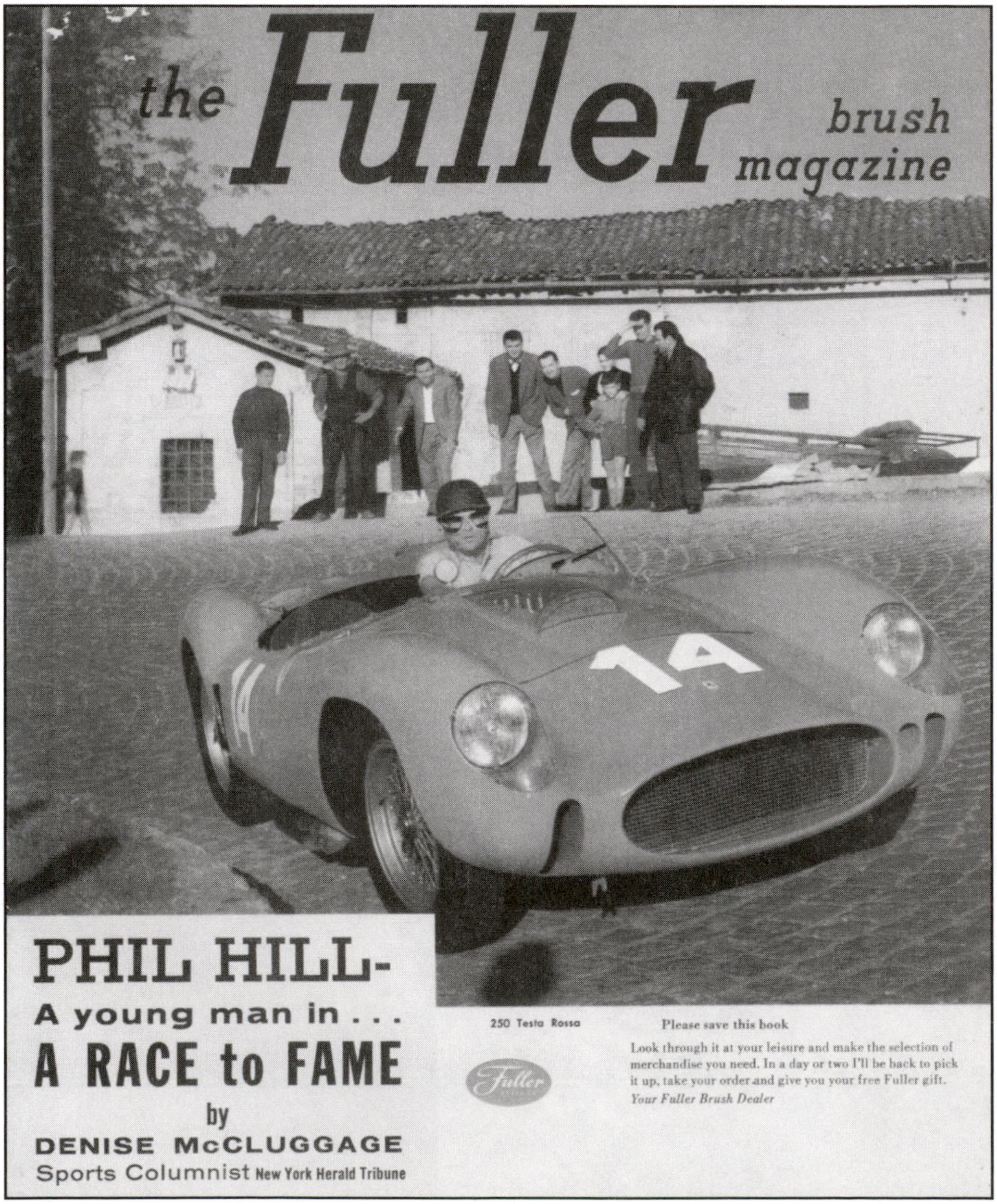

Federal Employees, Executive Departments	$5,921.00
Federal Military	$4,650.00
Finance, Insurance, and Real Estate	$6,239.00
Gas, Electricity, and Sanitation Workers	$7,801.00
Manufacturing, Durable Goods	$7,228.00
Manufacturing, Nondurable Goods	$6,172.00
Medical/Health Services Workers	$4,565.00
Miscellaneous Manufacturing	$5,548.00
Motion Picture Services	$7,397.00
Nonprofit Organization Workers	$4,280.00
Passenger Transportation Workers, Local and Highway	$5,737.00
Personal Services	$4,551.00
Private Industries, Including Farm Labor	$6,098.00
Public School Teachers	$6,142.00

Radio Broadcasting and Television Workers $8,833.00
Railroad Workers $7,708.00
State and Local Government Workers $5,834.00
Telephone and Telegraph Workers $6,858.00
Wholesale and Retail Trade Workers $7,345.00

Selected Prices

Antiques Magazine, Monthly for One Year $12.00
Black and Decker Drill, Electric $19.95
Bloomcraft Art Nouveau Cloth, per Yard $3.50
Custom 7 Transistor Radio $12.95
Delta Airline Fare, Miami $74.70
Englander Mattress, Full Size $59.95
Florient Disinfectant Spray $0.59
Fred Astaire Dance Lessons, Eight Lessons $13.95
Friden Model 132 Electronic Calculator $1,950.00
General Electric Alarm Clock $5.98
Goldblatts Air Conditioner $498.00
Honeywell Slide Projector $149.50
Kutmaster, Two-Bladed Knife $1.00
Magnavox Television $650.00
Major League Warm-Up Jacket $12.95
Old Patina Polish, per Pint $2.25
Pittsburgh Plate Glass Mirror $7.00
Polaroid Color Pack Camera $50.00
Proctor Ice Cream Maker $16.95
Sheffield Candelabra, 22" High $425.00
Simonize Car Wax $0.99
Stiffel Lamp, 22" Height $72.50
Tru-Dent Electric Toothbrush $12.50
Tyco Prairie Sante Fe Locomotive $16.77
Viking Chair $11.95
West Bend Coffee Maker $9.95

"College 'Sex Revolution' Overstressed," by Jean White, *The Washington Post*, May 1, 1966:

"'Nice girls do, and that's that.' (Student at Reed College)

'I don't think there's been a sex revolution in what people are doing—just in the amount they talk about it.' (Radcliffe Co-ed)

'Promiscuity isn't a matter of the pill. . . . It may be easier to have an affair, but just because she's safe from pregnancy doesn't mean a girl is going to sleep with two dozen guys. Female psychology just doesn't work that way.' (University of Texas Co-ed)

'Who cares about a sex revolution? The thing is, how many dates do you have?' (Blonde at Ohio State University.)

Perhaps no revolution in history has been so minutely and flamboyantly reported as the so-called 'sexual revolution' of our time.

It has been debated in magazines and newspapers and on television panels. The scope of concern has ranged from the morality of it all to this fine point of etiquette raised in a question to an advice-to-the-lovelorn columnist: Should the man or woman pay for the pills for an affair?

The discussion has necessarily focused on the campus, where the first Post-Pill Generation has come of sexual age. Now even a best-selling book can be patched together from the quotes of 600 co-eds talking about their sex life on campus.

On the other hand, 'I'm not at all convinced that the activity matches the conversation,' says Clark E. Vincent, a family-life professor at the Bowman Gray School of Medicine at Winston-Salem.

Paul H. Gebhard, one of the authors of The Kinsey Report and Kinsey's successor as director of the Institute for Sex Research at Indiana University, agrees. He points to what he wryly calls the 'terrific amount of verbalization about sex' these days. . . .

With all the present ferment about campus sex, Gebhard feels that there is a need for 'hard data' beyond talk to document any revolution that has occurred. He has applied for a quarter-million-dollar federal grant to study sexual behavior on college campuses.

He shouldn't have any trouble collecting both views and experiences from the students, a survey of college correspondents of the *Washington Post* shows. They supplied most of the quotations and other material for this article, which was rounded out with observations from several specialists.

The survey report points to these conclusions:

The modern 'sexual revolution' has been inflated and overreported. One distortion has come from the overexposure of the sex life of the single student—and the brashest are always the most quotable.

'No one ever seems to write about the sex life of the 41-year-old truck driver or the 30-year-old matron these days,' complains Gebhard, 'and whoever interviews the girl who sits around the dorm and studies?'

Sociologist Vincent points out that an interviewer could talk to a half-dozen girls at each of 20 colleges and conclude that the sex has broken wide open; then go back and choose sets of six other girls and conclude that this is an age of prudery.

Or as a 22-year-old English major at Harvard put it: 'It's not really the "new moralists" who are talking, but the "new blabbermouths".'

The 'sexual revolution' is not all talk, however. Campus sex morals have been changing, and these changes must be taken seriously in contrast to the sensationalism of the free-love exhibitionists whose dirty words match their discarded dirty clothes at naked sex orgies.

In sex ethics, as in many other areas, young men and women are honestly questioning the relevance of old codes to contemporary society. The move is from stern 'thou-shalt-not' morality to more permissiveness and self-determination.

These changes are evident in two main areas: (1) freer discussion of sex, and (2) more

(continued)

"College 'Sex Revolution' . . ." *(continued)*

premarital sex between 'serious' couples and more open living together before marriage. . . .

In a recent report on 'Sex and the College Student,' a committee of the Group for the Advancement of Psychiatry (GAP) has this to say about campus sex:

'There is general agreement that premarital sexual relations among undergraduate college students are more frequent than they were a generation ago. Certain students are more open in their activities and more vocal in their prerogatives.'

The report goes on to note a tolerance of behavior that would have been censured a few decades ago and even now is questioned in many quarters. Only 25 years ago, the GAP committee points out, the college boy went into 'town' for a sexual experience. Today, his partner is likely to be a college girl on campus."

"The Inside Story of The NFL-AFL Merger," by Bob Stewart, *Complete Sports*, November 1966:

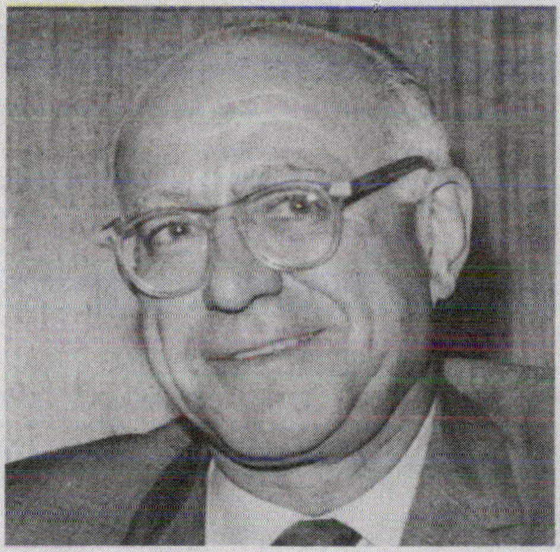
Sonny Werblin

"Sonny Werblin relaxed over his coffee. His luncheon date with one of the New York newspapermen this Tuesday afternoon of May 24 had run quite a bit longer than he had intended. But then, such affairs always take up more time than you anticipate, and he had enjoyed the session. He had had yet one more opportunity to preach his gospel of unrelenting war with the National Football League, just so long as that league chose to fight, rather than talk on sensible, business-like terms.

Werblin's spectacular success with the New York team in the American Football League had altered all concepts of the pro-football world. It has been axiomatic that no league in any sport can succeed without a profitable, going concern in New York. Even the National League in baseball had rued its decision to pull the Giants and Dodgers from the big town, and recouped only by installing the ridiculous but rich Mets back in the United States' prime market.

Werblin, with a career of success behind him in showmanship, had seen the staggering possibilities of a New York Football League franchise. When the ill-fated, mismanaged Titans of the new league provided an albatross of staggering weight, he had stepped in, purchased its assets and, to some extent liabilities, and proceeded to provide the franchise with the magic touch—money.

It had taken two years of unrelenting labor, but the green-clad team through unlimited money had become the strongest entry in a league which had been hanging on, even without a premier showcase in New York.

Acceptable finally as a going, solid concern, the AFL had been assured of financial stability through a multi-million-dollar virtual sponsorship by the National Broadcasting Company, which, as always, was locked in its rating war with the Columbia Broadcasting System. Pro-football had become as much an NBC-CBS struggle as an AFL-NFL battle for survival.

Over his coffee, Werblin now permitted himself a secret smile. He had, as ever, sounded off about the ultimate victory of his AFL and Jets over the NFL and the Giants. That that (sic) was even closer, he had not intimated. The newspapermen recapitulating his notes had not asked, nor could not know, that this very evening the owners of other AFL franchises were meeting in Werblin's apartment to hear what Lamar Hunt had to say about the peace terms being offered by Tex Schramm of the Dallas Cowboys, with the authority of Pete Rozelle and his NFL superiors.

Rozelle and his owners knew that continuation of the struggle was senseless. The AFL, through its TV package and the 50,000-plus attendance at Shea Stadium, as well as increased dates in its other cities—even those cities deemed 'bush'—could hold out for years, and in that time the savage cost could only lacerate those NFL teams that could not approach the blasé, happy circumstances which had made New York Giant season tickets an item for divorce settlements or last will and testament codicils.

Yet, the independence of the AFL owners could prove financially frightening. Wellington Mara of New York had signed Pete Gogolak, the

(continued)

"The Inside Story . . ." *(continued)*

astonishing field goal kicker who had played out his option with the Buffalo team of the AFL. This seemingly minor transaction in terms of cost had pried open the Pandora's Box, for now in retaliation the Werblins, the Wilsons, the Hunts of the AFL could and would go to NFL stars, offer them staggering contracts to be signed once said NFL greats had played out their options.

The college draft had been brutal, with All-Americans sitting back calmly with their attorneys while the two leagues bickered, bargained, and undercut each other. The bonus money proliferated, so much so that Joe Namath's $400,000 a year before was taken as the guideline to be surpassed."

LIFE
THE TEXAS SNIPER
Store window shattered by bullets fired from tower in background by Charles Whitman
AUGUST 12 · 1966 · 35¢

1968 Family Profile

Woody and Eva Duker operate a ski lodge in Winter Park, Colorado, providing food and lodging for the legions of skiers now coming to the Colorado Rockies each year.

Annual Income: $13,800

Annual Budget

The average per capita consumer expenditures in 1968 for all workers nationwide are:

Auto Parts	$22.92
Auto Usage	$338.80
Clothing	$178.87
Dentists	$19.93
Food	$605.86
Furniture	$39.36
Gas and Oil	$92.67
Health Insurance	$19.93
Housing	$397.09
Intercity Transport	$15.45
Local Transport	$11.96
New Auto Purchase	$122.07
Personal Business	$141.00
Personal Care	$52.81
Physicians	$54.31
Private Education	$49.33
Recreation	$182.85
Religion/Welfare Activities	$51.32
Telephone and Telegraph	$41.35
Tobacco	$46.83

Winter Park is now dotted with quality ski lodges.

Utilities $100.15
Per Capita Consumption $2,785.67

Life at Home

- The Dukers maintain a double room in the back of the lodge as their home, constantly commingling life at home with life at work.
- Their lodge is one of the oldest in the area, and though their facilities are aging, their customers are loyal.
- They are worried that if they do not install saunas, improve lighting, and upgrade the lodge, people will stop coming; if they do make all the improvements, they are unsure if they will make enough to stay in business.
- The skiing season extends from December through April, when they make all of their income for the year.
- In May and June they like to travel—if the ski season has been lucrative enough.
- Last year, this ski lodge and Winter Park in general experienced a 12-percent drop in business from the previous year.
- They are hoping that the 1968–69 season will be better.
- To ensure more business, this couple is part of a group lobbying for artificial snowmaking, a recent innovation in some ski areas.
- They believe it will help them create a longer season by laying a base earlier and help attract more skiers who know that an adequate base will always be available.
- Snowmaking is not only expensive, but requires tremendous quantities of water; some large Eastern ski areas spend $50,000 or more to produce snow during a season.
- Snowmaking is feasible only in locations where the nightly temperature range is from 20 to 25 degrees, and Winter Park certainly qualifies.
- In 1963, Ski Broadmoor and Geneva Basin in Colorado both installed snowmaking equipment; currently, snowmaking facilities are available on the lower practice slopes at seven ski areas.
- Communities such as Aspen and Vail are developing year-round recreation centers to attract visitors all year; Woody and Eva would love to be less dependent on just five months' activity to support them the entire year.
- A recent decision by the federal government to group holidays on Mondays, creating three-day weekends, looks like it may increase their business, but they are unsure.
- Winter Park has a long history as a ski resort; many in Denver consider Winter Park the "locals" place to ski.
- A current survey of skiers shows that Vail, Winter Park, Aspen, Stowe, and Mammoth are their favorite weekend ski areas.

- The survey shows that the skiers' favorite resorts are Vail, Aspen, Winter Park, Europe, Sun Valley, Alta, Jackson Hole, Squaw Valley, Steamboat, Stowe, and Breckenridge.
- The Dukers fear that the real action is now at Aspen's Buttermilk Mountain or Meadow Mountain near Vail.

Life at Work

- The ski industry of Colorado and Winter Park is experiencing phenomenal growth.
- The number of skiers visiting Colorado during the 1966-67 season increased by 14 times since the 1955–56 season.
- Non-resident skiers spent an estimated $41.3 million during the 1966-67 season compared with $3 million in 1955–56.
- Overall lift ticket sales throughout Colorado increased 15.2 percent from 1965–66 to 1966–67, but competition is cutting into income.
- Statewide, the ski lift ticket sales increased to $1,221,300.
- Unfortunately, last year the number of skiers using the Winter Park lifts dropped from 203,000 during the 1965–66 season to 179,200 in 1966–67, a drop of 11.8 percent.
- The Winter Park community is concerned; Arapahoe Basis, Buttermilk Mountain, Crested Butte, Monarch, and Snowmass all had a 20 percent or more increase in ski lift use.

- Some areas are experimenting with night skiing to improve revenues and increase usage; most of these areas are on the lower slopes such as Arapahoe Basis, Durango, Meadow Mountain, and Snowmass.
- As the number of ski areas increases, attracting more skiers, the number of lodges also swells.
- Currently, 20 lodges operate in Winter Park.
- Most tend to be geared to family skiers, offering a warm, friendly atmosphere with little emphasis on nightlife.
- Rates run from $3.50 for a single to $28 for a double.
- The Dukers' lodge charges $10 a night for a single and $18 for a double, breakfast and dinner included.
- Winter Park is the last ski area in America to be served by a genuine snow train, operated by the Rio Grande Railroad on Saturdays and Sundays during the season.
- Locals believe that one of the most awe-inspiring sights in skiing is seeing the train disgorge its load of 1,000 or more Denver skiers.
- This type of activity handicaps the ski lodge, which needs week-long visitors to maximize its profits; weekend guests only rent for one or two days, while the staff works all seven.
- Winter Park is known for grooming its slopes to withstand the onslaught of visitors, using the Bradley-Packer-Grader, which chops off moguls.

- Topography is Colorado's—and Winter Park's—greatest asset; its light-powder snow is extremely good and offers a great variety of experiences to the vacation skier. It is also high-altitude skiing, which for some takes a little getting used to.
- Winter Park attracts skiers who consider skiing a leisure activity; it also attracts big names in racing, both for training and actual races.
- On weekends, Winter Park is packed with Denver skiers who make the one-hour drive up the mountain—often on a whim.
- Many skiers, including tourists who arrive at Denver by air, make their skiing destination decision based on which area has the "best powder" for maximum skiing conditions.
- Many believe that Rocky Mountain Powder is easier to ski than any snow in the world.

Life in the Community: Winter Park, Colorado

- Skiing impacts every part of Colorado's, and Winter Park's, economy.
- Industries tied to the success of the season include the airlines, auto rental agencies, service stations, real estate developments, restaurants, lodging places, and ski clothing and equipment manufacturers and retailers.
- A skier will spend more than $300 on skiwear and equipment before hitting the slopes.
- Currently, the cost of skis is about $170; boots cost $80 and bindings, $30; gloves will cost $30 a pair, while ski poles run $35 a pair.
- The state now boasts 38 ski areas in operation; 22 are open daily and 16 operate on weekends only.
- Most are located below the timberline, at 7,000 to 11,000 feet in altitude; the altitude protects the slopes and makes them less susceptible to sudden thaws and freezes, giving Colorado a natural advantage over other ski areas.
- Last year, more than $41 million in Colorado was spent by non-resident skiers; Colorado accounts for more than 27 percent of all skiing expenditures in the 12 Western states.

"Why Ski Colorado?" *Colorado Skiing*, 1968:

"Colorado's light, silky powder snow is unique in the American West. It has to be skied to be believed. Powder snow is abundant in Colorado because of the dependable west winds that bring bounteous moisture from the Pacific. Colorado snow is dry and powdery because the wind's long journey over the desert has evaporated the excess moisture out of the clouds before the sharp cold of the Rockies makes it fall. Colorado powder remains sparkling and white because the dry, smog-free air keeps the snow crisp and white long after it falls.

Colorado ski lodges are new—built within the last five to 10 years, for the most part. This means up-to-date facilities: baths, saunas, comfortable beds, adequate heating, and heated swimming pools. It also means modern means of management, assuring prompt replies to your inquiries, and a minimum of confusion and reservations, even at peak seasons.

As a state, Colorado is less than 100 years old, scarcely two generations from frontier times. As a result, Colorado people still have much of the old-time frontier openness and friendliness to the stranger that is lost in many overcrowded parts of America. Sprinkled in with native Coloradans are many newcomers: Swiss, Austrian, German, Italian, and French skiers, as well as Eastern Americans who have 'gone West' to ski, and never returned."

- One quarter of a skier's expenditures goes to lodging and meals; another quarter is consumed by lift ticket fees and the rest is spent on transportation and after-skiing activities.
- Resident skiers spend an average of $20 per day during weekend trips, while the average for non-residents is about $57 a day.
- United Airlines is spending $1 million to promote ski travel, hoping to generate $22 million in business.
- Approximately 80 to 90 percent of the revenues will result in trips to Colorado; 100 percent of the advertising is displayed in Chicago and along the East and West coasts.
- United began its ski promotions in 1962 with a $100,000 promotional movie called *Ski Country U.S.A.*, which produced a return of $2.6 million in new business, and its commitment to ski-travel promotions has increased every year since.
- United is also adding a direct "snowbird" flight into Grand Junction from both Chicago and Los Angeles.
- For the past two years, the state has spent record amounts to promote Colorado as the nation's ski resort center of America; as a result, in 1966, the Burlington Railroad carried 1,837 out-of-state skiers into Colorado aboard 31 special ski trains from Illinois and Texas.
- Continental Airlines reported that it brought 1,262 sets of skis into Denver in special flight boxes during the holiday season, up 46 percent over last year.

Historical Snapshot
1968

- The Vietnam War became the longest war in U.S. history; protests against the war intensified
- Vietnam casualties exceeded the total for the Korean War
- BankAmericard holders passed 14 million, up 12 million in two years
- Automobile production reached 8.8 million cars
- Compact microwave ovens for home use became available
- Volkswagen captured 57 percent of the U.S. import market
- Television advertising revenues passed $2 billion, twice that of radio
- First-class postage increased to $0.06
- Robert Lehman bequeathed 3,000 works valued at more than $100 million to the Metropolitan Museum of Art
- The Uniform Monday Holiday law was enacted by Congress, creating three-day weekends
- Martin Luther King, Jr., was assassinated in Memphis, Tennessee; riots erupted in more than 100 cities
- The average farm subsidy was nearly $1,000; the average farm produced enough food for 47 people
- Shirley Chisholm of New York became the first black woman elected to the U.S. House of Representatives
- Protestors at the Miss America Pageant threw bras, girdles, curlers, false eyelashes, and wigs into the Freedom Trash Can
- Twenty thousand were added monthly to New York's welfare rolls; one fourth of the city's budget was allocated to welfare
- Celibacy of the priesthood became an issue in the Catholic Church; Pope Paul VI's ban on contraception was challenged by 800 U.S. theologians
- Violent crimes were up 57 percent since 1960
- Yale admitted women for the first time
- On the nightly TV news, the nation watched the Saigon chief of police calmly shoot a prisoner in the head
- Film courses and Black Studies programs were developed at many colleges
- The Poor People's Campaign, led by the Reverend Ralph Abernathy, arrived in Washington, DC
- IBM stocks split again; 100 shares purchased in 1914 for $2,750 now totaled 59,320 shares valued at more than $20 million
- The American Medical Association formulated a new standard of death: "brain dead"

1968 Economic Profile

Income, Standard Jobs

Bituminous Coal Mining	$8,169.00
Building Trades	$8,332.00
Domestic Industries	$6,759.00
Domestics	$3,254.00
Farm Labor	$3,327.00
Federal Civilian	$9,002.00
Federal Employees, Executive Departments	$6,520.00
Federal Military	$5,148.00
Finance, Insurance, and Real Estate	$6,994.00
Gas, Electricity, and Sanitation Workers	$8,666.00
Manufacturing, Durable Goods	$8,002.00
Manufacturing, Nondurable Goods	$6,849.00
Medical/Health Services Workers	$5,292.00
Miscellaneous Manufacturing	$6,252.00
Motion Picture Services	$7,946.00
Nonprofit Organization Workers	$4,655.00
Passenger Transportation Workers, Local and Highway	$6,279.00
Personal Services	$4,960.00
Private Industries, Including Farm Labor	$6,772.00
Public School Teachers	$7,129.00
Radio Broadcasting and Television Workers	$9,563.00
Railroad Workers	$8,663.00
State and Local Government Workers	$7,255.00
Telephone and Telegraph Workers	$7,506.00
Wholesale and Retail Trade Workers	$8,142.00

Selected Prices

Arrow Shirt	$7.50
Black & Decker Electric Drill	$10.99
Black & Decker Saw	$27.77
Bond's Famous "Executive Group" Hat	$7.99
Brach's Chocolate Covered-Cherries, 12 Ounces	$0.47
Folger's Coffee, Two-Pound Can	$1.27
Frigidaire, 12.3 Cubic Feet	$208.00

General Electric Dishwasher $119.25
Gillette Foamy Shaving Cream, 11-Ounce Can $0.59
Gillette Razor Blades $0.99
Hunts Catsup, 14-Ounce Bottle $0.22
Jarman Shoes $22.00
Just Wonderful Hairspray, 12-Ounce Can $0.47
Nu-Nails Artificial Fingernails, per 10 . . . . $0.49
Polaroid Color Pack Camera $50.00
Proctor Blender $13.49
Roller Pan Painting Set $0.49
Schlitz Beer, Six Pack $0.99
Speed Queen Dryer $178.00
Volkswagen Automobile $2,602.00

The Winter Park Ski Industry

- Up until the turn of the century, skiing was largely a means of survival, not recreation.
- Ski clubs formed in the 1920s, but in the days before rope tows or T-Bars, skiers walked up the trail for the privilege of a short ride down the mountain.
- The dream of creating a mountain ski area was assisted by the completion of a railway line in the 1930s.
- George E. Cranmer was the father of the Winter Park ski area; he dreamed of a mountain city park that could become a winter sports center.
- He envisioned this city park—60 miles from the city—as a recreational "gift to the children of Denver."
- He was supported by a group of prominent Denver businessmen who formed themselves into the Arlberg Club.
- A clubhouse was built on the Mary Jane Placer claim in 1933; the U.S. Forest Service cut trails by 1937.
- In 1938, the U.S. Forest Service granted the City of Denver a special-use permit for some 6,400 acres of land for winter sports and recreational development.

- That same year, the Denver City Council accepted a grant from the Federal Emergency Administration of Public Works to construct park improvements to include ski tows and ski-ways.
- In 1939, the city of Denver acquired 100 acres of land at the mouth of Jim Creek, adjacent to West Portal.
- To assist in the promotion of this new ski area, the name West Portal was changed to the more family-oriented "Winter Park."
- A crowd of 10,000 turned out for the first annual three-day "Winter Sports Festival."
- By 1942, a snow train carrying 500 Denver children began the tradition of weekend skiing Cranmer dreamed about.
- By 1946, with the war ending, skier volume broke all records; Winter Park was firmly established as a ski destination.

Survey of Vail (Colorado) Skiers: Conclusions, 1968:

"He is younger than we had previously believed—29.2 years, as compared with our hypothetical 35-year-old average skier. Even accounting for holiday and weekend incursions of students, this average age indicates a departure from the classic long-stay resort guest pattern. Apparently, higher incomes among young college graduates, greater mobility, and increased vacation time have allowed a younger crowd to enjoy the type of winter resort experience once reserved for the affluent middle-aged.

There is a curious inconsistency in the length of stay as compared to the type of (lift) tickets sold. The average stay is 5.2 days (6.4 days for the in-week guest). Yet only 22 percent of those surveyed bought five- or seven-day tickets and seven percent bought packages, while 46 percent bought single day tickets! It is obvious that many customers prefer to keep their options open, skiing when they wish, rather than locking themselves into a week of daily skiing. In this respect, the Vail skier is more like the European skier, whose activity pattern is relaxed and varied, than the traditional western resort customer, who skis determinedly, every day, during his vacation.

As might be expected, the Vail skier, like most other sportsmen, somewhat over-evaluates his abilities. Note that he has listed as his favorite slopes at Vail the three most difficult areas: The Bowls, Prima, and Riva Ridge. Yet 49 percent of all surveyed are beginning or intermediate skiers, who have no business skiing such slopes. Dreams of glory intrude even into the dry pages of a customer survey.

As brought into sharp focus by this survey, the Vail customer is nearly ideal from a ski resort marketing point of view. He is young, affluent, highly mobile, well-educated, largely white-collar in profession.

Even more significant, in view of the product Vail offers, is his dedication to skiing. A skier for nearly seven years, he intends to devote a month of each year to the sport. His family skis, too, and nearly everyone owns his ski equipment (88 percent).

He is largely undemanding, in terms of the more sophisticated frills of resort life, so long as the skiing is good. If lifts run smoothly, and slopes and snow are right, he is a happy, satisfied customer. Only a few small clouds darken his horizon. Because many others like him have discovered Vail, there are lift lines at peak holiday times, and prices for Vail-type facilities seem too high."

- Skiers could stay overnight in a bunkhouse for $0.50.
- By 1949, ski trains carrying up to 1,500 people were arriving in Winter Park for a week-end of fun.
- The *Chicago Tribune* praised the access to the area by train; skiing in the Denver area increased by 75 percent, with more than 26,500 skiing during the 1949–50 season.

- New lifts increased capacity in the 1950s; at the same time, Winter Park began grooming its slopes—an innovative feature.
- The popularity of Winter Park spread during the 1960s Olympics at Squaw Valley, where many of the area's ski patrols participated in the international event.
- By 1967, the Winter Park Ski School had grown to 28 instructors because of demand.

"Will Lift-Skiing Spoil Snowmass?" by John Henry Auran, *Skiing*, October 1967:

"Rather than starting off with a list of facilities to establish Snowmass' 'big, big mountain' image, a much more telling clue to the mountain's character is the little service which will provide snowcat tours from the top of lift Number 4 to just below Baldy Mountain, the highest summit in the Snowmass complex.

Snowcat tours are no longer a novelty. In the case of Snowmass, however, these tours have a special purpose—to keep alive the spirit of adventure and the sense of personal involvement that have characterized the area since the skiing public first got a look at it—via snowcat tours—in 1962. 'Almost by accident the tours gave Snowmass a special excitement,' Bill Janss, the major mover of the project, says. 'It's the sort of excitement the people in the 1930s felt when they first discovered skiing. Once lost, you can never recapture it. We're going to preserve that excitement.'

The snowcat tours came about because the vehicle used by the Aspen Skiing Corporation for the exploration and evaluation of the mountain had room for 10 riders. Since the evaluation crews usually consisted of only three men, including the driver, why not, it was reasoned, take along a few paying passengers ($10 a head) to defray some of the costs, and why not get some feedback from those who would eventually pay for the privilege of skiing at Snowmass?

The tours were a sparkling success from the start. Each party of six to eight skiers, accompanied by a guide, would make two or three long runs in the morning, the object being to ski fresh, uncut powder on every run. At midday, there was time out for a leisurely lunch—a combination of All-American camp-out and Renoiresque picnic—at a hut on Sam's Knob, a shoulder in the midsection of the mountain. After lunch, there was more skiing, more powder, but this time with emphasis on moving around to catch the last of the sinking sun.

The powder, of course, was the big attraction. And so was the opportunity to be among the first to ski what was to be an important new area. But what gave the tours their special character was the camaraderie and single-mindedness they would engender in an otherwise highly diverse group of people. What you were and what you did for a living receded into nothing. The mountain was everything."

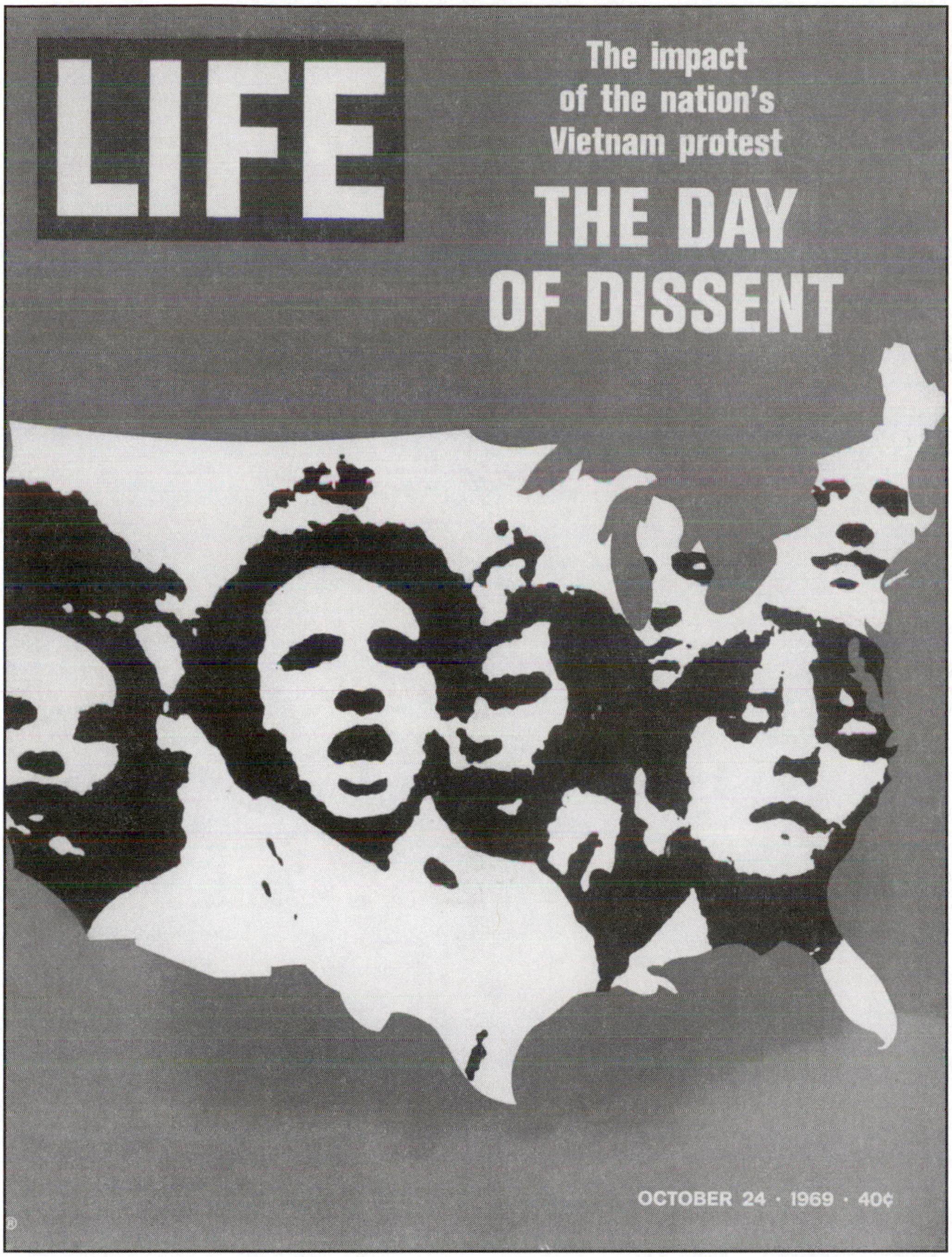
LIFE
The impact
of the nation's
Vietnam protest
THE DAY
OF DISSENT
OCTOBER 24 · 1969 · 40¢

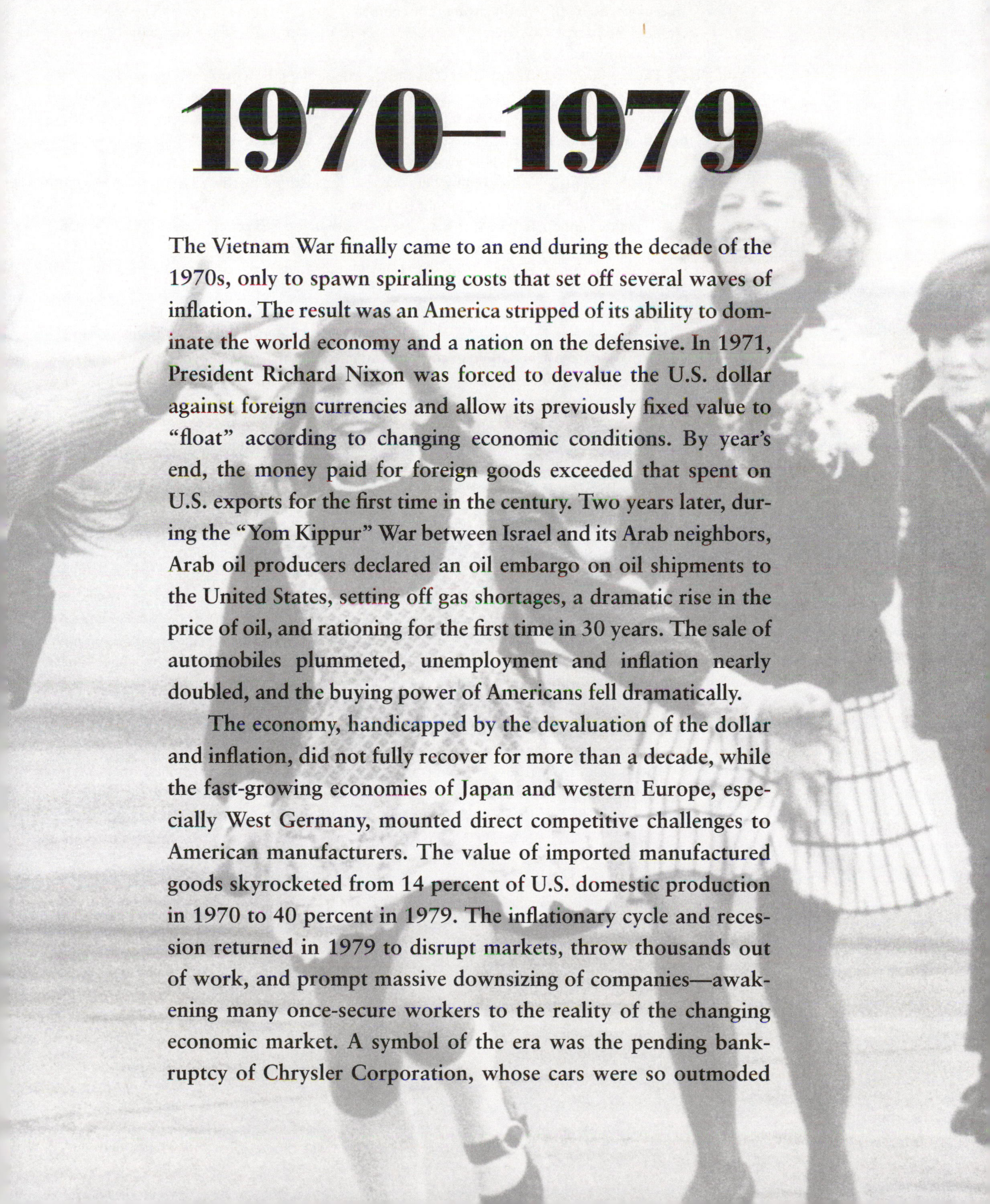

1970–1979

The Vietnam War finally came to an end during the decade of the 1970s, only to spawn spiraling costs that set off several waves of inflation. The result was an America stripped of its ability to dominate the world economy and a nation on the defensive. In 1971, President Richard Nixon was forced to devalue the U.S. dollar against foreign currencies and allow its previously fixed value to "float" according to changing economic conditions. By year's end, the money paid for foreign goods exceeded that spent on U.S. exports for the first time in the century. Two years later, during the "Yom Kippur" War between Israel and its Arab neighbors, Arab oil producers declared an oil embargo on oil shipments to the United States, setting off gas shortages, a dramatic rise in the price of oil, and rationing for the first time in 30 years. The sale of automobiles plummeted, unemployment and inflation nearly doubled, and the buying power of Americans fell dramatically.

The economy, handicapped by the devaluation of the dollar and inflation, did not fully recover for more than a decade, while the fast-growing economies of Japan and western Europe, especially West Germany, mounted direct competitive challenges to American manufacturers. The value of imported manufactured goods skyrocketed from 14 percent of U.S. domestic production in 1970 to 40 percent in 1979. The inflationary cycle and recession returned in 1979 to disrupt markets, throw thousands out of work, and prompt massive downsizing of companies—awakening many once-secure workers to the reality of the changing economic market. A symbol of the era was the pending bankruptcy of Chrysler Corporation, whose cars were so outmoded and plants so inefficient they could not compete against Japanese imports. The federal government was forced to extend loan guarantees to the company to prevent bankruptcy and the loss of thousands of jobs.

The appointment of Paul Volcker as the chairman of the Federal Reserve Board late in the decade gave the economy the distasteful medicine it needed. To cope with inflation, Volcker slammed on the economic brakes, restricted the growth of the money supply, and curbed inflation. As a result, he pushed interest rates to nearly 20 percent—their highest level since the Civil War. Almost immediately the sale of automobiles and expensive items stopped.

The decade also was marred by the deep divisions caused by the Vietnam War. For more than 10 years the war had been fought on two fronts: at home and abroad. As a result, U.S. policy makers conducted the war with one eye always focused on national opinion. When it ended, the Vietnam War had been the longest war in American history, having cost $118 billion and resulted in 56,000 dead, 300,000 wounded, and the loss of American prestige abroad.

The decade was a time not only of movements, but of moving. In the 1970s, the shift of manufacturing facilities to the South from New England and the Midwest accelerated. The Sunbelt became the new darling of corporate America. By the late 1970s, the South, including Texas, had gained more than a million manufacturing jobs, while the Northeast and the Midwest lost nearly two million. Rural North Carolina had the highest percentage of manufacturing of any state in the nation, along with the lowest blue-collar wages and the lowest unionization rate in the country. The Northeast lost more than traditional manufacturing jobs. Computerization of clerical work also made it possible for big firms such as Merrill Lynch, American Express, and Citibank to shift many of their operations to the South and West.

The largest and most striking of all the social actions of the early 1970s was the women's liberation movement; it fundamentally reshaped American society. Since the late 1950s, a small group of well-placed American women had attempted to convince Congress and the courts to bring about equality between the sexes. By the 1970s, the National Organization for Women (NOW) multiplied in size, the first issue of *Ms. Magazine* sold out in a week, and women began demanding economic equality, the legalization of abortion, and the improvement of women's role in society. "All authority in our society is being challenged," said a Department of Health, Education, and Welfare report. "Professional athletes challenge owners, journalists challenge editors, consumers challenge manufacturers . . . and young blue-collar workers, who have grown up in an environment in which equality is called for in all institutions, are demanding the same rights and expressing the same values as university graduates."

The decade also included the flowering of the National Welfare Rights Organization (NWRO), founded in 1966, which resulted in millions of urban poor demanding additional rights. The environmental movement gained recognition and momentum during the decade starting with the first Earth Day celebration in 1970 and the subsequent passage of the federal Clean Air and Clean Water acts. And the growing opposition to the use of nuclear power peaked after the near calamity at Three Mile Island in Pennsylvania in 1979. As the formal barriers to racial equality came down, racist attitudes became unacceptable and the black middle class began to grow. By 1972, half of all Southern black children sat in integrated classrooms, and about one third of all black families had risen economically into the ranks of the middle class.

The changes recorded for the decade included a doubling in the amount of garbage created per capita from 2.5 pounds in 1920 to five pounds. California created a no-fault divorce law, Massachusetts introduced no-fault insurance, and health food sales reached $3 billion. By mid-decade, the so-called typical nuclear family, with working father, housewife, and two children, represented only seven percent of the population and the family size was falling. The average family size was 3.4 persons compared with 4.3 in 1920.

1971 Family Profile

Just as Alex Haas's income as a life insurance agent in Omaha, Nebraska, has begun to accelerate, his wife Rebecca suffered a debilitating brain aneurysm, placing his career—and their lives—on hold. They have two children, both girls.

Annual Income: $45,000

Annual Budget

The average per capita consumer expenditures in 1971 for all workers nationwide are:

Auto Parts	$34.19
Auto Usage	$419.43
Clothing	$208.99
Dentists	$24.56
Food	$710.26
Furniture	$44.30
Gas and Oil	$111.72
Health Insurance	$23.59
Housing	$494.56
Intercity Transport	$21.19
Local Transport	$15.89
New Auto Purchase	$135.79
Personal Business	$169.51
Personal Care	$58.27
Physicians	$73.68
Private Education and Research	$65.97
Recreation	$221.51
Religion/Welfare Activities	$65.01

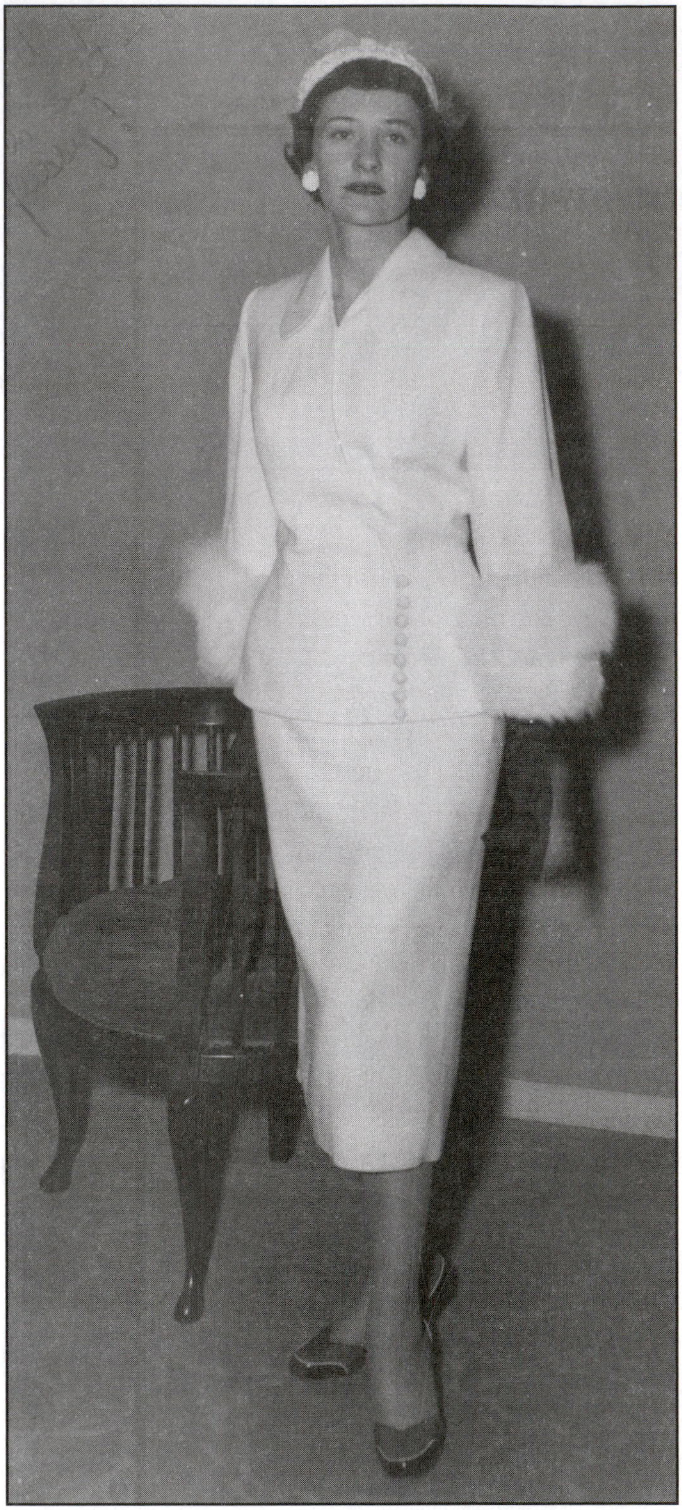

Rebecca's life has been reshaped by a brain aneurysm.

Telephone and Telegraph	$52.97
Tobacco	$54.42
Utilities	$119.43
Per Capita Consumption	$3,372.32

Life at Home

- Alex and Rebecca are living in their "dream home" in west Omaha.
- Their tri-level house, which cost $27,500, has three bedrooms, three baths, a living room, dining room, kitchen, and great room.
- Being the first owners allowed them to pick the wallpaper, the color of the kitchen cabinets, and other design features.
- Alex is proud of his home, but cautious about debt.
- His beliefs were heavily shaped by the Depression; he learned that when you lost your money, you had nothing.
- Born in 1915, his father was a district attorney; Alex had wanted to be a farmer, but was advised by his grandmother to avoid farming and attend college instead.
- Reluctantly he agreed, after the experience of the Depression; he did not want to work his entire life only to become destitute because of an economic whim he could not control.
- Now the Haas family is experiencing a catastrophe that insurance cannot solve.
- Their lives have been reshaped by a brain aneurysm suffered by Rebecca, who is 44 years old.
- Until recently, she was working as a receptionist at a plumbing and electrical engineering company in Omaha.
- She collapsed at work and was taken to the hospital.
- Following her surgery, she was provided intensive care in a private room for 10 days—the cost was $100 a day.
- Despite an eight-hour operation, she has lost the use of the left side of her body.
- Nearly four months were spent in physical therapy before coming home, and she is still adjusting to the need to wear a brace and take her daily medication.
- She is now having grand mal seizures, which began a month after she finally arrived home.
- The family has hired an aide to assist Rebecca, but having someone else in the house has not worked well; she does not like having someone else in her home.
- Despite excellent medical insurance, the family owes $20,000 in medical fees—a staggering burden.
- The oldest daughter is currently attending the University of Nebraska, while her younger sister is at an all-girls' Catholic high school run by the Sisters of the Sacred Heart.

Life at Work

The Haas' house is a gathering place for teenagers.

- Alex has been an insurance agent for Equitable Life of New York for 21 years.
- Before his wife's illness, he began his day at 5:30 a.m., eating breakfast alone; he enjoys his quiet time.
- After breakfast, he was joined by his younger daughter, who still lives at home, and his wife; he took them to school and work, respectively, in the family car.
- Rebecca never learned to drive.
- At the office, he reviews the work prepared by his secretary; he is proud that his volume justifies an assistant, since not everyone has this type of help.
- He then spends the morning attempting to set up appointments with families, whom he likes to meet at their homes after dinner at about 7:00 p.m. or 7:30 p.m.
- In mid-afternoon, he normally picks up his daughter, then goes home to fix the evening meal before going to his first sales call.
- He enjoys people and doing the insurance interviews.
- Although a very fastidious man, he has the ability to make nearly everyone comfortable, even when talking about the need for life insurance.
- Before a call begins, he is often served coffee and cake, which he must enjoy before discussing business, because to do otherwise would be considered rude.
- He never smokes or accepts an alcoholic drink while making a visit.
- Since Rebecca's illness, he spends more time at home caring for her.
- He also helps his younger daughter with her studies.
- Going to meet clients every night is causing problems, so he is thinking about taking a supervisory job that requires less selling, less night work, and probably less income overall.
- Currently, he puts about 500 miles a week on his car, a red Dodge Charger with four-on-the-floor.
- He knows that people buy life insurance for a variety of reasons, but most want to provide financial protection for their families in case they die prematurely.
- Martin Luther King, Jr.'s, "I have a dream" speech several years ago turned a light on in his life as he realized that the blacks of northern Omaha had been denied the right to own homes and buy insurance.
- He decided to bring about a change, and began providing life insurance policies to African-Americans, despite some disapproving signals from his company.
- When he sold a policy to St. Louis Cardinal all-star pitcher Bob Gibson, the company was particularly cautious and required the professional athlete to undergo a complete physical examination before they would approve the $1 million coverage Gibson requested.
- Americans bought about three fourths of their new protection in 1971 on an individual basis, by personal decision, usually through a life insurance agent.
- Purchases of life insurance totaled $132 billion in 1971; group life insurance purchases were $49 billion.
- Part of his success grows from his extensive record keeping; he maintains detailed records of all the clients' children and regularly checks the newspapers for births and deaths.
- Families tend to buy life insurance while going through a life change, such as the birth of a child.

- In 1961, the average new policy was $6,300; by 1966, the average was $8,750, and by 1971, $11,670.
- Forty-three percent of the adults who bought insurance have an income of less than $7,500.

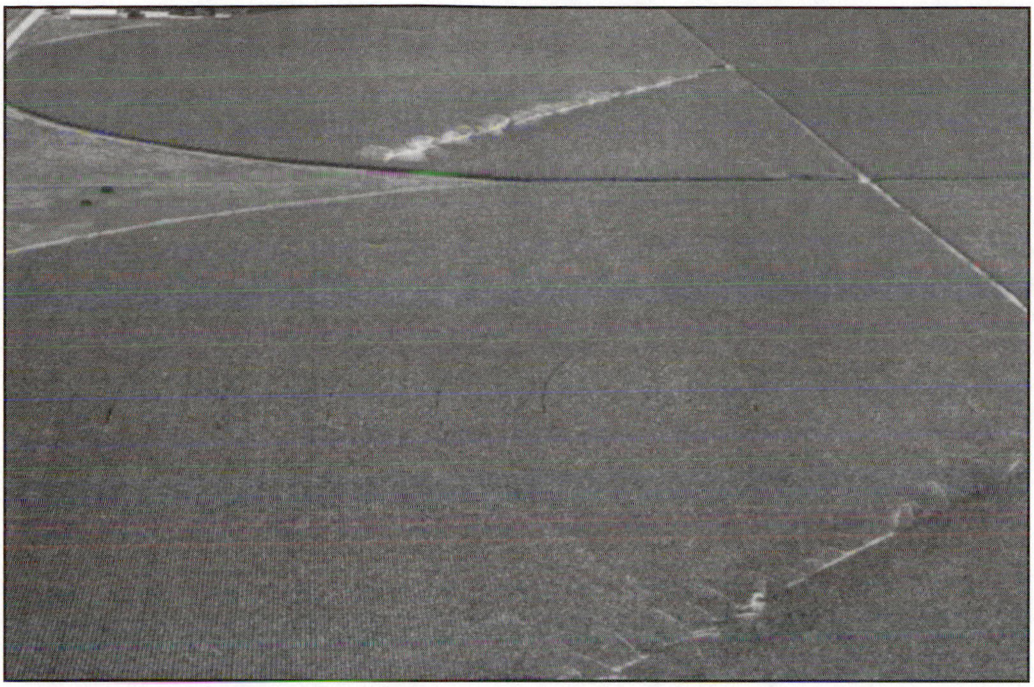

Nebraska is primarily an agricultural state.

- During the week, he attends mass on Wednesday and then again on Sunday; before his wife became ill, he was a member of the Catholic Men's Association and the men's choir.

Life in the Community: Omaha, Nebraska

- The river community of Omaha is known as the Gateway City.
- Founded in 1853 along the Missouri River, Omaha quickly became the cross point for rail traffic.
- With the resumption of regularly scheduled barge service in 1953, Omaha returned to its roots to become a river town again.
- Father Flanagan's Boys' Town, a famous refuge for homeless boys, sits on a hilltop 10 miles from the city.
- Omaha boasts three universities, three colleges, two schools of medicine, two pharmacy schools, one law school, eight nurses' training programs, 30 business and technical schools, and five Montessori preschools.
- Recently, just in time for the state's 100th anniversary, Omaha saw the resurgence of the Old Market into an artistic and cultural center.
- The dilapidated buildings were rescued by a combination of artists and businessmen; the Old Market now has artist's lofts, restaurants, shops, and boutiques.
- Although Nebraska is primarily an agricultural state, Omaha boasts more than 600 manufacturing concerns, which turn out everything from TV components to TV dinners.
- Statewide, 62 percent of Nebraska's 1.5 million people live in urban areas and only 18 percent are engaged in farming.

"Payroll Leadership the Key, UCAN Tries to Break Cycle," by Wes Iversen, *Omaha Sun*, April 1, 1971:

"Most people don't realize it, black contractor Boyd V. Galloway claims, but contractors and builders are 'the basic people to any community.'

'A community can't pull itself up by its bootstraps,' he goes on, until some of its members can 'develop some payroll leadership.'

Galloway is president of the United Contractors Association of Nebraska, Inc. (UCAN), a group of about 40 black general contractors, specialty contractors, craftsmen, and construction workers. The development of that payroll leadership, through helping members secure bonding and thus to be able to bid on larger, more meaningful contracts, is an immediate goal.

While UCAN has been around since the fall of 1969, Galloway says there's been a new enthusiasm just in the past four months.

One reason is the hope of a $61,000 federal grant to set up a training program and facilities for minority contractors and workers. With the aid of Paul B. Allen, minority representative with the Mayor's Committee for Economic Development with the Small Business Administration (SBA) under Section 406 of the Economic Opportunity Act of 1964 . . . under the UCAN proposal, the minority construction training program would be several-pronged. In addition to training the 'hard-core unemployed or underemployed,' the training encourages minority journeymen to set up their own contracting firms."

Rebecca worked as a receptionist at a plumbing and electrical engineering company before her illness.

"'71 Year of the Ballot for Midlands' Youth," *Omaha World-Herald*, December 31, 1971:

"It was a year of change for Midlands youth.

Mirrored in the pages of the 'Youth in the Midlands' section, young people moved into some areas that had been off-limits and began doing other things differently.

The vote for 18-year-olds probably will have the most lasting impact on teenagers.

Some Iowa and Nebraska youths already have voted, but only on local issues.

The arrival of the vote, however, brought the candidates' attention to young voters. Registration campaigns reached into the high schools for the first time. . . .

And girls, through their own efforts and those of teachers, took a step toward a full share of school programs by participating in more sports. Although inter-school basketball, common in Iowa, still is not allowed in Nebraska, state championship contests in other sports were available to Cornhusker girls.

Midlands' student councils vowed to be 'relevant' to rid themselves of the school dance organizer image and to become the leaders their fellow students elected them to be.

Many students took a look at pollution and decided to do something. Some youths began to help each other out of the mire of drug abuse, replacing the escape into the chemical world with the message of Jesus, or by finding something else for drug users to do with their lives."

- More than half of the industrial activity is devoted to the processing of food and food products; food processing is a $1 billion industry in Omaha alone.
- Omaha also has become the meat packer of the world, taking the crown from Chicago; the city has 12 meat packing plants, including the major names in meat packing such as Swift's and Swanson's.
- The city is also known for Mutual of Omaha, an insurance company whose history, stability, and advertising campaigns have brought pride to Omaha.

Historical Snapshot
1971

- President Richard Nixon ordered a 90-day freeze on wages and prices
- First-class postal rates rose to $0.08 per ounce
- The *New York Times* published the first installment of the "Pentagon Papers," a classified history of American involvement in the Vietnam War; 75 percent of those polled opposed publication of the secret papers
- Tennis player Billie Jean King became the first woman athlete to earn $100,000 in one year
- The Supreme Court mandated busing as a means of achieving school desegregation
- The average taxpayer gave the government $400 for defense, $125 to fight the war in Indochina, $40 to build roads, $30 to explore space, and $315 for health activities
- A poll showed that 34 percent of the population believed marriage obsolete, up from 24 percent in 1969
- *Look* magazine ceased publication
- Beef consumption per capita rose from 113 pounds to 128.5 pounds
- Cigarette advertising was banned from television
- Three fourths of all moviegoers were under age 30
- *Gourmet* magazine circulation doubled to 550,000 in just four years; the fancy food industry continued to expand
- The phrases "think tank," "body language," "gross out," and "workaholic" all entered the language
- The National Cancer Act was passed, providing $1.5 billion a year for research; the president urged an all-out attempt to find a cure
- The Supreme Court ruled that qualification for conscientious-objector status necessitated opposing all wars, not just the Vietnam War
- The Metropolitan Museum of Art paid a record $5.5 million for a Velásquez portrait
- The diamond-bladed scalpel was developed for eye microsurgery
- Young women were appointed U.S. Senate pages for the first time
- The U.S. Supreme Court ruled that companies may not refuse to hire women with small children if the same policy is not applied to men
- The United States Public Health Service no longer advised children to have a smallpox vaccination
- Direct dialing began between New York and London
- Snowmobiles, dune buggies, auto trains, and a law banning sex discrimination all make their first appearance

1971 Economic Profile

Income, Standard Jobs

Bituminous Coal Mining	$10,331.00
Building Trades	$10,473.00
Domestic Industries	$8,255.00
Domestics	$4,159.00
Farm Labor	$3,783.00
Federal Civilian	$11,767.00
Federal Employees, Executive Departments	$8,995.00
Federal Military	$7,139.00
Finance, Insurance, and Real Estate	$8,347.00
Gas, Electricity, and Sanitation Workers	$10,696.00
Manufacturing, Durable Goods	$10,473.00
Manufacturing, Nondurable Goods	$8,167.00
Medical/Health Services Workers	$7,043.00
Miscellaneous Manufacturing	$7,355.00
Motion Picture Services	$8,441.00

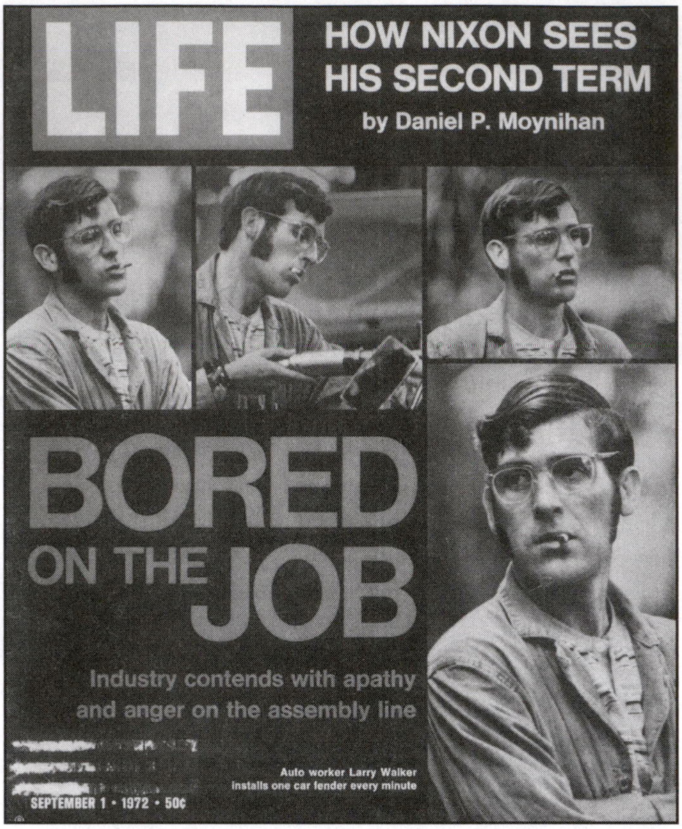

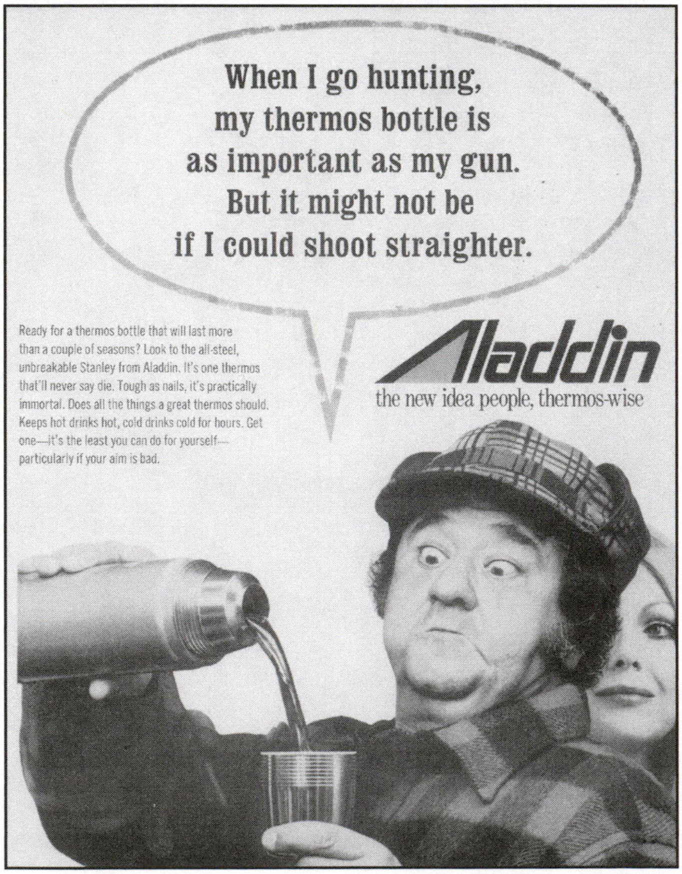

Nonprofit Organization Workers . . . $5,924.00
Passenger Transportation Workers, Local and Highway $7,309.00
Personal Services $5,892.00
Public School Teachers. $8,813.00
Radio Broadcasting and Television Workers. $10,885.00
Railroad Workers. $11,360.00
State and Local Government Workers $8,443.00
Telephone and Telegraph Workers . . $9,350.00

Selected Prices

Adorn Hard to Hold Hairspray, 13 Ounces $1.09
Alva Museum Pendant $6.50
Ban Roll-On Deodorant, 1.5-Ounce Size. $0.49
Bayer Aspirin, 100 Tablets $0.79
Calgon Bath Oil Beads, 16-Ounce Package. $0.98
Craftsman Tool Set $39.99
Dove Liquid Detergent, 22 Ounces $0.57
Downy Fabric Softener, 64 Ounces $0.99
Dynaflo Tropical Fish Motor Filter $13.50
Excedrin, 100 Count. $0.89
Laredo Tobacco. $1.00
Magna-Lite Shop Light $6.95
Relco Metal Detector $19.95
Sauna Belt Weight-Loss Pants $13.50
Sealy Posturepedic Mattress and Box Spring $249.95
Sunnybrook Eggs, Grade A, per Dozen $0.39
Used Oldsmobile Cutlass, 1968 Model $1,850.00
Valmor High Fashion Wig, Human Hair $29.99
Visine $0.99
Volkswagen Automobile $2,999.00
Western Electric Telephone $6.95

Letter from Robert H. Long, student at William and Mary College, to friend, November 16, 1971:

"Thank you for your letter. I so very much appreciate that you miss me because it is very mutual. I don't have but a handful of people that I miss and you're the number 1. I have had problems with Laurie, but now we aren't seeing each other or talking, which is so stupid. She just won't think about dropping or somewhat forgetting that boy back home. That has caused a weekly argument for the past month and a half, so now we're taking a breather. Maybe someone else will come up for me, or she'll have a change in heart. She's really so much of what I want in a girl. I hate to lose her completely.

John, Jere, and I went to the March on Washington yesterday. It was so unbelievable. We were there with 250,000-plus others. Though we weren't really expecting it, we were completely overwhelmed by the masses of people and no violence. I have never seen so many people—young, old, mainly college age—doing something in common. It was mainly believers and not teenybopper hangers-on and high schoolies. I'll never forget everything and am so glad we went. We stood on the Capital Mall for two hours before we could walk and then took another one and a half hours to walk the 14 blocks. I'll tell you about it at Thanksgiving.

Our moratorium could have gone over better. There was a march down Duke of Gloucester Street to the Capital. Speeches, silent vigil, and ended with a reading of war dead names in the Sunken Gardens by candlelight. It was nice, but could have been more effective. The majority up here doesn't like some of the pseudo-hippies that are influencing our leaders.

We have gotten permission for girls to be in boys' rooms on Friday and Saturday nights from 8:00 to 12:00 if we ask permission from the dean. That's really great. My roommate and I had a party last weekend. We decorated and entertained about seven couples from 8:00 to 1:30. Candlelight, Cold Duck, rum, etc. We cleaned up the next day for two hours. The party really started Friday night as a practice party and Saturday was the real thing. It was great. Laurie and I finished our fifth of rum and were really feeling good; then the next day her conscience got her and we argued and haven't seen each other for the last week.

I just don't know. I really hate to lose her completely. I don't think I will, though. Well, I must go to study now. Write soon. Be good. Bobby."

The Insurance Industry

- Despite an uncertain economic climate, approximately 145 million people were insured by one or more life insurance policies; this equals seven out of 10 people in the total population.
- The average ordinary life policy had a face value of $6,450 compared with $6,100 a year earlier.
- Purchases of new ordinary policies totaled $132 billion, an increase of $9.4 billion over 1970.
- The assets of legal reserve life insurance companies reached $222.1 billion, an increase of $14.8 billion over 1970; approximately $79 billion was in corporate bonds, $75 billion in mortgages, and only $20 billion in stocks.

- The new investments of life insurance companies during the year provided seven percent of the flow of financial capital from all investment sources in the nation that year.
- Nationwide, $789 billion in ordinary life insurance was in force; this represented a 7.9 percent increase over 1970 and a 116 percent increase during the past decade.
- Group life insurance represented another $581 billion, an increase of 202.5 percent over 1961.
- The average insured family nationwide had $25,700 in life insurance coverage; protection for all families was equivalent to 24 months of total disposable personal income per family.
- In Nebraska, the average amount of life insurance in force per family was $21,000.
- Approximately 86 percent of men and 74 percent of women had some type of life insurance protection.
- Ninety-two percent of men in the 45-54 age group had coverage.
- The western part of the United States had a lower incidence of life insurance ownership than did the rest of the nation.
- Benefit payments to beneficiaries and payments to policyholders passed $17 million in 1971—an increase of 94.9 percent during the past 10 years.
- That year, the industry was represented at the White House Conference on Aging, as it focused on retirement planning.

Alex (far right) grew up in Omaha.

"The Crucial Math of Motherhood," *Life*, May 19, 1972:

"This week there are two million more Americans than there were 12 months ago. In two huge metropolitan regions of the East and West, the population is shooting up even faster than it is in India. Although the national birthrate has actually been declining for the past decade, the inexorable mathematics of motherhood means that the U.S. is still growing by more than one percent a year. At this rate, there will be 280 million of us by the year 2000, enough to force a marked change in many of the ways we now live.

Both the Pill and easier abortion laws have helped lower the birthrate in recent years. So have inflation, job shortages, and the women's rights movement, all of which tend to encourage later marriages and fewer children. Last month, after an exhaustive two-year study, the Presidential Commission on Population Growth and the American Future recommended that we now seize the chance to stabilize our population. The commission, headed by John D. Rockefeller, III, favors abortion on request, free contraceptive information and supplies for all, including minors, and a national policy of zero population growth. Married couples would be encouraged to have an average of only two children (the present average is 2.3). President Nixon responded to his Commission's report by attacking both the legalization of abortion and the distribution of contraceptive supplies to minors. . . .

No less than 15 percent of all babies born to married couples between 1966 and 1970 were unwanted, reported the Population Commission. 'The incidence of unwanted fertility,' declared the commissioners, 'in terms of ordinary medical health criteria would qualify as epidemic proportions. One third of all conceive their first child before they are married, and among couples who decide they have had enough children, a third still go on to have at least one more. If every family were able to have only the number of children it wanted,' the Commission concluded, 'the U.S. would have gone a long way toward solving its population problem.'"

September 18, 1972
Newsweek
Terror at The Olympics

1973 News Profile

January 19, 1973. Going Home.

At last the doors would open, at the Hanoi Hilton, the Zoo Annex, and all the other North Vietnamese prisons where American servicemen had endured as much as eight and a half years under sometimes brutal conditions. Two days earlier, in Paris, U.S. and North Vietnamese representatives had signed a peace agreement freeing the POWs. Now was a time for rejoicing.

At the Hanoi Hilton, however, there were no shouts of joy, no backslapping among the Americans as the hated commandant, nicknamed Weasel by the prisoners, impassively informed them that they were to be released. Many simply were numb and gaunt, having lost a third of their weight on the meager diet ordered by the North Vietnamese commandant. Some had broken legs and arms that had not been set. Others did not want to be used in a propaganda event, fearing that communist cameras might be recording their emotions. Not a few remembered the hundreds of other Americans for whom there would be no homecoming, having died in captivity from lack of medical attention, starvation, and the brutality of the camps.

'Ten good men died in my arms, and I'm damned mad about that,' said Army Major Floyd Kushner, a physician who was a prisoner initially held in South Vietnam. 'It was all the result of maltreatment in South Vietnam. Our mortality rate in South Vietnam (among POWs) was 45 percent. I guess there was a parallel with Japanese treatment during World War II. . . .'

In order to extract propaganda statements from Colonel Robinson Risner of Oklahoma City, North Vietnamese jailers attached 60-pound bars to his ankles and trussed him with ropes. As the iron bars

Navy Lieutenant Commander John McCain II was shot down in 1967.

pressed for hours against his ankles, the pain slowly rose until it reached an excruciating level. Risner agreed to make the statement. 'I made one more tape,' said the 48-year-old Risner. 'I wrote what they told me to write after a torture session. If I was told to say the war was wrong, I said the war was wrong. . . . The pain became too severe. I myself have screamed all night. I have heard as many as four people holler at one time. . . .'

Navy Lieutenant Commander John McCain II, 36, shot down and captured in October 1967, said the North Vietnamese both saved his life and tortured him after they learned his father was an admiral who would command the United States forces in the Pacific. 'My leg was broken, and I had other injuries when I was shot down,' he said. 'After four days with no medical treatment whatever ... I realized I was dying . . . the Bug (the North Vietnamese jailer) came in and brought a doctor. I asked, "Are you going to take me to the hospital?" and they said, "Too late, too late." '

The Bug returned a short time later and told McCain, 'Your father is a big admiral.' McCain was then sent to the hospital, where he was treated. 'In mid-1968, a man in charge of all the camps tried to get me to accept release,' McCain said. 'I didn't know at the time that it coincided with my father's appointment as commander in the Pacific. When I refused to take release ahead of Commander Everett Alvarez and the others who had been there longer, the treatment became very bad.' McCain's leg was re-broken, one arm was broken, his teeth were smashed, and other injuries were inflicted in torture sessions. . . .

Navy Captain Jeremiah Denton, Jr., 48, of Virginia Beach, Virginia, said that beginning in October 1965, the North Vietnamese tried by torture and isolation to steamroller all of the POWs into tools of anti-Americanism and antiwar propaganda. . . .

Of the more than seven and a half years Denton was held captive, four were spent in solitary confinement. As with many of the other prisoners, he found the isolation and loneliness as difficult to handle as any of the physical torture.

'A man does a lot of thinking during seven years, seven months in enemy prisons,' he said. 'Mental exercise . . . helped the mind escape the confines of tiny cells. But even more than thinking, a man does a lot of praying in an enemy prison. Prayer, even more than sheer thought, is the firmest anchor to windward.'

Many of the prisoners turned to prayer, even those who had strayed from the church over the years. Although the Weasel only allowed captives to use the Bible on special religious holidays, they managed to make it an integral part of their lives. Major Norman McDaniel of Greensboro, North Carolina, and other prisoners memorized as much of the book as possible during religious holidays, then wrote down what they remembered when they were allowed pencil and paper.

America rejoiced when the POWs returned home, beginning in February. Navy Commander Brian Woods of San Diego, California, and Air Force Major Glendon Perkins of Orlando, Florida, the first two of the returning prisoners, stepped onto their native soil in San Diego with a salute. 'This homecoming is not only for myself and Glendon Perkins, but for all the POWs,' Woods said. 'We are grateful and overwhelmed.' "

1975 Family Profile

Gerard Keshian, a 41-year-old ear, nose, and throat doctor, moved to Fort Myers, Florida, to focus on bringing high-quality medicine to an underserved, small community in his native state. Recently, the dramatic growth of the area has begun to overwhelm him and his wife, Fay. They have four children.

Annual Income: $60,000

Annual Budget

The average per capita consumer expenditures in 1975 for all workers nationwide are:

Auto Parts	$47.69
Auto Usage	$550.53
Clothing	$279.66
Dentists	$37.97
Food	$1,011.70
Furniture	$59.27
Gas and Oil	$183.82
Health Insurance	$30.56
Housing	$680.64
Intercity Transport	$33.80
Local Transport	$18.52
New Auto Purchase	$135.67
Personal Business	$245.40
Personal Care	$77.32
Physicians	$108.81
Private Education and Research	$94.92
Recreation	$331.53

Energetic Dr. Keshian lives in downtown Fort Myers.

Fay is a native Floridian, a designation growing less common each year.

Religion/Welfare Activities	$91.22
Telephone and Telegraph	$81.95
Tobacco	$69.92
Utilities	$196.32
Per Capita Consumption	$4,745.50

Life at Home

- The Keshians live in downtown Fort Myers, Florida, on the scenic Caloosahatchee River.
- Their home, built in the 1920s, is within blocks of Thomas Edison's winter home, now a tourist attraction owned by the city.
- Both Gerard and Fay are native Floridians, a designation that is growing less common in this rapidly growing state.
- To help educate newcomers to the area, the couple has actively raised money for a nature center, complete with an extensive boardwalk for viewing the flora and fauna of Florida.
- When they began last year, no money was available for a brochure, so Gerard made individual pictures of the plans, location, and plants and then pasted the pictures on paper to create individualized brochures; after Fay wrote the copy, they distributed each personalized presentation to key members of the community.
- Gerard does not like fundraising, but their efforts have resulted in $85,000 being donated, and the boardwalk is now under way.

- As each stage of the boardwalk is completed, the Keshians go out to walk the new section; the children are less thrilled by this ritual than are their parents.
- The progress of the boardwalk is being charted by photographs from a helicopter provided by the publicly financed mosquito-control taxing district.
- Each May, Gerard and Fay take their three boys and one girl on a one-week driving tour of Florida.
- The parents are determined to teach the children about Florida before much of it disappears.
- The family often stays in Howard Johnson Hotels, which always have swimming pools and television sets.
- Since Gerard and Fay refuse to have a television set in their house, the children are often glued to the TV once they hit the motel room.
- Dr. Keshian believes that television is a poor influence and a time waster for all persons, particularly children.
- This year, the annual tour included a trip to Disney World, whose impact on tourism is tremendous.
- When Gerard is home, he and the children are often in his workshop making rockets, wooden boats, and electronic gadgets.

When Gerard is home, he and the children are often in the workshop.

The oldest girl enjoys modeling and dance.

- The family has also attached, from an Australian pine tree, a rope swing that attracts children—and sometimes adults—from miles around to the yard.
- Most weekends, the entire family goes 18 miles outside the city to a 30-acre tract of land purchased in 1966 for $1,000 an acre.
- The use of drugs is on the rise in the community; in the country, Gerard can keep the children away from their peers, many of whom he does not trust.

A special effort is made to have the entire family together for dinner.

Wading birds of Florida are often seen around the Keshian home.

- There they have devised catapults made from surgical tubing, and pipe cannons loaded with palm seeds propelled by homemade gunpowder and fuses.
- Also, they have worked as a family to identify most of the plants on the property, especially orchids and bromeliads, by common and Latin name.
- An out-of-state developer is currently digging canals near their property to create a housing development; the dredging is undercutting the water table and causing the land to dry up, so this family has formed a coalition of residents in the area to battle the company's expansion plans.

- Recently, Gerard acquired from a patient several used pinball machines, which he has stripped and made into flashing, blinking, noise-making, scary objects for the annual Junior Welfare League Haunted House Fundraiser at Halloween.
- No Junior League existed when the Keshians moved to Fort Myers; Fay helped establish the organization and has served on many of its most critical boards.
- Because of the various ages of the four children, their activities range from Cub Scouts to advanced ballet.
- Although most of the activities are near their home, Fay feels that she is constantly running a taxicab service for the children.
- The oldest child, the only girl, must be driven to school each morning; the other children are in private schools affiliated with either the Catholic Church or the Lutheran Church.
- Fay drives a five-year-old Oldsmobile, which her mother gave to her, while Gerard drives a Jeep Wagon with four-wheel drive.
- Both Gerard and Fay grew up in Tampa, Florida; after his father died in 1947, Gerard was determined to be a doctor despite the meager resources of the family.
- Fay also grew up without a father; she and her mother lived with her grandparents following her parents' divorce in the closing days of the Second World War.
- She attended Newcomb College in New Orleans, while Gerard attended nearby Tulane University in New Orleans, thanks to the generosity of a wealthy great-uncle who provided some tuition help; in addition, he had a work scholarship that required 20 hours of work a week in the physics lab.
- He graduated Phi Beta Kappa in 1956; they married that year and he began looking for a way to attend medical school.
- No money or scholarships were available for medical school and the rules forbade students from working.
- He eventually got $500 from his great-uncle, $500 from the Kiwanis Club, and a loan whose only guarantee was future earnings.
- After graduation from Tulane Medical, he served his internship in New Orleans, working 36 hours on and 12 hours off with a half-day off on either Saturday or Sunday.
- During this time, their first child was born, but with his work schedule, he participated little as a father in her early years.
- They next moved to Chicago to continue ear, nose, and throat specialty training, living in a garage apartment with a growing family, which then included two children.

"Length of Schoolboy's Hair Sharply Divides Community," *Fort Myers News-Press*, November 23, 1975:

"Saguache, Colorado—Le Seaman studies his fifth-grade lessons at home because he can't go to school with his hair touching his collar. But if he decides to fight, the issue may go to court on grounds he is a victim of sexual discrimination.

Le began his first year at Mountain Valley Elementary School in September. Three weeks ago, the Saguache School Board suspended him for violating the school's dress code. The action has sharply divided this community in the San Luis Valley of central Colorado.

Even the five-member School Board, which met Friday night with its attorney, is at odds on the issue. Board member Patricia Hills said the vote to suspend 10-year-old Le was four to one, 'but I don't know where we stand right now.'

'You wonder what kind of people, what kind of sense . . . where's their common sense regarding education, making a hassle for this child?' said Norman Aaronson, an attorney for Colorado Rural Legal Services, which represents Le. 'It would be different if he was a high-school senior and a troublemaker, but he's a good student. His teacher wants him back; she told me yesterday that the kids keep asking, "When's Le coming back?"' "

Their home on the Caloosahatchee River is surrounded by palm trees.

"Critical Area Study of Charlotte Harbor Delayed," *Fort Myers News-Press*, October 22, 1975:

"A lack of state staffing will delay study of the long-sought state critical area designation for the Charlotte Harbor Complex, state officials said Saturday in Fort Myers.

The Environmental Confederation of Southwest Florida struggled to organize its priorities and reasons for the protective state mandate, now in effect in Key West, the Green Swamp, and Big Cypress, but Eastern Tin, of the Division of State Planning, said more work is necessary.

The environmental group, composed of conservationists from about 40 organizations in five counties nominated a coastal stretch from Mantasota Key in Sarasota County to Wiggins Pass in Collier County last year. The proposal would include all barrier islands off the Lee County coast, but firm boundaries would not be drawn until after a nomination is accepted."

- In 1963, he made $270 a month as a resident; the family attempted to get a Sears charge card that year and were denied.
- By 1964, they moved to Fort Myers, where he was required to practice for three years before taking exams to become Board qualified.
- The tests were so stressful he began smoking cigarettes again.

Life at Work

- With the area growing so rapidly, the demand for the services of an ear, nose, and throat specialist has skyrocketed.
- This is especially true now that large numbers of families from the Midwest are retiring to the area, only to discover new allergies and ailments.
- Many live in newly established residential developments literally dredged out of the wetlands to create overnight, canal communities.
- The canal-based development technique allows the developer to use the dredged dirt to fill the land and make it higher above sea level; the residents who buy, as a result, have homes on a water-filled canal that connects to deeper water.
- Thousands of lots have been sold in this manner, waiting for the owner to retire; as a result, most of the lots are left barren to grow pollen-laden weeds and vegetation.
- Normally, he begins work at 6:45 a.m., usually at one of the two hospitals in the area, where he performs surgery starting about 7:30 a.m.
- The most common surgeries are tonsillectomies, nose repair, cosmetic reconstruction, and occasionally the "pinning back" of obtrusive ears.
- Most days, surgery is completed by mid-morning, after which he sees patients until 6 p.m.; many nights he attends medical meetings or civic functions before returning home.

On weekends the family goes to their cabin in the country.

- The three doctors in the office each treat from 12 to 20 patients during the afternoon, sometimes doing minor surgery in the office and treating a variety of skin cancers common in the heat-soaked environment of Florida.
- During the summers, much time is spent treating swimmer's ear.
- A typical office visit costs $20; subsequent visits are $11 to $15 each.
- This office does not participate in Medicare assignments, and most of its clients do not have insurance; 20 percent do not pay their bills.
- Dr. Keshian often does not charge patients, particularly those with families, who he knows are unable to afford his services.
- He takes every Thursday off, working on Thursday mornings at the Senior Friendship Center treating approximately a dozen patients each week for free.
- He got interested in the Center through a presentation made to the Tuesday afternoon Rotary Club, of which he is a member.
- As a result of the cancers Gerard has seen, most commonly found in retirees who have been heavy drinkers and smokers their entire life, he does not hesitate to tell his patients about the consequences of prolonged use of alcohol and cigarettes.
- Personally, he and Fay will occasionally have a glass of wine, rarely more than one.
- Dr. Keshian is turning more of these cases over to his partner in order to focus on the delicate specialty of ear surgery.
- He is treating a large number of male retirees who are experiencing hearing loss as a result of explosions and loud noises during their military service in World War II or the Korean War, since sound-protection was given little consideration in those days.
- Dinner is always at 7 p.m., prepared by Fay. The family rarely eats out; the fast food phenomenon sweeping the nation has been slow to reach this south Florida community.
- At work, he and his partners have started a pension plan that is forcing him to save money; with four children it is not always easy to set aside funds for the future.
- To help fund the children's future, the sale of hearing aids has been established as a separate corporation owned by his children, with all revenues going to their college funds.
- The office is staffed by one nurse who assists three doctors.
- Despite the conservative use of staff, the office overhead has risen from 15 percent of total costs in 1964 to 25 percent.

Life in the Community: Fort Myers, Florida

- The rapid growth of southwest Florida, especially the sensitive wetland areas, is causing many natives to question the wisdom of growth.
- Currently, the area is ranked as one of the top five fastest growing areas in the nation; at its current rate of approximately 20 percent per year, the population will double every five years.
- Throughout most of the century, Fort Myers was untouched by growth; at the end of War World II, the town claimed only 10,600 residents.
- Mosquitoes, poor roads, heat, and the lack of an industrial base held down growth until the 1960s.

- Air conditioning, sophisticated telephone sales programs by developers, and the dream of a "Florida retirement" attracted millions.
- Nearly 500 new residents have been settled in the state each day since the mid-1960s.
- Almost overnight, a frontier-like state became the largest and most urban state in the region.
- Many of the new residents are retired, with approximately 25 percent of the population—the highest in the nation—over 65 years of age.
- The new residents, while bringing cash from years of working in Michigan, Ohio, and Indiana, are also impacting social programs and schools throughout the state.
- The elderly have consistently voted against new tax initiatives, including school construction, to protect their income, often stating publicly, "No new taxes; I have educated my children up North."

"County Hikes Water Rates, Hookup Fees," by Lee Melsek, *Fort Myers News-Press*, November 20, 1975:

"Spurred to action by SOS signals from professional consultants, Lee County officials took emergency action Wednesday to bail out the county's troubled water service by hiking water rates and hookup fees.

Beginning in January, county water customers will be charged an additional 25 percent surcharge on their water bills and new customers will pay nearly double the current hookup fees.

Both hikes were labeled temporary until the county can establish new rates following more studies and the required public hearings necessary for utility rate increases. The emergency measure was taken by the Lee County Commission to avoid defaulting on the county's utility bond requirements, which consultants say could happen if the tangled financial problems of the water department are not straightened out soon."

- Throughout the coastal communities and barrier islands of Florida, Georgia, and South Carolina, battles are raging between developers who promise change and environmentalists who wish to preserve.
- Greater affluence nationally and improved technology are allowing the islands and marshes to be developed.
- Conservationists in Fort Myers are warning that the residential development is destroying the environmental characteristics people are flocking to see.
- The developers say that residents are simply trying to preserve the beauty for themselves and lock others out.
- Many communities, including nearby Sanibel Island, are attempting to control growth through comprehensive plans and tougher zoning laws.
- On the statewide level, environmental activism has resulted in the Environmental Protection Act, the Land and Water Management Act, and the State Comprehensive Planning Act.
- Florida has also begun a land acquisition program to preserve the most sensitive and endangered lands, including Cayo Costa Island in southwest Florida.

Historical Snapshot
1975

- The so-called typical nuclear family, with working father, housewife, and two children, represented only seven percent of the population; average family size was 3.4, down from 4.3 in 1920
- Harvard changed its five-to-two male to female admissions policy to equal admissions
- The first desktop microcomputer became available
- Pet rocks went on sale, featuring obedience, loyalty, and low maintenance costs
- Vandalism and violence increased in public schools; homicides increased nearly 20 percent, rapes and robberies were up 40 percent since 1965
- Unemployment reached 9.2 percent
- The Atomic Energy Commission was dissolved
- The Supreme Court ruled that the mentally ill cannot be hospitalized against their will unless they are dangerous to themselves or to others
- McDonald's opened its first drive-thru restaurant
- A record 120,000 Americans declared personal bankruptcy
- Chrysler, followed by other auto companies, offered rebates to counter record low sales
- Many cities were hit by strikes, including a police strike in San Francisco, teachers' strikes in Chicago and Charleston, West Virginia, and strikes by sanitation workers in New York
- Minnesota became the first state to require businesses, restaurants, and institutions to establish no-smoking areas
- The Brewers' Society reported that Americans consumed an average of 151 pints of beer per year, 11.5 pints of wine, and 9.1 pints of spirits
- *Penthouse* sales surpassed those of *Playboy*
- The Rolling Stones tour grossed $13 million; singer Stevie Wonder signed a record contract for $13 million
- A Massachusetts physician was convicted of manslaughter by a Boston jury for aborting a fetus and was sentenced to a year's probation
- California and New York doctors publicized their enormous malpractice insurance increases by withholding all but emergency services; premiums had risen 93.5 percent in one year
- New York City, under threat of default, was bailed out by union pension funds
- Rape laws were changed in nine states, narrowing the amount of corroborative evidence necessary for conviction and also restricting the trial questions permitted regarding the victim's past sex life
- An endangered whooping crane was born in captivity
- TV advertisements for tampons appeared for the first time

1975 Economic Profile

Income, Standard Jobs

Bituminous Coal Mining	$15,924.00
Building Trades	$13,447.00
Domestics	$5,774.00
Farm Labor	$5,073.00
Federal Civilian	$15,024.00
Federal Employees, Executive Departments	$12,446.00
Federal Military	$10,064.00
Finance, Insurance, and Real Estate	$10,609.00
Gas, Electricity, and Sanitation Workers	$14,231.00
Manufacturing, Durable Goods	$12,594.00

Editorial, "Southerners Happiest about Their Lives," *Fort Myers News-Press*, November 24, 1975:

"The research institute of a northern university recently announced it finds people in the South happiest of any region in the nation.

That may not be surprising to the 'Crackers' in our midst, or perhaps even to many transplanted Yankees who came to Dixie in search of happier (or cheaper) lives.

The study, undertaken by the Institute for Social Research of the University of Michigan, found that most Americans are satisfied with their lives, but that Southerners are more satisfied in almost every respect than their counterparts in the rest of the country.

This research, which is said to be the first scientific survey of how Americans evaluate their lives, might have a message for intellectual sociologists who have a tendency to put down the South.

For example, the South ranked at the bottom of the study of desirability done by the Environmental Protection Agency in 1973. That study, however, was based on data about socioeconomic factors, such as jobs, education, housing, and income. It didn't ask people how they felt about their lives, such as the Michigan study did.

Perhaps the sociologists assumed how people should feel about a region based on their own academically established criteria.

Interestingly, even Southern blacks are apparently more content than Northern blacks.

The report said 57 percent of Southern blacks said they were very well satisfied overall, compared with 43 percent of blacks in the rest of the nation.

Despite the griping that is heard and the negative outlook of many, the study found on a nationwide basis 63 percent of white Americans and 51 percent of blacks are generally 'very satisfied with their life as a whole.'

On a regional basis, the percentage of those satisfied with their lives broke down as follows: South, 67 percent; Central, 65 percent; East, 57 percent; West, 57 percent. It's a reminder that we live in a pretty fine area."

Manufacturing,
  Nondurable Goods $10,901.00
Medical/Health Services Workers . . . $9,624.00
Miscellaneous Manufacturing $9,407.00
Motion Picture Services $10,614.00
Nonprofit Organization Workers . . . $7,407.00
Passenger Transportation
  Workers, Local and Highway $9,462.00
Personal Services $7,459.00
Private Industries,
  Including Farm Labor $10,655.00
Public School Teachers. $11,182.00
Radio Broadcasting and
  Television Workers. $13,475.00
Railroad Workers. $14,987.00
State and Local
  Government Workers $10,831.00
Telephone and Telegraph
  Workers $13,948.00
Wages per Full-Time Employee $10,817.00
Wholesale and Retail
  Trade Workers $12,930.00

Selected Prices

Antartex Main Shop Coat. $175.00
Bravos Tank Shirt $2.99
Chanel No. 19 Bath Powder $7.00
Chisholm Classics Brief Bag $52.00
Colibri Cigarette Case. $34.95
Continental Quilt Shoppe Quilt $109.95
Dual 1225 Fully Automatic
  Turntable. $199.95
Edmund Newtonian Field
  Reflector Telescope $129.95
Espresso Maker $40.00
JS&A Remote-Control Racer $49.95
L.L. Bean Touring Cap $7.50
Lord & Taylor Blazer $50.00
Marty's Old-Fashioned Fruit Cake $6.00
Miss Dior Compact. $4.50
Revlon Ultima II Wrinkle Cream $15.00
Revlon Ultima II Makeup,
  1.5 Ounces. $8.50
Saks Happy Coat Kimono $35.00
Salton's Ice Cream Machine $24.95
St. Moritz on the Park Hotel
  Room, per Day $31.00
Volkswagen Rabbit $3,500.00

"All Glitter, But Some Are Truly Golden," by Joy Williams, *Sports Illustrated*, May 5, 1975:

"There are a great many visions, and places we haven't words for. It is in our nature perhaps—our Corvette nature, our Pulsar nature, our Disney World Tomorrowland nature—to be able to speak far more eloquently about sex and the movies than about wildernesses. We spend so much time inside our heads, marshaling abstractions, fondling our emotions, that we have no time for the world's uncluttered spaces and their peace. We fear silence. We have not become civilized, educated, and free enough for silence. Or perhaps we can nerve ourselves for just a moment of it, with a martini as the sun goes down. Certainly too much stillness, with its connotation of death, is not a good thing. We're not here for long, we haven't much time.

We must make our mark, build our houses, take our recreation. The concept of 'recreation' is a new one, and we love it. We've taken to the idea like puppies to pork chops. Land use has become an obsession. There's a developer on Hilton Head who refers to conservationists as 'druids.' For isn't it the developers with their slick hotels and condos and villas who really have our best interests at heart? They want us to have a little bit of tamed playground for our own, where we can watch the sea and the sky and maybe the last seabird flying home. We haven't much time. The developers make nature accessible, do they not? They're curbing the wilderness discreetly and at great expense. And then it is presented to us—the championship golf courses, the raked beaches, the sumptuous buffets. We take our city pleasures, our suburban pastimes along with us, and tell our friends we are getting away from it all.

It is still possible to get away from it all, on islands, for instance, islands that the spoilers have somehow overlooked. So far . . . half the marshes on the East Coast have been lost to pollution, sewage, dredging, filling, industrial effluent. There are those who still believe that saving the marshes is a luxury. In fact, our estuaries produce 20 times as much food as the open sea, and more efficiently than any other ecosystem; they combat man's insatiable desire to burn up the earth's store of fossil fuel, pollute the atmosphere, trap the earth's heat, melt the glaciers, flood the plains. Marshes produce much of the air we breathe, the living grasses and algae combining to release oxygen into the atmosphere, the dying grasses, feeding plankton, oysters, shrimp, clams, crabs, and fish. It is an intricate, delicate, powerful world, anciently working, curing, and correcting itself."

EXXON SHORELINES OF AMERICA
Text by Bern Keating
Photographs by Dan Guravich
THE GULF OF MEXICO

1977 Family Profile

The Reynolds family of four lives outside Atlanta, where Martin Reynolds practices real estate law and helps his wife Audrey manage a small antique store. They have a son who is 13 and a daughter who is eight.

Annual Income: $30,700

Their income includes $28,000 from the practice of law and profits of $2,700 from selling antiques and garden furniture, particularly to "snowbirds" moving from the North to Atlanta.

Annual Budget

The average per capita consumer expenditures in 1977 for all workers nationwide are:

Auto Parts	$58.57
Auto Usage	$748.73
Clothing	$326.01
Dentists	$46.77
Food	$1,161.92
Furniture	$74.76
Gas and Oil	$212.95
Health Insurance	$42.68
Housing	$815.02
Intercity Transport	$44.95
Local Transport	$21.79
New Auto Purchase	$201.59
Personal Business	$300.13
Personal Care	$93.99
Physicians	$134.39

Private Education and Research	$108.97
Recreation	$392.30
Religion/Welfare Activities	$112.60
Telephone and Telegraph	$97.62
Tobacco	$77.19
Utilities	$251.54
Per Capita Consumption	$5,773.33

Life at Home

- The Reynolds family own their own home in Smyrna, Georgia, a community north of rapidly expanding Atlanta.
- Martin and Audrey purchased the house five years after they were married, which was 10 years ago; they have talked about upgrading.
- Audrey thinks the time to buy a bigger home is now because prices in the community are rising rapidly; Martin wants to hold down his mortgage payments so he can invest in more land and take advantage of the growth coming their way.
- They own two cars—Martin's brand-new one and Audrey's four-year-old station wagon, which she uses to transport the children.

"Inflation Still Potent, '78 Slump Inevitable," by James L. Green, Professor of Economics, University of Georgia, 1977:

"Inflation—rising prices and surging costs—remains potent in today's uneasy business climate. Consumer prices moved up 0.8 percent in January, 1 percent in February, 0.6 percent in March, 0.8 percent in April, and 0.6 percent in May (an annual rate of 9.1 percent since the first of the year).

Since 1967, the consumer price index has risen an outrageous 80.7 percent. Your income gains are, as a result, almost worthless. For example, since May of last year, average weekly earnings have increased $13.97. But in terms of standard dollars, the real gain in purchasing power is only $0.69. More than half the price of inflation of the past 10 years has occurred since January 1, 1974, during a period of deep recession, high unemployment, and faltering economic recovery. Certainly, this reflects the new stagflation twist in economic affairs.

The Commerce Department reports that both personal income and consumer prices rose 0.6 percent in May. This would seem to leave consumers neither better nor worse off. Not so. The Commerce Department also advises that local units of government raised taxes some 12.1 percent on income, retail sales, and motor vehicles. Real estate taxes in 1976 were up 9.8 percent.

In fact, real discretionary incomes are lower. As higher money incomes push us into higher marginal brackets of the tax schedule we pay more federal income taxes. Also, Social Security taxes are taking a larger bite, leaving us with less real discretionary income to spend as we choose as individuals.

Actually, one dollar in four flowing into federal coffers comes from Social Security contributions. In May, our spendable discretionary income was down 0.4 percent from a year earlier. This doesn't augur well for a sustained recovery."

New housing is being built in the rapidly growing community.

- The wagon is also used for "tailgating parties" when they attend football games at the University of Georgia, where they both graduated.
- They have season tickets to all the Georgia football games because, he says, entertaining at football games is good for business; actually, cheering for the Bulldogs is an obsession.
- The family recently purchased an English bulldog, the mascot of the University of Georgia, as a sign of their devotion to the team.

- At 38, Martin is beginning to feel that he understands how to make money, make connections, and be included in key real estate deals. He thinks he is on the brink of a fortune and is convinced that Smyrna is about to explode with new growth, and he wants to be one of those that profit.

"Does Atlanta Want Good Theater?" by Barbara Thomas, *Atlanta Journal and Constitution*, July 17, 1977:

"Atlantans who wring their hands and moan about the state of the arts here seem to have a terminal case of 'Why can't we be like New York?' If it can be done in a fashion not sounding like a Chamber of Commerce type, I'd like to suggest that maybe many Atlantans don't want to be like Gotham, culturally or otherwise, and that if comparing ourselves to that urban center is our cultural yardstick, it's little wonder we're off the mark.

While Atlanta is constantly criticized for lack of good theater, good restaurants, and whatever has the populace irritated that week, the city does have a different set of 'plusses' that many urban areas do not have. The city is filled, either fortunately or unfortunately, depending on one's stance on a side of the fence, by leisure time activities that no other urban cultural center can claim.

Explains one native New Yorker transplanted to Atlanta, 'It's hard to imagine any excitement over the arts here at all, when 10 minutes away you have pools and tennis courts that are free, where you don't have to wait in line or pay $10 an hour to play on them. To expect Atlanta to have the same cultural dynamics as a city of glass and steel is like having your cake and eating it, too.'"

- He and several friends have formed an investment club to buy real estate, and for the past several years, they have been purchasing land—betting it will become valuable.
- They believe that by owning land, they can direct the growth of the town and earn substantial gains.
- None of the men is currently wealthy or is expecting his real estate investments to pay off quickly; right now, the monthly payments on raw land—which provides no income—are cutting down on each investor's cash flow.

The Omni in Atlanta has helped mark the city as a Southern powerhouse.

- Yet all of the men, including another attorney, a doctor, and a banker, are optimistic that their investments will pay off big.
- Their wives are not so sure, but the women were not asked their opinion.
- Audrey believes the family is overextended, and is concerned about the number of empty office buildings in Atlanta, which is a good sign that growth is slowing and that the "pot of gold" her husband dreams about is not around the corner as he claims.
- She is worried that inflation will eat up their savings before the land deals are closed.
- The monthly electricity bill for 1,000 kilowatt hours is now around $60 a month, nearly double the rate of a few years ago.
- A private telephone line costs $11.50 a month before long distance calls, while station-to-station calls cost $0.30 a minute; person-to-person calls are $1.75 for the first three minutes and $0.30 a minute thereafter.
- Some neighbors still have a two-party line costing $9.30 a month, but Martin's work is too confidential for that to be practical.
- The older black woman who helps clean the Reynolds' house is now demanding a raise to $3.00 an hour; babysitters for the youngest child want $1.00 an hour.
- Going out almost doesn't pay at those prices, Audrey has told her husband repeatedly; after all, regular gas has climbed to $0.64 per gallon and for the cars that need unleaded the price is even higher—$0.66 per gallon.
- President Carter just announced plans for a five-cent increase in federal gasoline taxes, which will raise costs even more.
- Just last month, the charges for the children's visit to the dentist were $15.00 each for cleaning their teeth; a filling is now $12.00.
- Haircuts for men are now $8.00–$10.00 in the city—and for women, a permanent now costs $35.00, a shampoo and set, $8.00, and a haircut, $10.00.
- To dry clean her husband's suits—and he always wears a suit—the dry cleaner charges $4.00 per suit, shirts are $1.50 each, and the dress she wore to a party last weekend ran $4.00.

Life at Work

- Up a flight of 29 wooden stairs in a bank building is Martin's office, where he and his two partners occupy half of the second floor.
- The bank, which occupies the first floor, was established at the turn of the century, and the building serves as its headquarters.
- Thanks to restrictive banking laws, few competitors have come into Cobb County, allowing the bank to grow quickly.

- Martin works closely with the bank to close deals, perfect titles, and meet the difficult deadlines often demanded by customers.
- He spends so much time at the courthouse researching titles, often working on Saturdays and at night, he has been given his own key to the building.
- Two days a week, he takes coffee and biscuits to the women who work in the records section of the courthouse.
- They call him the "Mayor of Smyrna" because he handles so many real estate transactions and loves to talk about how the town is going to grow.
- While travelling, he enjoys buying antiques for his wife's business; he especially likes Southern furniture made prior to the Civil War.

- The family has had three different wooden kitchen tables this year alone; after each new purchase, the earlier table goes to Audrey's antique store.
- Prices for quality furniture are rising quickly.
- He also collects Civil War bullets, belt buckles, and uniforms, and keeps a metal detector in the trunk of the car so he can search sites for artifacts.
- Audrey keeps her antique store open Tuesday through Friday from 10 a.m. to 3 p.m.; most of her business is by appointment only, and she never does business on Sundays.

Smyrna is not far from the state capital in Atlanta.

- Twice a year, she sponsors a booth at the Atlanta Flea Market—an enormous, one-story building with 83,000 square feet of space.
- Some days she is unsure whether she wanted the antique store, or if Martin did.

Life in the Community: Smyrna, Georgia

- The rapid growth of Atlanta is remolding this Southern town into an international community, but the changes are not without their conflicts.
- Atlantans constantly debate the merits of imitating New York or forging their own image.
- Atlanta, the largest city between New Orleans and Washington, DC, is the financial, commercial, and cultural capital of the Southeast.
- Atlanta serves as the headquarters for the Sixth Federal Reserve System, making the city the region's financial center; it is also the world headquarters of Coca-Cola.
- The city is proud of its 47 parks and three professional teams, covering baseball, football, and hockey.
- Atlanta's school system was the first in Georgia to integrate in the 1960s.
- In Atlanta, the price of a home sold through the Board of Realtors' Multiple Listing Service was $109,000; in Smyrna, the average is closer to $85,000.
- Condominiums are now being built and sold in Atlanta, costing an average of $66,000, though Martin does not believe his community is ready for "condos"; everyone in Smyrna takes great pride in their yards.
- Many of his neighbors now share a "yard man" to help with the grass and leaves, since few can afford their own help as in the old days.
- Not everyone in the Smyrna community is interested in growth and change; many enjoy the quiet pace of this Southern community.
- In Atlanta, foreclosures are rising; the Atlanta savings and loan associations report that foreclosures doubled in the past year.
- The Georgia Railroad Bank and Trust Company of Augusta is currently foreclosing on two pieces of property in the financially ailing Underground Atlanta.
- President Jimmy Carter has just declared 62 counties in the state eligible for federal assistance for farmers due to drought, making Georgia cattle farmers eligible now for grants to feed their herds.
- According to the Tax Foundation, the average family pays about 40 percent of its family income in taxes, with about 29 percent of the family income expended for direct taxes such as property tax, auto and gas taxes, and Social Security, state, and federal taxes, and about 11 percent for indirect taxes.

Coca-Cola is an important corporate citizen.

Historical Snapshot
1977

- American Express became the first service company to top $1 billion in sales
- *Li'l Abner* ceased publication
- Three major networks controlled 91 percent of prime-time audiences
- Cheryl Tiegs, the world's highest-paid model, earned $1,000 a day
- 1.9 million women operated businesses
- The U.S. and Canada signed a pact to build a gas pipeline from Alaska to the Midwest
- Because of soaring prices, consumers boycotted coffee
- The sale of imported cars broke all records, passing 1.5 million
- Balloon angioplasty was developed for reopening diseased arteries of the heart
- The Supreme Court reversed a New York law that prohibited the distribution of contraceptives to minors
- The FDA banned the use of the additive Red Dye # 2 in foods, drugs, and cosmetics
- Widespread looting occurred during a blackout in New York and Westchester that affected nine million people
- Pepsi topped Coca-Cola in sales for the first time
- 20,000 shopping malls generated 50 percent of total retail sales
- 45 million people watched the highest-rated TV interview in history, featuring former President Richard Nixon on the David Frost program; Nixon was paid $600,000, plus 10 percent of the show's profits
- The Supreme Court ruled that the spanking of schoolchildren by teachers was constitutional
- CBS anchor Walter Cronkite acted as an intermediary between Anwar Sadat and Menachem Begin to arrange a meeting in Israel
- Elvis Presley died, and within a day of his death, two million of his records sold; his funeral cost $47,000
- Fashion for men saw a return to conservatism marked by narrow, silk challis ties with small patterns and Oxford and broadcloth shirts
- More than 400,000 teenage abortions were performed, a third of the total in the United States; 21 percent of the unmarried teens gave birth and 87 percent kept their children
- The CB radio fad resulted in record sales
- Presidential call-ins, no-brand generic products, pocket TVs, and public automatic blood pressure machines all made their first appearance

1977 ECONOMIC PROFILE

Income, Standard Jobs

Bituminous Coal Mining	$18,292.00
Building Trades	$14,639.00
Domestics	$6,844.00
Farm Labor	$6,021.00
Federal Civilian	$17,488.00
Federal Employees, Executive Departments	$13,980.00

"Too Many Tigers, Boom in Metro Lawyers Population Could Help Public or Flood Courts," by Hyde Post, *The Atlanta Journal and Constitution*, July 17, 1977:

"Some Georgia bar members warn that the abundance of attorneys in the Atlanta area offers the potential for increases in unnecessary legal filings.

Others, however, suggest the surfeit of legal talent will prove a boon for currently under-represented middle-income groups, and for competition in general.

Whether they see gloom or boom on legal business horizons, though, lawyers and judges contacted recently seemed to agree on one point: the attorney population in greater metro-Atlanta is growing faster than a well-watered lawn.

In 12 judicial circuits that include all 15 metro-Atlanta counties, plus an additional 17 rural ones, the number of attorneys in the last six years has increased 70 percent, according to statistics from a 1976 Georgia Administrative Office of the Courts (AOC) report.

In contrast, the population of the circuits has grown by 11 percent over the same period.

Some bar members suggested that the abundance of attorneys, coupled with the U.S. Supreme Court's decision on advertising, could prove to be a blessing for the middle 70 percent of the population, which the American Bar Association has said 'is not being reached or adequately served by the legal profession.'

Others, however, said there was only so much legitimate legal business to be had in the greater metro area. An inordinate number of hungry attorneys, they warned, could bring an increase in unwarranted litigation. 'If you've got too many tigers in the jungle and they eat up all their natural prey, they start becoming mankillers because of hunger, and I think that's true of lawyers . . . and not just younger ones by any means,' said (attorney) Wayne Hyatt."

Federal Military	$10,854.00
Finance, Insurance, and Real Estate	$12,184.00
Gas, Electricity, and Sanitation Workers	$16,916.00
Manufacturing, Durable Goods	$14,730.00
Manufacturing, Nondurable Goods	$12,578.00
Medical/Health Services Workers	$11,248.00
Miscellaneous Manufacturing	$10,678.00
Motion Picture Services	$13,209.00
Nonprofit Organization Workers	$8,297.00
Passenger Transportation Workers, Local and Highway	$10,780.00
Personal Services	$8,322.00
Private Industries, Including Farm Labor	$12,222.00
Public School Teachers	$12,738.00
Radio Broadcasting and Television Workers	$15,708.00
Railroad Workers	$18,784.00
State and Local Government Workers	$12,359.00
Telephone and Telegraph Workers	$17,279.00

Atlanta's new airport is aiding the city's growth.

Wages per Full-Time
Employee $14,584.00
Wholesale and Retail Trade
Workers $12,930.00

Selected Prices

Big Slider Gym. $64.99
Catesbury Print $150.00
Chandis Lines Cruise,
Seven Nights, Eight Days $6.99
Citizens Band Transceiver
Car Stereo $269.99
Elizabeth Arden Gown $125.00
Firestone Forever Battery $59.00

Editorial, "Economy and Energy," *The Atlanta Journal and Constitution*, July 18, 1977:

"The headlines told good economic news. 'Building Boom to Hit 19 Percent,' said one; 'July Car Sales up 15 Percent,' said the other.

But is that good energy news?

The McGraw-Hill Information Systems Co. has reported that revenues in the U.S. construction industry will surge 19 percent over last year's total of $127.5 billion, with housing starts expected to total 1.75 million units in 1977. 'We expect a high plateau of housing activity for the remainder of 1977, and 1978 as well,' said a McGraw spokesman.

As for the automobiles, the four major U.S. auto makers reported combined new domestic car sales rose 15 percent during the first 10 days of July, compared with the same period in 1976. For the calendar year to date, new auto sales were up seven percent from a year ago.

There's no arguing that the new reports are good for the nation's economy and consumers. For now, at least. The boosts in housing starts and auto sales mean increased jobs and better payrolls, higher standards of living, reduced unemployment. The housing and auto industries are economic bellwethers, and when they are doing well, it indicates the rest of the economy is in fine health, also.

But—and this has become the important economic issue of all in the United States—how energy-efficient are these new cars being sold and new houses being built?

The energy crisis hasn't magically gone away. It's still with us and it's going to get worse. Our economy is rapidly moving into a new era—an era of energy shortage rather than energy abundance.

Historically, the U.S. economy has boomed, and Americans live the richest lives of any people of the world, in major part because of our energy abundance. But already, the growing shortages and higher prices and energy are forcing changes in our lifestyles, and much more drastic changes are ahead.

Surely today's new cars and new houses are more energy-efficient than they were just a couple of years ago, and further improvements are planned. But the improvements are coming too slowly; there's still too much emphasis on luxury rather than efficient use of energy. Meanwhile, Congress is too scared to take the strong action needed. While we mindlessly burn up energy, Congress fiddles."

Gamefisher Boat Motor $119.00
Lawn Valet Sweeper and Bagger $186.00
Motorcycle Helmet $30.99
Persian Baktiari Rug $1,850.00
Portalign Drill Stand $19.99
Presto Pressure Cooker, Six-Quart $10.88
Saxon Plain Paper Copier $2,995.00
Seal-N-Save Food Sealer $16.49
Singapore by Croscill Bedspread. $39.00
Sno-Cone Maker $5.66
Storm Windows, Triple-Track
  Insulating Aluminum Frame $32.95
Toughskin Jeans $6.39
United Airlines Roundtrip Fare
  to Los Angeles/San Francisco $342.00
Viewmaster 3-D Viewer $17.44

Craig and Tarlton, Inc.
122 Glenwood Avenue • Raleigh, North Carolina 27603
(919) 828-2559
Queen Anne walnut and gilt looking glass, circa 1720-40, retaining its original finish, gilt, and cut-decorated glass. Illustrated Nutting plate 2842.
Important American umbrella, circa 1790-1810, with handle depicting the U.S. Seal on one side and a bust of George Washington on the reverse. It retains its original whalebone stays.
Rare Philadelphia Chippendale walnut dressing table, circa 1770, with molded top, scalloped apron, and cabriole legs terminating in exceptionally handsome claw and ball feet. Height 28½", width 35¼", depth 20¼".
Massachusetts mahogany swell front chest retaining its original brasses, circa 1780. Height 35¼", width 40½", depth 22½".
Gallery hours are 10-5
Fine eighteenth and early nineteenth century American furniture, complementing accessories, and American paintings.
Closed Saturdays through Sept. 4

Retail Food Prices

Apples, All-Purpose, per Pound $0.64
Bread, White, One Pound $0.37
Butter, One Pound $1.40
Carrots, per Pound $0.23
Coffee, One-Pound Can $3.08
Cookies, Cream-Filled, One Pound $1.17
Corn Flakes, 12 Ounces $0.58
Eggs, Grade A, Large, per Dozen $0.73
Flour, White, All-Purpose $0.81
Frying Chicken, per Pound $0.74
Hamburger, per Pound $1.05
Ice Cream, Half-Gallon. $1.33
Lettuce, Head $0.63
Margarine, One Pound $0.64
Milk, Fresh, Half-Gallon $0.72
Pork Chops, per Pound $2.13
Potatoes, 10 Pounds $1.21
Rib Roast, per Pound $2.23
Steak, Round, per Pound $2.09
Sugar, White, Five Pounds. $1.11
Tomatoes, per Pound. $0.65
Tuna Fish, Six-Ounce Can $0.72

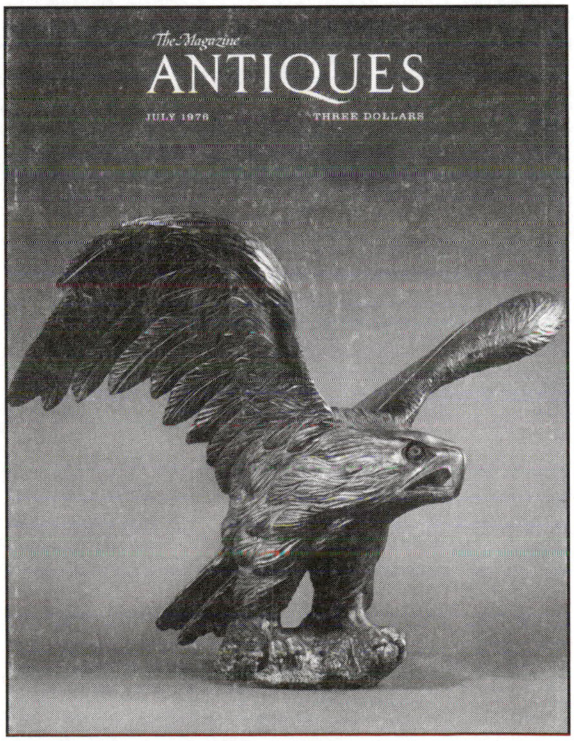

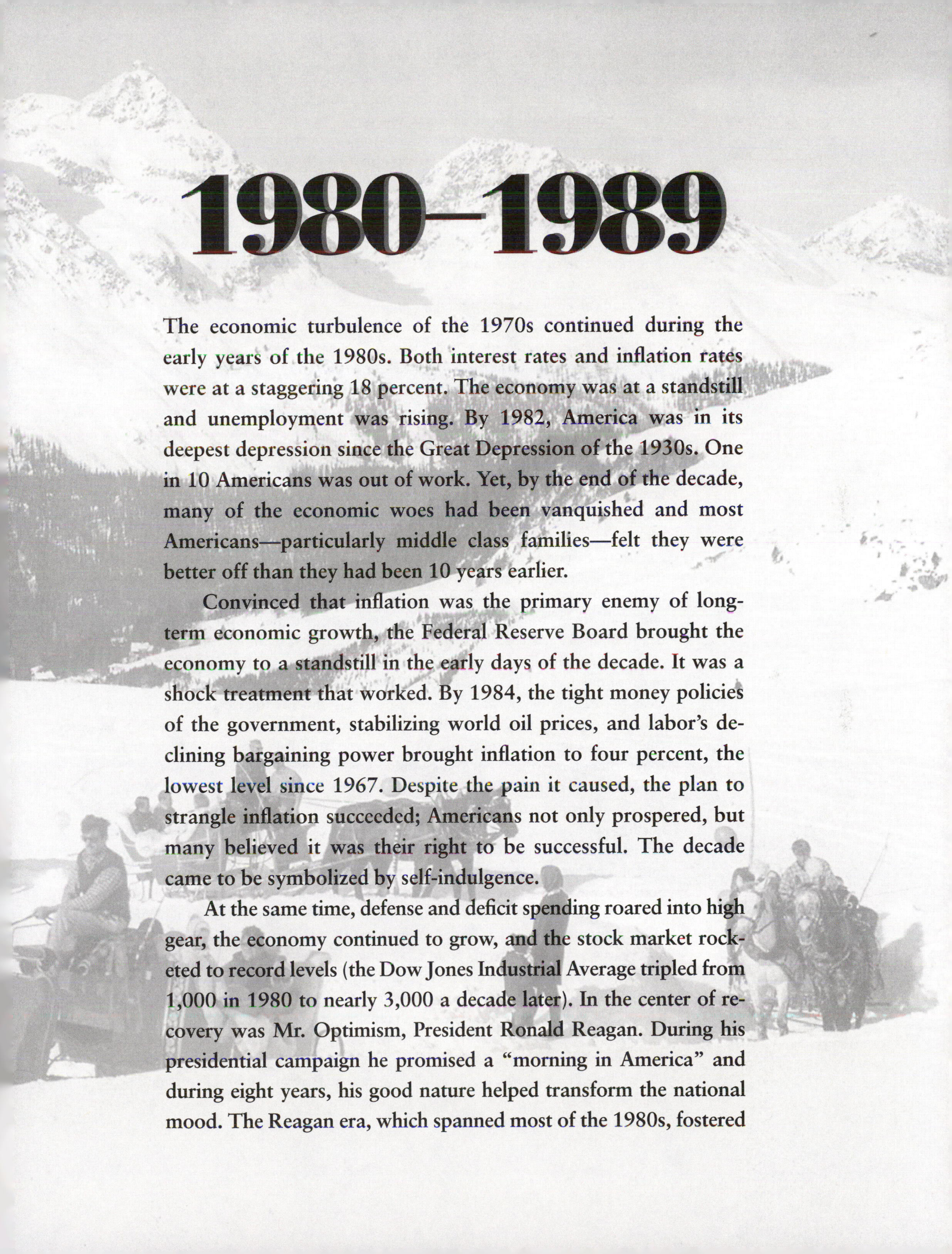

1980–1989

The economic turbulence of the 1970s continued during the early years of the 1980s. Both interest rates and inflation rates were at a staggering 18 percent. The economy was at a standstill and unemployment was rising. By 1982, America was in its deepest depression since the Great Depression of the 1930s. One in 10 Americans was out of work. Yet, by the end of the decade, many of the economic woes had been vanquished and most Americans—particularly middle class families—felt they were better off than they had been 10 years earlier.

Convinced that inflation was the primary enemy of long-term economic growth, the Federal Reserve Board brought the economy to a standstill in the early days of the decade. It was a shock treatment that worked. By 1984, the tight money policies of the government, stabilizing world oil prices, and labor's declining bargaining power brought inflation to four percent, the lowest level since 1967. Despite the pain it caused, the plan to strangle inflation succeeded; Americans not only prospered, but many believed it was their right to be successful. The decade came to be symbolized by self-indulgence.

At the same time, defense and deficit spending roared into high gear, the economy continued to grow, and the stock market rocketed to record levels (the Dow Jones Industrial Average tripled from 1,000 in 1980 to nearly 3,000 a decade later). In the center of recovery was Mr. Optimism, President Ronald Reagan. During his presidential campaign he promised a "morning in America" and during eight years, his good nature helped transform the national mood. The Reagan era, which spanned most of the 1980s, fostered a new conservative agenda of good feeling. During the presidential election against incumbent President Jimmy Carter, Reagan joked, "A recession is when your neighbor loses his job. A depression is when you lose yours. And recovery is when Jimmy Carter loses his."

The economic wave of the 1980s was also driven by globalization, improvements in technology, and willingness of consumers to assume higher and higher levels of personal debt. By the 1980s, the two-career family became the norm. Forty-two percent of all American workers were female, and more than half of all married women and 90 percent of female college graduates worked outside the home. Yet, their median wage was 60 percent of that of men. The rapid rise of women in the labor force, which had been accelerating since the 1960s, brought great social change, affecting married life, child rearing, family income, office culture, and the growth of the national economy.

The rising economy brought greater control of personal lives; homeownership accelerated, choices seemed limitless, debt grew, and divorce became commonplace. The collapse of communism at the end of the 1980s brought an end to the old world order and set the stage for a realignment of power. America was regarded as the strongest nation in the world and the only real superpower, thanks to its economic strength. As democracy swept across eastern Europe, the U.S. economy began to feel the impact of a "peace dividend" generated by a reduced military budget and a desire by corporations to participate in global markets—including Russia and China. Globalization was having another impact. At the end of World War II, the U.S. economy accounted for almost 50 percent of the global economic product; by 1987, the U.S. share was less than 25 percent as American companies moved plants offshore and countries such as Japan emerged as major competitors. This need for a global reach inspired several rounds of corporate mergers as companies searched for efficiency, market share, new products, or emerging technology to survive in the rapidly shifting business environment.

The 1980s were the age of the conservative Yuppie. Business schools, investment banks, and Wall Street firms overflowed with eager baby boomers who placed gourmet cuisine, health clubs, supersneakers, suspenders, wine spritzers, high-performance autos, and sushi high on their agendas. Low-fat and fiber cereals and Jane Fonda workout books symbolized much of the decade. As self-indulgence rose, concerns about the environment, including nuclear waste, acid rain, and the greenhouse effect declined. Homelessness increased and racial tensions fostered a renewed call for a more caring government. During the decade, genetic engineering came of age, including early attempts at transplantation and gene mapping. Personal computers, which were transforming America, were still in their infancy.

The sexual revolution, undaunted by a conservative prescription of chastity, ran head-on into a powerful adversary during the 1980s with the discovery and spread of AIDS, a frequently fatal, sexually transmitted disease. The right of women to have an abortion, confirmed by the Supreme Court in 1973, was hotly contested during the decade as politicians fought over both the actual moment of conception and the right of a woman to control her body. Cocaine also made its reappearance, bringing drug addiction and a rapid increase in violent crime. The Center on Addiction and Substance Abuse at Columbia University found alcohol and drug abuse implicated in three fourths of all murders, rapes, child molestations, and deaths of babies suffering from parental neglect.

For the first time in history, the Naval Academy's graduating class included women, digital clocks and cordless telephones appeared, and 24-hour-a-day news coverage captivated television viewers. Compact disks began replacing records, and Smurf and E.T. paraphernalia were everywhere, New York became the first state to require seat belts, Pillsbury introduced microwave pizza, and Playtex used live lingerie models in its ads for the "Cross Your Heart" bra. The Supreme Court ruled that states may require all-male private clubs to admit women, and 50,000 people gathered at Graceland in Memphis, Tennessee, on the tenth anniversary of Elvis Presley's death.

1982 Family Profile

Greg Tilsner is chief operating officer of Softec, a software company for personal computers in Los Angeles. His wife, Yukiko, who is second-generation Japanese, works alongside him. They have no house, no children, and a five-year-old car. Softec is their life.

Annual Income: $70,000
They pay themselves $35,000 each; Greg also received stock options during the past year, which are of an undetermined value.

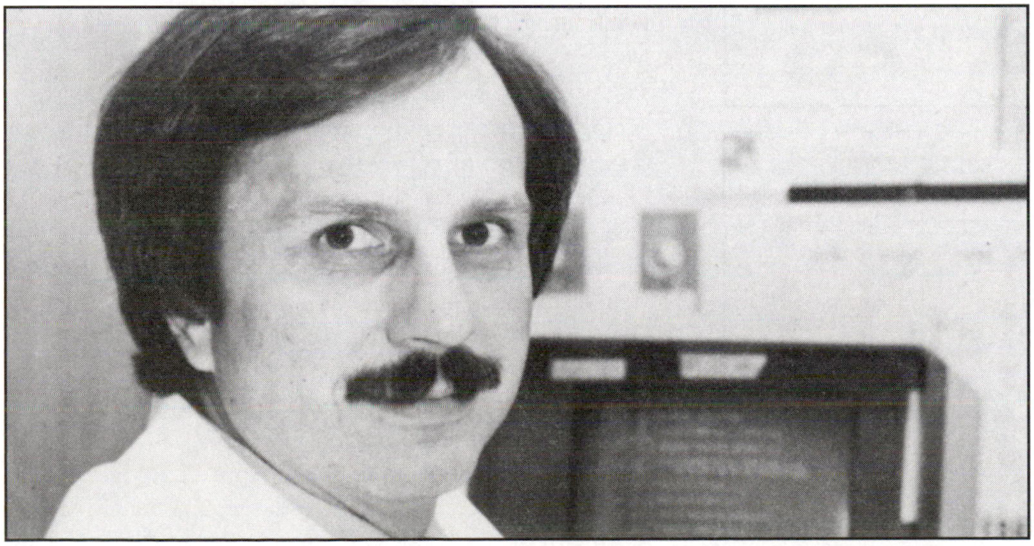

Most of Greg Tilsner's life revolves around Softec.

```
980  IF QUIZ$ = "Y" THEN  HTAB 1: PRINT "HANG IN  WHILE I CHOOSE THE STATE
     S...";: GOTO 225
990  GOSUB 30460: GOTO 225
995 :
999  END
1000 :
29000  REM                                          SET-UP & CHECKERS
29010 TITLE$ = LINE$ + ", " + STAET$(THIS)
29020  VTAB 15: HTAB 1: CALL  - 868
29030  GOSUB 34000
29040  VTAB 15
29050  HTAB HT%
29060  INPUT "";A$
29070  IF  LEN (TE$) > 0 AND  LEN (A$) = 0 THEN A$ = TE$
29080  IF A$ = "" THEN  PRINT  CHR$ (7): GOTO 29020
29090  GOSUB 30500: REM  LEAD/TRAIL SPACES
29100 A$ =  LEFT$ (A$,PL)
29110 TITLE$ = A$ + ", " + STAET$(THIS)
29120  VTAB 15: HTAB 1: CALL  - 868
29130  GOSUB 34000
29140  VTAB 22: HTAB 1: CALL  - 958
29150  INVERSE : PRINT "ARE YOU SURE? (Y/N RETURN=Y) ";
29160  NORMAL
29170  POKE  - 16368,0: GET QUIZ$
29180  IF QUIZ$ <  > "N" THEN 29280
29190  VTAB 22: HTAB 1: CALL  - 958
29200  PRINT "PLEASE TYPE IN YOUR NEW ANSWER"
29210  INVERSE : PRINT "RETURN";
29220  NORMAL : PRINT " KEEPS YOUR OLD ANSWER"
29230  VTAB 15: HTAB 1: CALL  - 868
29240  IF  LEN (A$) = PL THEN TITLE$ = A$ + ", " + STAET$(THIS): GOTO 2926
     0
29250 TITLE$ = A$ +  LEFT$ (LINE$,PL -  LEN (A$)) + ", " + STAET$(THIS)
29260 TE$ = A$
29270  GOTO 29030
29280 TE$ = ""
29290  RETURN
29299 :
30000  REM                                          TITLE PAGE
30010  TEXT : HOME :TITLE$ = "STATE CAPITALS":CHAR$ = "*":CT% = 40:L% =  LEN
     (TITLE$)
30070  VTAB 4
30080 HT% = (CT% - L%) / 2 - 1
30090  GOSUB 31000
30100  GOSUB 32000
30110  HTAB HT%: PRINT CHAR$;" ";: INVERSE : PRINT TITLE$;: NORMAL : PRINT
     " ";CHAR$
30170  GOSUB 32000
30180  GOSUB 31000
30190  VTAB 14
30200 RJ$ = "COPYRIGHT 1981"
30210  GOSUB 33000
30220 RJ$ = "BY SCOT KAMINS"
30230  GOSUB 33000
30240 RJ$ = "COML RIGHTS RESERVED"
30250  GOSUB 33000
30260  VTAB 21: HTAB 7: INVERSE : PRINT "RETURN";: NORMAL : PRINT " TO BEG
     IN"
30302  PRINT "PRESS";
```

Annual Budget

The average per capita consumer expenditures in 1982 for all workers nationwide are:

Auto Parts	$64.88
Auto Usage	$1,034.58
Clothing	$435.45
Dentists	$74.94
Food	$1,662.57
Furniture	$90.45
Gas and Oil	$405.30
Health Insurance	$77.09
Housing	$1,339.96
Intercity Transport	$77.09
Local Transport	$23.26
New Auto Purchase	$229.57
Personal Business	$525.91
Personal Care	$127.92
Physicians	$237.76
Private Education and Research	$179.61
Recreation	$603.00
Religion/Welfare Activities	$206.31
Telephone and Telegraph	$151.18
Tobacco	$104.66
Utilities	$425.55
Per Capita Consumption	$8,869.32

Life at Home

- Softec is this couple's life; together all day at work, they rarely go home to the apartment they rent nearby.
- All of their friends work at Softec; occasionally, Yukiko will take a break and fly to see her father in San Francisco, where she grew up.
- Most of Greg's waking hours are spent on the job.
- Working at Softec is like living in a college dormitory; the average age of the employees is 30 years old, and they are crammed into tiny offices two at a time.
- Blue jeans and work shirts are common, and most of the men wear beards and have sideburns.
- The company refrigerator is stocked with Coke, Pepsi, and an assortment of natural fruit juices.
- Every employee, including receptionists, has a computer terminal.
- All the interoffice mail is sent through the company's newest Prime minicomputer.
- Dozens of personal computers, Apples, Radio Shacks, IBMs, and others, are scattered throughout the office, most with their innards permanently exposed.

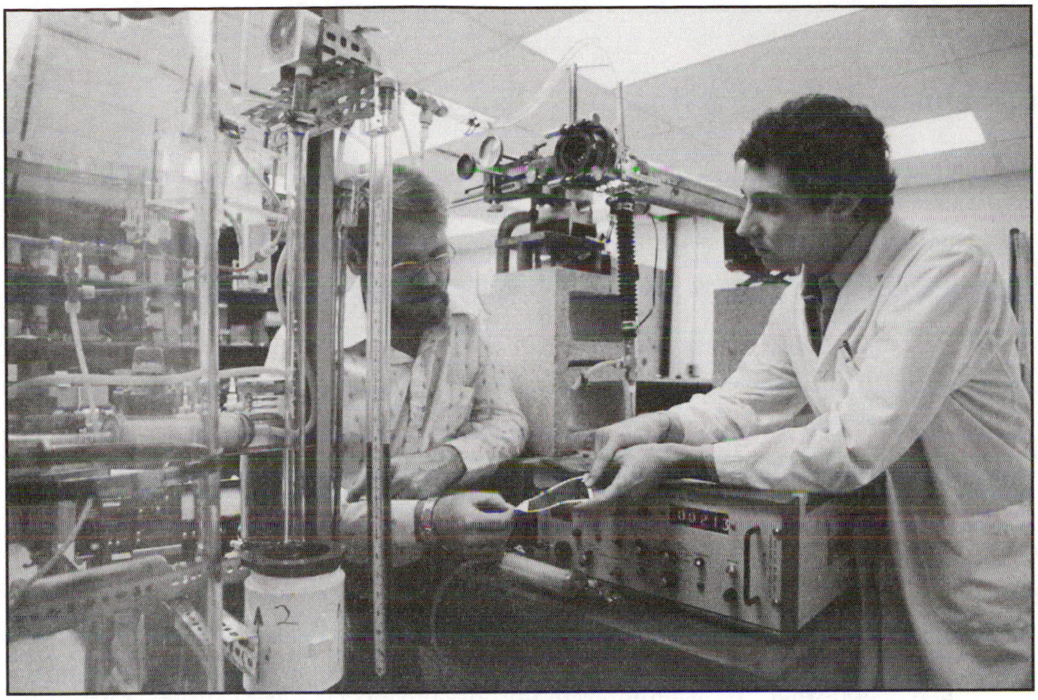

Life at Work

- Greg serves as the chief financial officer and day-to-day manager of a Los Angeles-based software company called Softec, which is focused exclusively on providing products for the personal computer market.
- His biggest worry at the moment is finding the type of management the company will need in a year if Softec continues to grow as quickly.
- The company's principal product is a home budgeting program that effectively crunches and organizes a large quantity of numbers; more than 200,000 copies have been sold.
- Initially, the program was designed exclusively for Apple computers; Apple believes the software has helped promote its hardware.
- Last year, the company adapted the program to other machines.
- The company was founded three years ago, and all of the management is under 30 years old.
- Two years ago, the revenues of Softec were $1 million; last year, the company planned for $2 million and ended with $3 million.
- Management is unsure of how to plan for this year, because in a company only three years old in an industry only five years old, there are few precedents to draw upon.
- The number of employees has grown from four to 35 in the first year, and now stands at 50.

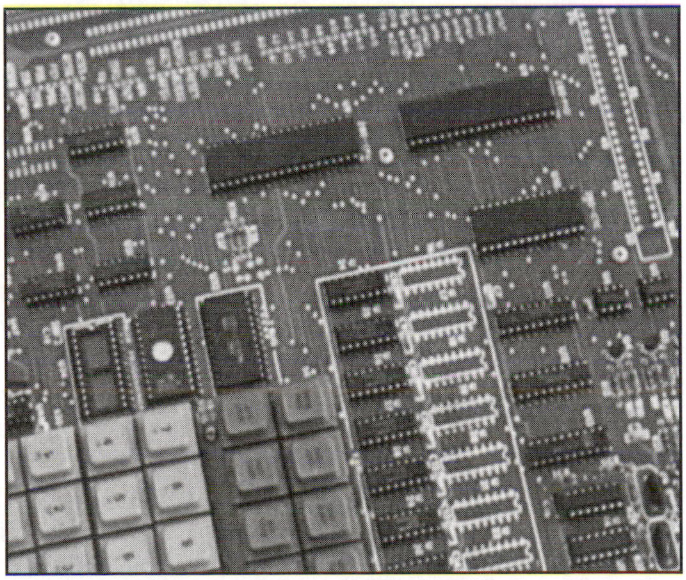

"How Software Is Manufactured," *Inc.*, January 1982:

"It is important to distinguish between software authors and publishers, though they may overlap. The author writes the program itself, which involves a dogged attention to detail that may require long stretches of 18-hour days until a program is completed.

The author writes step-by-step instructions telling the computer exactly how to execute a task. Computers operate by recognizing either the presence or absence of an electrical impulse, so they can only manipulate long strings of yes or no commands. That means the programmer can't leave anything to the imagination. Each step in a task must be spelled out in excruciating detail. The finished program ends up as a series of encoded lines of computer instructions that, if written out line by line, would fill dozens of pages of text; it's usually stored on a compact 5.5-inch magnetic disk.

'Once a program is completed to the programmer's satisfaction, he typically submits it on a disk to a publisher,' says Harris Landgarten, director of software applications at Lifeboat Associates. The program, along with the documentation (the manual that describes the program and how to use it), is evaluated for its sales potential, its probable markets, and its user-friendliness.

The author and publisher then negotiate a contract in which the author assigns the publication rights to the publisher for either a flat fee or a royalty of 15 percent to 30 percent of the retail price of the program. If they can come to an agreement, both parties work on perfecting the program (called 'working out the bugs,' in the jargon of the trade). The software is tested, usually by both an in-house staff (called alpha-testers) and by outsiders (called beta-testers), and the manual is typeset and printed. Finally, the program is mass-produced on disks or tapes in formats compatible with the operating systems of different microcomputers.

A software author may opt to self-publish. A number of authors have been successful enough to establish and build companies that specialize in writing programs and have started to publish their own products. And, with sophisticated programming languages like Microsoft BASIC and the increased accessibility of personal computers, many non-technical people have learned how to program computers well enough to create useful software for specialized purposes. Duplicating a diskette is a simple operation: In minutes just about anyone can turn a blank $2 disk into a $50 to $500 program disk."

- Management is trying to grow the company in a controlled way, but feels it is constantly out of control.
- Cautious about making public sales projections, they don't want too much hype to spoil their progress.
- Greg has a sense that time has sped up; he works 18-hour days, rarely accomplishing as much as he had hoped.
- He began development of the software during college with two partners, slowly developing the concept, often borrowing computers or renting time-sharing terminals to complete the programming.
- After several computer dealers showed little interest in their prototype, Greg and his partners scraped up $20,000 in cash, pledged a loan for $65,000, and bought a Prime 550 minicomputer for the final development of the Softec program.

"Oh, no. . . . It's Sunday."

Yukiko occasionally takes time off to visit her father in San Francisco.

Life in the Community: Los Angeles, California

- Despite the success of Softec, the general economy has been battered.
- The auto industry is burdened with debt, housing activity is slow, and retailers report sluggish sales.
- Gasoline prices are moving up again as OPEC attempts to push the price of oil to $34 a barrel.
- However, high tech is booming; both California's Apple Computer and New Jersey's Matrix, maker of diagnostic imaging systems, registered seven-fold increases in sales from 1977 to 1981.
- Los Angeles, the largest city area in the country, encompasses 450 square miles and boasts more than 10 million in the metropolitan area.
- It is the city of cars; day and night, the freeways and highways are choked with traffic.
- It is also a city of diversity.
- A recent report indicates that its large Spanish-speaking population is switching to English at about the same rate as the German, Italian, and Polish immigrants who came before them.

HISTORICAL SNAPSHOT 1982–1983

- The courts ordered the breakup of AT&T, the U.S. telephone monopoly, into AT&T long-distance lines and regional telephone companies
- The Japanese marketed the wristwatch-sized television with a 1.2 inch screen
- A mysterious disease that killed 40 percent of its victims was reported and named AIDS, acquired immune deficiency syndrome
- Prices for computers plummeted; Timex sold a personal computer for $99.95, while the Commodore VIC 20 sold for $199
- Computers reached 1.5 million homes—five times the number in 1980
- *USA Today*, the first national general-interest daily newspaper, was introduced
- 2.9 million women operated businesses
- Nationwide, 93 percent of homes had a telephone
- The first artificial heart was impacted in patient Barney Clark, age 61
- The Vietnam Veterans' Memorial, inscribed with the 57,939 names of American soldiers killed or missing in Vietnam, was dedicated in Washington, DC
- Braniff International Airlines and F.W. Woolworth declared bankruptcy
- Dun and Bradstreet reported a total of 20,365 bankruptcies by October, the highest figure since the Great Depression
- The United Auto Workers agreed to wage concessions with Ford Motor Company
- U.S. Steel acquired Marathon Oil
- Unemployment reached 10.8 percent
- Efforts at library censorship tripled; books under fire in New York included *The Adventures of Huckleberry Finn*, *The Grapes of Wrath*, and *The Catcher in the Rye*
- The computer "mouse" was introduced by Apple
- The first successful embryo transfer was performed
- Columbia, the last all-male college in the Ivy League, decided to begin accepting women in 1983
- NutraSweet was introduced as a synthetic sugar substitute
- President Ronald Reagan proclaimed May 6 "National Day of Prayer" and endorsed a constitutional amendment to permit school prayer; it was defeated
- In professional football, a strike cut the regular season to nine games
- The proposed equal rights amendment (ERA) ran out of time, receiving only 35 of the 38 state ratifications required
- The Dow experienced a one-day drop of a record 39 points; the high for the year was 1,070, while the low was 776
- Ocean Spray was introduced in paper bottles
- The compact disk, polyurethane car bumpers, the Honda Accord, and the NCAA major college basketball championship for women all made their first appearances

1982 Economic Profile

Income, Standard Jobs

Bituminous Coal Mining	$29,110.00
Building Trades	$21,868.00
Domestics	$10,260.00
Farm Labor	$8,781.00
Federal Civilian	$24,452.00
Federal Employees, Executive Departments	$20,689.00
Federal Military	$17,384.00
Finance, Insurance, and Real Estatez	$18,966.00
Gas, Electricity, and Sanitation Workers	$26,185.00
Manufacturing, Durable Goods	$22,256.00
Manufacturing, Nondurable Goods	$19,272.00

Inside the Family Business, the Misapplication of Time, by Leon A. Danco:

"The entrepreneur overspends his money, yes, and his health, yes, and the emotions of his family, yes, but other resources are wasted just as surely—mostly as a result of his misapplication and overassumption of his major asset, time.

Where the business owner puts his time is where he puts his heart, his dreams, and his thoughts. It can't be otherwise, because time steadily ticks by and every moment is just as important as the next. The minutes follow each other in relentless procession, and they can never be duplicated.

Yet the entrepreneur in his early years spends prodigiously of his time, with very little sense of priority. In doing so, he tends to waste his resources. All he gets every day is 24 hours. So to get everything done that he must get done, he steals from his sleep, he steals from his energies, he steals from his limited reservoirs, whatever he thinks he must do, in order to survive. He works 16–18 hours a day, seven days a week.

He abuses his health. He abuses his family and his friends. He doesn't have the patience, the understanding, and often, the guts to take time out of his relentless pursuit of survival. He is beset with the inevitable entrepreneurial disease called tunnel vision, the single-minded pursuit of objectives regardless of the cost to himself or to others."

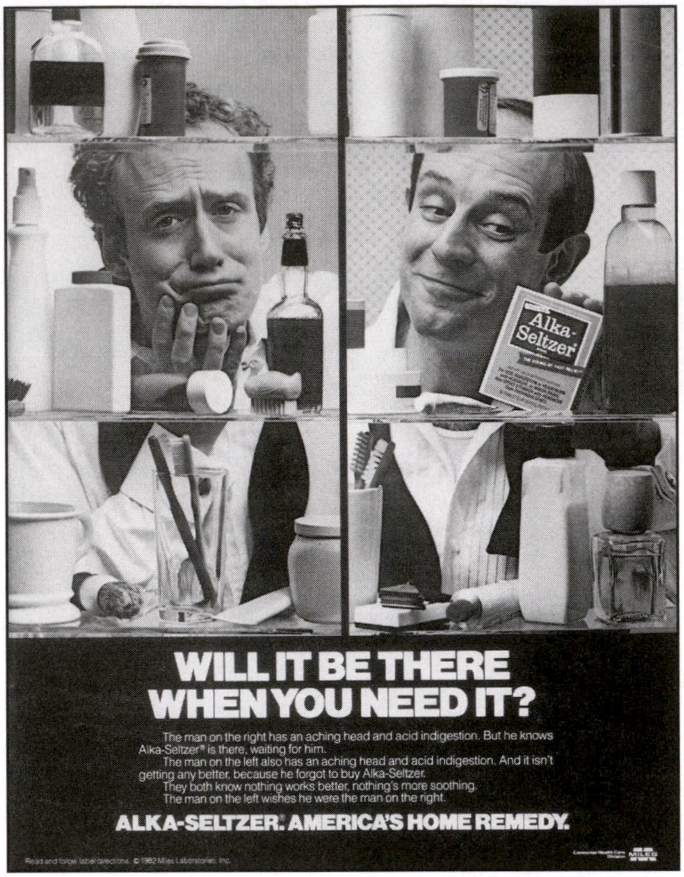

Medical/Health Services Workers	$17,861.00
Miscellaneous Manufacturing	$16,680.00
Motion Picture Services	$21,452.00
Nonprofit Organization Workers	$11,971.00
Passenger Transportation Workers, Local and Highway	$15,224.00
Personal Services	$11,752.00
Postal Employees	NR
Private Industries, Including Farm Labor	$15,721.00
Public School Teachers	$18,061.00
Radio Broadcasting and Television Workers	$22,550.00
Railroad Workers	$29,692.00
State and Local Government Workers	$17,762.00
Telephone and Telegraph Workers	$27,313.00
Wages per Full-Time Employee	$15,757.00
Wholesale and Retail Trade Workers	$21,694.00

"Top 100, 1982," *Inc.*:

"There is a bright side to the economy of the past year, however, and it can be found in the 1982 *Inc. 100*—fourth annual ranking of the fastest-growing publicly held smaller corporations in the United States. While the giants posted a 1981 sales gain of about 12 percent, the *Inc. 100* companies chalked up a vigorous 77 percent increase. . . . Sporting nameplates from the exotic, such as HemoTec and Healthdyne, to the simple such as Liz Claiborne and Taco Charley, the ranking represents a diverse range of manufacturing, mining, and service industries. It includes 24 computer and business equipment makers, 11 oil and gas producers, nine manufacturers in the medical field, three restaurant chains, and two airlines. The elite group is headquartered in 28 states: California is the front-runner with 17 companies, followed by New York and Texas with 15 each and Minnesota with seven.

Diverse as they are in industry and location, the *Inc. 100* share four qualities: youth, innovation, high productivity, and a healthy bottom line. Fifty-six have incorporated since 1972, 89 have increased since 1962. On average, the *Inc. 100* firms have been in business less than 12 years."

Selected Prices

Bass Tracker 1 Boat $3,795.00
Breyers Yogurt, Eight-Ounce Container. $0.89
Browning Featherweight Soft Leather Boots $102.95
Cabela Camouflage Hunting Suit $74.95
Cadillac Eldorado Automobile, 1981 . . . . $19,700.00
Canvas-Cloth Work Gloves $6.49

"Prab Robots Inc. Keeps It Simple," *Inc.*, June 1982:

"Prab Robots Inc. of Kalamazoo, Michigan, is noteworthy among robot manufacturers. It has been involved from the outset with smaller companies, and 60 to 80 percent of its business is with companies not in the automotive industries.

'I think we have as broad, if not a broader, base than anyone in the game,' says Prab president Jack Wallace. The company owes not only its success to smaller businesses—during 1981 it sold about 180 units, and had revenues of $17.8 million and net earnings of $740,000, a one-year increase of 161 percent—but its existence as well. In 1961, Wallace was fired from his job as general manager of the Hapman Corp., a small manufacturer of industrial conveyors. His response was to get together with another Hapman employee, Charles Larson, raise some money, and buy a competitor, Prab Conveyors, Inc.

The company, founded in 1959 by Peter Ruppe and Allen Bodycomb (whose initials yielded PRAB), specialized in the production of equipment used to transport and process scrap metal. Attempting to expand his market base, Wallace got involved in the die-casting industry, a fortuitous turn of events, since it exposed him to robotics technology.

'The classic scheme in die casting was to drop the hot parts from the die-casting machine into a water tank and have a conveyor down there to convey them to a trimming machine. We made a lot of conveyors like that,' says Wallace. 'The first robot we saw—it was a Unimate—was in a die-casting plant, and we were told it was going to put us out of the conveyor business.' Wallace was pretty sure that wouldn't happen, and he was also sure that the unit was overkill for the application. 'Our people came back and said, "Let's make something for half the price that will do the job." That's how we got started.'

The principle has remained intact as the company has grown. 'We don't believe in pushing technology,' says Wallace. 'We're pushing results.' The firm's current advertising slogan makes the same point: 'Prab Robots Inc. keeps it simple.'

It was natural that Prab sell to small companies. Its robots were uncomplicated, it had started out with smaller firms, and was a small company itself. 'An order for 200 robots would have killed us back then,' says Wallace.

'The other companies devoted most of their time to going after the automotive spot-welding lines; we've devoted our time to going after the one-here, two-there applications,' says Prab vice president Walt Weisel. 'Our biggest user doesn't have more than 20 machines.' "

"A Moon-Made Match, Two of the Reverend's Disciples Embark on a 'Spiritual Blind Date,'" by Anne Fadiman, *Life*, August 1982:

"It was a moment for misty eyes: the radiant, young bride-to-be, the homemade wedding dress, the hush of anticipation as she tried on the veil . . . but wait. What was the cloud of tulle on the floor? More veils? To be exact, 2,074 of them—and each one identical to her own. Nina Perry's wedding was going to be, as she says, 'a little different.' Nina is a Moonie, and along with 4,149 other Unification Church members, she would recite her vows at Madison Square Garden in the largest mass marriage in history. Moonies do not choose their own spouses. They are 'matched' by the Reverend Sun Myung Moon, often to people neither they nor Moon have ever met. A third of the couples were matched only seven days before their wedding. When Nina Perry modeled her gown, she did not yet know who her fiancé would be. When asked his name by an unenlightened relative, she called him Mr. X. 'Do you love him?' asked the relative. 'Yes,' replied Nina, 'I know I will.'

'Reverend Moon is directly guided by the Heavenly Father,' says Nina, 'so I was confident that he would choose better for me than I could choose myself.' Moon made all his decisions on the spur of the moment, allotting about two minutes per couple until 1,306 Moonies were matched. Sometimes he asked direct questions: How old are you? Where are you from? How many degrees do you have? Would you like to marry someone of a different race? Sometimes he merely looked—'right into your soul' says Nina. Moonies may reject their matches after talking for a few minutes, though few did, since they have been told the most perfect union may be with 'the ugly person, the hard-to-love person, the person you think you hate.' Nina was among the first to be matched. 'When Reverend Moon touched me,' she says, 'I thought, "I'm about to meet my spiritual partner, not just for the rest of my life but for eternity"—and I wasn't even nervous. We walked down a row of brothers and as soon as Father stopped I knew it was my whoever. "What's your name?" I asked. "Gil," he said.' Gilbert Alexander, a 33-year-old engineer from Perth, Australia, who had mentally prepared himself to accept 'a toad,' wrote in his diary that night: 'I felt great joy and excitement beyond anything I had ever experienced. I knew without a doubt that Nina was right for me.'"

Hotpoint Air Conditioner, 5950 BTUs	$299.00
Kero-Sun Omni Heater	$289.95
L.L. Bean Chamois Cloth Shirt	$18.25
Lady Wellco Mesh Walking Shoe	$19.99
Laura Lynn Baby Crib	$119.99
Lew Childre & Sons Casting Reel	$95.00
Macintosh Computer, 128 K	$1,788.00
Marples Chisel Set, Set of Six	$51.95
Ocean Spray Cranapple Juice, 32-Ounce Bottle	$0.93

"Cries of Plague for Mysterious AIDS," by Loudon Wainwright, *Life*, July 1983:

"Assured and neat in his dark blue suit, the young man testified before a New York State Senate committee about a new and terrifying disease. 'My life has become totally controlled by AIDS and my fight to recover,' he said. 'I am subject to fevers and night sweats and an unendurable fatigue. I live with the fear that every cold or sore throat or skin rash may be a sign of something more serious. At the age of 28, I wake up every morning to face the very real possibility of my own death.'

Michael Callen is one of more than 1,500 people who have been diagnosed since 1981 as having acquired immune deficiency syndrome, a complex disease of unknown origin about which fears of death are appropriate. There is no known treatment for it; only the diseases that come in its wake can be fought directly. According to some calculations, it eventually kills more than 80 percent of its victims, most within two to three years.

Like 70 percent of AIDS victims, Callen is a gay male who has had many sexual partners, which suggests to researchers that the disease is transmitted sexually. But there are other possibilities. The fact that many among the rest of the ill are drug users who use needles, or hemophiliacs, who require frequent blood transfusions, suggests that it is transmitted by blood. That five percent of those with AIDS are natives of Haiti with no clear hemophilic, homosexual, or drug-use background has almost everyone puzzled. And because a very few patients seem to fit into none of the categories, many people are badly frightened.

Their fear, of course, is that the disease, which has already been called an epidemic by authorities and is cropping up at the rate of three to five new cases a day, will be spread uncontrollably by casual, even unknowing, contacts with the general population. The fear, in fact, is quite possibly more dangerous and degrading than the pestilence."

Olin/Winchester Shotgun	$1,200.00
Pabst Blue Ribbon Beer, 12 Pack	$3.19
Ramada Inn Hotel Room, Lake Havasu City, Arizona, per Night	$27.00
Seiko Ladies' Wristwatch	$84.95
Sharp Video Camera	$359.50
Turco Saratoga Gas Grill	$179.99
Wing-Tip, Oxford Men's Shoes	$39.99

Nutcracker Sweet.
Who but Godiva could improve upon nature's subtle beauty? Our secret lies hidden in a nutshell. Where walnuts, hazelnuts and delectable treasures are carefully ensconced inside luscious morsels of chocolate. Each sculpted piece seems the diligent work of nature herself. And every crunchy taste opens up a world of discovery. As with our other varieties, all are available in elegant packages of three, two, one and one-half pound assortments.
GODIVA.
Chocolatier
BRUXELLES · NEW YORK
PARIS · COLOGNE
Godiva Chocolatier, 701 Fifth Avenue, New York, New York 10022

1985 Family Profile

Alex and Naomi Behr have returned to Switzerland for the second time to head European operations for Union Carbide. He is in charge of three country companies and five businesses. The full impact of an attempted takeover of the company is just becoming clear.

Annual Income $120,000

In addition to his salary, Alex receives bonuses, stock options, and European housing allowances that boost his total compensation to $180,000.

Annual Budget

The average per capita consumer expenditures in 1985 for all workers nationwide are:

Auto Parts	$75.90
Auto Usage	$1,398.52
Clothing	$542.22
Dentists	$92.68
Food	$1,891.67
Furniture	$119.93
Gas and Oil	$406.35
Health Insurance	$95.19
Housing	$1,645.94
Intercity Transport	$93.93
Local Transport	$31.03
New Auto Purchase	$366.51
Personal Business	$775.37
Personal Care	$167.32
Physicians	$319.96
Private Education and Research	$228.54

Recreation	$787.95
Religion/Welfare Activities	$265.45
Telephone and Telegraph	$179.48
Tobacco	$132.93
Utilities	$500.28
Per Capita Consumption	$11,185.00

Life at Home

- The Behrs live in a Swiss section of Geneva, Switzerland, avoiding the section of the city populated by "IAs" or Internationally Assigned foreigners, mostly Americans.
- They believe it is more exotic to live with Swiss neighbors.
- They are renting a home previously occupied by a company executive who recently retired.
- The home is a duplex, and large by European standards at 2,000 square feet.
- They are paying $1,600 a month in rent.
- He travels extensively in his job, often nine out of 10 weeks, and is rarely home.
- When he travels to the Middle East or eastern Europe on business, he does not even make it home on weekends.
- His wife Naomi is attempting to make friends, but their son, a sophomore in high school, is miserable.
- His son wants to return to the United States where he can play American football, see his girlfriend, and drive a car.
- Even though he has a driver's license from the United States, the laws of Switzerland do not permit the teenager to drive until he is 18 years old.

- Naomi returns occasionally to the United States to see her two oldest children, both of whom are in college.
- The couple also has taken several trips together, including an antique-buying spree in London, a cruise in the Mediterranean, and a trip to northern Africa to buy rugs.
- Recently, they purchased a vacation home on Cape Cod in Massachusetts.

- Each month, they mail $2,000 to the United States for mortgage and upkeep of the second home.
- The first of three children and the son of a salesman, Alex was born in the Boston community of Hyde Park in 1940, and was raised in that city.
- His father worked as a salesman at various times for the family lumber business, Bendix, during the Second World War, and for a company that manufactured commercial laundry equipment.
- His mother, who did not work, was active in the Episcopal Church in the altar guild as a Sunday school teacher, and also as a welcome hostess in the community.
- She enjoyed playing bridge and taking part in a "Thought Club" of women that gathered once a month to discuss current books.
- His father took his work seriously, rarely allowing himself time to participate in his children's activities and athletic events.
- His paternal grandparents and his maternal grandmother all live within a few blocks of his childhood home.
- Because a relative previously worked for Union Carbide, Alex interviewed with the company following his graduation from MIT.
- Until he was six years old, the family rented a home; after the third child was born, his parents bought the first and last home they would own.
- To accommodate the growing family, the house was expanded, adding a two-story addition that provided an additional bedroom upstairs and a breakfast room downstairs.

- After the addition, the house had four bedrooms, one bathroom upstairs, and a half-bathroom downstairs and also included a two-car garage.
- When the home was built, the streets within the city limits of Boston were still unpaved.
- In the 1950s, Alex's sister developed polio and nearly died.
- Only a few years later, the Salk vaccine was introduced, dramatically reducing the occurrence of the illness.
- Growing up, he walked to the area schools, which were often more than a mile away; in the seventh grade, he enrolled in West Roxbury Latin School, after which his father drove him to and from school.
- There he was required to participate in organized athletics and selected baseball, football, and wrestling as his sports.
- Prior to attending Roxbury Latin, he had never played football.
- His education included training in Greek, allowing him to read the Bible in Greek by his junior year; he had considered a career in the ordained clergy, but did not pursue the inclination.
- At MIT, he majored in beer, girls, and engineering, roughly in that order.
- During his sophomore year, he began specializing in chemical engineering because many of his friends were headed in that direction and it required less math.
- At MIT, he participated in the two years of mandatory ROTC training and then elected to participate in it his third and fourth years; his senior year he was a Senior Regional Commander of the Perishing Rifles, a subsidiary activity of ROTC.

Life at Work

- He is at the pinnacle of his career as a vice president at Union Carbide, with authority over five businesses and three country companies—Germany, Turkey, and Dubai.
- His home base is Geneva, Switzerland, although he travels nine weeks out of 10.
- He thinks nothing of making a day trip from Geneva to Dusseldorf, Germany, headquarters of the German operations.
- Chauffeurs drive him to and from the airport, occasionally the company's private plane flies him where he needs to be that day.

- A trip away from home may last a day, but often will take more than a week, especially when he visits customers throughout eastern Europe or the Middle East.
- Business meetings are held with suppliers of the raw materials used by the company, customers, and prospects.
- He often conducts business over dinner, and his days are frequently very long.
- The trips also allow him to review the business performance of the areas he manages, which include films for the food industry, metal coatings, proprietary catalysts, and engineering services.
- Language is rarely an issue; English is spoken well and freely by the people he meets, especially businessmen in developed countries.

Union Carbide's employment worldwide tops 100,000.

- Alex also speaks French, but not well enough, he believes, to negotiate sensitive deals in that language.
- Six times a year, he flies back to the United States for planning sessions and meetings in Connecticut at corporate headquarters.
- Even though Union Carbide's market reach is global, most strategic decision making is still centralized in the United States.
- Union Carbide's current employment worldwide tops 100,000.
- The company describes itself in annual reports as a "global powerhouse."
- It leads the world in polyolefin production, dry-cell batteries, and graphite electrodes for steel making, and is the largest producer of industrial gases in the United States.
- Its portfolio includes an agricultural products business, the world's largest-selling brand of antifreeze, and such specialty businesses as food-processing, silicones, molecular sieves, coating services, specialty chemicals, and specialty polymers.
- A Carbide associate's identity is built around reliability, responsibility, and stability.
- Many Wall Street analysts view Carbide as a dull, underperforming company and are growing more concerned about the impact of the chemical leak at Bhopal and a hostile takeover bid that is now under way.
- The December 3, 1984, tragedy of a chemical leak at Bhopal, India, changed the company.
- The release of the gas methyl isocyanate, used in the preparation of insecticides, resulted in the deaths of more than 3,500 people in India and 150,000 injuries.
- When stockholders met in the spring of 1985, the per-share stock price had fallen from $60 a share to $30.
- Union Carbide is currently attempting to fend off a hostile takeover by GAF Corporation.

- This has been one of the most turbulent years for Carbide, which began its operations in 1917 in the Kanawha Valley of West Virginia.
- Alex joined Union Carbide in 1961 in Charleston, West Virginia, the same year he married Naomi.
- Within a year, he returned to MIT to obtain a master's degree while Union Carbide held his job open; he did not believe himself equipped to handle the demands of the job without more education.
- Their first child was born in 1963 while he was studying at MIT.
- Once his master's degree was completed, he finished his military commitment in the Signal Corps and was assigned to Fort Gordon, Georgia, and Fort Monmouth, New Jersey, where he served on the radio and electrical engineering faculty.
- Their second child, a son, was born during this time.
- He returned to Union Carbide in 1965 in the Chemical and Plastics Division.
- There, Alex spent his time doing "rough appraisals," a new idea-evaluation process that linked engineering, research and development, and marketing; it was heavily layered in the bureaucracy for which Union Carbide is well known.
- Carefully constructed layers of bureaucracy within the company make every decision slow, safe, and often cumbersome.
- Shortly after returning to the company, Alex joined the agricultural chemicals business, known for its popular Sevin insecticide and Temik, a more toxic insecticide used only by professionals.

- For the next two years, he was involved in collaborative projects between the chemical engineering staff and research and development.
- Then he was asked to take a cross-training assignment for a year in production—the actual making of 10 different products at a plant in West Virginia.
- Most of the products were for metal crafting, paints, automotive fluids, or chemical intermediates.
- In 1967, he and Naomi purchased their first home, a split-entry home of 1,144 square feet, for which they paid $25,575; their house payments are $179 per month.
- The next year, he moved into engineering with the hydrocarbon group, where gas concentrates were cracked into chemical products.
- The company also assigned him to a team investigating a multi-million plant explosion in Texas; working with experts in production, research and development, and engineering, the team reconstructed the accident.
- The six-month investigation required frequent trips to the company's room-size IBM 360 computer; computer time was so precious, he was permitted only 20 to 30 minutes, often after midnight, to run his calculations.
- Once a computer run was completed and analyzed, a new set of computer cards was created so another set of calculations could be run—when time was available.
- The writing of software and running of calculations consumed half of the six-month investigation.
- He was then promoted and asked to move to New York, the corporate headquarters.
- There, at 31 years old, he served as a business analyst working for a business vice president.
- He, Naomi, and their three children lived in Norwalk, Connecticut, in a house near the commuter line.
- Each morning at 7:00 a.m., he rode the train to Manhattan, often not returning home until after 9 p.m.
- The workday sometimes included entertaining customers and party time after work—all considered part of the job.
- Union Carbide was in its heyday—a world leader in a variety of products and processes.
- After two years of long hours, frequent weekend projects, and close interaction with the leaders of the company, he was asked in 1973 to move to Geneva, Switzerland, and join the agricultural product marketing.
- It was a time of travel and adventure for his growing family.
- Two years later, he returned to Charleston, West Virginia, where his career had begun, to work in agricultural products, and then accepted a role as director of Engineering, establishing an engineering department in Jacksonville, Florida.
- When he and the family moved back to New York in 1979, he was head of engineering and operations at age 37, supervising half a dozen plants and dozens of engineers.
- In New York, he was named vice president over herbicide and plant growth regulators worldwide; it was an exciting time, but the company was changing, and when he was asked to return to Europe he jumped at the chance.
- He likes being with customers and having direct responsibility for day-to-day results.

"U.S. Court Bars Excluding People as Jurors Solely Because of Race," by David Margolick, *New York Times*, December 4, 1984:

"A divided federal appeals court in Manhattan ruled yesterday that prosecutors could not systematically exclude people from juries solely because of their race.

The two-to-one decision by the Court of Appeals for the Second Circuit marks the first time that a federal appellate court has invalidated such use of peremptory challenges, for which potential jurors can be rejected without cause. Such challenges have often been used to keep blacks and Hispanic people off juries."

Life in the Community: Geneva, Switzerland

- They live in a small community outside the city of Geneva, Switzerland.
- This scenic, affluent city sits on Lake Geneva, the largest Alpine Lake.

- The city is remarkably international; its non-Swiss population accounts for one third of its 165,000 residents
- Geneva is home to the European headquarters of the United Nations and the central offices of more than 200 international bodies from the Red Cross to the World Council of Churches.
- Natives are more likely to speak English as their second language, in addition to German, Italian, or French.
- Geneva's Old Town is an architectural gem of cathedrals and stately buildings, which attest to the city's wealth in the late Middle Ages and Renaissance periods.
- Crescent-shaped Lake Geneva is 45 miles long and two to nine miles wide.
- The city is known for its elegant cafés, lakeside promenades, and trees; there are at least three trees for every resident within the city limits.
- Characteristic of its opulence, two thirds of the 13,000 hotel beds in the city are in deluxe or first-class hotels.

Historical Snapshot
1985

- The AMA reported that medical malpractice suits had tripled since 1975; the average award increased from $95,000 to $333,000
- The U.S. Army ruled that male officers were forbidden to carry umbrellas
- Videocassette movie-rental income equaled movie theater receipts
- The "Live Aid" concert in Philadelphia and London was viewed on television by 1.6 billion people and grossed $70 million for famine-stricken Africa
- More than 2,000 people died in plane crashes, the worst year in civilian air travel
- The high for the Dow Jones Industrial Average for the year was 1,553; the low was 1,184
- A highly addictive, inexpensive cocaine derivative called "crack" became popular; it sold for $5 to $10 per vial
- Parents and local school boards fought over keeping AIDS-afflicted children in public schools
- The number of Barbie dolls surpassed the American population
- General Westmoreland dropped his $120 million 1982 libel suit against CBS for its documentary alleging that he deceived the public concerning Vietcong strength
- A single optic fiber carried 300,000 simultaneous phone calls in Bell Laboratory tests
- Capital Cities Communications bought television network ABC for $3.5 billion
- The Nobel peace prize went to the International Physicians for the Prevention of Nuclear War, founded by two cardiologists, one at Harvard, the other in Moscow
- The first genetically engineered microorganisms were licensed for commercial purposes
- The Supreme Court upheld affirmative-action hiring quotas
- World oil prices collapsed, bottoming out at $7.20 per barrel
- The U.S. national debt topped $1.8 trillion
- New York transit fares rose from $0.75 to $1.00
- Coca-Cola introduced new-formula Coke; public outcry forced Coke to bring back the old formula as Classic Coke one year later
- An estimated 27 million adults were functional illiterates
- Rock Hudson became one of the first public figures to acknowledge his battle with AIDS, raising public awareness of the disease
- The words golden parachute, leveraged buyout, and poison pill all entered the corporate language

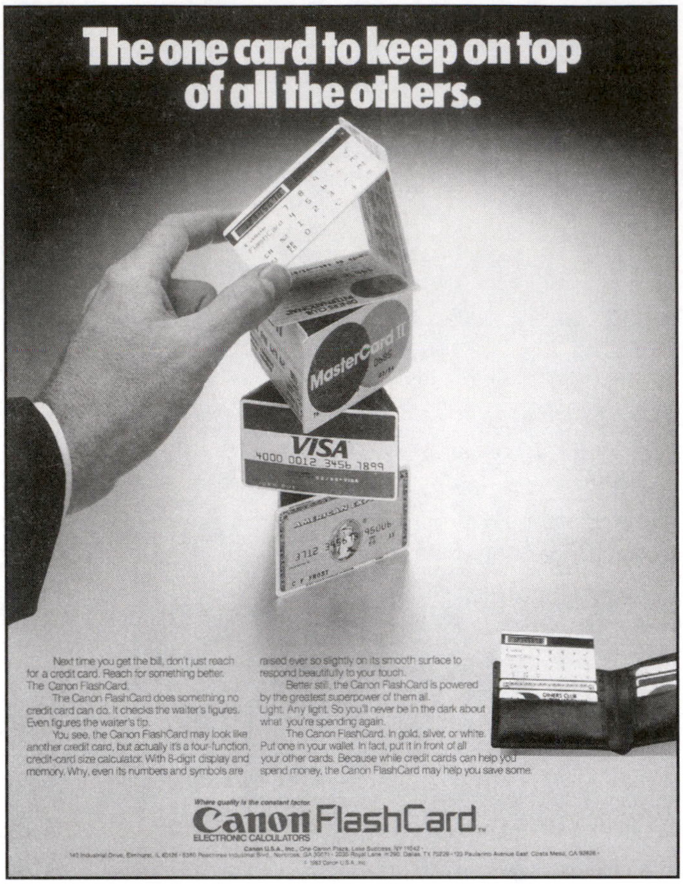

1985 Economic Profile

Income, Standard Jobs

Bituminous Coal Mining	$34,837.00
Building Trades	$23,590.00
Domestics	$7,072.00
Farm Labor	$7,228.00
Federal Civilian	$25,591.00
Federal Employees, Executive Departments	$26,598.00
Finance, Insurance, and Real Estate	$22,308.00
Gas, Electricity, and Sanitation Workers	$31,096.00
Manufacturing, Durable Goods	$23,868.00
Manufacturing, Nondurable Goods	$20,800.00
Medical/Health Services Workers	$18,668.00
Miscellaneous Manufacturing	$18,200.00
Motion Picture Services	$27,040.00
Nonprofit Organization Workers	$11,440.00
Passenger Transportation Workers, Local and Highway	$12,589.00
Personal Services	$10,088.00
Postal Employees	$26,995.00
Public School Teachers	$20,973.00
Radio Broadcasting and Television Workers	$25,064.00
Railroad Workers	$23,036.00
State and Local Government Workers	$18,363.00
Telephone and Telegraph Workers	$29,276.00
Wages per Full-Time Employee	$19,188.00
Wholesale and Retail Trade Workers	$23,764.00

Selected Prices

Apple IIGS Computer	$795.00
Arvin Heater, Fan-Forced Heat	$23.88
AT&T Reachout America, One Hour of Long-Distance Calls	$9.45
Baby's First Shoes, Bronze-Plated	$5.99
Ballet Ticket to *The Nutcracker*	$18.00
Bausch & Lomb Criterion 400 Telescope	$695.00

DieHard Lightbulb, Two per Pack $4.00
Dove Bar Ice Cream $1.45
Epson Printer. $429.00
Fuji Diskettes, 5.5" DS/DD, per Box $9.95
Kodak 3440 Camcorder $893.00
Master Mechanic 6' Pocket
Tape Rule. $8.99
Metrocom Car Phone, Hands-Free. . . . $995.00
Milk, Two Percent, Plastic Carton $1.59
Movie Ticket, *Lady and the Tramp* $2.00
Oneida Heirloom Flatware,
48 Pieces $229.95
Panasonic Portable Cassette
Player and Recorder $37.00

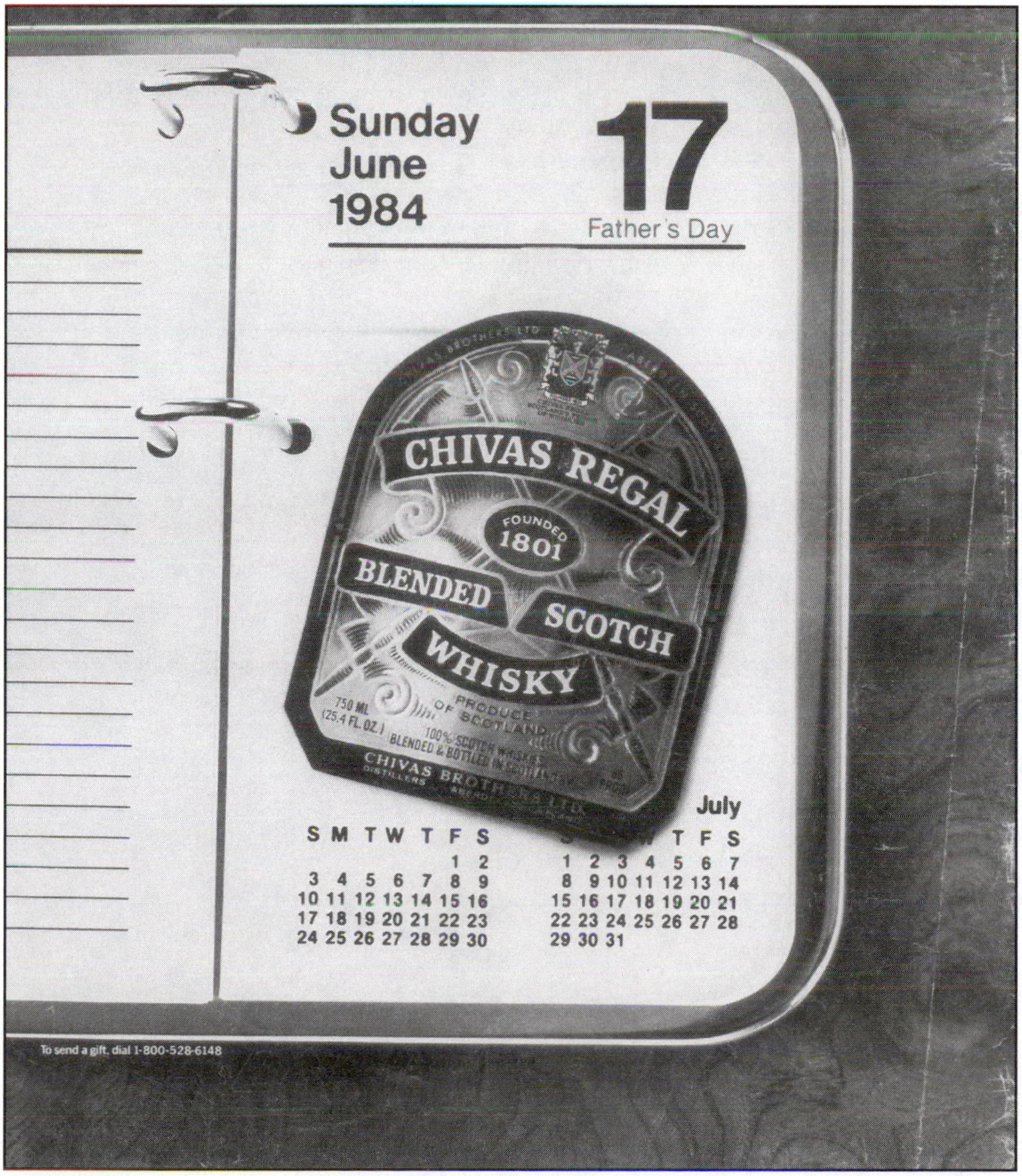

"A Language That Has Ausgeflippt," *Time*, June 16, 1986:

"The United States and Britain, George Bernard Shaw once remarked, are two nations separated by a common language. Today he might say much the same thing about the U.S. and the whole world. ICE CUBOS, says a sign in the Mexican resort of Acapulco. Lebanese audiences watching *Rambo* shout exhortations in English, and a Japanese rock-'n'-roll hit begins, 'Let's dancin' people/*Hoshi-kuzu nagarete* feel so good . . .

It was the British empire, on which the sun never set, that originally spread English around the world, along with tea breaks, cuffed trousers, and the stiff upper lip. But when the imperial sun finally did set after World War II, the American language followed American power into the vacuum. Key reason: the language has a rare forcefulness and flexibility. Even the authoritative *Oxford English Dictionary* last month incorporated such Americanisms as yuppie and zilch. Explained editor Robert Burchfield: 'Our language is changing slowly, and America is leading the way now, not Britain.'

Commerce is the driving force. The ads in Italy's *Corriere della Sera* for just one day included the words personnel administrator, quality audit, contract manager, and know-how. Germans routinely refer to their employer as der Boss, who is expected to be a good Manager. 'American English is definitely the model, not English—this is what we see looking through French advertising,' says Micheline Faure, organizing secretary of a Paris group called AGULF, which was formed to resist the linguistic invasion. Japanese ads, posters, and shopping bags are full of a special kind of American English, often starting with an enthusiastic 'Let's' as in 'Let's hiking' or 'Let's sex.'

Hand in hand with commerce goes technology, and the tools of technology were mostly baptized in the U.S. The French still cling to *ordinateur* instead of computer, but in Italy even schoolchildren call it by its American name. Also floppy disks, lasers, compact disks, software. Germans buy Tapes, not Magnetbander. In fact, they call the whole field HITEC. . .

This combination of money and technology, show biz, and sex appeal strikes many foreigners as the epitome of the American success story, and so they adopt English words that imply success itself: super, blue chip, boom, status symbol, summit. Some of that, clearly is just snobbery. Through U.S. television, says British grammarian Randolph Quirk, a foreigner can pick up an Americanized vocabulary 'if you want to show you're with it and talking like Americans, the most fashionable people on earth.'"

Radio Shack Television Satellite Dish $1,995.00
Ruffles Potato Chips, 6.5-Ounce Bag $1.19
Shop-Vac Mighty Mini-Vac $44.88
Sony Watchman Television, Pocket Size, Black and White $95.00
Technics Compact Disc Player $229.95
Weller Solderings Gun Kit. $19.99

Thanks to you, it
works. For all of us.
United Way

1986 News Profile

"Deep Pockets for Doing Good, Charitable Contributions are More Generous Than Ever," by Evan Thomas, *Time Special Issue, America's Best*, June 16, 1986

"At the turn of the century, when robber barons were amassing embarrassingly large fortunes, charity sometimes served as a form of atonement, a guilt tax for living so well. Nowadays, says David Rockefeller, who as chairman of the Rockefeller Brothers Fund has overseen the donation of $342 million of his family's immense wealth to worthy causes, philanthropy can be, well, 'a lot of fun. . . .'

Americans are digging deeper into their pockets than ever before. Last year charitable contributions in the U.S. reached a record high of some $80 billion, an 8.9 percent increase over 1984. As the Reagan Administration has cut back on social services, the citizenry has responded to President Reagan's call for a new voluntarism. Private charity, of course, will never be a substitute for the public welfare state. Still, last year, for the first time in 16 years, the average American donated more than two percent of his income to charity. Although precise comparisons are hard to come by, 'citizens in no other country come close,' asserts John J. Schwartz, president of the American Association of Fund-Raising Councils, Inc.

Giving in America is remarkably democratic. Nearly nine out of 10 Americans report making some contribution to charity. Those earning over $50,000 a year say they give away an average of 2.9 percent of their income.

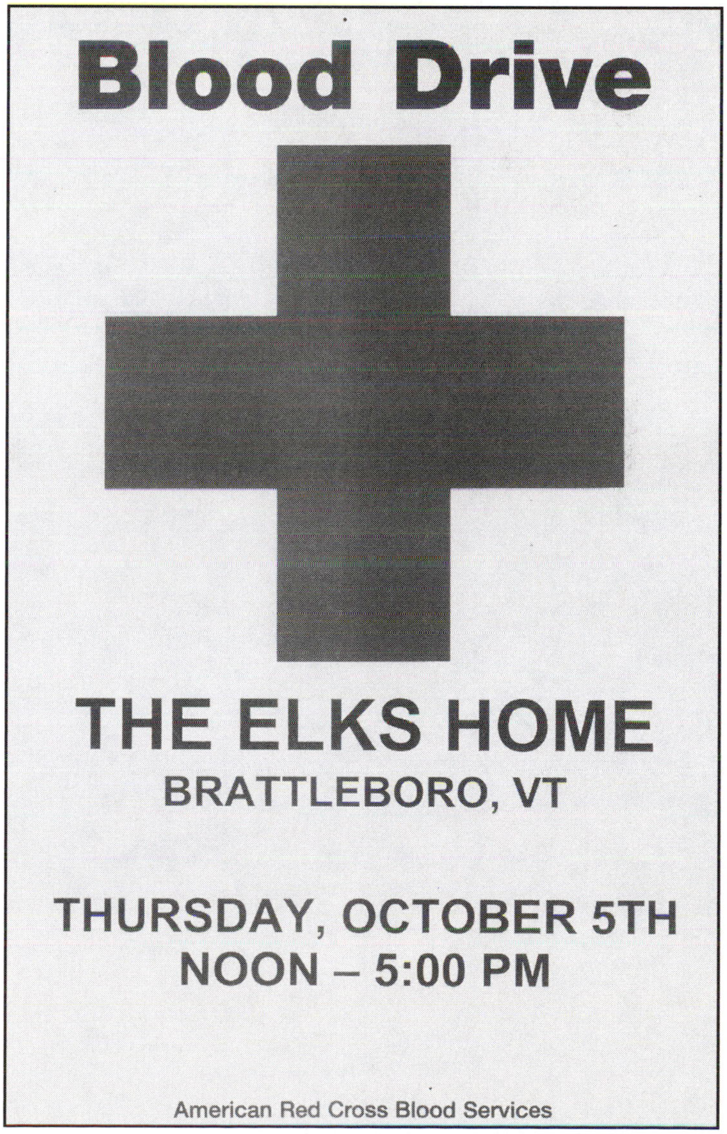
Blood Drive
THE ELKS HOME
BRATTLEBORO, VT
THURSDAY, OCTOBER 5TH
NOON – 5:00 PM
American Red Cross Blood Services

THE
UNITED WAY
IS A GIFT
WE GIVE
EACH OTHER
FOR BEING
HUMAN.

But those who make the least (under $10,000) give slightly more—about three percent of their income.

Churches remain the largest recipients of giving: $37.7 billion a year is raised by religious organizations and agencies. Corporations, with their stockholders to worry about, give far less (about $4 billion last year), but in the past decade some 1,600 U.S. companies have pledged to give two to 10 percent of their pretax profits to charity.

The young give comparatively little to charity: those ages 30 to 34 report giving 1.7 percent of their income, according to a 1985 Yankelovich poll. That may be because they have not yet reached their full earning capacity and have less disposable income than their elders. Still, baby boomers seem less willing to give than their parents—'a downward trend that bears serious watching,' says Richard Lyman, president of the Rockefeller Foundation. 'It would be a tragedy if it is an early sign that philanthropy in this country is losing some of its force.'

The pop-charity events like Live Aid could help get the young into the habit of giving. But organizers are already worrying about 'compassion fatigue.' Pop charity may turn out to be one more passing fad. At the upper end of the economic scale, some wonder if charity is in danger of succumbing to chic. New York financier Felix Rohatyn, who along with his wife Elizabeth has launched a small crusade against events that concentrate more on social glamour than helping worthy causes, is concerned that the pet charities of the New York rich, the favored museums and cultural institutions and hospitals, will sop up money that could be better used to help less fashionable but equally needy causes. 'Why should a program for the homeless be allowed to disintegrate,' he asks, 'if at the same time large institutions with professional fund-raising staffs can raise large amounts?'

American charity will never be an orderly or even-handed process. Even so, millions still depend on private largesse, not just at home but abroad. Last year Americans sent more than $2 billion in private donations to the peoples of foreign countries. The Rockefeller Foundation alone will spend up to $300 million over the next five years to promote economic development in Third World countries and focus on politically controversial goals like fostering contraception. 'Because philanthropy is not concerned with election returns or stockholders, we see ourselves deliberately moving into things that government and businesses are not picking up,' says Rockefeller Foundation Vice President Kenneth Prewitt. In America, charity is not just the fruit of compassion; it is a legacy of free choice."

Presents
FOR THE SMALL FRY

1990–1999

The 1990s were called the "Era of Possibilities" by *Fortune* magazine and were dominated by an economic expansion that became the longest in the nation's history. It was characterized by steady growth, low inflation, low unemployment, and dramatic gains in technology-based productivity, especially driven by computers and the emerging Internet.

The decade opened in an economic recession, a ballooning national debt, and the economic hangover of the collapse of much of the savings and loan industry. The automobile industry produced record losses; household names like Bloomingdale's and Pan Am declared bankruptcy. Housing values plummeted and factory orders fell. Media headlines were dominated by issues such as rising drug use, crime in the cities, racial tensions, and the rise of personal bankruptcies. Family values ranked high on the conservative agenda, and despite efforts to limit Democrat Bill Clinton to one term as president, the strength of the economy played a critical role in his re-election in 1996.

Guided by Federal Reserve Chair Alan Greenspan's focus on inflation control and Clinton's early efforts to control the federal budget, the U.S. economy soared, producing its best economic indicators in three decades. By 1999, the stock market produced record returns, job creation was at a 10-year high, and the federal deficit was falling. Businesses nationwide hung "Help Wanted" signs outside their doors and even paid signing bonuses to acquire new workers. Crime rates, especially in urban areas, plummeted to levels unseen in three decades, illegitimacy rates fell, and every year business magazines marvelled at the length of the recovery, asking, "Can it last another year?"

The stock market set a succession of records throughout the period, attracting thousands of investors to stocks for the first time, including the so-called glamour offerings of high-technology companies. From 1990 to the dawn of the twenty-first century, the Dow Jones Industrial Average rose 318 percent. Growth stocks were the rage; of Standard and Poor's 500 tracked stocks, almost 100 did not pay dividends. This market boom eventually spawned unprecedented new wealth, encouraging early retirement to legions of aging baby boomers. The dramatic change in the cultural structure of corporations continued to threaten the job security of American workers, who had to be more willing to learn new skills, try new jobs, and move from project to project. Profit sharing, which allowed workers to benefit from increased productivity, become more common. Retirement programs and pension plans became more flexible and transferable, serving the needs of a highly mobile work force. The emerging gap of the 1990s was not always between the rich and the poor, but the computer literate and the technically deficient. To symbolize the changing role of women in the work force, cartoon character Blondie, wife of Dagwood Bumstead, opened her own catering business which, like so many small businesses in the 1990s, did extremely well. For the first time, a study of family household income concluded that 55 percent of women provided half or more of the household income.

In a media-obsessed decade, the star attraction was the long-running scandal of President Bill Clinton and his affair with a White House intern. At its climax, while American forces were attacking Iraq, the full House of Representatives voted to impeach the president. For only the second time in American history, the Senate conducted an impeachment hearing before voting to acquit the president of perjury and obstruction of justice.

During the decade, America debated limiting abortion, strengthening punishment for criminals, replacing welfare for work, ending Affirmative Action, dissolving bilingual education, elevating educational standards, curtailing the rights of legal immigrants, and imposing warnings on unsuitable material for children on the Internet. Nationwide, an estimated 15 million people, including smokers, cross-dressers, alcoholics, sexual compulsives, and gamblers, attended weekly self-help support groups; dieting became a $33 billion industry as Americans struggled with obesity.

The impact of the GI Bill's focus on education, rooted in the decade following World War II, flowered in the generation that followed. The number of adult Americans with a four-year college education rose from 6.2 percent in 1950 to 24 percent in 1997. Despite this impressive rise, the need for a more educated population, and the rapidly rising expectations of the technology sector, the century ended with a perception that the decline in public education was one of the most pressing problems of the decade. Throughout the decade, school violence escalated, capturing headlines year after year in widely dispersed locations across the nation.

The '90s gave birth to $150 tennis shoes, condom boutiques, pre-ripped jeans, Motorola 7.7-ounce cellular telephones, rollerblading, TV home shopping, the Java computer language, digital cameras, DVD players, and Internet shopping. And in fashion, a revival of the 1960s' style brought back miniskirts, pop art prints, pants suits, and the A-line. Black became a color worn at any time of day and for every purpose. The increasing role of consumer debt in driving the American economy also produced an increase in personal bankruptcy and a reduction in the overall savings rate. At the same time, mortgage interest rates hit 30-year lows during the decade, creating refinancing booms that pumped millions of dollars into the economy, further fueling a decade of consumerism.

1991 Family Profile

This Chicago couple, Ben and Bridget Nichols, began the year confident, excited, and at the peak of their earnings. Bridget turned 40, Ben's daughter Meghan moved in with them, and they bought two new cars and an airplane. By year-end, however, Ben was out of work, the victim of a corporate bankruptcy.

Annual Income: $132,000
Bridget makes $68,000 as manager of underwriting with Chase Mortgage; Ben earns $64,000, despite the layoff.

One of Ben's three daughters, 16-year-old Meghan, moved in with the couple in Chicago.

Annual Budget

The average per capita consumer expenditures in 1991 for all workers nationwide are:

Auto Maintenance	$245.00
Auto Usage	$1,741.00
Clothing	$667.00
Entertainment	$566.00
Food	$2,651.00
Furniture	$113.00
Gas and Oil	$382.00
Health Care	$597.00
Health Insurance	$252.00
Housing	$1,996.00
New Auto Purchase	$414.00
Personal Business	$1,071.00
Personal Care	$153.00
Public Transportation	$116.00
Telephone	$237.00
Tobacco	$105.00
Utilities	$527.00
Per Capita Consumption	$11,390.00

Life at Home

- Bridget has just become an instant mother; Ben's 16-year-old daughter Meghan, who had been living with her natural grandmother in Charlotte, North Carolina, has moved in with them.
- Married for the first time, Bridget is excited by the chance to help raise his middle daughter and participate in her band competitions, homework, and dating.
- Active in band competitions, Meghan plays the flute and captured second chair.
- The couple was married in 1988; this is his fourth marriage and her first.
- He has just purchased his own airplane; life has never been better.
- At mid-year, in his new role of captain and instructor for Midway Airlines, he is on track to make $120,000 annually.
- Their home in the suburbs of Chicago was purchased last year for $176,000; they have a monthly mortgage payment of $1,100 per month.
- The house is a three-bedroom, split-level home with brick façade and sits on a half-acre lot.
- The walls are covered with pictures and paintings of airplanes, including the one he now owns and many he has flown during his career.
- Property taxes are $3,400 a year.
- Their New Ford Tempo, bought this year, cost $8,000.
- On his days off, Ben flies a biplane at a crop-dusting school; when flying for Midway, he pilots a DC-9.
- When crop dusting, usually with pesticides on corn and soybeans, he makes $1.00 per acre and sometimes earns up to $2,000 a weekend.

The Nichols' home is in the suburbs of Chicago.

Ben began flying when he was 14 years old.

- This year's vacation was spent at a fly-in at Oshkosh, Wisconsin, where hundreds of home-built and antique airplane buffs camp out and socialize every year.
- Born in 1944 in Norfolk, Virginia, Ben grew up loving airplanes.
- He took his first airplane flight at two years old, spent his summers around crop-dusting airplanes, and by the time he was 14, his life revolved around flying.
- He learned to fly before he learned to drive.
- As a teenager, to get the $8 he needed for each flight lesson, he washed airplanes, swept hangars, and did odd jobs in his neighborhood.

They attend the annual fly-in at Oshkosh, Wisconsin.

"Pilots Recall Anxiety, Adrenaline of First Air Raids,"
***Chicago Tribune*, February 10, 1991:**

"Central Saudi Arabia—In the early morning hours of January 17, a huge air armada circled over northern Saudi Arabia, lights out, radios off, every pilot waiting for the moment to cross the border and begin the war to liberate Kuwait.

Spread along the Iraqi and Kuwaiti borders were some of the most sophisticated planes in the Western arsenal, poised to catch the Iraqis by surprise and hit key communications and military targets in one staggering blow.

Twenty F-15C fighters would sweep the skies while radar-evading F-117 Stealth fighters and F-15E and F111 fighter-bombers, navy and marine A6E attack bombers, and British Tornado jets went into action against targets in Iraq and Kuwait.

'It was one massive, coordinated strike. They had a time-on-target window of 30 minutes,' said Capt. Alan Miller, who was leading a flight of four F-15C fighters. That meant all of the bombing was scheduled to start and end between 3:30 and 4:00 a.m.

From air bases throughout the kingdom, aircraft began crossing the Saudi border around 1:30 a.m. for the run to their targets.

The first planes to go in were about two dozen Stealth fighters. Their high-priority job was to knock out Iraqi communications. 'There's no use giving a guy a telephone in Baghdad to pick up and call out to all his planes and say, "Hey, look out for air strikes." If we can't get all his airplanes, at least we can kill the brain,' said Col. Hal Hornburg, commander of the 4th Tactical Fighter Wing Provisional."

- In 1961, using a technicality in the law, he joined the Marine Reserves on his seventeenth birthday so he would be eligible for a pilot's license without parental permission, which his father had refused to give; otherwise, Ben would have had to wait until he was 21.
- His father worked for Remington Rand Typewriter Company.
- Following high school, Ben served in the Marines becoming a flight engineer, spent time in Vietnam, and then left the Marines to marry his first wife.
- As a couple, they attended a Methodist Church dedication of an airplane for missionaries in Africa, an event which changed their direction.
- He realized that it was God's will for his life to be a missionary pilot.
- The couple lived and worked in Liberia; his job was to fly missionaries into remote locations in the underdeveloped country.
- When he returned from Africa, he worked a variety of jobs, all connected to flying; he crop-dusted, flew helicopters, and worked as a pilot for a private development company.
- His wife died at age 32; he married twice more, both times briefly, before moving to Chicago in 1986.

Much of their life revolves around airplanes.

- He met Bridget in Chicago, and they have been married three years.
- Born in Uniontown, Pennsylvania, she grew up in the suburbs of Chicago; when she was five, her parents divorced, after which she was raised by her mother and her grandfather.
- Her mother worked as a secretary for Ford Motor Company, and later for Clark Equipment.
- Many nights, while her mother worked late, Bridget heated a can of Spaghettios and dreamed of having a mom who stayed home and baked cookies.
- After high school, she attended community college at night, working her way through school at the First National Bank of Chicago.
- As a part of the secretarial pool, she used manual typewriters and carbon paper to prepare the reports dictated by the male managers.
- In 1974, she joined Fannie Mae, a private investor in second mortgages, taking a job as a paralegal, a new job in a new type of industry; her bosses said they were unsure a woman could do the work.
- By 1984, she was made a lender representative at Fannie Mae before moving to an aggressive savings and loan company as the manager of underwriting.
- She quickly discovered the financial institution was more interested in increasing sales than in making quality loans.
- To prevent the savings and loan from folding based on a badly performing commercial loan portfolio, Chase Manhattan acquired the company.
- By 1987, when the couple met, Bridget was vice president of underwriting for Chase; her lending authority was $750,000.
- Never married, she had been dating the same man for 16 years before she met Ben.

Life at Work

- Ben has been working for Midway Airlines for the past four years; his jobs have included pilot, instructor, and now instructor/captain—the job he has always wanted.
- Midway currently serves 40 cities nationwide.
- He typically works 17 days a month; following a three-day trip, he has two days off.
- For the past year, Midway has struggled with rising fuel prices, tight credit, and escalating debt.

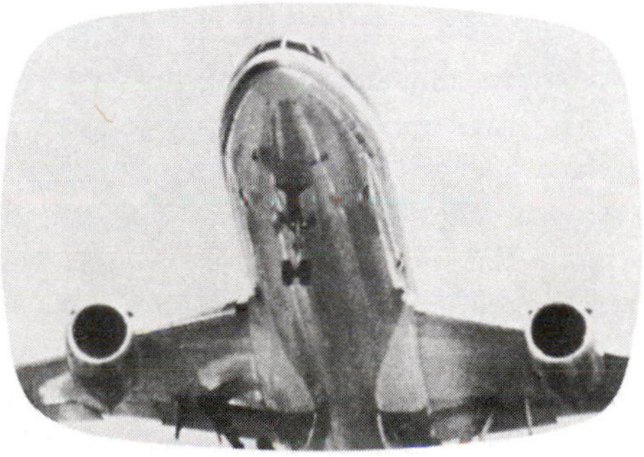

Ben is now an instructor/captain—the job he has always wanted.

- Airline rate wars have produced tremendous consumer demand in the midst of a recession; though airplanes are full, profits are still low.
- Northwest Airlines has said it plans to buy the discount airline, formed after deregulation of the airline industry.
- On his last day on the job with Midway, Ben flew from Chicago to Palm Springs, Florida, to Nassau and back not knowing if at the end of the day he would be a new employee of Northwest or out of a job.
- After he landed his plane in Chicago, he learned the purchase had fallen through.
- Midway passengers were stranded at airports across the country.
- A friend called from Midway to say, "They are shutting the airline down, do you want me to get your flight bag out of the airport?"
- His next-door neighbor called after the 10 p.m. news announcement of the bankruptcy and offered him a job with his company.
- For the last few months of the year, he has been learning about auto sprays and dreaming of ways to get back into the air.
- At Chase Manhattan Mortgage, Bridget has spent much of her year traveling and training; it has been a creative but difficult year.
- The economy is clearly slowing—its first major economic decline since 1982; unemployment is climbing.
- The year began with 30-year, fixed-rate mortgages hovering at 9.5 percent; during the year, driven by the recession, rates dropped steadily.

Life in the Community: Chicago, Illinois

- Ben and Bridget live in the suburbs of Chicago, the second-largest city and third-largest metropolitan area in the United States.
- Currently, 2,982,370 people work in the Chicago area, more than the total population of the city.
- The city was the birthplace of the skyscraper; the first steel-skeleton building was constructed in Chicago in 1885.
- After the construction of that modest 10-story building, the 110-story Sears Tower and the 100-story John Hancock Center followed.
- Thanks in part to the World's Columbian Exposition, Chicago is home to the largest number of medical associations of any other American city, including the American Medical Association, The American Hospital Association, the American College of Surgeons, The American College of Radiology, the American Society of Anesthesiologists,

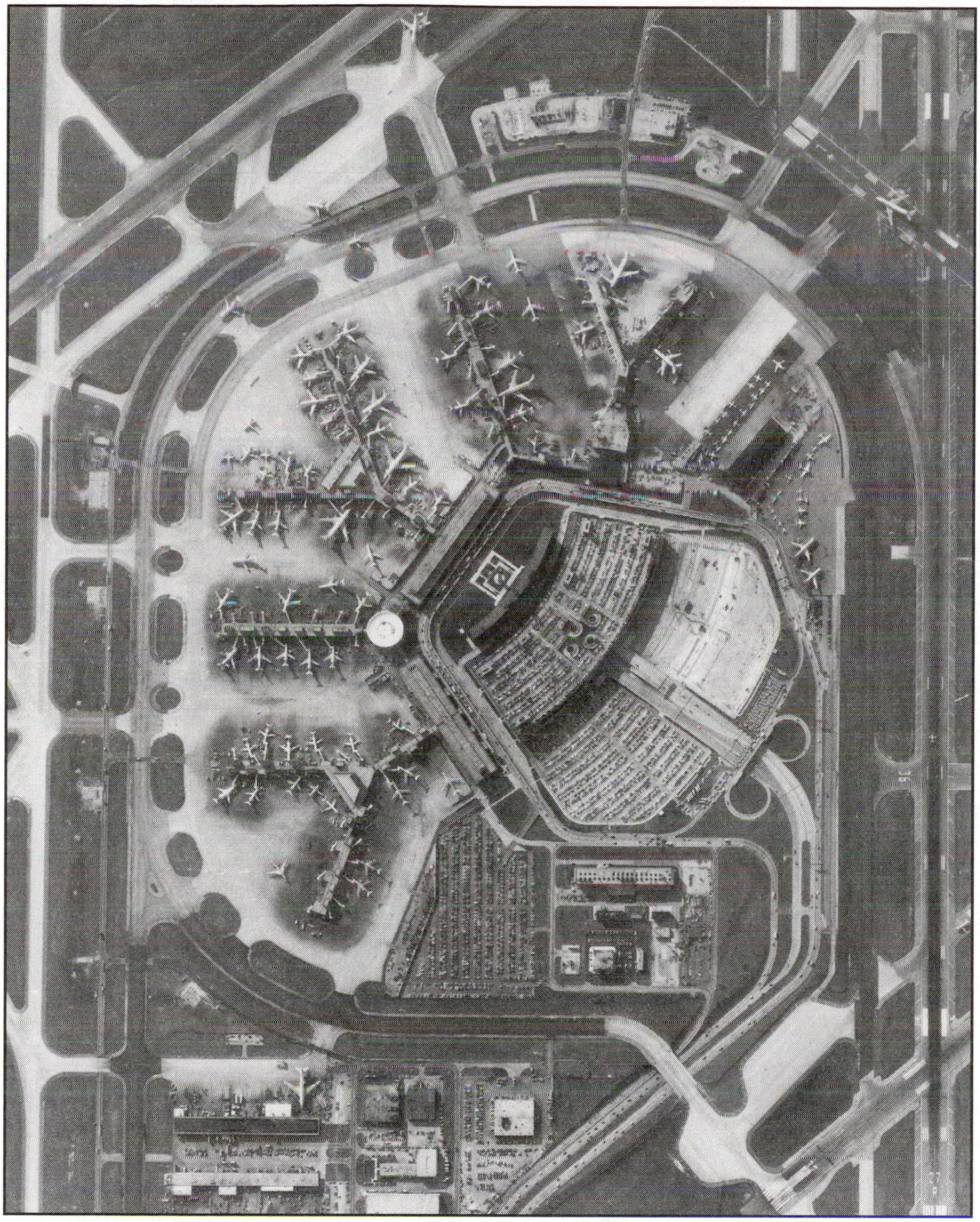

Midway serves 40 cities nationwide.

the Association of American Physicians & Surgeons, the American Association of Industrial Physicians & Surgeons, and the College of American Pathologists.

- The collection in the Field Museum storage vault has grown to 19 million biological specimens—9.8 million of which are insects.
- The *Chicago Tribune* reported that Joseph "Pops" Panczko, dean of Chicago's trunk poppers and lock pickers, retired at the age of 72 after serving time for his 200th arrest.
- Only two years earlier, the Chicago Cubs became the last major league team to introduce night baseball in their home field.

The Nichols love relaxing with friends at home, at the lake and at fly-ins.

"Signs of Life, Projects a Boost for Wicker Park," by J. Linn Allen, *Chicago Tribune*, February 10, 1991:

"Nancy Kapp's inexperience may be Wicker Park's gain.

'I'm doing two redevelopment projects simultaneously in the middle of a recession,' says Kapp, president of Renaissance Realty Group. 'They would be risky even if the economy were perfect. It shows the advantage of not knowing what we can't do.'

Kapp is the chief mover in the condominium conversion of a 41-unit courtyard apartment at 2108–18 W. North Ave. and the rehab of the ramshackle four-story Elm Park Hotel right on Wicker Park itself. The hotel has been the bane of the Near Northwest Side neighborhood, Kapp said.

That $2.5 million redevelopment, partly subsidized by the city, is to have its grand opening in late February as Wicker Park Place, a project with 112 units renting for $285 to $340 a month for low-and moderate-income residents.

The courtyard building several blocks away, called the Cloister of Wicker Park, received a $650,000 facelift and is offering two- and three-bedroom condos from $66,000 to about $94,000 with upgrades, and under $60,000 'as is.'

Kapp's projects may indicate that Wicker Park, which is roughly bounded by Milwaukee Avenue, Division Street, Wabansia Avenue, and Oakley Boulevard, is finally on the verge of fulfilling some 20 years of predictions that it was Chicago's next hot real estate neighborhood.

The last several years have seen the cleanup or razing of some of the big multi-unit buildings that as centers of neighborhood decay had, according to many observers, slowed the resurgence of Wicker Park while neighboring Bucktown, for instance, was growing in appeal.

'The big multi-unit buildings are probably the first to go when a neighborhood starts declining, and the last to be redone when it is gentrifying. Wicker Park has reached the point where that is happening,' said Barry Kreisler, president of Matanky Realty Group."

Chicago is the nation's second-largest city.

- The filming of the movie *Uncle Buck* recently was completed in Evanston; other movies shot in Chicago within the past few years include *Looking for Mr. Goodbar*, *The Blues Brothers*, *Ordinary People*, *Rich and Famous*, and *The Fury*.
- A three-bedroom, one-and-a-half-bath brick home in the Chicago Ridge section, featuring six rooms, full basement with recreation room and workshop, living room fireplace, and updated kitchen sells for $99,000; the qualifying income is $33,774.
- To purchase the home requires a down payment of $19,980; the monthly payment for the $79,020 loan at nine percent would be $788 per month.

Historical Snapshot
1991

- Allied forces attacked Iraq, dropping 2,232 tons of explosives the first day, the largest strike in history; all regular television programming was canceled for full coverage of the Gulf War
- The economy officially went into a recession for the first time since 1982; disposable income fell as unemployment rose
- A record 23,300 homicides were reported nationwide
- Arlette Schweitzer, 42, acted as surrogate mother for her daughter who was born without a uterus, giving birth to her own grandchildren—twins
- The number of single parents rose 41 percent from 1980, while the number of unmarried couples living together was up 80 percent
- One quarter of all newborns were born to single women
- Michael Jackson signed a $1.1 billion multi-year contract with Sony
- The U.S. Postal Service increased the first-class postage stamp rate from $0.25 to $0.29
- The U.S. trade deficit hit an eight-year low
- The median age for first marriages was 26.3 years for men and 24.1 years for women
- Cartoon character Blondie, wife of Dagwood Bumstead, announced her need for a career
- The U.S. Supreme Court ended forced busing, originally ordered to end racial segregation
- Congress approved family leave, allowing up to 12 weeks for family emergencies
- Eastern and Pan Am went into bankruptcy; Delta took over most Pan Am routes and became the leading carrier
- The Federal Reserve slashed interest rates to spur the economy
- A single sheet of the first printing of the Declaration of Independence sold for $2,420,000; it was found at a flea market for $4 in the backing of a painting
- School violence escalated; 25 percent of whites and 20 percent of blacks said they feared being attacked in school
- Walter H. Annenberg bequeathed his $1 billion art collection to the Metropolitan Museum of Art
- *Scarlett*, Alexandra Ripley's sequel to *Gone with the Wind*, sold a record 250,000 copies in one day
- Simon LeVay's study showed anatomical hypothalamic differences in gay and heterosexual men, lending credibility to the biological origin of sexual orientation
- Congress halted a nationwide rail strike after one day
- General Motors announced plans to close more than 20 plants over several years, eliminating more than 70,000 jobs
- Motorola introduced the 7.7-ounce cellular telephone
- The words and phrases date rape, boy toy, homeboy, and living will all entered the language

1991 Economic Profile

Income, Standard Jobs

Bituminous Coal Mining	$39,988.00
Building Trades	$25,945.00
Domestics	$9,527.00
Farm Labor	$14,493.00
Finance, Insurance, and Real Estate	$31,008.00
Gas, Electricity, and Sanitation Workers	$33,940.00
Manufacturing, Durable Goods	$25,112.00
Manufacturing, Nondurable Goods	$21,823.00
Medical/Health Services Workers	$18,522.00
Miscellaneous Manufacturing	$19,107.00
Motion Picture Services	$35,152.00
Nonprofit Organization Workers	$13,368.00
Passenger Transportation Workers, Local and Highway	$16,770.00
Postal Employees	$33,210.00
Private Industries, Including Farm Labor	$24,178.00

"Schaumburg Airport Expansion in Doubt," by David Ibata, *Chicago Tribune*, February 11, 1991:

"Efforts by local governments to get federal funds to buy and enlarge the Schaumburg Air Park have snagged over concerns that the airport might be too close to O'Hare International Airport to be expanded.

State aviation officials say they have asked the Federal Aviation Administration to review the grant application from the village and the Du Page Airport Authority.

'We're waiting for guidance from the FAA on under what conditions an airport expansion can be done, if at all,' said Roger Barcus, chief engineer of the Division of Aeronautics of the Illinois Department of Transportation.

To foot most of the expected $15.9 million bill to study, acquire, and expand the airport, Schaumburg and Du Page last fall filed a grant application with the state of $14.3 million in federal funds and $795,000 in state funds. The single-runway, 104-acre airport lies south of Irving Park Road on the Cook-Du Page County line at the southern end of Schaumburg.

It is the last privately owned airfield open to the public and Du Page County. Because it sits on prime land near the right-of-way of the Elgin-O'Hare Expressway, local officials fear that the airport may someday be lost to redevelopment."

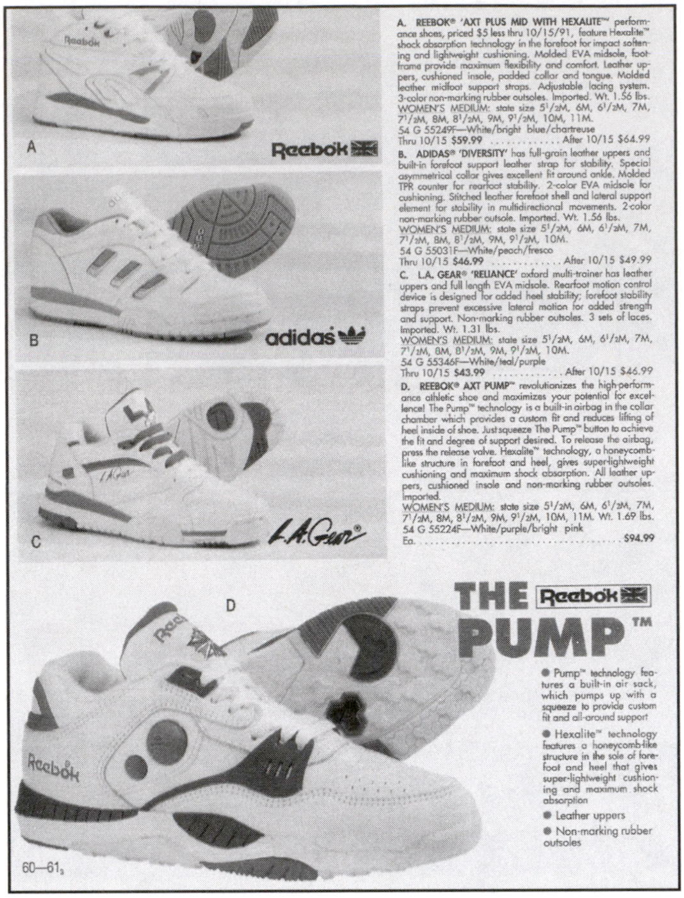

Public School Teachers. $24,561.00
Radio Broadcasting and
  Television Workers. $28,455.00
Railroad Workers. $36,772.00
State and Local Government
  Workers $25,863.00
Telephone and Telegraph
  Workers $31,034.00
Wages per Full-Time Employee $24,578.00
Wholesale and Retail
  Trade Workers $12,930.00

Selected Prices

Advil Caplets, 100-Count $6.68
Chrysler LeBaron, 1988 . . . . $8,495.00
Columbia Bugaboo Parka. $119.00
Goodyear 54S Tire $41.95
Hanes Men's Underwear,
  Three per Pack. $4.49

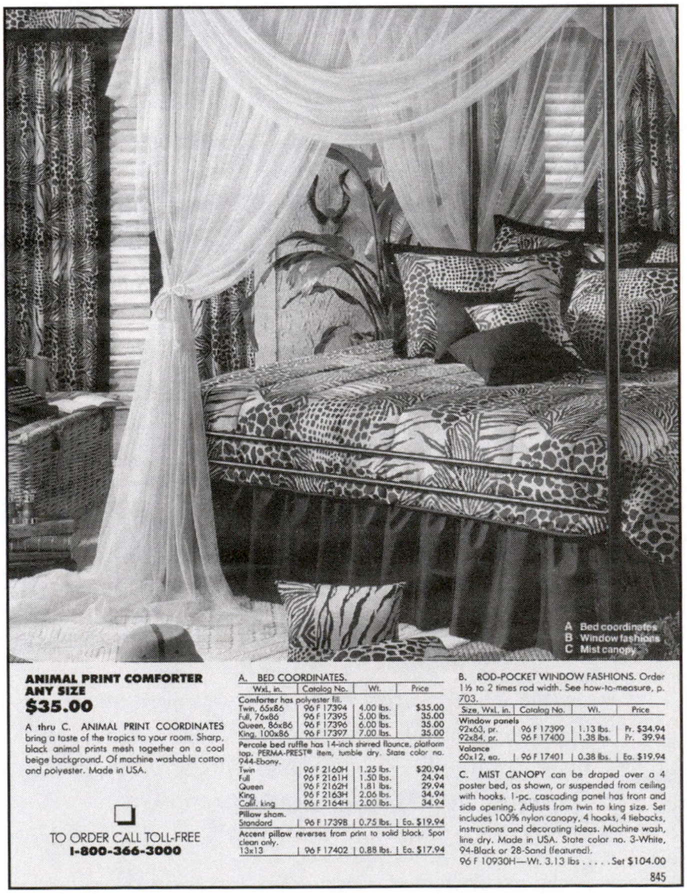

Hefty Trash Bags, 22 Bonus Size Bags $2.88
Ingraham Wood Alarm Clock $9.99
La-Z-Boy Recliner $599.99
Monsanto Round-Up Weed Killer $16.99
Nike Air Cross Trainer Shoes $58.99
Raymond Weil Men's Watch $750.00
RCA VCR $294.97
Regal Drip Coffeemaker, 10-Cup Capacity $7.99
Rubbermaid Laundry Basket $2.99
Sealy Queen Size Mattress $324.00
Shrimp, Cooked Tail on, 12 Ounces $8.99
Wild Bird Food, 20 Pounds $2.99
Wild Thunder Cotton Canvas Pants $19.99
Xerox Personal Photocopier $899.99

PACKARD BELL COMPUTERS
These computer models are only available from Sears!

- Our fastest computer at 33 MHz
- Huge 85 MB hard drive
- **Sears exclusive** 4 MB RAM memory and a limited 1 year on-site service warranty

1. PACKARD BELL LEGEND 833DX, $50 monthly on SearsCharge PLUS,* is a true 386 performer that processes information at speeds to 33 MHz, twice as fast as 286 models. It can operate in a graphic user interface mode with windows, pull-down menus, icons, and point-and-click mouse control. Multitasking ability so you can run multiple programs at once. The memory capacity is an impressive 4 MB of internal memory (RAM) with a 85 MB, fast 20ms (millesecond), hard disk drive. Plus, 5.25-inch 1.2 MB and a 3.5-inch 1.44 MB High density floppy drives. If you are confused 1 MB (Mega Byte) is equal to 1,000,000 characters of memory. You also get a 2400 baud modem to connect with on-line services like PRODIGY® which is included with 1 free month of service (see page 1435 for description). Mouse included to make good use of window programs. Software includes DOS 4.01, DOS shell, GW-BASIC, and PRODIGY start-up kit. Plus, LotusWorks integrated software that gives you word processing, spreadsheet, database, graphics, and telecommunications programs. Extended VGA card offers 1024 x 768 lines and supports (compatible with) Super VGA, VGA, EGA,CGA, and MDA monitors. Enhanced 101 key keyboard with 12 function keys. Real time clock/calendar with battery back-up and 2 serial ports, 1 parallel. 4 disk drive cavities (3 used) and 7 system expansion slots: one 32-bit, four 16-bit, two 8-bit slots (2 used) for expansion cards. RAM (internal memory) can be expanded to 8 MB on the mother board using SIMMs (chips). LIM EMS 4.0™/ Novell/OS2 compatible with proper expansion. 150 watt power supply. Imported. Limited 1 year on-site service warranty** with a 24 hour technical support hotline.
3 F [illegible]—Wt. 49 lbs **$2089.99**

2. PACKARD BELL SUPER VGA MONITOR, $13 monthly,* delivers 1024 x 768 resolution with 262,144 color range. Fine 0.28 mm pitch dots. 13-inch diagonal non-glare screen with tilt/ swivel base. Requires Super VGA card for maximum resolution but it also can use other VGA modes. Compatible with Packard Bell, IBM, and compatible computers. Controls include power, brightness, contrast, vertical center, vertical size, and horizontal width. 15 PIN interface cable. Limited 1 year on-site service warranty.**
3 F 32328—Wt. 38 lbs **$409.99**

3. PACKARD BELL 9815 LASER PRINTER, $21 monthly on SearsCharge PLUS,* prints type and graphics at a crisp 300 DPI (Dots Per Inch) for clear smooth lines at up to 8 pages per minute. Handles pages both horizontally and vertically (portrait and landscape) and can print letter, legal size, envelopes, transparencies, and labels. Eight internal fonts including Courier and capable of using downloadable soft fonts. 1.5 MB of RAM internally for a memory buffer and for greater font expandability. LCD control panel of printer functions. Uses HP Laserjet™ Series II and IBM Proprinter X24E/XL24E emulations to understand your software. Parallel and serial communication ports. 1 year Limited Warranty.**
3 F 32450—Wt. 35 lbs **$989.99**

REPLACEMENT DRUM for (3) above.
3 F 32470—Wt. 4 lbs **$119.99**

TONER/DEVELOPER KIT for (3) above includes 5 toner cartridges and 1 developing unit.
3 F 32471—Wt. 2 lbs . . . . Kit **$199.99**

*See page 459 for further credit information.
**Warranted by Sears or manufacturer, write for free copy, see page 476.

Our manufacturers may temporarily lower costs on some of our computer products. We would like to pass any savings on to you, so call 1-800-366-3000 for our current prices.

1436

Editorial: "Caller ID Poses Invasion of Privacy," by Jeffrey M. Shaman, *Chicago Tribune*, May 18, 1990:

"A new telephone device known as Caller ID is the latest technological innovation that at first blush seems to improve our lives, when in fact it may have disastrous consequences. Already available in a number of states, Caller ID is to be brought to Illinois if approved by the Commerce Commission.

Caller ID operates by displaying the phone number of an incoming call on a screen at the recipient's phone while it is ringing. Without an implement that allows callers to selectively block the display of their telephone numbers, Caller ID automatically reveals them, and perhaps their identity and location as well. In the absence of a blocking implement, Caller ID deprives individuals of the ability to decide when and to whom to give their telephone numbers.

This is an invasion of personal privacy and autonomy. Many individuals will be deterred from calling crisis centers that deal with suicide, rape, child abuse, or AIDS for fear of having their identities revealed. Psychiatrists, doctors, social workers, and lawyers will not be able to return emergency calls from home if they want to keep their numbers confidential."

"Just What Do Suburbs Want at O'Hare? Fewer Flights, Less Noise," by Patricia Szymczak, *Chicago Tribune*, May 20, 1990:

"If suburbia had its way at O'Hare International Airport, it would put the world's busiest air transportation center on a diet.

Here's the menu:

- Cut flights by 100,000 a year
- Put airlines on a noise budget to make them schedule their newest and quietest aircraft into O'Hare
- Impose a nighttime curfew
- Compensate homeowners nearest the airport for property value lost to jet noise and other pollution
- Phase all of the above in slowly and in coordination with the opening of a new third airport in 1995

Close O'Hare? Park Ridge Mayor Martin Butler, one of the most militant suburban voices in the O'Hare noise controversy, gets accused, in jest, of wanting to do that sometimes. 'It's stupid. It's unthinkable,' Butler says.

'O'Hare has been a tremendous engine driving the area's economy,' he says. 'But it is an engine that's running wild. The question is, what is the balance between O'Hare's impact on livability and its impact on economic vitality?'

Mary Rose Loney, Chicago's first deputy commissioner of aviation, estimates that O'Hare pumps $11 billion a year into the economy of the six-county region. There are 50,000 jobs on the field alone. . .

'Noise is not just a product of volume,' Loney said. 'But volume, a noise budget, and a nighttime curfew are on the table as solutions to the noise problem,' she said. Yet she added, 'Before we leap in we need to look at the impact in terms of jobs and dollars.'

The suburbs couldn't agree more. In fact, they contend a smaller O'Hare would be better for the region so far as jobs and economic muscle are concerned, if its downsizing were completed in tandem with the opening of another airport as big or bigger.

Consider this: The Federal Aviation Administration says O'Hare at its current size is inefficient and actually chases business away from Chicago if used by more than 700,000 flights a year. That's because above 700,000 flights, delays become so intolerable that air travelers who are only connecting in Chicago to another flight choose to connect in another city, FAA studies say."

"Airline Fare Wars Uncork Pent-up Consumer Interest," by John N. Maclean, *Chicago Tribune*, February 9, 1991:

"At 8 a.m., Friday, Chicago's United Airlines had 800 telephone calls on hold waiting to talk to reservation clerks. A round-trip ticket from Chicago to San Francisco on United was going for as little as $227.

At Phoenix's American West Airlines, calls were up by 50 percent, from 200,000 to 300,000. A round-trip ticket to Hawaii was going for as little as $336 from Phoenix.

At many of the nation's airlines, battered by months of Mid-East uncertainty and recession fears, a short-lived, short-notice fare sale was putting Americans back in the skies. By midnight, Saturday, it will be over.

But for now, said Laura DeMaio of the giant travel agency Thomas Cook Travel, 'It's made people lose their fear of flying.'

What began as a three-day, half-price promotion by American West has mushroomed to include hundreds of major routes across the country. But the sale's scope has grown so rapidly, it has angered some would-be flyers who find their desired routes unavailable at the special fares. . . .

The big half-price question: Will revenues go up enough to justify the deep discounting? It may be a while before the airlines know if they won or lost the gamble.

'We're not having a problem with cash flow,' said American West spokesman Dick Shimizu from Phoenix. 'Traffic has been down since the middle of last year. But we're finding people still want to travel and have the money.'

'What we need to do is strike a balance between revenues and traffic,' said Northwest Airlines' Christy Klapp. 'Traffic's been soft.'"

"Suburban Growth Is Finding Wildlife to Be a Formidable Foe," *Chicago Tribune*, March 9, 1991:

"After a platoon of raccoons invaded his attic last February, Burt Wright thought his Hinsdale home was becoming a barracks for wayward critters.

The five masked marauders, who apparently decided to relocate to the Wright's home after a development cleared a nearby vacant lot, gnawed on the insulation surrounding the air-conditioning ducts and plundered the garbage . . .

Whether it's a raccoon in the attic, beavers building dams in the drainage ditches, or coyotes in a St. Charles subdivision, encounters with wildlife are becoming more common these days, according to state statistics.

The primary reason, experts agree, is growth.

Du Page County alone has grown in population by 100,000 in the last 10 years, with subdivisions sprawling into territory once the exclusive province of beavers, raccoons, and deer."

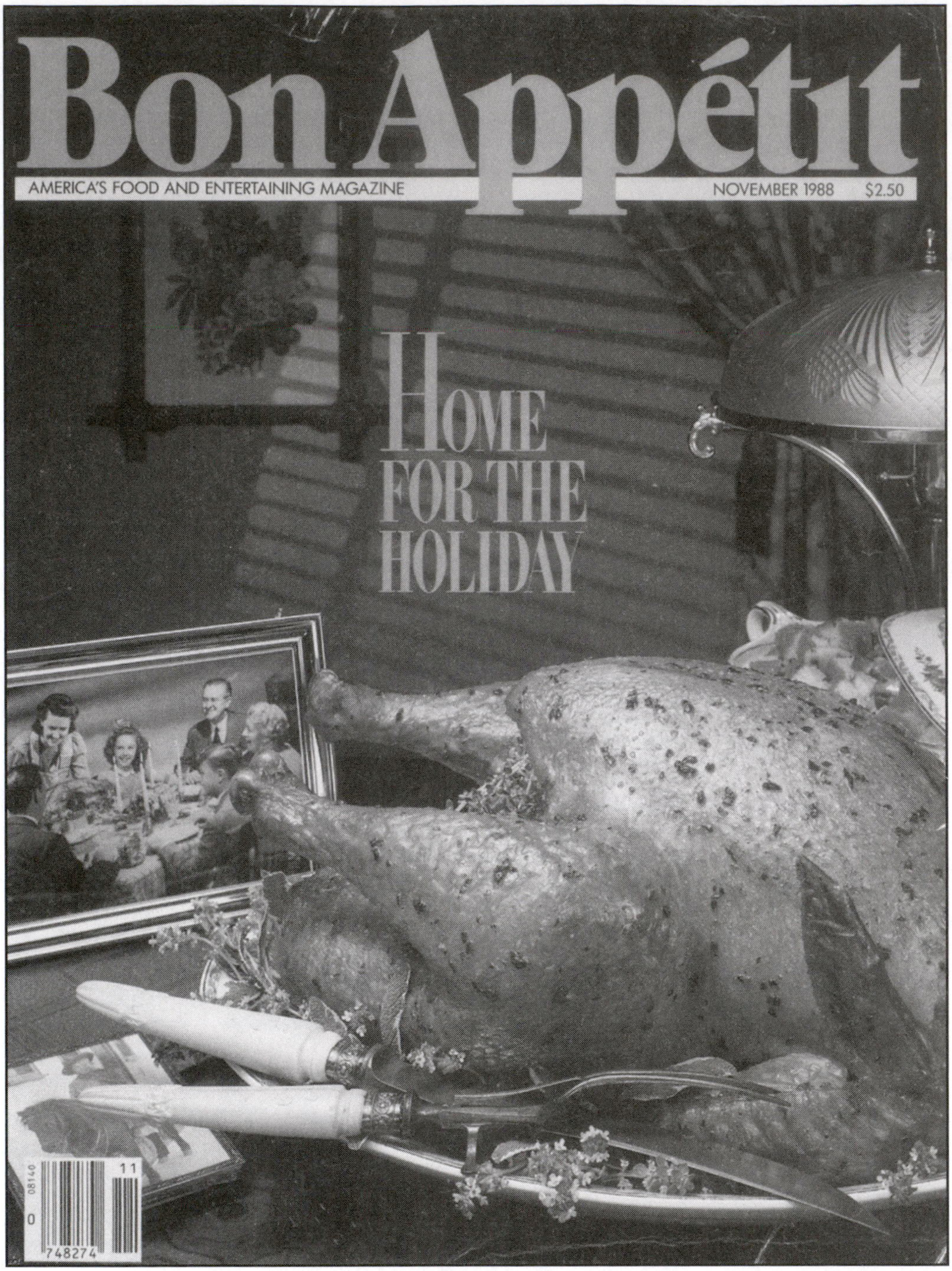
Bon Appétit
AMERICA'S FOOD AND ENTERTAINING MAGAZINE
NOVEMBER 1988
$2.50
HOME
FOR THE
HOLIDAY

1992 News Profile

The Overworked American, The Unexpected Decline in Leisure, by Juliet B. Schor, Basic Books, 1992:

"In the last 20 years the amount of time Americans have spent on their jobs has risen steadily. Each year the change is small, amounting to about nine hours, or slightly more than one additional day of work. In any given year, such a small increment has probably been imperceptible. But the accumulated increase over two decades is substantial. When surveyed, Americans report that they have only 16.5 hours of leisure a week, after the obligations of job and household are taken care of. Working hours are already longer than they were 40 years ago. If present trends continue, by the end of the century Americans will be spending as much time at their jobs as they did back in the 1920s.

The rise of worktime was unexpected. For nearly a hundred years, hours had been declining. When this decline abruptly ended in the late 1940s, it marked the beginning of a new era in worktime. But the change was barely noticed. Equally surprising, but also hardly recognized, has been the deviation from western Europe. After progressing in tandem for nearly a century, the United States veered off into a trajectory of declining leisure, while in Europe work has been disappearing. Forty years later, the differences are large. U.S. manufacturing employees currently work 320 more hours—the equivalent of over two months—than their counterparts in western Germany or France.

The decline in Americans' leisure time is in sharp contrast to the potential provided by the growth of productivity. Productivity measures the goods and services that result from each hour worked. When productivity rises, a worker can either produce the current output in less time, or remain at work the same amount of hours and produce more. Every time productivity increases, we are presented with the possibility of either more free time or more money. That's the productivity dividend.

Since 1948, productivity has failed to rise in only five years. The level of productivity of the U.S. worker has more than doubled. In other words, we could now produce our 1948 standard of living (measured in terms of marketed goods and services) in less than half the time it took in that year. We actually could have chosen the four-hour day. Or a working year of six months. Or, every worker in the United States could now be taking every other year off from work—with pay. Incredible as it may sound, this is just the simple arithmetic of productivity growth in operation.

But between 1948 and the present we did not use any of the productivity dividend to reduce hours. In the first two decades after 1948, productivity grew rapidly, at about three percent a year. During that period, worktime did not fall appreciably. Annual hours per labor force participant fell only slightly. And on a per-capita (rather than a labor force) basis, they even rose a bit. Since then productivity growth has been lower, but still positive, averaging just over one percent a year. Yet hours have risen steadily for two decades. In 1990, the average American owns and consumes more than twice as much as he or she did in 1948, but also has less free time.

How did this happen? Why has leisure been such a conspicuous casualty of prosperity? In part, the answer lies in the difference between the markets for consumer products and free time. Consider the former, the legendary American market. It is a veritable consumer's paradise, offering a dazzling array of products varying in style, design, quality, price, and country of origin. . . . In cross-country comparisons, Americans have been found to spend more time shopping than anyone else. They also spend a higher fraction of the money they earn. And with the explosion of consumer debt, many are now spending what they haven't earned.

After four decades of this shopping spree, the American standard of living embodies a level of material comfort unprecedented in human history. The American home is more spacious and luxurious than the dwellings of any other nation. Food is cheap and abundant. The typical family owns a fantastic array of household and consumer appliances: we have machines to wash our clothes and dishes, mow our lawns, and blow away our snow. On a per-person basis, yearly income is nearly $22,000 a year—or 65 times the average income of half the world's population.

On the other hand, the 'market' for free time hardly even exists in America. With few exceptions, employers (the sellers) don't offer the chance to trade off income gains for a shorter workday or the occasional sabbatical. They just pass on income in the form of annual pay raises or bonuses, or, if granting increased vacation or personal days, usually do so unilaterally. Employees rarely have the chance to exercise an actual choice about how they will spend their productivity dividend. The closest substitute for a 'market in leisure' is the travel and other leisure industries that advertise products to occupy our free time. But this indirect effort has been weak, as consumers crowd increasingly expensive leisure spending into smaller periods of time."

1993 Family Profile

Harry deBoer hopes that his company, Reflective, will lead the rebirth of industry in Connecticut. As a partner in the firm, he is committed to employee ownership as the modern vehicle for managing people and making money. He is married with three children, two of whom are in college.

Annual Income: $136,000
His annual salary is $95,000; the sale of a small portion of his stock options this year resulted in $41,000 more in income.

Annual Budget

The average per capita consumer expenditures in 1993 for all workers nationwide are:

Auto Maintenance	$248.00
Auto Usage	$1,843.00
Clothing	$670.00
Entertainment	$650.00
Food	$2,735.00
Furniture	$126.00
Gas and Oil	$390.00
Health Care	$710.00
Health Insurance	$320.00
Housing	$2,166.00
New Auto Purchase	$486.00
Personal Business	$1,163.00
Personal Care	$154.00
Public Transportation	$125.00
Telephone	$263.00

Harry deBoer moved to Connecticut from Detroit.

Tobacco........................$107.00
Utilities........................$581.00
Per Capita Consumption.........$12,276.00

Life at Home

- Harry and Nicole moved from Detroit, Michigan, several years ago and purchased a 150-year-old home they adore.
- The home was built in three stages, each addition approximately 30 years apart, with the last change in the 1930s.
- The house, which has six fireplaces, features tall ceilings, solid hand-made doors, and steep roofs.
- Nicole is carefully restoring the home; once a month, she goes to New York City with a decorator to discover new treasures.
- She has completely modernized the bathrooms and kitchen; the rest of the rooms are being restored to their original look.
- Harry enjoys watching the house being transformed; even though he has little time to pick colors or wallpaper for each room, he is fascinated by the changes under way.
- On a few occasions, he has assisted in the renovations, establishing a full woodworking shop in a barn on the property.
- When time permits, he slips into the shop to work on a shaker-style clock, based on a story he read in *Fine Woodworking* magazine.

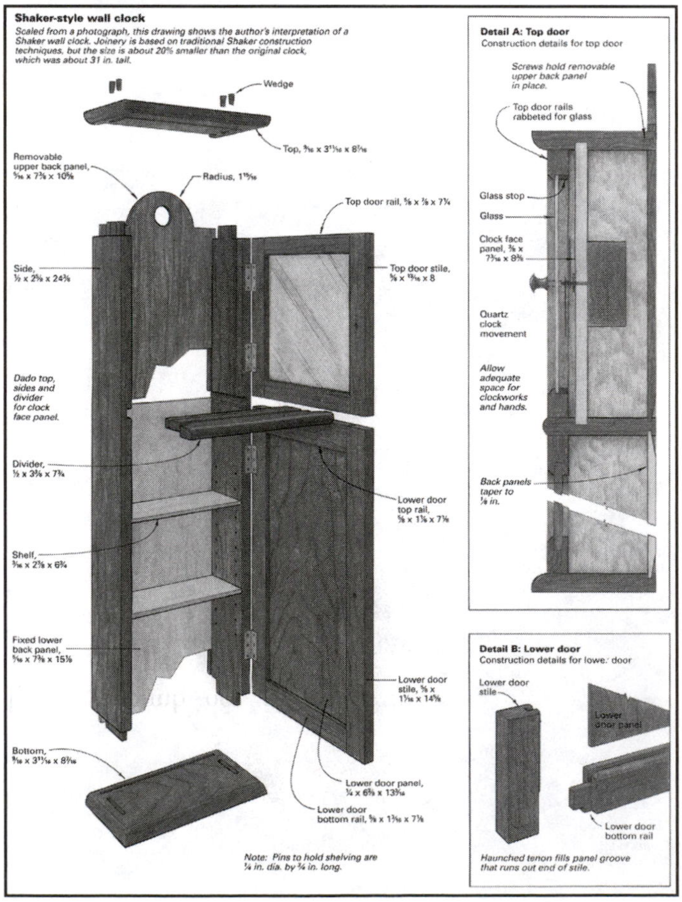

- Their youngest child is attending prep school at Hotchkiss; Connecticut is renowned for its long tradition of excellent prep schools, including Taft, Choate, Loomis, Westminster, and Ethel Walker.
- The oldest son is now at Yale; their daughter, a junior at Northwestern, is currently studying in France.
- Nicole is very pleased to be living in a state that would select the endangered sperm whale as its state animal.

Life at Work

- This small company has just weathered an economic downturn by shifting gears quickly to keep profits steady.
- Sales last year were more than $31 million, an increase of 200 percent since 1986; its work force has tripled to more than 300.
- Even though Harry's company competes with the giant 3M Corporation for customers, Reflective has been bold enough to expand into Canada, Europe, and Mexico.
- Reflective is owned by its employees, who own 59 percent of the company's stock.
- Harry has instituted an in-house technology-development capability to stay ahead of the competition.
- Under this system, Reflective engineers and technicians design and build the big multi-million-dollar machines that produce the prismatic material they need.

Reflective *is owned by its employees.*

***Practice Kaizen, New Work Habits for a Radically Changing World*, by Price Pritchett:**

"A strong organization is the best position to protect your career. If it's financially successful, your paycheck is more secure. If it keeps getting better and better in the way it does business, your future usually gets brighter.

But the organization doesn't improve unless its people do.

Continuous improvement—the Japanese call it kaizen—offers some of the best insurance for both your career and your organization. Kaizen is the relentless quest for a better way, for higher quality craftsmanship. Think of it as the daily pursuit of perfection.

Kaizen keeps you reaching, stretching to outdo yesterday. The continuous improvements may come bit by bit. But enough of these small, incremental gains will eventually add up to a valuable competitive advantage. Also, if every employee constantly keeps an eye out for improvements, major innovations are more likely to occur. The spirit of kaizen can trigger dramatic breakthroughs.

Without kaizen, you and your employer will gradually lose ground. Eventually, you'll both be 'out of business,' because the competition never stands still.

Tom Peters puts it this way: 'Good quality is a stupid idea. The only thing that counts is your quality getting better at a more rapid rate than your principal competitors. It's real simple. If we're not getting more, better, faster than they are getting more, better, faster, then we're getting less better or more worse.'

Nobody can afford to rest on a reputation anymore. Circumstances change too quickly. Competition gets tougher and more global all the time. What we consider 'good' today is seen as 'so-so' by tomorrow."

- Each new machine incorporates dozens of new process improvements, most of which will never appear in any patent.
- Some of their products require a complex blend of eight to 10 chemical layers.
- The company was started by two Connecticut-born brothers who both graduated from Yale in the 1940s.
- As engineers, they have for years been fascinated by new products, particularly in the plastics industry.
- In the 1960s, one of the brothers invented a new method for producing material that is retro-reflective, meaning reflecting light back to its source; it is often used to coat highway signs and barricades.
- The new method he created involved molding thousands of microscopic prisms onto every square inch of a plastic sheet.
- In the past, competitor 3M has attempted to buy the business, offering 42 times the earnings.
- The brothers would have made $5 million each; the sale would have resulted in the closing of the factory in New Britain, Connecticut.
- Harry was hired to make Reflective capable of competing worldwide against giants such as 3M; the employees know it is his job to keep the company from being gobbled up by a giant competitor.

- He must find new applications for his company's technology if it is to remain viable in the marketplace.
- He has previous experience in the corporate world, including stints with Anheuser-Busch and Container Corporation of America.
- The experience has crystallized a belief that traditional top-down management, left over from the days when immigrant workers might have no more than a strong back to offer an employer, was no longer the best way to run a company in the twentieth century.
- He believes that today's employee, because of education and background, has more to contribute than traditionally believed.
- He also believes employees want more than money from their employer; they want to be committed to something and also want some power over the decisions affecting their work lives.
- Creating an employee-owned company is more than a matter of altruism, Harry believes; it is smart business.
- The federally approved employee stock ownership plans (ESOPs) provided him with the way to convert the company from private ownership by a few to a company owned broadly by its workers.

Harry believes that today's employee has much to contribute.

The Good Life, The Meaning of Success for the American Middle Class, by Loren Baritz:

"What the middle-class employee owns is his skill—what working people have always offered employers—but now with a computer, legal brief, or ledge, not with a lathe. Because corporate fortunes are seen to be more dependent on the judgment of such employees than on the individual workers on the factory floor, the bureaucrats command commensurately higher salaries. Throughout the twentieth century, and even earlier, the skills that create the financial strength of corporations have been changing, and such evolution has created the opportunity for larger numbers of people to work their way upward. Job descriptions in middle management require specific forms of specialized 'education' increasingly accessible to middle-class students. Training has replaced the capital once required to start a business. Those with vocational training—professionals, they are called—are paid accordingly, and the nature and the quality of their private lives depends on the degree of their perceived value to their superior."

"More Signs of a Productive U.S.," by Sylvia Nasar, *The New York Times*, October 24, 1993:

"Contrary to a widely held view that the United States is an industrial has-been whose productivity in manufacturing has been surpassed in some other countries, a new study concludes that for manufacturing as a whole, the United States still holds a significant edge over the presumed world standard setters, Germany and Japan.

The year-long study combined research into nine industries with a wide array of available statistics. While other studies have also found that the United States was still the world's productivity leader in manufacturing, the new study provides a more detailed look at individual industries.

Perhaps the most provocative findings concern the probable causes of the productivity differences that do exist. It concludes that in industries where the United States has fallen behind, the reasons have more to do with how goods are produced than with the skills of workers or the quality of technology.

'If the United States is lagging behind Japan in certain manufacturing industries, it doesn't appear to be because of the failure of our schools of technology,' said Martin Baily, University of Maryland professor, who helped direct the study. 'We haven't put enough effort into organizing the workplace and designing products so that they are easy to manufacture. . . .'

The study, a sequel to a McKinsey report last year that found that American service industries had a large productivity lead over the German and Japanese industries, challenges the view of some influential economists—from Lester Thurow of MIT, author of *Head to Head: The Coming Economic Battle among Japan, Europe, and America*, to Laura D. Ahdrea Tyson, chief of the Council of Economic Advisors—who have argued that American manufacturing has been overtaken by German and Japanese industries."

Their oldest son is now at Yale.

- Economist Louis O. Kelso invented ESOPs in hopes of transforming society by making workers into capitalists.
- Most companies that have created ESOPs have experienced modest success.
- Harry believes an employee-owned company creates a different kind of culture; employees are more willing to move faster into new markets to protect themselves from competition.
- In addition, the longer employees work at Reflective, the more shares they receive and the more their nest egg grows.
- They are also more willing to run leaner, thus more profitably, because they share more equitably in the results.
- Currently, the median ESOP account contains more than $50,000; long-term employees' accounts are significantly higher.

"Pact Called Key to Lower Imports," by Robert D. Hershey, Jr., *The New York Times*, October 17, 1993:

"President Clinton, in his most vigorous promotion of the North American Free Trade Agreement since the formal signing of labor and environmental safeguards in mid-September, warned today that failure to ratify the deal could isolate the United States and flood it with imported goods.

'Without Nafta, one of our best markets, Mexico, could turn to Japan and Europe to make a sweetheart deal for trade,' the President said in his weekly radio address. 'Without Nafta, Mexico could well become an export platform allowing more products from Japan and Europe into America. Why would we want that to happen?'

Critics of the agreement have repeatedly argued that it would be American companies that would use Mexico as a platform from which to export goods after they move factories there, causing a substantial loss of jobs.

Mr. Clinton's renewed campaign for the agreement, which would gradually remove tariffs and other trade barriers among the United States, Mexico, and Canada, was the latest example of a shift in the drive to stress the consequences if it fails."

- Employees are also eligible to get a bonus once a month; three percent of the company's operating profit is divided up by shares.
- In a good month, the bonus adds several hundred dollars to the average, experienced worker's paycheck; in a bad month, nothing at all is paid out.
- All shareholders, including employee shareholders, get annual dividends amounting to 20 percent of pretax earnings.
- A middle manager with an average number of shares received about $1,000 in dividends last year.
- Quarterly plant meetings are being held to provide regular information about the company's performance and priorities.
- At the annual meeting, typically the same day as the company picnic, employee stockholders vote for the Board of Directors.
- The company and its employees are still running to stay ahead of competitor 3M.
- Current products include reflective traffic cones that change colors at night to provide a higher reflection value; they are also working with the Coast Guard on reflective buoys and even decorative stickers for children.
- Invention is only one part of the process; getting products into so many markets is both tricky and time-consuming.
- Reflective has been able to adapt and expand rapidly by finding entrepreneurs in the host company who know the industry, and then provide them with capital and technical

The deBoers love the older homes of the state.

expertise so they can run their own business; bonuses reflect how well they handle this responsibility.

- The business opportunities change daily; Harry likes to tell his teammates that a weekend edition of *The New York Times* contains more information than the average person was likely to come across in a lifetime during seventeenth-century England.
- He also reminds them that change is ever-present; during the decade of the 1980s, a total of 230 companies—46 percent—disappeared from the listing of the *Fortune 500*.

Life in the Community: New Britain, Connecticut

- New Britain is known as Hardware City; during its early history, the city was a manufacturing center for sleigh bells, locks, and saddlery gear.
- In recent years, tools, hardware, and machinery have been manufactured in the community, though several factories have closed in recent years.
- The huge former home of the defunct New Britain Machine is now dark and silent, "a mute testament to the decline and fall of yesterday's industrial economy," one magazine proclaimed.
- The growth of Reflective has been a point of community pride for many in New Britain.

- It symbolizes the new economy of technology-based businesses competing for a place in the world economy.
- Many in the community now believe that knowledge is becoming America's most important "product"; the Industrial Age has given way to the Information Age.
- As recently as the 1960s, almost one half of all workers in the industrialized countries were involved in manufacturing; currently, only one sixth of the work force of industrialized countries is involved in the traditional role of making and moving goods.
- In 1991, for the first time ever, companies spent more money on computing and communications gear than the combined money spent on industrial, mining, and farm and construction equipment.
- The community is dotted with homes that date to the days of the Declaration of Independence.

Restoring a 150-year-old home is a painstaking and exacting task.

- The state was shaped by its early history; the lack of a major crop—such as cod, rice, cotton, or tobacco to trade with the Old World—and the absence of a deep-water port caused Connecticut to remain isolated for two centuries.
- Those who made money reinvested in Connecticut; absentee ownership has never been the tradition of the state.

Historical Snapshot
1993

- A bomb blast injured hundreds in the World Trade Center bombing in New York City; Mohammed A. Salameh was arrested for the bombing when he attempted to reclaim his $400 car rental deposit
- Major League baseball owners announced new initiatives on minority hiring
- Law enforcement agents raided a religious cult in Waco, Texas, igniting a storm of protests
- U.S. pledged $1.6 billion in aid to assist in Russian reforms
- An Oregon law permitted physician-assisted suicide; Michigan's Dr. Jack Kevorkian was jailed twice for assisting patients' suicides
- President Bill Clinton promised "universal health coverage" comparable to that of *Fortune 500* companies; 64 million people lacked adequate coverage
- Women received combat roles in aerial and naval warfare
- Civil rights advocate Ruth Bader Ginsburg was named to the U.S. Supreme Court
- *Jurassic Park* became the highest-grossing movie of all time
- IBM announced an $8.9 billion restructuring of the world's largest computer maker; the firm eliminated 60,000 jobs
- President Clinton supported easing a ban on homosexuals in the military
- Chicago Bulls basketball star Michael Jordan retired to play professional baseball
- Work statistics showed that nearly one out of three American workers had been with their employer for less than a year, and almost two out of three for less than five years
- The brown uniform of the Brownies changed after 66 years to include pastel tops, culotte jumpers, and floral print vests
- The inflation rate remained at 2.7 percent, the lowest in seven years
- The U.S. began testing of the French abortion pill RU-486
- Cosmologists discovered that stars and other observable matter occupied less than 10 percent of the universe
- Sears ended its mail-order catalog business
- Thirty-year mortgages dropped to 6.7 percent, the lowest in 25 years
- The Ford Taurus topped the Honda Accord in total car sales
- The Pentium processor, one-pound personal digital assistant, and Mighty Max Toby Terrier all made their first appearances

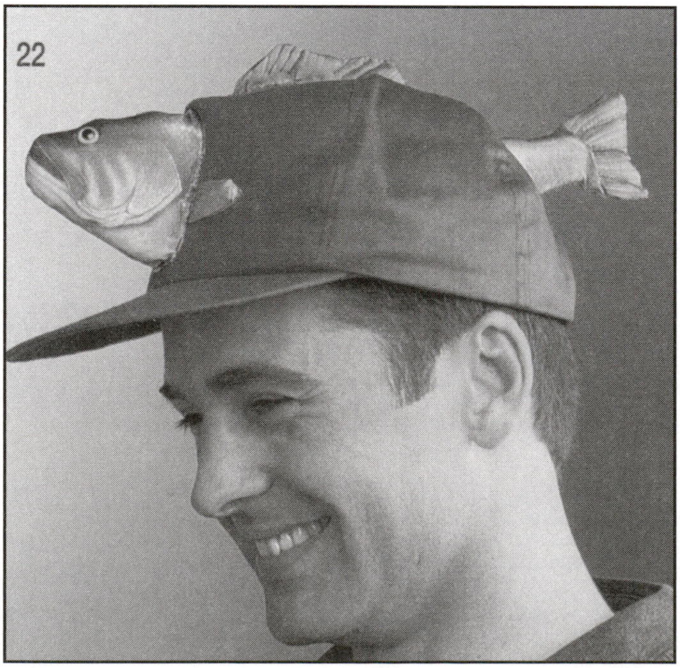

1993 Economic Profile

Income, Standard Jobs

Bituminous Coal Mining	$40,493.00
Building Trades	$26,739.00
Domestics	$10,275.00
Farm Labor	$15,019.00
Finance, Insurance, and Real Estate	$36,013.00
Gas, Electricity, and Sanitation Workers	$36,755.00
Manufacturing, Durable Goods	$26,992.00
Manufacturing, Nondurable Goods	$23,181.00
Medical/Health Services Workers	$20,091.00
Miscellaneous Manufacturing	$20,508.00
Motion Picture Services	$37,541.00
Nonprofit Organization Workers	$14,094.00
Passenger Transportation Workers, Local and Highway	$17,802.00
Postal Employees	$37,609.00
Public School Teachers	$25,816.00
Private Industries, Including Farm Labor	$25,934.00
Radio Broadcasting and Television Workers	$30,702.00
Railroad Workers	$40,672.00
State and Local Government Workers	$27,369.00
Telephone and Telegraph Workers	$33,871.00
Total Federal Government	$36,940.00
Wages per Full-Time Employee	$26,361.00
Wholesale and Retail Trade Workers	$13,597.00

Selected Prices

American Museum of Natural History Tour	$10.00
Apple Macintosh Powerbook, 180 4/80	$3,799.00
Artcarved High School Class Ring	$69.95
Brother Intellifax-600 Fax Machine with Cutter	$353.43

Camel Genesis Sixty-Second Tent, 7' x 8' $89.98
Etonic Stableair Base 11 Men's Running Shoes $49.96
Gold Medal Flour, Five-Pound Bag $0.79
"Insects of the New World" Wall Calendar $12.85
Loving Care Supreme Queen Size Mattress $189.95
Mardi Gras Paper Towels $0.50
New Orleans Jazz and Heritage Festival Ticket $25.00
Nissan Altima GXE, 1993 . . . . $14,484.00
Nyquil, 10-Ounce Bottle $4.93
Oki-810 Car Phone with Antenna and Installation $149.00
Philips Bag-A-Way, Two Bulbs $1.61
Shelby Women's Leather Shoe $68.00
Sheraton New York Hotel Room, per Night $169.00
Spalding Cotton Golf Shirt $14.98
Washington State Delicious Apples, per Pound $0.59
Wilson Tennis Racket, 3.0 Tennis Frame $129.97

"Scientist Clones Human Embryos, and Creates an Ethical Challenge," by Gina Kolata, *The New York Times*, October 19, 1993:

"A university researcher in Washington has, as an experiment, cloned human embryos, splitting single embryos into identical twins or triplets. This appears to be the first time such a feat has been reported.

The scientist, Dr. Jerry L. Hall of George Washington University Medical Center, reported his work at a recent meeting of the American Fertility Society. The experiment was not a technical breakthrough, since he used methods that are commonly used to clone animal embryos, but it opens a rank of practical and ethical questions.

For example, since human embryos can be frozen and used at a later date, parents could have a child and then years later, use a cloned embryo to give birth to an identical twin, possibly as an organ donor for the older child."

"Made in North America—Still; How Delat, Powermatic, and General Have Dealt with the Taiwanese Challenge," by Vincent Laurence, *Fine Woodworking*, July/August, 1993:

"The woodworking machinery market looked a lot different 15 years ago. A handful of European companies and a Japanese newcomer or two were all the competition North American manufacturers faced. Then, in the early 1980s, Taiwanese machines began to flow into the United States, and everything changed. Little more than a decade later, what at first was a trickle has long since become a torrent. Open any woodworking magazine and chances are you'll see more advertisements for Taiwanese-made machines than for American machines.

Despite the fact that American machines frequently cost twice as much as their Taiwanese counterparts, the American companies are thriving, which means they must be doing something right. Because every day we hear from readers who want advice on buying machinery—should I buy American or Taiwanese?—we thought it was a good idea to get reacquainted with the American manufacturers of stationary woodworking power tools. I wanted to know how the American companies have remained competitive, what they've had to do here and in some cases, overseas, and what it means to the average power-tool buyer like me. . . .

One of the most important questions anyone running a business can ask is, 'What market am I serving?' General Manufacturing Co. asked that question in the early '80s, and the answer was, 'We're manufacturers of industrial-grade woodworking machinery.' Unfortunately, the industrial market wasn't growing, labor and material costs were rising, and Taiwanese machinery was on the streets for a fraction of what a comparable U.S. or Canadian machine cost. Disaster wasn't imminent, but the handwriting was on the wall.

General's solution was two-fold: First, it was decided to continue building the same heavy-duty industrial equipment it has since 1946, but to market equipment to home-shop woodworkers as well as to professionals. Second, General increased the efficiency of its Drummondville, Quebec, plant and foundry. General upgraded its foundry with an electric furnace, allowing smaller, more consistent batches of iron to be poured more quickly. The firm also began buying CNC (computer numerically controlled) equipment for its machining and assembly plant.

CNC machines are flexible, programmable milling machines, capable of performing a whole spectrum of operations. They require far less monitoring than traditional machining stations, so one worker can operate a number of machines safely and effectively. Also, setup time for a new part or operation is all but eliminated because the bulk of setup is in the programming."

1997 Family Profile

Dan Stevens is the division administrator for the Iowa Division of the Federal Highway Administration, U.S. Department of Transportation. This is his eighth move in 21 years. He has promised the family it will be their last.

Annual Income: $81,734

Annual Budget

The average per capita consumer expenditures in 1997 are not available. The average per capita consumer expenditures in 1995 for all workers nationwide are:

Auto Maintenance	$266.00
Auto Usage	$2,015.00
Clothing	$681.00
Entertainment	$644.00
Food	$2,803.00
Furniture	$130.00
Gas and Oil	$402.00
Health Care	$692.00
Health Insurance	$344.00
Housing	$2,371.00
New Auto Purchase	$479.00
Personal Business	$1,185.00
Personal Care	$163.00
Public Transportation	$142.00
Telephone	$283.00
Tobacco	$107.00
Utilities	$593.00
Per Capita Consumption	$12,905.00

Iowa's long winters encourage family-oriented projects.

Life at Home

- To move up in the organization, Dan has asked his family to move eight times; he has told the family they will stay in Ames, Iowa, his current assignment.
- They are particularly happy with the public schools and the friendly atmosphere of the community.
- He designed their new home in Ames himself, and is extremely pleased with the craftsmanship and skills of the workers who built his house.
- Generally, he finds that workers in Iowa take great pride in their craftsmanship, whether they are building houses or roads.
- The home cost $280,000 to construct. The family has a $1,500 monthly house payment; for the first time he is using a 15-year mortgage to finance his home rather than a 30-year mortgage.
- The length of the winters, often seven months long, has surprised Dan; he enjoys being around his wife and three children, but feels confined.
- On weekends, he coaches youth soccer, which is in its infancy in the state; few of the parents played soccer as children, and struggle with the rules.
- He played soccer in high school and in a college intramural league at the Pennsylvania State University.
- His daughter's team travels throughout Iowa and Nebraska to find competition.
- He is also spending time building a deck on his new home and finishing the landscaping; new homes always require lots of touch-ups to get them right, he has learned.
- Both he and his wife Maura earned civil engineering degrees from the Pennsylvania State University.
- They met in college and married after graduation, when they both got jobs with the Federal Highway Administration.
- Once they were married, they were not allowed to work in the same office, but were assigned to areas near one another, particularly during the two-year training program.

On weekends, he coaches youth soccer.

- Maura worked for 10 years before electing to stay home with their two children.
- At the time, they were each making approximately $35,000 a year.
- The long winters have given her more time to cook; she has carefully designed the kitchen and often orders specialty items from kitchen catalogs.

He is extremely pleased with the craftsmanship of his house.

Dan designed his new home in Ames himself.

Dozens of mail order catalogs now arrive each month at the Stevens' home.

Life at Work

- Dan manages 17 employees in an office which handles approximately $200 million in Federal Highway Aid coming to Iowa.
- His role is to help highway projects move through their various stages to completion; from concept to completion nearly always takes several years.
- A typical project moves from planning to environmental evaluation, right-of-way acquisition, to design, and then construction.
- He sees his principal role as creating an environment in which his engineers can make quality decisions, despite political pressures.
- Twenty years of experience has taught him that problems will arise on complex, expensive Interstate projects, and without a good working relationship, problems quickly turn to crises.
- He believes that open and honest communication is the best way to forge partnerships.
- He encourages the people in his office to socialize with each other and their counterparts with the Iowa DOT.
- Getting to know each other will make communication easier, he believes.
- He also believes in having fun on the job, because confident people make better decisions, he feels.

They are pleased with the schools in Ames.

- He tries not to get involved in highway projects personally unless his agency is preparing to say "no" or planning to withhold federal funds on a project.
- He believes his staff needs to be empowered to make decisions.
- Because his agency controls millions of dollars, its decisions can often spark political debate and controversy.
- Much of his time is spent improving the relationship between the Federal Highway Administration and the Iowa Department of Transportation.
- When he arrived a year ago, an adversarial relationship existed; he was asked to move to Iowa to help breed a sense of partnership.
- Cooperation is especially critical now that the national staff of the Highway Administration has been cut from 5,500 employees to 2,800; without trust and a partnership, projects cannot be easily completed.
- The local newspapers editorialized against his department shortly after his arrival, saying the Federal employees did little for the community.
- Since then, Dan has demonstrated the community spirit of the federal agency, showing its involvement in the local Multiple Sclerosis Society, his role as a soccer coach, and various other community activities by his staff.
- Although trained as a civil engineer, he most enjoys his leadership role and working with people, projects, and problems.
- Unlike many engineers, he tests as an extrovert on the Myers Briggs Personality profile, while most engineers are more introverted.
- Recently, his department began working on widening the Interstate around Des Moines.
- His team is assisting with design and traffic analyses for the project, as well as traffic flow and safety during the construction phase.
- Managing existing traffic while building highways for future traffic has become increasingly important in recent years.

- The Federal Highway Department is also working on a new, four-lane bypass in Eddyville, Iowa.
- When designed several years earlier, planners failed to fully account for the environmental sensitivity of sand dunes in the area.
- Dan is now working with the Iowa DOT to review alternate routes for the highway without substantially increasing the cost of the project.
- To level the dunes will be environmentally controversial, as will changing the design plans at this stage.
- His staff is spending considerable time at public hearings and workshops looking for solutions.
- Normally, engineers involved with rights-of-way and property rights plan and attend public hearings to answer the public's questions.
- To gain promotions and positions with greater authority in the Federal Highway Administration often requires multiple moves.
- Dan has moved eight times, having lived in Massachusetts, Maryland, North Carolina, Georgia twice, Washington, DC, and now Iowa.

- In each location, he gained experience in state-federal relations, since each state's politics are unique.
- The Highway Department rarely promotes in place; to go up you must move.
- He has held a wide variety of jobs, including pavement design and in safety, and manager of field offices; he has also served as a district engineer.
- While assigned to the national headquarters in Washington, DC, he came to appreciate the complexity of national politics surrounding the Federal-Aid Highway system and its funding.
- He was ready to leave Washington, its politics, and paperwork behind when he moved to Iowa.
- He enjoys the day-to-day management of projects and seeing the results of his department; in Washington, it was more difficult to measure his progress each day.

Life in the Community: Ames, Iowa

- Many in the community have deep roots running back generations; they grew up in the town and have never seen a need or had a desire to move.
- Located in the center of the state, Ames still retains much of the ethnic flavor introduced by German, Dutch, and Scandinavian immigrants who first began arriving in large numbers in the 1850s.
- Small comments and reactions remind him that he will always be considered an outsider no matter how long he lives in the state.
- Friday nights in Ames are reserved for high school football; the stands are packed with adults who attended the school years before and whose children have long since graduated.

Dan enjoys coaching soccer and seeing young people learn the game.

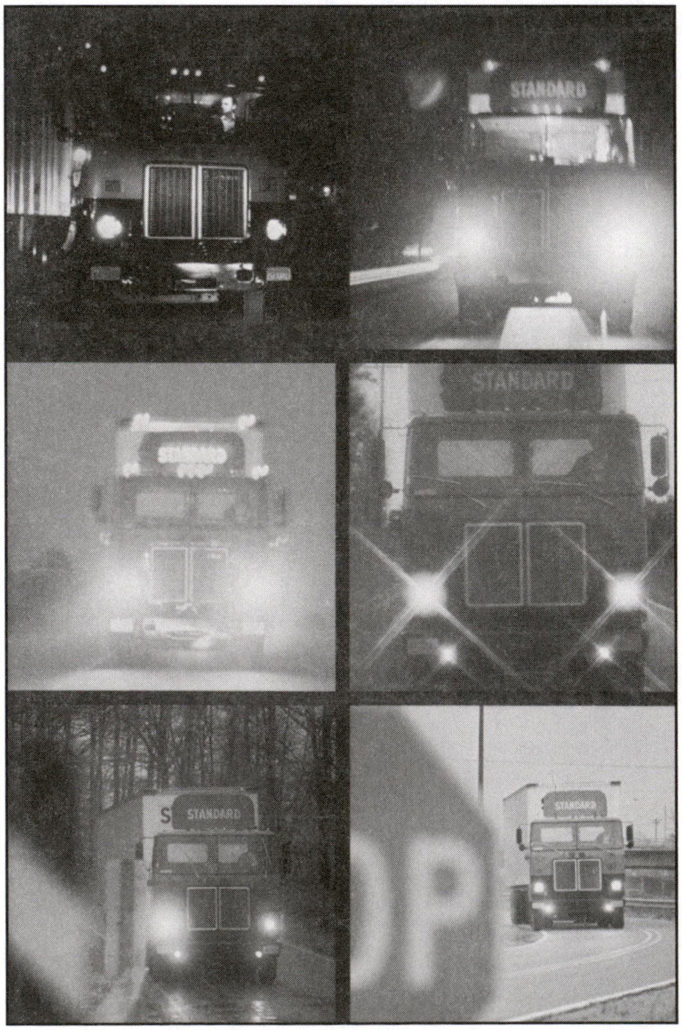

- Drug use within the community is beginning to rise; community leaders don't like to discuss the problem, but believe they must find more for teenagers to do before drug use gets worse.
- A socially conservative state, laws against Sunday dancing, hunting, and horse racing were not repealed until 1955.
- The flat, vast plains of Iowa, leveled off thousands of years ago by the glaciers of the Pleistocene epoch, are largely used for farming hogs, corn, and soybeans.
- Iowa is one of the few states in which the number of people still living on farms matches the number of city dwellers.
- The state raises seven percent of the nation's food supply, ranking second to California in agricultural output.
- Nearly 95 percent of Iowa's land is under cultivation—almost 34 million acres divided into more than 150,000 farms.

Historical Snapshot
1997

- Despite a one-day plunge of 554 points, the stock market soared, the Dow was up 20 percent for the third straight year, and job creation continued
- A record $920 billion in mergers created corporations of unprecedented size
- Princess Diana's death generated more press coverage than any event in the century as millions watched her televised funeral
- Controversy erupted over allegations that large contributors were invited by President Bill Clinton to stay overnight in the White House Lincoln Bedroom
- Oprah Winfrey launched a highly successful book club on her television program to encourage reading
- The price of personal computers (Compaq, Hewlett Packard, IBM) fell below $1,000
- Unemployment hit five percent, while inflation was at 2.5 percent
- The cost of a 30-year mortgage fell to seven percent
- A survey of grocery owners revealed that 64 percent of their customers ate cookies, chips, or candy without buying the product
- Children became so unsettled by the virtual Tamogotchi pet, which required constant attention to stay alive, that the toys were banned by many schools
- Jerry Seinfeld announced that this would be the last season for his television show, *Seinfeld*, despite a $5 million-per-episode offer to continue
- Violent crime in New York City was down by 38 percent; the city's count of 981 homicides was the lowest since 1968
- Microsoft came under antitrust scrutiny for insisting that its Internet browser was intrinsic to its Windows 95 product
- The newest Barbie doll introduction featured a larger waistline, smaller breasts, and more modest clothing; she also was provided a friend in a wheelchair
- The leading tobacco companies made a $368 billion settlement with the states to settle smoking death claims
- Scottish researchers announced the first cloning of an adult mammal, a sheep named Dolly
- Severe asthma, common in poor urban areas, was linked to cockroaches
- President Clinton gained line-item veto power for the first time
- Affirmative Action programs, designed to aid minorities, came under attack
- Digital cameras, DVD players, voice recognition software, and prosthetic knee joints all made their first appearances

1997 Economic Profile

Income, Standard Jobs

Bituminous Coal Mining	$42,711.00
Building Trades	$28,465.00
Domestics	$10,854.00
Farm Labor	$15,863.00
Finance, Insurance, and Real Estate	$38,577.00
Gas, Electricity, and Sanitation Workers	$38,936.00
Manufacturing, Durable Goods	$28,507.00
Manufacturing, Nondurable Goods	$24,387.00
Medical/Health Services Workers	$21,234.00
Miscellaneous Manufacturing	$21,798.00
Motion Picture Services	$39,585.00
Nonprofit Organization Workers	$15,016.00
Passenger Transportation Workers, Local and Highway	$18,525.00
Postal Employees	$35,797.00
Public School Teachers	$27,130.00
Radio Broadcasting and Television Workers	$32,223.00
Railroad Workers	$42,175.00
State and Local Government Workers	$29,023.00
Telephone and Telegraph Workers	$35,844.00
Wholesale and Retail Trade Workers	$14,412.00

Selected Prices

Bridgestone High Performance 65 HR Tire	$85.00
Cashmere-Blend Jacket	$69.99
Crest Gel Tartar Control Toothpaste, 6.4 Ounces	$2.00
Disney's *Lion King* Video	$29.97
Everyday Battery, D-Size, Two-Pack	$6.00
Hotel Room at The Talbot Hotel	$160.00

Kirium Chronometer
Men's Watch. $1,695.00
Lubriderm Lotion, 16 Ounces $7.00
Pink/White Lily Flowering
Tulip Bulbs, 100 . . . . $43.00
Rand Barbie 12" Girl's Bicycle $49.97
Robitussin DM Cough
Suppressant, Four Ounces. $3.00
Secret Deodorant, 1.7 Ounces $1.50
Sierra Four-Piece Setting,
Bakelite Handles $40.00
Sofa, Green Stripe Cover. $999.00
SOLO Radar and Laser
Cordless Detector $199.00
Ultra-Downy, 20 Ounces $2.00
Variflex Rollerblades. $34.97
Wing Chair, Floral Cover $699.00
Zenith 19" Color Television $139.00
Zinsser's Blend & Glaze
Decorative Paint, Gallon. $25.00

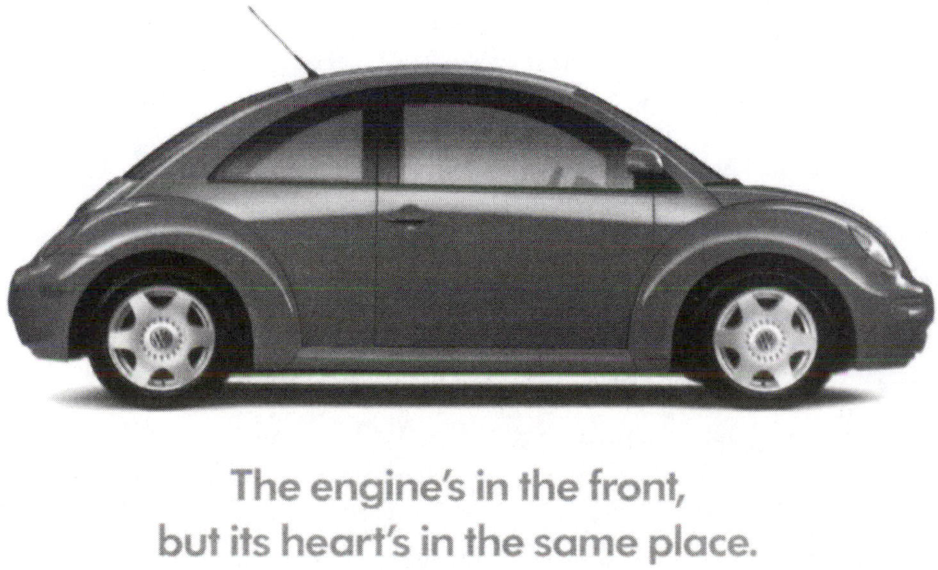
The engine's in the front,
but its heart's in the same place.

The Interstate System

- Created by Congress in 1956, the Interstate Highway System in America was now 41 years old.
- The Great Wall of China and the Interstate Highway System were among the only human creations that could be seen by astronauts from an orbiting spacecraft.
- The property that Highway authorities had acquired in order to site the Interstates equaled a land mass the size of Delaware.
- When created, politicians and writers celebrated the goal of "man's triumph over nature."
- President Eisenhower passionately believed in the need for a modern, interstate highway system to ensure the "personal safety, the general prosperity, the national security of the American people."
- Before the passage of the Federal-Aid Highway Act of 1956, the Bureau of Public Roads produced a 100-page book designating the 2,175 miles of proposed interstate highways.
- Congressmen, businessmen, and local politicians could study and anticipate the impact the Interstate Highway System would have on their communities.
- The Federal-Aid Highway Act of 1956 was signed by Eisenhower in June 1956 while he was recovering from surgery in Walter Reed Army Medical Center.
- The bill authorized $25 billion for 12 years to accelerate construction of a National System of Interstate and Defense Highways.
- It also created a Highway Trust Fund supported by increasing the federal tax on gas and diesel fuel from $0.02 to $0.03 cents, and increased the federal portion of construction of interstate highways to 90 percent.
- All standards were based on meeting the needs of American traffic in 1972, the year the System was slated for completion.
- Editorials nationwide lauded the legislation, since Americans valued their mobility
- At the time, 72 percent of American families owned an automobile; by 1970, the number would rise to 82 percent.

- Despite enthusiasm, early construction went slowly.
- Even though the federal government paid for 90 percent of the costs of the new highways and could veto expenditures, individual states had the responsibility of initiating construction projects and determining when and where to build particular sections of interstate.
- In many states, including Iowa, bid rigging was common enough that several county officials were convicted and sent to prison.
- Then, in the early 1960s, with the leadership of Rex Whitton, road construction was on schedule and honest.

makes you feel. It has the rare ability to thrill you. Exhilarate you. Rejuvenate you. While
protecting you. Making each day feel like an extended recess. www.bmwusa.com
BMW
The Ultimate Driving Machine

Divided Highways, by Tom Lewis:

"When a mild recession pushed unemployment over five percent (it had been as low as 2.9 percent at the height of the Korean War), President Dwight David Eisenhower looked to public works and defense procurement as a way to prevent another depression. At his direction the Undersecretary of Commerce for Transportation submitted a report in December 1953 entitled 'The Potential Use of Toll Road Development in a Business Depression.' He wanted a real public works program, the President told his Cabinet in February 1954, ready to use in the event of an economic setback. 'If we don't move rapidly, we could be in terrible trouble.' Highway construction would be the keystone of public works.

Simply put, the President knew he could not fail with highways. Highway building would be popular with the electorate, fiscally sound, and above all would give people jobs. Each federal dollar, so his Commission on Public Roads reported, generated close to a half-hour of employment, not only in construction, but in steel mills, cement plants, and mines, among various manufacturers. Like a stone cast into a pond, each mile of modern, four-lane, limited-access highway would produce ripples that would be felt throughout the country.

For that new mile of road, surveys would have to site its 200-foot-wide right-of-way across the landscape. Property would receive compensation for 24 and a quarter acres of land; bulldozer operators would have to level and prepare the road's surface; gravel contractors would have to haul in truckloads of rubble and fill; compactor operators would have to compress the materials and smooth them. The mile would consume 50 tons of cement to make up the concrete pavement, and 20 tons of steel for reinforcing screens and roads embedded in the concrete. The mile would give jobs to welders to secure the steel, and masons to spread the concrete. Each bridge or overpass, culvert or drainage line meant still more construction and more materials.

That mile of road would ripple through other parts of the economy too. Literally dozens of industries would grow by producing goods for the construction. Powder manufacturers like Hercules would profit from the sale of explosives. Lumber mills like Georgia-Pacific would produce plywood and wood for construction firms. Great companies like Allis-Chalmers, General Motors, Westinghouse, Caterpillar, and Ingersoll-Rand would get new orders to produce

- By the stated 1972 completion date for the Interstate System, enough roadways had been completed so that the wide bands of concrete were highly controversial.
- Mass transit advocates were lobbying for more mass transit dollars in the face of a gas crisis; many areas also feared that even more urban sprawl and white flight would result from building highly efficient and convenient Interstates from city to city.
- From the inception of the Highway Act, the control of expenditures and handling of federal dollars within each state had caused numerous political and financial tug-of-wars; by mid-1975, the question of control caused outright warfare in many cities and states.

heavy equipment, gargantuan bulldozers, and jumbo trucks and rollers. Rubber plants like Goodyear and Firestone would produce strips of expansion buffers between the sections of concrete pavement. And to keep all the equipment operating, companies like Standard Oil and Texaco and Phillips and Sinclair would supply a steady stream of fuel and grease.

The ripples continued to spread outward through the economy. Paint manufacturers like Pittsburgh and Sherwin Williams would receive orders for yellow and white traffic paint. Minnesota Mining and Manufacturing—3M—produced a unique reflecting material sign makers used for the huge letters on the traffic signs a high-speed road demanded. Lighting companies like Sylvania and General Electric would receive contracts to produce high-intensity mercury vapor lamps at interchanges. Still other steel companies would have to produce lampposts, dividing barriers, and signposts, all of which required a contractor to install them. Landscapers would provide trees and ground cover. Material laboratories would get contracts to test core samples of new concrete pavement. As construction workers often traveled a considerable distance to the job site, sometimes even from another state, hotels and motels as well as restaurants and diners would benefit. Still other vendors followed along with the workers, like Mother Courage behind the army, to sell coffee, sandwiches, and snacks.

The new mile of highway depended on the services of an average of eight engineers. State highway departments would increase their staffs. Behind all the engineers were colleges and universities across the nation that would benefit from the construction boom as they enlarged their faculties to teach the growing number of students.

Nor would the rippling cease when local politicians cut the ribbons and the automobiles cruised down the pavement. Drivers of that mile would have to purchase cars and trucks—and then gasoline, tires, and insurance—to ride on it. If that mile was in the Northeast, say New Hampshire or New York, road crews would have to spend many dollars to maintain it, including money for sand and plows to keep it open in the winter. Police would have to patrol it night and day. If the mile happened to be near an exit or entrance, businesses and small companies might locate there."

- Highways that cut through urban areas such as Boston or San Francisco were accused of destroying neighborhoods and dividing the city.
- Despite criticism, traffic on the nation's Interstates boomed; travel time from region to region dropped dramatically.
- Soon, skiers in St. Louis thought little of driving to Colorado for the weekend; winter-weary water lovers from Michigan shot down the Interstate to Florida in record time.
- By 1986, the building of 97 percent of the System had been completed.
- Even though the Interstate System accounted for about one percent of the nation's highways, it carried about 20 percent of the nation's traffic and 50 percent of its trucks.
- People and businesses placed their lives in relation to the highway, as in, "we are about three miles east of 77 on Highway 21."
- Relocating businesses began asking more about transportation routes than about labor forces; if the roads were available, the people would come.

The opening of new Interstates created excitement in the 1950s.

- In 1990, there were 115 million workers in the United States age 16 and older; fully 99.8 million of those workers rode a car, motorcycle, or truck to work, while six million used public transit, and five million walked or road a bike.
- Yet, despite the frenzy of activity, Highway System accidents actually fell.
- In 1990, just 4,941 people lost their lives on the Interstate System, which carried cars, trucks, and business 479 billion miles; the death rate per 100 million vehicle miles was 1.03.

"Where's the Panic? The Global Crisis May Not Be Over. But It Sure Feels Like It," *Newsweek*, November 30, 1998:

"Ahh, the sights and sounds of normalcy. On Wall Street, Internet stocks are again getting bid skyward—and deflating a week later like billion-dollar party balloons. Traders puffing on Montecristos are packing into tiny steak-and-cigar saloons like Angelo & Maxie's and talking trash to each other over the din. 'I've never seen a mood change this dramatic,' said one trader, Ralph Kartzman of First New York Securities, as the Dow finished at near-record levels above 9,000 last week. 'You don't hear about Russia, Brazil. Nobody cares, not even a bump.' Downtown at the New York Fed, which only six weeks ago orchestrated the bailout of a giant hedge fund to prevent global panic, officials will admit only to breathing easier. But they point out that money is flowing back into corporate junk bonds from the high, safe ground of U.S. treasuries. 'Stability,' says a Federal Reserve official, 'may yet break out.'"

1999 News Profile

"Silicon Valley Millionaires, They Have a Different Kind of Problem, Plenty of Money, No Time to Spend It," by Kim Curtis, Associated Press, February 5, 1999:

"For Silicon Valley's young entrepreneurs, the millions seem to come easy. Finding time to spend them is the hard part. These nouveau riche spend an hour or more in traffic getting to work, slog home 12 to 15 hours later, and can't remember their last vacation. Couple that with increasingly outrageous prices for homes and you've summarized the down side to the economic boom in this technology hot zone south of San Francisco.

'My friends didn't see me for three years,' says Dan Whaley, 32, co-founder and chief technology officer for GetThere.com, a Web site to provide travel services. 'The carrot's always just slightly in front of our nose. You're working your butt off, but you're living this incredible Silicon Valley dream.' Starting a business has always required long hours, but when the business seems to evolve daily—as does the Internet—the pace and workload are just that much tougher.

For some, cutting back to a 12-hour day actually represents relief. Whaley laughs when he thinks back to his company's infancy when he worked 18 to 20 hours a day, kept his possessions at his office and slept in a sleeping bag under his desk. 'I only happened to move into an apartment when I was walking down the street for coffee and saw a rental sign. I moved in, but I still ended up sleeping 50 percent of the time at the office because I was too tired to walk across the street,' he said.

Now, Whaley works 60 to 80 hours a week, 'which is great,' he says. He bought a home, which he shares with a roommate. 'I do go home at night and I haven't slept at the office in about a year.' Such workaholic lifestyles may sound unhealthy, but that's not necessarily the case, according to Catherine Chambliss, chairwoman of the psychology department at Ursinus College in Pennsylvania. The term

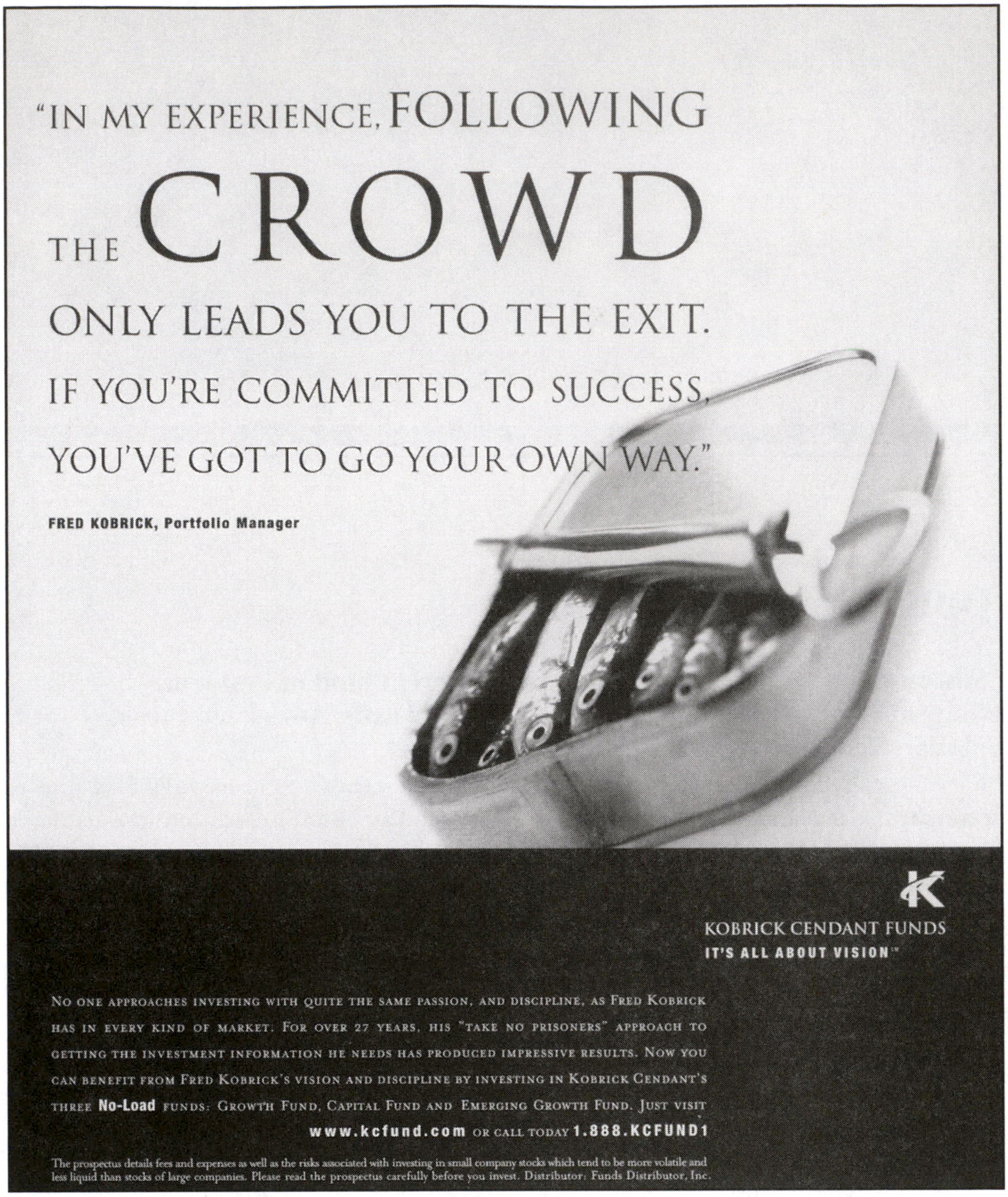

'workaholic' applies to 'neurotic, highly driven people who are opting to work excessively as a way of avoiding the personal sphere,' she said. 'This group seems to present something different. It's a real passionate blending of work and play.' For example, there's Joe Cha, 30, who co-founded Xuma, a company that builds and manages Web sites. 'I love this place and I love all the people here. It feels like a big drug,' he said. 'It's like if you're a chef and you love cooking. You cook at home.'

Of course, not everyone who works in high technology is a millionaire. Cha, who lives and works in San Francisco, earns about $175,000 a year. Business groups worry that housing costs there and in the Valley are too high for most people. 'Silicon Valley can only remain home to leading-edge companies to the extent we address the need for affordable homes for cutting-edge employees,' said Carl Guardino of the Silicon Valley Manufacturing Group, a

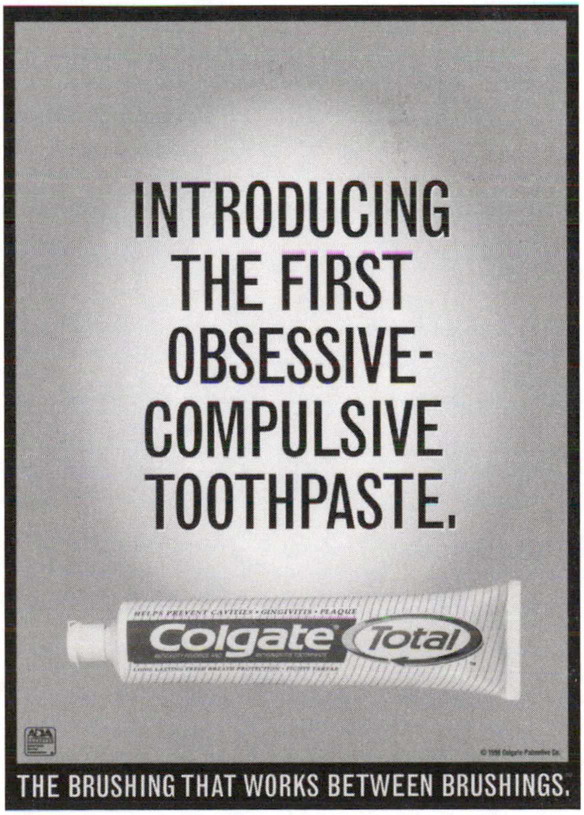

trade group. Despite a median income of $82,400 for a family of four, Guardino said home prices are out of reach for seven of every 10 families shopping for their first home. Between 1995 and 1999, housing prices rose 46 percent in the Silicon Valley—the median price is now $427,000, compared to a national median of about $136,000.

Not surprisingly, the frantic pace and the high costs have prompted some dropouts. Carl Sassenrath founded Rebol Technologies, a programming language company, in Vichy Springs, a mineral bath resort about two hours north of San Francisco. 'It was so congested, such a frenzy down there. I wanted to have a peaceful life and have found it to be a more productive and creative way to live.' He said Rebol's corporate philosophy calls for a slower pace. For Sassenrath and his 15 employees, a busy day may involve walking over to the massage cottage for an herbal facial or cruising down the road to a winery.

In older, more established technology companies like Microsoft, outside Seattle, a few have started calling it quits.

Brad Silverberg, an architect of Microsoft's success with Windows and the Web browser Internet Explorer, took a leave of absence two years ago and made it permanent late last year. 'Everyone talks about finding balance, and I'm inherently not a balanced kind of guy,' Silverberg said at the time. 'There's work, there's family, there's your personal life, and there's just not enough time in the day to do a great job on all three.' "

Sources

1880–1899

Charles Francis Adams, Jr., *Railroads, the Origin and Problems,* G.P. Putnam's Sons, The Knickerbocker Press, 1888

George H. Burgess and Miles C. Kennedy, *Centennial History of The Pennsylvania Railroad Company,* The Pennsylvania Railroad Company, Philadelphia, 1949

Neil Harris, *The Land of Contrasts, 1880–1901,* George Braziller, New York, 1970

Samuel Eliot Morison, *The Oxford History of the American People, Volume Three, 1869 through the Death of John F. Kennedy, 1963,* A Meridian Book, New York, 1994

Simon Sterne, *Railways of the United States,* G.P. Putnam's Sons, The Knickerbocker Press, New York, 1912

Nicholas B. Wainwright, *The Philadelphia National Bank, 1803–1953,* William F. Fell Co., Philadelphia, 1957

Nicholas B. Wainwright, *History of the Philadelphia Electric Company, 1881 to 1961,* Philadelphia Electric Company, Philadelphia, 1961

Stephen Ambrose and Douglas Brinkley, *Witness to America, An Illustrated Documentary History of the United States from the Revolution to Today,* Harper Collins Publishers, A Lou Reda Book, 1999

David R. Johnson, John A. Booth, and Richard J. Harris, *The Politics of San Antonio, Community, Progress, and Power,* University of Nebraska Press, Lincoln, 1983

Clyde A. Milner II, Carol A. O'Connor, Martha A. Sandweiss, *The Oxford History of the American West,* Oxford University Press, New York, 1996

Marion Patton and Mary Sherwin, *Know Your America, Volume II,* Doubleday & Company, Inc., Garden City, New York, 1978

Charles Ramsdell, *San Antonio, A Historical and Pictorial Guide,* University of Texas Press, Austin, 1959

Gordon B. Dodds, *The Salmon King of Oregon, R.D. Hume and the Pacific Fisheries,* The University of North Carolina Press, Chapel Hill, North Carolina, 1959

Dianne Newell, *The Development of the Pacific Salmon-Canning Industry, a Grown Man's Game,* McGill-Green's University Press, Montreal, 1989

Keith Wheeler, *The Alaskans, The Old West,* TIME-LIFE BOOKS, Alexandria, Virginia, 1977

William H. Wilson, *Railroad in the Clouds: The Alaska Railroad in the Age of Steam, 1914–1945,* Pruett Publishing Company, Boulder, Colorado, 1977

1900–1909

Thomas F. Campbell and Edward M. Miggins, *The Birth of Modern Cleveland, 1865–1930,* Western Reserve Historical Society, London, 1988

Susan Porter Benson, *Counter Cultures, Saleswomen, Managers, and Customers in American Department Stores, 1890–1940,* University of Illinois Press, Urbana, 1986

Boris Emmet and John E. Jeuck, *Catalogues and Counters, A History of Sears, Roebuck and Company,* The University of Chicago Press, 1950

John William Ferry, *A History of the Department Store,* The MacMillan Company, 1960

Godfrey M. Lebhar, *Chain Stores in America, 1859–1962,* Chain Store Publishing Corporation, New York, 1963

Carol Poh Miller and Robert A. Wheeler, *Cleveland: A Concise History, 1796–1996,* Indiana University Press, Bloomington, 1997

William Ganson Rose, *Cleveland: The Making of a City,* The World Publishing Company, Cleveland, Ohio, 1950

Joseph J. Schroeder, Jr., *1895 to 1930, the Wonderful World of Automobiles,* Follett Publishing Company, Chicago, 1971

Robert W. Twyman, *History of Marshall Field & Co.*, University of Pennsylvania Press, Philadelphia, 1954

1910–1919

William C. and Elizabeth B. Jones, *Buckwalter, The Colorado Scenes of a Pioneer Photojournalist, 1890–1920,* Pruett Publishing Company, Boulder, Colorado, 1989

Clyde A. Milner, Carol A. Connor, Martha A. Sandweiss, *The Oxford History of the American West,* Oxford University Press, New York, 1996

George Waldo Browne, *The Amoskeag Manufacturing Company, A History,* Amoskeag Manufacturing Company, 1915

Daniel Creamer and Charles W. Coulter, *Labor and the Shut-Down of the Amoskeag Textile Mills,* Anro & The New York Times, New York, 1971

Tamara K. Hareven and Randolph Langenbach, *Amoskeag, Life and Work in an American Factory-City,* Pantheon Books, New York, 1978

Henry Berry, "The Marine's Marine," *Make the Kaiser Dance, Living Memories of the Doughboys,* Arbor House, New York, 1978

Roger Butterfield, *The American Past, A History of the United States from Concord to the Great Society,* A Fireside Book, Published by Simon and Schuster, 1976

David M. Kennedy, *Freedom from Fear, the American People in Depression and War, 1929–1945,* Oxford University Press, New York, 1999

Frederick Lewis Allen, *Only Yesterday, An Informal History of the 1920s,* Harper and Brothers, New York, 1931

1920–1929

Scott Derks, *The Value of a Dollar, 1860–1999,* Grey House Publishing, Millerton, New York, 1999

Helen Kohn Hennig, *Columbia, Capital City of South Carolina, 1786–1936,* The Columbia Sesqui-Centennial Commission, Columbia, South Carolina, 1936

Harvey Green, *The Uncertainty of Everyday Life, 1915–1945,* Harper Collins Publishers, New York, 1992

Robert C. Harvey, *The Art of the Funnies, An Aesthetic History,* University Press of Mississippi, Jackson, Mississippi, 1994

Bevis Hillier, *The Style of the Century, 1900–1980,* E.P. Dutton, Inc., New York, 1983

Maurice Horn, *100 Years of American Newspaper Comics,* Gramercy Books, New York, 1996

Harry S. Linfield, Ph.D., *The Communal Organization of the Jews in the United States, 1927,* The American Jewish Committee, New York, 1930

Martin Sheridan, *Classic Comics and Their Creators,* Post-Era Books, Arcadia, California, 1942

William K. Klingaman, *1929, The Year of the Great Crash,* Harper & Row, New York, 1989

John B. Montville, *Mack,* Axtex Corporation, Tucson, Arizona, 1981

James A. Wren and Genevieve J. Wren, *Motor Trucks of America,* The University of Michigan Press, Ann Arbor, Michigan, 1979

1930–1939

Scott Derks, *The Value of a Dollar, 1860–1999*, Grey House Publishing, Millerton, New York, 1999

Full Range Radio Log, Published by General Electric Radio, 1931

David M. Kennedy, *Freedom from Fear, the American People in Depression and War, 1929–1945*, Oxford University Press, New York, 1999

Irving Settel and William Laas, *A Pictorial History of Television*, Grosset & Dunlap, Inc., New York, 1969

A Social-Economic Grouping of the Gainful Workers of the United States, 1930, U.S. Department of Commerce, Bureau of the Census

Carter Goodrich, *The Miner's Freedom, A Study of the Working Life of a Changing Industry*, Marshall Jones Company, Boston, 1925

Homer Lawrence Morris, Ph.D., *The Plight of the Bituminous Coal Miner*, University of Pennsylvania Press, Philadelphia, 1934

Isabel Leighton, *The Aspirin Age, 1919–1941*, A Clarion Book, New York, 1949

Gary M. Walton and Ross M. Robertson, *History of the American Economy*, Harcourt Brace Jovanovich, New York, 1983

John Brooks, *The Great Leap, The Past Twenty-Five Years in America*, Harper Books, New York, 1966

David Gelernter, *1939, The Lost World of the Fair*, The Free Press, New York, 1995

Helen A. Harrison, *Dawn of a New Day, The New York World's Fair, 1939–1940*, New York University Press, New York, 1980

1940–1949

Connie Goddard and Bruce Hatton Boyer, *The Great Chicago Trivia & Fact Book,* Cumberland House Publishing, Nashville, Tennessee, 1996

Jay Lovinger, Editor, *Life Celebrates 1945,* Time Inc., June 1995

Stevenson Swanson, Editor, *Chicago Days, 150 Defining Moments in the Life of a Great City,* Cantigny First Division Foundation, 1997

Lee Finkle, *Forum for Protest, The Black Press During World War II,* Fairleigh Dickinson University Press, London, 1975

Stefan Lorant, Pittsburgh, *The Story of an American City,* Authors Edition, Inc., Lenox, Massachusetts, 1975

Charles A. Simmons, *The African-American Press,* McFarland & Company, Inc., Publishers, Jefferson, North Carolina, 1998

Michael Gannon, Editor, *The New History of Florida*, University Press of Florida, Gainesville, 1996

Victor Bondi, *American Decades, 1940–1949*, A Manly, Inc., Book, Gale Research Inc., Detroit, 1995

1950–1959

Michael E. Brown, *Flying Blind, the Politics of the U.S. Strategic Bomber Program*, Cornell University Press, Ithaca, New York, 1992

Robert D. Loomis, *The Story of the U.S. Air Force*, Random House, New York, 1959

Lislie A. Rose, *The Cold War Comes to Main Street*, University Press of Kansas, Lawrence, Kansas, 1999

Lois Gordon and Alan Gordon, *American Chronicle, Year by Year through the Twentieth Century*, Yale University Press, New Haven, 1999

James B. Edwards, D.M.D., *The Southeast's Oldest Medical School, Now a Leading Research and Treatment Center*, The Newcomen Society of the United States, New York, 1986

Walter J. Fraser, Jr., *Charleston, The History of a Southern City*, University of South Carolina Press, Columbia, South Carolina, 1989

1960–1969

Harry Castleman and Walter J. Podrazik, *Watching TV, Four Decades of American Television*, McGraw-Hill Book Company, New York, 1982

John L. Chapman, *Incredible Los Angeles*, Harper & Row, New York, 1967

Scott Derks, *The Value of a Dollar, 1860–1999*, Grey House Publishing, Millerton, New York, 1999

Richard Levinson and William Link, *Stay Tuned, An Inside Look at the Making of Prime-Time Television*, St. Martin's Press, New York, 1981

Christopher Rand, *Los Angeles, The Ultimate City*, Oxford University Press, New York, 1967

1970–1979

Scott Derks, *The Value of a Dollar, 1860–1999*, Grey House Publishing, Millerton, New York, 1999

Marion Patton and Mary Sherwin, Editors, *Know Your America, A Guide to Every State in the Union, Volume II*, Doubleday & Company, Inc., Garden City, New York, 1978

The Eyewitness History of the Vietnam War, 1961–1975, by George Esper and The Associated Press

Michael Gannon, *The New History of Florida*, University Press of Florida, Gainesville, 1996

1980–1989

Sheila Jasanoff, *Learning from Disaster, Risk Management after Bhopal*, University of Pennsylvania Press, Philadelphia, 1994

Horne, *Congress—Committee on Education & Labor*, OSHA Oversight-Worker Health, Washington, DC, 1985

EPA, *Promoting Chemical Recycling*, Washington, DC, 1999

Adam Cohen, Elizabeth Taylor, *American Pharaoh: Mayor Richard T. Daley: His Battle for Chicago and the Nation*, Little Brown, Boston, 2000

Gordon M. Bethune, *From Worst to First: Behind the Scenes of Continental's Remarkable Comeback*, Newcomen Society of the United States, New York, 1999

1990–1999

Loren Baritz, *The Good Life, The Meaning of Success for the American Middle Class*, Alfred A. Knopf, New York, 1989

Charles Sigismund, *Champions of Silicon Valley*, John Wiley, New York, 2000

Randy Komisar, *The Monk and the Riddle*, Harvard Business School Press, Boston, Massachusetts, 2000

Tom Lewis, *Divided Highways: Building the Interstate Highways*, Viking, New York, 1997

William Lipford, *The Nation's Highway System*, Congressional Research Service, Library of Congress, 1994

Daiva E. Edgar, *Performance of Specular Reflectors used for Lighting Enhancement*, U.S. Army Corps of Engineers, Springfield, Virginia, 1999

Scott W. Richter, *Technology Development for an Advanced Microsheet Glass Concentrator*, National Aeronautics and Space Administration, Springfield, Virginia, 1990

INDEX

Photographs, figures, and illustrations are indicated by *italic* page numbers.